WOMEN'S AMERICA

Refocusing the Past

WOMEN'S AMERICA

Refocusing the Past

VOLUME 1

EIGHTH EDITION

Edited by

Linda K. Kerber
University of Iowa

Jane Sherron De Hart
University of California, Santa Barbara

Cornelia Hughes Dayton
University of Connecticut

Judy Tzu-Chun Wu
University of California, Irvine

New York   Oxford
Oxford University Press

Oxford University Press is a department of the University of Oxford.
It furthers the University's objective of excellence in research,
scholarship, and education by publishing worldwide.

Oxford   New York
Auckland   Cape Town   Dar es Salaam   Hong Kong   Karachi
Kuala Lumpur   Madrid   Melbourne   Mexico City   Nairobi
New Delhi   Shanghai   Taipei   Toronto

With offices in
Argentina   Austria   Brazil   Chile   Czech Republic   France   Greece
Guatemala   Hungary   Italy   Japan   Poland   Portugal   Singapore
South Korea   Switzerland   Thailand   Turkey   Ukraine   Vietnam

For titles covered by Section 112 of the US Higher Education
Opportunity Act, please visit www.oup.com/us/he for the
latest information about pricing and alternate formats.

Published by Oxford University Press
198 Madison Avenue, New York, New York 10016
http://www.oup.com

Library of Congress Cataloging-in-Publication Data
Women's America / edited by Linda K. Kerber, University of Iowa, Jane Sherron
De Hart, University of California, Santa Barbara, Cornelia Hughes Dayton, University
of Connecticut, Judy Tzu-Chun Wu, Ohio State University. -- Eighth edition.
    pages cm
  ISBN 978-0-19-934935-7
  1. Women--United States--History--Sources. 2. Women--Employment--United States--
History--Sources. 3. Women--Political activity--United States--History--Sources.
4. Women--Health and hygiene--United States--History--Sources. 5. Feminism--United
States--History--Sources. I. Kerber, Linda K.
  HQ1426.W663 2015
  305.40973--dc23
                                                                        2014033991

Printing number: 9 8 7 6 5 4 3 2 1

Printed in the United States of America
on acid-free paper

with admiration + gratitude,

Nina + Linda

For our teachers

Annette Kar Baxter (1926–1984)

Mary Maples Dunn

Lilia Fernández

Estelle Freedman

Susan Hartmann

John Atlee Kouwenhoven (1909–1990)

Gerda Lerner (1920–2013)

Peggy Pascoe (1954–2010)

Susan Porter Benson (1943–2005)

Leila J. Rupp

Anne Firor Scott

Christine Stansell

Eleanor M. Tilton (1913–1994)

Teaching Workshop in Women's History (UCLA)

and

our own cohorts of pioneering women's historians

and, of course,

the present and future generations of women's and gender history scholars

ILLUSTRATIONS

CONTENTS

PREFACE

To our readers:

Twenty-seven years ago, writing the preface for the second edition of *Women's America*, we observed that in the few years since the first edition, "an extraordinary amount of new scholarship has appeared, changing the way in which professional historians address the major issues in the field. . . . The pace of scholarly development is so rapid that comparisons can appropriately be made to scientific fields, which are expected to change overnight, rather than to the leisured pace of traditional history." That observation is even truer today, as the history of women in the United States reaches out to embrace changing understandings of gender and to engage comparisons with other national histories.

Recognizing the wider range of new scholarship, this eighth edition of *Women's America* includes some 23 new items, many on subjects new to these volumes, with enhanced coverage of women's transnational contacts and activities; sexual choices and dilemmas, including transsexuality; and women's lives in the West, the Midwest, and the South. Even more than all previous editions, *Women's America* gives fresh attention to the challenges of citizenship and its grounding in the law, now in global context.

We have written a new, more succinct Introduction, reflecting on the book's purposes and its readers' questions in the 32 years since *Women's America* was first published. We continue to offer an account of different stages in historians' inquiries into the history of women and gender in the United States. In it, we explain key terms and concepts, such as feminism, the social construction of gender, and intersectionality (the understanding that categories of difference, of race, ethnicity, class, able-bodiedness, sexual expression, culture, nationality, religion, and historical memory intersect and define one another). We give a few examples of how mainstream ideas about proper gender roles and women's and men's differing sexual drives have changed dramatically over the four centuries of U.S. history. For example, today, sex (male/female) is increasingly seen as a spectrum. We stress that varied activism aimed at improving women's lives, expanding rights, and fulfilling goals of liberation occurred continuously throughout the nation's history—and sometimes in unexpected places and ways. The introduction contains tips on using the book and a roadmap in terms of the book's major themes. Here and throughout the book, we invite students to join us in asking how we can find equality in an American society shaped, like all human societies, by differences. Repeatedly we encourage students to ask their own questions and to embark on their own research, especially by doing local and oral histories.

Recognizing the richness of new scholarship on the twentieth century, and wanting to accommodate the different shapes of upper-division courses, *Women's America* now gathers its essays, documents, and images into five chronological sections. Part I: Early America, 1600–1820, and Part II: America's Many Frontiers, 1820–1880, retain the same temporal bounds as previous editions, although new readings have been added. We introduce a new bridge section, Part III: Modern America Emerges, 1880–1920. In the two-volume version, Part III appears in each volume. Instructors of *early* U.S. women's history can use Part III to extend their course to the passage of women's suffrage, if they wish to. Instructors of *modern* U.S. women's history can extend their course back to the late nineteenth century. A new Part IV: A Transforming World, 1920–1945, focuses on women's history from suffrage to the end of World War II. Part V: A Transforming World, 1945–2014, includes emerging scholarship along with some key primary sources on the decades since World War II.

xvi PREFACE

For instructors perhaps the most salient innovation is that that the materials in each Part are now arranged in thematic clusters, such as Workplace and Household Scenes, Sexuality and the Body, Gender and the Armed Forces. These vary in each part, but reflect six core themes of *Women's America*: *family/household/sexuality, labor/economy/class, race/ethnicity/religion, law and citizenship, women's activism*, and the *global context of U.S. women's history*. And don't forget the two Photo Essays, each of which ranges over the full sweep of U.S. history, offering a running commentary on visual materials relating to the broad themes of Women in Public and Adorning the Body. These images and text can serve as independent readings and as supplements to other items in *Women's America*. We have also added a list of illustrations to the volume's table of contents so that all visual materials can be better identified by readers.

ACKNOWLEDGMENTS

We are delighted to welcome Judy Tzu-Chun Wu to our quartet of editors. And although the best part of the collaboration is meeting in person, we are grateful for the many means of electronic communication that carry our daily exchanges—Dropbox, e-mail, SKYPE—that enable the rich, three- and four-way conversations among us.

We are lucky to have had the advice of nearly seven users of previous editions, who offered their advice anonymously to Oxford University Press.

We are grateful for the good counsel of friends and colleagues as we prepared this edition. Among them are Alexis Boylan, Judith Carney, Catherine Denial, Estelle Freedman, Allison Horrocks, Omar Jimenez-Valerio, Katherine Marino, Stephanie McCurry, Micki McElya, Tracy McQueen, Daniel Rivers, Terri Snyder, Amy Sopcak-Joseph, Lisa Wilson, and Sharon Wood. Karissa Haugeberg shared her deep knowledge of the history of reproductive rights and pitched in at crucial moments. We benefitted from the ideas and advice of students in Lisa Wilson's classes at Connecticut College and Dayton's at the University of Connecticut. We are especially grateful to Mike Limberg and Philip Moore, who assisted Nina Dayton at the University of Connecticut, and to law librarians Druet Cameron Klughmand and Noëlle Sinclair at the University of Iowa College of Law.

James Boster unflaggingly cheered us on and was a fount of invaluable computer know-how. We are grateful to archivist Jenny Gotwals at the Schlesinger Library for the History of Women in America at the Radcliffe Institute. We thank Brian Wheel, Brianna Provenzano, and Taylor Pilkington of Oxford University Press; India Gray and Christian Holdener for shepherding the manuscript through copy-editing; and our thoughtful agent, Anne Borchardt.

Linda K. Kerber
Jane Sherron De Hart
Cornelia Hughes Dayton
Judy Tzu-Chun Wu

INTRODUCTION

Linda K. Kerber
Jane Sherron DeHart
Cornelia Hughes Dayton
Judy Tzu-Chun Wu

... all men are created equal.
—Declaration of Independence, 1776

No State shall . . . deny to any person within its jurisdiction equal protection of the laws.
—Fourteenth Amendment to the U.S. Constitution, 1868

Equality of rights under the law shall not be denied or abridged by the United States or by any State on account of sex.
—Proposed Equal Rights Amendment
Submitted to the states, 1972; failed to be ratified, 1982

Recalling that discrimination against women violates the principles of equality of rights and respect for human dignity, . . . [signers of this convention agree] to embody the principle of the equality of men and women in their national constitutions . . . and to ensure, through law and other appropriate means, the practical realization of this principle.
—UN Convention on the Elimination of Forms of Discrimination Against
Women, Entered into force, 1981. Not ratified by the United States.

The first edition of *Women's America* was published in 1982, in the midst of intense national debate about what equality means. At the time, women of all ages were deeply engaged in or by the women's liberation movement of the 1960s and 1970s, challenging the many dimensions of unequal treatment of women and men that pervaded American law and cultural practices. They wanted to know why most women worked in jobs in which their coworkers were generally women and in which their wages were substantially lower than the wages of men who did roughly similar work. They wanted to know why women could not be hired as police officers or firefighters. They wanted to know why women were regularly excluded from professional training—medical and law schools generally had strict quotas that held women to 10 percent of the class. They wanted to know why only 2 percent of military officers could be women. On college campuses they wanted to know why they were so frequently discouraged from fields of study marked as "men's fields"—for example, mathematics, engineering, and astronomy. They wanted to know why men's sports teams were generally funded from student fees but women's sports teams had to hold bake sales to raise their own funds for travel to competitions.

And they wanted to know why they learned so little in courses in literature, political science, and history about women's experiences. When they examined the indexes of high school and college textbooks, they found the witches of seventeenth-century Salem, Massachusetts; a few women reformers scattered throughout the 1800s and 1900s; and Ethel Rosenberg, executed for treason in 1953. (Among the reasons that President Dwight Eisenhower offered for refusing to commute her sentence was, as he wrote in a letter to his son John, "if there would be any commuting of the woman's sentence without the man's then from here on the Soviets would simply recruit their spies from among women."[1]) Virtually everything else of consequence in the past seemed to have been accomplished by men. Could that really be true?

The first edition of *Women's America* was a result of young women's demands for their own history.

When they searched the past for evidence of changing relations between men and women, inquirers found that the practices of silencing women as authors, lawmakers, and voters that European settlers had brought to the American colonies contrasted with traditions among the many indigenous American groups where women were important storytellers, religious leaders, and clan elders. Scanning the history of American politics, they found that the promise of equality has been central to American identity since the founding of the nation. But equality can be a complex and elusive concept. It is tangled with the hierarchies of race, class, religion, and sexual identity. In the new nation, adult women, whatever their class or perceived racial heritage, were barred from voting and holding political office, but class and race privilege gave some the power of mastery over household dependents—enslaved persons, servants, and children. After the passage of the Nineteenth Amendment to the Constitution in 1920, adult women were entitled to suffrage, but if they were black and lived in the segregated South they were generally excluded from the polls. Women in Japanese and Japanese-American families living in California and other states in the 1910s and 1920s were acutely aware of the unjust Alien Land laws that barred Asian-origin residents (who were ineligible for U.S. citizenship) from owning the land they tended as proficient farmers. Throughout the nineteenth and twentieth centuries, long before women's liberation took form in the 1960s, women in these and countless other communities all over the continent protested and worked against inequalities that riled them. Once you start looking for evidence of their activities, you find a great deal.

In response to student demand, some faculty invented new courses: others, like Anne Firor Scott at Duke University, "bootlegged women's history into the two-semester introductory American History course." The very earliest such courses were offered in the early and mid-1960s. "Women's history," Scott observed, "developed in close association with women's activism."[2] In the 1970s new courses were flooding into the curricula— in history, literature, philosophy, sociology, and other fields—and in the same decade women's studies programs took root, stressing interdisciplinary methods and knowledge. But none of these changes came easily. College and university faculties, accustomed to defining what was appropriate for students to learn, were generally slow to appreciate the compliment that was being paid. The new courses and programs were sometimes denounced as "feminist propaganda"—or as overtly political or inappropriately polemical.

Women's studies programs, like the African American studies initiated a few years before, were typically the result of protracted negotiations; in extreme cases these came about only after sit-ins and other disruptive protests.[3]

The 8th edition of *Women's America* appears at another time of anxiety about the meanings of equality in the twenty-first century. Some of the inequalities with which women have long struggled have been eliminated; others have emerged. What changes would you count as eliminating inequalities? What do you see as new and persisting problems?

As we seek to retrieve the history of women's experience, we are strengthened by the work that women and their male allies have done to protect historical records. Women activists in the nineteenth century self-consciously created an historical archive. Fearing that women would be denied knowledge of their own history and predicting that pioneering campaigners on behalf of women's rights would die before their experiences had been recorded, Elizabeth Cady Stanton and Susan B. Anthony energetically collected evidence of some of the women's movements of their own time. The rich collection of documents that they published—six large volumes, entitled *History of Woman Suffrage*—was intended to be "an arsenal of facts" for the next generation of activists and historians.[4] But, starting in the early twentieth century, most writers of history ignored it. "[I]f women were doing any thinking . . . ," the historian Mary Beard acidly observed in 1946, "it is difficult to find out [from college textbooks] . . . what it was."[5] In 1933 she edited a documentary collection, *America through Women's Eyes*, in which she argued that an accurate understanding of the past required that women's experiences be analyzed with as much care as historians devoted to the experiences of men. Despite the existence of these documents, books that treated women's history were rare.[6]

STAGES IN WOMEN'S HISTORY

The historian Gerda Lerner suggested that the writing of women's history can be arranged in stages of development, each stage more complex and sophisticated than the last, but all useful and necessary.[7] The first stage she called *"compensatory history,"* in which the historian seeks to identify women and their activities. In the 1970s, some historians began to search for women whose work and experiences deserved to be more widely known. The accomplishments of these women ranged from feats of exploration and endurance to scientific discoveries, artistic achievements, and humanitarian reforms. They included such pioneers as Amelia Earhart, the pilot whose solo flight across the Atlantic in 1933 dramatically demonstrated women's courage and daring; Alice Hamilton, the social reformer and physician whose innovative work in the 1920s on lead poisoning and other toxins made her a world authority on industrial disease and a strong critic of American industries; Maria Goeppert-Mayer, the brilliant theoretical physicist whose research on the structure of the atom and its nucleus won her the Nobel Prize; and Zora Neale Hurston, the novelist and folklorist who mastered African American folk idiom and depicted independent black women.

One result of this early search for women in the historical record was the publication of *Notable American Women*, five volumes of fascinating biographies of over 2,200 remarkable individuals.[8] This project inspired many people to collect the neglected histories of other women—by searching family papers, store accounts, and business records that had been archived or thought of as men's history; and by eliciting oral histories of many women whose experiences had been deemed trivial. In this work, amateur historians and professionals, newcomers and long-time practitioners, students and the friends they recruit, make important contributions.[9] We hope that you may be inspired to add to the histories we tell here.

"The next level of conceptualizing women's history," in Lerner's taxonomy, is *contribution history.*" In this stage, historians describe women's contribution to events, arenas, and themes that storytellers of the nation's past had already determined important. The main actors in the historical narrative remain men; women are subordinate, "helping" or "contributing" to the work of men. If the tone of "compensatory history" is delighted discovery of previously unknown women, the tone of contributory history can often be reproachful: how is it that men did not acknowledge women's help? Still, the work of contributory history can be very important in connecting women to major movements in the past: the women of Hull House in Chicago, such as Jane Addams, "contribute" to Progressive reforms; the women in cotton factories in Lowell, Massachusetts, are an important part of the story of early industrialization. Another example is the grassroots, behind-the-scenes activism of Ella Baker, a key civil rights organizer who worked with black ministers as well as the student movement. People know of Martin Luther King, Jr. but less frequently of Baker, Fannie Lou Hamer, Anne Moody, and others who were crucial to the mobilizing around racial justice and human rights in the 1950s and 1960s.[10]

Once major examples of women's "contributions" were identified, familiar historical narratives were no longer reliable. Lerner saw rewriting historical narratives as a third stage in the development of women's history—one that was more transformative than stages one and two. Things we thought we "knew" about American history turn out to be more complex than we had suspected. For example, most textbooks suggest that frontier lands meant opportunity for Americans—"a gate of escape from the bondage of the past." But it was white men who more readily found on the frontiers compensation for their hard work; many pioneering women found only drudgery. (In fact, white women were more likely to find economic opportunity in cities than on the frontier.) When the United States acquired Texas and New Mexico in 1848, the inhabitants, who were mostly indigenous and Mexican, experienced the changes as encroachment and loss of political control. But not all outcomes were negative. For example, as there was virtually no divorce in Mexico, women trapped in unhappy marriages often welcomed the opportunities offered by the U.S. courts.[11]

Over a decade after Gerda Lerner identified these phases of studying women's history, Joan Wallach Scott and others argued for the importance of using gender as an analytical category that helps reveal power relationships.[12] Gender refers to the socially constructed nature of sex roles. One example of this is that earlier in U.S. history (but not among all groups or with one understanding) concepts of womanhood or manhood were understood as biologically determined and unchanging. As Supreme Court Justice David Brewer put it in 1908, "The two sexes differ in the structure of the body, in the functions to be performed by each, in the amount of physical strength, in the capacity for long continuing labor . . . , [in] the self reliance which enables one to assert full rights, and in the capacity to maintain the struggle for subsistence." Woman's "physical structure and a proper discharge of her maternal functions" place her at a disadvantage in that struggle, he continued, and justify legislation to protect her.[13] The assumption that men are self-reliant and that women are not, that men struggle for subsistence and women do not, that women nurture their children and men cannot, reflects the ways in which Justice Brewer and most of his generation understood the implications of being male or female.

More recent thinking about gender challenges biologically essentialist understandings of maleness and femaleness, asserting instead that normative understandings of masculinity and femininity are socially defined ideas projected onto perceived biological differences. It also makes it easy to grasp that, as a social construction, gender has history. Gender practices and ideas about gender change over time and space. Historians ask how the concepts of womanhood and manhood were created, sustained, contested, and altered.

Historians also argue that gendered differences exemplify broader power hierarchies. These social differences and hierarchies have been *systemically created* over time. Economics, law, politics, religion—each has been permeated by assumptions, practices, and expectations that are deeply gendered (as well as shaped by understandings of race, class, and what is understood to be able-bodied).[14] These are so widely shared and so much a part of the ordinary, everyday experience that they acquire an aura of naturalness, rightness, and even inevitability. Common sense dictates that "this is simply the way things are." The price of comprehending the world in this way—whether in the past or in the present—is that it obscures the workings of systems in which economic, political, and cultural forces interact and reinforce each other in ways that benefit some groups and disadvantage others.

Just as historians have argued that gender is a social construction, scholars find that concepts of sex and sexuality change over time. In her study of transsexuality, Joanne Meyerowitz points out that biological differences between men and women are not always clearly distinct. Some people are born with characteristics of more than one sex, as traditionally defined. Furthermore, among experts and medical researchers, understandings of sex difference have not been static. In recent decades, people who desire to alter their sex have been able to do so through surgery and taking hormones. The multiplicity of approaches and the regulations established to reinforce sex differences suggest that the boundaries between male and female can change over time.[15]

And of course sexuality has its own history. Concepts of sexual feelings and behavior, including attitudes toward how erotic desire should be expressed, with whom, and where, vary among cultural groups and, in mainstream Euro-American society, have morphed over time. In the seventeenth century, for example, women were believed to be more lustful and carnal than men. Female sexuality was seen as a source of power and corruption to be feared and controlled. By the nineteenth century, sexuality was redefined. Women—at least white, native-born, middle- and upper-class women—were viewed as having weaker sexual desires than men. Sensuality was attached to working-class and "darker" women—who, so the assumption went, "invited" male advances.[16]

In addition to highlighting women, gender, sex, and sexuality, scholars of women also emphasize the importance of an intersectional approach to studying women. *Intersectionality* reminds us that categories of difference intersect and mutually define one another.[17] In other words, the category of "woman" has different meanings depending on the race, class, citizenship status, sexuality, and able-bodiedness of an individual.

Differences among women are multiple. Differences of culture, nationality, and historical memory are exacerbated by distinctions of race, class, ethnicity, ability, and sexual preference. Each of these differences carries with it implications of hierarchy. As Martha Minow writes, "Women are compared to the unstated norm of men, 'minority' races to white, handicapped persons to the able-bodied, and 'minority' religions to 'majorities.'" Difference is not a neutral term: "A short person is different only in relation to a tall one."[18]

How can we find equality within a society shaped—like all societies—by differences? That is a challenge we continue to face. We may find it helpful to think about two forms of law that coexist in Anglo-American legal tradition. There is "law"—the rules that are understood to apply to every person on the same terms, whatever their sex. When two coworkers do the same job, their wages should be the same. As one judge famously observed in comparing the wages of a maid and a janitor, "dusting is dusting is dusting."[19] And there is a parallel system that we call "equity"—in which courts search for outcomes that have equal impact even though the specifics may be different. What is equal treatment of two coworkers when one can become pregnant and the other cannot? Is maternity leave best understood as vacation leave, sick leave, or something else entirely? What is equality when one partner does the work of maintaining the household and the other does not? In the 1970s, full-time employed women packed an additional twenty-five hours of work—housework and child care—into evenings and weekends each week. While there is evidence that men are doing considerably more than they used to, the gender disparity in housework persists in the twenty-first century, not only in the United States but throughout the world.[20]

Although one provision (Title VII) of the 1964 Civil Rights Act squelched employers' routine habit of limiting certain jobs to one sex (see pp. 745–746), most men and women workers are still employed in occupations where substantial majorities of their coworkers are the same sex. The following statistics reveal how difficult it is to effect structural changes in the labor market. Barely 5 percent of the chief executives at large corporations are women. Historically, once a form of work has been identified with women, it has invariably become associated with low pay and minimal prestige. The overwhelming majority of women are employed in the retail, clerical, and service sectors of the economy. In 2013, for every dollar earned by men, women earned seventy-eight cents; this pay gap has not changed much for the past decade.[21] Finally, juxtapose these facts about the opposite ends of the economic spectrum in the United States: (a) women make up nearly two-thirds of those who hold minimum wage jobs; and (b) a survey of the 2014 graduates of an elite university revealed that among those who had accepted job offers, 19 percent of men and only 4 percent of women were destined to receive the highest starting salaries ($90,000 or more).[22] Much as we would like to think that women and men now occupy level playing fields, the evidence presented here reflects a persistent, societal devaluing of women's work. Why is this so?

HOW TO READ *WOMEN'S AMERICA?*

Women's America invites you to join the continuing expansion of our knowledge by exploring the field of U.S. women's history. Our book offers both *primary sources* (materials that were created during the historical period being studied, e.g., diaries, newspaper articles, letters, government records, photographs), and *secondary sources* (articles or books published by scholars who study history). We encourage you to read both *primary* and *secondary* sources with a critical eye. As you read, ask questions:

- Who wrote or created these sources?
- When and why did they create them?
- How did the historical and legal contexts of their time shape what they recorded and what they did not record? What might we learn from the silences in historical documents and historical writing?
- What assumptions informed these writings?
- Using the primary and secondary sources in this volume, what questions do you think require further research? What subjects do you think have been neglected? When do you see parallels and applications to your communities?

The changing interpretations of the past are referred to as *historiography*—or the history of history writing. Scholars' interpretations vary, based not only on the information they gather, but also on the subtlety of their analysis, the cultural context in which they work, and, to some extent, their own life experiences. That is why we use endnotes—to place the evidence where readers can see it and assess whether the author's interpretations are reasonable and persuasive. You can advance women's history by evaluating previous interpretations, asking new questions, and thinking creatively about sources.

Women's America also encourages you to hone and demonstrate your skills at analyzing images. We have placed visual sources throughout the book—mostly photographs, but also engravings, prints, and posters. Some appear in the essays and documents they are relevant to; for example, in Ruth Milkman's essay on the sexual division of labor during World War II, you will find a photograph of the Women's Airforce Service pilots who named their plane *Pistol Packin' Mama*. Others are grouped in the two Photo Essays, each of which provocatively addresses a big theme over the centuries. Women in Public offers examples of women who placed themselves in the public eye, sometimes risking serious attack. Adorning the Body considers the meanings of appearance. Each image in the book is itself a historical document, adding to what we learn from texts. Each is accompanied by some reflections, to which much can be added by you. With a modest amount of investigation, readers of this book have discovered a great deal about individual images—their creators, the circumstances of their creation, the response or backlash after the image circulated. We hope that scrutinizing these images will prompt you to raise your own questions.

MAJOR THEMES IN *WOMEN'S AMERICA*

Women's America seeks to capture the burgeoning and rich field of U.S. women's history by focusing on six main themes.

- *Family/household/sexuality*: how women and girls are situated in relation to their familial roles and household responsibilities, as well as women's experiences of sexuality and reproduction.
- *Labor/economy/class*: women's engagements in both unpaid and paid labor; women's secondary status within the dominant economy; and the class positions and divisions among women.

- *Race/ethnicity/religion*: how these categories of difference have an impact on women's experiences, identities, and their relationships to one another.
- *Law and citizenship*: how laws, including those governing marriage, reproduction, work, and taxation, shape the choices open to women and men; how changing definitions of citizenship affect women's national identity and their rights and obligations.
- *The global context of U.S. women's history*: how women's lives are intertwined with peoples and developments around the world, including migrations, trade, diplomacy, and war.
- *Women's activism*: how women of diverse backgrounds have been present in virtually all social, cultural, and political movements whether or not these were specifically focused on women; how U.S. women's activism has been in dialogue with allies in other countries and places.

Women's activism has often been described using the metaphor of a wave. The first wave commonly refers to the campaign for women's rights, including suffrage, that stretched from the 1840s to 1920. The second wave describes the women's liberation movement of the 1960s and 1970s. The third wave is used to capture feminist activism of the 1990s and onward. To speak of waves is to oversimplify. Important political work by and on behalf of women occurred outside the so-called wave periods. *Women's America* challenges the wave metaphor by presenting a broad understanding of women's activism.

What are some useful ways to think about feminism? The term came into use in the United States around 1910 when women were engaged in the fight for suffrage and a wide range other reforms. Historian Linda Gordon has offered this definition: "Feminism is a critique of male supremacy, formed and offered in the light of a will to change it, which in turn assumes a conviction that it is changeable."[23] Some of the outspoken women and change agents who appear in this book recognized themselves as feminists; others did not. U.S. history has been populated not by one feminism but by many feminisms.

We invite you to study women's history critically, to take part in a bold enterprise that can eventually lead us to new histories and new pathways of historical investigation. Let's think creatively together about the treasure trove of historical materials presented here. We encourage you to seek out new sources that await discovery in libraries, digital databases, auction houses, museums, family keepsakes, and people's memories.

NOTES

1. Stephen E. Ambrose, *Ike's Spies: Eisenhower and the Espionage Establishment* (New York, 1981; reprint 2012), pp. 182–83.

2. Anne Firor Scott to Linda K. Kerber, May 17, 2009, e-mail communication. Scott first offered such a course at a 1971 University of Washington summer session; her syllabus for GIS 468, "The Search for the American Woman," is in the Mary Aikin Rothschild Papers, Sophia Smith Collection, Smith College, Northampton, Mass. Scott would teach women's history at Duke for the rest of her career.

3. For primary documents that chronicle the founding of a women's studies program at Harvard University (late in the game), including the "propaganda" charge by Harvey C. Mansfield, professor of government, see *Yards and Gates: Gender in Harvard and Radcliffe History*, ed. Laurel Thatcher Ulrich (New York, 2004), pp. 299–302.

4. Elizabeth Cady Stanton, Susan B. Anthony, and Matilda Joslyn Gage, eds., *History of Woman Suffrage*, vol. 1 (New York, 1881), pp. 7–8.

5. Mary R. Beard, *Woman as Force in History: A Study in Traditions and Realities* (New York, 1946), pp. 59–60.

6. For one of the rare ones, see Eleanor Flexner, *Century of Struggle: The Woman's Rights Movement in the United States* (Cambridge, Mass., 1959).

7. Gerda Lerner, "Placing Women in History: Definitions and Challenges," *Feminist Studies* 3 (1975): 5–14; reprinted in Gerda Lerner, *The Majority Finds Its Past: Placing Women in History* (New York, 1979), pp. 145–59. Lerner's essay on the Seneca Falls Convention appears in *Women's America* on pp. 221–227.

8. Edward T. James, Janet Wilson James, and Paul Boyer, eds., *Notable American Women: A Biographical Dictionary*, vols. 1–3: *1607–1950* (Cambridge, Mass., 1971); Barbara Sicherman and Carol Hurd Green, eds., *Notable American Women: A Biographical Dictionary*, vol. 4: *The Modern Period* (Cambridge, Mass., 1980); Susan Ware and Stacy Braukman, eds., *Notable American Women: A Biographical Dictionary*, vol. 5: *Completing the Twentieth Century* (Cambridge, Mass., 2005).

9. For other models, see Barbara Bennett Peterson, ed., *Notable Women of Hawaii* (Honolulu, 1984); Linda K. Kerber, "The 40th Anniversary of *Roe v. Wade*: A Teachable Moment," *Perspectives on History* 50 (October 2012): 65–67; Nicola Foote, Frances Davey, and Kristine De Welde, "Teaching and Researching *Roe vs. Wade*: Responding to Linda Kerber's Call for Historical Action Through a Service-Learning Undergraduate Project," *Perspectives on History* (forthcoming, 2015); and "Weaving Women's Words: Seattle Stories," online at the Jewish Women's Archive, http://jwa.org/communitystories/seattle.

10. Barbara Ransby, *Ella Baker and the Black Freedom Movement: A Radical Democratic Vision* (Chapel Hill, N.C., 2005); Anne Moody, *Coming of Age in Mississippi* (New York, 1968); Chana Kai Lee, *For Freedom's Sake: The Life of Fannie Lou Hamer* (Athens, 1999). Learn why the Ella Baker Center for Human Rights in Oakland, Calif. took her name, and see one of the many biographical accounts available on the web, http://ellabakercenter .org/.

11. Johnny Faragher and Christine Stansell, "Women and Their Families on the Overland Trail to California and Oregon, 1842—1867," *Feminist Studies* 2 (1975): 150–66; Omar S. Valerio-Jiménez, "New Avenues for Domestic Dispute and Divorce Lawsuits Along the U.S. Mexico Border, 1832–1893," *Journal of Women's History* 21 (Spring 2009): 10–33.

12. Joan Wallach Scott, "Gender: A Useful Category of Historical Analysis," *American Historical Review* 91 (Dec. 1986): 1053–75.

13. *Muller v. Oregon*, 208 U.S. 412.

14. On able-bodiedness, see Barbara Young Welke, *Law and the Borders of Belonging in the Long Nineteenth Century United States* (New York, 2010), and Kim E. Nielsen, *A Disability History of the United States* (Boston, 2012).

15. Joanne J. Meyerowitz, *How Sex Changed: A History of Transsexuality in the United States* (Cambridge, Mass., 2002). See the related essay, pp. 615–629.

16. For an overview, see John D'Emilio and Estelle Freedman, *Intimate Matters: A History of Sexuality in America*, 3rd ed. (Chicago, 2012).

17. Kimberle Crenshaw, "Demarginalizing the Intersection of Race and Sex: A Black Feminist Critique of Antidiscrimination Doctrine, Feminist Theory and Antiracist Politics," *University of Chicago Legal Forum* (1989): 139–67; Crenshaw, "Mapping the Margins: Intersectionality, Identity Politics, and Violence Against Women of Color," *Stanford Law Review* 43 (July 1991): 1241–99; Evelyn Brooks Higginbotham, "African American Women's History and the Metalanguage of Race," *Signs* 17 (Winter 1992): 251–74.

18. Martha Minow, "The Supreme Court—1986 Term. Foreword: Justice Engendered," *Harvard Law Review* 101 (1987): 13. Minow points out that "'minority' itself is a relative term. . . . Only in relation to white Westerners are [people of color] minorities."

19. *Equal Employment Opportunities Commission v. Rhode Island*, 549 F. Supp. 60, 66 (1982).

20. Statistics on these matters are reliably kept by the Organisation for Economic Co-Operation and Development (OCED), a nonprofit sponsored by 34 developed countries that collaborate in comparing common policy experiences and identifying good practices. In 2014, the OCED reported that U.S. women spend an average of 126 minutes per day in routine housework; men spend 82 minutes. See http://www.oecd .org/gender/data/balancingpaidworkunpaidworkandleisure.htm.

21. Claire Cain Miller, "Pay Gap Shrinks, but is Still Stubborn," *New York Times*, Sep. 19, 2014, p. B4. See also the American Association of University Women, "The Simple Truth about the Gender Pay Gap" (2014), http://www.aauw.org/research/the-simple-truth-about-the-gender-pay-gap. There is great variability among regions. In 2012, in Washington D.C., women earn 90 percent of what men earn; in Wyoming they earn 64 percent. The gaps are greatest for women of color; Hispanic women earned 53 percent of what white men earned.

22. Claire Cain Miller, "An Elusive Jackpot," *New York Times*, June 8, 2014, p. BU1; The White House, "The Impact of Raising the Minimum Wage on Women," March 2014 Report, http://www.whitehouse.gov/sites/ default/files/docs/20140325minimumwageandwomenreportfinal.pdf. David Madland and Keith Miller, "Raising the Minimum Wage Would Boost the Incomes of Millions of Women and Their Families," Center for American Progress, Dec. 9, 2013, http://americanprogress.org/issues/labor/news/2013/12/09/80497/raising- the-minimum-wage-would-boost-the-incomes-of-millions-of-women-and-their-families. Starting salaries: Rebecca D. Robbins et al., "The Class of 2014 by the Numbers," *Harvard Crimson*, Commencement 2014 issue, Senior Section, http://features.thecrimson.com/2014/senior-survey/. For a perceptive essay on the origins of this pattern, see pp. 128–139.

23. Linda Gordon, quoted in Nancy F. Cott, "What's in a Name? The Limits of 'Social Feminism'; or, Expanding the Vocabulary of Women's History," *Journal of American History* 76 (Dec. 1989): 826.

I

EARLY AMERICA

1600–1820

GENDER FRONTIERS

KATHLEEN M. BROWN
The Anglo-Indian Gender Frontier

The first American women were Native American women. The religious, economic, and political roles that they played in their own societies prior to the arrival of Europeans indicate that Europeans and Native Americans held dramatically different ideas about what women and men should be and should do. The difficulties that Europeans had in understanding the alternative gender realities to which they were exposed tells us how strong is the impulse to view established gender definitions in one's own culture as natural rather than socially constructed. Kathleen M. Brown calls this chasm of understanding a "gender frontier." How did Pocahontas and her father, Powhatan, try to cross those divides to reach common understandings or alliances? If you were assigned to do research in the vast area of Indian women and gender relations before and during contact with visiting and colonizing Europeans, what questions and sources would you pursue?

On a January evening in London in 1617, Pocahontas, daughter of a powerful Virginia *werowance* (paramount chief), sat in attendance with James I and Queen Anne to watch the pageantry of Ben Jonson's masque *The Vision of Delight* unfold. Pocahontas had traveled a long way for this performance. Nine years earlier, as a young girl, she had participated in the first Anglo-Indian contact on the mainland the English called "Virginia." Now, as an adult, she continued the encounter by traveling to London with an entourage of Algonquian-speaking Indians. After making a favorable impression on their royal hosts, the Virginia Algonquians had been invited to join the annual Twelfth Night festivities. One Virginia Company investor noted that Pocahontas and her Indian escort Uttamatomakkin were "well placed" at the masque, meaning that they were not only well positioned for viewing the

spectacle but could easily be seen by other spectators. Seated next to the king and queen, the two visitors became part of the glittering display presented to other guests on this evening of costumed entertainment, an integral part of *The Vision of Delight*.[1]

Part of the appeal of Pocahontas for curious London notables was her reputed transformation to English gentility. The daughter of an Indian werowance . . . [and] a recent convert to Christianity, Pocahontas had relinquished her Indian name, Matoaka, and taken the new name Rebecca. She also spoke English, impressing her hosts with her fluency. Her marriage to English man John Rolfe and the birth of their son completed her [perceived] conversion. . . .

In contrast to Pocahontas, Uttamatomakkin, the trusted councillor of her father who accompanied her to the masque, retained his

Excerpted and slightly revised by the author from "The Anglo-Algonquian Gender Frontier" by Kathleen M. Brown in *Negotiators of Change: Historical Perspectives on Native American Women*, ed. Nancy Shoemaker (London: Routledge, 1995), pp. 26–48, and ch. 2 of *Good Wives, Nasty Wenches, and Anxious Patriarchs: Gender, Race, and Power in Colonial Virginia* (Chapel Hill: University of North Carolina Press, 1996). Reprinted by permission of the author and publishers. Notes have been edited and renumbered.

Indian dress and stubbornly refused to give ground in conversations with English ministers about Christian theology. He remained a skeptic about English symbols of royal authority, moreover, and persisted in judging the English by Indian standards of generosity in gift giving. When James I failed to offer a gift at their meeting, Uttamatomakkin doubted that he was king of the English. . . . Uttamatomakkin was appalled that James lacked the manners and wealth to treat visiting strangers appropriately. When he returned to Virginia, he fulminated against the shortcomings of the English.[2]

With their visit to London in 1616–1617, Pocahontas and Uttamatomakkin traveled along an Anglo-Indian gender frontier they had actively participated in making. During the early English voyages to Roanoake and Jamestown Island, English male adventurers, accompanied by few English women, confronted Indian men and women in their native land. In this cultural encounter, the gender performances of Virginia Algonquians challenged English gentlemen's assumptions about the naturalness of their own gender identities. In the responses of both groups to the other came exchanges, new cultural forms, discoveries of common ground, painful deceptions, bitter misunderstandings, and bloody conflicts.[3]

In both Indian and English societies, differences between men and women were critical to social order. Ethnic identities formed along this "gender frontier," the site of creative and destructive processes resulting from the confrontations of culturally-specific manhoods and womanhoods. In the emerging Anglo-Indian struggle, gender symbols and social relations signified claims to power. Never an absolute barrier, however, the gender frontier also produced sources for new identities and social practices.[4]

In this essay, I explore in two ways the gender frontier that evolved between English settlers and the indigenous peoples of Virginia's tidewater. First, I assess how differences in gender roles shaped the perceptions and interactions of both groups. Second, I analyze the "gendering" of the emerging Anglo-Indian power struggle. While the English depicted themselves as warriors dominating a feminized native population, Indian women and men initially refused to acknowledge [these] claims to military supremacy, treating the foreigners as they would subject peoples,

cowards, or servants. When English warrior discourse became unavoidable, however, Indian women and men attempted to exploit what they saw as the warrior's obvious dependence upon others for the agricultural and reproductive services that ensured group survival.

The indigenous peoples who engaged in this struggle were residents of Virginia's coastal plain, a region of fields, forests, and winding rivers that extended from the shores of the Chesapeake Bay to the mountains and waterfalls near present-day Richmond. Many were affiliated with Powhatan, the werowance who had consolidated several distinct groups under his influence at the time of contact with the English. Most were Algonquian-speakers whose distant cultural roots in the Northeast distinguished them from peoples further south and west where native economies depended more on agriculture and less on hunting and fishing.[5] Although culturally diverse, tidewater inhabitants shared certain features of social organization, commonalities that may have become more pronounced with Powhatan's ambitious chiefdom-building and the arrival of the English. . . .

English gender differences manifested themselves in primary responsibilities and arenas of activity, relationships to property, ideals for conduct, and social identities. Using plow agriculture, rural Englishmen cultivated grain while women oversaw household production, including gardening, dairying, brewing, and spinning. Women also constituted a flexible reserve labor force, performing agricultural work when demand for labor was high, as at harvest time. While Englishmen's property ownership formed the basis of their political existence and identity, most women did not own property [unless] they were no longer subject to a father or husband.[6]

. . . Early seventeenth century, advice-book authors enjoined English women . . . to maintain a modest demeanor. Publicly punishing shrewish and sexually aggressive women, communities enforced this standard of wifely submission as ideal and of wifely domination as intolerable. The sexual activity of poor and unmarried women proved particularly threatening to community order; these "nasty wenches" provided pamphleteers with a foil for the "good wives" female readers were urged to emulate.[7]

How did one know an English good wife when one saw one? Her body and head would be modestly covered. The tools of her work, such as the skimming ladle used in dairying, the distaff of the spinning wheel, and the butter churn reflected her domestic production. When affixed to a man, as in community-initiated shaming rituals, these gender symbols communicated his fall from "natural" dominance and his wife's unnatural authority over him.[8]

Advice-book authors described men's "natural" domain as one of authority derived from his primary economic role. A man's economic assertiveness, mirrored in his authority over wife, child and servant, was emblematized by the plow's penetration of the earth, the master craftsman's ability to shape his raw materials, and the rider's ability to subdue his horse. Although hunting and fishing supplemented the incomes of many Englishmen, formal group hunts . . . remained the preserve of the aristocracy and upper gentry.

The divide between men's and women's activities described by sixteenth- and seventeenth-century authors did not capture the flexibility of gender relations in most English communities. Beliefs in male authority over women and in the primacy of men's economic activities sustained a perception of social order even as women marketed butter, cheese and ale, and cuckolded unlucky husbands.

Gender roles and identities were also important to the Algonquian speakers whom the English encountered along the three major tributaries of the Chesapeake Bay. Like indigenous peoples throughout the Americas, Virginia Algonquians invoked a divine division of labor to explain and justify differences between men's and women's roles on earth. . . . Tidewater Indians described several creator gods, including a malevolent deity named Okeus, who appeared to worshippers as a hunter-warrior. With the right side of his head shaved so that hair would not catch in his bowstring and the left side grown long—a style adopted by Indian men—Okeus epitomized the virility of the Indian bowman.[9]

Although the English collected little information about female deities from the Indian men they questioned, they did take note of at least one goddess. The Patawomeck werowance Iopassus described a divine woman who lived along the road traveled by dead Indians as they approached the home of their creator, a giant hare god. She "hath alwaies her doores open for hospitality," related Iopassus, "and hath at all tymes ready drest greene *Uskatahomen* and *Pokahichary,*" an Indian delicacy made from bruised unripe corn and walnut milk. The consummate Indian hostess, this goddess provided "all manner of pleasant fruicts" and stood in "readines to entertayne all such as do travell to the great hares howse." For the Patawomecks and perhaps for other Virginia Algonquians as well, goddesses set the standard for gracious entertainment and unlimited hospitality.[10]

. . . Indian women's tasks centered on cultivating and processing corn, which provided up to 75 percent of the calories consumed by residents of the coastal plain. In addition, women grew squash, peas, and beans and tended the fires needed for cooking stews and cakes. Women also were responsible for providing much of the material culture of daily life, including clothing, jewelry, and domestic tools and furnishings like pots, baskets, and bedding. Indian women appear to have been active in housebuilding. Their practice of maintaining their own homes, providing kinsmen with basic household necessities, transporting belongings, and building winter houses makes it likely that women provided much of the labor of household construction.[11] . . . Bearing and raising children and mourning the dead rounded out the range of female duties. All were spiritually united by life-giving and its association with earth and agricultural production, sexuality and reproduction. Lineage wealth and political power passed through the female line. Among certain peoples, women may also have had the power to determine the fate of captives, the nugget of truth in the much-embellished tale of Pocahontas's intervention on behalf of Captain John Smith.[12]

Indian women were responsible not only for reproducing the traditional features of their culture, but for much of its adaptive capacity as well. As agriculturalists, women must have had great influence over decisions to move to new grounds, to leave old grounds fallow, and to initiate planting. As producers and consumers of vital household goods and implements, women may have been among the first to feel the impact of new technologies, commodities, and trade. And as accumulators of lineage property, Indian women may have been forced to change strategies as subsistence opportunities shifted.

Indian men assumed a range of responsibilities that complemented those of women. Men cleared new planting grounds of trees. During the spring and summer months, they periodically left villages to fish and hunt, providing highly valued protein. After the final corn harvest, whole villages traveled with their hunters to provide support throughout the winter. Women carried furnishings, cooking implements, and other belongings, setting up temporary winter headquarters. Men's pursuit of game shaped the rhythms of village life during these cold months, just as women's cultivation of crops determined feasts and the allocation of labor during the late spring and summer.[13]

Indian men's social and work roles became distinct from women's at the moment of the *huskanaw*—a male rite of passage—and remained so until the men were too old to hunt or go to war. Young boys chosen by priests to participate in the ceremonial test of manhood endured a physical and psychological trial of several weeks. The English were under the impression that many boys did not survive the ordeal in the woods, which may have included the near-starvation, drug-induced hallucinations, and frequent beatings that later-seventeenth-century observers described. Those who withstood the journey's harrowing approximation of social and physical death began their lives as men with all memories ritually (if not actually) erased. According to Spelman, women attended these ceremonies carrying funeral accoutrements and mourning loudly for the "death" of their young boys. Men departed from the event "merily," having witnessed the ritual male birthing of a new generation of hunters and warriors.[14]

During the prime of manhood, the period of greatest divergence in gender roles, men continued to live in households with women and children. Higher-status men, including local werowances, were recorded by English men as eating separately from the women of the household. In extremely wealthy homes, such as those of polygynous regional werowances, women served meals to seated men. When ordinary men needed to adopt a more virile identity, they may have slept away from women and children, even leaving the village. By ritually separating themselves from women through sexual abstinence, hunters periodically became warriors, taking revenge for killings or initiating their own raids. This adult leave-taking reenacted the separation celebrated in the

huskanaw, in which young boys left their mothers' homes to become men.[15]

Men's hunting and fighting were associated with life-taking, with its ironic relationship to the life-sustaining acts of procreation, protection, and provision. Whereas earth and corn symbolized women, the weapons of the hunt, the trophies taken from the hunted, and the predators of the animal world represented men. Men displayed their status as hunters by wearing bucks' antlers on their heads, claw earrings, bears' teeth necklaces, and snake and weasel skin headdresses. The ritual use of *pocones*, a blood-colored dye, also reflected this gender division. Women anointed their bodies with pocones for sexual encounters and ceremonies celebrating the harvest; men wore it during hunting, warfare, or the ritual celebrations of successes in these endeavors.[16]

The exigencies of the winter hunt, the value placed on meat, and intermittent warfare among native peoples may have been the foundation of male dominance in politics and religious matters. Women were not without their bases of power in Algonquian society, however; their important roles as agriculturalists, reproducers of Indian culture, and caretakers of lineage property kept gender relations in rough balance. Indian women's ability to choose spouses motivated men to be "paynefull" in their hunting and fishing. These same men warily avoided female spaces in which menstruating women may have gathered. By no means equal to men, whose political and religious decisions directed village life, Indian women were perhaps more powerful in their subordination than English women.[17]

Even before the English sailed up the river they renamed the James, however, Indian women's power may have been waning, eroded by Powhatan's chiefdom-building tactics. A "goodly old-man, not yet shrincking," with gray hair and weather-beaten-skin, Powhatan was probably in his seventies when the English met him. During the last quarter of the sixteenth century, perhaps as a consequence of early Spanish forays into the region, he began to add to his inherited chiefdom, coercing and manipulating other coastal residents into economic and military alliances. Powhatan also subverted the matrilineal transmission of political power by appointing his kinsmen to be werowances of villages recently consolidated into his chiefdom. The central military force under his command created opportunities for male recognition in which acts of bravery, rather than matrilineal property or political inheritance, determined privileges. . . . [Powhatan extracted] tribute for promise[d] protection or non-aggression [from him]. He [was thus] appropriating corn, the product of women's labor, from the villages he dominated. He also communicated power and wealth through conspicuous displays of young wives. Through marriages to women drawn from villages throughout his chiefdom, Powhatan emblematized his dominance over the margins of his domain and created kinship ties to strengthen his influence over these villages. With the arrival of the English, the value of male warfare and the symbolism of corn as tribute only intensified, further strengthening the patriarchal tendencies of Powhatan's people.[18]

Conquest seemed justifiable to many English because Native Americans had failed to tame the wilderness according to English standards. Writers claimed they found "only an idle, improvident, scattered people . . . carelesse of anything but from hand to mouth." Most authors compounded impressions of sparse indigenous populations by listing only numbers of fighting men, whom they derided as impotent for their failure to exploit the virgin resources of the "bowells and womb of their Land." The seasonal migration of native groups and the corresponding shift in diet indicated to the English a lack of mastery over the environment, reminding them of animals. John Smith commented, "It is strange to see how their bodies alter with their diet; even as the deare and wild beastes, they seem fat and leane, strong and weak."[19]

The English derision of Indian dependence on the environment and the comparison to animals . . . contained implicit gender meanings. Women's bodies, for example, showed great alteration during pregnancy from fat to lean, strong to weak. English authors often compared female sexual appetites and insubordination to those of wild animals in need of taming. Implicit in all these commentaries was a critique of indigenous men for failing to fulfill the responsibility of economic provision with which the English believed all men to be charged. Lacking private property in the English sense, Indian men, like the Gaelic Irish, appeared to the English to be feminine and not yet civilized to manliness.[20]

For many English observers, natives' "failure" to develop an agricultural economy or dense population was rooted in their gender division of labor. Women's primary responsibility for agriculture merely confirmed the abdication by men of their proper role and explained the "inferiority" of native economies in a land of plenty. [John] Smith commented that "the land is not populous, for the men be fewe; their far greater number is of women and children," a pattern he attributed to inadequate cultivation. Of the significance of women's work and Indian agriculture, he concluded, "When all their fruits be gathered, little els they plant, and this is done by their women and children; neither doth this long suffice them, for neere 3 parts of the yeare, they only observe times and seasons, and live off what the Country naturally affordeth from hand to mouth." In Smith's convoluted analysis, the "failure" of Indian agriculture, implicitly associated in other parts of his text with the "idleness" of men and the reliance upon female labor, had a gendered consequence; native populations became vulnerable and feminized, consisting of many more women and children than of "able men fitt for their warres."[21]

English commentators reacted with disapproval to seeing women perform work relegated to laboring men in England while Indian men pursued activities associated with the English aristocracy. Indian women, George Percy claimed, "doe all their dru[d]gerie. The men takes their pleasure in hunting and their warres, which they are in continually." Observing that the women were heavily burdened and the men only lightly so, John Smith similarly noted "the men bestowe their times in fishing, hunting, wars and such manlike exercises, scorning to be seene in any woman like exercise," while the "women and children do the rest of the worke." Smith's account revealed his discomfort with women's performance of work he considered the most valuable.[22]

The English were hard pressed to explain other Indian behavior without contradicting their own beliefs in the natural and divinely-sanctioned characteristics of men and women. Such was the case with discussions of Indian women's pain during childbirth. . . . Many English writers claimed that Indian women gave birth with little or no pain. Their relatively easy labor appeared to contradict Judeo-Christian traditions in which all women, as products of an original and single divine creation, paid for the sins of Eve. The belief that

The wyfe of an Herowan of Secotan.

Carolina Algonquin woman, drawing by John White, 1585.
This portrait of an Algonquin woman was drawn at her home settlement during the summer of 1585 by John White, the official artist of the English expedition to Roanoke. His drawings are rare representations of Algonquin life before extensive European contact. The woman, who looks skeptically at the viewer, is the wife of a leading male chief or counselor. Her body is decorated with gray, brown, and blue tattoos on the face, neck, arms, and legs. Women's tattoos simulated elaborate necklaces and other ornamentation; men used body paint for ceremonial purposes. (Courtesy of the British Museum. See also Paul Hulton, America 1585: The Complete Drawings of John White *[Chapel Hill: University of North Carolina Press and British Museum Publications, 1984].)*

indigenous women were closer to nature than English women—which implied that English women had labor pains because they were civilized—allowed the English to finesse Indian women's seeming exemption from Eve's curse.[23]

The English were both fascinated and disturbed by other aspects of Native American society through which gender identities were communicated, including hairstyle, dress and make-up. The native male fashion of going clean-shaven, for example, clashed with English associations of beards with male political and sexual maturity, diminishing Indian men's claims to manhood in the eyes of the English. . . . It probably did not enhance English respect for Indian manhood that female barbers sheared men's facial hair.[24]

Most English writers found it difficult to distinguish between the sexual behavior of Chesapeake dwellers and what they viewed as sexual potency conveyed through dress and ritual. English male explorers were particularly fascinated by indigenous women's attire, which seemed scanty and immodest compared to English women's multiple layers and wraps. John Smith described an entertainment arranged for him in which "30 young women came naked out of the woods (only covered behind and before with a few greene leaves), their bodies al painted." Several other writers commented that Native Americans "goe altogether naked," or had "scarce to cover their nakednesse." Smith claimed, however, that the women were "alwaies covered about their midles with a skin and very shamefast to be seene bare." Yet he noted, as did several other English travelers, the body adornments, including beads, paintings, and tattoos, that were visible on Indian women's legs, hands, breasts, and faces. Perhaps some of the "shamefastness" reported by Smith resulted from Englishmen's close scrutiny of Indian women's bodies.[25]

For most English writers, Indian manners and customs reinforced an impression of sexual passion. Hospitality that included sexual privileges, for instance sending "a woman fresh painted red with *Pocones* and oile" to be the "bedfellow" of a guest, may have confirmed in the minds of Englishmen that Indians were licentious. Smith's experience with the thirty women, clad in leaves, body paint, and buck's horns and emitting "hellish cries and shouts," undoubtedly strengthened the English association of Indian culture with unbridled passion: "they solemnly invited Smith to their lodging, but no sooner was hee within the house, but all these Nimphes more tormented him than ever, with crowding, and pressing, and hanging upon him, most tediously crying, *love you not mee*."[26] Such incidents left the English with a vivid impression of unconstrained sexuality that in their own culture could mean only promiscuity. . . .

Although the dominant strand of English discourse about Indian men denounced them for being savage and failed providers, not all Englishmen shared these assessments of the meaning of cultural differences. Throughout the early years of settlement, male laborers deserted military compounds to escape puny rations, disease and harsh discipline, preferring to take their chances with local Indians whom they knew had food aplenty. Young boys like Henry Spelman, moreover, had nearly as much to fear from the English, who used him as a hostage, as he did from his Indian hosts. Spelman witnessed and participated in Indian culture from a very different perspective than most Virginia chroniclers. While . . . John Smith described Indian entertainments as horrible antics, Spelman coolly noted that Patawomeck dances bore a remarkable resemblance to the Darbyshire hornpipe. . . .

. . . After a period of homesickness provoked him to escape his duties as a hostage among the Powhatans, Spelman returned to live in relative security among [the group he was assigned to live with,] the Patawomecks. He formed close bonds with the Patawomeck werowance and at least one of his children, whom he could reputedly quiet better than any other person in the werowance's household.[27]

Even among men more elite and more widely traveled than Spelman, a lurking and disquieting suspicion that Indian men were men like the English disrupted discourses about natural savagery and inferiority. Smith, the only Jamestown leader of yeoman background, often explained Indian complexions and superior resistance to the elements as a result of conditioning and daily practice rather than of nature. Indian women had trained their children from early infancy to endure cold river baths, Smith believed, thus enabling their sons (although presumably the same could have been said of daughters) to withstand physical discomforts in later life: "They are very strong, of an able body and full of agilitie, able to endure to lie in the woods under a tree by the fire, in the worst of winter, or in the weedes and grasse, in Ambuscado in the Sommer."[28] . . .

English leaders at Jamestown also created areas of common ground with Algonquians through exchanges of gifts, shared entertainments, and feasts. The need to deal with Indians on Indian terms and in Indian ways enhanced the overlap between the two cultures during the first two years of English settlement. Drawn into Indian cultural expressions despite himself, Smith gave gifts when he would have preferred to barter. . . . Despite flamboyant rhetoric about savage warriors lurking in the forests like animals, Smith soon had English men learning to fight in the woods. He clearly thought his manly English, many of whom could barely fire a gun, had much to learn from their Indian opponents.[29] . . .

Most English writers did not dwell on these areas of similarity and exchange, but emphasized the "wild" and animalistic qualities of tidewater peoples. Descriptions of Indian warfare, sexual behavior, and religion inspired fear and supported English claims to dominance and superiority. As much as animals fell below humans in the hierarchy of the natural world, so the Indians of English chronicles inhabited a place that was technologically, socially, and morally beneath that of the civilized English. Through depictions of feminized, impotent, male "naturalls," English men reworked Anglo-Indian relations, portraying themselves as the "naturally" dominant men of gender relations. In so doing, they contributed to an emerging male colonial identity that was deeply rooted in English gender discourses.

The gendering of Anglo-Indian relations in English writing was not without contest and contradiction, nor did it lead inevitably to easy conclusions of English dominance. Englishmen incorporated Indian ways into their diets and military tactics, and Indian women into their sexual lives. Some formed close bonds with Indian companions, while others lived to father their own "naturall" progeny. . . . Colonial domination was a complex process involving sexual intimacy, cultural incorporation, and self-scrutiny.

The Englishmen who landed on the shores of Chesapeake Bay and the James River were not the first European men that Virginia Algonquians had seen. During the 1570s, Spanish Jesuits established a short-lived mission near the James River tributary that folded with the murder of the clerics. The Spaniards who revenged the Jesuit deaths left an unfavorable impression upon local Chickahominy, Paspegh, and Kecoughtan Indians. [In addition,] at least one English ship also predated the 1607 arrival of the Jamestown settlers; its captain was long remembered for killing a Rappahannock river werowance.[30]

The maleness of English explorers' parties and early settlements undoubtedly raised Indian suspicions of bellicose motives. Interrogating Smith at their first meeting about the purpose of the English voyage, Powhatan was apparently satisfied with Smith's answer that the English presence was temporary. Smith claimed his men sought passage to "the backe Sea," the ever elusive water route to India which they believed lay beyond the falls of the Chesapeake river system. . . . The explanation may have initially seemed credible to Powhatan because the English expedition consisted only of men and boys. Frequent English military drills in the woods and the construction of a fort at Jamestown, however, may have aroused his suspicions that the English strangers planned a longer and more violent stay.[31]

Equipped with impressive blasting guns, the English may have found it easy to perpetuate the warrior image from afar; up close was a different matter, however. English men were pale, hairy, and awkward compared to Indian men. They also had the dirty habit of letting facial hair grow so that it obscured the bottom part of their faces where it collected food and other debris. Their clumsy stomping through the woods announced their presence to friends, enemies, and wildlife alike and they were forced, on at least one very public occasion, to ask for Indian assistance when their boats became mired in river ooze. Perhaps worst of all from the perspective of Indian people who valued a warrior's stoicism in the face of death, the Englishmen they captured and killed died screaming and whimpering. William Strachey recorded the mocking song sung by Indian men sometime in 1611, in which they ridiculed "what lamentation our people made when they kild him, namely saying how they [the Englishmen] would cry whe, whe."[32]

Indian assumptions about masculinity may have led Powhatan to over-estimate the vulnerability of Smith's men. The gentlemen and artisans who were the first to arrive in Virginia proved to be dismal farmers, remaining wholly dependent upon native corn stores during their first three years and partially dependent thereafter. They tried, futilely, to persuade Indians to grow more corn to meet their needs, but their requests were greeted with scorn by Indian men who found no glory in the "woman-like exercise" of farming. Perhaps believing that the male settlement would always require another population to supply it, Powhatan tried to use the threat of starvation to level the playing field with the English. During trade negotiations with Smith in January 1609, Powhatan held out for guns and swords, claiming disingenuously that corn was more valuable to him than copper trinkets because he could eat it.[33]

When Powhatan and other Indian peoples reminded Smith of his dependence upon Indian food supplies, Smith reacted with anger. In his first account of Virginia, he recalled with bitterness the scorn of the Kecoughtan Indians for "a famished man": they "would in derision offer him a handfull of Corne, a peece of bread." Such treatment signified both indigence and female vulnerability to the English, made worse by the fact that the crops they needed were grown by women. At Kecoughtan, Smith responded by "let[ting] fly his muskets" to provoke a Kecoughtan retreat and then killing several men at close range. The survivors fell back in confusion, allowing the image of their god Okeus to fall into English hands. After this display of force, he found the Kecoughtan "content" to let the English dictate the terms of trade: Kecoughtan corn in exchange for copper, beads, hatchets, and the return of Okeus. The English thus used their superior weaponry to transform themselves from scorned men into respected warriors and to recast the relationship: humble agriculturists became duty-bound to produce for those who spared their lives.[34]

Powhatan's interactions with Englishmen may also have been guided by his assessment of the gender imbalance among them. His provision of women to entertain English male guests was a political gesture whose message seems to have been misunderstood as sexual license by the English. . . . Powhatan may also have believed that by encouraging English warriors' sexual activity, he might diminish their military potency . . . Ultimately, Powhatan may have hoped that intimacy between native women and English men would lead to an integration of the foreigners and a diffusion of

the threat they presented. . . . Powhatan's gesture, however, only reinforced the English rationale for subjugating the "uncivilized" and offered English men an opportunity to express the Anglo-Indian power relationship sexually with native women.[35]

Indian women were often more successful than Powhatan in manipulating Englishmen's desires for sexual intimacy. At the James River village of Appocant in late 1607, the unfortunate George Cawson met his death when village women "enticed [him] up from the barge into their howses." Oppossunoquonuske, a clever *werowansqua* of another village, similarly led fourteen Englishmen to their demise. Inviting the unwary men to come "up into her Towne, to feast and make Merry," she convinced them to "leave their Armes in their boat, because they said how their women would be afrayd ells of their pieces."[36]

Although both of these accounts are cautionary tales that represent Indians literally as feminine seducers capable of entrapping Englishmen in the web of their own sexual desires, the incidents suggest Indian women's canny assessment of the men who would be colonial conquerors. Exploiting Englishmen's hopes for colonial pleasures, Indian women dangled before them the opportunity for sexual intimacy, turning a female tradition of sexual hospitality into a weapon of war. Acknowledging the capacity of English "pieces" to terrorize Indian women, Oppossunoquonuske tacitly recognized Englishmen's dependence on their guns to construct self-images of bold and masculine conquerors. Her genius lay in convincing them to rely on other masculine "pieces." When she succeeded in getting Englishmen to set aside one colonial masculine identity—the warrior—for another—the lover of native women—the men were easily killed. . . .

. . . Algonquians tried to maneuver the English into positions of political subordination. Smith's account of his captivity, nearexecution, and rescue by Pocahontas was undoubtedly part of an adoption ritual in which Powhatan defined his relationship to Smith as one of patriarchal dominance. Smith became Powhatan's prisoner after warriors easily slew his English companions and then "missed" with nearly all of the twenty or thirty arrows they aimed at Smith himself. Clearly, Powhatan wanted Smith brought to him alive. Smith reported that during his captivity he was offered "life, libertie, land and women," prizes Powhatan must have believed to be very attractive to Englishmen, in exchange for information about how best to capture Jamestown: After ceremonies and consultations with priests, Powhatan brought Smith before an assembly where, Smith later claimed, Pocahontas risked her own life to prevent him from being clubbed to death by executioners. It seems that Smith understood neither the ritual adoption taking place nor the significance of Powhatan's promise to make him a werowance and to "for ever esteeme him as [he did] his son Nantaquoud."[37]

After returning Smith to Jamestown, Powhatan showered him with gifts of food and entreaties to take up his kingdom as a subordinate werowance. Although interested in both the land and the corn, Smith wanted to avoid making gestures of obeisance. Upon a subsequent visit to Powhatan, the werowance assured Smith he would receive his due but that "he expected to have all these [Smith's] men lay their armes at his feet, as did his subjects." Smith demurred at the implied subordination, claiming that only an enemy of the English would expect them to disarm. Powhatan again repeated his offer to Smith, urging the adoptive relationship upon him. Pronouncing him "a werowanes of Powhatan, and that all his subjects should so esteeme us," Powhatan integrated Smith and his men into his own chieftancy, declaring "no man account us strangers nor Paspaheghans, but Powhatans, and that the Corne, weomen and Country, should be to us as to his owne people."[38] . . .

That Smith's rejection of Powhatan's claims to benevolent fatherhood was not simply an attempt to retain the upper hand but also a refusal to accept the implied obligation of the relationship as Indians perceived it became evident only much later, during Smith's final conversation with Pocahontas in 1617. Having been in England for nearly six months, Pocahontas was surprised to see Smith for the first time only near the end of her stay [there]. According to Smith's account, she upbraided him for his rudeness and failure to reciprocate the hospitality the Algonquians had shown him. After "remembr[ing] [Smith] well what courtesies shee had done," she focused on Smith's betrayal of her father. "You did promise Powhatan what was yours should bee his, and he the like to you," Smith recalled her saying. "You called him father being in his land a stranger, and by the same reason so must

I doe you." Recounting the words with which the two men had become fictive kin, Pocahontas noted that Smith had failed to do for her, a stranger to his land, what her father had done for him. Also, he had reneged on his promise to share with Powhatan all that was his. . . .[39]

With false modesty and calculated deference, Smith demurred that a king's daughter should call him father. Pocahontas, he noted, responded angrily, taunting Smith, asking him how it was that in the safety of his own country he should fear being called father when he had shown no qualms about invading Powhatan's country, causing "feare in him and all his people (but mee)." Pocahontas insisted: "I tell you then I will [call you father], and you shall call mee childe, and so I will bee for ever and ever your Countrieman." With this remark, Pocahontas recast the politics and the meaning of her conversion to Englishness. No longer simply the adoption of a new language, strange religion, and foreign manners, Pocahontas's transformation implied mutual obligations that originated with the promises exchanged by Powhatan and Smith. She interpreted her Englishness as a consequence of the relationship between the two men, through which Smith as well as the daughter of Powhatan should have been transformed.[40]

Despite her fashionable English dress and hat, Pocahontas held Smith to an Indian standard of reciprocity and exchange. By transferring the burden of obligation to Smith, she challenged depictions of Powhatan's daughter as indebted to the English for the gift of civilization. Her words, undoubtedly altered somewhat by the self-serving Smith, nonetheless suggest that her own view of her conversion was considerably more complicated than either Smith or the Virginia Company would ever understand.

The first decade of encounter between English and Indian peoples wrought changes in the gender relations of both societies. Contact bred trade, political reshuffling, sexual intimacy, and warfare, [and, for the indigenous, unfamiliar illnesses and a spike in deaths due to diseases spread by Europeans]. The very process of confrontation between two groups with male-dominated political and religious systems initially may have strengthened the value of patriarchy for each.

The rapid change in Indian life and culture had a particularly devastating impact upon women. Many women, whose office it was to bury and mourn the dead, may have been relegated to perpetual grieving. Corn was also uniquely the provenance of women; economically it was the source of female authority, and religiously and symbolically they were identified with it. The wanton burning and pillaging of corn supplies, through which the English transformed their dependence into domination, may have represented to indigenous residents an egregious violation of women.

English dominance in the region [especially after 1644] ultimately led to the decline of the native population and its way of life. As a consequence of war, nutritional deprivation, and disease, Virginia Indians were reduced in numbers from the approximately 14,000 inhabitants of the Chesapeake Bay and tidewater in 1607 to less than 3,000 by the early eighteenth century. White settlement forced tidewater dwellers farther west, rupturing the connections between ritual activity, lineage, and geographic place. [Indigenous] priests lost credibility as traditional medicines failed to cure new diseases, while confederacies such as Powhatan's declined and disappeared. Uprooted tidewater peoples also encountered opposition from piedmont [inland] inhabitants upon whose territory they encroached. Ironically, the destruction of Powhatan's carefully nurtured political institutions and of Indian societies themselves opened up opportunities for individual women to assume leadership over tribal remnants by the mid-seventeenth century.[41]

The English, meanwhile, emerged from these early years of settlement with gender roles more explicitly defined in English, Christian, and yeoman terms. This core of English identity proved remarkably resilient, persisting through seventy years of wars with neighboring Indians and continuing to evolve as English settlers imported Africans to work the colony's tobacco fields. Initially serving to legitimate the destruction of traditional Indian ways of life, this concept of Englishness ultimately constituted one of the most powerful legacies of the Anglo-Indian gender frontier.

NOTES

1. Philip L. Barbour, *Pocahontas and Her World: A Chronicle of America's First Settlement* (Boston, 1970), 176–176, 179.

2. John Smith, *The Generall Historie of Virginia, New-England, and the Summer Isles . . .* (1624), in *The*

Complete Works of Captain John Smith (1580–1631), ed. Philip L. Barbour, 3 vols. (Chapel Hill, N.C., 1986) (hereafter, *CWJS*), II, 261.

3. For "performances" as used here, see Judith Butler, "Gender Trouble," in Linda J. Nicholson, ed., *Feminism/Postmodernism* (New York, 1990), 336–339.

4. For analyses of economic, linguistic, and religious "frontiers," see James Merrell, "'The Customes of Our Country': Indians and Colonists in Early America," in *Strangers Within the Realm: Cultural Margins of the First British Empire*, ed. Bernard Bailyn and Phillip D. Morgan (Chapel Hill, N.C., 1991), 117–156. In no way separate or distinct, the gender frontier infiltrated other frontiers we usually describe as economic, social, or cultural. See Kathleen M. Brown, "Brave New Worlds: Women's and Gender History," *William and Mary Quarterly*, 3rd ser., 50 (April 1993), 311–328.

5. See, for example, Ben C. McCary, *Indians in Seventeenth Century Virginia* (Williamsburg, Va., 1957); Helen C. Rountree, *The Powhatan Indians of Virginia: Their Traditional Culture* (Norman, Okla., 1989), 17–31, 151–52; Helen C. Rountree, *Pocahontas's People: The Powhatan Indians of Virginia through Four Centuries* (Norman, Okla., 1990); G. Melvin Herndon, "Indian Agriculture in the Southern Colonies," *North Carolina Historical Review* 44 (1967), 283–297; and Nancy Oestreich Lurie, "Indian Cultural Adjustment to European Civilization," in *Seventeenth-Century America: Essays in Colonial History*, ed. James Morton Smith (Chapel Hill, N.C., 1959), 40–42. The groups under Powhatan's mantle of authority included the Pamunkey, Kecoughtan, Mattaponi, Appamattuck, Rappahannock, Piankatank, Chiskiack, Werowocomoco, Nansemond, and Chesapeake.

6. Among the most useful accounts of English agriculture are Joan Thirsk, ed., *The Agrarian History of England and Wales*, 6 vols. (Cambridge, 1967), vol. 4; K. D. M. Snell, *Annals of the Laboring Poor: Social Change and Agrarian England, 1660–1900* (Cambridge, 1985); and Ann Kussmaul, *Servants in Husbandry in Early Modern England* (Cambridge, 1981).

7. See Susan Dwyer Amussen, *An Ordered Society: Gender and Class in Early Modern England* (New York, 1988), ch. 2; William Gouge, *Domesticall Duties* (London, 1622); Richard Brathwait, *The English Gentlewoman* (London, 1631); Gervase Markham, *Country Contentments or the English Housewife* (London, 1623). For the terms "good wives" and "nasty wenches," see John Hammond, *Leah and Rachel, or the Two Fruitfull Sisters* (London, 1656).

8. Martin Ingram, "Ridings Rough Music, and the 'Reform of Popular Culture,' in Early Modern England," *Past and Present* 105 (Nov. 1984), 78–113; D. E. Underdown, "Taming of the Scold: The Enforcement of Patriarchal Authority in Early Modern England," in *Order and Disorder in Early Modern England*, ed. Anthony Fletcher and John Stevenson (New York, 1985), 116–136.

9. Smith, *Generall Historie*, in *CWJS*, II, 121–125; William Strachey, *The Historie of Travell into Virginia Britania*, ed. Louis B. Wright and Virginia Freund (London, 1953), 89, 103 (hereafter, *HTVB*); Rountree, *Powhatan Indians*, 135–138; Charles Hudson, *The Southeastern Indians* (Knoxville, Tenn., 1976), 148–149.

10. *HTVB,* 103. The dearth of information about female goddesses may have resulted from the relative uninterest of English Protestants and their habit of talking mainly to Indian men.

11. Edwin Randolph Turner III, "An Archaeological and Ethnohistorical Study on the Evolution of Rank Socieites in the Virginia Coastal Plain" (Ph.D. diss., Pennsylvania State University, 1976), 182–187; Rountree, *Powhatan Indians,* 45–54, 63–65, 90; Rountree, *Pocahontas's People,* 88. For primary accounts of Algonquian agriculture and women's work, see Henry Spelman, *Relation of Virginea,* in *Travels and Works of Captain John Smith,* ed. Edward Archer and A. G. Bradley, 2 vols. (Edinburgh, 1910) (hereafter *TWJS*), I, cvii, cxi–cxii; and John Smith, *Map of Virginia . . . ,* in *CWJS,* I, 157–159.

12. Rountree, *Powhatan Indians,* 84, 86, 88 n. 2.

13. Smith, *Generall Historie,* in *CWJS,* II, 118, 178; *HTVB,* 81; Spelman, *Relation of Virginea,* in *TWJS,* I, cvii; Rountree, *Powhatan Indians,* 32–35.

14. Smith, *Generall Historie,* in *CWJS,* II, 124–125, 178; Spelman, *Relation of Virginea,* in *TWJS,* I, cvi.

15. Smith, *Generall Historie,* in *CWJS,* II, 124–125; Rountree, *Powhatan Indians,* 88, 94; J. Leitch Wright, Jr., *The Only Land They Knew: The Tragic Story of the American Indians in the Old South* (New York, 1981), 8–14; Hudson, *Southeastern Indians,* 148–156, 258–260.

16. Hudson, *Southeastern Indians,* 259; Smith, *Generall Historie,* in *CWJS,* II, 147–148, 155.

17. *HTVB,* 83, 84.

18. Ibid., 40, 44, 57 (description of Powhatan), 62, 65–69; Spelman, *Relation of Virginea,* in *TWJS,* I, cxiv.

19. John Smith, *The Proceedings of the English Colony in Virginia . . .* (London, 1612), in *CWJS,* I, 257; *HTVB,* 24; Smith, *Map of Virginia,* in *CWJS,* I, 162–163.

20. V. G. Kiernan, "Private Property in History," in *Family and Inheritance: Rural Society in Western Europe, 1200–1800,* ed. Jack Goody et al. (Cambridge, 1976), 361–398.

21. Smith, *Generall Historie,* in *CWJS,* II, 114; Smith, *Map of Virginia,* ibid., I, 146–148.

22. George Percy, *Observations by Master George Percy, 1607* (1607), in *Narratives of Early Virginia, 1606–1625,* ed. Lyon Gardiner Tyler (New York, 1907) (hereafter, *NEV*), 18; Smith, *Map of Virginia,* in *CWJS,* II, 162, 164. See also David D. Smits, "'The Squaw Drudge': A Prime Index of Savagism," *Ethnohistory* 29 (1982), 281–306.

23. John Smith, *Description of Virginia and Proceedings of the Colonie* (London, 1612), in *NEV,* 99; Anne Laurence, "The Cradle to the Grave: English Observation of Irish Social Customs in the Seventeenth Century," *The Seventeenth Century* 3 (Spring 1988), 66–75; Jo Murphy-Lawless, "Images of Poor Women in the Writings of Irish Men Midwives," in *Women in Early Modern Ireland,* ed. Margaret MacCurtain and Mary O'Dowd (Edinburgh, 1991), 291–303.

24. Smith, *Generall Historie,* in *CWJS,* II, 173. For the deeper reverberations of different clothing and naming practices, see James Axtell, *The European and the Indian: Essays in the Ethnohistory of Colonial North America* (New York, 1981), 45, 47–55, 57–60.

25. Smith, *Proceedings of the English Colonies,* in *CWJS,* I, 235–236; Thomas Hariot, *A Briefe and True Report of the New Found Land of Virginia* (London, 1588; reprint, New York, 1903), E2–E3; Percy, *Observations,* in *NEV,* 12; Smith, *Map of Virginia,* in *CWJS,* I, 161.

26. Smith, *Proceedings of the English Colonies,* in *CWJS,* I, 236.

27. Spelman, *Relation of Virginea,* in *TWJS,* I, cviii, cxiv.

28. Smith, *Map of Virginia,* in *CWJS,* I, 160.

29. John Smith, *A True Relation of Such Occurences and Accidents of Note, as Hath Hapned in Virginia . . . ,* in *CWJS,* I, 54–55, 85.

30. James Axtell, *Beyond 1492: Encounters in Colonial North America* (New York, 1992), 104; Rountree, *Powhatan Indians,* 142; Rountree, *Pocahontas's People,* 15–18.

31. Smith, *True Relation,* in *CWJS,* I, 39, 91.

32. Axtell, *Beyond 1492,* 101; *HTVB,* 86.

33. Rountree, *Powhatan Indians,* 89; Smith, *Proceedings of the English Colonies,* in *CWJS,* I, 246.

34. Smith, *Proceedings of the English Colonies,* in *CWJS,* I, 248. See ibid., II, 247, for allusions to English dependence in Powhatan's speech to Smith. See Smith, *Proceedings of the English Colonies,* in *CWJS,* I, for Smith's admission of dependence on native corn supplies. For Smith on the engagement with the Kecoughtan, see *Generall Historie,* ibid., II, 144–145.

35. See Axtell, *Beyond 1492,* 31–32, 39, 45, and 102, for the claim that, whereas Europeans stressed sharp distinctions between Europeans and non-Europeans, Indians tended to stress the similarities.

36. *HTVB,* 60, 64.

37. Smith, *True Relation,* in *CWJS,* I, 45; Smith, *Generall Historie,* ibid., II, 147–151.

38. Smith, *True Relation,* in *CWJS,* I, 61–67.

39. Smith, *Generall Historie,* in *CWJS,* II, 260–262.

40. Ibid., 261; Peter Hulme, *Colonial Encounters: Europe and the Native Caribbean, 1492–1797* (London, 1986), 146–147, 151–152, 156.

41. Hudson, *Southeastern Indians,* ch. 8; Timothy Silver, *A New Face on the Countryside: Indians, Colonists, and Slaves in South Atlantic Forests, 1500–1800* (New York, 1990), 72, 74–83, 87–88, 91, 102; Alfred W. Crosby, *Ecological Imperialism: The Biological Expansion of Europe, 900–1900* (Cambridge, 1986), 195–216; Wright, *Only Land They Knew,* 24–26; Peter Wood, "The Changing Population of the Colonial South," in Peter Wood et al., eds., *Powhatan's Mantle: Indians in the Colonial Southeast* (Lincoln, Nebr., 1989), 38, 40–42. See Martha McCartney, "Cockacoeske, Queen of the Pamunkey: Diplomat and Suzeraine," in ibid., 173–195; Robert Steven Grumet, "Sunsquaws, Shamans, and Tradeswomen: Middle Atlantic Coastal Algonqian Women during the Seventeenth and Eighteenth Centuries," in *Women and Colonization: Anthropological Perspectives,* ed. Mona Etienne and Eleanor Leacock (New York, 1980), 43–62.

JENNIFER L. MORGAN

"Some Could Suckle over Their Shoulder": European Depictions of Indigenous Women, 1492–1750

Of all the women who crossed the Atlantic east to west between 1492 and 1800, four-fifths made the journey from African homelands. They were fully one-third of the Africans compelled to embark on the infamous Middle Passage. White European women were a small proportion of female migrants—forced or voluntary—because of the insatiable demand of New World planters, especially in Brazil and the Caribbean (then referred to as the West Indies), for laborers to harvest profitable crops like sugarcane. These taskmasters were not averse to using girls and women as laborers.* Thus, while middling-status European women were likely to experience the hope, anxiety, and exhilaration that could come with establishing a homestead in a new land, far more African women were fated to associate the American continent with severe trauma, ongoing despair, and cultural loss.

The merchant capitalists, investors, and planters who promoted New World colonization had little compunction about subjecting poor, uneducated European working men, women, and children to a host of exploitative, coercive labor systems. But they forced upon the eight million Africans carried off in the transatlantic slave trade even more degrading conditions—both on slave ships and on American plantations. How did they justify this behavior to themselves? We cannot point simply to racism, because a concept of race as a biologically hereditable set of traits congealed only in the nineteenth century. In the sixteenth century, educated Europeans believed that all humans descended from a common ancestor and thus shared a common humanity. "Race" was used mostly to indicate national origin or lineage. Skin color was not seen as an immutable marker of difference; many believed one's complexion would change according to how close one lived to the equator. Jennifer Morgan's essay forces us to grapple with how Europeans and Africans alike called into being the categories of blackness and whiteness.

To understand the process, Morgan argues, we must pay attention to Europeans' depictions of women's bodies and sexuality in the travel narratives of the time. The narratives' authors, European adventurers of the sixteenth to eighteenth centuries, can be thought of as early ethnographers in that they engaged in the close description of human cultures. Travelers to Africa borrowed tropes (i.e., significant themes or motifs) from earlier accounts written about indigenous American women. How did European depictions of African women change between the

---

*Jennifer L. Morgan, "Slavery and the Slave Trade," in *A Companion to American Women's History*, ed. Nancy A. Hewitt (Malden, Mass.: Blackwell, 2002), pp. 20–34.

1550s and the 1770s? Do you agree that these imaginary presentations amounted to "porno-tropical writings"? Does Morgan convince you about their boundary-making power? Morgan's analysis helps us understand not only the impact of these texts and their accompanying pictures on English readers, but also the enduring legacy they created for African and African-descended women and men in the Americas.*

Ideas about black sexuality and misconceptions about black female sexual behavior formed the cornerstone of Europeans' and Euro-Americans' general attitudes toward slavery.[1] Arguably, the sexual stereotypes levied against African-American women in the nineteenth and twentieth centuries were so powerful because of the depth and utility of their roots. Before they came into contact with enslaved women either in West Africa or on American plantations, slaveowners' images and beliefs about race and savagery were indelibly marked on the women's bodies. . . . For European travelers, both those who settled in the Americas and those who did not, the enslavement of African laborers required a sense of moral and social distance over those they would enslave. They acquired that distance in part through manipulating symbolic representations of African women's sexuality. In so doing, European men gradually brought African women into focus—women whose pain-free reproduction (at least to European men) indicated that they did not descend from Eve and who illustrated their proclivity for hard work through their ability to simultaneously till the soil and birth a child. Such imaginary women suggested an immutable difference between Africans and Europeans, a difference ultimately codified as race. . . .

Prior to their entry onto the stage of New World conquests, women of African descent lived in bodies unmarked by what would emerge as Europe's preoccupation with physiognomy—skin color, hair texture, and facial features presumed to be evidence of cultural deficiency. Not until the gaze of European travelers fell upon them would African women see themselves, or indeed one another, as defined by "racial" characteristics. During the decades after European arrival to the Americas, as

various nations gained and lost footholds, followed fairytale rivers of gold, traded with and decimated Native inhabitants, and ignored and mobilized Christian notions of conversion and just wars, English settlers constructed an elaborate edifice of forced labor on the foundation of emerging categories of race and reproduction. The process of calling blackness into being and causing it to become inextricable from brute labor took place in legislative acts, laws, wills, bills of sale, and plantation inventories just as it did in journals and adventurers' tales of travels. Indeed, the gap between intimate experience (the Africans with whom one lived and worked) and ideology (monstrous, barely human savages) would be bridged in the hearts and minds of prosaic settlers rather than in the tales of worldly adventurers. . . . I turn here to travel narratives to explore developing categories of race and racial slavery. . . .

The connections between forced labor and race became increasingly important. . . . A concept of "race" rooted firmly in biology is primarily a late eighteenth- and early nineteenth-century phenomenon. . . . As travelers and men of letters thought through the thorny entanglements of skin color, complexion, features, and hair texture [over the course of the sixteenth and seventeenth centuries], they constructed weighty notions of civility, nationhood, citizenship, and manliness on the foundation of the amalgam of nature and culture. Given the ways in which appearance became a trope for civility and morality, it is no surprise to find gender located at the heart of Europeans' encounter with and musings over the connection between bodies and Atlantic economies.

In June 1647, Englishman Richard Ligon left London on the ship *Achilles* to establish himself as a planter in the newly settled colony

---

*A set of the illustrations analyzed by Morgan appears in an earlier version of this essay, "'Some Could Suckle over Their Shoulder': Male Travelers, Female Bodies, and the Gendering of Racial Ideology, 1500–1770," *William and Mary Quarterly*, 3rd ser., 54 (Jan. 1997): 167–92 (accessible online in some college libraries via the database JSTOR).

of Barbados. En route, Ligon's ship stopped in the Cape Verde islands for provisions and trade. There Ligon saw a black woman for the first time. He recorded the encounter in his *True and Exact History of Barbadoes*: she was a "Negro of the greatest beauty and majesty together: that ever I saw in one woman. Her stature large, and excellently shap'd, well favour'd, full eye'd, and admirably grac'd . . . [I] awaited her comming out, which was with far greater Majesty and gracefulness, than I have seen Queen Anne, descend from the Chaire of State." Ligon's rhetoric must have surprised his English readers, for seventeenth-century images of black women did not usually evoke the monarchy as the referent. . . .[2]

[But] over the course of his journey, Richard Ligon came to another view of black women. He wrote that their breasts "hang down below their Navels, so that when they stoop at their common work of weeding, they hang almost to the ground, that at a distance you would think they had six legs." In this context, black women's monstrous bodies symbolized their sole utility—the ability to produce both crops and other laborers.[3] It is this dual value, sometimes explicit and sometimes lurking in the background of slaveowners' decision-making processes, that would come to define women's experience of enslavement most critically. . . .

As Ligon penned his manuscript while in debtors prison in 1653, he constructed a layered narrative in which the discovery of African women's monstrosity helped to assure the work's success. Taking the female body as a symbol of the deceptive beauty and ultimate savagery of blackness, Ligon allowed his readers to dally with him among beautiful black women, only to seductively disclose their monstrosity over the course of the narrative. Ligon's narrative is a microcosm of a much-larger ideological maneuver that juxtaposed the familiar with the unfamiliar—the beautiful woman who is also the monstrous laboring beast. As the tenacious and historically deep roots of racialist ideology become more evident, it becomes clear also that, through the rubric of monstrously "raced" African women, Europeans found a way to articulate shifting perceptions of themselves as religiously, culturally, and phenotypically superior to the black or brown persons they sought to define. In the discourse used to justify the slave trade, Ligon's beautiful Negro woman was as important as her "six-legged" counterpart.

Both imaginary women marked a gendered. . . . whiteness on which European colonial expansionism depended. . . .[4]

Travel accounts produced in Europe and available in England provided a corpus from which subsequent writers borrowed freely, reproducing images of Native American and African women that resonated with readers. Over the course of the second half of the seventeenth century, some eighteen new collections with descriptions of Africa and the West Indies were published and reissued in England; by the eighteenth century, more than fifty new synthetic works, reissued again and again, found audiences in England.[5] Both the writers and the readers of these texts learned to dismiss the idea that women in the Americas and Africa might be innocuous or unremarkable. Rather, indigenous women bore an enormous symbolic burden, as writers from Walter Raleigh to Edward Long used them to mark metaphorically the symbiotic boundaries of European national identities and white supremacy. The conflict between perceptions of beauty and assertions of monstrosity such as Ligon's exemplified a much larger process through which the familiar became unfamiliar as beauty became beastliness and mothers became monstrous, all of which ultimately buttressed racial distinctions. Writers who articulated religious and moral justifications for the slave trade simultaneously grappled with the character of a contradictory female African body—a body both desirable and repulsive, available and untouchable, productive and reproductive, beautiful and black. By the time an eighteenth-century Carolina slaveowner could look at an African woman with the detached gaze of an investor, travelers and philosophers had already subjected her to a host of taxonomic calculations.

Europe had a long tradition of identifying Others through the monstrous physiognomy or sexual behavior of women. Armchair adventurers might shelve Pliny the Elder's ancient collection of monstrous races, *Historia Naturalis*, which catalogued the long-breasted wild woman, alongside Herodotus's *History*, in which Indian and Ethiopian tribal women bore only one child in a lifetime. They may have read Julian's arguments with Augustine in which he wrote that "barbarian and nomadic women give birth with ease, scarcely interrupting their travels to bear children." . . . Images of female devils included sagging breasts as part of the iconography of danger and monstrosity. The medieval wild woman, whose breasts dragged on the ground when she walked and could be thrown over her shoulder, was believed to disguise herself with youth and beauty in order to enact seductions. . . .[6]

Writers . . . easily applied similar modifiers to Others in Africa and the Americas in order to mark European boundaries. According to *The Travels of Sir John Mandeville*, "in Ethiopia and in many other countries [in Africa] the folk lie all naked . . . and the women have no shame of the men." Furthermore, "they wed there no wives, for all the women there be common . . . and when [women] have children they may give them to what man they will that hath companied with them." Deviant sexual behavior reflected the breakdown of natural laws—the absence of shame, the inability to identify lines of heredity and descent. This concern with deviant sexuality, articulated almost always through descriptions of women, is a constant theme in the travel writings of early modern Europe. . . . Indeed, Columbus used his reliance on the female body to articulate the colonial venture at the very outset of his voyage when he wrote that the earth was shaped like a breast with the Indies composing the nipple; his urge for discovery of new lands was inextricable from language of sexual conquest.[7]

Richard Eden's 1553 English translation of Sebastian Münster's *A Treatyse of the Newe India* presented Amerigo Vespucci's 1502 voyage to English readers for the first time. Vespucci did not use color to mark the difference of the people he encountered; rather, he described them in terms of their lack of social institutions ("they fight not for the enlargeing of theyr dominion for asmuch as they have no Magistrates") and social niceties ("at theyr meate they use rude and barberous fashions, lying on the ground without any table clothe or coverlet"). Nonetheless, his descriptions are not without positive attributes, and when he turned his attention to women his language bristled with illuminating contradiction:

> Theyr bodies are verye smothe and clene by reason of theyr often washinge. They are in other thinges fylthy and withoute shame. Thei use no lawful coniunccion of mariage, and but every one hath as many women as him liketh, and leaveth them agayn at his pleasure. The women are very fruiteful, and refuse no laboure al the whyle they are with childe. They travayle in maner withoute payne, so that the nexte day they are cherefull and able to walke. Neyther have they theyr bellies wimpeled or loose, and hanginge pappes, by reason of bearinge manye chyldren.[8]

The passage conveys admiration for indigenous women's strength in pregnancy and their ability to maintain aesthetically pleasing bodies, but it also illustrates the conflict at the heart of European discourse on gender and difference. It hinges on both a veiled critique of European female weakness and a dismissal of Amerindian women's pain. Once English men and women were firmly settled in New World colonies, they too would struggle with the notion of female weakness; they needed both white and black women for hard manual labor, but they also needed to preserve a notion of white gentlewomen's unsuitability for physical labor. . . .

Despite his respect for female reproductive hardiness, at the end of the volume Vespucci fixed the indigenous woman as a dangerous cannibal:

> There came sodeynly a woman downe from a mountayne, bringing with her secretly a great stake with which she [killed a Spaniard.] The other wommene foorthwith toke him by the legges, and drewe him to the mountayne. . . . The women also which had slayne the yong man, cut him in pieces even in the sight of the Spaniardes, shewinge them the pieces, and rosting them at a greate fyre.

Vespucci later made manifest the latent sexualized danger inherent in the man-slaying woman in a letter in which he wrote of women biting off the penises of their sexual partners, thus linking cannibalism—an absolute indicator of savagery and distance from European norms—to female sexual insatiability.[9]

The label "savage" was not uniformly applied to Amerindian people. Indeed, in the context of European national rivalries, the indigenous woman became somewhat less savage. In the mid to late sixteenth century, the bodies of women figured at the borders of national identities. . . .

In "Discoverie of the . . . Empire of Guiana" (1598), [Sir Walter] Ralegh stated that he "suffered not any man to . . . touch any of [the natives'] wives or daughters: which course so contrary to the Spaniards (who tyrannize over them in all things) drewe them to admire her [English] majestie." Although he permitted himself and his men to gaze upon naked Indian women, Ralegh accentuated the restraint they exercised. In doing so, he used the untouched bodies of Native American women to mark national boundaries and signal the civility and superiority of English colonizers in contrast to the sexually violent Spaniards. Moreover, in linking the eroticism of indigenous women to the sexual attention of Spanish men, Ralegh signaled the Spaniards' "lapse into savagery."[10] . . .

[Visual depictions of Native women were always in flux]. . . . [E]arly volumes of Theodor de Bry's *Grand Voyages* (1590) depicted the Algonkians of Virginia and the Timucuas of Florida as classical Europeans: Amerindian bodies mirrored ancient Greek and Roman statuary, modest virgins covered their breasts, and infants suckled at the high, small breasts of young attractive women. . . .

In the third de Bry volume, *Voyages to Brazil*, published in 1592, the Indian was portrayed as aggressive and savage, and the representation of women's bodies changed. The new woman is a cannibal with breasts that fell below her waist. She licks the juices of grilled human flesh from her fingers. . . . The absence of a suckling child in these . . . depictions . . . signified the women's cannibalism—they consumed rather than produced. Although women alone did not exemplify cannibalism, women with long breasts came to mark such savagery in Native Americans for English readers. As depictions of Native Americans traversed the gamut of savage to noble, the long-breasted women became a clear signpost of savagery in contrast to her high-breasted counterpart . . .[11]

English travelers to West Africa drew on American narrative traditions as they too worked to establish a clearly demarcated line that would ultimately define them. Richard Hakluyt's collection of travel narratives, *Principal Navigations* (1589), brought Africa into the purview of English readers. *Principal Navigations* portrayed Africa and Africans in both positive and negative terms. . . . In response, Hakluyt presented texts that, through an often-conflicted depiction of African peoples, ultimately differentiated between Africa and England and erected a boundary that made English expansion in the face of confused and uncivilized peoples reasonable, profitable, and moral. . . .[12] [To] write of sex was also to define and expand the boundaries of profit through productive and reproductive labor.

The symbolic weight of indigenous women's sexual, childbearing, and childrearing practices moved from the Americas to Africa and continued to be brought to bear on England's literary imagination in ways that rallied familiar notions of gendered difference for English readers. John Lok's account of his 1554 voyage to Guinea, published forty years later in Hakluyt's collection, . . . described all Africans as "people of beastly living." He located the proof of this in women's behavior: among the Garamantes, women "are common: for they contract no matrimonie, neither have respect to chastitie." This description of the Garamantes first appeared in Pliny, was reproduced again by Iulius Solinus's sixth century *Polyhistor* and can be found in travel accounts through the Middle Ages and into the sixteenth and seventeenth centuries. . . .[13]

William Towrson's narrative of his 1555 voyage to Guinea, also published by Hakluyt in 1589, further exhibits this kind of distillation. Towrson depicted women and men as largely indistinguishable. They "goe so alike, that one cannot know a man from a woman but by their breastes, which in the most part be very foule and long, hanging downe low like the udder of a goate." This was, perhaps, the first time an Englishman in Africa explicitly used breasts as an identifying trait of beastliness and difference. He went on to maintain that "diverse of the women have such exceeding long breasts, that some of them will lay the same upon the ground and lie downe by them."[14] Lok and Towrson represented African women's bodies and sexual behavior in order to distinguish Africa from Europe. Towrson in particular gave readers only two analogies through which to view and understand African women—beasts and monsters. . . .

. . . After Hakluyt died, Samuel Purchas took up the mantle of editor and published twenty additional volumes in Hakluyt's series beginning in 1624.[15] . . . [including] a translation of Pieter de Marees's *A description and historicall declaration of the golden Kingedome of Guinea.* This narrative was first published in Dutch in 1602, was translated into German and Latin for the de Bry volumes (1603–1634), and appeared in French in 1605. Plagiarism by seventeenth- and eighteenth-century writers gave it still wider circulation. Here, too, black women embody African savagery. De Marees began by describing the people at Sierra Leone as "very greedie eaters, and no lesse drinkers, and very lecherous, and theevish, and much addicted to uncleanenesse; one man hath as many wives as

Women in Africa, engraving by Theodor de Bry, 1604.
Appearing in a much-reproduced travel narrative, this engraving purported to show representative examples of women's clothing and personal decoration in four regions of western Africa. (Women in Africa, *from* Verum et Historicam Descriptionem Avriferi Regni Guineaa, *in* Small Voyages, *vol. 6, by Theodor de Bry [Frankfurt am Main, 1604], p. 3. Courtesy of the John Work Garrett Library, Johns Hopkins University.)

hee is able to keepe and maintaine. The women also are much addicted to leacherie, specially, with strange Countrey people . . . [and] are also great Lyers, and not to be credited." As did most of his contemporaries, de Marees invoked women's sexuality to castigate the incivility of both men and women. Women's savagery does not stand apart. Rather, it indicts the whole: all Africans were savage. The passage displays African males' savagery alongside their access to multiple women. Similarly, de Marees located evidence of African women's savagery in their sexual desire. . . .

[He] further castigated West African women: they delivered children surrounded by men, women, and youngsters "in most shamelesse manner . . . before them all." This absence of shame (evoked explicitly, as here, or implicitly in the constant references to nakedness in

other narratives) worked to establish distance. Readers, titillated by the topics discussed and thus tacitly shamed, found themselves further distanced from the shameless subject of the narrative. De Marees dwelled on the brute nature of shameless African women. He marveled that "when the child is borne [the mother] goes to the water to wash and make cleane her selfe, not once dreaming of a moneths lying-in . . . as women here with us use to doe; they use no Nurses to helpe them when they lie in child-bed, neither seeke to lie dainty and soft. . . . The next day after, they goe abroad in the streets, to doe their businesse."[16] . . .

De Marees goes on to inscribe an image of women's reproductive identity whose influence persisted long after his original publication. "When [the child] is two or three monethes old, the mother ties the childe with a peece of cloth at her backe. . . . When the child crieth to sucke, the mother casteth one of her dugs backeward over her shoulder, and so the child suckes it as it hangs."[17] Frontispieces for the de Marees narrative and the African narratives in de Bry approximate the over-the-shoulder breast-feeding de Marees described, thereby creating an image that could symbolize the continent . . .

The image, in more or less extreme form, remained a compelling one, offering in a single narrative-visual moment evidence that black women's difference was both cultural (in this strange *habit*) and physical (in this strange *ability*). The word "dug," which by the early seventeenth century meant both a woman's breasts and an animal's teats, connoted a brute animality that de Marees reinforced through his description of small children "lying downe in their house, like Dogges, [and] rooting in the ground like Hogges" and of "boyes and girles [that] goe starke naked as they were borne, with their privie members all open, without any shame or civilitie.[18] . . .

As Englishmen traversed the uncertain ground of nature and culture, African women became a touchstone for physical and behavioral curiosity both within Africa and in the Americas and Europe. Fynes Moryson wrote of Irish women in 1617 that they "have very great Dugges, some so big as they give their children suck over their Shoulders." But it is important that he connects this to being "not laced at all," or to the lack of corsetry.[19] While nudity—a state in which the absence of corsetry is certainly implicit—is constantly at play in descriptions of African women, the overwhelming physicality of the image is disaggregated from culture and instead becomes part of African female nature; something no amount of corsetry would set right . . .

African women's Africanness became contingent on the linkages between sexuality and a savagery that fitted them for both productive and reproductive labor. . . . [D]escriptions of African women in the Americas almost always highlighted their fecundity along with their capacity for manual labor. Erroneous observations about African women's propensity for easy birth and breast-feeding reassured colonizers that these women could easily perform hard labor in the Americas; at the same time, such observations erected a barrier of difference between Africa and England. Seventeenth-century English medical writers, both men and

women, equated breast-feeding and tending to children with difficult work, and the practice of wealthy women forgoing breast-feeding in favor of sending their children to wet nurses was widespread. English women and men anticipated pregnancy and childbirth with extreme uneasiness and fear of death, but they knew that the experience of pain in childbirth marked women as members of a Christian community.[20] . . .

. . . By about the turn of the seventeenth century, however, as England joined in the transatlantic slave trade, assertions of African savagery began to be predicated less on consumption and cannibalism and more on production and reproduction. African women came into the conversation in the context of England's need for productivity. Descriptions of these women that highlighted the apparent ease and indifference of their reproductive lives created a mechanistic image. . . . Whereas English women's reproductive work took place solely in the domestic economy, African women's reproductive work embodied the developing discourses of extraction and forced labor at the heart of England's design for the Americas. . . .

By the eighteenth century, English writers rarely used black women's breasts or behavior for anything but concrete evidence of barbarism in Africa. In *A Description of the Coasts of North and South-Guinea*, begun in the 1680s and completed and published almost forty years later, John Barbot "admired the quietness of the poor babes, so carr'd about at their mothers' backs . . . and how freely they suck the breasts, which are always full of milk, over their mothers' *shoulders, and sleep soundly in that odd posture." William Snelgrave introduced his New Account of Some Parts of Guinea and the Slave-trade* with an anecdote designed to illustrate the benevolence of the trade. He described himself rescuing an infant from human sacrifice and reuniting the child with its mother, who "had much Milk in her Breasts." He accented the barbarism of those who had attempted to sacrifice the child and claimed that the reunion cemented his goodwill in the eyes of the enslaved, who, thus convinced of the "good notion of White Men," caused no problems during the voyage to Antigua.[21] . . .

Eighteenth-century abolitionist John Atkins similarly adopted the icon of black female bodies in his writings on Guinea. "Childing, and their Breasts always pendulous, stretches them to so unseemly a length and Bigness that some . . . could suckle over their shoulder." Atkins then considered the idea of African women copulating with apes. He noted that "at some places the Negroes have been suspected of Bestiality." . . . The evidence lay mostly in apes' resemblance to humans but was bolstered by "the Ignorance and Stupidity [of black women unable] to guide or controll lust." Abolitionists and anti-abolitionists alike accepted the connections between race and black women's monstrous and fecund bodies . . .

The visual shorthand of the sagging-breasted African savage held sway for decades . . . When William Smith embarked on a voyage to map the Gold Coast for the Royal Africa Company in 1727, he was initially uninterested in ethnography. His first description of people comes more than halfway through the narrative when he writes "but before I describe the Vegetables, I shall take Notice of the Animals of this Country; beginning with the Natives, who are generally speaking a lusty strong-bodied People, but are mostly of a lazy idle Disposition." His short description, followed by a section on "Quadrepedes," is organized primarily around accusations of polygamy and promiscuity in which "hot constitution'd Ladies" are put to work by husbands who treat them like slaves. As the narrative continues, his ethnographic passages, while always brief, are also always organized around sexually available African women. In Whydah, for example, the reader encounters female Priests inclined to whoredom, and he tells of an anomalous Queen in Agonna who satisfies her sexual needs with male slaves, hands down her crown to the resulting female progeny and sells any male children into slavery.[23] . . .

One of a very few English women in late eighteenth-century West Africa, abolitionist Anna Falconbridge . . . noted that women's breasts in Sierra Leone were "disgusting to Europeans, though considered *beautiful* and ornamental here." But such weak claims of sisterly sympathy could hardly interrupt 300 years of porno-tropical writing. By the 1770s, Edward Long's *History of Jamaica* presented readers with African women whose savagery was total, for whom enslavement was the only means of civilization. . . . Long used women's bodies and behavior to justify and promote the mass enslavement of Africans. By the time he wrote, the Jamaican economy was fully

invested in slave labor and was contributing more than half of the profits obtained by England from the West Indies as a whole. The association of black people with beasts—via African women—had been cemented: "Their women are delivered with little or no labour; they have therefore no more occasion for midwifes than the female oran-outang, or any other wild animall. . . . Thus they seem exempted from the course inflicted upon Eve *and her daughters.*"[24] If African women gave birth without pain, they somehow sidestepped God's curse upon Eve. If they were not Eve's descendants, they were not related to Europeans and could therefore be forced to labor on England's overseas plantations with impunity. . . .[25]

When [Richard] Ligon arrived in Barbados and settled on 500-acre sugar plantation with 100 slaves, his notion of African beauty—if it had ever really existed—dissolved in the face of racial slavery. He saw African men and women carrying bunches of plantains: "Tis a lovely sight to see a hundred handsom Negroes, men and women, with every one a grasse-green bunch of these fruits on their heads . . . the black and green so well becoming one another." Here in the context of the sugar plantation, where he saw African women working as he had never seen English woman do, Ligon struggled to situate African women as workers. Their innate unfamiliarity as laborers caused him to cast about for a useful metaphor. He compares African people to vegetation; now they are only passively and abstractly beautiful as blocks of color. Ligon attested to their passivity with their servitude: They made "very good servants, if they be not spoyled by the English."[26]

But . . . he ultimately equated black people with animals. He declared that planters bought slaves so that the "sexes may be equall . . . [because] they cannot live without Wives," although the enslaved choose their partners much "as Cows do . . . for, the most of them are as near beasts as may be." Like his predecessors, Ligon offered further proof of Africans' capacity for physical labor—their aptitude for slavery—through ease of childbearing. "In a fortnight [after giving birth] this woman is at worke with her Pickaninny at her back, as merry a soule as any is there."[27] In the Americas, African women's purportedly pain-free childbearing thus continued to be central. When Ligon reinforced African women's animality with descriptions of breasts "hang[ing] down below their Navels," he tethered his narrative to familiar images of black women that—for readers nourished on Hakluyt and de Bry—effectively naturalized the enslavement of Africans . . .

By the time the English made their way to the West Indies, decades of ideas and information about brown and black women predated the actual encounter. In many ways, the encounter had already taken place in parlors and reading rooms on English soil, assuring that colonists would arrive with a battery of assumptions and predispositions about race, femininity, sexuality, and civilization. Confronted with an Africa they needed to exploit, European writers turned to black women as evidence of a cultural inferiority that ultimately became encoded as racial difference. Monstrous bodies became enmeshed with savage behavior as the icon of women's breasts became evidence of tangible barbarism. African women's "unwomanly" behavior evoked an immutable distance between Europe and Africa on which the development of racial slavery depended. By the mid-seventeenth century, what had initially marked African women as unfamiliar—their sexually and reproductively bound savagery—had become familiar. To invoke it was to conjure a gendered and racialized figure that marked the boundaries of English civility even as she naturalized the subjugation of Africans and their descendants in the Americas.

NOTES

1. Deborah Gray White, *Ar'n't I A Woman? Female Slaves in the Plantation South* (New York and London: W.W. Norton, 1985), 29–46; Barbara Bush, *Slave Women in Caribbean Society, 1650–1838* (Bloomington: Indiana University Press, 1990), 11–12.

2. Richard Ligon, *A True and Exact History of the Island of Barbados* (London, 1657), 12–13.

3. Ligon, *True and Exact History of Barbados*, 51.

4. Kim F. Hall, *Things of Darkness: Economies of Race and Gender in Early Modern England* (Ithaca, N.Y.: Cornell University Press, 1995), 29–61.

5. Anthony J. Barker, *The African Link: British Attitudes to the Negro in the Era of the Atlantic Slave Trade, 1550–1807* (London: Frank Cass, 1978), 22.

6. Pliny the Elder, *Natural History*, 10 vols., trans. H. Rackham (Cambridge, Mass., Harvard University Press, 1938–63), 2: 509–27; Herodotus, *The History*, trans. David Grene (Chicago: University of Chicago Press, 1987), 4, 180, 191; Elizabeth A. Clark, "Generation, Degeneration, Regeneration: Original Sin and the Conception of Jesus in the Polemic Between Augustine and Julian of Eclanum," in *Generation and Degeneration: Tropes of Reproduction in*

Literature and History from Antiquity to Early Modern Europe, ed. Valeria Finucci and Kevin Brownlee (Durham, N.C.: Duke University Press, 2001), 30; Richard Bernheimer, *Wild Men in the Middle Ages: A Study in Art, Sentiment, and Demonology* (Cambridge, Mass.: Harvard University Press, 1952), 33–41, 34.

7. *The Travels of Sir John Mandeville: The Version of the Cotton Manuscript in Modern Spelling*, ed. A.W. Pollard (London: Macmillan, 1915), 109, 119; Sharon W. Tiffany and Kathleen J. Adams, *The Wild Woman: An Inquiry into the Anthropology of an Idea* (Cambridge: Schenkman, 1985), 63.

8. *A Treatyse of the Newe India by Sebastian Münster (1553)*, trans. Richard Eden (microprint) (Ann Arbor, Mich., 1966), 57.

9. Münster, *Treatyse*, trans. Eden, quoted in Louis Montrose, "The Work of Gender in the Discourse of Discovery," *Representations* 33 (1991): 1–41, 4, 5.

10. Ralegh, "The Discoverie of the large rich and beautifull Empire of Guiana," in Richard Hakluyt, *The Principal Navigations, Voyages, Traffiques & Discoveries of the English Nation*, 12 vols. (1598–1600; reprint Glasgow, 1903–5), 10, 39; Karen Robertson, "Pocahantas at the Masque," *Signs* 21 (1996): 561.

11. Theodore de Bry, ed., *Grand Voyages*, 13 vols. (Frankfurt am Main, 1590–1627); Bernadette Bucher, *Icon and Conquest: A Structural Analysis of the Illustrations of de Bry's Great Voyages*, trans. Basia Miller Gulati (Chicago: University of Chicago Press, 1981).

12. Emily C. Bartels, "Imperialist Beginnings: Richard Hakluyt and the Construction of Africa," *Criticism* 34 (1992): 517–38, 519.

13. "The second voyage [of Master John Lok] to Guinea . . . 1554," in Richard Hakluyt, *The Principal Navigations, Voyages, Traffiques, and Discoveries of the English Nation*, 12 vols. (London, 1598–1600), 6: 167, 168; Barker, *African Link*, 121.

14. "The first voyage made by Master William Towrson Marchant of London, to the coast of Guinea . . . in the yeere 1555," in Hakluyt, *Principal Navigations*, 6: 184, 187.

15. Samuel Purchas, *Hakluytus Posthumus, or Purchas His Pilgrimes: Contayning a History of the World in Sea Voyages and Land Travells by Englishmen and Others*, 20 vols. (1624; reprint Glasgow: J. MacLehose and Sons, 1905).

16. De Marees, "Description and historicall declaration of the golden Kingdome of Guinea," in *Purchas His Pilgrimes*, 6: 251, 258–59. This testimony to African women's physical strength and emotional indifference is even more emphatic in the original Dutch. In the most recent translation from the Dutch, the passage continues: "This shows that the women here are of a cruder nature and stronger posture than the Females in our Lands in Europe." Pieter de Marees, *Description and Historical Account of the Gold Kingdom of Guinea*, trans. and ed. Albert van Dantzig and Adam Jones (1602; reprint Oxford: Oxford University Press, 1987), 23.

17. De Marees, "Description and historicall declaration of the Golden Kingdome," 259.

18. De Marees, "Description and historicall declaration of the Golden Kingdome," 261. *Oxford English Dictionary*, 2nd ed., 1989.

19. Fynes Moryson, *Shakespeare's Europe: A survey of the Condition of Europe at the end of the Sixteenth Century, Being unpublished chapters of Fynes*

Moryson's Itinerary, 2nd ed. (1617; reprint New York: Benjamin Blom, 1967), 485.

20. Jordan, *White over Black*, 39; Marylynn Salmon, "The Cultural Significance of Breastfeeding and Infant Care in Early Modern England and America," *Journal of Social History* 28 (1994): 247–70; Linda Pollock, "Embarking on a Rough Passage: The Experience of Pregnancy in Early Modern Society," in *Women as Mothers in Pre-Industrial England*, ed. Valerie Fildes (New York: Routledge, 1990), 45.

21. Barbot, *A Description of the Coasts of North and South-Guinea, in A Collection of Voyages*, ed. A. Churchill (London, 1732), 36; William Snelgrave, "Introduction," *A New Account of Some Parts of Guinea and the Slave Trade* (1734; reprint London: Cass, 1971).

22. John Atkins, *A Voyage to Guinea, Brazil, and the West-Indies* (1735; reprint London: Cass, 1970), 50, 108.

23. William Smith, *A New Voyage to Guinea* (London, 1744), 142–43, 195, 208.

24. Anna Maria Falconbridge, *Two Voyages to Sierra Leone, During the Years 1791–2–3*, in *Maiden Voyages and Infant Colonies: Two Women's Travel Narratives of the 1790s*, ed. Deirdre Coleman (London: Leicester University Press, 1999), 45–168, 74, emphasis in the original; Edward Long, "History of Jamaica, 2, with notes and corrections by the Author" (1774), Add. Ms., 12405, p364/f295, p380/f304; Robin Blackburn, *The Making of New World Slavery: From the Baroque to the Modern, 1492–1800* (London: Verso, 1997), 527–45.

25. Early modern European women were so defined by their experience of pain in childbirth that an inability to feel pain was considered evidence of witchcraft. Lyndal Roper, *Oedipus and the Devil: Witchcraft, Sexuality and Religion in Early Modern Europe* (London: Routledge, 1994), 203–4.

26. Ligon, *True and Exact History of Barbadoes*, 44, 47, 51.

27. Ligon, *True and Exact History of Barbadoes*, 47, 51.

EUROPEAN SETTLERS: GENDER PUZZLES, GENDER RULES

MARY BETH NORTON

An Indentured Servant Identifies as "Both Man and Woeman": Jamestown, 1629

The story that Mary Beth Norton tells is one that demonstrates that gender is a social as well as a biological construction. It is very rare that a newborn is hermaphrodite, or intersexed, displaying "some combination of 'female' and 'male' reproductive and sexual features." Later in life, hormonal abnormalities may mask clear distinctions between male and female. In our own time, "sexual reassignment" surgery is generally performed while an intersexed child is an infant; for adults, hormonal treatments, sometimes accompanied by surgery, can be used to clarify the gender identity of an individual.*

In one seventeenth-century Virginia community, the presence of a person who dressed as a man and also as a woman, who behaved alternately like a woman and like a man, and whose physical formation was vulnerable to multiple interpretations was deeply disconcerting. How did T. Hall's neighbors respond to gossip that this person's sex was unclear? What authority did women claim in assessing the situation? What authority did men claim? What does the struggle to mark T. Hall's gender identity suggest about the structure of community life and the roles of men and women?

On April 8, 1629, a person named Hall was brought before the General Court of the colony of Virginia. Hall was not formally charged with a crime, although witnesses alluded to a rumor about fornication. Yet Hall's case is one of the most remarkable to be found in the court records of any colony. If no crime was involved, why was Hall in court?

Hall had been reported to the authorities for one simple reason: people were confused about Hall's sexual identity. At times Hall dressed as a man; at other times, evidently, as

---

* Suzanne Kessler, "The Medical Construction of Gender: Case Management of Intersexed Infants," *Signs: Journal of Women in Culture and Society* 16 (1990): 3–26. For other interpretations of the Hall case, see Kathleen Brown, "'Changed . . . into the fashion of a man': The Politics of Sexual Difference in a Seventeenth-Century Anglo-American Settlement," *Journal of the History of Sexuality* 6 (1995): 171–93; and Elizabeth Reis, *Bodies in Doubt: An American History of Intersex* (Baltimore: Johns Hopkins University Press, 2009), 10–16, 22, 29.

Excerpted from the prologue to sec. 2 of *Founding Mothers and Fathers: Gendered Power and the Forming of American Society* by Mary Beth Norton (New York: Alfred A. Knopf, 1996). Reprinted by permission of the author and publisher. Notes have been edited and renumbered. For transcripts of the court records in the Hall case see H. R. McIlwaine, ed., *Minutes of the Council and General Court of Colonial Virginia, 1622–1632, 1670–1676* (Richmond, Va.: Colonial Press/Everett Waddey, 1924), 194–195, via www.archive.org.

a woman. What sex was this person? Other colonists wanted to know. The vigor with which they pursued their concerns dramatically underscores the significance of gender distinctions in seventeenth-century Anglo-America. The case also provides excellent illustrations of the powerful role the community could play in individuals' lives and of the potential influence of ordinary folk, both men and women, on the official actions of colonial governments.

The Hall case offers compelling insights into the process of defining gender in early American society. Hall was an anomalous individual, and focusing on such anomalies can help to expose fundamental belief systems. Since in this case sex was difficult to determine, so too was gender identity. Persons of indeterminate sex, such as the subject of this discussion, pose perplexing questions for any society. The process through which the culture categorizes these people is both complex and revealing. The analysis here will examine the ways in which seventeenth-century Virginians attempted to come to grips with the problems presented to them by a sexually ambiguous person.[1] . . .

Describing my usage of personal pronouns and names is essential to the analysis that follows. The other historians who have dealt with the case have referred to Hall as "Thomas" and "he," as do the court records (with one significant exception). Yet the details of the case, including Hall's testimony, make such usage problematic. Therefore the practice here shall be the following: when Hall is acting as a female, the name "Thomasine" and the pronoun "she" will be used. Conversely, when Hall is acting as a male, "Thomas" and "he" are just as obviously called for. In moments of ambiguity or generalization (as now) "Hall," or the simple initial "T" will be employed (the latter as an ungendered pronoun).

Thomasine Hall was born "at or neere" the northeastern English city of Newcastle upon Tyne.[2] As the name suggests, Hall was christened and raised as a girl. At the age of twelve, Thomasine went to London to stay with her aunt, and she lived there for ten years. But in 1625 her brother was pressed into the army to serve in an expedition against Cadiz. Perhaps encouraged by her brother's experience (or perhaps taking his place after his death, for that expedition incurred many casualties), Hall subsequently adopted a new gender identity.

Thomas told the court that he "Cut of[f] his heire and Changed his apparell into the fashion of man and went over as a souldier in the Isle of Ree being in the habit of a man."[3] Upon returning to Plymouth from army service in France, probably in the autumn of 1627, Hall resumed a feminine identity. Thomasine donned women's clothing and supported herself briefly by making "bone lace" and doing other needlework. That she did so suggests that Thomasine had been taught these valuable female skills by her aunt during her earlier sojourn in London.

Plymouth was one of the major points of embarkation for the American colonies, and Hall recounted that "shortly after" arriving in the city Thomasine learned that a ship was being made ready for a voyage to Virginia. Once again, Hall decided to become a man, so he put on men's clothing and sailed to the fledgling colony. Thomas was then approximately twenty-five years old, comparable in age to many of the immigrants to Virginia, and like most of his fellows he seems to have gone to the Chesapeake as an indentured servant.

By December, Hall was settled in Virginia, for on January 21, 1627/8, a man named Thomas Hall, living with John and Jane Tyos (T's master and mistress), was convicted along with them for receiving stolen goods from William Mills, a servant of one of their neighbors. According to the testimony, Hall and the Tyoses had encouraged Mills in a series of thefts that began before Christmas 1627. Some of the purloined items—which included tobacco, chickens, currants, a shirt, and several pairs of shoes—were still in the possession of Hall and the Tyoses at the time their house was searched by the authorities on January 14. Although Thomas Hall is a common name (indeed, John Tyos knew another Thomas Hall, who had arrived with him on the ship Bona Nova in 1620), a significant piece of evidence suggests that T and the man charged with this crime were one and the same. William Mills had difficulty carrying the currants, which he piled into his cap during his initial theft. Since that was clearly an unsatisfactory conveyance, when Mills was about to make a second foray after the desirable dried fruits he asked his accomplices to supply him with a better container. Thomas Hall testified that Jane Tyos then "did bring a napkin unto him and willed him to sowe it & make a bagg of it to carry currants." It is highly unlikely that an ordinary male servant would have had better seamstressing skills than his mistress, but Thomasine was an expert at such tasks.[4]

Although thus far in Hall's tale the chronology and the sequence of gender switches have been clear—for T specifically recounted the first part of the tale to the Virginia General Court, and the timing of the thefts and their prosecution is clearly described in court testimony—the next phase of the story must be pieced together from the muddled testimony of two witnesses and some logical surmises.

A key question not definitively answered in the records is: what happened to raise questions in people's minds about Hall's sexual identity? Two possibilities suggest themselves. One is that John and Jane Tyos, who obviously recognized that Hall had "feminine" skills shortly after T came to live with them, spoke of that fact to others, or perhaps visitors to their plantation observed Hall's activities and drew their own conclusions. Another possibility is that, after traveling to Virginia as a man, Hall reverted to the female clothing and role that T appears to have found more comfortable. The court records imply that Hall did choose to dress as a woman in Virginia, for Francis England, a witness, reported overhearing a conversation in which another man asked T directly: why do you wear women's clothing? T's reply—"I goe in weomans aparell to gett a bitt for my Catt"—is difficult to interpret and will be analyzed later. In any event, a Mr. Stacy (who cannot be further identified) seems to have first raised the issue of T's anomalous sexual character by asserting to other colonists that Hall was "as hee thought a man and woman." Just when Mr. Stacy made this statement is not clear, but he probably voiced his opinion about a year after T arrived in the colony.

In the aftermath of Mr. Stacy's statement, a significant incident occurred at the home of Nicholas Eyres, perhaps a relative of Robert Eyres, who had recently become John Tyos's partner. "Uppon [Mr Stacy's] report," three women—Alice Longe, Dorothy Rodes, and Barbara Hall—scrutinized Hall's body. Their action implied that T was at the time dressed as a woman, for women regularly searched other women's bodies (often at the direction of a court) to look for signs of illicit pregnancy or perhaps witchcraft. They never, however, performed the same function with respect to men—or anyone dressed like a man. Moreover, John Tyos both then and later told Dorothy Rodes that Hall was a woman. Even so, the

female searchers, having examined Hall, declared that T was a man. As a result of the disagreement between Tyos and the women about T's sex, T was brought before the commander of the region, Captain Nathaniel Basse, for further examination.[5]

Questioned by Mr. Basse, T responded with a description of a unique anatomy with ambiguous physical characteristics. (The text of the testimony is mutilated, and the remaining fragments are too incomplete to provide a clear description of T's body.) Hall then refused to choose a gender identity, instead declaring that T was "both man and woeman." Captain Basse nevertheless decided that Hall was female and ordered T "to bee putt in weomans apparell"—thus implying that T was, at that moment at least, dressed as a man. The three women who had previously searched T's body were shaken by the official ruling that contradicted their own judgment; after being informed of the commander's decision, they reportedly "stood in doubte of what they had formerly affirmed."

John Tyos then sold Hall, now legally a maidservant named Thomasine, to John Atkins, who was present when Captain Basse questioned T. Atkins must have fully concurred with Mr. Basse's decision; surely he would not have purchased a female servant about whose sex he had any doubts. Yet on February 12, 1628/9, questions were again raised about T, for Alice Longe and her two friends went to Atkins's house to scrutinize Thomasine's body for a second time. They covertly examined her while she slept and once more decided that the servant was male. But Atkins, though summoned by the searchers to look at his maid's anatomy, was unable to do so, for Hall's "seeming to starre as if shee had beene awake" caused Atkins to leave without viewing her body.

The next Sunday, the three women returned with two additional female helpers.[6] On this occasion, the searchers had the active cooperation and participation of John Atkins, who ordered Thomasine to show her body to them. For a third time the women concluded that Hall was a man. Atkins thereupon ordered his servant to don men's clothing and informed Captain Basse of his decision.

By this time not only Hall but also everyone else was undoubtedly confused. Since Hall was now deemed to be male, the next curiosity-seekers to examine T's body were also male.

One of them was Roger Rodes, probably the husband of Dorothy, who had joined in all the previous searches of Hall's body. Before forcefully throwing Thomas onto his back and checking his anatomy, Roger told Hall, "thou hast beene reported to be a woman and now thou art proved to bee a man, i will see what thou carriest." Like the female searchers before them, Roger and his associate Francis England concluded that T was male.

A rumor that Hall "did ly with a maid of Mr Richard Bennetts called greate Besse" must have added considerably to the uncertainty. Hall accused Alice Longe, one of the persistent female searchers, of spreading the tale. She denied the charge, blaming the slander instead on an unnamed male servant of John Tyos's. If the story was true, what did it imply about Hall's sexual identity? Whether Hall was male or female would obviously have a bearing on the interpretation of any relationship with Bennett's maid Bess. Clearly, Virginians now had reason to seek a firm resolution of the conflict. Since Captain Basse, the local commander, had been unable to find an acceptable solution, there was just one remaining alternative— referring the dilemma to the General Court.

That court, composed of the governor and council, was the highest judicial authority in the small colony. The judges heard from Hall and considered the sworn depositions of two male witnesses (Francis England and John Atkins), who described the events just outlined. Remarkably, the court accepted T's own self-definition and, although using the male personal pronoun, declared that Hall was "a man and a woman, that all the Inhabitants there may take notice thereof and that hee shall goe Clothed in mans apparell, only his head to bee attired in a Coyfe and Crosecloth with an Apron before him." Ordering Hall to post bond for good behavior until formally released from that obligation, the court also told Captain Basse to see that its directives were carried out. Since most court records for subsequent years have been lost (they were burned during the Civil War), it is impossible to trace Hall's story further.

What can this tale reveal about gender definitions and the role of the community in the formative years of American society? Six different but related issues emerge from the analysis of Hall's case.

First, the relationship of sexual characteristics and gender identity. All those who examined T,

be they male or female, insisted T was male. Thus T's external sex organs resembled male genitals. Roger Rodes and Francis England, for example, pronounced Thomas "a perfect man" after they had "pulled out his members." Still, T informed Captain Basse "hee had not the use of the mans parte" and told John Atkins that "I have a peece of an hole" (a vulva). Since T was identified as a girl at birth, christened Thomasine, and raised accordingly, T probably fell into that category of human beings who appear female in infancy but at puberty develop what seem to be male genitalia. Such individuals were the subjects of many stories in early modern Europe, the most famous of which involved a French peasant girl, Marie, who suddenly developed male sex organs while chasing pigs when she was fifteen, and who in adulthood became a shepherd named Germain. It is not clear whether early Virginians were aware of such tales, but if they understood contemporary explanations of sexual difference, the narrative of Marie-Germain would not have surprised them. Women were viewed as inferior types of men, and their sexual organs were regarded as internal versions of male genitalia. In the best scientific understanding of the day, there was just one sex, and under certain circumstances women could turn into men.[7]

What, then, in the eyes of Virginia's English residents, constituted sufficient evidence of sexual identity? For the male and female searchers of T's body, genitalia that appeared to be normally masculine provided the answer. But that was not the only possible contemporary response to the question. Leaving aside for the moment the persons who saw T as a combination of male and female (they will be considered later), it is useful to focus on those who at different times indicated that they thought T was female. There were three such individuals, all of them men: Captain Nathaniel Basse, who ordered T to wear women's clothing after T had appeared before him; John Atkins, T's second master, who purchased Thomasine as a maidservant and referred to T as "shee" before bowing to the contrary opinion of the female searchers and changing the pronoun to "him"; and, most important of all, T's first master, John Tyos.

It is not clear from the trial record why Captain Basse directed T to dress as a woman, for T asserted a dual sexual identity in response to questioning and never claimed to be exclusively female. Perhaps the crucial fact was T's admission that "hee had not the use of the mans parte." Another possibility was that Mr. Basse interpreted T's anatomy as insufficiently masculine. As was already indicated, the partial physical description of T included in this portion of the record survives only in fragmentary form and so is impossible to interpret, especially in light of the certainty of all the searchers.

John Atkins acquired T as a servant after Captain Basse had issued his order, and he at first accepted Thomasine as a woman, referring to how "shee" seemed to awaken from sleep. Yet Atkins changed his mind about his servant after he and the five women subjected T's body to the most thorough examination described in the case record. It involved a physical search by the women, then questioning by Atkins, followed by an order from Atkins to Hall to "lye on his backe and shew" the "peece of an hole" that T claimed to have. When the women "did again find him to bee a man," Atkins issued the directive that contradicted Captain Basse's, ordering T to put on men's clothes. For Atkins, Hall's anatomy (which he saw with his own eyes) and the women's testimony were together decisive in overriding his initial belief that T was female, a belief presumably based at least in part on his presence at Mr. Basse's interrogation of T.

Unlike Atkins, John Tyos had purchased T as Thomas—a man. And for him the interpretive process was reversed. After just a brief acquaintance with Thomas, John and his wife learned that he had female skills. Approximately a year later Tyos "swore" to Dorothy Rodes that Hall "was a woman," a conclusion that contradicted the opinion of the female searchers. It also seemingly flew in the face of what must have been his own intimate knowledge of Hall's physical being. The lack of space in the small houses of the seventeenth-century Chesapeake is well known to scholars.[8] It is difficult to imagine that Tyos had never seen Hall's naked body—the same body that convinced searchers of both sexes that T was male. So why would Tyos insist that T was Thomasine, even to Dorothy Rodes, who forcefully asserted the contrary? The answer must lie not in T's sexual organs but in T's gender—that is, in the feminine skills and mannerisms that would have been exhibited by a person born, raised, and living as a female until reaching the age of twenty-two, and which would have

been immediately evident to anyone who, like John Tyos, lived with T for any length of time.

Thus, for these colonists, sex had two possible determinants. One was physical: the nature of one's genitalia. The other was cultural: the character of one's knowledge and one's manner of behaving. The female and male searchers used the former criterion, John Tyos, the latter. John Atkins initially adopted the second approach, but later switched to the first. Nathaniel Basse may have agreed with Tyos, or he may have refused to interpret T's anatomy as unambiguously as did the searchers: it is not clear which. But it is clear that two quite distinct tests of sexual identity existed in tandem in early Virginia. One relied on physical characteristics, the other on learned, gendered behavior. On most occasions, of course, results of the two tests would accord with each other. Persons raised as females would physically appear to be females; persons raised as males would look like other males. Hall acted like a woman and physically resembled a man. Thus in T's case the results of the two independent criteria clashed, and that was the source of the confusion.

Second, the importance of clothing. Many of the key questions about Hall were couched in terms of what clothing T should wear, men's or women's. Captain Basse and John Atkins did not say to T, "you are a man," or "you are a woman," but instead issued instructions about what sort of apparel T was to put on. Likewise, although the General Court declared explicitly that Hall was both male and female, its decision also described the clothing T was to wear in specific detail. Why was clothing so important?

The answer lies in the fact that in the seventeenth century clothing was a crucial identifier of persons. Not only did males and females wear very different garb, but persons of different ranks also were expected to reveal their social status in their dress. In short, one was supposed to display visually one's sex and rank to everyone else in the society. Thus, ideally, new acquaintances would know how to categorize each other even before exchanging a word of greeting. In a fundamental sense, seventeenth-century people's identity was expressed in their apparel. Virginia never went so far as Massachusetts, which passed laws regulating what clothing people of different ranks could wear, but the Virginia colonists were clearly determined to uphold the same sorts of rules.[9]

Clothing, which was sharply distinguished by the sex of its wearer, served as a visual trope for gender. And gender was one of the two most basic determinants of role in the early modern world (the other was rank, which was never at issue in Hall's case—T was always a servant). People who wore skirts nurtured children; people who wore pants did not. People who wore aprons could take no role in governing the colony, whereas other people could, if they were of appropriate status. People who wore headdresses performed certain sorts of jobs in the household; people who wore hats did other types of jobs in the fields. It is hardly surprising, therefore, that Virginians had difficulty dealing with a person who sometimes dressed as a man and other times as a woman—and who, on different occasions, did both at the direction of superiors. Nor, in light of this context, is it surprising that decisions about T's sexual identity were stated in terms of clothing.[10]

Third, the absence of a sense of personal privacy throughout the proceedings. To a modern sensibility, two aspects of the case stand out. First, seventeenth-century Virginians appear to have had few hesitations about their right to examine the genitalia of another colonist, with or without official authorization from a court and regardless of whether that activity occurred forcibly, clandestinely, or openly. The physical examinations were nominally by same-sex individuals (women when T was thought to be female, men when T had been declared to be male), with one key exception: John Atkins joined the women in scrutinizing the body of his maidservant. A master's authority over the household, in other words, extended to the bodies of his dependents. If a master like Atkins chose to search the body of a subordinate of either sex, no barrier would stand in his way.

Second, Hall seems not to have objected to any of the intrusive searches of T's body nor to the intimate questioning to which T was subjected by Captain Basse and the General Court. Hall too appears to have assumed that T's sexual identity was a matter of concern for the community at large. Such an attitude on Hall's part was congruent with a society in which the existing minimal privacy rights were seen as accruing to households as a unit or perhaps to their heads alone. Subordinates like Hall neither expected nor received any right to privacy of any sort.

Fourth, the involvement of the community, especially women, in the process of determining sexual identity. One of the most significant aspects of Hall's story is the initiative taken throughout by Hall's fellow colonists. They not only brought their doubts about Hall's sex to the attention of the authorities, they also refused to accept Captain Basse's determination that Hall was female. Both men and women joined in the effort to convince Virginia's leaders that T was male. Nearly uniformly rejecting T's self-characterization as "both" (the only exception outside the General Court being Mr. Stacy), Virginians insisted that Hall had to be either female or male, with most favoring the latter definition. They wanted a sexual category into which to fit T, and they did not hesitate to express their opinions about which category was the more appropriate.

Women in particular were active in this regard. Three times groups of women scrutinized T's body, whereas a group of men did so only once. After each examination, women rejected T as one of their number. Because of the vigorous and persistent efforts of female Virginians, Hall was deprived of the possibility of adopting unambiguously the role with which T seemed most comfortable, that of Thomasine. Here Hall's physical characteristics determined the outcome. Accustomed to searching the bodies of other females, women thought T did not physically qualify as feminine— regardless of the gendered skills T possessed— and they repeatedly asserted that to any man who would listen. For them, T's anatomy (sex) was more important than T's feminine qualities (gender).

Male opinion, on the other hand, was divided. The three male searchers of T's body— Roger Rodes, Francis England, and John Atkins—agreed with the women's conclusion. Other men were not so sure. John Tyos and Nathaniel Basse thought T more appropriately classified as a woman, while Mr. Stacy and the members of the General Court said T displayed aspects of both sexes. It seems plausible to infer from their lack of agreement about T's sex that men as a group were not entirely certain about what criteria to apply to create the categories "male" and "female." Some relied on physical appearance, others on behavior.

Moreover, the complacency of the male searchers can be interpreted as quite remarkable.

They failed to police the boundaries of their sex with the same militance as did women. That T, if a man, was a very unusual sort of man indeed did not seem to bother Rodes, Atkins, and England. For them, T's physical resemblance to other men was adequate evidence of masculinity, despite their knowledge of T's feminine skills and occasional feminine dress. That opinion was, however, in the end overridden by the doubts of higher-ranking men on the General Court, who were not so willing to overlook T's peculiarities.

Fifth, the relationship among sex, gender, and sexuality. Twice, and in quite different ways, the case record raises issues of sexuality rather than of biological sex or of gendered behavior. Both references have been alluded to briefly: the rumor of Thomas's having committed fornication with "greate Besse," and T's explanation for wearing women's clothing—"to gett a bitt for my Catt."

A judgment about T's body would imply a judgment about T's sexuality as well. Yet was it possible to reach a definitive conclusion about T's sexuality? If T were Thomas, then he could potentially be guilty of fornicating with the maidservant Bess; if T were Thomasine, then being in the same bed with Bess might mean nothing—or it could imply "unnatural" acts, the sort of same-sex coupling universally condemned when it occurred between men. The rumor about Bess, which for an ordinary male servant might have led to a fistfight (with the supposed slanderer, Tyos's servant), a defamation suit, or a fornication presentment, thus raised perplexing questions because of T's ambiguous sexual identity, questions that had to be resolved in court.[11]

T's phrase "to gett a bitt for my Catt," as reported by Francis England, was even more troubling. What did it mean, and was that meaning evident to England and the members of the General Court? As an explanation for wearing female apparel, it could have been straightforward and innocent. One historian reads it literally, as indicating that Hall wore women's clothing to beg scraps for a pet cat. Hall might also have been saying that because T's skills were feminine, dressing as a woman was the best way for T to earn a living, "to get a bit (morsel) to eat." But some scholars have read erotic connotations into the statement. Could T, speaking as a man, have been saying that wearing women's clothing allowed T to get close to women, to—in modern slang—"get a piece of pussy" by masquerading as a female?[12]

There is another more likely and even more intriguing erotic possibility. Since Hall had served in the English army on an expedition to France, T could well have learned a contemporary French slang phrase—"pour avoir une bite pour mon chat"—or, crudely put in English, "to get a penis for my cunt." Translating the key words literally into English equivalents (bite=bit, chat=cat) rather than into their metaphorical meanings produced an answer that was probably as opaque and confusing to seventeenth-century Virginians as it has proved to be to subsequent historians.[13] Since much of Francis England's testimony (with the exception of his report of this statement and the account of his and Roger Rodes's examination of T's anatomy) duplicated John Atkins's deposition, England could have been called as a witness primarily to repeat such a mysterious conversation to the court.

If T was indeed employing a deliberately misleading Anglicized version of contemporary French slang, as appears probable, two conclusions are warranted. First, the response confirms T's predominantly feminine gender, for it describes sexual intercourse from a woman's perspective. In light of the shortage of women in early Virginia, it moreover would have accurately represented T's experience: donning women's garb unquestionably opened sexual possibilities to Thomasine that Thomas lacked. Second, at the same time, Hall was playing with T's listeners, answering the question about wearing women's apparel truthfully, but in such an obscure way that it was unlikely anyone would comprehend T's meaning. In other words, Hall was having a private joke at the expense of the formal and informal publics in the colony. Hall's sly reply thus discloses a mischievous aspect of T's character otherwise hidden by the flat prose of the legal record.

Sixth, the court's decision. At first glance, the most surprising aspect of the case is the General Court's acceptance of Hall's self-definition as both man and woman. By specifying that T's basic apparel should be masculine, but with feminine signs—the apron and the coif and cross-cloth, a headdress commonly worn by women at the time—Virginia officials formally recognized that Hall contained elements of both sexes. The elite men who sat as judges thereby demonstrated their ability to transcend the dichotomous sexual categories that determined the thinking of ordinary Virginians. But their superficially astonishing verdict becomes explicable when the judges' options are analyzed in terms of contemporary understandings of sex and gender.

First, consider T's sexual identity. Could the court have declared Hall to be female? That alternative was effectively foreclosed. Women had repeatedly scrutinized T's anatomy and had consistently concluded that T was male. Their initial determination that T was a man (in the wake of Mr. Stacy's comment that T was both) first brought the question before Captain Basse. Subsequently, their adamant rejection of Captain Basse's contrary opinion and their ability to convince John Atkins that they were correct, coupled with the similar assessment reached by two men, were the key elements forcing the General Court to consider the case. A small community could not tolerate a situation in which groups of men and women alternately stripped and searched the body of one of its residents, or in which the decisions of the local commander were so openly disobeyed. Declaring T to be female was impossible; ordinary Virginians of both sexes would not accept such a verdict.

Yet, at the same time, could anyone assert unconditionally that Hall was sexually a man? Francis England, Roger Rodes, John Atkins, and the five female searchers thought so, on the basis of anatomy; but John Tyos, who was probably better acquainted with T than anyone else, declared unequivocally that Hall was a woman. And T had testified about not having "the use of the mans parte." Hall, in other words, revealed that although T had what appeared to be male genitalia, T did not function sexually as a man and presumably could not have an erection. To Captain Basse and the members of the General Court, that meant that (whatever T's physical description) Hall would not be able to father children or be a proper husband to a wife.

. . . The ability to impregnate a woman was a key indicator of manhood in seventeenth-century Anglo-America. Childless men were the objects of gossip, and impotence served as adequate grounds for divorce. A person who could not father a child was by that criterion alone an unsatisfactory male. T had admitted being incapable of male orgasm. Given that admitted physical incapacity and its implications,

declaring Hall to be a man was as impossible as declaring T to be a woman.[14]

Second, consider T's gender identity. In seventeenth-century Anglo-America, as in all other known societies, sexual characteristics carried with them gendered consequences. In Hall's life history those consequences were especially evident, because what T did and how T did it were deeply affected by whether T chose to be Thomas or Thomasine.

Whenever Hall traveled far from home, to France in the army or to Virginia, T became Thomas. Men had much more freedom of movement than did women. Unlike other persons raised as females, Hall's unusual anatomy gave T the opportunity to live as a male when there was an advantage to doing so. Even though T seemed more comfortable being Thomasine—to judge by frequent reversions to that role—the option of becoming Thomas must have been a welcome one. It permitted Hall to escape the normal strictures that governed early modern English women's lives and allowed T to pursue a more adventurous lifestyle.[15]

Thus whether T chose to be male or female made a great difference in T's life. As Thomas, Hall joined the army and emigrated to the colonies; as Thomasine, Hall lived quietly in London with an aunt, did fancy needlework in Plymouth, and presumably performed tasks normally assigned to women in Virginia. T's most highly developed skills were feminine ones, so T was undoubtedly more expert at and familiar with "women's work" in general, not just seamstressing.

It was, indeed, Hall's feminine skills that convinced some men that T was female; and those qualities, coupled with Hall's physical appearance, must have combined to lead to the court's decision. T's gender was feminine but T's sex seemed to be masculine—with the crucial exception of sexual functioning. Given T's sexual incapacity, all indications pointed to a feminine identity—to Thomasine. But Virginia women's refusal to accept T as Thomasine precluded that verdict. On the other hand, the judges could not declare a person to be male who had admitted to Captain Basse an inability to consummate a marriage. Ordinary men might possibly make a decision on the basis of physical appearance alone, but the members of the General Court had a responsibility to maintain the wider social order. If they said Hall was a man, then Thomas theoretically could marry and become a household head once his term of service was complete. That alternative was simply not acceptable for a person of T's description.

So, considering sex (incompletely masculine) and gender (primarily feminine), the Virginia General Court's solution to the dilemma posed by Hall was to create a unique category that combined sex and gender for T alone. Unable to fit Hall into the standard male/female dichotomy, the judges preferred to develop a singular definition that enshrined T's dual identity by prescribing clothing that simultaneously carried conflicting messages.

The court's decision to make Hall unique in terms of clothing—and thus gender identity—did not assist the community in classifying or dealing with T. After the verdict, Virginians were forced to cope with someone who by official sanction straddled the dichotomous roles of male and female. By court order, Hall was now a dual-sexed person. T's identity had no counterpart or precedent; paradoxically, a society in which gender—the outward manifestation of sex—served as a fundamental dividing line had formally designated a person as belonging to both sexes. Yet at the same time it was precisely because gender was so basic a concern to seventeenth-century society that no other solution was possible.

Hall's life after the court verdict must have been lonely. Marked as T was by unique clothing, unable to adopt the gender switches that had previously given T unparalleled flexibility in choosing a way of life, Hall must have had a very difficult time. T, like other publicly marked deviants—persons branded for theft or adultery or mutilated for perjury or forgery—was perhaps the target of insults or assaults. The verdict in T's case, in its insistence that T be constantly clothed as both sexes rather than alternating between them, was therefore harsh, though it nominally accorded with T's own self-definition. Hall's identity as "both" allowed movement back and forth across gender lines. The court's verdict had quite a different meaning, insisting not on the either/or sexual ambiguity T had employed to such great advantage, but rather on a definition of "both" that required duality and allowed for no flexibility.

It is essential to re-emphasize here what necessitated this unusual ending to a remarkable case: the opinions and actions of the female neighbors of John Tyos and John Atkins. Captain Nathaniel Basse, confronted with basically the same information that the General Court later considered, concluded that Hall should be dressed and treated as a woman. In a sexual belief system that hypothesized that women were inferior men, any inferior man—that is, one who could not function adequately in sexual terms—was a woman. Thus, charged the women at an Accomack cow pen in 1637, John Waltham "hade his Mounthly Courses as Women have" because his wife had not become pregnant.[16] Undoubtedly the General Court's first impulse would have been the same as Captain Basse's: to declare that T, an inferior man, was female and should wear women's clothing. But Virginia women had already demonstrated forcefully that they would not accept such a verdict. Hall's fate therefore was determined as much by a decision reached by ordinary women as it was by a verdict formally rendered by the elite men who served on the General Court.

Notes

1. Anthropologists have been in the forefront of the investigation of the various relationships of sex and gender. A good introduction to such work is Sherry Ortner and Harriet Whitehead, eds., *Sexual Meanings: The Cultural Construction of Gender and Sexuality* (New York: Cambridge University Press, 1981). . . . For an account of how contemporary American society handles sexually ambiguous babies at birth, see Suzanne J. Kessler, "The Medical Construction of Gender: Case Management of Intersexed Infants," *Signs*, XVI (1990), 3–26.

2. Unless otherwise indicated, all quotations and details in the account that follows are taken from the record in the case, *Va Ct Recs*, 194–95.

3. The expedition in which Thomas took part was an ill-fated English attack on the Isle de Ré during the summer of 1627. The troops who futilely tried to relieve the French Protestants besieged in the city of La Rochelle embarked on July 10, 1627; most of them returned to Plymouth in early November.

4. *Va Ct Recs*, 159, 162–64 (quotation 163). Yet it is possible that the Thomas Hall in this case was the other man, the one who came to Virginia in 1620. For him, see Virginia M. Meyer and John F. Dorman, eds., *Adventurers of Purse and Person Virginia 1607–1624/5*, 3d ed. [Richmond: Order of First Families of Virginia, 1987]. The Virginia muster of 1624/5 (ibid., 42) lists Thomas Hall and John Tyos as residents of George Sandys's plantation in James City. . . .

5. Little can be discovered about the three women. . . .

6. The two newcomers were the wife of Allen Kinaston and the wife of Ambrose Griffen. . . .

7. The best discussion of the one-sex model of humanity and its implications is Thomas Laqueur, *Making Sex: Body and Gender from the Greeks to Freud*

(Cambridge, Mass.: Harvard University Press, 1990). See 126–30 for an analysis of Marie-Germain.

8. See Lois Green Carr et al., *Robert Cole's World: Agriculture and Society in Early Maryland* (Chapel Hill: University of North Carolina Press, 1991), 90–114, on "the standard of life" in the early Chesapeake.

9. See *Mass Col Recs*, IV, pt 1, 60–61, IV, pt 2, 41–42. . . .

10. Laqueur observes, in *Making Sex*, 124–25, that "in the absence of a purportedly stable system of two sexes, strict sumptuary laws of the body attempted to stabilize gender—woman as woman and man as man—and punishments for transgression were quite severe." A relevant recent study is Marjorie Garber, *Vested Interests: Cross-Dressing and Cultural Anxiety* (New York: Routledge, 1991).

11. A good general discussion of the colonists' attitudes toward sexuality is John D'Emilio and Estelle B. Freedman, *Intimate Matters: A History of Sexuality in America* (New York: Harper & Row, 1988), 1–52, especially (on the regulation of deviance) 27–38.

12. Brown interprets the statement literally in her "Gender and the Genesis of Race and Class System," I, 88. The suggestion that the phrase might have meant

"earning a living" is mine, developed after consulting the *OED* (s.v. "bit"). Katz speculates that T's phrase had the erotic meaning suggested here, though he recognizes that such an interpretation is problematic (*Gay/Lesbian Almanac*, 72).

13. I owe the identification of the probable French origin of this phrase to Marina Warner and, through her, to Julian Barnes, whom she consulted (personal communication, 1993). My colleague Steven Kaplan, a specialist in the history of early modern France (and scholars he consulted in Paris), confirmed that "bite" and "chat" were used thus in the late sixteenth century and that the interpretation appears plausible.

14. On the importance of marital sexuality in the colonies: D'Emilio and Freedman, *Intimate Matters*, 16–27.

15. See, on this point, Rudolf M. Dekker and Lotte C. van de Pol, *The Tradition of Female Transvestism in Early Modern Europe* (London: Macmillan, 1989).

16. Susie M. Ames, ed., *County Court Records of Accomack-Northampton, Virginia, 1632–1640* (American Legal Records, VII) (Washington, D.C., 1954), p. 85.

LAUREL THATCHER ULRICH
Three Inventories, Three Households

One of the greatest barriers to an accurate assessment of women's role in the community has been the habit of assuming that what women did was not very important. Housekeeping has long been women's work, and housework has long been regarded as trivial. Laurel Thatcher Ulrich shows, however, that housekeeping can be a complex task and that real skill and intelligence might be exercised in performing it. The services housekeepers perform, in early as well as in contemporary America, are an important part of the economic arrangements that sustain the family and need to be taken into account when describing any community or society. Note the differences Ulrich finds between rural and urban women, and between middle-class and impoverished women.

By English tradition, a woman's environment was the family dwelling and the yard or yards surrounding it. Though the exact composition of her setting obviously depended upon the occupation and economic status of her husband, its general outlines were surprisingly similar regardless of where it was located. The difference between an urban "houselot" and a rural "homelot" was not as dramatic as one might suppose.

If we were to draw a line around the housewife's domain, it would extend from the kitchen and its appendages, the cellars, pantries, brewhouses, milkhouses, washhouses,

Excerpted from ch. 1 of *Good Wives: Image and Reality in the Lives of Women in Northern New England, 1650–1750,* by Laurel Thatcher Ulrich (New York: Alfred A. Knopf, 1982). Reprinted by permission of the author and publisher. Notes have been edited and renumbered.

and butteries which appear in various combinations in household inventories, to the exterior of the house, where, even in the city, a mélange of animal and vegetable life flourished among the straw, husks, clutter, and muck. Encircling the pigpen, such a line would surround the garden, the milkyard, the well, the hen-house, and perhaps the orchard itself—though husbands pruned and planted trees and eventually supervised the making of cider, good housewives strung their wash between the trees and in season harvested fruit for pies and conserves.

The line demarking the housewife's realm would not cross the fences which defined outlying fields of Indian corn or barley, nor would it stretch to fishing stages, mills, or wharves, but in berry or mushroom season it would extend into nearby woods or marsh and in spells of dearth or leisure reach to the shore. Of necessity, the boundaries of each woman's world would also extend into the houses of neighbors and into the cartways of a village or town. Housewives commanded a limited domain. But they were neither isolated nor self-sufficient. Even in farming settlements, families found it essential to bargain for needed goods and services. For prosperous and socially prominent women, interdependence took on another meaning as well. Prosperity meant charity, and in early New England charity meant personal responsibility for nearby neighbors. . . .

. . . For most historians, as for almost all antiquarians, the quintessential early American woman has been a churner of cream and a spinner of wool. Because home manufacturing has all but disappeared from modern housekeeping, many scholars have assumed that the key change in female economic life has been a shift from "production" to "consumption," a shift precipitated by the industrial revolution.[1] This is far too simple, obscuring the variety which existed even in the preindustrial world. . . .

. . . Beatrice Plummer, Hannah Grafton, and Magdalen Wear lived and died in New England in the years before 1750. One of them lived on the frontier, another on a farm, and a third in town. Because they were real women, however, and not hypothetical examples, the ways of their households were shaped by personal as well as geographic factors. A careful examination of the contents of their kitchens and chambers suggests the varied complexity as well as the underlying unity in the lives of early American women.

Let us begin with Beatrice Plummer of Newbury, Massachusetts.[2] Forgetting that death brought her neighbors into the house on January 24, 1672, we can use the probate inventory which they prepared to reconstruct the normal pattern of her work.

With a clear estate of £343, Francis Plummer had belonged to the "middling sort" who were the church members and freeholders of the Puritan settlement of Newbury. As an immigrant of 1653, he had listed himself as a "linnen weaver," but he soon became a farmer as well.[3] At his death, his loom and tackling stood in the "shop" with his pitchforks, his hoes, and his tools for smithing and carpentry. Plummer had integrated four smaller plots to form one continuous sixteen-acre farm. An additional twenty acres of salt marsh and meadow provided hay and forage for his small herd of cows and sheep. His farm provided a comfortable living for his family, which at this stage of his life included only his second wife, Beatrice, and her grandchild by a previous marriage. . . .

The house over which Beatrice presided must have looked much like surviving dwellings from seventeenth-century New England, with its "Hall" and "Parlor" on the ground floor and two "chambers" above. A space designated in the inventory only as "another Roome" held the family's collection of pots, kettles, dripping pans, trays, buckets, and earthenware. . . . The upstairs chambers were not bedrooms but storage rooms for foodstuffs and out-of-season equipment. The best bed with its bolster, pillows, blanket, and coverlet stood in the parlor; a second bed occupied one corner of the kitchen, while a cupboard, a "great chest," a table, and a backless bench called a "form" furnished the hall. More food was found in the "cellar" and in the "dairy house," a room which may have stood at the coolest end of the kitchen lean-to.[4]

The Plummer house was devoid of ornament, but its contents bespeak such comforts as conscientious yeomanry and good huswifery afforded. On this winter morning the dairy house held four and a half "flitches" or sides of bacon, a quarter of a barrel of salt pork, twenty-eight pounds of cheese, and four pounds of butter. Upstairs in a chamber were more than twenty-five bushels of "English" grain—barley, oats, wheat, and rye. (The Plummers apparently reserved their Indian corn, stored in another location, for their animals.) When made into malt by a village specialist, barley would become the basis for beer. Two bushels of malt were already stored in the house. The oats might appear in a variety of dishes, from plain breakfast porridge to "flummery," a gelatinous dish flavored with spices and dried fruit.[5] But the wheat and rye were almost certainly reserved for bread and pies. The fine hair sieves stored with the grain in the hall chamber suggest that Beatrice Plummer was particular about her baking, preferring a finer flour than came directly from the miller. A "bushell of pease & beans" found near the grain and a full barrel of cider in the cellar are the only vegetables and fruits listed in the inventory, though small quantities of pickles, preserves, or dried herbs might have escaped notice. Perhaps the Plummers added variety to their diet by trading some of their abundant supply of grain for cabbages, turnips, sugar, molasses, and spices. . . .

Since wives were involved with early-morning milking, breakfast of necessity featured prepared foods or leftovers—toasted bread, cheese, and perhaps meat and turnips kept from the day before, any of this washed down with cider or beer in winter, with milk in summer. Only on special occasions would there be pie or doughnuts. Dinner was the main meal of the day. Here a housewife with culinary aspirations and an ample larder could display her specialties. After harvest Beatrice Plummer might have served roast pork or goose with apples, in spring an eel pie flavored with parsley and winter savory, and in summer a leek soup or gooseberry cream; but for ordinary days the most common menu was boiled meat with whatever "sauce" the season provided—dried peas or beans, parsnips, turnips, onions, cabbage, or garden greens. A heavy pudding stuffed into a cloth bag could steam atop the vegetables and meat. The broth from this boiled dinner might reappear at supper as "pottage" with the addition of minced herbs and some oatmeal or barley for thickening. Supper, like breakfast, was a simple meal. Bread, cheese, and beer were as welcome at the end of a winter day as at the beginning. . . .

Preparing the simplest of these meals required both judgment and skill. . . . The most basic of the housewife's skills was building and regulating fires—a task so fundamental that it must have appeared more as habit than

craft. Summer and winter, day and night, she kept a few brands smoldering, ready to stir into flame as needed. The cavernous fireplaces of early New England were but a century removed from the open fires of medieval houses, and they retained some of the characteristics of the latter. Standing inside one of these huge openings today, a person can see the sky above. Seventeenth-century housewives did stand in their fireplaces, which were conceived less as enclosed spaces for a single blaze than as accessible working surfaces upon which a number of small fires might be built. Preparing several dishes simultaneously, a cook could move from one fire to another, turning a spit, checking the state of the embers under a skillet, adjusting the height of a pot hung from the lug-pole by its adjustable trammel. The complexity of firetending, as much as anything else, encouraged the one-pot meal.[6]

The contents of her inventory suggest that Beatrice Plummer was adept not only at roasting, frying, and boiling but also at baking, the most difficult branch of cookery. Judging from the grain in the upstairs chamber, the bread which she baked was "maslin," a common type made from a mixture of wheat and other grains, usually rye. She began with the sieves stored nearby, carefully sifting out the coarser pieces of grain and bran. Soon after supper she could have mixed the "sponge," a thin dough made from warm water, yeast, and flour. Her yeast might have come from the foamy "barm" found on top of fermenting ale or beer, from a piece of dough saved from an earlier baking, or even from the crevices in an unwashed kneading trough. Like fire-building, bread-making was based upon a self-perpetuating chain, an organic sequence which if once interrupted was difficult to begin again. Warmth from the banked fire would raise the sponge by morning, when Beatrice could work in more flour, knead the finished dough, and shape the loaves, leaving them to rise again.

Even in twentieth-century kitchens with standardized yeast and thermostatically controlled temperatures, bread dough is subject to wide variations in consistency and behavior. In a drafty house with an uncertain supply of yeast, bread-making was indeed "an art, craft, and mystery." Not the least of the problem was regulating the fire so that the oven was ready at the same time as the risen loaves. Small cakes or biscuits could be baked in a skillet or directly on the hearth under an upside-down pot covered with coals. But to produce bread in any quantity required an oven. Before 1650 these were frequently constructed in door-yards, but in the last decades of the century they were built into the rear of the kitchen fireplace, as Beatrice Plummer's must have been. Since her oven would have had no flue, she would have left the door open once she kindled a fire inside, allowing the smoke to escape through the fireplace chimney. Moving about her kitchen, she would have kept an eye on this fire, occasionally raking the coals to distribute the heat evenly, testing periodically with her hand to see if the oven had reached the right temperature. When she determined that it had, she would have scraped out the coals and inserted the bread—assuming that it had risen enough by this time or had not risen too much and collapsed waiting for the oven to heat.[7]

Cooking and baking were year-round tasks. Inserted into these day-by-day routines were seasonal specialities which allowed a housewife to bridge the dearth of one period with the bounty of another. In the preservation calendar, dairying came first, beginning with the first calves of early spring. In colonial New England cows were all-purpose creatures, raised for meat as well as for milk. Even in new settlements they could survive by browsing on rough land; their meat was a hedge against famine. But only in areas with abundant meadow (and even there only in certain months) would they produce milk with sufficient butterfat for serious dairying.[8] Newbury was such a place.

We can imagine Beatrice Plummer some morning in early summer processing the milk which would appear as cheese in a January breakfast. Slowly she heated several gallons with rennet dried and saved from the autumn's slaughtering. Within an hour or two the curd had formed. She broke it, drained off the whey, then worked in a little of her own fresh butter. Packing this rich mixture into a mold, she turned it in her wooden press for an hour or more, changing and washing the cheesecloth frequently as the whey dripped out. Repacking it in dry cloth, she left it in the press for another thirty or forty hours before washing it once more with whey, drying it, and placing it in the cellar or dairy house to age. As a young girl she would have learned from her mother or a mistress the importance of thorough pressing and the virtues of cleanliness. . . .

The Plummer inventory gives little evidence of the second stage of preservation in the housewife's year, the season of gardening and gathering which followed quickly upon the dairy months. But there is ample evidence of the autumn slaughtering. Beatrice could well have killed the smaller pigs herself, holding their "hinder parts between her legs," as one observer described the process, "and taking the snout in her left hand" while she stuck the animal through the heart with a long knife. Once the bleeding stopped, she would have submerged the pig in boiling water for a few minutes, then rubbed it with rosin, stripped off the hair, and disemboweled it. Nothing was lost. She reserved the organ meats for immediate use, then cleaned the intestines for later service as sausage casing. Stuffed with meat scraps and herbs and smoked, these "links" were a treasured delicacy. The larger cuts could be roasted at once or preserved in several ways.[9] . . .

Fall was also the season for cider-making. The mildly alcoholic beverage produced by natural fermentation of apple juice was a staple of the New England diet and was practically the only method of preserving the fruit harvest. With the addition of sugar, the alcoholic content could be raised from five to about seven percent, as it usually was in taverns and for export. . . .

Prosaic beer was even more important to the Plummer diet. Although some housewives brewed a winter's supply of strong beer in October, storing it in the cellar, Beatrice seems to have been content with "small beer," a mild beverage usually brewed weekly or bi-weekly and used almost at once. Malting—the process of sprouting and drying barley to increase its sugar content—was wisely left to the village expert. Beatrice started with cracked malt or grist, processing her beer in three stages. "Mashing" required slow steeping at just below the boiling point, a sensitive and smelly process which largely determined the success of the beverage. Experienced brewers knew by taste whether the enzymes were working. If it was too hot, acetic acid developed which would sour the finished product. The next stage, "brewing," was relatively simple. Herbs and hops were boiled with the malted liquid. In the final step this liquor was cooled and mixed with yeast saved from last week's beer or bread. Within twenty-four hours—if all had gone well—the beer was bubbling actively.[10]

. . . A wife who knew how to manage the ticklish chemical processes which changed milk into cheese, meal into bread, malt into beer, and flesh into bacon was a valuable asset, . . . [though some men were too churlish to admit it]. After her husband's death, Beatrice married a man . . . who not only refused to provide her with provisions, [but insisted on doing his own cooking]. He took his meat "out of ye pickle" and broiled it directly on the coals, and when she offered him "a cup of my owne Sugar & Bear," he refused it. When the neighbors testified that she had been a dutiful wife, the Quarterly Court fined him for "abusive carriages and speeches." Even the unhappy marriage that thrust Beatrice Plummer into court helps to document the central position of huswifery in her life.[11] . . .

Beatrice Plummer represents one type of early American housewife. Hannah Grafton represents another.[12] Chronology, geography, and personal biography created differences between the household inventories of the two women, but there are obvious similarities as well. Like Beatrice Plummer, Hannah Grafton lived in a house with two major rooms on the ground floor and two chambers above. At various locations near the ground-floor rooms were service areas—a washhouse with its own loft or chamber, a shop, a lean-to, and two cellars. The central rooms in the Grafton house were the "parlour," with the expected featherbed, and the "kitchen," which included much of the same collection of utensils and iron pots which appeared in the Plummer house. Standing in the corner of the kitchen were a spade and a hoe, two implements useful only for chipping away ice and snow on the December day on which the inventory was taken, though apparently destined for another purpose come spring. With a garden, a cow, and three pigs, Hannah Grafton clearly had agricultural responsibilities, but these were performed in a strikingly different context than on the Plummer farm. The Grafton homelot was a single acre of land standing just a few feet from shoreline in the urban center of Salem.[13]

Joshua Grafton was a mariner like his father before him. His estate of £236 was modest, but he was still a young man and he had firm connections with the seafaring elite who were transforming the economy of Salem. When he died late in 1699, Hannah had three living children—Hannah, eight; Joshua, six; and

Priscilla, who was just ten months.[14] This young family used their space quite differently than had the Plummers. The upstairs chambers which served as storage areas in the Newbury farmhouse were sleeping quarters here. In addition to the bed in the parlor and the cradle in the kitchen, there were two beds in each of the upstairs rooms. One of these, designated as "smaller," may have been used by young Joshua. It would be interesting to know whether the mother carried the two chamber pots kept in the parlor upstairs to the bedrooms at night or whether the children found their way in the dark to their parents' sides as necessity demanded. But adults were probably never far away. Because there are more bedsteads in the Grafton house than members of the immediate family, they may have shared their living quarters with unmarried relatives or servants.

Ten chairs and two stools furnished the kitchen, while no fewer than fifteen chairs, in two separate sets, crowded the parlor with its curtained bed. The presence of a punch bowl on a square table in the parlor reinforces the notion that sociability was an important value in this Salem household. Thirteen ounces of plate, a pair of gold buttons, and a silverheaded cane suggest a measure of luxury as well—all of this in stark contrast to the Plummers, who had only two chairs and a backless bench and no discernible ornamentation at all. Yet the Grafton house was only slightly more specialized than the Newbury farmhouse. It had no servants' quarters, no sharp segregation of public and private spaces, no real separation of sleeping, eating, and work. A cradle in the kitchen and a go-cart kept with the spinning wheels in the upstairs chamber show that little Priscilla was very much a part of this workaday world.

How then might the pattern of Hannah Grafton's work have differed from that of Beatrice Plummer? Certainly cooking remained central. Hannah's menus probably varied only slightly from those prepared in the Plummer kitchen, and her cooking techniques must have been identical. But one dramatic difference is apparent in the two inventories. The Grafton house contained no provisions worth listing on that December day when Isaac Foot and Samuel Willard appeared to take inventory. Hannah had brewing vessels, but no malt; sieves and a meal trough, but no grain; and a cow, but no cheese. What little milk her cow gave in winter probably went directly into the children's mugs.

Perhaps she would continue to breast-feed Priscilla until spring brought a more secure supply. . . . Trade, rather than manufacturing or agriculture, was the dominant motif in her meal preparations.

In colonial New England most food went directly from processer or producer to consumer. Joshua may have purchased grain or flour from the mill near the shipbuilding center called Knocker's Hole, about a mile away from their house. Or Hannah may have eschewed bread-making altogether, walking or sending a servant the half-mile to Elizabeth Haskett's bakery near the North River. Fresh meat for the spits in her washhouse may have come from John Cromwell's slaughterhouse on Main Street near the Congregational meetinghouse, and soap for her washtubs from the soap-boiler farther up the street near the Quaker meetinghouse.[15] Salem, like other colonial towns, was laid out helter-skelter, with the residences of the wealthy interspersed with the small houses of carpenters or fishermen. Because there was no center of retail trade, assembling the ingredients of a dinner involved many transactions. Sugar, wine, and spice came by sea; fresh lamb, veal, eggs, butter, gooseberries, and parsnips came by land. Merchants retailed their goods in shops or warehouses near their wharves and houses. Farmers or their wives often hawked their produce door to door.[16] . . .

In such a setting, trading for food might require as much energy and skill as manufacturing or growing it. One key to success was simply knowing where to go. Keeping abreast of the arrival of ships in the harbor or establishing personal contact with just the right farmwife from nearby Salem village required time and attention. Equally important was the ability to evaluate the variety of unstandardized goods offered. An apparently sound cheese might teem with maggots when cut.[17] Since cash was scarce, a third necessity was the establishment of credit, a problem which ultimately devolved upon husbands. But petty haggling over direct exchanges was also a feature of this barter economy.

Hannah Grafton was involved in trade on more than one level. The "shop" attached to her house was not the all-purpose storage shed and workroom it seems to have been for Francis Plummer. It was a retail store, offering door locks, nails, hammers, gimlets, and other hardware as well as English cloth, pins, needles, and thread. As a mariner, Joshua Grafton may well have sailed the ship which brought these goods to Salem. In his absence, Hannah was not only a mother and a housewife but, like many other Salem women, a shopkeeper as well.

There is another highly visible activity in the Grafton inventory which was not immediately apparent in the Plummer's—care of clothing. Presumably, Beatrice Plummer washed occasionally, but she did not have a "washhouse." Hannah did. The arrangement of this unusual room is far from clear. On December 2, 1699, it contained two spits, two "bouldishes," a gridiron, and "other things." Whether those other things included washtubs, soap, or a beating staff is impossible to determine. . . .

But on any morning in December the washhouse could . . . have been hung with the family wash. Dark woolen jackets and petticoats went from year to year without seeing a kettle of suds, but linen shifts, aprons, shirts, and handkerchiefs required washing. Laundering might not have been a weekly affair in most colonial households, but it was a well-defined if infrequent necessity even for transient seamen and laborers. One can only speculate on its frequency in a house with a child under a year. When her baby was only a few months old, Hannah may have learned to hold little Priscilla over the chamber pot at frequent intervals, but in early infancy, tightly wrapped in her cradle, the baby could easily have used five dozen "clouts" and almost as many "belly bands" from one washing to another. Even with the use of a "pilch," a thick square of flannel securely bound over the diaper, blankets and coverlets occasionally needed sudsing as well.[18]

Joshua's shirts and Hannah's own aprons and shifts would require careful ironing. Hannah's "smoothing irons" fitted into their own heaters, which she filled with coals from the fire. As the embers waned and the irons cooled, she would have made frequent trips from her table to the hearth to the fire and back to the table again. At least two of these heavy instruments were essential. A dampened apron could dry and wrinkle while a single flatiron replenished its heat.

As frequent a task as washing was sewing. Joshua's coats and breeches went to a tailor, but his shirts were probably made at home. Certainly Hannah stitched and unstitched the tucks which altered Priscilla's simple gowns and petticoats as she grew. The little dresses which the baby trailed in her go-cart had once clothed her brother. Gender identity in childhood was less important in this society than economy of effort. It was not that boys were seen as identical to girls, only that all-purpose garments could be handed from one child to another regardless of sex, and dresses were more easily altered than breeches and more adaptable to diapering and toileting. At eight years of age little Hannah had probably begun to imitate her mother's even stitches, helping with the continual mending, altering, and knitting which kept this growing family clothed.[19]

In some ways the most interesting items in the Grafton inventory are the two spinning wheels kept in the upstairs chamber. Beatrice Plummer's wheel and reel had been key components in an intricate production chain. The Plummers had twenty-five sheep in the fold and a loom in the shed. The Graftons had neither. Children—not sheep—put wheels in Hannah's house. The mechanical nature of spinning made it a perfect occupation for women whose attention was engrossed by young children. This is one reason why the ownership of wheels in both York and Essex counties had a constancy over time unrelated to the ownership of sheep or looms. In the dozen inventories taken in urban Salem about the time of Joshua Grafton's death, the six nonspinners averaged one minor child each, the six spinners had almost four. Instruction at the wheel was part of the almost ritualistic preparation mothers offered their daughters.[20] Spinning was a useful craft, easily picked up, easily put down, and even small quantities of yarn could be knitted into caps, stockings, dishcloths, and mittens.

. . . [A] cluster of objects in the chamber over Hannah Grafton's kitchen suggests a fanciful but by no means improbable vignette. Imagine her gathered with her two daughters in this upstairs room on a New England winter's day. Little Priscilla navigates around the end of the bedstead in her go-cart while her mother sits at one spinning wheel and her sister at the other. Young Hannah is spinning "oakum," the coarsest and least expensive part of the flax. As her mother leans over to help her wind the uneven thread on the bobbin, she catches a troublesome scent from downstairs. Have the turnips caught on the bottom of the pot? Has the maid scorched Joshua's best shirt? Or has a family servant returned from the wharf and spread his wet clothes by the fire? Hastening

down the narrow stairs to the kitchen, Hannah hears the shop bell ring. Just then little Priscilla, left upstairs with her sister, begins to cry. In such pivotal but unrecorded moments much of the history of women lies hidden.

The third inventory can be more quickly described.[21] Elias Wear of York, Maine, left an estate totaling £92, of which less than £7 was in household goods—including some old pewter, a pot, two bedsteads, bedding, one chest, and a box. Wear also owned a saddle, three guns, and a river craft called a gundalow. But his wealth, such as it was, consisted of land (£40) and livestock (£36). It is not just relative poverty which distinguished Elias Wear's inventory from that of Joshua Grafton or Francis Plummer. Every settlement in northern New England had men who owned only a pot, a bed, and a chest. Their children crowded in with them or slept on straw. These men and their sons provided some of the labor which harvested barley for farmers like Francis Plummer or stepped masts for mariners like Joshua Grafton. Their wives and their daughters carded wool or kneaded bread in other women's kitchens. No, Elias Wear was distinguished by a special sort of frontier poverty.

His father had come to northern New England in the 1640s, exploring and trading for furs as far inland in New Hampshire as Lake Winnipesaukee. By 1650 he had settled in York, a then hopeful site for establishing a patrimony. Forty years later he died in the York Massacre, an assault by French and Indians which virtually destroyed the town, bringing death or captivity to fully half of the inhabitants. Almost continuous warfare between 1689 and 1713 created prosperity for the merchant community of Portsmouth and Kittery, but it kept most of the inhabitants of outlying settlements in a state of impecunious insecurity.[22]

In 1696, established on a small homestead in the same neighborhood in which his father had been killed, Elias Wear married a young widow with the fitting name of Magdalen. When their first child was born "too soon," the couple found themselves in York County court owning a presentment for fornication. Although New England courts were still sentencing couples in similar circumstances to "nine stripes a piece upon the Naked back," most of the defendants, like the Wears, managed to pay the not inconsequential fine. The fifty-nine shillings which Elias and Magdalen pledged the court amounted to almost half of the total value of two steers. A presentment for fornication was expensive as well as inconvenient, but it did not carry a permanent onus. Within seven years of their conviction Elias was himself serving on the "Jury of Tryalls" for the county, while Magdalen had proved herself a dutiful and productive wife.[23]

Every other winter she gave birth, producing four sons—Elias, Jeremiah, John, and Joseph—in addition to the untimely Ruth. A sixth child, Mary, was just five months old when her father met his own death by Indians in August of 1707 while traveling between their Cape Neddick home and the more densely settled York village. Without the benefits of a cradle, a go-cart, a spinning wheel, or even a secure supply of grain, Magdalen raised these six children. Unfortunately, there is little in her inventory and nothing in any other record to document the specific strategies which she used, though the general circumstances of her life can be imagined.

Chopping and hauling for a local timber merchant, Elias could have filled Magdalen's porridge pot with grain shipped from the port of Salem or Boston. During the spring corn famine, an almost yearly occurrence on the Maine frontier, she might have gone herself with other wives of her settlement to dig on the clam flats, hedging against the day when relief would come by sea.[24] Like Beatrice Plummer and Hannah Grafton, she would have spent some hours cooking, washing, hoeing cabbages, bargaining with neighbors, and, in season, herding and milking a cow. But poverty, short summers, and rough land also made gathering an essential part of her work. We may imagine her cutting pine splinters for lights and "cattails" and "silkgrass" for beds. Long before her small garden began to produce, she would have searched out a wild "sallet" in the nearby woods, in summer turning to streams and barrens for other delicacies congenial to English taste—eels, salmon, berries, and plums. She would have embarked on such excursions with caution, however, remembering the wives of nearby Exeter who took their children into the woods for strawberries "without any Guard" and narrowly avoided capture.[25] . . .

. . . The Wears probably lived in a single-story cottage which may or may not have been subdivided into more than one room. A loft above provided extra space for storage or sleeping. With the addition of a lean-to, this house could have sheltered animals as well as humans, especially in harsh weather or in periods of Indian alarm. Housing a pig or a calf in the next room would have simplified Magdalen's chores in the winter. If she managed to raise a few chickens, these too would have thrived better near the kitchen fire.[26]

Thus, penury erased the elaborate demarcation of "houses" and "yards" evident in yeoman inventories. It also blurred distinctions between the work of a husbandman and the work of his wife. At planting time and at harvest Magdalen Wear undoubtedly went into the fields to help Elias, taking her babies with her or leaving Ruth to watch them as best she could.[27] A century later an elderly Maine woman bragged that she "had dropped corn many a day with two governors: a judge in her arms and a general on her back."[28] None of the Wear children grew up to such prominence, but all six of them survived to adulthood and four married and founded families of their own. Six children did not prevent Magdalen Wear from remarrying within two years of her husband's death. Whatever her assets—a pleasant face, a strong back, or lifetime possession of £40 in land—she was soon wed to the unmarried son of a neighboring millowner.[29]

Magdalen Wear, Hannah Grafton, and Beatrice Plummer were all "typical" New England housewives of the period 1650–1750. Magdalen's iron pot represents the housekeeping minimum which often characterized frontier life. Hannah's punch bowl and her hardware shop exemplify both the commerce and the self-conscious civilization of coastal towns. Beatrice's brewing tubs and churn epitomize home manufacturing and agrarian self-sufficiency as they existed in established villages. Each type of housekeeping could be found somewhere in northern New England in any decade of the century. Yet these three women should not be placed in rigidly separate categories. Wealth, geography, occupation, and age determined that some women in any decade would be more heavily involved in one aspect of housekeeping than another, yet all three women shared a common vocation. Each understood the rhythms of the seasons, the technology of fire-building, the persistence of the daily demands of cooking, the complexity of home production, and the dexterity demanded from the often conflicting roles of housekeeper, mother, and wife.

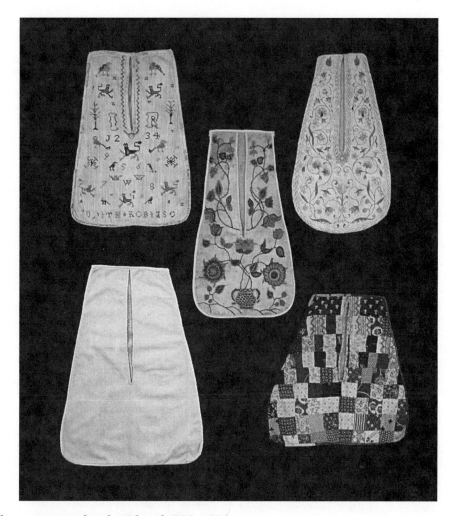

Pockets, sewn and embroidered 1720–1830.
Laurel Thatcher Ulrich suggests that the pocket, not the spinning wheel, is the best icon for colonial European women. Pockets were tied around the waist, and hidden between the skirt and the petticoat. They were handy for carrying small objects on one's daily circuit. Women typically made their own pockets—sometimes in a plain style and sometimes embroidered or pieced. Here are five examples ranging in date from roughly the 1720s to the 1820s. Clockwise from top left: Pocket with lions, made by Judith Robinson, Pennsylvania, 1780–1820; Pocket with flowers and vase, New England, 1720–1750; Floral pocket, Britain, 1737; Pieced pocket, New York, probably Albany, ca. 1810; White pocket, New York, Scotia area, 1780–1820. (Courtesy of the Colonial Williamsburg Foundation.)

The thing which distinguished these women from their counterparts in modern America was not, as some historians have suggested, that their work was essential to survival. "Survival," after all, is a minimal concept. Individual men and women have never needed each other for mere survival but for far more complex reasons, and women were essential in the seventeenth century for the very same reasons they are essential today—for the perpetuation of the race. . . . Nor was it the narrowness of their choices which really set them apart. Women in industrial cities have lived monotonous and confining lives, and they may have worked even harder than early American women. The really striking differences are social.

. . . [T]he lives of early American housewives were distinguished less by the tasks they performed than by forms of social organization which linked economic responsibilities to family responsibilities and which tied each woman's household to the larger world of her village or town.

For centuries the industrious Bathsheba has been pictured sitting at a spinning wheel—"She layeth her hands to the spindle, and her hands hold the distaff." Perhaps it is time to suggest a new icon for women's history. Certainly spinning was an important female craft in northern New England, linked not only to housework but to mothering, but it was one enterprise among many. Spinning wheels are such intriguing and picturesque objects, so resonant with antiquity, that they tend to obscure rather than clarify the nature of female economic life, making home production the essential element in early American huswifery and the era of industrialization the period of crucial change. Challenging the symbolism of the wheel not only undermines the popular stereotype, it questions a prevailing emphasis in women's history.

An alternate symbol might be the pocket. In early America a woman's pocket was not attached to her clothing, but tied around her waist with a string or tape. (When "Lucy Locket lost her pocket, Kitty Fisher found it.") Much better than a spinning wheel, this homely object symbolizes the obscurity, the versatility, and the personal nature of the housekeeping role. A woman sat at a wheel, but she carried her pocket with her from room to room, from house to yard, from yard to street. The items which it contained would shift from day to day and from year to year, but they would of necessity be small, easily lost, yet precious. A pocket could be a mended and patched pouch of plain homespun or a rich personal ornament boldly embroidered in crewel. It reflected the status as well as the skills of its owner. Whether it contained cellar keys or a paper of pins, a packet of seeds or a baby's bib, a hank of yarn, or a Testament, it characterized the social complexity as well as the demanding diversity of women's work.

NOTES

1. [See] William H. Chafe, *Women and Equality: Changing Patterns in American Culture* (New York: Oxford University Press, 1977), p. 17; . . . and Nancy F. Cott, *The Bonds of Womanhood* (New Haven and London: Yale University Press, 1977), p. 21.

2. Unless otherwise noted, the information which follows comes from the Francis Plummer will and inventory, *The Probate Records of Essex County* (hereafter *EPR*) (Salem, Mass.: Essex Institute, 1916–1920), II: 319–22.

3. Joshua Coffin, *A Sketch of the History of Newbury, Newburyport, and West Newbury* (Boston, 1845; Hampton, N.H.: Peter E. Randall, 1977), p. 315.

4. Abbott Lowell Cummings, *The Framed Houses of Massachusetts Bay, 1625–1725* (Cambridge, Mass., and London: Harvard University Press, 1979), pp. 29–32.

5. Darrett B. Rutman, *Husbandmen of Plymouth* (Boston: Beacon Press, 1967), pp. 10–11. . . . *Records and Files of the Quarterly Courts of Essex County, Massachusetts* (hereafter *ECR*) (Salem, Mass.: Essex Institute, 1911–1975), III:50; . . . Massachusetts Historical Society (hereafter MHS) *Collections*, 5th Ser., I:97; and Jay Allen Anderson, "A Solid Sufficiency: An Ethnography of Yeoman Foodways in Stuart England" (Ph.D. diss., University of Pennsylvania, 1971), pp. 171, 203–04, 265, 267, 268.

6. Cummings, *Framed Houses*, pp. 4, 120–22; . . . Jane Carson, *Colonial Virginia Cookery* (Charlottesville: University Press of Virginia, 1968), p. 104. . . .

7. Carson, *Colonial Virginia Cookery*, pp. 104–06.

8. Anderson, "Solid Sufficiency," pp. 63, 65, 118; . . . New Hampshire Historical Society Collections, V (1837), p. 225.

9. Anderson, "Solid Sufficiency," pp. 99–108, 120–32.

10. Sanborn C. Brown, *Wines and Beers of Old New England* (Hanover, N.H.: University Press of New England, 1978). . . .

11. *ECR*, IV:194–95, 297–98.

12. Unless otherwise noted, the information which follows comes from the Joshua Grafton will and inventory, Manuscript Probate Records, Essex County Probate Court, Salem, Mass. (hereafter Essex Probate), vol. CCCVII, pp. 58–59.

13. "Part of Salem in 1700," pocket map in James Duncan Phillips, *Salem in the Seventeenth Century* (Boston: Houghton Mifflin, 1933), H-6.

14. Sidney Perley, *The History of Salem, Massachusetts* (Salem, 1924), I:435, 441.

15. Phillips, *Salem in the Seventeenth Century*, pp. 314, 317, 318, 328; and James Duncan Phillips, *Salem in the Eighteenth Century* (Boston: Houghton Mifflin, 1937), pp. 20–21.

16. [See] Karen Friedman, "Victualling Colonial Boston," *Agricultural History* XLVII (July 1973): 189–205, and . . . Benjamin Coleman, *Some Reasons and Arguments Offered to the Good People of Boston and Adjacent Places, for the Setting Up Markets in Boston* (Boston, 1719), pp. 5–9.

17. . . . *The Salem Witchcraft Papers*, ed. Paul Boyer and Stephen Nissenbaum (New York: Da Capo Press, 1977), I:117–29.

18. [See] . . . e.g., *Province and Court Records of Maine* (hereafter *MPCR*) (Portland: Maine Historical Society, 1928–1975), IV:205–06; . . . and Essex Probate, CCCXXI:96. . . .

19. Susan Burrows Swan, *Plain and Fancy: American Women and Their Needlework, 1700–1850* (New York: Holt, Rinehart and Winston, 1977), pp. 18–19, 34–38.

20. "Letter-Book of Samuel Sewall," MHS *Collections*, 6th Ser., I:19. . . .

21. Unless otherwise noted, the information which follows comes from the Elias Wear will and inventory, Manuscript Probate Records, York County Probate Court, Alfred, Me., . . . II:26.

22. Charles Clark, *The Eastern Frontier* (New York: Alfred A. Knopf, 1970), pp. 67–72.

23. *MPCR*, IV:91–92, 175, 176, 206, 263, 307, 310.

24. Maine Historical Society *Collections*, IX: 58–59, 457, 566; MHS *Collections*, 6th Ser., I:126–65, 182–84, 186–89. . . .

25. Cotton Mather, *Decennium Luctuosum* (Boston, 1699), reprint Charles H. Lincoln, ed., *Narratives of the Indian Wars* (New York: Charles Scribner's Sons, 1913), pp. 266–67.

26. Richard M. Candee, "Wooden Buildings in Early Maine and New Hampshire: A Technological and Cultural History, 1600–1720" (Ph.D. diss., University of Pennsylvania, 1976), pp. 18, 42–48. . . .

27. . . . MHS *Proceedings* (1876), p. 129. Also see *ECR*, II: 372–73, 22, 442. . . .

28. Sarah Orne Jewett, *The Old Town of Berwick* (Berwick, Me.: Old Berwick Historical Society, 1967), n.p. . . .

29. Sybil Noyes, Charles Thornton Libby, and Walter Goodwin Davis, *A Genealogical Dictionary of Maine and New Hampshire* (Portland, Me.: Southworth-Anthoensen Press, 1928), pp. 726, 729.

CAROL F. KARLSEN

The Devil in the Shape of a Woman: The Economic Basis of Witchcraft

Puritan ministers stressed the equality of each soul in the eyes of God and the responsibility of each believer to read the Bible. They urged women as well as men toward literacy and taking responsibility for their own salvation. One distinguished minister, Cotton Mather, writing at the end of the seventeenth century, observed that since women came close to the experience of death in repeated childbirth, their religiosity was likely to be greater than that of men. In being "helpmeets" to their husbands, women were encouraged to strengthen their ability to be competent and capable. There was much in Puritan thought that could be appealing to women.

But, as we have seen in the case of Anne Hutchinson, the Puritan community was unforgiving to women who failed to serve the needs of godly men in their strictly hierarchical community. Lurking in their imagination—as it lurked throughout the Judeo-Christian tradition—was the cautionary biblical story of Eve, who, by her disobedience, brought evil into the world. (Puritans paid no attention to other elements of that complicated tale: Eve's disobedience, after all, was in quest of Knowledge; the biology of birth is reversed, with Eve emerging from Adam's body.) Witchcraft prosecutions were rare in English colonies outside of New England; there, they occurred individually or in small clusters, numbering under 100 until the famous outbreak in and near Salem, Massachusetts, in 1692, during which nearly 200 people, three-quarters of whom were women, were accused, and 13 women and 6 men were executed. Carol F. Karlsen argues that in early colonial New England culture, an older view of women as a necessary evil had been only superficially superseded by a new, Protestant view of women as a necessary good. Note that fear of women-as-witches was endemic at this time in Europe, where between 1450 and 1750 roughly 90,000 trials occurred, including 3,000 in the British Isles.

Excerpted from "The Economic Basis of Witchcraft," ch. 3 of *The Devil in the Shape of a Woman: Witchcraft in Colonial New England* by Carol F. Karlsen (New York: W. W. Norton, 1987). Reprinted by permission of the author and publisher. Notes have been edited and renumbered and tables renumbered.

In her essay, Karlsen provides in-depth, biographical profiles of several women who faced accusations both prior to and during the Salem witch-hunt. This research technique led her to make a startling and truly innovative discovery involving the category of "inheriting women." Her findings help to answer a frequently asked question: even though everyone in the society believed that witches existed and supernatural forces were operating in their lives, why did neighbors and aquaintances launch accusations against particular persons?

Anthropologists have long understood that communities define as witches people whose behavior enacts the things the community most fears; witchcraft beliefs, wrote Monica Hunter Wilson, are "the standardized nightmare of a group, and . . . the comparative analysis of such nightmares . . . [is] one of the keys to the understanding of society."* Have witch-hunts (using the word metaphorically) occurred in your lifetime or the lifetimes of your parents or grandparents?

Most observers now agree that witches in the villages and towns of late sixteenth- and early seventeeth-century England tended to be poor. They were not usually the poorest women in their communities, one historian has argued; they were the "moderately poor." Rarely were relief recipients suspect; rather it was those just above them on the economic ladder, "like the woman who felt she ought to get poor relief, but was denied it."[1] This example brings to mind New England's Eunice Cole, who once berated Hampton selectmen for refusing her aid when, she insisted, a man no worse off than she was receiving it.[2]

Eunice Cole's experience also suggests the difficulty in evaluating the class position of the accused. Commonly used class indicators such as the amount of property owned, yearly income, occupation, and political offices held are almost useless in analyzing the positions of women during the colonial period. While early New England women surely shared in the material benefits and social status of their fathers, husbands, and even sons, most were economically dependent on the male members of their families throughout their lives. Only a small proportion of these women owned property outright, and even though they participated actively in the productive work of their communities, their labor did not translate into financial independence or economic power. Any income generated by married women belonged by law to their husbands, and because occupations open to women were few and wages meager, women alone could only rarely support themselves. Their material condition, moreover, could easily change with an alteration in their marital

status. William Cole, with an estate at his death of £41 after debts, might be counted among the "moderately poor," as might Eunice Cole when he was alive. But the refusal of the authorities to recognize the earlier transfer of this estate from husband to wife ensured, among other things, that as a widow Eunice Cole was among the poorest of New England's poor. . . .

Despite conceptual problems and sparse evidence, it is clear that poor women, both the destitute and those with access to some resources, were surely represented, and very probably overrepresented, among the New England accused. Perhaps 20 percent of accused women . . . were either impoverished or living at a level of bare subsistence when they were accused.[3] Some, like thirty-seven-year-old Abigail Somes, worked as servants a substantial portion of their adult lives. Some supported themselves and their families with various kinds of temporary labor such as nursing infants, caring for sick neighbors, taking in washing and sewing, or harvesting crops. A few, most notably Tituba, the first person accused during the Salem outbreak, were slaves. Others, like the once-prosperous Sarah Good of Wenham and Salem, and the never-very-well-off Ruth Wilford of Haverhill, found themselves reduced to abject poverty by the death of a parent or a change in their own marital status.[4] Accused witches came before local magistrates requesting permission to sell family land in order to support themselves, to submit claims against their children or executors of their former husbands' estates for nonpayment of the widow's lawful share of the estate, or simply to ask for food and fuel from

* Quoted in Carol F. Karlsen, *The Devil in the Shape of a Woman* (New York: W. W. Norton, 1987), p. 181.

the town selectmen. Because they could not pay the costs of their trials or jail terms, several were forced to remain in prison after courts acquitted them. The familiar stereotype of the witch as an indigent woman who resorted to begging for her survival is hardly an inaccurate picture of some of New England's accused.

Still, the poor account for only a minority of the women accused. Even without precise economic indicators, it is clear that women from all levels of society were vulnerable to accusation.... Wives, daughters, and widows of "middling" farmers, artisans, and mariners were regularly accused, and (although much less often) so too were women belonging to the gentry class. The accused were addressed as Goodwife (or Goody) and as the more honorific Mrs. or Mistress, as well as by their first names.

Prosecution was a different matter. Unless they were single or widowed, accused women from wealthy families—families with estates valued at more than £500—could be fairly confident that the accusations would be ignored by the authorities or deflected by their husbands through suits for slander against their accusers. Even during the Salem outbreak, when several women married to wealthy men were arrested, most managed to escape to the safety of other colonies through their husbands' influence. Married women from moderately well-off families— families with estates valued at between roughly £200 and £500—did not always escape prosecution so easily, but neither do they seem, as a group, to have been as vulnerable as their less prosperous counterparts. When only married women are considered, women in families with estates worth less than £200 seem significantly overrepresented among convicted witches—a pattern which suggests that economic position was a more important factor to judges and juries than to the community as a whole in its role as accuser.[5]

Without a husband to act on behalf of the accused, wealth alone rarely provided women with protection against prosecution. Boston's Ann Hibbens, New Haven's Elizabeth Godman, and Wethersfield's Katherine Harrison, all women alone, were tried as witches despite sizable estates. In contrast, the accusations against women like Hannah Griswold of Saybrook, Connecticut, Elizabeth Blackleach of Hartford, and Margaret Gifford of Salem, all wives of prosperous men when they were accused, were simply not taken seriously by the courts.[6]...

Economic considerations, then, do appear to have been at work in the New England witchcraft cases. But the issue was not simply the relative poverty—or wealth—of accused witches or their families. It was the special position of most accused witches vis-à-vis their society's rules for transferring wealth from one generation to another. To explain why their position was so unusual, we must turn first to New England's system of inheritance.

Inheritance is normally thought of as the transmission of property at death, but in New England, as in other agricultural societies, adult children received part of their father's accumulated estates prior to his death, usually at the time they married.[7] Thus the inheritance system included both pre-mortem endowments and post-mortem distributions. While no laws compelled fathers to settle part of their estates on their children as marriage portions, it was customary to do so. Marriages were, among other things, economic arrangements, and young people could not benefit from these arrangements unless their fathers provided them with the means to set up households and earn their livelihoods. Sons' portions tended to be land, whereas daughters commonly received movable goods and/or money. The exact value of these endowments varied to a father's wealth and inclination, but it appears that as a general rule the father of the young woman settled on the couple roughly half as much as the father of the young man.[8]

Custom, not law, also guided the distribution of a man's property at his death, but with two important exceptions. First, a man's widow, if he left one, was legally entitled "by way of dower" to one-third part of his real property, "to have and injoy for term of her natural life." She was expected to support herself with the profits of this property, but since she held only a life interest in it, she had to see that she did not "strip or waste" it.[9] None of the immovable estate could be sold, unless necessary for her or her children's maintenance, and then only with the permission of the court. A man might will his wife more than a third of his real property—but not less. Only if the woman came before the court to renounce her dower right publicly, and then only if the court approved, could this principle be waived. In the form of her "thirds," dower was meant to provide for a woman's support in widowhood. The inviolability of dower protected the widow from the claims of her children against the estate and protected the community from the potential burden of her care.

The second way in which law determined inheritance patterns had to do specifically with intestate cases.[10] If a man died without leaving a will, several principles governed the division of his property. The widow's thirds, of course, were to be laid out first. Unless "just cause" could be shown for some other distribution, the other two-thirds were to be divided among the surviving children, both male and female.[11] A double portion was to go to the eldest son, and single portions to his sisters and younger brothers. If there were no sons, the law stipulated that the estate was to be shared equally by the daughters. In cases where any or all of the children had not yet come of age, their portions were to be held by their mother or by a court-appointed guardian until they reached their majorities[12] or married. What remained of the widow's thirds at her death was to be divided among the surviving children, in the same proportions as the other two-thirds.

Although bound to conform to laws concerning the widow's thirds, men who wrote wills were not legally required to follow the principles of inheritance laid out in intestate cases. Individual men had the right to decide for themselves who would ultimately inherit their property. . . . [T]he majority seem to have adhered closely (though not always precisely) to the custom of leaving a double portion to the eldest son. Beyond that, New England men seem generally to have agreed to a system of partible inheritance, with both sons and daughters inheriting.

When these rules were followed, property ownership and control generally devolved upon men. Neither the widow's dower nor, for the most part, the daughter's right to inherit signified more than access to property. For widows, the law was clear that dower allowed for "use" only. For inheriting daughters who were married, the separate but inheritance-related principle of coverture applied. Under English common law, "feme covert" stipulated that married women had no right to own property—indeed, upon marriage, "the very being or legal existence of the woman is suspended."[13] Personal property which a married daughter inherited from her father, either as dowry or as a post-mortem bequest, immediately became the legal possession of her husband, who could exert full powers of ownership over it. A married daughter who inherited land from her father retained title to the land, which her husband could not sell without her consent. On her husband's death such land became the property of her children, but during his life her husband was entitled to the use and profits of it, and his wife could not devise it to her children by will.[14] The property of an inheriting daughter who was single seems to have been held "for improvement" for her until she was married, when it became her dowry.[15]

This is not to say that women did not benefit when they inherited property. A sizable inheritance could provide a woman with a materially better life; if single or widowed, inheriting women enjoyed better chances for an economically advantageous marriage or remarriage. But inheritance did not normally bring women the independent economic power it brought men.

The rules of inheritance were not always followed, however. In some cases, individual men decided not to conform to customary practices; instead, they employed one of several legal devices to give much larger shares of their estates to their wives or daughters, many times for disposal at their own discretion. Occasionally, the magistrates themselves allowed the estate to be distributed in some other fashion. Or, most commonly, the absence of male heirs in families made conformity impossible. In all three exceptions to inheritance customs, but most particularly the last, the women who stood to benefit economically also assumed a position of unusual vulnerability. They, and in many instances their daughters, became prime targets for witchcraft accusations.

Consider first the experience of witches who came from families without male heirs. . . . [T]hese histories begin to illuminate the subtle and often intricate manner in which anxieties about inheritance lay at the heart of most witchcraft accusations.

KATHERINE HARRISON

Katherine Harrison first appears in the Connecticut colonial records in the early 1650s, as the wife of John Harrison, a wealthy Wethersfield landowner.[16] Her age is unknown[17] and her family background is obscure. We know that she called John, Jonathan, and Josiah Gilbert, three prominent Connecticut Valley settlers, her cousins, but her actual relationship to them is ambiguous.[18] . . . She may have been the daughter or niece of Lydia Gilbert, who was executed as a witch in Hartford in 1654, but we can be reasonably certain only that the two

THE DEVIL IN THE SHAPE OF A WOMAN: THE ECONOMIC BASIS OF WITCHCRAFT

women were members of the same Connecti-cut family.[19] . . .

It has been said that Katherine Harrison was first tried as a witch in October 1668.[20] If so, then she must have been acquitted, because she was indicted in the Court of Assistants in Hartford on 25 May 1669, on the same charge.[21] The jury was unable to agree upon a verdict, however, and the court adjourned to the next session. Meantime, Harrison was supposed to remain in jail, but for some reason she was released in the summer or early fall, and she returned home to Wethersfield. Shortly there-after, thirty-eight Wethersfield townsmen filed a petition, complaining that "shee was suf-fered to be at libertie," since she "was lately prooved to be Deaply guiltie of suspicion of Wichcrafte" and that "the Juerie (the greater part of them) judged or beleaved that she was guilty of such high crimes" and "ought to be put to death." Among the petition's signers were several of the town's most prominent citi-zens, including John Blackleach, Sr., who had "taken much paines in the prosecution of this cause from the beginninge," and John Chester, who was then involved in a legal controversy with Harrison concerning a parcel of land.[22] When the Court of Assistants met again in Oc-tober, all of the jury members found her guilty of witchcraft.[23]

The Hartford magistrates, however, were reluctant to accept the verdict. Perhaps remem-bering how accusations had gotten out of hand during the Hartford outbreak seven years before, they put Harrison back in prison and appealed to local ministers for advice on the use of evidence. The response was ambiguous enough to forestall execution.[24] At a special session of the Court of Assistants the following May, the magistrates reconsidered the verdict, determined that they were not able to concur with the jury "so as to sentance her to death or to a longer continuance in restraynt," and or-dered Harrison to pay her fees and leave the colony for good.[25]

If witnesses testifying against her in her 1669 trial can be believed, Katherine Harrison's neighbors had suspected that she was a witch sixteen or eighteen years earlier. Elizabeth Simon deposed that as a single woman, Harrison was noted to be "a great or notorious liar, a Sabbath breaker and one that told fortunes"—and that her predictions frequently came to pass. Simon was also suspicious of Harrison for another reason: because she "did often spin so great a quantity of fine linen yarn as the said Elizabeth did never know nor hear of any other woman that could spin so much."[26] Other witnesses testified to the more recent damage she did to individuals and their property. Harrison was also a healer, and although many of her neigh-bors called upon her skills, over the years some of them came to suspect her of killing as well as curing.[27] Or so they said in 1668–69; she was not formally accused of any witchcraft crimes until after her husband's death.

John Harrison had died in 1666, leaving his wife one of the wealthiest, if not *the* wealth-iest woman in Wethersfield. In his will he be-queathed his entire estate of £929 to his wife and three daughters. Rebecca, age twelve, was to have £60, and his two younger daughters, eleven-year-old Mary and nine-year-old Sarah, were to have £40 each. The remaining £789 was to go to his widow.[28] Unlike many widows in colonial New England, Katherine Harrison chose not to remarry. Instead she lived alone, managing her extensive holdings herself, with the advice and assistance of her Hartford kinsman, Jonathan Gilbert.

In October 1668, not long after her adver-saries began gathering their witchcraft evi-dence against her, Harrison submitted a lengthy petition to "the Fathers of the Comonweale" asking for relief for the extensive vandalism of her estate since her husband's death. Among other damage, she spoke of oxen beaten and bruised to the point of being "altogether un-serviceable"; of a hole bored into the side of her cow; of a three-year-old heifer slashed to death; and of the back of a two-year-old steer broken. Her corn crop was destroyed, she said, "damnified with horses, they being staked upon it," and "30 poles of hops cutt and spoyled." Twelve of her relatives and neigh-bors, she said, including Jonathan and Josiah Gilbert, could testify to the damage done. The response of the court went unrecorded, but there is no indication that provision was made for the "due recompense" Harrison requested or that her grievances were even investigated.[29]

The Court of Assistants also seems to have been unsympathetic to another petition Harrison submitted in the fall of 1668, in which she complained that the actions of the magis-trates themselves were depleting her estate.[30] Indeed, the local court had recently fined her £40 for slandering her neighbors, Michael and Ann Griswold—a fine greatly in excess of the normal punishment in such cases.[31] The exact circumstances of the incident are unknown, but the Griswolds were among Harrison's witchcraft accusers, and she apparently considered Michael Griswold central in the recruiting of additional witnesses against her, for she said that "the sayd Michael Griswold would Hang her though he damned a thousand soules," adding that "as for his own soule it was damned long agoe." Griswold, a member of Wethersfield's elite, but not as wealthy as Harrison, sued her for these slanderous remarks and for calling his wife Ann "a savadge whore."[32] Besides levying the fine, the court ordered Harrison to confess her sins publicly.[33] She made the required confession, but she appealed the exorbitant fine.

Harrison's petition, which she filed within the month, was a peculiar mixture of justification for her actions, concession to the magistrates' insistence on deference in women, determination in her convictions, and desperation in her attempt to salvage her estate. Acknowledging herself to be "a female, a weaker vessell, subject to passion," she pleaded as the source of her frustration and anger the vicious abuse to which she had been subjected since her husband's death. She admitted her "corruption," but pointed out that it was well known that she had made "a full and free confession of [her] fault" and had offered "to repaire the wound that [she] had given to [the Griswolds'] names by a plaster as broad as the sore, at any time and in any place where it should content them." At the same time, she indicated Michael Griswold for being less interested in the reparation of his name than in her estate and did not hesitate to call the fine oppressive, citing the laws of God and the laws of the commonwealth as providing "that noe mans estate shal be deminished or taken away by any colony or pretence of Authority" in such an arbitrary manner. In her final statements, however, she returned to a more conciliatory stance: "I speake not to excuse my fault," she said, "but to save my estate as far as Righteousness will permit for a distressed Widow and Orphanes."[34]

Fear of losing her estate is a recurring theme in the records of Harrison's life during this period. Almost immediately after her husband's death in 1666, she petitioned the court to change the terms of her husband's will. Arguing that the bequests to the children were "inconsiderate" (by which she probably meant inconsiderable), she asked that the magistrates settle on her eldest daughter £210, and £200 on

each of her younger daughters, reserving the house and lot for herself during her lifetime.[35] Since her husband had left her full ownership of most of his estate, she could simply have given her daughters larger portions, but she must have felt that the court's sanction rendered the inheritances less vulnerable. Several months later, she appealed directly to Connecticut's governor, John Winthrop, Jr., requesting that Hartford's John and Jonathan Gilbert, and John Riley of Wethersfield, be appointed overseers of her estate.[36] Winthrop must not have granted her request, because in 1668 Harrison signed over the rest of the estate she had inherited from her husband to her daughters and appointed Jonathan and John Gilbert her daughters' guardians.[37] By the following year, her neighbors reported, she had "disposed of great part of her estate to others in trust."[38]

In June 1670, Katherine Harrison moved to Westchester, New York, to begin her life anew. Her reputation for witchcraft followed her, however, in the form of a complaint, filed in July by two of her new neighbors, that she had been allowed to resettle in Westchester. Noting that suspicion of her in Connecticut "hath given some cause of apprehension" to the townspeople, in order to "end their jealousyes and feares" a local New York magistrate told her to leave the jurisdiction.[39] Harrison refused. Before any action could be taken against her, her eldest daughter was fortuitously betrothed to Josiah Hunt, a son of Thomas Hunt, one of the men who had protested her presence in Westchester. The elder Hunt became a supporter and appeared in court on her behalf, with his son and three other influential men. Though she was required to give security for her "Civill carriage and good behaviour," the General Court of Assizes in New York ordered "that in regard there is nothing appears against her deserving the continuance of that obligacion shee is to bee release from it, and hath Liberty to remaine in the Towne of Westchester where shee now resides, or any where else in the Government during her pleasure."[40]

Evidently Harrison continued to live with recurring witchcraft suspicion, but after 1670 there is no further evidence of official harassment.[41] Early in 1672, she reappeared in Hartford to sue eleven of her old Connecticut Valley neighbors, in most cases for debt, and to release her "intrusted overseer" Jonathan Gilbert from his responsibilities for her estate (although he continued to act as guardian to her two younger daughters).[42] A month later, she signed at least some of her remaining Wethersfield land over to Gilbert.[43] After that, she fades from view. She may have returned to Connecticut for good at that time, for some evidence suggests that she died at Dividend, then an outlying section of Wethersfield, in October 1682.[44]

SUSANNA MARTIN

Born in England in 1625, Susanna North was the youngest of three daughters of Richard North. Her mother died when Susanna was young and her father subsequently remarried. The family migrated to New England in or just prior to 1639, the year in which Richard North was listed as one of the first proprietors of Salisbury, Massachusetts. Susanna's sister Mary had married Thomas Jones and was living in Gloucester by 1642. Of her sister Sarah we know only that she married a man named Oldham, had a daughter named Ann, and died before the child was grown. In August 1646, at the age of twenty-one, Susanna married George Martin, a Salisbury man whose first wife had recently died. In June of the following year, she gave birth to her son Richard, the first of nine children. One of these children, a son, died in infancy.[45] . . .

Early in 1668, less than a year after the birth of her last child, Susanna Martin's father died, leaving a modest estate of about £150. As the only surviving children, the then forty-three-year-old Susanna and her sister Mary anticipated receiving a major portion of the property, to posses either immediately or after the death of their stepmother, Ursula North. They were disappointed. According to the will probated shortly after he died, Richard North had voided all previous wills and written a new one—*nearly two decades* before his death. In this document, dated January 1649, he left all but £22 of his estate directly to his wife. Twenty-one pounds was to be divided among Mary Jones, Susanna Martin, and Ann Bates (Sarah Oldham's daughter). Susanna's share was 20 shillings and the cancellation of a £10 debt George Martin owed his father-in-law. Listed as witnesses to this will were Thomas Bradbury of Salisbury and Mary Jones's daughter, Mary Winsley.[46] But the will raised problems. In 1649, Ann Bates was still Ann Oldham (she did not marry Francis Bates until 1661) and the Mary Winsley listed as witness to the will was still Mary Jones, at most eleven or twelve years old

when it was allegedly written.[47] Despite the obvious irregularities, Thomas Bradbury and Mary Winsley attested in court that this was indeed Richard North's last will and testament.

Whether Susanna Martin and her sister saw or protested this will when it was probated cannot be determined. Susanna, at least, may have had more pressing concerns on her mind. In April 1669, a bond of £100 was posted for her appearance at the next Court of Assistants "upon suspicion of witchcraft." That was the same day that George Martin sued William Sargent for slandering his wife. According to George Martin, Sargent had not only said that Susanna "was a witch, and he would call her witch," but also accused her of having "had a child" while still single and of "wringing its neck" shortly after. George Martin also sued William Sargent's brother Thomas for saying "that his son George Marttin was a bastard and that Richard Marttin was Goodwife Marttin's imp."[48] . . .

Meanwhile, the magistrates bound Susanna Martin over to the higher court to be tried for witchcraft. Although the records have not survived, she must have been acquitted, because several months later she was at liberty. In October 1669, George Martin was again bound for his wife's appearance in court, not for witchcraft this time but for calling one of her neighbors a liar and a thief.[49]

By April 1671, George and Susanna Martin (Susanna's sister Mary Jones would later join them) were involved in what would become protracted litigation over the estate of Susanna's father. Ursula North had died a month or two before, leaving a will, dated shortly after her husband's death, that effectively disinherited her two stepdaughters by awarding them 40 shillings apiece. She left the rest of the original North estate first to her granddaughter, Mary Winsley, and secondarily to Mary and Nathaniel Winsley's only child, Hepzibah.[50]

The exact sequence of the numerous court hearings that followed is less clear. Evidently, Susanna and George Martin initiated legal proceedings against Mary and Nathaniel Winsley in April 1671, for unwarranted possession of the North estate. . . . In October 1672, the General Court responded, giving Susanna Martin liberty to sue for her inheritance a second time at the local level.

In April 1673, the recently widowed Mary Jones and George Martin, acting for his wife, sued Nathaniel Winsley "for withholding the inheritance of housing, lands and other estate ... under color of a feigned or confused writing like the handwriting of Mr. Thomas Bradbury and seemingly attested by him, and Mary Winsly." The court declared the case nonsuited, and again Susanna Martin appealed to the General Court, requesting that the case be reheard at the local level. The General Court consented in May 1673, and the following October, Susanna and George Martin instituted proceedings against the Winsleys for the third time. Again the county court decided for the defendants, and the Martins appealed to the Court of Assistants. For a while it looked as though things were finally going their way. The higher court, which "found for the plaintiff there being no legall prooffe of Richard North's will," ordered that "the estate the said North left be left to the disposall of the county court." ...

[In 1674] Susanna, George, and Mary appealed a final time to the General Court, this time for "a hearing of the whole case" by the highest court itself. The magistrates agreed to hear the case, remitting the usual court fees, as they had done before, on the basis of Susanna's pleas of poverty. But in October 1674, after "perusall of what hath binn heard and alleadged by both parties," the court found for Nathaniel Winsley.[51] In what Susanna Martin and Mary Jones believed was a flagrant miscarriage of justice, they had lost what they considered their rightful inheritances.

For almost the next two decades, Susanna Martin's name rarely appears in the public records of the colony. Her sister Mary died in 1682, followed by her husband George in 1686.[52] Early in 1692, she was again accused of witchcraft, this time by several of the possessed females in Salem. They claimed that her apparition "greviously afflected" them, urging them to become witches themselves. Summoned before the court as witnesses against her were eleven men and four women, all old neighbors of the now sixty-seven-year-old widow.[53]

Unnerved by neither the agonies of the possessed or the magistrates' obvious belief in her guilt, Martin insisted that she was innocent. To Cotton Mather, she "was one of the most impudent, scurrilous, wicked Creatures in the World," who had the effrontery to claim "that she had lead a most virtuous and holy life."[54] Years of living as a reputed witch had left Martin well-versed on the subject of the Devil's powers. "He that appeared in sam[uel]s

shape, a glorifyed saint," she said, citing the Bible in her own defense, "can appear in any ones shape." She laughed at the fits of her young accusers, explaining: "Well I may at such folly." When asked what she thought the possessed were experiencing, she said she did not know. Pressed to speculate on it, she retorted: "I do not desire to spend my judgment upon it" and added (revealing what must have been her long-standing opinion of the magistrates' bias), "my thoughts are my own, when they are in, but when they are out they are anothers."[55] ...

Susanna Martin was found guilty of witchcraft and was one of five women executed on 19 July 1692. One week later, another Salisbury woman was indicted on the same charge. She was Mary Bradbury, the now elderly wife of the man Susanna Martin believed had written her father's "will" nearly twenty-five years before. Mary Bradbury was sentenced to hang too, but friends helped her to escape. No explicit connection between the accusations of the two women is discernible. Rumors circulated, however, that because Thomas Bradbury had friends in positions of authority, there had been little real effort to capture his fugitive wife.[56] ...

These ... short histories ... suggest the diverse economic circumstances of witches in early New England. ... The ... women featured in these histories were either (1) daughters of parents who had no sons (or whose sons had died), (2) women in marriages which brought forth only daughters (or in which the sons had died), or (3) women in marriages with no children at all. These patterns had significant economic implications. Because there were no legitimate male heirs in their immediate families, each of these ... women stood to inherit, did inherit, or were denied their apparent right to inherit substantially larger portions of their fathers' or husbands' accumulated estates than women in families with male heirs. Whatever actually happened to the property in question— and in some cases we simply do not know— these women were aberrations in a society with an inheritance system designed to keep property in the hands of men.

These ... cases also illustrate fertility and mortality patterns widely shared among the families of accused witches. A substantial majority of New England's accused females were women without brothers, women with daughters but no sons, or women in marriages with no children at all (see Table 1). Of the 267 accused females, enough is known about 158 to identify them as either having or not having brothers or sons to inherit: only 62 of the 158 (39 percent) did, whereas 96 (61 percent) did not. More striking, once accused, women without brothers or sons were even more likely than women with brothers or sons to be tried, convicted, and executed: women from families without male heirs made up 64 percent of the females prosecuted, 76 percent of those who were found guilty, and 89 percent of those who were executed.

These figures must be read with care, however, for two reasons. First, eighteen of the sixty-two accused females who had brothers or sons to inherit were themselves daughters and granddaughters of women who did not. It appears that these eighteen females, most of whom were young women or girls, were accused because their neighbors believed that their mothers and grandmothers passed their witchcraft on to them. Therefore they form a somewhat ambiguous group. Since they all had brothers to inherit, it would be inaccurate to exclude them from this category in Table 1, yet including them understates the extent to which inheritance-related concerns were at issue in witchcraft accusations. At the same time, the large number of cases in which the fertility and mortality patterns of witches' families are unknown (109 of the 267 accused females in New England) makes it impossible to assess precisely the proportion of women among the accused who did not have brothers or sons.

Table 2 helps clarify the point. It includes as a separate category the daughters and granddaughters of women without brothers or sons and incorporates the cases for which this information is unknown. Although inclusion of the unknowns renders the overall percentages meaningless, this way of representing the

available information shows clearly the particular vulnerability of women without brothers or sons. Even if *all* the unknown cases involved women from families *with* male heirs—a highly unlikely possibility—women from families without males to inherit would still form a majority of convicted and executed witches. Were the complete picture visible, I suspect that it would not differ substantially from that presented earlier in Table 1—which is based on data reflecting 60 percent of New England's witches and which indicates that women without brothers and sons were more vulnerable than other women at all stages of the process.

Numbers alone, however, do not tell the whole story. More remains to be said about what happened to these inheriting or potentially inheriting women, both before and after they were accused of witchcraft.

It was not unusual for women in families without male heirs to be accused of witchcraft shortly after the deaths of fathers, husbands, brothers, or sons. Katherine Harrison [and] Susanna Martin . . . exemplify this pattern. So too does elderly Ann Hibbens of Boston, whose execution in 1656 seems to have had a profound enough effect on some of her peers to influence the outcome of subsequent trials for years to come. Hibbens had three sons from her first marriage, all of whom lived in England; but she had no children by her husband William Hibbens, with whom she had come to Massachusetts in the 1630s. William died in 1654; Ann was brought to trial two years later. Although her husband's will has not survived, he apparently left a substantial portion (if not all) of his property directly to her: when she wrote her own will shortly before her execution, Ann Hibbens was in full possession of a £344 estate, most of which she bequeathed to her sons in England.[57]

Similarly, less than two years elapsed between the death of Gloucester's William Vinson and the imprisonment of his widow Rachel in 1692. Two children, a son and a daughter, had been born to the marriage, but the son had died in 1675. Though William Vinson had had four sons (and three daughters) by a previous marriage, the sons were all dead by 1683. In his will, which he wrote in 1684, before he was certain that his last son had been lost at sea, William left his whole £180 estate to Rachel for her life, stipulating that she could sell part of the lands and cattle

TABLE 1. Female Witches by Presence or Absence of Brothers or Sons, New England, 1620–1725 (A)

Action	Women without Brothers or Sons	Women with Brothers or Sons	Total
Accused	96 (61%)	62 (39%)	158
Tried	41 (64%)	23 (36%)	64
Convicted	25 (76%)	8 (24%)	33
Executed	17 (89%)	2 (11%)	19

TABLE 2. Female Witches by Presence or Absence of Brothers or Sons, New England, 1620–1725 (B)

Action	Women without Brothers or Sons	Daughters and Granddaughters of Women without Brothers or Sons	Women with Brothers or Sons	Unknown Cases	Total
Accused	96 (36%)	18 (7%)	44 (16%)	109 (41%)	267
Tried	41 (48%)	6 (7%)	17 (20%)	22 (26%)	86
Convicted	25 (56%)	0 (0%)	6 (13%)	12 (27%)	45
Executed	17 (61%)	0 (0%)	2 (7%)	9 (32%)	28

if she found herself in need of resources. After Rachel's death, "in Case" his son John "be Living and returne home agayne," William said, most of the estate was to be divided between John and their daughter Abigail. If John did not return, both shares were to be Abigail's.[58] . . .

In other cases, many years passed between the death of the crucial male relative and the moment when a formal witchcraft complaint was filed.

. . . Mary English of Salem was charged with witchcraft seven years after she came into her inheritance. Her father, merchant William Hollingworth, had been declared lost at sea in 1677, but at that time Mary's brother William was still alive. Possibly because the younger William was handling the family's interests in other colonies, or possibly because the father's estate was in debt for more than it was worth, the magistrates gave the widow Elinor Hollingworth power of attorney to salvage what she could. With her "owne labor," as she put it, "but making use of other mens estates," the aggressive and outspoken Mistress Hollingworth soon had her deceased husband's debts paid and his wharf, warehouse, and tavern solvent again.[59] She had no sooner done so, however, than she was accused of witchcraft by the wife of a Gloucester mariner.[60] Though the magistrates gave little credence to the charge at the time, they may have had second thoughts later. In 1685, her son William died, and Elinor subsequently conveyed the whole Hollingworth estate over to Mary English, who was probably her only surviving child.[61]

Elinor Hollingworth had died by 1692, but Mary English was one of the women cried out upon early in the Salem outbreak. Her husband, the merchant Philip English, was accused soon after. Knowing their lives were in grave danger, the Englishes fled to the safety of New York. But as one historian of witchcraft has pointed out, flight was "the legal equivalent of conviction."[62] No sooner had they left than close to £1200 of their property was confiscated under the law providing attainder for witchcraft.[63]

Not all witches from families without male heirs were accused of conspiring with the Devil after they had come into their inheritances. On the contrary, some were accused prior to the death of the crucial male relative, many times before it was clear who would inherit. . . . [O]ne of these women . . . was Martha Corey of Salem, who was accused of witchcraft in 1692 while her husband was still alive. Giles Corey had been married twice before and had several daughters by the time he married the widow Martha Rich, probably in the 1680s. With no sons to inherit, Giles's substantial land holdings would, his neighbors might have assumed, be passed on to his wife and daughters. Alice Parker, who may have been Giles's daughter from a former marriage, also came before the magistrates as a witch in 1692, as did Giles himself. Martha Corey and Alice Parker maintained their innocence and were hanged. Giles Corey, in an apparently futile attempt to preserve his whole estate for his heirs, refused to respond to the indictment. To force him to enter a plea, he was tortured: successively heavier weights were placed on his body until he was pressed to death.[64]

What seems especially significant here is that most accused witches whose husbands were still alive were, like their counterparts who were widows and spinsters, over forty years of age—and therefore unlikely if not unable to produce male heirs. Indeed, the fact that witchcraft accusations were rarely taken seriously by the community until the accused stopped bearing children takes on a special meaning when it is juxtaposed with the anomalous position of inheriting women or potentially inheriting women in New England's social structure.

Witches in families without male heirs sometimes had been dispossessed of part or all of their inheritances before—sometimes long before—they were formally charged with witchcraft. Few of these women, however, accepted disinheritance with equanimity. Rather, like Susanna Martin, they took their battles to court, casting themselves in the role of public challengers to the system of male inheritance. In most instances, the authorities sided with their antagonists. . . .

. . . The property of women in families without male heirs was vulnerable to loss in a variety of ways, from deliberate destruction by neighbors (as Katherine Harrison experienced) to official sequestering by local magistrates. In nearly every case, the authorities themselves seem hostile or at best indifferent to the property claims of these women. One final example deserves mention here, not only because it indicates how reluctant magistrates were to leave property in the control of women, but because it shows that the property of convicted witches was liable to seizure even without the benefit of an attainder law.

Rebecca Greensmith had been widowed twice before her marriage to Nathaniel Greensmith. Her first husband, Abraham Elsen of Wethersfield, had died intestate in 1648, leaving an estate £99. After checking the birth dates of the Elsens' two children, three-year-old Sarah and one-year-old Hannah, the court initially left the whole estate with the widow. When Rebecca married Wethersfield's Jarvis Mudge the following year, the local magistrates sequestered the house and land Abraham Elsen had left, worth £40, stating their intention to rent it out "for the Use and Benefit of the two daughters."[65] The family moved to New London shortly after, but Jarvis Mudge died in 1652 and Rebecca moved with Hannah and Sarah to Hartford. Since Rebecca was unable to support herself and her two daughters, the court allowed her to sell the small amount of land owned by her second husband (with whom she had had no children) "for the paing of debts and the Bettering the Childrens portyons."[66]

Sometime prior to 1660, Rebecca married Nathaniel Greensmith. During the Hartford outbreak, Rebecca came under suspicion of witchcraft. After Nathaniel sued his wife's accuser for slander, Nathaniel himself was named. Both husband and wife were convicted and executed.[67]

Respecting Nathaniel's £182 estate, £44 of which was claimed by the then eighteen-year-old Sarah and seventeen-year-old Hannah Elsen, the court ordered the three overseers "to preserve the estate from Waste" and to pay "any just debts," the only one recorded being the Greensmiths' jail fees. Except for allowing the overseers "to dispose of the 2 daughters," presumably to service, the magistrates postponed until the next court any decision concerning the young women's portions. First, however, they deducted £40 to go "to the Treasurer for the County."[68] No reason was given for this substantial appropriation and no record of further distribution of the estate has survived.

Aside from these many women who lived or had lived in families without male heirs, there were at least a dozen other witches who, despite the presence of brothers and sons, came into much larger shares of estates than their neighbors would have expected. In some cases, these women gained full control over the disposition of property. We know about these women because their fathers, husbands, or other relatives left wills, because the women themselves wrote wills, or because male relatives who felt cheated out of their customary shares fought in the courts for more favorable arrangements.

Grace Boulter of Hampton, one of several children of Richard Swain, is one of these women. Grace was accused of witchcraft in 1680, along with her thirty-two-year-old daughter, Mary Prescott. Twenty years earlier, in 1660, just prior to his removal to Nantucket, Grace's father had deeded a substantial portion of his Hampton property to her and her husband Nathaniel, some of which he gave directly to her.[69]

Another witch in this group is Jane James of Marblehead, who left an estate at her death in 1669 which was valued at £85. While it is not clear how she came into possession of it, the property had not belonged to her husband Erasmus, who had died in 1660, though it did play a significant role in a controversy between her son and son-in-law over their rightful shares of both Erasmus's and Jane's estates. Between 1650 and her death in 1669, Jane was accused of witchcraft at least three times by her Marblehead neighbors.[70] . . .

Looking back over the lives of these many women—most particularly those who did not have brothers or sons to inherit—we begin to understand the complexity of the economic dimension of New England witchcraft. Only rarely does the actual trial testimony indicate that economic power was even at issue. Nevertheless it is there, recurring with a telling persistence once we look beyond what was explicitly said about these women as witches. Inheritance disputes surface frequently enough in witchcraft cases, cropping up as part of the general context even when no direct link between the dispute and the charge is discernible, to suggest the fears that underlay most accusations. No matter how deeply entrenched the principle of male inheritance, no matter how carefully written the laws that protected it, it was impossible to insure that all families had male offspring. The women who stood to benefit from these demographic "accidents" account for most of New England's female witches.

The amount of property in question was not the crucial factor in the way these women were viewed or treated by their neighbors, however. Women of widely varying economic circumstances were vulnerable to accusation and even to conviction. Neither was there a direct line from accuser to material beneficiary of the accusation: others in the community did sometimes profit personally from the losses sustained by these women . . . , but only rarely did the gain accrue to the accusers themselves. Indeed, occasionally there was no direct temporal connection: in some instances several decades passed between the creation of the key economic conditions and the charge of witchcraft; the charge in other cases even anticipated the development of those conditions.

Finally, inheriting or potentially inheriting women were vulnerable to witchcraft accusations not only during the Salem outbreak, but from the time of the first formal accusations in New England at least until the end of the century. . . . The Salem outbreak created only a slight wrinkle in this established fabric of suspicion. If daughters, husbands, and sons of witches were more vulnerable to danger in 1692 than they had been previously, they were mostly the daughters, husbands, and sons of inheriting or potentially inheriting women. As the outbreak spread, it drew into its orbit increasing numbers of women, "unlikely" witches in that they were married to well-off and influential men, but familiar figures to some of their neighbors nonetheless. What the impoverished Sarah Good had in common with Mary Phips, wife of Massachusetts's governor, was what Eunice Cole had in common with Katherine Harrison. . . . However varied their backgrounds and economic positions, as women without brothers or women without sons, they stood in the way of the orderly transmission of property from one generation of males to another.

Notes

1. Alan Macfarlane, *Witchcraft in Tudor and Stuart England: A Regional and Comparative Study* (New York, 1970), pp. 149–51. See also Keith Thomas, *Religion and the Decline of Magic* (New York, 1971), pp. 457, 520–21, 560–68.

2. See Trials for Witchcraft in New England (unpaged), dated 5 September 1656 (manuscript volume, Houghton Library, Harvard University, Cambridge, Mass.).

3. Relying on very general indicators (a married woman who worked as a servant, a widow whose husband had left an estate of £39, and so forth), I was able to make rough estimates about the economic position of 150 accused women. Twenty-nine of these women seem to have been poor. . . .

4. For Abigail Somes, see *The Salem Witchcraft Papers: Verbatim Transcripts of the Legal Documents of the Salem Witchcraft Outbreak of 1692*, 3 vols., eds. Paul Boyer and Stephen Nissenbaum (New York, 1977), 3:733–37 (hereafter cited as *Witchcraft Papers*). For Tituba, see *Witchcraft Papers* 3:745–57. Documents relating to Ruth Wilford are in *Witchcraft Papers* 2:459; 3:961; *The Probate Records of Essex County, Massachusetts, 1635–1681*, 3 vols. (Salem, 1916–20), 3:93–95 (hereafter cited as *Essex Probate Records*).

5. Most families in seventeenth-century New England had estates worth less than £200. However, since only a very small proportion of convicted witches who were married seem to have come from families with estates worth *more* than £200, it seems reasonable to conclude that married women from families with less than £200 estates were overrepresented among the accused. Nearly all of the convictions of married women from families with estates worth more than £200 occurred during the Salem outbreak. . . .

6. For accusations against Hannah Griswold and Margaret Gifford, see Norbert B. Lacy, "The Records of the Court of Assistants of Connecticut, 1665–1701" (M.A. thesis, Yale University, 1937), pp. 6–7 (hereafter cited as "Conn. Assistants Records"); and *Records and Files of the Quarterly Courts of Essex County, Massachusetts*, 9 vols. (Salem, 1912–75), 7:405; 8:23 (hereafter cited as *Essex Court Records*).

7. This discussion of the inheritance system of seventeenth-century New England is drawn from the following sources: *The Book of the General Lawes and Libertyes Concerning the Inhabitants of the Massachusetts*, ed. Thomas G. Barnes (facsimile from the 1648 edition, San Marino, Calif., 1975); *The Colonial*

Laws of Massachusetts. Reprinted from the Edition of 1672, with the Supplements through 1686, ed. William H. Whitmore (Boston, 1887); John D. Cushing, comp., *The Laws and Liberties of Massachusetts, 1641–91: A Facsimile Edition*, 3 vols. (Wilmington, Del., 1976); *Massachusetts Province Laws, 1692–1699*, ed. John D. Cushing (Wilmington, Del., 1978); *New Hampshire Probate Records; Essex Probate Records: A Digest of the Early Connecticut Probate Records*, vol. 1, ed. Charles W. Manwaring (Hartford, 1904) (hereafter cited as *Conn. Probate Records*); Marylynn Salmon, *Women and the Law of Property in Early America* (Chapel Hill, 1986); George L. Haskins, "The Beginnings of Partible Inheritance in the American Colonies," in *Essays in the History of American Law*, ed. David H. Flaherty (Chapel Hill, 1969); Edmund S. Morgan, *The Puritan Family: Religion and Domestic Relations in Seventeenth-Century New England* (1944; reprint New York, 1966).

8. See Morgan, *The Puritan Family*, pp. 81–82.

9. Barnes, *Book of the General Lawes*, pp. 17–18. . . .

10. Since only a small proportion of men left wills during the colonial period, intestacy law played a significant role in determining inheritance practices. See Salmon, *Women and the Law of Property*, p. 141.

11. Barnes, *The Book of the General Lawes*, p. 53.

12. Young women officially came of age in New England when they reached 18; young men when they reached 21.

13. William Blackstone, *Commentaries on the Laws of England*, 4 vols. (Oxford, 1765–69), 1:433.

14. Once widowed, a woman who inherited land from her father (or who had bought land with her husband in both of their names) could make a will of her own, as could a single woman who came into possession of land. . . . See Salmon, *Women and the Law of Property*, pp. 144–45 and passim.

15. Evidence suggests that in seventeenth-century New England, daughters of fathers who died relatively young (and possibly most sons) did not normally come into their inheritances until they married. If daughters had received their shares when they came of age, we would expect to find probate records for single women who died before they had the opportunity to marry. Though there are many existing intestate records and wills for single men who died in early adulthood, I have located only one record involving a young, single woman.

16. Wethersfield Land Records (manuscript volume, Town Clerk's Office, Town Hall, Wethersfield, Conn.) 1:19, 38.

17. Given the ages of her children, Katherine Harrison had to have been between her late twenties and her mid-fifties when she was first accused of witchcraft in 1668. I suspect that she was in her forties.

18. See Wethersfield Land Records 2:149; Katherine Harrison to John Winthrop, Jr., undated letter (probably early 1667), and Katherine Harrison's Testimony, undated document (probably October 1669), in the Winthrop Papers, Massachusetts Historical Society, Boston (hereafter cited as Winthrop Papers). . . .

19. Samuel Wyllys Papers: Depositions on Cases of Witchcraft, Assault, Theft, Drunkenness and Other Crimes, Tried in Connecticut, 1663–1728 (manuscript volume, Archives, History and Genealogy Unit, Connecticut State Library, Hartford, doc. 15) (hereafter cited as Wyllys Papers).

20. See Sherman W. Adams and Henry R. Stiles, *The History of Ancient Wethersfield*, 2 vols. (New York, 1904), 1:682; and Lacy, "Conn. Assistants Records," p. 12.

21. Lacy, "Conn. Assistants Records," p. 13.

22. Petition for the Investigation of Katherine Harrison, Recently Released after Imprisonment, Signed by John Chester and Thirty-Eight Other Citizens of Wethersfield (Manuscript Collections, Connecticut Historical Society, Hartford [hereafter cited as Petition for the Investigation of Katherine Harrison]) (emphasis mine). See also Order about Katherine Harrison's Land, in the Winthrop Papers. . . .

23. Lacy, "Conn. Assistants Records," pp. 13–14, 18–19.

24. "The Answers of Some Ministers to the Questions Propounded to Them by the Honored Magistrates," dated 20 October 1669, Samuel Wyllys Papers, Supplement: Depositions on Cases of Witchcraft Tried in Connecticut, 1662–1693, photostat copies of original documents from the Wyllys Papers, Annmary Brown Memorial Brown University Library, Providence, R.I. . . .

25. Lacy, "Conn. Assistants Records," p. 23. . . .

26. Wyllys Papers Supplement, p. 11.

27. Depositions submitted against Harrison in 1668 and 1669 are in the Wyllys Papers, docs. 6–17; Wyllys Papers Supplement, pp. 46–63. . . . For Harrison's response to these accusations, see Katherine Harrison's Testimony, Winthrop Papers.

28. Manwaring, *Conn. Probate Records* 1:206.

29. "A Complaint of Severall Greevances of the Widdow Harrison's," Wyllys Papers Supplement, p. 53.

30. "The Declaration of Katherine Harrison in Her Appeal to This Court of Assistants," dated September 1668, in Connecticut Archives, Crimes and Misdemeanors, 1st ser. (1662–1789) (manuscript volume, Archives, History and Genealogy Unit, Connecticut State Library, Hartford), vol. 1 (pt. 1):34 (hereafter cited as Crimes and Misdemeanors).

31. Connecticut Colonial Probate Records 56:80; Records of the Colony of Connecticut, Connecticut Colonial Probate Records, County Court, vol. 56, 1663–77 (Archives, History and Genealogy Unit, Connecticut State Library, Hartford, 56:79–81 (hereafter cited as Connecticut Colonial Probate Records).

32. Ibid., pp. 78–79. For the Griswolds as accusers, see Katherine Harrison's Testimony, Winthrop Papers.

33. Connecticut Colonial Probate Records 56:80.

34. "The Declaration of Katherine Harrison," Crimes and Misdemeanors, 1 (pt. 1):34.

35. Manwaring, *Connecticut Probate Records*, p. 206.

36. Katherine Harrison to John Winthrop, Jr., "Letter," Winthrop Papers.

37. Wethersfield Land Records 2:149.

38. Petition for the Investigation of Katherine Harrison.

39. See "The Cases of Hall and Harrison," in *Narratives of the Witchcraft Cases, 1648–1706*, ed. Charles Lincoln Burr (New York, 1914), pp. 48–49.

40. Ibid., pp. 48–52.

41. See Samuel D. Drake, *Annals of Witchcraft in New England* (New York, 1869), pp. 133–34.

42. Connecticut Colonial Probate Records 56:118; Wethersfield Land Records 2:249.

43. Wethersfield Land Records 2:210.

44. See Gilbert Collection.

45. See Joseph Merrill, *History of Amesbury, Including the First Seventeen Years of Salisbury....* (Haverhill, Mass., 1880), pp. 11–13, 28; *Vital Records of Salisbury . . .* (Topsfield, Mass., 1915), pp. 151, 415.

46. *Essex Probate Records* 2:125–27.

47. James Savage, *A Genealogical Dictionary of the First Settlers of New England*, 4 vols. (Boston, 1860–62), 1:138; 4:483.

48. See *Essex Court Records* 4:129, 133.

49. *Essex Court Records* 4:184, 187, 239.

50. *Essex Probate Records* 2:223–24.

51. See *Records of the Governor and Company of the Massachusetts Bay in New England*, 6 vols., ed. Nathaniel B. Shurtleff (Boston, 1853–54), 5:6, 26–27.

52. Savage, *Genealogical Dictionary* 2:566. . . . When he died, George Martin left an estate valued at £75, most of which he left to Susanna "during her Widowhood."

53. See *Witchcraft Papers* 2:549–79.

54. Cotton Mather, *The Wonders of the Invisible World* (1693; facsimile of the 1862 London edition, Ann Arbor, Mich., 1974), p. 148.

55. *Witchcraft Papers* 2:551.

56. *Witchcraft Papers* 1:115–29.

57. Ann Hibbens' will is reprinted in *New England Historical and Genealogical Register*, vol. 6 (1852), pp. 287–88.

58. See *Witchcraft Papers* 3:880–81.

59. *Essex Probate Records* 3:191–93.

60. *Essex Court Records* 7:238.

61. *New England Historical and Genealogical Register*, vol. 3 (1849), p. 129.

62. Marion L. Starkey, *The Devil in Massachusetts* (New York, 1949), p. 185.

63. *Witchcraft Papers* 3:988–91.

64. For Martha and Giles Corey and Alice Parker, see *Witchcraft Papers* 1:239–66; 2:623–28, 632–33; 3:985–86, 1018–19.

65. Manwaring, *Conn. Probate Records* 1:7–8.

66. *Records of the Particular Court of Connecticut, 1639–1663, Collections of the Connecticut Historical Society*, vol. 22 (1928), p. 119.

67. Ibid., p. 258.

68. Manwaring, *Conn. Probate Records* 1:121–22.

69. Norfolk Deeds (manuscript volume, Registry of Deeds, Essex County Courthouse, Salem, Mass.), 1:116, 154.

70. *Essex Probate Records* 1:314–16; 2:160; *Essex Court Records* 1:199, 204, 229; 2:213; 3:292, 342, 413.

ANN M. LITTLE

Captivity and Conversion: Daughters of New England in French Canada

Ann Little's essay introduces us to the geopolitics of the second half of the colonial period. Protestant England and Catholic France, along with their independent-minded Indian allies, engaged in a succession of imperial wars involving North American territory from the late seventeenth century through the Seven Years' War of 1756–63. In 1700, English settlers far outnumbered the 15,000 French soldiers, missionaries, fur traders, and habitants (farmers) clustered chiefly in settlements along the St. Lawrence River. However, the English occupied only a narrow sliver along the eastern seaboard, while the French claimed authority (and established mutually advantageous relations with native groups) from Louisiana to Canada along the Mississippi River and around the Great Lakes. It was not at all clear if one European power (France, Spain, or England) could gain ascendancy over the continent as a whole.

The author takes us on a detective's journey to recover the voices of and find out what happened to the children, teenagers, and grown women who were

Excerpted from Ann M. Little, "'A Jesuit will ruin your Body & Soul!': Daughters of New England in Canada," ch. 4 of *Abraham in Arms: War and Gender in Colonial New England by Ann M. Little* (Philadelphia: University of Pennsylvania Press, 2007). Reprinted by permission of the author and publisher. Notes have been edited and renumbered.

captured from New England towns and farms in wartime raids by Abenaki allies of the French. On arrival in Canada, English girls were typically schooled at Ursuline convents in New France's principal northern towns, Montreal, Québec (City), and Trois Rivières. Finding these New England women in the thorough records kept by French notaries—baptisms, marriages, deaths—means that they converted to Catholicism. Letters exchanged with their birth families in New England confirm that a high proportion of them chose not to be redeemed or ransomed so as to return to their onetime homes.

A good way to assess the author's evidence is to construct a list or table profiling the life courses of the captives who stayed. What do you find are the most compelling factors explaining why New England women remained in New France?

In the 1690s in the midst of the first war with New France, English depictions of frontier warfare and captivity shifted dramatically from identifying Indians as the primary danger to New England to portraying the French and their Catholicism as the chief threat to the New England way. While Indians were still formidable opponents in the battle, in New England they came to be feared more as agents of the French than as actors in their own right ... Even more threatening ... were European enemies who had studied the tactics of their Native allies so well. French Catholics proved more successful than Indians at encouraging English people to cross cultural borders and live among them for the rest of their lives. European Catholics were perhaps even more disturbing than Indian enemies because they were not all that different from English Protestants. They dressed the same, they did the same work, they ate the same food, they worshipped the same God—and thus they could be plotting and scheming just about anywhere and at any time. . . . Thus New Englanders began to worry less about Indian captivity and more about the vulnerability of captives in the hands of dedicated missionaries like the Jesuits, Ursulines, Sulpicians, and the Sisters of the Congregation of Notre Dame. Captivity narratives began to discuss the dedicated efforts that French priests and nuns made to convert their English prisoners of war, a theme that was . . . a feature of the genre through the Seven Years' War (1756–63).[1]

What was perhaps additionally disturbing about French successes in getting and keeping English captives is that the majority of the captives were New England's daughters, sisters, wives, and widows. While male captives always comprised the majority of New Englanders in captivity (mostly as prisoners of war, sometimes as adopted captives), female captives were vastly more likely to remain in Canada, convert to Catholicism, and marry.[2] This apparent danger to female captives jibed with long-standing puritan fears of women's greater vulnerability to spiritual corruption, as well as their specific susceptibility to the seductions of Catholicism. The sensually rich experiences of the Mass were believed to be powerfully attractive to unlearned, undisciplined women, as they had already proved to be to the Indians living in the French mission villages like Odanak (St. Francis), Kahnawake, La Montaigne, and Lorette.[3] Girls and women who remained in Canada became the focus of a great deal of familial and cultural anxiety in New England, as they lived lives that openly rejected the faith, language, and laws of their fathers. The following pages offer some explanations for their decisions to stay in Canada, choices that so baffled, wounded, and disturbed their families and communities in New England.

While for a time they were the subjects of intense diplomacy and worry on the part of their families and New England officials alike, these girls and women have been largely forgotten in the histories of the northeastern borderlands. This is partly because they did not write narratives about their experiences the way returned captives did, but it may also be due in part to their families' shame of daughters or sisters who stayed in Canada even when they were free to return to New England, and even in the face of parental and brotherly pleading and admonitions to come home. Because these women chose to remain in Canada, the sources for understanding their motivations and their lives in Canada are very thin. Furthermore, once these girls and women decided to remain in Canada, their New England families apparently had very little to say about them. . . . [M]ost New England families evidently disinherited and turned their backs on their disobedient daughters. . . .

Why is it that the usually prolific, expansive, and furious New England writers like Cotton Mather had so little to say about these girls and women who did not come home? Perhaps the shame and anger they felt both at being bested by the French, as well as because of their daughters' defiance, explains why these women's stories have been largely deleted from the family histories of New England.

New England's paranoia about the designs of the French and their successful alliances with Indians emerged in local writings and publications as early as King Philip's War (1675–78). Reports on the war's progress on the Maine and western Massachusetts frontiers note the presence and influence of the French among the Indians. By the time of the first war with New France, the English came to see the French as their major—if not yet their only— rivals for the control of North America.[4] The clear success of the French in creating political and diplomatic alliances with Indians (particularly with the Eastern Abenaki and the mission Iroquois) made a formidable European foe truly frightening to the English living in the northeastern borderlands at the end of the seventeenth century.

Fear and loathing of the French as enemies went hand-in-glove with the strong anti-Catholicism that was a foundational part of New England's sense of its historical and religious mission. Because religion and nationalism were so intertwined for English Protestants in the early modern era, it is impossible to separate New Englanders' fears of French political and military victories and their fear of being compelled to embrace Catholicism. . . . New England was founded by people who were especially zealous adherents to several versions of reformed Protestantism. They and their descendants believed that warfare and Indian captivity in the northeastern borderlands were evidence, variously, of God's disfavor or his willingness to test their faith. New Englanders who saw Indian warfare as an opportunity to test and prove their faith were even more willing to see wars against Catholic New France as an extension of Christ's struggle against the Devil for worldwide dominations.[5]

. . . [A]nti-Catholicism in Old and New England was . . . a strongly gendered phenomenon. Ever since the struggles between Elizabeth and Mary Queen of Scots for the English throne in the 1560s and 1570s, Protestant propagandists had effectively linked Catholicism with femininity and claimed that this feminization was both the cause and result of political and spiritual corruption. By the seventeenth century, xenophobia and misogyny were knit into the fabric of transatlantic English nationalism. All English people were in theory united by their collective struggle against the "Scarlet Whore of Babylon," the foreign and feminized Roman church.[6]

With King William's War under way (1688–97), New England writers and publishers of the 1690s produced some of its first virulently anti-French and anti-Catholic books and pamphlets. . . . [The Puritan minister] Cotton Mather was one of the most enterprising purveyors of this propaganda. . . . Mather's books and other contemporary pamphlets show that both the Roman empire and the Church of Rome represented despotic power in the minds of New Englanders and stood only for the power to compel people of the true faith to worship false gods.[7]

. . . [W]e cannot dismiss Mather's fears as mere paranoia, as the French had purposefully and determinedly sought to bring their religion to the Indians. Led chiefly by the energetic Catholic Reformation orders of the Jesuits and the Ursulines, religious men traveled down the St. Lawrence River to the Great Lakes, up to Hudson's Bay, and down the Mississippi to spread their faith, and they established successful Indian missions throughout New France and its borderlands from modern-day Maine and Nova Scotia westward to Ontario, Michigan, and the Mississippi River valley. Religious women established schools in Québec, Montreal, and Three Rivers that served as vital centers for the preservation and transmission of French language and culture as well as religion. The work of these French men and women stood in direct contrast to the distinctly underfunded efforts of the English to convert Indians and establish "praying towns." Only a minority of English ministers and settlers expended any efforts whatsoever on preaching to and converting Native Americans. . . .[8]

Cotton Mather agreed with other frontier observers that New England had failed grievously in its neglect of the souls of the Indians, and he argued that King William's War was in part God's punishment of New England for failing their duty to spread the gospel as energetically as French priests had brought their religion to the New World: "This is the Vengeance of God upon you, because you did no more, for the Conversion of those Miserable Heathen." But Mather's concern about Protestant missionary work was not simply for fear of the Lord's judgment; he also saw how French missionary work had paid off in their strong military alliances with the Eastern and Western Abenaki in particular. "Had we done, but half so much as the French Papists have done, to Proselyte the Indians of our East, unto the Christian Faith, instead of being, Snares and Traps unto us, and Scourges in our Sides, and Thorns in our Eyes they would have been, A wall unto us, both by Night and Day." Mather supports this observation with the claim that English captives of the Indians had been told by their captors that "had the English been as careful to Instruct us, as the French, we had been of your Religion!" While at other times in the same book Mather scorns the close association between the French and the Indians, disdaining the "Frenchified Indians" and "Indianized French" that were the result of such New World alliances, in the end he recognizes the advantage of their cooperation and blames New England for not reaching out to the Indians. "[I]f the Salvages had been Enlightened with The Christian Faith, from us, the French Papists could never have instill'd into them those French Poisons."[9]

. . . Mather played a key role in introducing explicitly anti-Catholic themes to captivity narratives with the publication of Hannah Swarton's story in 1697. Even amidst her difficult removes with the Indians after her capture from Casco in 1690, she reports, "yet I dreaded going to Canada, to the French, for fear lest I should be overcome by them, to yield to their Religion; which I had Vowed unto God, That I would not do. But the Extremity of my Sufferings were such, that at length I was willing to go, to preserve my Life." Like many New England captives who were brought to Canada, she was relieved to receive the hospitality of the French and gloried in eating familiar foods and dressing in European clothing once again. But this was the danger of consorting with the French— their way of life was so comfortable to English captives, especially after months or even years

with the Indians, that it made captives all the more susceptible to seduction by "popery." After being taken to Québec and so "kindly Entertained" and "courteously provided for . . . so that I wanted nothing for my Bodily Comfort, which they could help me unto," she was inevitably cast into a conflict that caused her intense spiritual discomfort. (Many readers might have assumed that as a woman, she was naturally more easily seduced by creature comforts that appealed to her carnal nature.) But Swarton, as we hear her through Mather's pen, was all too aware of the dangers that faced her: "Here was a great and comfortable Change, as to my Outward man, in my Freedom from my former Hardships, and Hard hearted Oppressors. But here began a greater Snare and Trouble to my Soul and Danger to my Inward man." Her mistress in Québec, and several priests and nuns "set upon me . . . to perswade me to Turn Papist." Swarton, through Mather's narrative, claims that they sometimes used scriptural arguments, "which they pressed with very much Zeal, Love, Intreaties, and Promises," and sometimes "Hard Usages," even threatening to send her "to France, and there I should be Burned, because I would not Turn to them." This kind of rhetoric served two purposes: it would stir up the emotions of the New England reading public to hear of the allegedly barbarous methods of French proselytizers, but it also gave Swarton and Mather the opportunity to demonstrate the steadfastness of her faith and prove herself a worthy model for other New Englanders to emulate . . . Through her ordeal [Swarton] . . . was comforted by Psalm 118:17–18, "I shall not Dy but live, and Declare the works of the Lord.". . .[10]

. . . The gaping hole in Swarton's narrative of triumph over French priestly designs is the fact that Swarton's own daughter Mary remained in Montreal after she herself returned to New England. She and Mather end her narrative with an earnest request for the "prayers of my Christian Friends, that the Lord will deliver" her [daughter]. Captured with her mother when she was fourteen, at the age of twenty-two Mary married an Irish fellow convert, John Lahey (more often rendered in the French records as Jean LaHaye) in 1697, the same year Mather published her mother's narrative. They presented eleven children for baptism over the next twenty years, three of whom had New England-born godmothers, Christine Otis, Freedom French, and Mary

Silver. As eloquent as Mather and Swarton are about her heroic efforts to resist conversion, they are silent about the decision her daughter made to become a French *bonne femme* instead of an English goodwife.[11]

As Swarton's narrative and personal experiences with captivity suggest, children (and especially daughters) were more vulnerable to the various cultural and religious conversions that might be required of them in captivity. Elizabeth Hanson was grateful when she was purchased by the French in 1725, whom she reports "were civil beyond what I could either desire or expect." "But," she reports with some alarm, "the next Day after I was redeemed, the Romish Priests took my Babe from me, and according to their custom, they baptized it." The priests explained that "if it died before [baptism], it would be damned, like some of our modern pretended reformed Priests." Hanson, a Quaker, worked in an insult aimed at other Protestants in her discussion of priestly intervention. Significantly, Hanson also reports that the priests gave her daughter a new Catholic name: "Mary Ann Frossways" (actually Françoise, or French).[12]

The captivity narrative of John Gyles, published in 1736, nearly fifty years after his boyhood capture and captivity among the Maliseet (Eastern Abenaki) in 1689, illustrates how completely French Catholics had replaced Indians as the enemies of New England and highlights particular fears of the vulnerability of children to conversion. After his initial capture, his Indian "master" shows him to a Jesuit missionary, who Gyles says "had a great mind to buy me. . . . I saw the Jesuit shew him Pieces of Gold, and understood afterward, that he tendered them for me." The politics of the mid-eighteenth century surely shaped his memories of 1689, as he reports a great deal of anxiety about conversion. "The Jesuit gave me a Bisket, which I put into my Pocket, and dare not eat; but buried it under a Log, fearing that he had put something in it, to make me Love him: for I was very Young, and had heard much of the Papists torturing the Protestants &c. so that I hated the sight of a Jesuit."

Fear of being made to "love" a priest may also reflect other dangers Catholic clergy represented in the minds of English people: their sexual ambiguity, and the possibility that they may replace English mothers and fathers, as Indian men and women had for many captives. Just as Catholicism itself was suspect because of its allegedly feminized nature and its

greater appeal to women, so priests were often held in suspicion by Protestants as "unnatural" or feminized men. Men who lived intimately together and shunned marriage were suspect in a culture that elevated heterosexuality to a near-sacrament and regularly depicted Catholicism as a shield for all manner of sexual improprieties. Additionally, New Englanders may have feared that French priests (or nuns) might offer their captive children another alternative family. . . .

A poignant moment in Gyles's narrative suggests that priests might represent both of these kinds of danger, sexual and familial, at the same time. The last time Gyles saw his mother alive, he told her that he might be sold to a Jesuit, and he reports that she reacted with great alarm: "Oh! my dear Child! If it were GOD's Will, I had rather follow you to your Grave! Or never see you more in this World, than you should be Sold to a Jesuit: for a Jesuit will ruin you Body & Soul!". . .[13]

. . . [W]e have almost no direct testimony from captives who remained in Canada. What little evidence we have of these people, their lives in Canada, and their reasons for remaining there comes from their slight communications with their New England families and their chance encounters with other captives who returned to New England to author narratives of their captivity among the Indians and the French. The numbers and demography of those who remained in Canada speak powerfully to the notion that their fates were not accidental. While they were always in the minority of those taken during the border wars (approximately 392 of 1,579 total captives, or less than a quarter of the captive population), girls and women were much likelier to remain in Canada, convert to Catholicism, marry French men, and (presumably) fill Canada's need for European housewifery. Of ninety-five captives taken between 1689 and 1755 who can be reliably traced through the Canadian notarial records, sixty-five (nearly 70 percent) were girls and women. While overall only about one captive in twenty stayed in Canada, female captives were nearly seven times as likely to stay in Canada as their male peers. . . . [A] bare majority of the female captives who remain in Canada were abducted as children; almost a third of them were adolescents or adults—a few women were even married mothers or widows in their thirties and forties. . . .[14]

What made these (mostly) girls and young women remain in Canada? More than half of them (thirty-four out of sixty-five) were taken into captivity before their thirteenth birthday, many of them as very young children. These captives, who frequently lost all memories of their English families and mother tongue, were the most easily assimilated into Canadian life. William Pote tells the sad story of Rachael Quackenbush, whom he saw while in prison in Québec during King George's War (1744–48). "This Child had been with ye French Ever since she was Taken with her Parents which is about 18 months. There was her Father & mother, Grandfather and Grandmother In this prison. They Endeavour'd to make her speak with ym, But she would not Speak a word Neither in Dutch nor English." Even for those captive girls who remembered their families and their native language, after spending several years in Canada, learning French, converting to Catholicism, and marrying a French man, it may have been simply unimaginable to return to a home a family they no longer knew nor remembered well. However, twenty of these captives were adolescents or adults when taken into captivity, young women who were almost fully grown and fully acculturated as English-speaking Protestants, and who would have been unlikely candidates to forget their native language and homeland. The choices of these twenty women are difficult to untangle, although given their age, it is appropriate to call their remaining in Canada a choice. [By the time they were free to return to New England], many of these older captives—especially the older teenagers—had probably adapted to life in Canada and perhaps had already converted to Catholicism. Many may have met a French man they fancied . . . Some of them may have resented or disliked their natal families; surviving court records indicate that at least one of them was eager to escape an abusive home in New England, as we will see.[15] . . .

There are some broad economic and legal facts that might have made New France a more attractive place for women. In stark contrast to the English common law tradition, French Canadian laws governing the "communauté de biens," or the "marriage community" of husband and wife, followed the Custom of Paris, which said that except for wealth in land owned by either partner prior to marriage, husbands and wives owned marital property equally. Although husbands were designated

"masters of the community," neither husbands nor their wives could sell, mortgage, or alienate their joint property without the written consent of the other. . . . Upon the death of either spouse, the widow or widower inherited half of all real and personal property, as well as half the debts; the other half of the property and debts went to the children. Thus, women in French Canada were not economically disenfranchised in marriage as were their sisters in the English colonies. We will never know the extent to which French marital laws were major factors in these women's decisions to turn their backs on New England. However, these property laws may be indicative of a culture that was generally more welcoming and tolerant of women as economic producers and decision makers. This autonomy might have been especially attractive to former captives, as many of them would have spent significant time among Indians before they were purchased by French masters, and they may have come to expect the authority over family resources exercised by their Indian mothers.[16]

Beyond this legal framework, it is clear that New France had very good reasons to want to recruit and retain New England girls and women in the late seventeenth and early eighteenth centuries. French agricultural settlements in the St. Lawrence River valley had long suffered from an imbalanced sex ratio and they were desperate for women trained in European housewifery skills like dairying, baking, and working with textiles (spinning, knitting, weaving, and sewing). Censuses of seventeenth-century New France are unreliable and vary greatly, but they indicate that the scarcity of women was a problem in colonial New France. One historian has put the overall percentage of women among French immigrants to Canada at 12.3 percent for the seventeenth century. . . .[17]

Women skilled in European housewifery would have made the lives of male habitants more comfortable, to be sure, but these skills were also central to European identity in a place that was dominated by other people and other cultural ways. Indians in the colonial northeastern borderlands did not keep cows or consume dairy products; they did not bake European bread; and they did not produce their own thread or cloth. Furthermore, in the later seventeenth century, French officials came to see that the more obvious fruits of marriage might be important to the colony's political future. Observing the rapidly increasing English population along the Atlantic seaboard and in the Connecticut and Hudson River valleys, Canadian officials concluded that recruiting and retaining women with strong bodies and European skills was not just a personal convenience for male habitants; it was a political necessity if the French were going to best their rivals for the control of North America.[18]

Officials in New France spent considerable money and energy recruiting French women for Canadian settlement or, alternatively, training Indian girls to become like French wives and mothers, and religious women played a key role in these efforts in the 1670s and 1680s. Teaching not just French girls but English captives and Indian girls and women in their convent schools, the nuns instructed them in academic subjects, religion, and women's domestic skills that were in such scarce supply in early New France. This dedication to girls' education resulted in a literacy rate higher among French women than men before the British conquest, although in the end few Indian girls and women crossed over to become French housewives—the majority of Native women trained in French schools assumed Indian ways when they returned to their villages and married there. . . .[19]

One of the most striking things about the treatment of English female captives in Canada was the attention and personal involvement of the colony's highest officials. Governor of Montreal (1698–1703) and then governor general of New France from 1703 to his death in 1725, Philippe de Rigaud, Marquis de Vaudreuil, was a powerful central player in the politics and diplomacy of the first two intercolonial wars. Thus it is revealing that he took a personal interest in several female captives during his governorship, even bringing some of them into his household and looking after their educations. He was the godfather of Mary Silver when she was baptized in 1710 among the Sisters of the Congregation of Notre Dame in Ville-Marie (near Montreal), and he placed Mary Scammon among the Ursulines in Three Rivers in 1725. . . . [T]he girls and women that Vaudreuil took such a personal interest in were high-status captives. In order to preserve diplomatic relations, he would have had a strong interest in ensuring these young women's health and happiness as much as possible, given their circumstances. However, the measures he took—putting them into convent schools and witnessing their baptisms and

marriages—doubtlessly served to bind them closer to their adopted home. Other officials of New France also served as godfathers and witnesses at the marriages of English captives, as the notarial records are full of references to "Intendants" performing these duties. In contrast, no New England governors ever expended equal funds or political capital to get these young women back.[20]

Vaudreuil's son Pierre de Rigaud, Marquis de Vaudreuil-Cavagnal, who was governor of Three Rivers and then Louisiana before he became governor general of New France in 1755, carried on his father's tradition of looking after English captives, especially the girls. He witnessed their baptisms, put them into convent schools, and took them into his home. He placed Jemima Howe's daughters Mary and Submit Phipps in the Ursuline convent school in Québec during the Seven Years' War with the instructions that "they should both of them together, be well looked after, and carefully educated, as his adopted children." When he brought Mary Phipps to France with him after the French capitulation in 1760, her mother reports that she was married there "to a French gentleman, whose name is Cron Lewis." Submit became so enthusiastic about her new faith that she refused to leave her convent. "[S]he absolutely refused," wrote her frustrated mother, "and all the persuasions and arguments I could use with her, were to no effect." Only because the younger Vaudreuil himself insisted that she be returned to her mother did Submit finally live up to her name, but she returned to her mother quite unwillingly. This very personal touch was doubtlessly influential in the lives of the young women taken in by the Vaudreuil family over a half-century, but perhaps more significantly, it suggests how important these girls and women were to their new country.[21]

Beyond this personal and official encouragement of English captives, the French crown also directly assisted their assimilation into Canadian society by offering naturalization and even cash payments to male and female captives alike. In 1702, Canadian officials secured two thousand livres of crown support for thirty-eight Catholicized English captives (twenty-one women and seventeen men). In May of 1710, Louis XIV naturalized twenty-eight male and thirty-eight female war captives, and again in 1713 he naturalized another thirty-four men and four women. . . .

The interest of government officials in the fates of these captive girls and women was important, but they relied heavily on Church officials to bring the young women over to French language, culture, and religion. While priests alone had the power to administer the sacraments of baptism and marriage that were so important to bringing ex-captives into Canadian society, much of the daily hard work of these multiple conversions was done by the nuns of Québec, Montreal, and Three Rivers through their convent schools. As we have seen, these female-run institutions were central to seventeenth-century efforts to bring Native girls and women into French society, so adding English girls to their lists of pupils required little adjustment on the part of the sisters who gloried in their evangelical work.[22]

We know that all of the captives who stayed to make lives in Canada were persuaded by this evangelism—or, at least that they accepted the necessity of converting to Catholicism in order to be naturalized. There is too little evidence on the religious opinions of former captives in Canada for us to generalize about their religious experiences. Renouncing Protestantism and converting to Catholicism was an enormous ideological leap, as religion and nationalism were so tightly bound to each other in New England. Even English families on the far borderlands of New England had a strong sense of the moral and intellectual superiority of English Protestantism versus their perceptions of the so-called despotism and corruption of French Catholicism, although they may not have appreciated the finer points of doctrinal difference. Nevertheless, many former captives may have become earnestly devout Catholics. . . . For those who had spent months or years among Indian families who were not living in mission towns, they may have felt a welcome familiarity upon seeing a cross, hearing European music sung, or taking communion again. Some might have come to Catholicism through the practice of Indian families who adopted them. . . .

While officials of both the church and the state clearly played an important role in acculturating English captives, the girls and women themselves established bonds with one another that appear to have eased their adoption into Canadian society. The fact that English captives created and maintained their own networks that lasted decades is further evidence that remaining in New France was a choice, not a fate, for most of them. Canadian notarial records show that ex-captives witnessed one another's baptisms, weddings, and children's baptisms; . . . these women were friends and neighbors who continued to support one another through their lives. . . .

We get only a haphazard picture of these networks through the captivity narratives of returned New Englanders . . . Susanna Johnson reports being approached by two ex-captives turned Ursuline nuns when Johnson and her sister as captives went to the Ursuline convent in Québec to visit Jemimah Howe's daughters, Mary and Submit Phipps. "We here found two aged English ladies, who had been taken in former wars." One of them was Esther Wheelwright (now La Mère Marie-Joseph de l'Enfant Jésus), and the other perhaps Sarah Davis, who took the name Marie-Anne Davis de Saint-Benoit. Mother Esther (as she called herself) was taken in the same 1703 raid on Wells, Maine, along with the Storer cousins Mary and Priscilla, including Priscilla's sister Rachael who also married a French man but settled in Québec rather than Montreal. Mother Esther too expressed interest in the English visitors to her convent, and she told Johnson that she had "a brother in Boston, on whom she requested me to call, if ever I went to that place." After she was redeemed and returned to New England, Johnson followed up on the connection. "I complied with her request afterwards, and received many civilities from her brother." Mother Esther, Mary St. Germaine, and other captives clearly had the connections to go home if they wanted to. They were interested in and affectionate toward their New England friends and families, but they had made their home in Canada. . . .[23]

[A]t least one of the women who stayed in Canada fled some of the more dramatic consequences of New England patriarchy. Abigail Willey (or Willy) stands out . . . because of her age and her marital status: taken in 1689 from Oyster River, New Hampshire, she was a married woman of 32 with two daughters who were about thirteen and eight. Her young daughters were prime candidates to stay in Canada, but why would someone of such a relatively advanced age, and with a husband and other children remaining in New Hampshire, choose baptism and (eventually) remarriage in New France? In a 1683 statement to the New Hampshire colony court, Abigail Willey outlined the harsh reality of her life as an English goodwife. She complained of her husband's chronic violence against her and her isolation as an abused woman: "I have for several years past lived and spent, without making my addresses to any in authority, with Stephen Willy, my husband, often suffering much by sore and heavy blows received from his hand, too much for any weak woman to bear." She also related his frequent threats "to take away my life by the evil disposition of his own mind, seeing that neither his own relations, neither my own natural brothers, dare countenance in any way of natural friendship [with Stephen]." Abigail Willey described herself, in short, as "the suffering subject of his insatial jealousy." Her claims in this petition were supported by an accompanying deposition by a neighbor, Joseph Hill, who one night heard Stephen Willey yell, "I will kill her or whore." (Perhaps Hill meant to indicate that Willey said either, "I will kill her," or "I will kill the whore.") He apparently went into the Willey home to intervene in the violent affair, and found "John Willy, his brother, standing between the said Stephen and his wife, to prevent them from danger."

She had not brought her situation to the attention of local officials and instead suffered for years in silence, perhaps because she believed herself to be the victim of the English courts as well as of her husband. An earlier experience before the bar was grievously humiliating: when Stephen Willey brought her before Judge Edgerly, Willey reports that her husband "at his own request procured of said judge the shameful sentence of ten strips, to be laid upon me at a post." The judge later reversed himself and cancelled the whipping, accepting a twenty-shilling fine instead. But then, when Willey went to visit her sister in Kittery, she reports "said judge sent after me as a runaway, to be procured; the second time to be dealt with according to law." . . . Clearly, she saw this English magistrate and English law as operating at the whim of her disreputable and abusive husband. Perhaps she chose to remain in Canada because she saw an opportunity to escape not just a despotic husband but a legal system that did not operate in her interest.[24]

Colonial Anglo-American women's historians have shown how difficult it was for woman to procure a divorce on any grounds other than desertion, [adultery,] or sexual insufficiency on the part of the husband. Catholic Canada was hardly a libertine's playground—in fact, divorce was nonexistent—but French

Canadian women could claim greater economic self-sufficiency when their marriages broke down, and for a wider variety of reasons. There were two types of legal separation available to aggrieved couples: division of the marital property without physical separation, or a separation of bed and board in addition to the division of all assets. Of 149 petitions for separation in the seventeenth- and eighteenth-century St. Lawrence Valley, most were filed by wives, and most focused on the profligacy of the husband and his inability to manage domestic affairs, situations that were frequently linked to drunkenness and domestic violence. . . . New France, like New England, tolerated wife-beating, but evidence from separation petitions suggests that repeated spousal abuse, death threats, insanity, and venereal infection could gain wives a bed and board separation from men like Stephen Willey. The differences between the New France and New England legal systems are telling, with Canada offering women more flexibility and control in both happy and unhappy marriages. New France's legal tradition offered abused wives more economic rights and autonomy in marital separations than . . . New England.[25]

We know comparatively little of Willey's life in Canada and can glean only a few details from the notarial records that note her transformation from English wife and mother, to French servant, and eventually to wife of a Montreal habitant. Willey was baptized as a Catholic in 1693, took the name Marie Louise Pilman (presumably a transcription error, after her maiden name Pitman), and was described as a servant to Hector de Callières, a Montreal official; apparently even servitude was preferable to her life as an abused New England wife. Her husband Stephen's 1696 will made no mention of her name or her existence whatsoever; neither did he recognize or remember his two daughters in Canada. He died sometime in or before 1700; Mary Louise Pilman married Edouard de Flecheur in 1710 and was naturalized the same year, at the age of fifty-three. Her two daughters had preceded her in marriage to French men . . .[26]

English families used inheritances and inheritance law to compel their captive children and siblings to return to New England, although this tactic was used differently depending on the sex of the captive. Based on the fragmentary evidence available in wills and probate records, it appears that daughters' inheritances were more likely to be contingent upon their return to New England, while New England's captive sons were twice as likely to receive their inheritances without returning to New England. . . . The fact that female captives in Canada fared worse than their male counterparts when it came to their inheritances may be unsurprising, given the patriarchal nature of inheritance law in general: eldest sons reaped great privileges that eldest daughters did not. Furthermore, property ownership was itself a gendered phenomenon, because the law of coverture meant that Anglo-American women might easily spend the majority of their lives as *femes couverts*, and thus not as property owners. But even beyond this, evidence indicates that parents of children who remained in Canada of their own choice used the power of inheritance to communicate disapproval of their children's decisions, or to compel a return to New England, especially when it came to their daughters. . . . [T]he legal structures of Anglo-American society communicated very clearly whose work was valued and whose was not; and whose interests were directly represented and whose were not. We will never know to what extent the concepts of coverture versus the marriage community (in New France) influenced the thinking of captive girls and women, but it was a difference that they were likely aware of, especially those daughters who were threatened with disinheritance.

The way in which William and Mary Moore's parents' estate was settled in 1694 reveals a clear double standard of male and female captives' inheritance. Whereas brother William could receive his portion of the estate "provided said William be alive & demand it," sister Mary could receive hers only if she returned to New England: "if Mary More doo not return from captivity, then her redemption money and her portion to be equally devided among the rest of her brethren and sisters." . . . The language parents used could be very specific: daughters could not simply come home to claim their inheritance (like William Moore would have been permitted to); they had to renounce French law, language, and religion, and come home to stay. Joseph Storer wrote in his 1721 will: "I Give & Bequeath to my beloved Daughter Mary St. Germain Fifty pounds in good Contrey pay upon Condition that She return from under the French Government & Settle in New England.". . . Esther Wheelwright

was . . . disinherited by her mother's 1750 will, unless she "by the Wonder working Providence of God be returned to her Native Land and tarry & dwell in it."[27]

Captive sons fared much better. . . . Even when their claims on inheritance were disputed, returned male captives had good luck in court, especially with the help of a mother's testimony. William Hutchins, taken from Kittery, Maine, in 1705 when he was nine, was apparently presumed dead when the state ordered the division of his late father's estate in 1721, as he was left entirely out of the proceedings. When he returned to Maine in 1733 to claim his inheritance, . . . his brothers denied his identity, so he decided to sue them for his inheritance. Many neighbors testified that he was in fact the real William Hutchins; in the end his mother's judgment that "he is the first born of my Body" prevailed. Hutchins not only received an inheritance, he won the double portion due him as the eldest brother. Conveniently settled, he married a New England woman in 1734 and remained for some time in Kittery. Clearly, English male captives who remained in French Canada were still seen as legitimate heirs, by their families and by the courts, even decades after they had left New England. Their sisters were not so lucky. . . .[28]

The case of Mary Storer and her contested relationship with her English family bears close examination, both for what it suggests about the female captives who remained in Canada and for one family's reaction to this exercise of daughterly will and determination. The surviving correspondence of Mary Storer St. Germaine consists of nine letters to her eldest brother, Ebenezer, one letter each to her mother and another brother, five letters from her husband, Jean St. Germaine, to Ebenezer, and two letters from Ebenezer, one addressed to Mary, the other to her husband, a total of eighteen letters that span nearly thirty years, from 1725 to 1754. Read together, these letters offer valuable glimpses into family relationships in colonial New England. More importantly, they are almost the only direct words we have from a female captive who remained in Canada, and thus offer us some insight into the mind of one captive as she attempts to reconcile the English and the French sides of her family and her own identity. Mary's brother Ebenezer seems to have functioned as the go-between for his sister and the rest of their family in these letters, performing as the executor of not only his father's will but also his family's wishes regarding Mary in general.[29]

The correspondence begins twenty-two years after Mary was taken by the Indians, when both she and Ebenezer were middle-aged parents. Mary Storer was taken in the 1703 Abenaki raid on Wells, Maine, when she and her cousins Rachael and Priscilla Storer were taken in the same attack as Aaron Little-field and Esther Wheelwright. . . . [T]he Storer girls were teenagers: Mary was eighteen, Pris-cilla nineteen, and Rachael about sixteen. All three Storers were therefore young women at the time of their captivity, not children, which may have contributed to greater resentment among the Storer family of their daughters' choices. All three married French men and re-mained in Canada—Mary and Priscilla . . . lived near each other in Montreal the rest of their lives, and Rachael (baptized "Marie Fran-çoise") settled in Québec with her husband, Jean Berger.

The occasion for what seems to have been a new or renewed epistolary relationship with Mary's brother Ebenezer was a visit she made to Boston in the late spring and summer of 1725, as the first letters she writes are posted from Newport, Rhode Island, where she was awaiting the ship that would return her to Montreal. These first letters, all but one ad-dressed to Ebenezer, communicate her distress at having been so long separated from her birth family and indicate that like the Williams family, her family wanted to return her and her children to New England and thus to the Prot-estant faith. In her own handwriting and crude spelling, she assures brother Ebenezer, "my harte is alwais full of sorey and my eyes full of ters to think that I have toke sech a grate jorney to come to se my deare father and mother and had no coumforte to staye longe with them." In another letter she repeats the same sentiments in similar language: "[While] I am not with you my harte and tender love is alwaise with you I shall never for git what every good peple has sead to me becaus I know that is for my good and I pray to god onley that it maie be so an if I can sende one of my childrine I will." Another letter, which was probably intended for her brother Seth, a congregational minister in Watertown, Massachusetts, also gives thanks for some good counsel she received during her visit: "I had but a litel time with you

who I thought woulde show and teach me more then aney bodey [sir?] but what you have saide to me I will not forgett it and I hope god will in able me in all my aflections and that it may be for the best and good of my soule deare brother." Clearly, Mary's natal family had urged her to the Protestant fold, as well as tried to convince her to return to New England. Her notation to Ebenezer that "if I can sende one of my childrine I will" seems to indicate that the Storers were interested in taking in and evan-gelizing her Catholic children as well. . . .

Although Mary wrote that she under-stood that the Storer family's counsel to return to New England and to puritanism was "for the goode of my soule and bodey," she had no intention of remaining with them. Her contin-uing correspondence with Ebenezer suggests that she was adept at shifting between identi-fying with her natal family in Boston and with her husband and children in Montreal. Con-tinuing to address herself to Ebenezer before her return home, she writes, "Dear brother it grievs me to thinke of my father and mother that I had soe litel time to staye with theme but I finde the time very longe with strangers and longe to be with my famelie." Thus by calling her natal family "strangers," as opposed to her "famelie" in Montreal, she makes it clear that her family of first allegiance was in Montreal, not in Boston. And while she implies that her Boston family are "strangers" to her, her emo-tional attachment to them was quite powerful immediately after her 1725 visit. "Deare brother I remember what you have saide to me I thanke you and all that has spoke for my goode." Then again using formulaic language, she writes, "I desier your prayers for me who is youre sister til death with a harte full of sorey and my eyes full of tears fearewell my deare brother and sister I remaine your loving and sorrowful sister," and signs herself, as she did through most of their correspondence, "Mary St. Germaine, Mary Storer," as though to sig-nify her awareness of her two families and her two identities. With only a few notable excep-tions, however, her married name was written above her maiden name.

. . . For eight years after her visit to Boston, Mary and Ebenezer continued to exchange letters every year or two, updating each other on family news and sending along formulaic but apparently warm good wishes. When Ebenezer sent news of their father's death, Mary [wrote]. . . "I pray to god to comforte us all wee are father les children [while] I am hear [in Montreal], you may beleive my harte love is with you all we are al the same blode you can not denie it."

. . . In a letter to her mother, she writes that Ebenezer told her, "my dear father maide his will that I [might?] be equal to my sisters you may believe my dear mother [while] I am far of[f] from you and my deare familei I belave that is not cappable to kep it frome me in conseonc that is for me who is youre [own] child." Regarding her father's command that she remove herself from "French government" in order to receive her inheritance, Mary then claims it is impossible for her even to visit Boston: "wee have a governer & he will nat give any permission to goe in [New] Ingland to our contre[y]," she writes, and names the merchant in Boston whom she had designated to receive and convey her inheritance. . . . [S]he signs her letter, "your dutifull daughter," a departure from her usual practice, and a maneuver that suggests an effort to recast herself as a properly obedient and submissive daughter.

There exists no letter of reply from Mary's mother, but brother Ebenezer's reply underscores the differences her New England family drew between Mary and her siblings. . . . Ebenezer does not promise [her] her inheritance, but he writes that he will remind their mother of her request, and assures Mary, "I know she will do any thing yt is proper & it be not against ye will of our Father deceas'd." The problem was that what Mary was requesting was clearly against her father's will. Joseph Storer had decreed that "if She doth not returne [to New England] Then I Give & bequeath to her the Sum of Tenn Shillings in Countrey pay." This paltry remembrance stood as a rebuke to Mary's resistance of her father's will, and her mother and brother were apparently willing to let the rebuke stand. Legally they could not have directly sent Mary St. Germaine her portion directly from her father's estate, but they could have chosen to give her her portion out of their own fortunes.

Perhaps not surprisingly, there is no record of Mary St. Germaine ever receiving her inheritance, and the surviving correspondence between her and her brother ceases for several years. Only in the autumn of 1739, nearly six and a half years since her last surviving letter to Ebenezer, Mary wrote to him, and the tone

of that letter suggests that she is still annoyed with him and his role in her non-inheritance. Whereas before she had always written him in English in her own hand, this letter appears to have been written by an amanuensis; it is also, significantly, written in French. She opens this letter with a standard, if cooler, salutation to Ebenezer, and then quickly announces the purpose of her letter: "I desire the favour to Let me hear from you & your family for as I have not heard any knews of mother I dont know whether she is on the Land of the Living which obliges me to adress my self to you to lett me hear from her." Notice how her language has changed since her fervent correspondence around the time of her father's death. . . . "If you still have any Love for me I hope you will not refuse me that Comfort," she adds, in further confirmation of her alienation from her natal family. She passes on news of her family, briefly reporting her children's marriages and sadly noting the death of her youngest son the previous year. We do not know if she ever received a reply. . . .

This may well have been the last letter Mary St. Germaine wrote to her brother Ebenezer, for the next letter in the collection is by her husband, Jean, dated eight and a half years after Mary's last letter. Like Mary's last letter, it too is written in French. Seven months after the fact, he wrote the man he addressed as his "very dear brother" to let Ebenezer know of his sister's death. "She died with all possible resignation to the will of God, that is to say as a perfect Christian, and as she had been here 39 years that we were together we had a blessed union and we never had a single difficulty. You know well my dear brother that her death is a great affliction to me, but I must submit to the will of our Creator, as it was he who gave me one of the best women in the world." . . .

Stories like that of Mary Storer St. Germaine show the effects that choices like hers had on the workings of patriarchal power within New England families. The Storer family was typical of other New England families, . . . who also went to great lengths to recover their daughters and save them from the twin evils of French government and Catholicism, or to punish them for their rejection of New England government and Protestantism, or both. Any captives who turned their backs on New England by converting to Catholicism and remaining in Canada represented a painful and shameful failure of the New England way, boys and men as well as girls and women. But New England communities and colonial governments actively courted the return of male ex-captives by offering them cash and jobs, whereas former female captives were offered little if any incentive to return. Instead, it was the government of New France that went out of its way to retain female captives from New England, especially in the years 1689–1713. Mary Storer St. Germaine's story demonstrates that New England families interpreted their daughters' conversion to Catholicism and marriage to French men and Indians as a rejection of New England patriarchal authority. Instead of dutiful obedience and submission to their fathers' (or brothers') household government, women like Mary Storer St. Germaine set themselves against New England's prescribed gender roles when they refused to come home and return to puritanism. While their own decision to abandon New England is no doubt part of the reason they have been written out of New England history, perhaps their families' shame and desire to forget these daughters are also responsible for the fact that so many of them have disappeared from the New England record.

NOTES

1. Frances E. Dolan, *Whores of Babylon: Catholicism, Gender, and Seventeenth-Century Print Culture* (Ithaca, N.Y.: Cornell University Press, 1999).

2. James Axtell, *The Invasion Within: The Contest of Cultures in Colonial North America* (New York: Oxford University Press, 1985), 287–301; Barbara E. Austen, "Captured . . . Never Came Back: Social Networks Among New England Female Captives in Canada, 1689–1763," and Alice N. Nash, "Two Stories of New England Captives: Grizel and Christine Otis of Dover, New Hampshire," both in *New England/New France, 1600–1850*, ed. Peter Benes (Boston: Boston University, 1992), 28–48; William Foster, *The Captors' Narrative: Catholic Women and Their Puritan Men on the Early American Frontier* (Ithaca, N.Y.: Cornell University Press, 2003).

3. On women's alleged vulnerability to the devil's blandishments, see Carol Karlsen, *The Devil in the Shape of a Woman: Witchcraft in Colonial New England* (New York: Norton, 1987), especially chs. 4 and 5; Elizabeth Reis, *Damned Women: Sinners and Witches in Puritan New England* (Ithaca, N.Y.: Cornell University Press, 1997).

4. For reports of French collaboration with the Abenaki during King Philip's War, see Henry Jocelyn and Joshua Scottow to Gov. John Leverett, September 15, 1676, Coll. S-888, misc. box 33/21, Maine Historical Society, Portland, Maine; *Documentary History of the State of Maine* (Portland, Maine: Lefavor-Tower, 1869–1916), 4:377–79.

5. Francis D. Cogliano, *No King, No Popery: Anti-Catholicism in Revolutionary New England* (Westport, Conn.: Greenwood Press, 1995), introduction and chs. 1–2.

6. Anne McLaren, "Gender, Religion, and Early Modern Nationalism: Elizabeth I, Mary Queen of Scots, and the Genesis of English Anti-Catholicism," *American Historical Review* 107 (June 2002): 739–67; Dolan, 6–27.

7. Cotton Mather, *Humiliations follow'd with Deliverances* (Boston, 1697), 30–31. He made the same historical argument a few years later in *Decennium Luctuosum: an History of Remarkable Occurences in the long war which New England hath had with the Indian Salvages, 1688–1698* (Boston, 1699).

8. Francis Jennings, *The Invasion of America: Indians, Colonialism, and the Cant of Conquest* (Chapel Hill: University of North Carolina Press, 1975), 228–53. On the praying Indians more generally, see Ann Marie Plane, *Colonial Intimacies: Indian Marriage in Early New England* (Ithaca, N.Y.: Cornell University Press, 2000).

9. Mather, *Decennium Luctuosum*, 81, 215–16.

10. Mather, *Humiliations follow'd with Deliverances*, 59–71; Emma Lewis Coleman, *New England Captives Carried to Canada* (Portland, Maine: The Southworth Press, 1925; reprint, Bowie, Md.: Heritage Books, 1989), vols. 1 and 2.

11. Mather, *Humiliations follow'd with Deliverances*, 72; Coleman, *New England Captives*, 1:204–08.

12. Elizabeth Hanson, *God's Mercy Surmounting Man's Cruelty* (Philadelphia, 1729), 34; Coleman, *New England Captives*, 2:163.

13. John Gyles, *Memoirs of Odd Adventures* (Boston, 1736), 4–5; Dolan, 85–93.

14. Alden T. Vaughan and Daniel K. Richter, "Crossing the Cultural Divide: Indians and New Englanders, 1605–1763," *American Antiquarian Society Proceedings*, 90 (April 16, 1980), 23–99; author's database compiled from the cases documented by Coleman, *New England Captives*, vols. 1 and 2.

15. William Pote, Jr., original ms. journal kept by him 1745–47 during captivity among the French & Indians, Ayer Collection, Newberry Library, Chicago, Ill., 15; Axtell, *Invasion Within*, 291–94; Laurel Thatcher Ulrich, *Good Wives: Image and Reality in the Lives of Women in Northern New England, 1650–1750* (New York: Oxford University Press, 1983), 208–13.

16. Louise Dechêne, *Habitants and Merchants in Seventeenth Century Montreal* (Montreal: McGill-Queens University Press, 1992), 240–49; Trevor G. Burnard and Ann M. Little, "Where the Girls Aren't: Women as Reluctant Migrants but Rational Actors in Early America," in *The Practice of U.S. Women's History: Narratives, Intersections, and Dialogues*, ed. Eileen Boris, Jay Kleinberg, and Vicki Ruiz (New Brunswick, N.J.: Rutgers University Press, 2007), 12–29.

17. Peter Moogk, "Manon's Fellow Exiles: Emigration from France to North America before 1763," in *Europeans on the Move: Studies on European Migration, 1500–1800*, ed. Nicholas Canny (Oxford: Clarendon Press, 1994), 236–60; Leslie Choquette, "French and British Emigration to the North American Colonies: A Comparative Overview," *New England/New France, 1600–1850*, ed. Peter Benes (Boston: Boston University, 1992), 49–59.

18. For evidence of the state's drive to bring more properly trained housewives into Canada, see, for example, the correspondence of Governor Frontenac and Minister Colbert, *Rapport de L'Archiviste de la Province de Québec* (Québec: Ls- A. Proulx, 1927), 7:44, 60, 65–66, 82 (1673–74); and the correspondence of Governor Frontenac and Intendant Bochart Champigny to the Minister, 8:351, 359, 377 (1697–98).

19. Leslie Choquette, "'Ces Amazones du Grand Dieu': Women and Mission in Seventeenth-Century Canada," *French Historical Studies* 17 (1992): 627–55; Clark Robenstine, "French Colonial Policy and the Education of Women and Minorities: Louisiana in the Early Eighteenth Century," *History of Education Quarterly* 32 (1992): 193–211; Natalie Zemon Davis, "Marie de l'Incarnation: New Worlds," in *Women on the Margins: Three Seventeenth-Century Lives* (Cambridge, Mass.: Harvard University Press, 1995), 63–139.

20. Coleman, *New England Captives*, 1:316–17, 330–31, 356–57, 425–35, 2:44–58, 147, 390–91; SC1 45X, Massachusetts Archives Collection, 51:212–13, and 72:13–15, Massachusetts State Archives, Boston; Ann M. Little, "The Life of Mother Marie-Joseph de L'Enfant Jesus, or, How a little English Girl from Wells became a Big French Politician," *Maine History* 40 (Winter 2002), 276–308.

21. Coleman, *New England Captives*, 2: 320–21, 391, 396; Bunker Gay, *A genuine and correct account of the captivity, sufferings & deliverance of Mrs. Jemima Howe, of Hinsdale in New Hampshire* (Boston, 1792), 16–18.

22. Coleman, *New England Captives*, 1:121–29; Choquette, "Ces Amazones du Grand Dieu"; Little, "Mother Marie-Joseph."

23. Susanna Johnson, *A Narrative of the Captivity of Mrs. Johnson, together with a Narrative of James Johnson*, 3rd ed. (Windsor, Vt., 1814; reprint, Bowie, Md.: Heritage Books, 1990), 89–90.

24. Coleman, *New England Captives*, 1:255–61; Nathaniel Bouton, ed., *Collections of the New Hampshire Historical Society*, vol 8 (Concord: McFarland & Jenks, 1866), 146–48; Ulrich also cites domestic violence as a reason why Willey might have wanted to remain in Canada, *Good Wives*, 209.

25. Cornelia Hughes Dayton, *Women Before the Bar: Gender, Law, and Society in Connecticut, 1639–1789* (Chapel Hill: University of North Carolina Press, 1995), ch. 3; Nancy Cott, "Divorce and the Changing Status of Women in Eighteenth- Century Massachusetts," *William and Mary Quarterly* 3rd ser., 33 (1976): 586–614; Peter Moogk, *La Nouvelle France: The Making of French Canada—A Cultural History* (East Lansing: Michigan State University Press, 2000), 229–33.

26. Coleman, *New England Captives*, 1:255–61.

27. Evidence taken from Coleman, *New England Captives*, vols. 1 and 2, passim. Specific cases from vol. 1: 234–35, 418–19, 431.

28. Coleman, *New England Captives*, 1:391–93.

29. Mary Storer Papers, Massachusetts Historical Society, Boston, Mass. All letters discussed below are in this collection.

The Trial of Anne Hutchinson, 1637

In 1989, in a solemn ceremony soaked with irony and bitter humor, the leaders of the Newport Rhode Island Congregational Church announced that injustice had been done more than 350 years before when Anne Hutchinson had been expelled from Boston's Congregational Church for blasphemy and perjury. The minister who took the initiative, and who coincidentally bore the same name as the John Wilson who had read the formal excommunication in the seventeenth century, thought that the Hutchinson affair raised questions that remained central to religion in the present: questions "of spiritual freedom, the role of women in the church, the issue of individual freedom versus being part of a covenant community, and the church-state issue." In a public ceremony, the president of the Rhode Island Conference of the United Church of Christ burned a copy of the writ of excommunication.*

The Antinomian heresy of 1637–38 threw the Puritan colony of Massachusetts Bay into turmoil for years and forced its leaders to reconsider the nature of their experiment. Antinomians placed greater emphasis on religious feeling than did orthodox Puritans. They tended to be suspicious (*anti*) of law (*nomos*) or formal rules and came close to asserting that individuals had access to direct revelation from the Holy Spirit. They criticized ministers who seemed to argue that it was possible to earn salvation by good deeds rather than leaving it to God freely to decide who was to be saved by their faith, a distinction between the "covenant of works" and a "covenant of faith" which they thought separated authentic Puritans from ones who remained too close to the Anglican Church.

One such Antinomian critic, clergyman John Wheelwright (Anne Hutchinson's brother-in-law) was tried in early 1637 for giving a controversial sermon, found guilty of sedition, and banished. The close relationship between church and state in early New England meant that such challenges to the majority's theological views were interpreted as threatening to established authority of all kinds.

One leading dissenter was Anne Hutchinson, a high-status, well-educated woman in her mid-forties who had migrated to the colony with her merchant husband in 1634, four years after its founding, and who commanded great respect for her competence as a midwife. At meetings held in her home after Sunday church services, she summarized, discussed, and criticized ministers' sermons. Initially attended by five or six women, the meetings became very popular; soon Hutchinson was holding separate gatherings for men and women. The women who followed Hutchinson were often those who respected her medical knowledge and shared her theological ideas. The men who attended were often those

* Madeline Pecora Nugent, "Apologizing to Anne Hutchinson," *Christian Century* 106 (Mar. 22, 1989): 304–5.

Excerpted from "Examination of Mrs. Anne Hutchinson before the court at Newton, 1637," in *The Antinomian Controversy, 1636–1638: A Documentary History*, ed. David D. Hall (Middletown, Conn.: Wesleyan University Press, 1968), pp. 312–16. Copyright © 1968 by David D. Hall. Reprinted by permission of the editor. Notes have been edited and renumbered.

who were critical of the colony's leadership on political and economic as well as religious grounds. Tensions were high in Massachusetts Bay through 1636 and 1637 as colonists violently attacked the Pequot Indians, decimating the tribe and capturing and enslaving the women and children. In a context in which pastor John Wilson linked the destruction of "barbarous Indians" with God's will, religious and political dissent seemed to merge easily. Rumor spread that criticism of the governor and council, the majority of ministers, and the Pequot War had been voiced in the Hutchinsons' house. This led to Anne's being grilled, first by a convocation of ministers and then, in November 1637, by the magistrates and legislators of the colony, in a court held in Newtown (now Cambridge).

The proceedings were not a trial in the contemporary sense with due process safeguards; instead they followed the format of the early modern magisterial examination, an inquisition without a jury. Hutchinson, who was pregnant, had no lawyer. Her trial was conducted by the governor of the colony, John Winthrop. (His house was directly across the path from the Hutchinsons' dwelling; he could not have avoided seeing the people coming and going to her meetings.) Winthrop was joined in his questioning by the deputy governor and other members of the legislature (called the General Court). Only very late in the interrogation did Anne make an incautious statement—that God had directly revealed things to her—which provided her judges with a rationale to convict her of heresy and sentence her banishment from the colony.

Hutchinson's secular trial was followed by a disciplinary hearing in the Boston church to which she belonged. This second trial covered much of the same ground as the first; one of the ministers present spoke for many of the men in the room when he declared: "You have stept out of your place, you have rather bine a Husband than a Wife and a preacher than a Hearer; and a Magistrate than a Subject." After the members voted to excommunicate her, pastor Wilson pronounced the judgment: "Forasmuch as you, Mistress Hutchinson, have highly transgressed and offended and forasmuch as you have so many ways troubled the Church with your Errors and have drawn away many a poor soul and have upheld your Revelations: . . . I command you . . . as a Leper to withdraw your self out of the Congregation." At this, Hutchinson rose, walked to the meetinghouse door, turned, and spoke directly to her accusers: "The lord judgeth not as man judgeth, better to be cast out of the Church then [than] to deny Christ."

After Hutchinson was exiled, at least ten more women were banished or excommunicated for being outspoken. Thus, a clear message was sent that explicit dissent by women was not to be tolerated in the Massachusetts Bay Colony. In Winthrop's memoir of the events, published in 1644, miscarriages suffered by Hutchinson and her closest colleague, Mary Dyer, were interpreted as evidence of God's "displeasure against their opinions and practices, as clearly as if he had pointed with his finger, in causing the two fomenting women in the time of the height of the Opinions to produce out of their wombs, as before they had out of their braines, such monstrous births as no Chronicle . . . hardly ever recorded the like."*

---

* Sandra F. VanBurkleo, "'To Bee Rooted Out of Her Station': The Ordeal of Anne Hutchinson," in *American Political Trials*, rev. ed., ed. Michael R. Belknap (Westport, Conn.: Greenwood Press, 1994), pp. 1–24; *The Antinomian Controversy, 1636–1638: A Documentary History*, ed. David D. Hall (quotes on pp. 214, 382–83, 388); and *Winthrop's Journal, "History of New England": 1630–1649*, vol. 1, ed. James Kendall Hosmer (New York: Charles Scribner's Sons, 1908), p. 251.

Hutchinson and her husband fled to Rhode Island, a colony with a policy of religious toleration. Several years later, they moved to Dutch territory north of what is now New York City. Widowed, Anne Hutchinson died in an Indian raid on her settlement, in 1643.

In reading this excerpt from Anne Hutchinson's 1637 trial, note the extent to which criticism of her religious and political behavior merges with the complaint that she is challenging gender roles. It will help to know that by "rule," Protestants of the era meant a biblical passage that stipulated how Christians should behave. What strategies did Hutchinson use to defend her actions and challenge the proceedings? Which points of the dialogue best reveal colonial leaders' fear of independent women?

NOVEMBER 1637

The Examination of Mrs. Ann Hutchinson at the Court at Newtown

Mr. Winthrop, governor. Mrs. Hutchinson, you are called here as one of those that have troubled the peace of the commonwealth and the churches here; you are known to be a woman that hath had a great share in the promoting and divulging of those opinions that are causes of this trouble, and to be nearly joined not only in affinity and affection with some of those the court had taken notice of and passed censure upon, but you have spoken divers things as we have been informed very prejudicial to the honour of the churches and ministers thereof, and you have maintained a meeting and an assembly in your house that hath been condemned by the general assembly as a thing not tolerable nor comely in the sight of God nor fitting for your sex, and notwithstanding that was cried down you have continued the same, therefore we have thought good to send for you to understand how things are, that if you be in an erroneous way we may reduce you that so you may become a profitable member here among us, otherwise (if you be obstinate in your course that then the court may take such course that you may trouble us no further) therefore I would intreat you to express whether you do not hold and assent in practice to those opinions and factions that have been handled in court already, that is to say, whether you do not justify Mr. Wheelwright's sermon and the petition.[1]

Mrs. Hutchinson. I am called here to answer before you but I hear no things laid to my charge.

Gov. I have told you some already and more I can tell you.

Mrs. H. Name one, Sir.

Gov. Have I not named some already?

Mrs. H. What have I said or done?

Gov. Why for your doings, this you did harbour and countenance those that are parties in this faction that you have heard of.

Mrs. H. That's matter of conscience, Sir.

Gov. Your conscience you must keep or it must be kept for you. . . . Say that one brother should commit felony or treason and come to his other brother's house, if he knows him guilty and conceals him he is guilty of the same. It is his conscience to entertain him, but if his conscience comes into act in giving countenance and entertainment to him that hath broken the law he is guilty too. So if you do countenance those that are transgressors of the law you are in the same fact.

Mrs. H. What law do they transgress?

Gov. The law of God and of the state.

Mrs. H. In what particular?

Gov. Why in this among the rest, whereas the Lord doth say honour thy father and thy mother.

Mrs. H. Ey Sir in the Lord.

Gov. This honour you have broke in giving countenance to them. . . .

Mrs. H. What law have I broken?

Gov. Why the fifth commandment.

Mrs. H. I deny that for [Mr. Wheelwright] saith in the Lord.

Gov. You have joined with them in the faction.

Mrs. H. In what faction have I joined with them?

Gov. In presenting the petition . . .

Mrs. H. But I had not my hand to the petition.

Gov. You have councelled them.

Mrs. H. Wherein?

Gov. Why in entertaining them.

Mrs. H. What breach of law is that Sir?

Gov. Why dishonouring of parents.

Mrs. H. But put the case Sir that I do fear the Lord and my parents, may not I entertain them that fear the Lord because my parents will not give me leave?

Gov. If they be the fathers of the commonwealth, and they of another religion, if you entertain them then you dishonour your parents and are justly punishable.

Mrs. H. If I entertain them, as they have dishonoured their parents I do.

Gov. No but you by countenancing them above others put honor upon them.

Mrs. H. I may put honor upon them as the children of God and as they do honor the Lord.

Gov. We do not mean to discourse with those of your sex but only this; you do adhere unto them and do endeavour to set forward this faction and so you do dishonour us.

Mrs. H. I do acknowledge no such thing neither do I think that I ever put any dishonour upon you.

Gov. Why do you keep such a meeting at your house as you do every week upon a set day?

Mrs. H. It is lawful for me so to do, as it is all your practices and can you find a warrant for yourself and condemn me for the same thing? [I]t was in practice before I came therefore I was not the first.

Gov. For this, that you appeal to our practice you need no confutation. If your meeting had answered to the former it had not been offensive, but I will say that there was no meeting of women alone, but your meeting is of another sort for there are sometimes men among you.

Mrs. H. There was never any man with us.

Gov. Well, admit there was no man at your meeting and that you was sorry for it, there is no warrant for your doings, and by what warrant do you continue such a course?

Mrs. H. I conceive there lyes a clear rule in Titus, that the elder women should instruct the younger[2] and then I must have a time wherein I must do it.

Gov. All this I grant you, I grant you a time for it, but what is this to the purpose that you Mrs. Hutchinson must call a company together from their callings to come to be taught of you?

Mrs. H. Will it please you to answer me this and to give me a rule for then I will willingly submit to any truth. If any come to my house to be instructed in the ways of God what rule have I to put them away?

Gov. But suppose that a hundred men come unto you to be instructed will you forbear to instruct them?

Mrs. H. As far as I conceive I cross a rule in it.

Gov. Very well and do you not so here?

Mrs. H. No Sir for my ground is they are men.

Gov. Men and women all is one for that, but suppose that a man should come and say Mrs. Hutchinson I hear that you are a woman that God hath given his grace unto and you have knowledge in the word of God I pray instruct me a little, ought you not to instruct this man?

Mrs. H. I think I may.—Do you think it not lawful for me to teach women and why do you call me to teach the court?

Gov. We do not call you to teach the court but to lay open yourself.

Mrs. H. I desire you that you would then set me down a rule by which I may put them away that come unto me and so have peace in so doing.

Gov. You must shew your rule to receive them.

Mrs. H. I have done it.

Gov. I deny it because I have brought more arguments than you have.

Mrs. H. I say, to me it is a rule.

Mr. Endicot. You say there are some rules unto you. I think there is a contradiction in your own words. What rule for your practice do you bring, only a custom in Boston.

Mrs. H. No Sir that was no rule to me but if you look upon the rule in Titus it is a rule to me. If you convince me that it is no rule I shall yield.

Gov. . . . [T]his rule crosses that in the Corinthians.[3] But you must take it in this sense that elder women must instruct the younger about their business, and to love their husbands and not to make them to clash.

Mrs. H. I do not conceive but that it is meant for some publick times.

Gov. Well, have you no more to say but this?

Mrs. H. I have said sufficient for my practice.

Gov. Your course is not to be suffered for, besides that we find such a course as this to be greatly prejudicial to the state, besides the occasion that it is to seduce many honest persons that are called to those meetings and your opinions being known to be different from the word of God may seduce many simple souls that resort unto you, besides that the occasion which hath come of late hath come from none but such as have frequented your meetings, so that now they are flown off from magistrates and ministers and this since they have come to you, and besides that it will not well stand with the commonwealth that families should be neglected for so many neighbours and dames and so much time spent, we see no rule of God for this, we see not that any should have authority to set up any other exercises besides what authority hath already set up and so what hurt comes of this you will be guilty of and we for suffering you.

Mrs. H. Sir I do not believe that to be so.

Gov. Well, we see how it is we must therefore put it away from you, or restrain you from maintaining this course.

Mrs. H. If you have a rule for it from God's word you may.

Gov. We are your judges, and not you ours and we must compel you to it.

Mrs. H. If it please you by authority to put it down I freely let you for I am subject to your authority.

Notes

1. The petition the Antinomian party presented to the General Court in March 1637.

2. Titus 2.3, 4, 5.

3. 1 Corinthians 14.34, 35.

European Women and the Law: Examples from Colonial Connecticut

---

Marriage is an intimate relationship that is a result of private choice. But marriage is also a public act and has important social, political, and legal implications for both women and men. Indeed, deep into our own time, the law of marriage has shaped how men and women relate to each other and how they act in the world; when people want to change those relationships, they often begin by challenging the rules of marriage. If we want to understand the systems of gender in a culture, the rules of marriage are the place to begin.

Europeans were startled by the patterns of intimate relations among Native Americans. Although there were many differences among native cultures, marriage was generally situated within complex matrifocal systems of kinship in which husbands moved into the dwellings of the wife's kin; in which sisters and brothers remained close even in adulthood; and in which uncles and aunts could play important roles in the upbringing of nieces and nephews. In these kin networks, premarital sex, polygamy, marital separation, and divorce were not necessarily frowned upon, and there was often a space for a third gender or homosexual practice. For Europeans, such different rules of intimacy were signs of weakness and lack of civilization.

"Husband and wife are one person in law, that is, the very being or legal existence of the woman is suspended during the marriage, or at least is incorporated and consolidated into that of the husband; under whose wing, protection, and cover, she performs every thing; and is therefore called . . . *a feme covert*." This understanding, known as *coverture*, was the foundation of the English law of domestic relations. When an Englishwoman married, her husband became the owner of all the movable things she possessed and of all the property or wages she might earn during their marriage. He also received the right to manage and collect the rents and profits on any real estate she owned; if they had a child, the child could not inherit the dead mother's lands until after the death of the father. (For more details of the system of coverture, see Kerber, pp. 110–117.)

All colonies placed in their statutes a law regulating marriage. This step reflected a concern that marriage be celebrated publicly in order to guard against bigamy. Connecticut did not forbid interracial marriage, but many other colonies did.

Early America was for the most part a divorceless society. South Carolina boasted that it granted no divorce until 1868. Most colonies followed the British practice of treating marriage as a moral obligation for life. Occasional special dissolutions of a marriage were granted by legislatures in response to individual petitions or by courts of equity, but these were separations from bed and board, which normally did not carry with them freedom to marry again.

The Puritan settlers of Massachusetts and Connecticut were unusual in treating marriage as a civil contract, which might be broken if its terms were not carried out. Connecticut enacted the earliest divorce law in the colonies. It made divorce available after a simple petition to the superior court under certain circumstances. People who did not fit these circumstances were able to present special petitions to the legislature.

Most petitioners for divorce in early America were women. What sorts of troubled marriages could women in colonial Connecticut exit by getting a judicial divorce? If you were a legislator, what grounds for divorce would you add? Scholars call the eighteenth and nineteenth centuries a period of "fault divorce." One spouse was seen as guilty of having breached the contract, while the other was innocent; thus, divorce due to incompatibility or irreconcilable differences was not available. Identify the language in the Connecticut statute that reflects this outlook.

AN ACT RELATING TO BILLS OF DIVORCE, 1667

Be it enacted . . . that no bill of divorce shall be granted to any man or woman, lawfully married, but in case of adultery, or fraudulent contract, or wilful desertion for three years with total neglect of duty; or in case of seven years absence of one party not heard of: after due enquiry is made, and the matter certified to the superior court, in which case the other party may be deemed and accounted single and unmarried. And in that case, and in all other cases aforementioned, a bill of divorce may be granted by the superior court to the aggrieved party; who may then lawfully marry or be married again.

Perhaps no statutes were more important to women in the first 250 years after settlement of the English colonies than the laws protecting their claims to dower. The "widow's dower" should be distinguished from the dowry a bride might bring with her into marriage. "The widow's dower" or the "widow's third" was the right of a widow to use one-third of the real estate that her husband held at the time of his death. She was also entitled to one-third of the personal property he had owned, after the debts were paid. It was an old English tradition that he might leave her more in his will, but he could not leave her less. If a man died without a will, the courts would ensure that his widow received her "thirds."

It is important to note that she only had the right to use the land and buildings. She might live on this property, rent it out, farm the land, and sell the produce. But she could not sell or bequeath it. If the real estate was simply the family home and her children were adults, she had a claim only to a portion of the house. After the widow's death, the property reverted to her husband's heirs, who normally would be their children, but in the event of a childless marriage was likely to revert to his brothers or nephews.

A contrasting situation existed in the community property jurisdictions, including Louisiana, New Mexico, and California. There, "dotal" property, or dowry that came with the bride, was intended to help with the expenses of the marriage; the husband could manage this property and spend its income, but at the end of the marriage it was restored to the wife or her heirs, thus keeping it in her own family line of succession. She also kept her own "paraphernalia"—personal clothing and other items—which she could trade as a merchant (without her husband's consent) and dispose of in her own will.

In the Connecticut statute, which follows, note the provisions protecting the widow's interests. Normally colonial courts were scrupulous about assigning the widow's portion. Observe, however, that widows could not claim dower in "movable" property, which might represent a larger share of their husband's wealth than real estate. As time passed and the American economy became more complex, it became increasingly likely that a man's property would not be held in the form of land. If the land were heavily mortgaged, the widow's prior right to her "third" became a barrier to creditors seeking to collect their portion of a husband's debts. By the early nineteenth century, courts were losing their enthusiasm for protecting widows' thirds. By the middle of the century, the married women's property acts began to reformulate a definition of the terms by which married women could claim their share of the property of wife and husband. But between 1790 and 1840, when the right to dower was more and more laxly enforced and the new married women's property acts had not yet been devised, married women were in a particularly vulnerable position. (See Keziah Kendall, pp. 242–244.)

AN ACT CONCERNING THE DOWRY OF WIDOWS, 1672

That there may be suitable provision made for the maintenance and comfortable support of widows, after the decease of their husbands, Be it enacted . . . that every married woman, living with her husband in this state, or absent elsewhere from him with his consent, or through his mere default, or by inevitable providence; or in case of divorce where she is the innocent party, that shall not before marriage be estated by way of jointure in some houses, lands, tenements or hereditaments for term of life . . . shall immediately upon, and after the death of her husband, have right, title and interest by way of dower, in and unto one third part of the real estate of her said deceased husband, in houses and lands which he stood possessed of in his own right, at the time of his decease, to be to her during her natural life: the remainder of the estate shall be disposed of according to the will of the deceased. . . .

And for the more easy, and speedy ascertaining such rights of dower, It is further enacted, That upon the death of any man possessed of any real estate . . . which his widow . . . hath a right of dower in, if the person, or persons that by law have a right to inherit said estate, do not within sixty days next after the death of such husband, by three sufficient freeholders of the same county; to be appointed by the judge of probate . . . and sworn for that purpose, set out, and ascertain such right of dower, that then such widow may make her complaint to the judge of probate . . . which judge shall decree, and order that such woman's dowry shall be set out, and ascertained by three sufficient freeholders of the county . . . and upon approbation thereof by said judge, such dower shall remain fixed and certain. . . .

And every widow so endowed . . . shall maintain all such houses, buildings, fences, and inclosures as shall be assigned, and set out to her for her dowry; and shall leave the same in good and sufficient repair.

HIDDEN TRANSCRIPTS
WITHIN SLAVERY

JUDITH A. CARNEY
The African Women Who Preceded Uncle Ben: Black Rice in Carolina

"When most of us think about the origin of rice, we think of Asia. But there is another species of rice whose history is less well known—a rice of African origin, *Oryza glaberrima*." So explains historical geographer Judith A. Carney. Until the 1970s, scholars assumed that the rice grown in England's southern mainland colonies was of Asian origin. Then, historian Peter Wood, in 1974, argued that the rice initially cultivated in the Carolina colony was *glaberrima* and that its success as an export crop was possible only because of the knowledge system of the many enslaved Africans charged with planting, weeding, harvesting, and milling it—especially women's knowledge.*

In colonial North America, "the most lucrative plantation system was not based on the crops we traditionally associate with slavery, such as cotton, sugar, and tobacco. Rather, it was based on rice, for which there was a considerable demand in Europe," Carney writes. But when the Carolina colony was first established by English planters in 1670, they were intent on growing sugar. The enslaved persons who accompanied them began cultivating rice in the subsistence plots where they grew provisions to feed themselves. Within a few decades, rice shifted from a local food crop to a plantation export crop. On the eve of the American Revolution, over the years 1768–1772, rice exports from South Carolina exceeded 66 million pounds annually. Already rice had become the first cereal to be globally traded.

Two points of orientation should help when reading Carney's essay. First, early European settlers in the Carolina colony (which later became North and South Carolina) and Georgia (founded in 1733) used the terms tidewater and low country to describe the territory along the rivers that ran to the Atlantic Ocean as far upstream as the fall-line—the point above which boats could not navigate. Second, rice growers in Carolina and Georgia worked under a task system, with enslaved women, men, and children assigned specific tasks they were expected to get done by the end of the day. Although they were not constantly supervised by

---

* Peter Wood, *Black Majority: Negroes in Colonial South Carolina from 1670 through the Stono Rebellion* (New York: Knopf, 1974)

Excerpted from ch. 4 *of Black Rice: The African Origins of Rice Cultivation in the Americas* by Judith A. Carney (Cambridge, Mass.: Harvard University Press, 2001). Copyright 2001 Judith A. Carney. Reprinted by permission of the author. Notes have been edited and renumbered.

white overseers, and although they managed to find time to grow a variety of African and other foods to either consume or take to market, they faced grueling physical requirements in rice cultivation, as you will see.

Carney's research tells us about one of many African food contributions to the Americas. To this day, rice retains its prominence in the foodways of many former plantation societies. Her essay reminds us, too, that although we tend to take the cultivation of food crops for granted, each one requires a body of information and skills—a system of knowledge—that is neither simple nor self-evident. Like the white women of free status in early New England colonies described by Laurel Thatcher Ulrich (see pp. 43–53), the female protagonists of Carney's essay brought a complicated skill set to the annual cycle of rice cultivation. But they and their African kinfolk did not profit or benefit from the hard physical labor they performed. As you read, see if you can list the preconditions and steps necessary to make rice into an export crop that enriched the white planters of this rice-growing region.

Over much of the northern portion of the West African rice region, rice has long been a woman's crop. . . . Wherever rice is grown in West Africa, women are involved. They display sophisticated knowledge in recognizing soil fertility by plant indicators, which reveal, for instance, soil impoverishment or recovery. Females are responsible for seed selection, sowing, hoeing, and rice processing. Seed selection in particular requires a sophisticated understanding of the specific demands made by diverse rice micro-environments, such as water availability, the influence of salinity, flooding levels, and soil conditions.

Women's expertise in African rice culture extended beyond knowledge of the crop's cultivation to include the processing of rice. . . . To what extent did the gendered knowledge systems of African rice culture diffuse to South Carolina? Did the institution of slavery reproduce any of the gendered forms of African cultivation and processing systems on Carolina rice plantations?

The hoe is the primary agricultural tool throughout the entire West African rice region. Indispensable to women's work in rice culture are a long- and short-handled version, the former used for field preparation and the latter for detailed work and weeding. Several colonial-period engravings and paintings of American rice plantations depict slaves, often females, carrying or working with the long-handled hoe. Its significance in field preparation continued after Emancipation [in 1863]. Written accounts of Carolina rice culture also mention the use of short-handled hoes, with handles four and eight inches in length, for detailed plot work.[1]

During the colonial period the use of hand tools predominated in southern agriculture. The clearing of forests resulted in fields full of stumps and roots, which could not be worked by draft animal traction. However, by the close of the period hoes were being replaced, as stump removal and decay facilitated the use of horse- and ox-drawn plows. The exception to this pattern occurred on Carolina rice plantations, where the use of hand tools continued into the antebellum period. Historian Lewis Gray calls the use of hoes in Carolina low-country agriculture the "West Indian method," which he claimed to be fixed in local custom rather than technological necessity. [The] method links the continuance of hoe agriculture in South Carolina to the system of planting in islands of the West Indies, such as Barbados, whence migrated some of the first European and black settlers to the Carolina low country. The West Indian tradition of using hand tools likely has its roots in West Africa.[2] . . .

As an agricultural implement the hoe actually played a minor role in eighteenth-century European farming systems, which relied principally on draft animal traction. Hoes were typically used for work in the corners of fields, on small parcels, or for specialized crops like grapes. In Africa, the hoe took on a preeminent role since much of the continent potentially favored for draft animal traction suffered adversely from trypanosome infection lethal to cattle. On no other continent but Africa does the hoe figure so centrally or take so many forms.[3]

Three cultivation techniques on Carolina plantations suggest African antecedents. Throughout West Africa women are the sowers of rice. On Carolina and Georgia rice plantations, sowing was typically the work of female slaves. The method of planting additionally reveals an African basis. Sowing usually involved dropping seeds onto the trenched ground and covering them with the foot. African antecedents are also evident in a second, though less common, method in which seeds are enveloped with marsh clay before planting. The technique is similar to one long used in West Africa, where women wrap seeds in cow dung and/or mud to protect them against birds, insects, and microbial parasites. The documentary *Family across the Sea*, which profiled many of the similarities in rice cultivation between South Carolina and Sierra Leone, filmed African women dropping the encased seeds in the soil for cultivation. In South Carolina and Georgia this method of sowing became known as open-trench planting.[4] . . .

Another technique in Carolina rice cultivation that indicates the transfer of a gendered knowledge system across the Atlantic relates to the method used for cultivating freshwater river floodplains. Rice cultivation in this environment is often a West African female farming system with transplanting practiced only in areas beset by high tides or when variability in the onset of precipitation delays the return of the flood. . . . [This was] one of the features distinguishing African from Asian rice systems. Tidal rice cultivation in South Carolina and Georgia developed on freshwater rivers and seldom involved transplanted seedlings, relying instead upon direct seeding of floodplains, as in Africa.[5]

Another group of techniques that testify to the transfer of female knowledge systems to the Americas relates to the manner of milling and cooking rice. For most of the colonial period rice was milled with a wooden mortar and pestle, with winnowing accomplished with fanner baskets. Thus until the advent of water-driven mechanical devices during the second half of the eighteenth century, rice milling was performed in the African manner with an upright wooden mortar and pestle. . . .

The processing of rice also involves the removal of the indigestible hulls or chaff, a process known as winnowing. In West Africa, winnowing occurs by placing the hand-milled rice, a mixture of grains and empty hulls, in circular and shallow straw baskets as much as two feet in diameter. During a breeze the grains and hulls are rotated inside and repeatedly tossed in the air. By tossing the grains and hulls up and down, the lighter chaff is carried off into the air, leaving the heavier husked grains inside the basket. Winnowing on South Carolina plantations followed the same method. The winnowing baskets, known on rice plantations as fanner baskets, were shallow disks with a raised lip about two feet across. They could hold about a pound of rice at a time.

Even the weaving style used in making fanner baskets displays an African origin. . . . The fanner baskets used for winnowing on Carolina and Georgia plantations [were always coiled and have been linked] to a tradition derived from the West African rice area. . . . Those marketed as folk craft by female African-American vendors in the Charleston area today are woven in the identical manner.[6] . . .

Methods of cooking reveal additional linkages to Africa. The characteristic way of preparing rice in the Carolina plantation kitchen favored grain separation, the way African dishes based on *glaberrima* rice are typically cooked. In South Carolina and elsewhere in the Americas this culinary tradition could be achieved with sativa rice by using medium- to long-grained varieties that tended not to clump together. Then the plate of rice was prepared so that it appeared "white, dry, and every grain separate." The method involves steaming and absorption, boiling rice first for 10–15 minutes, draining off excess water, removing the pan from direct heat so the grains can absorb the moisture, and leaving the pot covered for at least an hour before eating. Often the product was encased in a thick residue of crust on the inner edges of the pot: "Around the pot there is a brown rice-cake, in the center of which are the snow-white grains, each thoroughly done and each separate. Unless one has eaten rice cooked in this way, he knows nothing about it. The stuff called rice—soft and gluey—may do to paper a wall, but not to feed civilized man." This is the same manner in which rice is traditionally prepared throughout the West African rice region.[7] . . .

Despite the familiar logo of Uncle Ben on the converted rice marketed by that name in the United States, it was African women who perfected rice cooking. . . . They also developed the method of parboiling, another name for converted rice. In newly harvested rice, which has not properly dried for milling, parboiling facilitates the removal of hulls. While the steaming of rice in its hull improves nutritional value by concentrating vitamins in the grain's center, parboiling causes the oils to migrate to the bran, a process that eases milling. As partial cooking reduces storage loss from mold, parboiled rice additionally confers superior keeping qualities.

For such reasons parboiling continued as a method of rice preparation in some rural southern communities well into this century. The method was undoubtedly known to the black Texas rice farmers symbolized by Uncle Ben, whose trademark was established when the process was industrialized during the 1940s.[8] Although the passage of time would divorce the image of Uncle Ben from its historical context to mere product icon, his representation on a well-known consumer product speaks to a deeper social and cultural memory of the early twentieth century, which associated black Americans with rice culture. The method of parboiling represents the diffusion of a female knowledge system from Africa, which survived slavery in the cooking practices of their free male and female descendants.

Thus more than the cultivation of rice took root in the Americas. Rice culture embodied a sophisticated knowledge system that spanned field and kitchen, one that demanded understanding the diverse soil and water conditions of seed survival along with cooking methods for consumption. The transformation of rice from field grain to food depended on yet another knowledge system perfected by African women, that of milling the cereal by hand. During the colonial period rice milling involved a skilled tapping motion for removing hulls without grain breakage. This female knowledge system served as the linchpin for the entire development of the Carolina rice economy. For without a means to mill rice, the crop could not be exported.

The issue of milling on Carolina plantations raises one remaining and pertinent question. To what degree, if any, did the gender division of labor characterizing African rice cultivation reappear under slavery in South Carolina? Since slavery could dissolve any preexisting pattern of work, what were the broader implications of the transfer of a knowledge system both African and gendered? An examination of the work cycle regulating life on rice plantations illuminates these issues

while bringing attention to the colonial milling method, which involved use of the mortar and pestle. The brutality of slave labor during the colonial period vividly portrays the complexity of the demeaning shift of work that blacks experienced under slavery.

Rice cultivation was arduous, requiring slaves to labor under strenuous and insalubrious conditions year-round. Slaves worked in knee-deep water, which exposed them to malaria, dysentery, and other waterborne diseases that in turn contributed to high mortality rates. . . . During the hot and humid summers of South Carolina and Georgia, where temperatures average over 90 degrees Fahrenheit, slaves labored mightily to keep up with the demands made upon their bodies. Partly to avoid the summer heat, the slaves' day began at sunrise on rice plantations. The pernicious conditions of rice cultivation and slaves' presumed racial predisposition to working in heat and humidity were captured by one planter descendant, Duncan Heyward: "For there was at that time in the province no white labor which could perform the work of reclaiming the river swamps. The white man could not stand the summer heat, nor could he endure working in the water. Negroes alone had to be relied upon."[9]

The rice calendar involved year-round work, and most of it was done completely by hand. Only in the last decades of slavery were animals brought into use for plowing and transport of materials. Even the harvest was carried out from the fields, typically in baskets placed on the head. Slaves began preparing for a new cycle of rice cultivation almost immediately after the harvest of the previous crop. The agricultural calendar got under way with land preparation from December to March. This involved burning the stubble from the previous harvest, digging out ditches, and fortifying the sides of canals that had slumped as well as removing excess mud from ditches. Slaves found especially odious the strenuous work involved in the digging, cleaning, and repair of ditches, where they were forced to labor over vast acreages with just their hands, buckets, and simple tools. Then in the spring the fields were cleared, leveled, and clods were broken apart with hoes in preparation for cultivation.[10]

. . . The sowing of seed was staggered in two planting periods, one from mid-March to early April and the other in late May through early June. The full moon regulated both sowing periods because its stronger tides facilitated germination by spreading water over the entire field.[11] Sowing was immediately followed by the first of four protracted floodings. The first or "sprout flow" aimed at seed germination, a period that lasted between three to six days. Then the water was drained off to allow the cleaning of debris, which was followed by hoeing and weeding. Next came the second irrigation flow, known as the "point or stretch" flow. Water remained on the field for another three to seven days, after which hoeing and weeding again took place.

Over the period from mid-July through August the field was once more flooded, the "deep flow" lasting for about three weeks. Hoeing and weeding again followed the draining off of water before the fourth and final period of field flooding, the "lay by or harvest flow." This referred to the irrigation phase when the plant began to joint so that the stalks supported clusters of rice. Water now stayed on the field until the rice crop reached maturity. The staggered sowings of rice enabled the cultivation of two rice crops and, as in Africa, reduced the labor bottlenecks in hoeing, weeding, and harvesting. The cycle of rice cultivation spanned a period from six to seven months. Once ripened, the crop was harvested with a sickle, usually over a six- to eight-week period from late August or early September into October.

Evidence from archival and historical sources yields clues on the division of labor underlying rice culture in South Carolina and Georgia. These include reminiscences by planter descendants and elderly ex-slaves of the Depression-era Federal Writers' Project, planter records ... , and drawings that depict slave labor in rice cultivation, such as those of Alice Huger Smith for Elizabeth Allston Pringle's 1914 plantation memoir. Such evidence indicates that female slaves composed the majority of "prime hands" on Carolina and Georgia rice plantations. Rice cultivation was characterized by a field labor force that was disproportionately female, with the less arduous artisanal "skilled" work such as making barrel staves for the crop's shipment, blacksmithing, and cooperage monopolized by male bondsmen.[12]

... [All of this evidence attests] to the necessity of revising conceptions of slavery that display a gender bias, such as those that undervalue agricultural and women's work by designating it as unskilled. ...

... The institution of slavery meant that the preexisting gender division of labor that characterized production of a crop in Africa could be disassembled in the Americas to accord with the dictates of the market and requirements of the plantation owner. Early accounts, however, do reveal the contours of a gendered system of production. Writing about rice cultivation in Georgia during the colonial period, Johan Martin Bolzius noted that with the exception of milling, there was no difference in the labor demanded of male and female slaves. However, men usually repaired rice embankments and ditches while the sowing of rice was principally performed by women. The association of rice sowing with female labor continued throughout the antebellum period, as planter descendant Duncan Heyward remarked: "Women always did this work, for the men used to say this was 'woman's wuck,' and I do not recall seeing one of the men attempt it." ... Women wielding long-handled hoes, the "human hoeing machine" as Frances Kemble described them at work in rice fields during the 1830s, provided crucial labor for land preparation and weeding. Following patterns established in West African rice culture, women typically performed the tasks of sowing, hoeing, and weeding on Carolina plantations.[13] ... The expertise of female slaves in rice culture must have proved of [great] value for adapting the crop to new conditions in the Americas.

As the cultivation cycle drew to a close with harvest in late September or early October, rice milling got under way. The processing of rice dominated the agricultural calendar until the resumption of cultivation in March or April. Although the actual period of farming was concentrated in the months from mid-March through October, production of rice for international markets in fact demanded work every month of the year. Nor was rice the only plantation crop cultivated. Its agricultural calendar was superimposed upon the planting, weeding, and harvest of subsistence crops like corn, beans, potatoes, and greens. The work of slaves on rice plantations intensified even more from the mid-eighteenth century with the cultivation of an additional export crop, indigo. Over the same period plantation labor demands were increasing with the expansion of tidal rice cultivation, which necessitated swamp reclamation and the construction of irrigation infrastructure. Such factors strained the endurance of slaves on rice plantations and undoubtedly contributed to their abbreviated life expectancy.[14]

But no work was as demanding as the toil of the postharvest period. Once the crop was harvested, rice stubble required plowing-under, then burning. Next the land was hoed to break up the soil. Field embankments, ditches, and fences needed repair, the canals cleaning and digging. But most important, the international market demanded a crop already milled. Once harvested, rice required threshing, winnowing, and pounding prior to shipment overseas. During the months from December to May work on a rice plantation intensified. In 1765 one Charleston visitor commented on the "active" work pace of slaves during winter and spring, when the "crops of rice and indigo [were] brought to town and shipped off." But the activity involved a great deal more than harvesting and loading the ships. Millions of pounds of rice required processing before shipment and this fact set the pace for the season's activity. The work regime of a Carolina rice plantation was thus more rigorous and sustained throughout the year than that on comparable cotton or sugar plantations.[15]

The principal demand for the rice crop in the colonial era was in Catholic Europe, with peak market prices prevailing during Lent. Aiming production at this southern European market, planters sought to complete rice milling by early winter in time for the transatlantic voyage that would deliver the grain in February. . . .[16] But the goal of punctual delivery to Europe was often not met, as is evident from one Charleston merchant's complaint in January 1726 about the shortage of milled grain for loading his waiting vessels: "Here thirty seven barrels of Rice and two Chest of Dearé Skin Ship by me Richard Splatt on board the *Lovely Polly* Michael Bath Master bound for London on my proper account and . . . goes Consigned to Mr. William Crisp . . . that there is not rice to load the ½ of 'em."[17] . . .

A Carolina rice plantation during the colonial period represented a stark departure in the work rhythms known to slaves who grew rice in West Africa. Instead of signaling the end of an agricultural cycle, the harvest marked the prelude to even more grueling work routines associated with milling. No wonder that cases of barn burnings as acts of sabotage increased in the fall, when the huge rice harvest had been gathered from thousands of acres and impatient planters were demanding that the crop be cleaned quickly and transported in heavy barrels to waiting ships. The intensified work effort required to process millions of pounds of rice by hand during the postharvest period brutalized slaves while transforming the colonial plantation system into a factory in the field.[18]

On the eve of the American Revolution exports of rice from South Carolina reached over sixty million pounds annually. This represented a staggering growth of the rice economy since 1700, when less than half a million pounds had been exported. The shift in rice cultivation from inland swamps to fertile floodplains had dramatically increased yields. Growing the crop with irrigation reduced the amount of weeding needed, which greatly improved labor productivity. From the first to the second half of the eighteenth century the per capita output of milled rice produced by slaves climbed from 2,250 pounds to an average that reached between 3,000 and 3,600 pounds.[19] But improved productivity scarcely ameliorated the work burdens facing slaves, for following the harvest, rice had to be milled. The exertions required by the rice harvest were negligible compared with the Herculean toil that awaited slaves milling the crop for export. For most of the eighteenth century this crucial step in preparing rice for export markets depended upon processing the crop by hand, with a mortar and pestle. . . .

. . . An examination of the milling process . . . reveals the effects of enslavement and mass production of rice on an African knowledge system, male and female identities, and slave culture. [On the one hand] active involvement in developing rice culture on Carolina plantations provided slaves the means to negotiate the conditions of their labor. But [on the other hand,] the very success of rice transfer to the low-country region resulted in one of the most profitable economies of the Americas, thereby consolidating planter power. With economic success, planters exerted greater control over slave lives. They made new claims on the bodies of enslaved persons, demands that tested human endurance. The expansion of the rice culture came at great cost to black lives.

. . . The method used in Africa to prepare rice for daily subsistence became transformed under slavery into a grueling labor regime in which millions of pounds of rice were processed in just a few months of the year. The story of this plantation crop and its milling, deeply rooted in West African culture and history, reveals the changing relationship of time, labor, and market that characterized the commodification of rice during the eighteenth century. The pounding of rice resonated through African communities as the heartbeat of daily life, the echo of cultural identity. Under slavery it was compressed into a seasonal activity, where each stroke of the pestle made inhuman demands on labor. . . .

The mortar was made by taking a tree trunk (usually cypress or pine), and using fire to burn a cavity or receptacle for placing the unmilled grain. With the mortar hollowed out to waist height, unprocessed rice was then milled with a wooden pestle (about one to one and a half meters long) that weighed between seven and ten pounds. Processing requires standing over the mortar, taking the pestle in hand and repeatedly lifting it up and down to remove the hulls that enclose the grain. . . . In recalling the process of making a mortar and pestle, an Alabama woman earlier this century drew attention to the steps involved in . . . [this skilled operation]:

> . . . [With the rice in the hollowed-out stump] we would take that maul [pestle] and beat it up and down on the top of the rice . . . Every once in a while we'd put our hands through it to see if all the husks, all the rice had gotten outa the husks . . . So a big windy day then we'd take that rice and spread a sheet out and then take it in a bucket and hold it up high. Let the rice fall down on the sheet and the husks would blow off. The wind would blow. We did that mo' one time to get all the husks and the rice was just as pretty and white as the rice you buy at the sto'.[20]

The processing of rice by hand with a mortar and pestle is known as pounding, which is really a misnomer, since the desire to obtain whole, in preference to broken, grains requires a skilled tapping and rolling motion, where loosening the pestle grip at the right moment prior to striking the rice minimizes grain breakage. This is a delicate operation that demands care and skill, especially when the objective is to produce white rice. Pounding by hand unfolds in two distinct stages. The first step takes off the grain's hull; the second step removes the bran and nutrient-bearing germ from the softer endosperm, which polishes or whitens the rice. Following each pounding, rice is winnowed to remove unwanted materials. . . .

The grade of rice produced by hand milling varied considerably with the skill level of the person carrying out the processing. An experienced person could obtain between 65 percent and 75 percent whole grains; half the rice might end up broken with a less-skilled, careless, or fatigued operator. While observers of rice processing during the colonial period commented upon the variability in the percentage of whole to broken rice with hand milling, the uneven quality was viewed as the result of worker apathy rather than of the brutal labor demanded by processing. . . . In fact, different rates of milled to broken rice among slaves probably had less to do with indifference than with the skill level and other plantation duties of individual slaves.[21]

Concern over obtaining a high percentage of whole grains from processing figure[d] prominently in planter concerns. In eighteenth-century world markets, as in those of the present day, broken rice sold at a much-reduced price. Merchant lists from the colonial period indicate that the export market favored "very clean, bright and whole grains." Higher market prices depended on milling the whole grains to remove the protein-bearing bran and then polishing them to whiteness. While this process reduced the nutritional value of white rice, it had the advantage of minimizing grain spoilage on long transatlantic voyages. Such market preferences required Carolina planters to separate milled rice production into three grades: whole grains, those partially broken, and small broken ones. . . . The broken rice, not as salable in international markets, was either sold at a lower price or reserved for local consumption.[22]

However, given the labor regimen facing rice plantation slaves in the eighteenth century, achieving a high percentage of whole grains with hand milling would have proved difficult. The abbreviated time period allotted for rice processing and the stress it placed on slave labor resulted in sacrificing quality for completion of the task. Slavery additionally forced men to process rice with the mortar and pestle. A skill of African women became with slavery male as well as female work due to the high demand for Carolina rice in international markets and the intensive labor required for its processing. Men's inexperience in milling rice with a mortar and pestle would have also resulted in a higher concentration of shattered grains. With slavery the division of labor characterizing

African farming systems dissolved, subjecting both male and female slaves to the radically different and demanding work regime of hand milling.

During the eighteenth century the percentage of broken rice likely remained high. Mortality rates kept the slave population from reproducing itself well into the century. Reliance on continuous slave imports from Africa meant males had to learn the skill upon arrival, the outcome resulting in high levels of broken rice. Differences in skill level between males and females directly imported from Africa partially explains some of the variability in quality of the output commented upon by numerous observers. For reasons such as these, planters deliberately sought slaves with expertise in rice culture. Women's skills in rice processing must have figured among the desired qualities in the unusual planter demand for female slaves on Carolina rice plantations. But slave markets could not always respond to such demands. Planters would take any able-bodied laborer, male or female, with or without previous experience growing rice, to complete their labor force.[23] . . .

Milling rice with a mortar and pestle was grueling, for the worker had to stand for hours at a time, repeatedly lifting a pestle that weighed as much as ten pounds to remove the hulls and bran. The task demanded strength and endurance as well as care and finesse. . . . [Women at the mortar and pestle] worked alone. Each one would have stood upright for hours at a time lifting the heavy pestle to meet a daily production quota. . . .

Since at least the 1750s the task of processing rice was divided into two sessions, morning and evening work, as Johan Martin Bolzius observed: "They [slaves] gather the rice, thresh it, grind it into wooden mills, and stamp [pound] it mornings and evenings." . . . Slaves worked late into the night during the winter months, beating the rice in large mortars to free the grain.[24] . . .

The pressures brought to bear on the slaves by market forces tested their physical endurance to its limits. Death was too frequently the result, as South Carolina scientist Alexander Garden noted in 1755: "Labour and the Loss of many of their lives testified the fatigue they underwent in Satiating the Inexpressible Avarice of their Masters . . . but the worst comes last for after the Rice is threshed, they beat it all in large Wooden Mortars to clean it from the

Women hulling rice with mortar and pestles, Sapelo Island, Georgia, between 1915 and 1934. (Courtesy of Georgia Archives, Vanishing Georgia Collection.)

Husk . . . [planters who work their slaves so much] often pay . . . dear for their Barbarity, by the Loss of many . . . Valuable Negroes."[25]

Technical progress on the second step of milling, removal of the inner skin of the rice grain or its bran, lagged until 1787 when Jonathan Lucas, the "Eli Whitney" of rice, invented a water-driven mill for polishing. The Lucas mill successfully husked the grain with minimal breakage and polished it to the desired whiteness. His machine achieved excellent results with the Carolina gold *sativa* variety then being planted in the colony. The tidal rivers used for irrigating rice fields during the spring and summer cultivation season served in the fall and winter as the source of water power for milling. With the diffusion of water mills throughout low-country rice plantations during the remaining decade of the century, slaves were for the most part finally relieved of the burden involved in processing the entire export crop by hand.[26]

Like all aspects of the plantation rice system, processing was "tasked," with each slave expected to deliver a fixed amount of polished rice daily until the plantation crop was completely milled. [Scientist] Alexander Garden provide[d] an early estimate of the amount of rice each slave was expected to clean: "Each Slave is tasked at Seven Mortars for One Day, and each Mortar Contains three pecks of Rice." [A peck weighed about eleven pounds.] While Garden placed the task as equal for men and women, later commentators like planter R. F. W. Allston, who drew upon family records, wrote that the daily task for milling differed between females and males, with six pecks required for men and four for women: "The method was, that each male laborer had three pecks of rough rice in a mortar, and each female two pecks, to pound before day or sun-rise; and the same at night, after finishing the ordinary task in the field." . . . Research on the Lowndes' rice plantation in South Carolina from the first decades of the nineteenth century show[s] that the daily task for an individual man working alone was one and one-half bushels while that for a woman was one bushel, approximately 67 and 45 pounds respectively.[27] . . .

By dividing processing into two daily work periods, before sunrise and after sunset, planters improved the "efficiency" of labor expended while intensifying it on a daily basis. Rice processing contributed to lengthening the number of days worked in rice cultivation during the calendar year. The addition of rice milling to a full day's plantation work starkly illustrates the dramatic rupture in labor relations slavery represented over the precapitalist agricultural system known in West Africa. A task performed daily by African women in less than an hour became transformed with commodity production into extended hours of daily toil by male and female slaves over an abbreviated period of the year.

The pounding of rice, the preparation of a food that signals daybreak and the re-creation of community life in West Africa, underwent a radical transformation on eighteenth-century rice plantations. As workers arose to the first of two pounding periods, the striking of the pestle represented a new conception of time and labor, calibrated by the dictates of planter and market. Commodity production transformed the mortar and pestle into a device that harnessed human arms to a measurement of rice required by planters for processing.

The pestle represented a powerful symbol of bondage for slaves on Carolina rice plantations as well as in other areas of plantation slavery in the Americas. . . . Only in areas of the Americas where slaves had escaped, as among rice-growing maroons of the Guianas, did the mortar and pestle reassert its African meaning. For Suriname's maroons, as in other free communities of blacks, the rhythms of food preparation still heralded the dawn of a new day. The striking of the pestle in a mortar became again the heartbeat of village life, a daily reminder of the significance of rice for daily culture. . . .[28]

During the period of slavery in the United States the market pressures to satisfy an increased international demand for rice shattered this aspect of African daily existence. Rice plantations ruptured and then transformed the traditional cultural associations of hand milling into an insatiable demand for labor that was forced to work faster to complete the processing of rice as quickly as possible. . . .

Women's indigenous knowledge, transmitted from one generation to another and from mother to daughter, forms a significant aspect of rice culture in West Africa. With enslavement, this knowledge crossed the Middle Passage and reemerged in the way rice was grown and processed and in the cooking styles that mark the African diaspora in the Americas. Among all the African crops that transferred to the New World, none proved as significant as rice in affirming African cultural identity. Rice became a dietary staple wherever blacks settled in environments amid social conditions favorable for its cultivation. Slaves as well as maroons adopted the crop, and their descendants planted it in freedom throughout tropical and subtropical America. . . .

In South Carolina, however, where rice became a plantation crop, slavery dismantled this gender division of labor as both men and women were forced to work in its cultivation and milling. The rice plantation economy necessitated the resolution of several problems associated with hand processing. Slavery shifted the temporal pattern of rice milling in Africa, characterized by women pounding the cereal for a short period of time each day of the year, to one that compressed milling into just a few months. The shift demanded that slaves spend grueling hours processing rice. Then, as the rice export economy placed ever greater demands on labor, rice processing required dissolving its African basis as a female responsibility so that both men and women processed the crop.

African knowledge of rice farming [especially women's knowledge] established, then, the basis for the Carolina economy. But by the mid-eighteenth century rice plantations had increasingly come to resemble those of sugar, imposing brutal demands on labor. Slaves with knowledge of growing rice had to submit to the ultimate irony of seeing their traditional agriculture emerge as the first food commodity traded across oceans on a large scale by capitalists who then took complete credit for discovering such an "ingenious" crop for the Carolina and Georgia floodplains. For this reason, the words "black rice" fittingly describe their struggle to endure slavery amid the enormity of the travail they faced to survive.

NOTES

1. Lewis Gray, *History of Agriculture in the Southern United States to 1860*, 2 vols. (Gloucester, Mass.: Peter Smith, 1958), 1:194–195; Leslie Schwalm, *A Hard Fight for We: Women's Transition from Slavery to Freedom in South Carolina* (Urbana: University of Illinois Press, 1997), p. 21.

2. Gray, *History of Agriculture*, 1:195; R. Berleant-Schiller and R. and L. Pulsipher, "Subsistence Cultivation in the Caribbean," *New West Indian Guide*, 60, nos. 1–2 (1986): 1–40.

3. See three essays in a special issue of *Cahiers ORSTOM*, série Sciences Humains, 20, nos. 3–4 (1984): H. M. Raulin, "Techniques agraires et instruments aratoires au sud de Sahara," pp. 339–58, esp. p. 350; F. Sigaut, "Essai d'identification des instruments à bras de travail de sol," pp. 360–67; and A. Lericollais and J. Schmitz, "La calebasse et la houe," p. 438.

4. Ibid. See the memoir of a plantation descendant: Theodore Ravenal, "The Last Days of Rice Planting," in David Doar, *Rice and Rice Planting in the South Carolina Low Country* (1936; Charleston: Charleston Museum, 1970), pp. 43–50, esp. pp. 49–50. And note this description: "Young men brought the clay water . . . while young girls, with bare feet and skirts well tied up, danced and shuffled the rice about with their feet until the whole mass was thoroughly clayed"; Elizabeth Allston Pringle, *A Woman Rice Planter* (1914; Cambridge, Mass.: Harvard University Press, 1961), pp. 11–12. *Family Across the Sea*, 57 minutes, directed by Tim Carrier, 1990, South Carolina ETV Commission.

5. See Doar, *Rice and Rice Planting*; R. F. W. Allston, "Essay on Sea Coast Crops," *De Bow's Review*, 16 (1854): 589–615, and Allston, "Memoir of the Introduction and Planting of Rice in South Carolina," *De Bow's Review*, 1 (1846): 320–357; Duncan Heyward, *Seed from Madagascar* (Chapel Hill: University of North Carolina Press, 1937), pp. 9–10.

6. Dale Rosengarten, "Social Origins of the African-American Lowcountry Basket" (Ph.D. dissertation, Harvard University, 1997), esp. pp. 273–311. These fanner baskets were woven from bullrush and sweet grass. On the Gullah tradition of fanner baskets, see Joseph Opala, *The Gullah* (Freetown, Sierra Leone: U.S. Information Service, 1987).

7. Karen Hess, *The Carolina Rice Kitchen: The African Connection* (Columbia: University of South Carolina Press, 1992), esp. pp. 2–26; Ntozake Shange, *If I Can Cook/You Know God Can* (Boston Beacon Press, 1998), pp. 33, 48–49; Jacob Motte Alston, cited in Charles Joyner, *Down by the Riverside* (Urbana: University of Illinois, 1984), p. 96.

8. For instance, elderly informants who lived in Oklahoma, descendants of Black Seminoles who settled there after their removal from Florida in the early 1840s, remember the method. Linda Salmon, pers. comm., March 20, 2000. Kate Sheehan, in Janice Jorgensen, ed., *Encyclopedia of Consumer Brands*, vol. 1 (Washington, D.C.: St. James Press, 1994), pp. 608–609.

9. Heyward, *Seed from Madagascar*, p. 55; Peter Wood, *Black Majority* (New York: Knopf, 1974); Peter Coclanis, *The Shadow of a Dream* (New York: Oxford University Press, 1989); William Dusinberre, *Them Dark Days* (Oxford: Oxford University Press, 1996).

10. Ira Berlin, *Many Thousands Gone: The First Two Centuries of Slavery in North America* (Cambridge, Mass.: Harvard University Press, 1998), p. 167.

11. On the rice calendar, see J. H. Easterby, "The South Carolina Factor as Revealed in the Papers of Robert F. W. Allston," *Journal of Southern History*, 7, no. 2 (1941): 160–172; Doar, *Rice and Rice Planting*; Daina L. Ramey, "'She Do a Heap of Work': Female Slave Labor on Glynn County Rice and Cotton Plantations," *Georgia Historical Quarterly* 82, no. 4 (1998), 707–734.

12. Schwalm, *Hard Fight*; Leigh Ann Pruneau, "All the Time is Work Time: Gender and the Task System on Antebellum Low Country Rice Plantations" (Ph.D. dissertation, University of Arizona, 1997), p. 15; Berlin, *Many Thousands Gone*, p. 168. Pringle's memoir can be found at www. http://docsouth.unc.edu/fpn/pringle/pringle.html.

13. Bolzius, quoted in Klaus G. Loewald, Beverly Starika, and Paul Taylor, "Johan Bolzius Answers a Questionnaire on Carolina and Georgia," *William and Mary Quarterly*, 3rd ser., 14 (1957): 257; Heyward, *Seed from Madagascar*, p. 31; Frances Kemble, *Journal of a Residence on a Georgia Plantation in 1838–1839* (Athens: University of Georgia Press, 1984; orig. pub. 1863), p. 156. See Joyner, *Down by the Riverside*, p. 48, for a drawing by one planter descendant of women sowing rice in the African manner of covering the seed by foot. Elizabeth Pringle, one of the last Carolina planters, wrote in 1913 that among male laborers: "The hoe they consider purely a feminine implement"; *Woman Rice Planter*, p. 79. See also Schwalm, *Hard Fight*, 9, 23, 37.

14. Doar, *Rice and Rice Planting*, pp. 13–15; Joyner, *Down by the Riverside*, pp. 46–47. Indigo, planted on the higher lands behind the riverine rice fields, got under way in the 1740s but declined as a cash crop after the American Revolution. Joyce Chaplin, *An Anxious Pursuit: Agricultural Innovation and Modernity in the Lower South, 1730–1815* (Chapel Hill: University of North Carolina Press, 1993), pp. 191–208.

Indigo cultivation and dyeing diffused to West Africa from the Nile Valley circa a.d. 700–1100. See George Brooks, *Landlords and Strangers: Ecology, Society, and Trade in Western Africa, 1000–1630* (Boulder: Westview Press, 1993), p. 56. On female slaves and indigo dyeing in West Africa, see Claire Robertson and Martin Klein, "Women's Importance in African Slave Systems," in Robertson and Klein, eds., *Women and Slavery in Africa* (Madison: University of Wisconsin Press, 1983), pp. 3–28, esp. pp. 15–16.

15. Pelatiah Webster, "Journal of a Visit to Charleston, 1765," in H. Roy Merrens, ed., *The Colonial South Carolina Scene: Contemporary Views, 1697–1774* (Columbia: University of South Carolina Press, 1977), p. 221; Henry C. Dethloff, *A History of the American Rice Industry, 1685–1985* (College Station: Texas A&M Press, 1988), p. 23.

16. James Clifton, "The Rice Industry in Colonial America," *Agricultural History*, 55 (1981): 266–283, esp. pp. 280–281; M. Eugene Sirmans, *Colonial South Carolina: A Political History, 1662–1763* (Chapel Hill: University of North Carolina Press, 1966), pp. 107–108; Clifton, "The Rice Industry," pp. 280–281. Demand for rice expanded during the eighteenth century throughout Europe since it was used for brewing beer and to make paper.

17. Richard Splatt, Charles Towne, to William Crisp, London, January 17, 1726, quoted in Dethloff, *American Rice Industry*, p. 11.

18. Barn burnings, Peter Wood, pers. comm., August 31, 1999; Michael Mullin, *American Negro Slavery: A Documentary History* (Columbia: University of South Carolina Press, 1976).

19. Dethloff, *American Rice Industry*, p. 10; estimates appear in Coclanis, *Shadow*, p. 97.

20. Onnie Lee Logan, as told to Katherine Clark, *Motherwit: An Alabama Midwife's Story* (New York: Dutton, 1989), p. 9.

21. Converse Clowse, *Economic Beginnings in Colonial South Carolina, 1670–1730* (Columbia: University of South Carolina Press, 1971), p. 129; Gray, *History of Agriculture*, 1:278.

22. Merchant demand list of Josiah Smith, Jr., quotes Leila Sellers, *Charleston Business on the Eve of the American Revolution* (Chapel Hill: University of North Carolina Press, 1934), p. 68. On spoilage of cereal grains, see Dethloff, *American Rice Industry*, p. 35, and Carville Earle, *Geographical Inquiry and American Historical Problems* (Stanford: Stanford University Press, 1992), p. 114. On rice grades, see U. B. Phillips, *American Negro Slavery* (New York: D. Appleton, 1918), p. 90; Gray, *History of Agriculture*, 1:278.

23. On slave imports directly from Africa, see Berlin, *Many Thousands Gone*, pp. 313–315. On planter preferences for slaves familiar with rice growing with the shift to tidal production, see Daniel C. Littlefield, *Rice and Slaves* (Baton Rouge: Louisiana State University Press, 1981); and D. Richardson, "The British Slave Trade to Colonial South Carolina," *Slavery and Abolition*, 12 (1991), 135–172.

24. Loewald, Starika, and Taylor, "Johan Bolzius," p. 259; Berlin, *Many Thousands Gone*, p. 147.

25. Samuel G. Stoney, *Plantations of the South Carolina Low Country* (Charleston: Carolina Art Association, 1938), pp. 33–34.

26. Dethloff, *American Rice Industry*, p. 29; Chaplin, *An Anxious Pursuit*, p. 254. Mortar-and-pestle processing continued, however, with rice retained for plantation consumption. It also continued in areas where the main plantation crop was cotton but slaves planted rice as a provision crop. See Amelia Wallace Vernon, *African Americans at Mars Bluff, South Carolina* (Baton Rouge: Louisiana State University Press, 1993).

27. Correspondence between Alexander Garden, M.D., and the Royal Society of Arts, quoted in Wood, *Black Majority*, p. 79; Allston, "Memoir of the Introduction," p. 342; J. Drayton, *A View of South Carolina* (Columbia: University of South Carolina Press, 1972; orig. pub. 1802), p. 151; Pruneau, "All the Time," pp. 68, 97, 155.

28. Melville Herskovits and Frances Herskovits, *Rebel Destiny: Among the Bush Negroes of Dutch Guiana* (New York: McGraw-Hill, 1934), p. 185.

ANNETTE GORDON-REED
The Hemings-Jefferson Treaty: Paris, 1789

From 1787 to 1789, Sally Hemings lived in Paris, becoming familiar with the city, learning French, and earning wages. She had been only fourteen years old when she made the Atlantic transit from Virginia, accompanying eight-year-old Polly Jefferson whose father, Thomas, wished his youngest child to join him in France. Three years earlier, Jefferson had taken up his diplomatic post in France,

Excerpted from chs. 14–17 of *The Hemingses of Monticello: An American Family* by Annette Gordon-Reed (New York: W. W. Norton, 2008). Reprinted by permission of the author and publisher. Notes have been edited and renumbered.

arriving with his teenage daughter Martha (called Patsy) and Sally's older brother James. By the time Polly and Sally joined him, the diplomat was renting an elegant, twenty-four-room house known as the Hôtel de Langeac; it was on the Champs-Elysées at some remove from the city center.

Sally and her brothers were born slaves, the legal property of Virginia planter John Wayles whose daughter Martha became Thomas Jefferson's first and only wife. At the Wayles-Jefferson wedding in 1772, various enslaved Hemingses, including Sally, James, and their mother Elizabeth, were added to Jefferson's human assets. John Wayles was actually Sally's biological father as well as her master; Sally was therefore the half sister of Jefferson's wife. Sally and other Hemings women were at Martha Wayles Jefferson's deathbed in 1782, where Martha, weeping, asked her husband to promise not to remarry and impose a stepmother on their then-living four children. Afterward, the young Sally lived with, and attended, the Jeffersons' youngest daughters; thus, she in effect grew up alongside her nieces. What she thought about this situation, we do not know.

Sally was still a slave girl when she lived in Paris. She remained an enslaved person until several years before her death in 1835. But those who observed her in Paris would not have associated her with the strenuous, debasing, and exhausting field labor that many African-descended women had to endure on New World plantations. She undertook light household duties such as sewing; she accompanied Patsy and Polly on daytime urban promenades and to evening receptions and balls. She wore fine clothes, as circumstances dictated. She did not have her femininity denied her.

Annette Gordon-Reed's essay pivots on a dramatic and private agreement that Sally Hemings and Thomas Jefferson made just before Jefferson was to leave his post and return to Monticello, his beloved Virginia plantation. Being under French law gave the Hemings siblings the opportunity to claim free status; Sally, the teenager, understood it as an extraordinary moment of leverage.

Until very recently, major Jefferson biographers (except for Fawn Brodie) refused to believe that Thomas Jefferson, slave owner, founding father, and two-term president, had a sexual relationship, or, as Gordon-Reed calls it, a long-term, possibly loving concubinage arrangement, with Sally Hemings. Even before there was DNA evidence to support this, Gordon-Reed, a lawyer as well as a scholar, wrote a book carefully laying out the evidence, pro and con. Appalled by decades of scholarly obfuscations and willed ignorance about the agency of African Americans, she pointed out the curious disconnect between the popular appeal of the Hemings-Jefferson story in the 1970s and 1980s and the historians' vehement, sometimes irrational denials.*

What do you make of the author's suggestion that for Sally Hemings, being female was more at the core of her identity than being enslaved? Some skeptics will argue that the existence of the 1789 treaty rests on slim evidence—Hemings family lore and an inkwell. How do you assess Gordon-Reed's reasoning?

Postscript to the story told here: the child that Sally Hemings was carrying in 1789 did not survive. Later, at Monticello where they continued their relationship, she gave birth to seven children, five of whom survived infancy. For these children, Thomas Jefferson abided by the terms of the treaty of 1789.

---

* Annette Gordon-Reed, *Thomas Jefferson and Sally Hemings: An American Controversy* (Charlottesville: University Press of Virginia, 1997); Dinitia Smith and Nicholas Wade, "DNA Test Finds Evidence of Jefferson Child by Slave," *New York Times*, Nov. 1, 1998, p. A1.

When we think of the young Sally Hemings, . . . we acknowledge that she was born into a cohort—eighteenth-century enslaved black women—whose humanity and femininity were constantly assaulted by slavery and white supremacy. While the experiences typical to that cohort are highly relevant as a starting point for looking at Hemings, they can never be an end in themselves. For Hemings lived in her own skin, and cannot simply be defined through the enumerated experiences of the group—enslaved black females.

Taking account of the larger social context in which Hemings lived is essential. . . . There is . . . no one context to consult in regard to [her] . . . she had the multiple identities that are the normal part of the human makeup. The people and places she encountered gave her multiple personal contexts—the circle of her mother and siblings, her extended family, the larger enslaved community at Monticello, her community in Paris, Jefferson, his white family, and, finally, her own children. Those associations . . . shaped her inner life and outlook. . . .

Sally Hemings . . . spent her first fourteen years in a country that defined her as human chattel. In her fifteenth and sixteenth years, she was in a place (France) where a court would . . . transform her status, turning her into a legally recognized free person. Sometime between 1787 and 1789, this teenager learned the difference between law in Virginia and law in France. The power of the former could reenslave her, while the power of the latter could set her free. So she stood poised between the reality of life in the place of her birth and the moment when she had to decide whether to take the step toward freedom in a new land. She could make her journey alone or with her older brother, leaving not only slavery behind but also a large and intensely connected family in Virginia. . .

[The years in Paris were also the time when Hemings became Jefferson's "concubine."] How is it possible to get at the nature of a relationship between a man and a woman like Jefferson and Hemings when neither party specifically writes or speaks to others about that relationship or their feelings? Even written words can be quite deceptive and seldom tell the whole story, for people sometimes choose, for whatever reason, to tell a story of their lives that is rosier, or grimmer, than it actually was. In the absence of words, actions may be quite telling. An event in the life of Hemings's oldest sister Mary that took place at the same time that Hemings was in Paris dealing with Jefferson offers some insight into the varied nature of the veiled relationships between enslaved women and white men. . . .

[Due to mounting family debts, Jefferson was under pressure to hire out some of his slaves. Thus, in the late 1780s] Mary Hemings, Sally's oldest sibling, was hired out to a prosperous merchant named Thomas Bell . . . She moved, along with three of her children—Molly, Joseph, and Betsy—to Bell's home on Main Street [in Charlottesville]. . . .

We do not know the circumstances surrounding the origins of the Bell-Hemings connection: Did he notice her and lease her for the purpose of making her his concubine, or was it something that developed after the leasehold? In either event, things moved quickly, for her children were born soon after she was leased. However matters started, in Mary Hemings we get a rare sense, from her own actions, of an enslaved woman's preferences regarding her choice of mate and the course of her life. Not long after Jefferson returned from Paris, Hemings specifically asked to be sold to Bell. Jefferson complied with her request and gave Nicholas Lewis, still overseeing his affairs, "power to dispose of Mary according to her desire, with such of her younger children as she chose."[1] In an ironic twist on his practice of selling or buying slaves to unite them with family members from other plantations, Jefferson sold Mary Hemings to unite her to her white partner and their children. He knew the couple's situation very well, and he acted in deference not just to the wishes of an enslaved woman but also to the desires of the white father of her children.

Within the extremely narrow constraints of what life offered her—ownership by Thomas Jefferson or ownership by Thomas Bell—Mary Hemings took an action that had enormous, lasting, and, in the end, quite favorable consequences for her, her two youngest children, and the Hemings family as a whole. She found in Bell a man willing to live openly with her, and to treat her and their children as if they were bound together as a legal family. She must have seen that capacity in him during the early stages of their time together. Over the years she would be able to compare notes on her life with a white man with her youngest sister, whom she honored by giving her own youngest daughter the name Sarah (also called Sally), known by the time of her marriage, in the early 1800s, as Sarah Jefferson Bell.[2] . . .

... Both Hemings sisters had very firm internal understandings about how they might influence the course of their lives so that they could have what many of the women of their day, black and white, wanted—the ability, during their measured time on earth, to associate with a man who would take care of them and provide the best possible lives for their children with some chance of stability in an unstable world. Mary Hemings experienced firsthand what this instability meant. Although she found a place for herself with Bell, unlike her sister Sally, she experienced one of the harshest aspects of enslaved motherhood. . . . [F]our of her six children were taken from her. The liaison with Bell ensured that any new children she had would be protected. The contingencies of the lives of Sally and Mary Hemings were such that Jefferson and Bell, for whatever reason—their personalities, their feelings about the women involved—supported these sisters' aspirations. As a result both women, in their own way, achieved exactly what they wanted. That their very elemental desires as women were met in the context of slavemaster, black-white relationships is troubling because they mix something that seems almost sacred (the human desire for a secure family life) with something deeply profane (slavery). . . .

The title . . . [of] historian Walter Johnson's *Soul by Souls*[3] captures the enormity of slavery's inhumanity and suggests at least one way to go about illuminating it in the pages of history. Slavery was not just one, enormous act of oppression against a nameless, interchangeable mass of people. It was millions of separate assassinations and attempted assassinations of individual spirits carried out over centuries. When we encounter some of those spirits responding to their circumstances as human beings respond and using whatever means available to them to maintain or assert their humanity in the face of the onslaught, their individual efforts should not be minimized or ignored, because they could never alone have killed off the institution of slavery. That is far too heavy a load to place on people whose burdens in life were already almost unimaginably heavy. . . .

PARIS, 1789

James and Sally Hemings had many months to contemplate their possible return to Virginia. Jefferson had, in fact, been preparing to go home long before he received official word that his request for a leave of absence had been granted; he had packed his bags to be ready to go on a moment's notice.[4] The Hemingses, as well as his daughters, were expected to return with him, and were likely as much on tenterhooks as he, for they, too, had to be ready to leave as soon as word arrived. When it was clear that return to America was imminent, Sally Hemings was pregnant, and her pregnancy created a problem that she and Jefferson had to address and sort out. [In a memoir recorded in 1873,] Madison Hemings, [a son of Sally Hemings,] described what happened:

> But during that time my mother became Mr. Jefferson's concubine, and when he was called back home she was enciente by him. He desired to bring my mother back to Virginia with him, but she demurred. She was just beginning to understand the French language well, and in France she was free, while if she returned to Virginia she would be re-enslaved. So she refused to return with him. To induce her to do so he promised her extraordinary privileges, and made a solemn pledge that her children should be freed at the age of twenty-one years. In consequence of his promises, on which she implicitly relied, she returned with him to Virginia.[5]

There is much to consider about this very simple, yet powerful, explanation of what happened between Sally Hemings and Thomas Jefferson in France. First, it could only have been a shorthand version of all that actually happened, all the words that passed between these two. . . . The stakes were extremely high for both, but highest for Hemings. She knew all too well what slavery meant, and she lived with the hard knowledge that, were she to return to Virginia, every child from her womb would follow her condition. In this moment and place, she was in the best position she would ever be in to walk away from *partus sequitur ventrem* [meaning the status of the child follows the status of the mother,] forever. . . .

We cannot know what Hemings thought about abortion for herself or whether the thought of not keeping her baby even crossed her mind. She was away from the network of her mother and female siblings who could counsel her and, as far as we know, without a network of women of color to confide in and discuss a matter so personal. . . .

Hemings's son described his mother as "implicitly" relying on his father, which goes to the mystery at the heart of Sally Hemings's life: Why would she trust Jefferson, and why would she, under any circumstances, return to Virginia with him? Trading immediate freedom for herself and her progeny for a life at Monticello with him and a promise of eventual freedom for her children was not an even exchange. There was something in the gap between those two conditions—some desired prospect on the other side of the ocean—that motivated her.

It is all too easy to ignore how being female shaped Hemings's desires and expectations and focus in on the thing that makes her so different from us today: she was born enslaved. By the time they were in France together, Jefferson had already helped set the terms for the development of Hemings's view of herself as a female. As the authority figure at Monticello, he sent a strong message to her when he acted to protect what he considered to be the femininity of Hemings and her female relatives, while failing to show similar concerns for other enslaved women on his plantations. Hemings watched every female go to the fields at harvest time, except her sisters, mother, and whatever white females were at the plantation.[6] She learned from all this that, in Jefferson's eyes, she was a female to be protected from certain things, when most women of her same legal status received no protection at all. . . .

Even without Jefferson's intervention, it is doubtful that Hemings thought being a slave was more at the core of her existence than being female; she could cease to be the one, never the other. Their numbers were still small when she was growing up, but there were free black people in Virginia, and their numbers would grow in the years after she returned to America.[7] The world sent her a very definite and hard message about enslavement at the same time as it conveyed another powerful message about what was to be her role in life as a woman—partner to a man and a mother. Those roles were tenuous because the law did not protect her in either of them. They were not, however, meaningless to her.

Having a child was perhaps the most serious matter that confronted women. Females who faced motherhood during Hemings's time—enslaved, free, black, white, and red—confronted the immediate issue of surviving the ordeal of pregnancy. They knew that even if they survived, at least some of their children would likely die because no society had figured out how to save its children from deadly

childhood diseases that are of little import in the developed world today. The death of children was not the only stalker of slave mothers and potential mothers like Hemings. She and other enslaved women faced the added, unspeakable reality that they could be separated from their children by sale. Above all of slavery's depredations, the separation of children from their families crystallized the system's barbarity so clearly that slave owners claimed that it rarely happened or spent endless time talking about how loath they were to do it— just before they did it. . . . [S]eparation from children by sale . . . shaped . . . [enslaved women's] identities as women. Hemings, like other enslaved girls, must have dreamed of a future in which her motherhood would never be blighted by such a moment. . . .

Had Hemings never been in Paris, her choice of mates at Monticello would have been perhaps even more limited than that of other enslaved women on the plantation. Her racial background contributed to her identity and undoubtedly affected her views about who would be attractive as a companion and as father of her children. . . . In slavery and outside of it, members of Hemings's family—female and male—developed a practice of having children with, and marrying when that was available, people who looked something like themselves, which is what most people in the world tend to do.[8] Jefferson probably resembled Hemings more than the average male slave on the plantation did, in terms of hair texture, skin color, and eye color. This is not to say that she would never under any circumstances have welcomed a partner with skin darker than her own or tightly curled hair, as allowances must always be made for the vagaries of attraction. It is human beings we are dealing with, after all, and no one has devised a precise formula or foolproof predictor of personal taste, and black couples and families come in all shades.

Although Hemings was probably not thinking in strictly legal terms about the racial makeup of the child she was carrying in Paris when she was deciding whether to come home with Jefferson, Virginia statutory law on racial categorizations, as Jefferson noted many years later, would make all of her children by him legally white [Virginia law provided that a person who was seven-eighths white was to be considered white]. We know Hemings wanted to free her children from slavery, and Jefferson's actions show he wanted that as well. No one has ever said that Hemings thought it important to free them from blackness, too. However, that is exactly the route that three of her four children took when they left both slavery and the black community to live as white people. The one child of hers who did remain in the black community, Madison Hemings, married a woman who was fair-skinned enough that some of their children were able to pass into the white world. We do not know whether the Hemings-Jefferson offspring were raised to do that, but it would not be surprising, particularly given their father's stated values, if that was a part of a plan or at least a very strong hope. . . .

Under the circumstances of Hemings's life, given her society and her family history, what type of man would be most able to end slavery for her children along with all the problems associated with being a person with black skin in America? If not Thomas Jefferson, who? She may have thought him as good a white man as any other, perhaps even better in some ways. That was a judgment to ponder. . . .

Unlike the vast majority of her enslaved cohort back in Virginia, freedom was within . . . [Sally Hemings'] grasp [in Paris], and she ended up using the unique opportunity she possessed, not as an end in itself, but as a starting point for a discussion with the man who wanted to take her home with him. That Jefferson desired that at all, a further contingent element in Hemings's life, gave her leverage under their particular circumstances. Another man might not have cared enough to try to persuade her or would have dared her (and her brother) to do their worst: take their claim to the Admiralty Court. . . .

Hemings had not only her own observations of Jefferson to draw upon; a wealth of family history supplemented her knowledge. Whether she had had time in her young life to learn this fact about him or not, the truth is that few things could have disturbed the very thin-skinned, possessive, and controlling Jefferson more deeply than having persons in his inner circle take the initiative and express their willingness to remove themselves from it. To have this come from a young female, the kind of person he thought was supposed to be under the control of males, whether they were enslaved or not, was likely doubly upsetting. . . . This challenge was a far greater threat to his self-esteem and emotions than to his

wallet. He had great confidence in his ability to charm and in his capacity to bring people to his side and keep them there. . . .

[Furthermore,] Hemings knew how Jefferson viewed women, and implicitly understood that if she were paired with an enslaved man [at Monticello] she would have two men over her: her enslaved husband and Jefferson. She would be one step removed from the man who held power over both of them, and Jefferson would have no personal stake in her or the children she bore with another man. . . .

Like other enslaved people when the all too rare chance presented itself, Hemings seized her moment and used the knowledge of her rights to make a decision based upon what she thought was best for her as a woman, family member, and a potential mother in her specific circumstances.

Visitors to the Hôtel de Langeac toasted Jefferson as the "apostle of liberty" and made much of his progressivism in the face of those who wanted to maintain the status quo in society. Imagine the stir if a slave of the "apostle" had shown up at the Admiralty Court in Paris, forced there because he had refused her request for freedom. Jefferson's image, which he so assiduously cultivated throughout his entire public career, would have been left in tatters. . . . To have Jefferson, of all people, act in direct opposition to France's Freedom Principle so that he could keep control over a sixteen-year-old enslaved girl would have been a spectacle for the ages. The word "irony" does not even begin to approach doing the situation justice. If the court had gotten the chance to see her, all would have been revealed instantly. . . . That was an outcome to be avoided at all costs. . . . Aside from whatever he felt for her, the Parisian Admiralty Court and Jefferson's special position and reputation in France gave Sally Hemings latitude to say, "I will go home with you, but only on certain conditions."[9]

Jefferson may have pointed out to Hemings and her brother the potential problems they might face by remaining in Paris. . . . [But] by this time, whatever sense of entitlement [Sally] had as a Hemings had been added to all her experiences to date—traveling across an ocean, . . . learning a new language, . . . and being a handsomely paid employee. The last experience was probably the most important. She worked alongside other French servants at the Hôtel de Langeac and knew she could work elsewhere. The fashion of having African and mixed-race servants gave her an advantage if she sought work as a *femme de chambre.* . . .

And then there was Paris' small community of color. . . . Sally Hemings had a special reason for thinking of this community. She did not likely consider staying in France without thinking of what the future might hold in the way of marriage and companionship. Although only around a thousand gens de couleur lived in all of Paris, the vast majority of them, concentrated in a small number of neighborhoods, were males in their late teens and early twenties—exactly suitable for a young woman approaching her seventeenth birthday.[10]

. . . [H]ad Hemings decided to break away from Jefferson and start a new life with her brother, she would have had the chance to be the mother of children who were free at birth and she could have had a legal marriage and the social respectability that would elude her totally in Virginia living with Jefferson. None of her children would have felt compelled to leave her, one another, and their family history behind in order to escape the racism of nineteenth-century America. . . .

. . . With no opportunity for legal marriage, Sally Hemings . . . was operating without the benefit of any written rules. The plan for her life at Monticello with Jefferson . . . depended . . . upon Hemings's ability to hold Jefferson in some serious fashion over the years and, more importantly, the quality of his personal character and his willingness to remain committed to her. It is not all surprising, therefore, that Hemings and Jefferson talked [in Paris] of the very matters that were among the core issues addressed in the basic marriage contract for free couples in the world in which they lived: the treatment of the woman, the man's duties and obligations toward the children, and what the children would receive from the man when they became adults, questions that men and women in every type of society from time immemorial have had to address. That the two would be having sex was implicit in the understanding that Hemings was going to have more children and that provision would be made for them as well as the one about to be born—the particular one that Hemings most wanted: their freedom.

[For the past decade, I have traveled the country, speaking about Hemings and Jefferson. I do not

recall a setting where this question was not asked explicitly or implicitly: "Did they love each other?"] The most intimate of situations, the one least likely to be observed by others—sexual compatibility—can . . . be a form of love. But in our Western culture (and some others, to be fair) sex is considered, if not exactly dirty or shameful, a somewhat guilty pleasure that must always be separated from more exalted love. This is especially true when a couple, like Hemings and Jefferson, for reasons of race, status, or gender are not supposed to be together, as if partners who do not have the imprimatur of law, society, and custom could never feel the emotion of love for one another. The invariable charge against such pairs is that they are inauthentic per se, because they are bound together purely for sex, rather than love.

[A] Jefferson great-granddaughter through the Hemings line told a . . . story about Hemings and Jefferson's origins in France when explaining why her great-grandmother gave up the chance for freedom and came back to Virginia, saying, "Jefferson loved her dearly."[11] In other words, she and other family members answered the questions why Hemings trusted Jefferson and came back to Virginia with him, by referencing her confidence in her knowledge of that fact, a confidence that allowed her to take what seems a breathtakingly large risk. . . .

Jefferson wanted Hemings to come back to Virginia with him, so much so that he took to bargaining with her about this. He well knew that in Virginia there were many other women, enslaved and not, who could satisfy any merely carnal impulses as soon as he returned to America. The problem was, however, that they would not actually have been Sally Hemings herself, a requirement that was evidently very important to him. Her siblings and other relatives seemed to have gauged this. . . . [T]heir attitude toward Jefferson after Hemings's return to Virginia is in perfect keeping with the idea that they believed he cared for her. If what had happened between them in France had been along the lines of more typical master-female slave sex, Hemings's expressed desire to stay in the country, especially after she became aware that she was pregnant, would have been exactly what Jefferson needed. He could have left her in Paris with her quite capable older brother, helped the pair financially, . . . thus ridding himself of a potentially embarrassing problem in a way that actually bolstered, instead of hurt, his image. History, and his philosophc friends of the moment, would have recorded that Jefferson (breathing the rarefied air of Enlightenment France) so identified with the Freedom Principle that he let go of two of his own slaves. He would have been a veritable hero.

Instead of doing that, Jefferson insisted on setting up an arrangement with a young woman that he knew could easily result in a houseful of children whose existence would be easily tied to him. . . . During the decades that followed their time in France, . . . this most thin-skinned of individuals persisted on his course, . . . having more children with her who were named in the same fashion as the older ones: for his important and favorite family members and his best friends.[12] . . . Jefferson continued on, guided by his own internal compass and, no doubt, his awareness that the woman being vilified in the press had given up to him a thing whose value he understood: her freedom. He knew very well that these people, really, did not know what, and whom, they were talking about.

If sex had been the only issue, it would have been a far simpler and more practical matter, for himself and his white family when they returned to Monticello, for Jefferson to have installed Hemings in one of his nearby quarter farms . . . and visited her there when the mood hit him. . . . Instead, Jefferson arranged his life at Monticello so that Hemings would be in it every day that he was there, taking care of his possessions, in his private enclave.

What most disturbed contemporary commentators about the arrangement at Monticello was not that the master had a slave mistress but that she was not sufficiently hidden away.[13] Hemings was a visible presence in his home when everyone knew that Jefferson had the resources to have her be someplace else. The racism and sexual hysteria this unleashed among white Americans was a thing to behold. . . . Yet, through all the talk during Jefferson's lifetime of his "Congo Harem," "Negro Harem," and "African Harem," only one woman's name emerged: Sally. Jefferson's enemies of the day could list each of Hemings's children, their order of birth and ages, what her duties were at Monticello, but they could never produce the name of another specific woman to be a part of his alleged seraglio.

From her side, it was Hemings who backed down from her decision to stay in France in return for a life at Monticello in which Jefferson would be a very serious presence. . . . [D]uring an almost twenty-year period of child-bearing, she conceived no children during Jefferson's sometimes prolonged absences from Monticello as he acted as a public servant, indicating that she had no other sexual partners.[14] That could well have been at his insistence as much as her own personal desires. Still, the expectation of fidelity—on her part at least—suggests something about the nature of their relationship. . . . Hemings's connection to Jefferson, held together totally by whatever was going on between them, was her children's way out of slavery, so long as her children were his, too. She was apparently unwilling to do anything (as in having babies by other men) that might jeopardize that connection and bring the effects of *partus sequitur ventrem* back into her life.

Before Hemings died, she gave one of her sons as heirlooms personal items that had belonged to Jefferson, a pair of his eyeglasses, a shoe buckle, and an inkwell that she had kept during the nine years after his death. These artifacts—things she saw him wear and a thing he used to write words that would make him live in history—were seemingly all that she had left of him. Monticello and virtually all its contents were sold to pay debts or were in the control of his legal white family. These items were quietly passed down in the Hemings family until well into the twentieth century.[15] . . . Hemings's action, which at the very least exhorted her descendants to both remember Jefferson and her connection to him, indicate that she wanted them to know he meant something to her. She had, after all, lived with him for decades, and he had given her valued children whom he had let go to make their way in the world. . . . Jefferson had kept his promises to her.

. . . Working backward to 1789 from either her death in 1835 or Jefferson's death in 1826, one can say that sixteen-year-old Hemings's instincts about how she might best shape her future in the context of her particular circumstances and needs were as sound as her older sister Mary's instincts about Thomas Bell, developing at the same time on another continent. Hemings could not have known this as she treated with Jefferson at the Hôtel de Langeac, but at the end of her life she would be able to say that she got the important things that she most wanted.

NOTES

1. TJ to Nicholas Lewis, April 12, 1792, *The Papers of Thomas Jefferson*, ed. Julian P. Boyd et al., 35 vols. to date (Princeton, 1950–), 23:408.

2. Lucia Stanton, "Monticello to Main Street: The Hemings Family and Charlottesville," *Magazine of Albemarle County History* 55 (1997): 100.

3. Walter Johnson, *Soul by Soul: Life inside the Antebellum Slave Market* (Cambridge, Mass., 1999).

4. TJ to Andre Limozin, May 3, 1789, *Papers*, 16:86.

5. [Reproduced in] Annette Gordon-Reed, *Thomas Jefferson and Sally Hemings: An American Controversy* (Charlottesville: University Press of Virginia, 1997), 246.

6. Lucia Stanton, *Free Some Day: The African-American Families of Monticello* (Charlottesville, 2000), 105.

7. Philip D. Morgan, *Slave Counterpoint: Black Culture in the Eighteenth-Century Chesapeake and Lowcountry* (Chapel Hill: University of North Carolina Press, 1998), 665–66; "An Act to Authorize the Manumission of Slaves," Laws of Virginia, 1782, chap. 61.

8. Stanton, *Free Some Day*, 106; Lucia Stanton and Dianne Swann Wright, "Bonds of Memory Identity and the Hemings Family," in *Sally Hemings and Thomas Jefferson: History, Memory and Civic Culture*, eds. Jan Ellen Lewis and Peter S. Onuf (Charlottesville, 1999), 170–72.

9. Sue Peabody, "There Are No Slaves in France": *The Political Culture of Race and Slavery in the Ancient Régime* (New York: Oxford University Press, 1996), 101–3.

10. Pierre H. Boulle, "Les Gens de couleur à Paris à la veille de la Révolution" in *L'Image de la Révolution française*, ed. Michel Vovelle. Vol 1 (Paris: Pergamon Press, 1989), 160–61.

11. Stanton and Swann Wright, "Bonds of Memory Identity," 176.

12. Gordon-Reed, *Thomas Jefferson and Sally Hemings*, 196–201.

13. Ibid., 170–71.

14. Ibid., 100–2, 216.

15. Nellie Jones to Stuart Gibboney, July 29, 1938, Aug. 10, 1938; Stuart Gibboney to Nellie Jones, Aug. 1, 1938, Nov. 1, 1938, correspondence in the University of Virginia Library, Accession No. 6636-a-b, Box No. Control Folder, Folder Dates 1735–1961. Nellie Jones was Madison Hemings's granddaughter. She wrote to Gibboney, the then president of the Thomas Jefferson Memorial Foundation, offering to donate mementos that her great-grandmother Sally Hemings had saved and given to their son: a pair of his glasses, an inkwell, and a silver buckle.

Virginia Establishes a Double Standard in Tax Law

Tax policy was the site of one of the earliest and most significant interventions made by English colonial lawmakers to cordon off black women from white, practically and symbolically. In the 1643 law that follows, the Virginia Assembly made one of its first discriminations according to race. The provision clarified the tithing system—by which Anglican ministers in each parish would be paid. European colonists paid a variety of taxes based not on income but "per poll" (per person) or according to the property they owned. Given the scarcity of circulating coins or paper currency, taxes were typically paid in goods including foodstuffs. From 1643 forward, heads of household would be required to pay annually the designated amount for each male over fifteen in the household (whether free, indentured, or enslaved)—and for what other category of person? We can think of the distinction that the law silently made between "negro" and other women as a continuation, or a second act, in the process of sexual stereotyping described by Jennifer L. Morgan (pp. 24–33). The Virginia law not only placed an extra financial burden on free black families, but also broadcast the ruling class's dictum that African and African-descended women were assumed to be field laborers, thus denying their domesticity.

The 1643 statute was tested in the colony's lower courts. Would authorities permit any exceptions to be made? Two examples are given here. In the first case, white male colonist Francis Stripes had recently married; probably a neighbor or tax assessor complained to the court that Stripes had not been paying the proper tithe. In Susannah's case, we do not know how the petitioner made a living, but it was not necessarily as a farm laborer. What do you imagine she argued in her plea (which was likely made orally) to the bench of local gentlemen who served as justices? How did they justify their ruling to themselves and to her? The court clerk's omission of Susannah's surname reflected a common colonial tendency to erase the chosen identities of people of color.

Be it further enacted and confirmed That there be tenn pounds of tob[acco]o per poll & a bushel of corne per poll paid to the ministers within the severall parishes of the colony for all tithable persons, that is to say, as well for all youths of sixteen years of age as upwards, as also for all negro women at the age of sixteen years.

1671 case, Lower Norfolk County: It is the opinion and Judgement of the Court that francis Stripes ought to pay Leavyes and tythes for his wife (shee being a negro) It being according to Law; and therefore ordered that he pay the Same for the Last year past, as well as this present [year] and so for the future.

Assembly of Virginia, act 1, March 1643, in William Waller Hening, *The Statutes at Large: Being a Collection of All the Laws of Virginia, from the First Session of the Legislature, in the Year 1619*, 13 vols. (New York: R. & W. & G. Bartow, 1823), 1:242; Lower Norfolk County Order Book, 1665–75, vol. 73, and Charles City County Order Book, 1677–79, 216, reproduced in *The Old Dominion in the Seventeenth Century: A Documentary History of Virginia, 1606–1689*, rev. ed., ed. Warren M. Billings (Chapel Hill: University of North Carolina Press, 2007), p. 183. The cases are reprinted with the kind permission of the author and publisher.

1677 case, Charles City County: Upon the petition of Susannah a free Negro-Woman that she may be Exempted from paying Levyes, And Whereas the Worshipful Courte is informed of her strength and ability It is thereupon thought fit that she be not Exempted but pay Levyes.

"According to the condition of the mother . . ."

The North American system of slavery relied heavily on marking differences of status (slave or free)—by visible bodily difference (black or white). Free black people and enslaved mulattoes undermined the simplicity of these signals, displaying in their very beings the fact that it was power, not nature, that placed any particular individual in one status or another.

In defining slavery—a condition not then recognized in English law—colonial lawmakers faced the question of how to interpret the status of children born to parents who were not married to each other, and whose fathers were white and mothers were black. Might such offspring claim free status? Could white fathers be obliged to take responsibility for the children's upbringing? In Spanish colonies in Central and South America, a complex system of godparenting made it possible for white fathers to maintain a wide variety of relationships with their mixed-blood children.

The Virginia law of 1662 shows how English colonists settled the question (Maryland had passed a similar statute two years earlier). Along with other laws passed at mid-century, it marked a turning point—from a period when blacks' status was often ambiguous and freedom was not foreclosed to a long era in which the default assumption would be that African-descended persons were enslaved and had few opportunities to become free. The Latin phrase for the rule enshrined in the colonial slave codes was *partus sequitur ventrem*, meaning that the status of the child (slave or free) would follow the mother's status. How did the 1662 law conflict with traditional English inheritance practices? What do the statute's two sections reveal about how Virginia legislators wished to shape interracial sexual relations? (With regard to the second section, note that the usual fine for fornication was 500 pounds of tobacco.) What are the implications of the law for children whose fathers were free black men and whose mothers were enslaved?

Whereas some doubts have arrisen whether children got by any Englishman upon a negro woman should be slave or free, *Be it therefore enacted and declared by this present grand assembly*, that all children borne in this country shalbe held bond or free only according to the condition of the mother, *And* that if any christian shall committ fornication with a negro man or woman hee or shee soe offending shall pay double the [usual] fines. . . .

Assembly of Virginia, act 16, December 1691, in William Waller Hening, *The Statutes at Large: Being a Collection of All the Laws of Virginia, from the First Session of the Legislature, in the Year 1619*, 13 vols. (New York: R & W & G Bartow, 1823), 2:170.

> "For prevention of that abominable mixture . . ."

Late in the seventeenth century, Virginia and Maryland lawmakers imposed harsh disincentives for whites and blacks who wished to marry such as Francis Stripes and his wife in the earlier document extract, stopping just short of an outright ban like the one that would later be enacted and would stand until the 1967 U.S. Supreme Court ruling in *Loving v. Virginia* (p. 670). What interracial relationships are omitted in Virginia's 1691 law? How would you characterize the legal status of mixed-race children born out of wedlock to free white women? Why did legislators think this set of laws would be self-enforcing?

[1691] . . . for prevention of that abominable mixture and spurious issue which hereafter may encrease in this dominion, as well by negroes, mulattoes, and Indians intermarrying with English, or other white women, as by their unlawful accompanying with one another, *Be it enacted* . . . that . . . whatsoever English or other white man or woman being free shall intermarry with a negroe, mulatto or Indian man or woman bond or free shall within three months after such marriage be banished and removed from this dominion forever. . . .

And be it further enacted . . . That if any English woman being free shall have a bastard child by any negro or mulatto, she pay the sume of fifteen pounds sterling, within one moneth after such bastard child shall be born, to the Church wardens of the parish . . . and in default of such payment she shall be taken into the possession of the said Church wardens and disposed of for five yeares, and the said fine of fifteen pounds, or whatever the woman shall be disposed of for, shall be paid, one third part to

their majesties . . . and one other third part to the use of the parish . . . and the other third part to the informer, and that such bastard child be bound out as a servant by the said Church wardens untill he or she shall attaine the age of thirty yeares, and in case such English woman that shall have such bastard child be a servant, she shall be sold by the said church wardens, (after her time is expired that she ought by law to serve her master) for five yeares, and the money she shall be sold for divided as is before appointed, and the child to serve as aforesaid.

[1705] *And be it further enacted*, That no minister of the church of England, or other minister, or person whatsoever, within this colony and dominion, shall hereafter wittingly presume to marry a white man with a negro or mulatto woman; or to marry a white woman with a negro or mulatto man, upon pain of forfeiting or paying, for every such marriage the sum of ten thousand pounds of tobacco; one half to our sovereign lady the Queen . . . and the other half to the informer. . . .

> *A Massachusetts Minister's Slave Marriage Vows*

Although Africans and African-descended people made up a much smaller proportion of the population and labor force in northern than in southern colonies, few white northerners took issue with the assumptions that undergirded the slave system. In fact, the merchants of Newport, Rhode Island, made

Assembly of Virginia, act 16, April 1691, in William Waller Hening, *The Statutes at Large: Being a Collection of All the Laws of Virginia, from the First Session of the Legislature, in the Year 1619*, 13 vols. (New York: R & W & G Bartow, 1823), 3:86–87; and Assembly of Virginia, ch. 49, sec. 20, October 1705 in Hening, *Statutes at Large*, 3:453.

enormous profits as the most active slave traders in the English colonies. For a gentleman, having one or two enslaved persons among his dependents was seen as a status symbol. Clergymen—who were respected for their learnedness, but were rarely wealthy—were sometimes presented with the gift of an enslaved youth or adult by their wealthy parishioners. By the eighteenth century, New England elites did not hesitate to encourage enslaved men and women to acculturate by embracing Christianity. Church records contain scattered entries for blacks—free and enslaved—receiving baptism, owning the covenant, marrying, having their children baptized, and being buried.

This is the "form of a Negro-Marriage" used by Congregational clergyman Samuel Phillips of Andover, Massachusetts, when enslaved men and women came to him, asking to be wed, during his sixty-year pastorate (1710–71). Similar vows were used in other churches. Read the vows aloud, and imagine what the marriage ceremony was like. How would you characterize the marriage contract that is being made? Which Christian rules is the Reverend Phillips selectively invoking? Some years later, in the famous *Jennison v. Walker* case that is often cited as ending slavery in Massachusetts, attorney Levi Lincoln confirmed and challenged the paradox at the core of these vows: "The master has a right to separate the Husband and wife—is this consistent with the law of nature[?] Is it consistent with the law of nature to separate what God has joined and no man can put asunder?"*

Minister: "You,—do now in the Presence of God, and these Witnesses, Take—: to be your Wife; Promising that so far as shall be consistent with the Relations which you now sustain, as a Servant, you will Perform the Part of an Husband towards her; And in particular, you Promise, that you will Love her: And that, as you shall have the Opportunity & Ability, you will take a proper Care of her in Sickness and Health, in Prosperity & Adversity: And that you will be True & Faithfull to her, and will Cleave to her only, so long as God, in his Providence, shall continue your and her abode in Such Place (or Places) as that you can conveniently come together:—Do you thus Promise?"

Then the same Vow was declared for the woman to agree to.

Minister: "I then agreeable to your Request, and with the Consent of your Masters & Mistresses, do Declare, that you have Licence given you to be conversant and familiar together, as Husband and Wife, so long as God shall continue your Places of abode as aforesaid; and so long as you shall behave yourselves as it becomes Servants to doe: For you must, both of you, bear in mind, that you Remain Still, as really and truly as ever, your Master's Property, and therefore it will be justly expected, both by God and Man, that you behave and conduct yourselves, as Obedient and faithfull Servants towards your respective Masters & Mistresses for the Time being. . . ."

"I shall now conclude with Prayer for you, that you may become good Christians, and that you may be enabled to conduct as such; and in particular, that you may have Grace to behave suitably towards each Other, as also dutifully towards your Masters & Mistresses, not with Eye-Service, as Men-pleasers, but as the Servants of Christ, doing the will of God from the heart."

---

* "Brief of Levi Lincoln in the Slave Case Tried 1781," *Collections of the Massachusetts Historical Society*, 5th ser., 3 (1877): 441.

George E. Howard, *A History of Matrimonial Institutions . . .* (London, 1904), vol. 2, pp. 225–26, quoting George H. Moore, "Slave Marriages in Massachusetts," *Dawson's Historical Magazine*, 2nd ser., 5 (1869): 137. We have modernized spelling and expanded abbreviated words.

Philadelphia Women Raise Money Door to Door

This broadside of 1780 announced a women's campaign to raise contributions for patriot soldiers. Organized and led by Esther DeBerdt Reed, wife of the president of Pennsylvania, and by Benjamin Franklin's daughter Sarah Franklin Bache, the campaign was large and effective. "Instead of waiting for the Donations being sent the ladys of each Ward go from dore to dore and collect them," wrote one participant. Collecting contributions this way invited confrontation. One loyalist wrote to her sister, "Of all absurdities, the ladies going about for money exceeded everything; they were so extremely importunate that people were obliged to give them something to get rid of them."* The campaign raised $300,000 in paper dollars in inflated war currency. Rather than let George Washington merge it with the general fund, the women insisted on using it to buy materials for making shirts so that each soldier might know he had received an extraordinary contribution from the women of Philadelphia. The broadside itself is an unusually explicit justification for women's intrusion into politics.

On the commencement of actual war, the Women of America manifested a firm resolution to contribute . . . to the deliverance of their country. Animated by the purest patriotism, they are sensible of sorrow at this day, in not offering more than barren wishes for the success of so glorious a Revolution. They aspire to render themselves more really useful; and this sentiment is universal from the north to the south of the Thirteen United States. Our ambition is kindled by the fame of those heroines of antiquity, who have rendered their sex illustrious, and have proved to the universe, that, if the weakness of our Constitution, if opinion and manners did not forbid us to march to glory by the same paths as the Men, we should at least equal, and sometimes surpass them in our love for the public good. I glory in all that which my sex has done great and commendable. I call to mind with enthusiasm and with admiration, all those acts of courage, of constancy and patriotism, which history has transmitted to us: The people favoured by Heaven, preserved from destruction by the virtues, the zeal and the resolution of Deborah, of Judith, of Esther! The fortitude of the mother of the Macchabees, in giving up her sons to die before her eyes: Rome saved from the fury of a victorious enemy by the efforts of Volumnia, and other Roman Ladies: So many famous sieges where the Women have been seen forgetting the weakness of their sex, building new walls, digging trenches with their feeble hands, furnishing arms to their defenders, they themselves darting the missile weapons on the enemy, resigning the ornaments of their apparel, and their fortune, to fill the public treasury, and to hasten the deliverance of their country; burying themselves under its ruins;

---

*Mary Morris to Catharine Livingston, June 10 [1780], Ridley Family Papers, Massachusetts Historical Society, Boston; Anna Rawle to Rebecca Rawle Shoemaker, June 30, 1780, in *Pennsylvania Magazine of History and Biography* 35 (1911), 398.

Excerpted from *The Sentiments of an American Woman* ([Philadelphia]: John Dunlap, 1780).

throwing themselves into the flames rather than submit to the disgrace of humiliation before a proud enemy.

Born for liberty, disdaining to bear the irons of a tyrannic Government, we associate ourselves to the grandeur of those Sovereigns, cherished and revered, who have held with so much splendour the scepter of the greatest States, The Batildas, the Elizabeths, the Maries, the Catharines, who have extented the empire of liberty, and contented to reign by sweetness and justice, have broken the chains of slavery, forged by tyrants in times of ignorance and barbarity. . . .

We know that at a distance from the theatre of war, if we enjoy any tranquility, it is the fruit of your watchings, your labours, your dangers. . . . Who, amongst us, will not renounce with the highest pleasure, those vain ornaments, when she shall consider that the valiant defenders of America will be able to draw some advantage from the money which she may have laid out in these. . . . The time is arrived to display the same sentiments which animated us at the beginning of the Revolution, when we renounced the use of teas, however agreeable to our taste, rather than receive them from our persecutors; when we made it appear to them that we placed former necessaries in the rank of superfluities, when our liberty was interested; when our republican and laborious hands spun the flax, prepared the linen intended for the use of our soldiers; when [as] exiles and fugitives we supported with courage all the evils which are the concomitants of war. . . .

Sarah Osborn, "The bullets would not cheat the gallows . . ."

Sarah Osborn was eighty-one years old when Congress made it possible for dependent survivors of Revolutionary war veterans to claim their pensions. She testified to her own service as well as to her husband's in the following deposition, sworn before the Court of Common Pleas in Wayne County, New Jersey, in 1837. Osborn's husband was a commissary guard; like many thousands of women, Osborn traveled with him, cooking and cleaning for troops at a time when there was no formal quartermaster corps and in which cleanliness was virtually the only guard against disease. Her account tells of working when the army was at West Point in 1780; of the long expedition south, marching proudly on horseback into Philadelphia, and then continuing to Yorktown. Osborn is the only one of the "women of the army" who has left us a narrative of her experiences. At Yorktown she brought food to soldiers under fire. When she told George Washington that she did not fear the bullets because they "would not cheat the gallows," she was conveying her understanding that her challenge to royal authority was congruent with his; if the soldiers risked being hanged for treason, so would she.

[In the march to Philadelphia in 1781?] Deponent was part of the time on horseback and part of the time in a wagon. Deponent's . . . husband was still serving as one of the commissary's guard. . . . They continued their march to Philadelphia, deponent on horseback through the streets. . . . Being out of bread, deponent was employed in baking the afternoon and evening . . . they continued their march . . . [at Baltimore she] embarked on board a vessel and sailed . . . until they had got up the St. James River as far as the tide would carry them. . . . They . . . marched for Yorktown. . . . Deponent was on foot. . . . Deponent took her stand just back of the American tents, say about a mile from the town, and busied herself washing, mending, and cooking for the soldiers, in which she was assisted by the other females; some men washed their own clothing. She heard the roar of the artillery for a number

Excerpted from *The Revolution Remembered: Eyewitness Accounts of the American Revolution*, ed. John C. Dann (Chicago: University of Chicago Press, 1980), pp. 240–45.

Deborah Sampson, who served in the Fourth Massachusetts Regiment as Robert Shurtleff, painted by Joseph Stone, 1797.

In 1782, Deborah Sampson, who was already notable in her community of Middleborough, Massachusetts, for her height and strength, adopted men's clothing and the name of Robert Shurtleff. She enlisted for service with the Fourth Massachusetts Regiment. Like many young women from impoverished families, Deborah Sampson had been bound out to domestic service as a young teenager. When her term was up, she taught school briefly in Middleborough and joined the First Baptist Church there. She was expelled from the church before her enlistment. She served with her regiment in New York and possibly in Pennsylvania until she was wounded at a battle near Tarrytown, New York.

After her return to Massachusetts, Sampson married and bore three children. The fame of her exploits persisted. After a fictionalized biography was published by Herman Mann in 1797, she went on a wide-ranging speaking tour, perhaps the first American woman to undertake such an enterprise, and applied for the pensions to which her wartime service entitled her. These were awarded slowly and grudgingly, and she died impoverished in 1827. (Joseph Stone, Deborah Sampson [Gannett], 1797, oil on paper, later pasted on wood. Courtesy of the Rhode Island Historical Society.)

of days. . . . Deponent's . . . husband was there throwing up entrenchments, and deponent cooked and carried in beef, and bread, and coffee (in a gallon pot) to the soldiers in the entrenchment.

On one occasion when deponent was thus employed carrying in provisions, she met General Washington, who asked her if she "was not afraid of the cannonballs?"

She replied, "No, the bullets would not cheat the gallows," that "It would not do for the men to fight and starve too."

They dug entrenchments nearer and nearer to Yorktown every night or two till the last. While digging that, the enemy fired very heavy till about nine o'clock next morning, then stopped, and the drums from the enemy beat excessively. Deponent was a little way off in Colonel Van Shaick's or the officers' marquee and a number of officers were present. . . .

The drums continued beating, and all at once the officers hurrahed and swung their hats, and deponent asked them, "What is the matter now?"

One of them replied, "Are not you soldier enough to know what it means?" Deponent replied, "No."

They then replied, "The British have surrendered."

Deponent, having provisions ready, carried the same down to the entrenchments that morning, and four of the soldiers whom she was in the habit of cooking for ate their breakfasts.

Deponent stood on one side of the road and the American officers upon the other side when the British officers came out of the town and rode up to the American officers and delivered up [their swords, which the deponent] thinks were returned again, and the British officers rode right on before the army, who marched out beating and playing a melancholy tune, their drums covered with black handkerchiefs and their fifes with black ribbands tied around them, into an old field and there grounded their arms and then returned into town again to await their destiny. . . . The British general at the head of the army was a large, portly man, full face, and the tears rolled down his cheeks as he passed along.

Rachel Wells, "I have Don as much to Carrey on the Warr as maney . . ."

Rachel Wells was probably sixty-five years old when she wrote the following words. She had bought loan office certificates from the state of New Jersey during the Revolution: subsequently she had moved to Philadelphia, but returned to Bordentown, New Jersey, after the war. In an effort to curb speculation, the New Jersey legislature decided that only state residents had a claim on interest payments; Rachel Wells's claim on her money was turned down because she had not been in the state at the war's end in 1783. She appealed directly to the Continental Congress. Although her petition was tabled, it remains—despite its bad spelling—as perhaps the most moving witness to the Revolution left to us by a woman. What did Rachel Wells think had been her contribution to the Revolution? What did she think the government owed to her?

To the Honnorabell Congress I rachel do make this Complaint Who am a Widow far advanced in years & Dearly have ocasion of ye Interst for that Cash I Lent the States. I was a Sitisen in ye jersey when I Lent ye State a considerable Sum of Moneys & had I justice dun me it mite be Suficant to suporte me in ye Contrey whear I am now, near burdentown. I Leved hear then . . . but Being . . . so Robd by the Britans & others i went to Phila to try to

Rachel Wells, Petition to Congress, May 18, 1786, Microfilm Papers of the Continental Congress, National Archives, Washington, D.C., M247, roll 56, item 42, vol. 8, pp. 354–55.

get a Living . . . & was There in the year 1783 when our assembley was pleasd to pas a Law that No one Should have aney Interest that Livd out of jearsey Stats . . .

Now gentelmen is this Liberty, had it bin advertised that he or She that Moved out of the Stat should Louse his or her Interest you mite have sum plea against me.

But I am Innocent Suspected no Trick. I have Don as much to Carrey on the Warr as maney that Sett now at ye healm of government. . . . your asembly Borrowed £300 in gould of me jest as the Warr Comencd & Now I Can Nither git Intrust nor principall Nor Even Security. . . . My dr Sister . . . wrote to me to be thankfull that I had it in my Power to help on the Warr which is well enough but then this is to be Considerd that others gits their Intrust & why then a poor old widow to be put of[f]. . . . I hartely pity others that ar in my Case that Cant Speak for themselves. . . .

god has Spred a plentifull table for us & you gentelmen are ye Carvers for us pray forgit Not the Poor weaklings at the foot of the Tabel ye poor Sogers has got Sum Crumbs That fall from their masters tabel. . . . Why Not Rachel Wells have a Little intrust?

if She did not fight She threw in all her mite which bought ye Sogers food & Clothing & Let Them have Blankets & Since that She has bin obligd to Lay upon Straw & glad of that . . .

Grace Galloway, Loyalist

Because the Revolution was a civil war, each adult had to assume a political identity and maintain it with sufficient clarity to satisfy the local authorities. Women had an advantage. Because they were not being recruited into the conflicting armies, their political choices were less carefully scrutinized than those of men; they might even shift back and forth between enemy camps. One patriot complained that the British "were informed of every thing that passed among us and that Women were the most proper persons for that purpose."[*]

Despite the presence of women spies and informant, the belief that politics was somehow no part of the woman's domain persisted throughout the war, expressed even by women whose own lives were in fact directly dependent on political developments. Grace Growden Galloway reveals this cluster of contradictory traits. She was a formidable woman, and not surprisingly her biographers tend to describe her as "imperious." The daughter of one of the wealthiest and most powerful men in colonial Pennsylvania, she married another, Joseph Galloway, who became Speaker of the Pennsylvania Assembly in the decade before war broke out. It was not a happy marriage. In one of the poems she inscribed in her diary she warned:

Never get tied to a man
    for when once you are yoked
'Tis all a mere joke
    of seeing your freedom again.

---

[*]Testimony of Henry Livingston, Feb. 5, 1777, *Minutes of the . . . Committee . . . for Detecting and Defeating Conspiracies . . .* (New York, 1924), I:120.

Excerpted from "Diary of Grace Growden Galloway, Kept at Philadelphia . . ." *Pennsylvania Magazine of History and Biography,* 55 (1931), 50ff. See also Linda K. Kerber, *Women of the Republic: Intellect and Ideology in Revolutionary America* (Chapel Hill: University of North Carolina Press, 1980), pp. 49, 74–76.

When the war began, Philadelphia was in rebel hands. Joseph Galloway fled the city to join the British army stationed to the north. When the British occupied Philadelphia in 1777, he returned with them, serving as Superintendent of the Port and the Police, a role in which he could make life hard for rebels. When the patriots regained control early in 1778 he left again, taking the couple's daughter (and only surviving child) with him.

Grace grimly stayed on in occupied Philadelphia, hoping by her presence to maintain her claim not only to the city property on which they lived but other property—several thousand acres—that she stood to inherit from her father. In the meantime, as a leading male loyalist, Galloway was singled out by Pennsylvania's governing patriots. He was convicted in absentia for high treason and his property was confiscated. His wife's dower right in it was ignored. (Wives, on their husbands' deaths, were entitled to the use and income of one-third of land and buildings; being a convicted traitor was a political form of death.)

When her husband and daughter left with the British, Grace Galloway began a diary. It is a marvelously opinionated document in which she registered her emotions as well as the weather and the names of her visitors. Her spelling is often informal (e.g., "Embassell'd" for "embezzled") but her voice is clear. Despite her open scorn for the patriot cause (in the diary and in public), she was surprised when her house was seized along with other loyalists' property, and she was stunned when the patriots evicted her, refusing to honor her dower rights.

WEDNESDAY JULY 22, 1778

Was ill in ye morn. . . . sent for Mr. Dickinson last Night & he tole Me he wou'd look over ye law to see if I cou'd recover My own estate & this evening he came & he told Me I cou'd Not recover dower & he fear'd my income in My estate was forfeited likewise & ye no tryal wou'd be of service: but advised Me to draw up a peti'on to ye Chief Judge Mccean for the recovery of my estate & refused a fee in ye Politest Manner but begg'd I wou'd look on him as My sincere friend & told me he would do me any service to ye Utmost of his power & I think he behaves much better than Chew. So I find I am a beggar indeed I expect every hour to be turn'd out of doors & where to go I know not. No one will take me in & all ye Men keeps from Me. . . . But I am fled from as a Pestilence. Mrs Jones here in the morn: sent nurse to Parson Combs to desire him to [tell] Mr G of my unhappy situation.

MONDAY, AUGUST 10, 1778

Peggy Johns & Becky Redman came in ye Morn, Lewis sent Me word Smith had gave his honour not to Molest Me till the Opinion of ye executive council was known but in a short time after came Peel[e], . . . [and others] took

Possession of my house. I was taken very ill & obliged to Lay down & sent them word I cou'd not see them; they went every Where below stairs & [one man] . . . offer'd to Me chuse My own bed chamber; but I sent them no Message but was very ill Up stairs. But between 2 & 3 o'clock the last went away. Peel[e] told Nurse now they had given [one] . . . Gentle Man possession they had nothing More to do with it. But they took the Key out of ye front parlor door & locked Me out & left the windows Open . . .

SUNDAY AUGUST 16, 1778 [THE COMING EVICTION HAS BEEN ANNOUNCED]

Mrs Redman & Mrs Montgomery drank tea here. I desired Mrs Montgomery to desire Mr McKean to drank tea with me or let me know when it Wou'd be Agreeable for me to Wait on him & I find [Samuel] Shoemaker . . . had been before me. The quakers all Assist her but they wou'd let me fall. I sent twice to Lewise for a sight of ye petition but he wou'd not let me see it & as I have No friends they treat me as they please. So much for Mr G [Galloway's] great friends. He has not one who will go out of ye way to serve him. I am in hopes they will let me have my Estate but that will be on my own

Account. No favour shown to J G [Joseph Galloway] or his Child: Nor has he a friend that will say now word in his favour. I am tired with sending after a set of men that allways keeps from me when I most need them. Am vex'd.

[Galloway was highly indignant when Charles Willson Peale (who later would be known as one of the greatest artists of the new nation) came to evict her.]

THURSDAY, AUGUST 20, 1778
[EVICTION DAY]

. . . Lewise sent me word that I must shut my doors & windows & if they wou'd come to let them Make a forcible Entry. Accordingly I did so & a little after 10 o'clock they Knocked Violently at the door three times. The Third time I sent Nurse & call'd out myself to tell them I was in possession of my own House & wou'd keep so & that they shou'd gain No admittance Hereupon which they went round in ye yard & Try'd every door but cou'd None Open. Then they went to the Kitchen door & with a scrubbing brush which they broke to pieces they forced that open, we Women standing in ye Entry in ye Dark. They made repeated strokes at ye door & I think was 8 or 10 Minuets before they got it open. When they came in I had ye windows open'd they look'd very Mad. Their was Peel[e], [Charles Willson Peale] Smith, ye Hatter, & a Col. Will, a pewterer in Second Street. I spoke first & told them I was Used ill: & show'd them the Opinion of ye Lawyers. Peel read it: but they all despised it & Peel said he had studyed ye Law & knew they did right. I told them Nothing but force shou'd get me out of My house. Smith said they knew how to Manage that & that they wou'd throw my cloaths in ye street: & told Me that Mrs Sympson & forty others [loyalist women] ware put out of ye lines in one day. . . . He . . . hinted that Mr G had treated people Cruely. I found the Villan wou'd say anything so I stop'd after hearing several insulting things. . . . In ye Mean While Peel & Will went over ye House to see Nothing was Embassell'd & Locking Up the things[. A]t last Smith went away & Mrs Irwin & he sat talking [in] ye Kitchen as they took my things to her House.

Peel went to the generals & asked for his Chariot & then returned & told me ye General was so kind as to let me have it & he, Mr Peel, was willing to Accommodate Me as well as he cou'd. I told him he Need not give himself the Troble for if I wanted ye Chariot I cou'd send to ye General myself. Just after ye General sent in his Housekeeper with His compliments & to let me know that I was wellcome to His Chariot & he wou'd have it ready any hour I pleased. I then Accepted of it & told her [that] I . . . after every Mortifying treatment [I] was tired & wanted to be turn'd out. Peel went Upstairs & brought down My Work bag & 2 bonnets & put them on the side table. At last we went in the Entry to sit. . . . Two of ye Men went out & after staying some time return'd & said they had been with the council & that they had done right [by ordering the eviction] & must proceed. I did not hear this myself but ye rest of ye Women did.

Mrs Craig asked for My Bed but they wou'd let Me Have Nothing & as I told them acted entirely from Malice: after we had been in ye Entry some time Smith & Will went away & Peel said ye Chariot was ready but he would not hasten me. I told him I was at home & in My own House & nothing but force shou'd drive me out of it. He said it was not ye first time he had taken a Lady by the Hand [he is] an insolent wretch. This speech was made some time in the room; at last he becon'd for ye Chariot for ye General wou'd not let it come till I wanted it & as the Chariot drew up Peel fetched My Bonnets & gave one to me ye other to Mrs Craig: then with [the] greatest air said come Mrs Galloway give me your hand. I answer'd I will not nor will I go out of my house but by force. He then took hold of my arm & I rose & he took me to the door. I then Took hold on one side & Look round & said pray take Notice I do not leave my house of My own accord or with my own inclination but by force & Nothing but force shou'd have Made Me give up possession. Peel said with a sneer very well Madam & when he led me down ye step I said now Mr Peel let go My Arm I want not your Assistance. He said he cou'd help me to ye Carriage. I told him I cou'd go without & you Mr Peel are the last Man on earth I wou'd wish to be Obliged to.

Mrs Craig then step'd into ye Carriage & we drove to her house where we din'd. It was neer two o'clock . . . Distress'd in ye afternoon when I reflected on the Occurences of ye day & that I was drove out of my house distitute & without any maintenance . . . Sent for Mr Chew. He came & told me I must sue them for a forcible Entry. I am just distracted but Glad it is over.

As litigation to recover her property continued, Grace Galloway's scorn for patriots was as vigorous and emphatic as any patriot castigation of the loyalists. "Nothing reigns here but interess[t],"
she wrote of Philadelphia. But despite her pride and her assertiveness, she continued to define
herself in private terms. "I . . . laughed at the whole wig [Whig—the name of the British opposi-
tion] party," she wrote on April 20, 1779. "I told them I was the happiest woman in town for I had
been strip[p]ed and Turn'd out of Doors yet I was still the same and must be Joseph Galloway's
Wife and Lawrxence Growdens daughter and that it was not in their power to humble Me."

Grace Galloway was a resentful woman to the end. Her husband, safely in London with their
daughter, never asked her to join him. She boarded with Quaker friends, fending for herself with
devalued Continental currency. The war seemed an intrusion into a private—and luxurious—
world in which she had expected to enjoy her inheritance safely. She did not particularly love her
husband, but she proudly claimed his identity. Though she made no secret of her hostility to the
patriots or her admiration for the Crown, she failed to comprehend why she—a woman—should
be expected to account for her views or why her views had any more significance than a preference
for silver over pewter. Even in the midst of the struggle over the possession of her house, she persisted in serving tea, a beverage that patriots had given up at the time of the Boston Tea Party in
1773 and that marked her as a proud Loyalist. Galloway was not a stupid woman, but she failed to
recognize that her political gestures went beyond merely private behavior, and she never came to
terms with the invasion of the political world into her private and material life.

The United States was formed in a revolution that claimed that "it is the right of the people to
alter or abolish" a government when they understand it to be destructive of their rights to "Life,
Liberty and the Pursuit of Happiness" (quoting the Declaration of Independence). The British
claimed that subjects owe permanent allegiance to the Crown; the patriots insisted that allegiance
must be voluntary. Grace Galloway never consented to change her allegiance. What do her diary
entries and the violence she experienced suggest about the nature of the Revolution? About her
conception of womanhood?

LINDA K. KERBER

Why Diamonds Really Are a Girl's Best Friend: The Republican Mother and the Woman Citizen

A kiss on the hand may be quite continental
But diamonds are a girl's best friend
A kiss may be grand . . . but it won't pay the rental
on your humble flat
Or help you at the automat . . .
  Jules Styne, 1950, sung by Carol Channing
  in the Broadway musical "Gentlemen Prefer
  Blondes"

"I expect to see our young women forming
a new era in female history," wrote Judith
Sargent Murray in 1798. Her optimism was part
of a general sense that all possibilities were
open in the post-Revolutionary world. The experience of war had given words like independence and self-reliance personal as well as

This essay has been prepared by the author for *Women's America*, 8th edition. It is drawn from *Women of the
Republic: Intellect and Ideology in Revolutionary America* (Chapel Hill: University of North Carolina Press, 1980),
chs. 7 and 9; *No Constitutional Right to Be Ladies: Women and the Obligations of Citizenship* (New York: Hill and
Wang, 1998), introduction and ch. 1; and "Why Diamonds Really Are a Girl's Best Friend: Another American
Narrative," *Daedalus* 141, no. 1 (Winter 2012), 89–100; all by Linda K. Kerber.

political overtones; among the things that ordinary people had learned from wartime had been that the world could, as the song played during the British surrender at Yorktown put it, turn upside down. The rich could quickly become poor; wives might suddenly have to manage farms and businesses; women might even, as the famous Deborah Sampson Gannett had done, shoulder a gun. Revolutionary experience taught that it was useful to be prepared for a wide range of unusual possibilities; political theory taught that republics rested on the virtue of their citizens. The stability and competence on which republican government relied required a highly literate and politically sophisticated constituency. Maintaining the republic was an intellectual and educational as well as a political challenge.

Murray herself, born into an elite family in Salem, Massachusetts, had felt the dislocations of the Revolution severely. Widowed, remarried to a Universalist minister of modest means, she understood what it was to be thrown on her own resources. "I would give my daughters every accomplishment which I thought proper," she wrote,

> and to crown all, I would early accustom them to habits of industry and order. They should be taught with precision the art economical; they should be enabled to procure for themselves the necessaries of life; independence should be placed within their grasp. . . . The SEX should be taught to depend on their own efforts, for the procurement of an establishment in life.[1]

The model republican woman was competent and confident. She could resist the vagaries of fashion; she was rational, independent, literate, benevolent, and self-reliant. Nearly every writer who described this paragon prepared a list of role models, echoing the pantheon of heroines admired by the fund-raising women of Philadelphia in 1780 (see pp. 110–111). There were women of the ancient world, like Cornelia, the mother of the Gracchi; rulers like Elizabeth of England and the Empress Catherine the Great of Russia; and a long list of British intellectuals: Lady Mary Wortley Montagu, Hannah More, Mary Wollstonecraft, and the historian Catherine Macaulay. Those who believed in these republican models demanded that their presence be recognized and endorsed and that a new generation of young women be urged to find in them patterns for their own behavior.

The Revolutionary years had brought some women close to direct criticism of political systems. Women had signed petitions, they had boycotted imported tea and textiles, they had made homespun and "felt nationly," as one young woman put it. In some places they had signed oaths of loyalty to patriot or loyalist forces. Rachel Wells bought £300 of government bonds to support the war and had a keen sense of her own contribution: "I did my Posabels every way . . . Ive Don as much to help on this war as Though I had bin a good Soger," she told the New Jersey legislature.[2]

Women were citizens of the new republic. They could be naturalized; they were required to refrain from treason on pain of punishment; if single, they paid taxes. Women could develop their own agendas; when Abigail Adams wrote the now-famous letter in which she urged her husband and his colleagues in the Continental Congress to "remember the ladies," she urged that domestic violence should be on the republican agenda: "Put it out of the power of our husbands to use us with impunity," she demanded. "Remember all men would be tyrants if they could."[3]

Expressions of women's desire to play a frankly political role were regularly camouflaged in satire, a device that typically makes new ideas and social criticism seem less threatening. (Think of the recent example of Jon Stewart's and Stephen Colbert's satirical political commentary on the Comedy Channel.) In 1791, for example, a New Jersey newspaper published a pair of semiserious satires in which women discuss the politics of excise taxes and national defense. "Roxana" expresses a feminist impatience:

> In fifty quarto volumes of ancient and modern history, you will not find fifty illustrious female names; heroes, statesmen, divines, philosophers, artists, are all of masculine gender. And pray what have they done during this long period of usurpation? . . . They have written ten thousand unintelligible books. . . . They have been cutting each other's throats all over the globe.[4]

Some years later, the students at Sarah Pierce's famous school for girls in Litchfield, Connecticut, prepared a "Ladies Declaration of Independence" for the Fourth of July. Alongside the frivolous phrasing is earnest comment on the unfilled promises of the republic. Less than ten years after that, Elizabeth Cady Stanton would use the same technique. "When in the Course of Human Events," the Litchfield declaration begins,

> it becomes necessary for the Ladies to dissolve those bonds by which they have been subjected

to others, and to assume among the self styled Lords of Creation that separate and equal station to which the laws of nature and their own talents entitle them, a decent respect to the opinions of mankind requires, that they should declare the causes which impel them to the separation.

We hold these truths to be self evident. That all mankind are created equal.

The Litchfield women wished to change "social relations." They complained about men who "have undervalued our talents, and disparaged our attainments; they have combined with each other, for the purpose of excluding us from all participation in Legislation and in the administration of Justice."[5]

As these young women understood, American revolutionaries had brilliantly and radically challenged the laws governing the relationship between ruler and ruled, subjects and the king. Republican ideology was antipatriarchal. It voiced the claim of adult men to be freed from the control of kings and political "fathers" in an antique monarchical system. "Is it in the interest of a man to be a boy all his life?" Tom Paine asked in *Common Sense*, the great political manifesto of the era.

But the men who modeled the new American republic after the war remodeled it in their own image. They did not eliminate the political father immediately or completely. George Washington quickly became the "Father of his Country"; at the Governor's Palace in Williamsburg, Virginia, the life-size portrait of George III was quickly replaced by a life-size portrait of George Washington in a similar pose. American revolutionary men understood that two major elements of prerevolutionary social and political life—the system of slavery and the system of domestic relations—directly clashed with the egalitarian principles of the Revolution. But they kept both systems in place. By embedding the three-fifths compromise and the Fugitive Slave Law in the federal Constitution of 1787, the founders actually strengthened and stabilized the system of slavery. And they left virtually intact the old English law governing relations between husbands and wives.

These codes (what we now call family law) are not well known nowadays, even by otherwise well-informed historians and lawyers. They were not written into the U.S. Constitution of 1787; unlike the fugitive slave clause or the three-fifths compromise, they were not publicly debated. White men—plantation masters,

merchants, ministers, farmers, laborers, Northerners, Southerners—were differently situated in relation to slavery, so they had real reason to debate it. But every free man, rich or poor, whatever their race, benefited from the structures of traditional family law. They had no need to debate it. As a result, we have to search hard to find the details of the old law of domestic relations embedded in old state statutes, outdated treatises, and judges' reasoning in humdrum cases from state and local courts.

The old law of domestic relations began with the principle that at marriage the husband controlled the physical body of his wife. He had unfettered sexual access to her body. (There was no concept of rape within marriage in U.S. law until feminists put it there, beginning in the 1970s.) The system was known as *coverture*: a married woman was understood to be "covered" by her husband's civic identity, as though they were walking together under an umbrella that the husband held. She was absorbed by her husband's civil identity in much the same way that children were subject to their parents. At the moment of marriage, the husband gained "absolute title" to the personal property a wife brought to the marriage as well as ownership of whatever she earned during it. He gained extensive authority over the real estate she brought to the marriage or inherited (perhaps from her father) once married. It followed that he could easily pressure her into agreement with him on all other matters. As Tapping Reeve, author of the treatise on which large numbers of lawyers would rely through much of the nineteenth century, put it, she gained no advantage "in point of property" from marriage.[6]

The rules of coverture made it seem logical that husbands manage the property that wives brought to the marriage and earned during it. As long as she was married, an adult woman could not make a contract without her husband's permission, because she had no property with which to guarantee that she would honor her commitments. Since she controlled no property to convey, she could not make a will until after she was a widow. The father was the guardian of the children: the mother could not make choices—for example, to whom a child was to be apprenticed—that challenged the choices made by her husband.

When Tapping Reeve explained why it was logical that wives could not enter into contracts, he added the point that wives could not enter into contracts involving their own labor.

"The right of the husband to the person of his wife," Reeve observed, "is a right guarded by the law with the utmost solicitude; if she could bind herself by her contracts, she would be liable to be arrested, taken in execution [of her bond], and confined in a prison; and then the husband would be deprived of the company of his wife, which the law will not suffer." If a husband were banished from the realm, however, then his wife "could contract, could sue and be sued in her own name; for in this case. . . . he was already deprived of the company of his wife."[7]

The rules of coverture made it seem logical that husbands determine where the family would live. Deep into the twentieth century, Oklahoma, like many states, was still using the traditional wording: "The husband is the head of the family. He may choose any reasonable place or mode of living and the wife must conform thereto." That law was not repealed until 1988, and then only after six years of vigorous debate.[8]

By giving fathers responsibility for children born within marriage (that's why fathers in the early republic had custody of children in case of divorce, which was rare), but leaving to mothers the responsibility for children born outside marriage, the old law of domestic relations excused all fathers from serious responsibility for children born out of wedlock—a principle that was largely unquestioned in American law until the twentieth century. It also ensured that children born to a free father and an enslaved mother followed the condition of the mother into slavery, not only binding enslaved men and women to labor but also making them permanently vulnerable to the sexual appetites of their masters. (Thus Sally Hemings was born into slavery; Thomas Jefferson married her half-sister.)

Since married women did not control property, and since at the time of the Revolution there were property requirements for voting, it seemed to follow that married women should not vote. (The reasoning, for both propertyless men and women, was that they could be too easily pressured by propertied husbands or employers.) No one has yet found a reasonable explanation for why unmarried propertied women were not permitted to vote. And although men had long served on juries in England and the United States even if they were not qualified to vote, women were barred from juries. Even after women won the right to vote, it did not automatically follow that they could serve on juries or hold office. In many states, new statutes were required.

Coverture gave husbands property rights in their wives' "services." These services included the right to "consortium"—understood not only as housekeeping but also love, affection, companionship, and sexual relations. If a married woman were injured by the negligence of another person, her husband could sue for damages, which included a monetary estimate of his loss of consortium. If he were injured, she had no claim for the loss of his companionship and sexual relations. This imbalance between the sexes in marriage was rarely tested, but when it was, as in the case of major accidents, the impact was severe. Not until the early 1950s were married women successful in making such a claim—in Washington D.C. in 1950, in Iowa in 1951—yet it took until the 1990s for all states to recognize the claim.

Because the civil law treated husband and wife as one, it seemed to follow that they could not sue each other—a situation known as "interspousal tort immunity." Thus a husband could not be convicted of larceny for theft of his wife's property; to do so, explained one New York judge (presumably with a straight face), would be to sow "the seeds of perpetual discord and broil." Interspousal tort immunity also means that married women could not claim civil damages for assault and battery by their husbands or for which their husbands were at fault.[9]

The rules of coverture were taken to imply that a married woman could not have a nationality independent of her husband's. It seemed to follow that a foreign woman who married an American man was "deemed a citizen" at marriage, but an American woman who married a foreign man lost her U.S. citizenship. Marriage to a foreign man was ruled "as voluntary and distinctive as expatriation," according to the U.S. Supreme Court during World War I. (Once the United States entered World War I, hundreds of U.S. women who had married German men were forced to register as enemy aliens. See *MacKenzie v. Hare*, pp. 413–15.) American men have never put their own citizenship at risk by their marriages.

In return for submitting their bodies and property to their husbands, women were assured that, if widowed, they could expect an inheritance. If a man died without a will, the probate courts would ensure that his widow received her "thirds": he could leave her more, but not less. The widow's dower right was grudging: it allowed her *to make use of one-third of the real estate* that her husband held at the time of his death. It was generally recognized that this could well be less than the property she had brought to the marriage. She usually could not sell it (or, if woodland, could not cut down the trees to sell to support herself) and was required to pass it down unscathed to her husband's heirs. A widow was also usually entitled to claim outright one-third of the personal property her husband had owned, *after* debts were paid, and to claim outright her personal "paraphernalia"—her clothing and cooking pots and featherbed—suitable to her station, as judged by probate officers.

So finally we get to diamonds. The jewelry a woman had been given was the last asset vulnerable to being seized as payment for her late husband's debts. The diamonds about which Carol Channing sings are a reference to the jewelry—generally pearls or opals—of the old law. In the late nineteenth and early twentieth centuries, especially after the marketing campaigns that accompanied the opening of diamond mines in South Africa, valuable jewels came to carry an additional value when given as an engagement present. The jilted fiancée no longer needed to face the humiliation of soothing her aching heart with money awarded to her in a breach of promise lawsuit. She got to keep the diamonds.

Yet the fact of women's citizenship in a democratic republic contained deep within it an implicit challenge to coverture. The revolutionary republic had promised to protect "life, liberty and property," but under the old law a married woman was deprived of her property and had none to protect. Patriot men rarely spoke about this contradiction, but their actions speak for them. In England, the killing of a husband by a wife was *petit treason,* analogous to regicide, although the killing of a wife by a husband was murder. The penalties for *petit treason* were worse than those for murder. The concept was not much enforced in colonial America, but it remained in the statutes. It was the only element of the old law of domestic relations that legislators of the early republic eliminated. Legislators were conscious of what they intended; they carefully retained the concept of *petit treason* for the killing of a master by a slave. With that single exception, neither the Revolutionary government under the Articles of Confederation nor the federal government of

the Constitution directly challenged the legal system of coverture.[10]

Instead of revising the law to remove its coercive elements, jurists simply ensured that the coerced voices would not speak. Husbands were responsible for crimes committed by their wives in their presence or with their approval—except in the case of treason, a crime so severe that responsibility for it overrode the obligation to a husband. Another exception was in the event that a wife kept a brothel with her husband's knowledge, since keeping a brothel "is an offense of which the wife is supposed to have the principal management."[11]

That the system of marriage contradicted the basic tenets of revolutionary thinking was obvious. But women who named the contradictions invited extraordinary hostility and ridicule. Among the most persistent themes was the link of female intellectual activity and political autonomy to an unflattering masculinity. "There is a *sex of soul*," announced the prominent Boston minister John Gardiner. "Women of masculine minds, have generally masculine manners. . . . Queen Elizabeth understood Latin and Greek, swore with the fluency of a sailor, and boxed the ears of her courtiers. . . . " A "mild, dove-like temper is so necessary to Female beauty, is so natural a part of the sex," reflected Parson Mason Locke Weems wistfully. "A masculine air in a woman frightens us."[12]

Selections from Mary Wollstonecraft's *Vindication of the Rights of Women* were published in the American press shortly after the book was published in London in 1792. She had borne one illegitimate daughter (Fanny Imlay) and lived with William Godwin before marrying him; after marriage she maintained lodgings in another house so that she could be free to write. Once her life history became generally known, it could be used to link intellectual women to political feminism and to aggressive sexuality, as one Federalist writer did in his bitter "Morpheus" essays, which ran in a Boston newspaper in 1802. In a dream sequence in "Morpheus," Wollstonecraft has arrived in America and sets out to teach its inhabitants wisdom.

> Women . . . are entitled to all the rights, and are capable of all the energies of men. I do not mean merely mental examples. . . . They can naturally run as fast, leap as high, and as far, and wrestle, scuffle, and box with as much success, as any of the . . . other sex.

That is a mistake (said an old man). . . [W]omen always feebler than men[—why]?

Because (said MARY) they are educated to be feeble; and by indulgence . . . are made poor, puny, baby-faced dolls; instead of the manly women they ought to be.

Manly women! (cried the wag). Wheu! A manly woman is a hoyden . . . a strumpet.[13]

Thus political behavior, like abstract thought, continued to be specifically proscribed as a threat to sensual attractiveness.

Only the mother who promised to use her political knowledge to serve the republic was spared this hostility. The concept was a variant of the argument for the improved education of women that republicans such as Judith Sargent Murray and Wollstonecraft herself had demanded. It defended education for women not only for their autonomy and self-realization but also so that they could be better wives, rational household managers, and better mothers for the next generation of virtuous republican citizens—especially sons. In a widely reprinted speech, "Thoughts upon Female Education," originally given at the new Young Ladies Academy of Philadelphia, the physician and politician Benjamin Rush addressed the issue directly: "The equal share that every citizen has in the liberty, and the possible share he may have in the government of our country, make it necessary that our ladies should be qualified to a certain degree, by a peculiar and suitable education, to concur in instructing their sons in the principles of liberty and government."[14] The Republican Mother was an educated woman who could be spared the criticism normally directed at the intellectually competent woman because she placed her learning at her family's service. That she had the leisure and opportunity for study located her solidly in the middle class.

It was commonly believed that republican government was fragile and rested on the presence of virtuous citizens. The Republican Mother was also a Republican Wife.[15] She chose a virtuous man for her husband; she condemned and corrected her husband's lapses from civic virtue; she educated her sons for it. The creation of virtuous citizens required wives and mothers who were well informed, "properly methodical," and free of "invidious and rancorous passions." The word virtue was derived from the Latin word for man, with its connotations of virility. Political action was ideologically marked as masculine; as we have seen, if political voice required independent property holding, it was legally marked masculine as well. Virtue in a woman required another theater for its display. To that end, writers created a mother who had a political purpose and argued that her domestic behavior had a direct political function in the republic.

As one college orator put it,

Let us then figure to ourselves the accomplished woman, surrounded by a sprightly band, from the babe that imbibes the nutritive fluid, to the generous youth. . . . Let us contemplate the mother distributing the mental nourishment to the fond smiling circle . . . watching the gradual openings of their minds . . . see, under her cultivating hand, reason assuming the reins of government, and knowledge increasing gradually to her beloved pupils. . . . Yes, ye fair, the reformation of a world is in your power. . . . It rests with you to make this retreat [from the corruptions of Europe] doubly peaceful, doubly happy, by banishing from it those crimes and corruptions, which have never yet failed of giving rise to tyranny, or anarchy. While you thus keep our country virtuous, you maintain its independence.[16]

Defined this way, the educated woman ceased to threaten the sanctity of marriage; the intellectual woman need not be masculine.

The ideology of Republican Motherhood was deeply ambivalent. On the one hand, it was a progressive ideology, challenging those who opposed women in politics by the proposal that women could—and should—play a political role through influencing their husbands and raising patriotic children. Within the dynamic relationships of the private family—between husbands and wives, mothers and children—it allocated an assertive role to women. Those who shared the vision of the Republican Mother usually insisted upon better education, clearer recognition of women's economic contributions, and a strong political identification with the republic. This ideology could complement the "fertility transition" under way in the postwar republic, a rapid fall in birthrates that would continue into our own time, and that was first found in urban areas that had experienced commercial and industrial as well as political revolution. Free women, the historian Susan Klepp has recently suggested, "applied egalitarian ideas and a virtuous, prudent sensibility to their bodies and to their traditional images of self as revolutions inspired discussion and debate. . . . On the household level, restricted fertility and high rates of literacy or years of education were persistently linked: the higher the educational attainment of women, the lower fertility rates."[17]

The idea that a mother can perform a political function represents the recognition that a citizen's political socialization takes place at an early age, that the family is a basic part of the system of political communication, and that patterns of family authority influence the general political culture. Most premodern political societies—and even some fairly modern democracies—maintain unarticulated, but nevertheless very firm, social restrictions that seem to isolate the family's domestic world from politics. The willingness of the American woman to overcome this ancient separation brought her into the political community.[18] In this sense, Republican Motherhood was an important and progressive invention congruent with revolutionary politics and the demographic transition. It altered the female domain in which most women had lived out their lives; it justified women's claims for participation in the civic culture. The ideology was strong enough to rout commentators such as "Morpheus" by redefining female political behavior as valuable rather than abnormal, as a source of strength to the republic rather than an embarrassment. The ideology would be revived as a rallying point for many twentieth-century women reformers, who saw their commitment to honest politics, efficient urban sanitation, and pure food and drug laws as an extension of their responsibilities as mothers.

But Republican Motherhood flourished in the context of coverture. The old law of domestic relations hemmed it in at every turn. Republican motherhood could legitimize only a minimum of political sophistication and interest. It was an extension into the republic of conservative traditions, stretching back at least as far as the Renaissance, that put narrow limits on women's assertiveness.[19] Captured by marriage, which not only secured their intimate relations but also their relationship to the public authority, for most of their lives most women had no alternative but to perform the narrow political role they managed to claim for themselves. Just as white planters claimed that democracy in the antebellum South necessarily rested on the economic base of black slavery, so male egalitarian society was said to rest on the moral base of deference among a class of

people—women—who would devote their efforts to service by raising sons and disciplining husbands to be virtuous citizens of the republic. The learned woman, who might very well wish to make choices as well as to influence attitudes, was a visible threat to this arrangement. Women were to contain their political judgments within their homes and families; they were not to bridge the world outside and the world within. The Republican Wife was not to tell her husband for whom to vote. She was a citizen but not really a constituent.

Restricting women's politicization was one of a series of conservative choices that Americans made in the postwar years as they avoided the full implications of their own Revolutionary radicalism. By these decisions Americans may well have been spared the agony of the French cycle of revolution and counterrevolution, which spilled more blood and produced a political system more regressive than had the American war. Nevertheless, the impact of these choices was to leave race equality to the mercies of a bloody century that stretched from the Civil War through Reconstruction and lynching into the civil rights movement of our own time. And the impact of these choices was also to leave in place the system by which marriage stood between women and civil society. When the revolutionary war made thousands of women widows, and hundreds of desperate military widows begged Congress for support, they found no one to listen when they claimed that they had served the nation's war effort. (See Rachel Wells' petition, pp. 113–114). But if they begged for recognition as wives and mothers who had been deprived , as one Congressman put it, "of their natural and civil protectors," women's pleas reached sympathetic ears. The unprecedented system of cash pensions developed in the decades before the civil war was distinctive in that for women marriage was the route to entitlement; "marriage," explains historian Kristin A. Collins, was "the source of legitimacy for women's citizenship." This practice continued to shape government programs for more than a century.[20] For most of the history of the United States, deep into the twentieth century, the legal traditions of marriage would be used to deny women citizens juries drawn from a full cross-section of the community, deny them control over their own property and their own earnings, sometimes deny them custody of their children, even deny them their rights as citizens should they marry a foreign man.

The 1960s and 1970s are distinctive for a remarkable shift in the way the law treats women's rights and obligations. Pressed by increasing public impatience with the ascriptive dependence of adult women on laws that disempowered women, legislatures and courts began to acknowledge that laws embodying gendered stereotypes harm not only women but also men and society as a whole. Indeed, they recognized that it is possible (something not imagined in the coverture regime) for men to be economically dependent on women, and therefore that it could be in men's interest for women to be independent civil actors.

Air Force Captain Sharron Frontiero had to press her argument all the way to the U.S. Supreme Court before she was authorized to draw a dependent's allowance for her husband in 1973. In a landmark decision, Justice William Brennan wrote in support of Frontiero: "Our nation has had a long and unfortunate history of sex discrimination . . . rationalized by an attitude of 'romantic paternalism,' which, in practical effect, put women, not on a pedestal but in a cage." (*Frontiero v. Richardson*, pp. 452–53). In a now classic series of opinions issued in the 1970s, the U.S. Supreme Court established the principle that laws based on gender stereotypes about the way men and women behave are unfair and unconstitutional. Ruth Bader Ginsburg argued these cases dazzlingly well as an attorney for the Women's Rights Project of the American Civil Liberties Union (ACLU). Even when stereotypes about women's or men's behavior might accurately predict what a majority of people will do, she argued, those individuals whose behavior does not conform to the stereotype ought not to be penalized. In 1975, Ginsburg argued *Weinberger v. Wiesenfeld*, leading the Supreme Court to agree unanimously that a Social Security law providing benefits to widows with small children, but not to similarly situated widowers, was based on the stereotype that imagined only bereft mothers, not bereft fathers. Many years later, in 1988, Ginsburg, now a U.S. Supreme Court Justice, would preside over the marriage of Jason Wiesenfeld, the little boy whose father had wanted to stay home and care for him.[21]

Laws that were once viewed as protective of women are now viewed as discriminating against them. It often startles people to learn that the Supreme Court did not regard discrimination on the basis of sex as a denial of the equal protection guaranteed of the Fourteenth Amendment (p. 289) until 1971, and then only very narrowly, in a case involving a teenager's cornet and a bank account worth $200. Other decisions followed in legislatures and in state and federal courts, reshaping the rules by which men and women make choices. It is no longer a reasonable defense against a charge of rape to claim that the victim dressed provocatively (although criminal charges of rape remain notoriously hard to prosecute successfully; the old suspicion of women's word remains). Discrimination on the basis of pregnancy, sexual harassment on the job, and exclusion from jobs on the basis that they are too harsh or dangerous: any of these actions can now count as a denial of equal protection.

It is now unreasonable to claim that women do not possess fully equal status, or that they lack the competence to make responsible choices. Nevertheless, while the legacy of coverture has been generally repudiated, it has not been eradicated. Distrust of women's claims to autonomy, cultural beliefs about the primacy of women's domestic obligations, and opinions about women's need to be protected from certain situations all reveal the lingering effects of coverture. Not until 1992 did the U.S. Supreme Court rule that as a general principle, "Women do not lose their constitutionally protected liberty when they marry."[22] As recently as the year 2000, dozens of state attorneys general called for passage of a new Violence Against Women Act, arguing that long-established laws against assault and battery have proven ineffective to protect women. As this volume goes to press, a grassroots movement among college women has revitalized the protections promised by Title IX (pp. 750–51) and the President of the United States has named sexual violence on campus as one of the key challenges facing the nation.

An antique story about how the world works, a story grounded in English legal practice and continued in the great narrative that we Americans have told ourselves about how we came to be what we are, continues to lurk in American law and practice. In that story, a husband could not kill his wife—that would be murder—but the only other guarantee she had was that he could not thrust her out naked into the world. She had her paraphernalia— her petticoats and her cooking pots. And the last thing he could take from her in order to pay his debts was her jewels—the diamonds that she could keep as her best friend. Those diamonds still gleam, but few among us know quite why.

NOTES

1. Murray's newspaper essays were reprinted in a collected edition, *The Gleaner* (Boston, 1798). These comments appear in vol. III, pp. 167–68, 189. See also Sheila L. Skemp, *First Lady of Letters: Judith Sargent Murray and the Struggle for Female Independence* (Philadelphia, 2009).

2. "Rachel Wells Petition for Relief," Nov. 15, 1785, New Jersey Archives, Trenton.

3. Abigail Adams to John Adams, Mar. 31, 1776, *Adams Family Correspondence* (Cambridge, Mass., 1963), I:370.

4. *Burlington (N.J.) Advertiser*, Feb. 1, 1791.

5. Miss Pierce's School Papers, 1839, Litchfield Historical Society, Litchfield, Conn.

6. Tapping Reeve, *The Law of Baron and Femme, Parent and Child, Guardian and Ward, Master and Servant* . . . (New Haven, Conn., 1816; Burlington, Vt., 1846), 37.

7. Ibid., ch. viii, pp. 98–99.

8. *Revised Laws of Oklahoma, 1910* . . . (St. Paul, Minn.: The Pioneer Co., 1912), I:837; Chris Casteel, "Husband-Wife Law Won't Stand, Opinion Advises," NewsOK, July 18, 1986, via www.newsok .com; *Annual Review of Population Law* 15 (1988): 81.

9. *Longendyke v. Longendyke*, 44 Barb. 366 (1863) (quotation at 369).

10. See, for example, "An Act for Annulling the Distinction between the Crimes of Murder and Petit Treason," Mar. 16, 1785, in Asahel Stearns et al., eds., *The General Laws of Massachusetts* . . . (Boston, 1823), I:188.

11. Reeve, *Law of Baron and Femme*, ch. v, p. 73.

12. "The Restorator" on "Rights of Woman," *Mercury and New-England Palladium*, Sept. 16, 1801, p. 1; Parson Mason Locke Weems, *Hymen's Recruiting Sergeant* (Philadelphia, 1800).

13. [Timothy Dwight], "Morpheus, Part 2, No. 1," *Mercury and New-England Palladium*, Mar. 2, 1802, p. 1.

14. Benjamin Rush, *Thoughts upon Female Education, Accommodated to the Present State of Society, Manners, and Government* . . . (Boston, 1787), p. 6.

15. See Linda K. Kerber, "The Republican Mother: Women and the Enlightenment—An American Perspective," *American Quarterly* 28 (Summer 1976): 187–205; Jan Lewis, "The Republican Wife: Virtue and Seduction in the Early Republic," *William and Mary Quarterly*, 3rd ser., 44 (Oct. 1987): 689–721.

16. *New York Magazine*, May 1795, pp. 301–305.

17. Susan E. Klepp, *Revolutionary Conceptions: Women, Fertility, and Family Limitation in America, 1760–1820* (Chapel Hill: University of North Carolina Press, 2009), p. 14.

18. See Gabriel Almond and Sidney Verba, *The Civic Culture* (Princeton, N.J.: Princeton University Press, 1963), pp. 377–401.

19. Elaine Forman Crane emphasizes this dimension; see *Ebb Tide in New England: Women, Seaports, and Social Change, 1630–1800* (Boston, 1998).

20. "'Petitions Without Number': Widows' Petitions and the Early Nineteenth-Century Origins of Public Marriage-Based Entitlements," *Law and History Review*, 31 (2013): 1–60.

21. *Coral Gables* [FL] *Sun-Journal*, Sept. 16, 1998.

22. *Planned Parenthood of Pennsylvania v. Casey*, 112 S. Ct. 2791 (1992).

II

AMERICA'S MANY FRONTIERS

1820–1880

WORKPLACE AND HOUSEHOLD SCENES

JEANNE BOYDSTON
The Pastoralization of Housework

Having read fiction and advice literature directed to women in the years before the Civil War, in 1966 the historian Barbara Welter identified a pervasive stereotype, which she called the "Cult of True Womanhood." Women were encouraged to cultivate the virtues of domesticity, piety, purity, and submissiveness. Home was referred to as women's "proper sphere" and understood to be a shelter from the outside world in which men engaged in hard work and cutthroat competition. Other historians agreed that men's and women's spheres of activity were separated and suggested that this separation was somehow linked to the simultaneous growth of capitalism and industrialization. Historian Gerda Lerner argued, by contrast, that stressing the shelter of home was a way by which middle-class women distinguished themselves from mill girls, and so maintained class boundaries.

How does Jeanne Boydston describe the relationship between home and work in antebellum America? How does she describe the relationship between women's work and men's work? What does she think were the uses of the ideology of separate spheres? How do the middle-class households described by Boydston differ from the households in which Harriet Jacobs and Rachel Davis lived (pp. 179–188)?

In the colonial period, family survival had been based on two types of resources: the skills of the wife in housewifery, and the skills and property of the husband in agriculture. Both sets of skills involved the production of tangible goods for the family—such items as furnishings, food, and fabrics. Both were likely to involve some market exchange, as husbands sold grain and wives sold eggs or cheese, for example. And both involved services directly to the household. By the early nineteenth century, however, husbands' contributions to their households were focused disproportionately on market exchange—on the cash they brought into the family—while their direct activities in producing both goods and services for the family had vastly decreased.

The meaning of this shift has often been misread, interpreted as an indication that households were no longer dependent on goods and services provided from within but had instead become reliant upon the market for their survival. . . . [But] consumerism was sharply curtailed by the amount of available cash. Choices constantly had to be made: to purchase a new cloak or try to refurbish the

Excerpted from *Home and Work: Housework, Wages, and the Ideology of Labor in the Early Republic* by Jeanne Boydston. Copyright © 1991 by Jeanne Boydston. Used by permission of Oxford University Press, Inc. Notes have been renumbered and edited. We mourn the death of Jeanne Boydston on November 1, 2008. For more on her life and career, see the tribute by Lori D. Ginzberg, http://www.historians.org/publications-and-directories/perspectives-on-history/february-2009/in-memoriam-jeanne-boydston.

old one for another season, to hire a woman to help with the wash or lay aside some money to buy a house. In these patterns of mundane decisions lay the essential economic character of antebellum households: they were in fact "mixed economies"—economic systems that functioned on the bases of both paid and unpaid labor and were dependent upon both. They required paid labor for the cash to purchase some goods and services. Equally, they depended on unpaid labor in the household to process those commodities into consumable form and to produce other goods and services directly without recourse to the cash market. . . .

[The] antebellum era was the last period during which most adult women shared the experience of having been, at some point in their lives, paid household workers. To an extent never repeated, even middle-class wives were likely to have worked as hired "help" in their youth. . . . [It is therefore possible to make a rough calculation] of the cost to a family to replace the unpaid labor of the wife by purchasing it on the market.[1] . . .

In northeastern cities in 1860, a woman hired both to cook and to do the laundry earned between $3 and $4 a week. Seamstresses and maids averaged two-and-a-half dollars a week. On the market, caring for children was at the lower end of the pay scale, seldom commanding more than $2 a week. If we assume that a woman did the full work of a hired cook and child's nurse, and also spent even an hour a day each sewing and cleaning (valued at about three cents an hour apiece), the weekly price of her basic housework would approximate $4.70. Even if we reduce this almost by half to $3 a week (to allow for variations in her work schedule and for the presence of assistance of some sort), taken at an average, this puts the price of a wife's basic housework at about $150 dollars a year.[2] . . .

To this should be added the value of goods a wife might make available within the family for free or at a reduced cost. Among poorer households, this was the labor of scavenging. A rag rug found among the refuse was worth half a dollar in money saved, an old coat, several dollars. Flour for a week, scooped from a broken barrel on the docks, could save the household almost a dollar in cash outlay.[3] In these ways, a wife with a good eye and a quick hand might easily save her family a dollar a week—or $50 or so over the course of the year. In households with more cash, wives found

other ways to avoid expenditures. By shopping carefully, buying in bulk, and drying or salting extra food, a wife could save ten to fifty percent of the family food budget . . . this could mean a saving of from 40 cents to over $2 a week. Wives who kept kitchen gardens or chickens . . . could . . . produce food worth a quarter a week (the price of 1/4 bushel of potatoes in New York in 1851).[4]

But there was also the cash that working-class wives brought into the household, by their needlework, or vending, or by taking in boarders, running a grocery or a tavern from her kitchen, or working unpaid in her husband's trade. A boarder might pay $4 a week into the family economy. Subtracting a dollar and a half for food and rent, the wife's labor-time represented $2.50 of that amount, or $130 a year.[5] . . .

The particular labor performed by a given woman depended on the size and resources of her household. . . . Yet we can estimate a general market price of housework by combining the values of the individual activities that made it up: perhaps $150 for cooking, cleaning, laundry, and childrearing; another $50 or so saved through scavenging or careful shopping, another $50 or so in cash brought directly into the household. This would set the price of a wife's labor-time among the laboring poor at roughly $250 a year beyond maintenance. . . . In working-class households with more income, where the wife could focus her labor on money-saving and on taking in a full-time boarder, that price might reach over $500 annually. . . . These shifts in the nature of a wife's work, and in the value of that work, as a husband's income increased seems not to have been entirely lost on males, who advised young men that if they meant to get ahead, they should "get married."[6] . . .

But husbands were not the sole beneficiaries of the economic value of housework, or of its unique invisibility. Employers were enabled by the presence of this sizeable but uncounted labor in the home to pay both men and women wages which were, in fact, below the level of subsistence. The difference was critical to the development of industrialization in the antebellum Northeast.[7] . . . Occasionally, mill owners acknowledged that the wages they paid did not cover maintenance. One agent admitted: "So long as they can do my work *for what I choose to pay them*, I keep them, getting out of them all I can. . . . [H]ow they fare outside my walls

I don't know, nor do I consider it my business to know. They must look out for themselves."[8] . . .

Even when employers paid high enough salaries to provide present security for a family, they seldom provided either the income or the job security to ensure a household's well-being against the erratic boom-and-bust cycles of business and the unemployment consequent upon those cycles. . . . Women's unremunerated labor in the household provided the needed "safety net," enabling middle-class families to maintain some degree of both material stability and healthfulness in a volatile economic environment. . . . Put simply, a wife was a good investment for a man who wanted to get ahead.

THE PASTORALIZATION OF HOUSEWORK

The culture of the antebellum Northeast recognized the role of wives in the making of contented and healthy families. Indeed, the years between the War of 1812 and the Civil War were a period of almost unabated celebration of women's special and saving domestic mission. "Grant that others besides woman have responsibilities at home. . . ." wrote the Reverend Jesse Peck in 1857, "[s]till we fully accord the supremacy of domestic bliss to the wife and mother."[9] . . .

As recent historians have recognized, this glorification of wife and motherhood was at the heart of one of the most compelling and widely shared belief systems of the early nineteenth century: the ideology of gender spheres. An elaborate set of intellectual and behavioral conventions, the doctrine of gender spheres expressed a worldview in which both the orderliness of daily social relations and the larger organization of society derived from and depended on the preservation of an all-encompassing gender division of labor. Consequently, in the conceptual and emotional universe of the doctrine of spheres, males and females existed as creatures of naturally and essentially different capacities. As the Providence-based *Ladies Museum* explained in 1825:

Man is strong—woman is beautiful. Man is daring and confident—woman is diffident and unassuming. Man is great in action—woman i[n] suffering. Man shines abroad—woman at home. Man talks to convince—woman to persuade and please. Man has a rugged heart—woman a soft and tender one. Man prevents misery—woman

relieves it. Man has science—woman taste. Man has judgment—woman sensibility. Man is a being of justice—woman of mercy.

These "natural" differences of temperament and ability were presumed to translate into different social roles and responsibilities for men and women. Clearly intended by the order of nature to "shine at home," Woman was deemed especially ill-equipped to venture into the world of nineteenth-century business, where "cunning, intrigue, falsehood, slander, [and] vituperative violence" reigned and where "mercy, pity, and sympathy, are vagrant fowls."[10]

. . . [T]he ideology of gender spheres was partly a response to the ongoing chaos of a changing society—an intellectually and emotionally comforting way of setting limits to the uncertainties of early industrialization. . . . The traits that presumably rendered Woman so defenseless against the guiles and machinations of the business world not only served to confine her to the home as her proper sphere but made her presence there crucial for her family, especially for her husband. Even the most enthusiastic boosters of economic expansion agreed that the explosive opportunism of antebellum society created an atmosphere too heady with competition and greed to engender either social or personal stability. However great his wisdom or strong his determination, to each man must come a time

when body, mind, and heart are overtaxed with exhausting labor; when the heavens are overcast, and the angry clouds portend the fearful storm; when business schemes are antagonized, thwarted by stubborn matter, capricious man, or an inauspicious providence; when coldness, jealousy, or slander chills his heart, misrepresents his motives, or attacks his reputation; when he looks with suspicion on all he sees, and shrinks from the frauds and corruptions of men with instinctive dread.[11] . . .

Whatever the proclivities or ambitions of individual women, the presumed contrasts between the sexes permitted Woman-in-the-abstract to be defined as the embodiment of all that was contrary to the values and behaviors of men in the marketplace, and thus, to the marketplace itself. Against its callousness, she offered nurturance. Against its ambition, she pitted her self-effacement and the modesty of her needs. Against its materialism, she held up the twin shields of morality and spiritual solace. If business was a world into which only men traveled and where they daily risked losing their souls, then wherever Woman was, was sanctuary. And Woman was in the Home.

The contrast between Man and Woman melted easily into a contrast between "workplace" and "home" and between "work" as Man engaged in it and the "occupations" of Woman in the home. Most writers of prescriptive literature did acknowledge that women were involved in activities of some sort in their households. For example, T. S. Arthur worried that a woman would be unable to keep the constant vigilance required to be a good mother if she also had to attend to "the operations of the needle, the mysteries of culinary science, and all the complicated duties of housekeeping." His language is revealing, however: housework consisted of "mysteries" and "duties"; it was a different order of activity from the labor that men performed. Indeed, some observers cautioned that the wife and mother should deliberately stay clear of employments which might seem to involve her in the economy. . . . William Alcott was among this group. Noting that a woman ". . . has duties to perform to the sick and to the well—to the young and to the aged; duties even to domestic animals," Alcott nevertheless cautioned that "[v]ery few of these duties are favorable to the laying up of much property, and some are opposed to it. So that while we commend industry—of the most untiring kind, too—we would neither commend nor recommend strong efforts to lay up property." The advice was not only consistent with, but reflected a critical aspect of the ideology of spheres: to the extent that workers in the household identified themselves with the labor of the marketplace, the function of the home as a place of psychological refuge would be undermined.[12]

Thus, the responsibilities of wives in their households were generally described in the prescriptive literature less as purposeful activities required and ordered by the welfare of their individual families than as emanations of an abstract but shared Womanhood. As Daniel C. Eddy explained:

> Home is woman's throne, where she maintains her royal court, and sways her queenly authority. It is there that man learns to appreciate her worth, and to realize the sweet and tender influences which she casts around her; there she exhibits the excellences of character which God had in view in her creation.

Underscoring the essentially passive nature of women's functions, Eddy concluded: "Her life should be a calm, holy, beautiful walk."[13]

. . . The consequence of this conflation of ideology with behavior was to obscure both the nature and the economic importance of women's domestic labor. It was not only Woman-in-the-abstract who did not labor in the economy, but also, by extension, individual women. It was not only Woman-in-the-abstract, but presumably, real women who guided the on-going functions of the home through the effortless "emanations" of their very being, providing for the needs of their families without labor, through their very presence in the household. As romantic narrative played against lived experience, the labor and economic value of housework ceased to exist in the culture of the antebellum Northeast. It became work's opposite: a new form of leisure. . . .

William Alcott's description of the wife's labors in *The Young Wife* provides a striking illustration of the pastoralization of housework in descriptions of the antebellum home:

> Where is it that the eye brightens, the smile lights up, the tongue becomes flippant, the form erect, and every motion cheerful and graceful? Is it at home? Is it in doing the work of the kitchen? Is it at the wash-tub—at the oven—darning a stocking—mending a coat—making a pudding? Is it in preparing a neat table and table cloth, with a few plain but neat dishes? Is it in covering it with some of nature's simple but choice viands? Is it in preparing the room for the reception of an absent companion? Is it in warming and lighting the apartments at evening, and waiting, with female patience, for his return from his appointed labor? Is it in greeting him with all her heart on his arrival?[14]

Clearly, Alcott was quite familiar with the types of work performed by women in their own families, and his description is all the more interesting on this account: cooking, baking, washing clothes, mending and darning, serving meals, building fires, attending to lamps—it is a surprisingly accurate catalogue. It is also incomplete, of course. Missing from this picture is the making of the soap that the wash might be done, the lugging and heating of the water, the tiresome process of heating and lifting cast-iron irons, the dusting and sweeping of rooms, the cleaning of the stove, and the making of the stocking and the coat now in need of repair.

Even the domestic tasks which Alcott acknowledges, however, are not to be contemplated as true work, a point which is made explicit in his identification of only the husband's employments as "labor." With "labor," indeed, the wife's activities have no truck, for there is no labor here to perform. . . . the food appears virtually as a gift of nature, and the compliant fires and lamps seem to light and tend themselves. . . . All is ordered, and the ordering of it is not only *not* burdensome or tiring, but the certain vehicle of good health and a cheerful disposition. Far from labor, housework is positively regenerating. . . .

The pastoralization of housework, with its emphasis on the sanctified home as an emanation of Woman's nature, required the articulation of a new way of seeing (or, more exactly, of *not* seeing) women as actors, capable of physical exertion. Most specifically, this applied to women as laborers, but the "magical extraction" of physical activity from the concept of Womanhood in fact proceeded in much larger terms and was most apparent in the recurrent celebrations of female "influence." Typically invoked as the female counterpart to the presumably *male* formal political power,[15] the concept of indirect womanly "influence" supplanted notions of women as direct agents, and thus as laborers. [In an article entitled "Woman's Offices and Influences," J. H. Agnew argued that] the contrast between presumably male "power" (physical as well as moral) and female "influence" could be drawn quite explicitly:

> We may stand in awe, indeed, before the exhibition of *power*, whether physical or moral, but we are not won by them to the love of truth and goodness, while *influence* steals in upon our hearts, gets hold of the springs of action, and leads us into its own ways. It is the *inflowing* upon others from the nameless traits of character which constitute woman's idiosyncrasy. Her heart is a great reservoir of love, the water-works of moral influence, from which go out ten thousand tubes, conveying the ethereal essences of her nature, and diffusing them quietly over the secret chambers of man's inner being.

Woman does not herself *act*. Rather, she "gets hold of the springs of action." An idiosyncrasy in the human order, she is not so much a physical as an ethereal being. Agnew concluded: "Let man, then, exercise power; woman exercise influence. By this she will best perform her offices, discharge her duties." It is the crowning touch on the pastoralization of housework: the home is not the setting of labor, but of "offices" and "duties." Therefore, what is required

for the happy home is not a worker, but rather "a great reservoir of love."[16]

The pastoralization of household labor became a common feature of antebellum literature, both private and published. . . . [It] shaped much of the fiction of the period. In a piece entitled "The Wife" (published in the *Ladies' Literary Cabinet* in July of 1819 and included in *The Sketch Book* the following year), Washington Irving described the plight of a young couple forced by the husband's disastrous speculations to give up their fashionable life in the city and move to a modest country cottage. One might anticipate numerous headaches and a good deal of hard work in such a move, especially for the wife, but such was not the case for Irving's "Wife." Mary goes out to the cottage to spend the day "superintending its arrangement," but the substance of that process remains a mystery, for the packing and unpacking, cleaning, hanging of curtains, arranging of furniture, putting away of dishes, sorting of clothes, and adjusting of new domestic equipment which one might expect to be required under such circumstances remain undisclosed in the text. Indeed, all we learn is that, when next encountered by the narrator, Mary "seems in better spirits than I have ever known." Transformed into a creature who is far more sylvan nymph than human female, Mary greets her husband and the narrator "singing, in a style of the most touching simplicity. . . . Mary came tripping forth to meet us; she was in a pretty rural dress of white, a few wild flowers were twisted in her fine hair, a fresh bloom was on her cheek, her whole countenance beamed with smile—I have never seen her look so lovely." To complete the pastoral scene, nature has obligingly provided "a beautiful tree behind the cottage" where the threesome picnic on a feast of wild strawberries and thick sweet cream.[17] . . .

In both its briefer and its more extended forms in fiction and in exposition, in prescription and in proscription, the pastoralization of housework permeated the culture of the antebellum Northeast. Often, it was expressed simply as a truism, as when the Reverend Hubbard Winslow reminded his Boston congregation that "[t]he more severe manual labors, the toils of the fields, the mechanics, the cares and burdens of mercantile business, the exposures and perils of absence from home, the duties of the learned professions devolve upon man. . . ." [H]e considered women's occupations to be of a "more delicate and retired nature." That same year, the shocked and angered Congregational clergy of Massachusetts drew upon the same assumptions and the same imagery of Womanhood to denounce the abolitionist activities of Sarah and Angelina Grimké. Reminding their female congregants that "the power of woman is in her dependence," the clergy spoke of the "unobtrusive and private" nature of women's "appropriate duties" and directed them to devote their energies to "those departments of life that form the character of individuals" and to embodying "that modesty and delicacy which is the charm of domestic life. . . ."[18]

As we have seen, working class husbands appear to have embraced the view that paid labor was economically superior to unpaid labor. They shared, too, a tendency to pastoralize the labor of their wives. The speeches of early labor activists, for example, frequently invoked both the rhetoric of the ideology of spheres and pastoral images of the household, implying a sharp contrast between "the odious, cruel, unjust and tyrannical system" of the factory, which "compels the operative Mechanic to exhaust his physical and mental powers," with the presumably rejuvenating powers of the home. Discouraging women from carrying their labor "beyond the home," working men called upon women to devote themselves to improving the quality of life within their families. . . . [A]s William Sylvis put it, it was the proper work of woman "to guide the tottering footsteps of tender infancy in the paths of rectitude and virtue, to smooth down the wrinkles of our perverse nature, to weep over our shortcomings, and make us glad in the days of our adversity. . . ."[19]

African-American newspapers of the antebellum Northeast also reflected and reaffirmed the pastoral conventions of women's domestic labor. *The Rights of All* compared women to ornamental creatures of nature, "as various in decorations as the insects, the birds, and the shells. . . ." In 1842, *The Northern Star and Freeman's Advocate* approvingly reprinted an article from the *Philadelphia Temperance Advocate* in which wives were described as deities "who preside over the sanctities of domestic life, and administer its sacred rights. . . ." That this perception ill fit the experiences of those female readers whose home was also their unpaid workplace, as well as those women who worked for money in someone else's home, appears not to have disturbed the paper's editors. Rather than as a worker, Woman was represented as a force of nature—and presumably one intended for man's special benefit: "The morning star of our youth—the day star of our manhood—the evening star of our age."[20]

For both middle-class and working-class men, the insecurities of income-earning during the antebellum period struck at the very heart of their traditional roles as husbands and fathers. Particularly since the late eighteenth century, manhood had been identified with wage-earning—with the provision of the cash necessary to make the necessary purchases of the household. In the context of the reorganization of paid work in the antebellum Northeast, the growing dependency of households on cash, and the roller-coaster business cycles against which few families could feel safe, that identification faced almost constant challenge. And as it was challenged, it intensified.

By the antebellum period, the late-eighteenth century association of manhood with wage-earning had flowered into the cult of the male "breadwinner." A direct response to the unstable economic conditions of early industrialization, this association crossed the lines of the emerging classes, characterizing the self-perceptions and social claims of both laboring and middle-class men.

Among laboring men, the identification of manhood with wage-earning melded easily with the traditional emphasis on the "manliness" of the crafts. . . . General Trades' Union leader Ely Moore warned that the unchecked industrial avarice of employers would create a class of "breadless and impotent" workers. When they struck for higher wages in 1860, the shoemakers of Massachusetts linked the encroachments of capital with an attack upon their manhood; in the "Cordwainers' Song," they called upon each other to "stand for your rights like men" and "Resolve by your fathers' graves" to emerge victorious and "like men" to "hold onto the last!"[21] Gender also provided the language for belittling the oppressor, for working men often expressed their rage—and reaffirmed the importance of their own manhood—by impugning the masculinity of their employers. The "Mechanic" sneered at "[t]he employers and those who hang on their skirts."[22]

In the midst of the upheavals of the antebellum economy, however, it was not only employers who threatened the old artisan definitions of manhood. Because an entire way of life was being undermined, so the dangers seemed to arise from everywhere in the new social order—including from wage-earning women themselves. In fact, women seldom directly imperiled men's jobs. The young women who went to Lowell were entering an essentially new industry. Moreover, in their families and hired out on an individual basis, carding, spinning, fulling, and even, to some extent, weaving had long been a part of women's work. . . .

But if wage-earning women did not directly challenge men's jobs, their very presence in the new paid labor force may have underscored the precariousness of men's position as wage-earners. Particularly given the post-Revolutionary emphasis on the importance of women's remaining in the home to cultivate the private virtues, females who were visible as outworkers and operatives may have seemed to bespeak an "unnaturalness" in society—an inability of wage-earning men to establish proper households. Like the witches of the seventeenth century, wage-earning women became symbols of the threats posed to a particular concept of manhood—in this instance, a concept that identified male claims to authority and power with the status of sole wage-earner. As they grappled with the precariousness of their own positions, laboring-class men focused their anxieties on the women who were their wives, daughters, and sisters, as well as on the men who were their employers.

They expressed these anxieties in two forms. First, wage-earning men complained that women were taking jobs—and thus the proper masculine role—away from men. An 1836 report of the National Trades' Union charged that because women's wages were so low, a woman's "efforts to sustain herself and family are actually the same as tying a stone around the neck of her natural protector, Man, and destroying him with the weight she has brought to his assistance." Not uncommonly, working men suggested that women did not really need to work for money and castigated "the girl, or the woman, as the case may be, who being in a condition to live comfortably at home by proper economy" selfishly took work from the truly needy. In 1831, the *Working Man's Advocate* called upon "those females who . . . are not dependent on their labor for a living" to withdraw from paid work so that men might have the jobs.[23]

At the same time, working men organized to call for "the family wage"—a wage packet for the male "breadwinner" high enough to permit his wife and children to withdraw from paid work. As Martha May has pointed out, the family wage "promised a means to diminish capitalists' control over family life, by allowing workingmen to provide independently for their families." But the demand for the family wage also signalled the gendering of the emerging class system, and, in this, the gendering of early industrial culture. Identifying the husband as the proper and "natural" wage-earner, the family wage ideal reinforced a distinctive male claim to the role of "breadwinner." By nature, women were ill-suited to wage-earning, many laboring-class men insisted. The National Trades' Union called attention to Women's "physical organization" and "moral sensibilities" as evidence of her unfitness for paid labor, and the anonymous "mechanic" focused on "the fragile character of a girl's constitution, [and] her peculiar liability to sickness."[24] Presumably, only men had the constitution for regular, paid labor.

It is tempting to see in the antebellum ideology of spheres a simple extension of the Puritan injunction to wives to be keepers at home and faithful helpmates to men. Certainly, the two sets of beliefs were related. The colonists brought with them a conviction that men and women were socially different beings, so created by God and so designated in the order of nature. Both were meant to labor, but they were meant to labor at different tasks. Perhaps even more important, they were meant to occupy quite different stations in social life and to exercise quite different levels of control over economic life. . . . "Labor" may have been a gender-neutral term in colonial culture, but "authority" and "property" were masculine concepts, while "dependence" and "subordination" were clearly feminine conditions. . . .

The origins of the antebellum gender culture were as much in the particular conditions of early industrialization as in the inherited past, however. . . . [T]he specific character of the nineteenth-century gender culture was dictated less by transformations in women's experience than by transformations in men's. To be sure, the principle of male dominance persisted into the nineteenth century. . . . Social power in the antebellum Northeast rested increasingly on the ability to command the instruments of production and to accumulate and reinvest profits. From these activities wives were legally barred, as they were from formal political processes that established the ground rules for the development of industrial capitalism. While most men were also eliminated from the contest on other grounds (race, class, and ethnicity, primarily), one had to be male to get into the competition at all. . . .

. . . With the demise of the artisan system, and so of a man's hopes to pass along a trade to his sons, the practical grounds on which a laboring man might lay claim to the role of male head-of-household had altered. Increasingly, it was less his position as future benefactor of the next generation than his position as the provider of the present generation (that is, the "breadwinner") that established a man's familial authority.

For men of the emerging middle class, the stakes were equally high but somewhat different. Many of these were the sons and grandsons of middling farmers, forebears who, while not wealthy, had established their adulthood through the ownership of land, and whose role within the family had been centrally that of the "father." Their power residing in their control of inheritance to the next generation, these were men who might have been described with some degree of accuracy as "patriarchs." But by the second decade of the nineteenth century middling farms throughout much of the Northeast were scarcely capable of supporting the present generation; much less were they sizeable or fertile enough to establish patriarchal control of the family. Simultaneously, the emergence of an increasingly industrialized and urbanized society rendered the inheritance of land a less useful and less attractive investment in the future for sons. Even successful businessmen and professionals experienced diminishing control over their sons' economic futures. A son might still read the law with his father, but new law schools, like medical schools, foreshadowed the time when specialized education, rather than on-the-job training with his father or his father's friends, would offer a young man the best chance for success. . . .

Early industrialization preserved the principle of male dominance, then, but in a new form: the "husband" replaced the "father." Men claimed social authority—and indeed exercised economic control—not because they owned the material resources upon which subsequent generations would be founded, but

because they owned the resources upon which the present generations subsisted. More important, they had established hegemony over the definition of those resources. In the gender culture of the antebellum Northeast, subsistence was purchased by wages—and men were the wage-earners.

Early industrialization had simultaneously redefined the paradigm that guided the social and economic position of women. . . . [T]he paradigm of womanhood shifted from "goodwife" to "mother"—that is, from "worker" to "nurturer." . . . [W]hat-ever cultural authority women gained as "mothers" was at the direct cost of a social identity in the terms that counted most in the nineteenth century—that is, as workers. As Caroline Dall noted in 1860, most Americans cherished "that old idea, that all men support all women. . . ." Dall recognized this to be "an absurd fiction," but it was a fiction with enormous social consequences. Even when women did enter paid work, their preeminent social identity as "mothers" (in distinct contrast to "workers") made their status as producers in the economy suspect: the predisposition to consider women "unfit" helped justify underpaying them.[25]

In all of this, the pastoralization of housework implicitly reinforced both the social right and the power of husbands and capitalists to claim the surplus value of women's labor, both paid and unpaid. It accomplished this by rendering the economic dimension of the labor invisible, thereby making pointless the very question of exploitation: one cannot confiscate what does not exist. Since the ideology of spheres made the non-economic character of housework a simple fact of nature, few observers in the antebellum Northeast felt compelled to argue the point.

The ideology of spheres did not affect all women in the same way, of course. Insisting that the domestic ideal was founded in the nature of Woman (and not in the nature of society), prescriptive writers saw its embodiments everywhere—from the poorest orphan on the streets, to the mechanic's daughter, to the merchant's wife. But their models transparently were meant to be the women of the emerging middle class. It was, after all, in the middle classes that women had presumably been freed from the necessity for labor that had characterized the colonial helpmate; there, that mothers and wives had supposedly been enabled to express their fullest capacities in the service of family formation. In celebrations of middle-class "Motherhood" lay the fullest embodiments of the marginalization of housewives as workers.

But if middle-class women were encased in the image of the nurturant (and nonlaboring) mother, working-class women found that their visible inability to replicate that model worked equally hard against them. As historian Christine Stansell has vividly demonstrated, the inability (or unwillingness) of working-class women to remain in their homes—that is, their need to go out into the streets, as vendors, washerwomen, prostitutes, or simply as neighbors helping a friend out—provided the excuse for a growing middle-class intrusion into working-class households, as reformers claimed that women who could not (or did not wish to) aspire to middle-class standards were defined as poor mothers.[26] . . .

In addition to its specific implications for women, the ideology of spheres, and the pastoralization of housework which lay at the heart of that ideology, both represented and supported larger cultural changes attendant upon the evolution of early industrial capitalism. The transition of industrialization was not purely material: it was ideological as well, involving and requiring new ways of viewing the relationship of labor to its products and of the worker to his or her work. In its denial of the economic value of one form of labor, the pastoralization of housework signaled the growing devaluation of labor in general in industrial America. Artisans were discovering, and would continue to discover, what housewives learned early in the nineteenth century: as the old skills were debased, and gradually replaced by new ones, workers' social claims to the fruits of their labor would be severely undercut. Increasingly, productivity was attributed, not to workers, but to those "most wonderful machines."[27] It was in part against such a redefinition that the craft workers of New York and the shoemakers of Lynn, Massachusetts, struggled.[28]

The denial of the economic value of housework was also one aspect of a tendency, originating much earlier but growing throughout the eighteenth and nineteenth centuries, to draw ever-finer distinctions between the values of different categories of labor, and to elevate certain forms of economic activity to a superior status on the grounds of the income they produced. As with housework, these distinctions were rarely founded on the actual material value of the labor in question. Rather, they were based on contemporary levels of power and wealth, and served to justify those existing conditions. An industrialist or financier presumably deserved to earn very sizeable amounts of money, because in accumulating capital he had clearly contributed more labor and labor of a more valuable kind to society than had, for example, a drayman or a foundry worker. . . .

Finally, the ideology of spheres functioned to support the emergence of the wage system necessary to the development of industrial capitalism. The success of the wage system depends upon a number of factors—among them the perception of money as a neutral index of economic value and the acceptance of the wage as representing a fair "livelihood." The devaluation of housework was a part of a larger process of obscuring the continuation of and necessity for barter-based exchanges in the American economy. In this, it veiled the reliance of the family on resources other than those provided through paid labor and heightened the visibility of the wage as the source of family maintenance.

But how did women respond to the growing devaluation of their contributions as laborers in the family economy? . . . [I]n their private letters and diaries, wives quietly offered their own definition of what constituted the livelihood of their families, posing their own perception of the importance of conservation and stewardship against the cash-based index of the marketplace and easily integrating the family's periodic needs for extra cash into their understanding of their own obligations.

Nevertheless, among the public voices affirming that Woman was meant for a different sphere than Man, and that the employments of Woman in the home were of a spiritual rather than an economic nature, were the voices of many women. In *Woman in America,* for example, Mrs. A. J. Graves declared: ". . . home is [woman's] appropriate sphere of action; and . . . whenever she neglects these duties, or goes out of this sphere . . . she is deserting the station which God and nature have assigned to her." Underscoring the stark contrast between Woman's duties in the household and Man's in "the busy and turbulent world," Graves described the refuge of the home in terms as solemn as any penned by men during the antebellum period: ". . . our husbands and our sons ... will rejoice to return to its sanctuary of rest," she averred, "there to refresh their wearied spirits, and renew their strength for the toils and conflicts of life."[29]

Graves was not unusual in her endorsement of the ideology of spheres and of the pastoralization of housework. Even those women who most championed the continuing importance of women's household labor often couched that position in the language of spheres. No one more graphically illustrates this combination than Catharine Beecher, at once probably the most outspoken defender of the importance of women's domestic labor and one of the chief proponents of the ideology of female domesticity.... Beecher was clear and insistent that housework was hard work, and she did not shrink from suggesting that its demands and obligations were very similar to men's "business." In her *Treatise on Domestic Economy*, Beecher went so far as to draw a specific analogy between the marriage contract and the wage labor contract:

> No woman is forced to obey any husband but the one she chooses for herself; nor is she obliged to take a husband, if she prefers to remain single. So every domestic, and every artisan or laborer, after passing from parental control, can choose the employer to whom he is to accord obedience, or, if he prefers to relinquish certain advantages, he can remain without taking a subordinate place to any employer.

Nevertheless, Beecher regularly characterized women's work in the home as the occupation merely of administering "the gentler charities of life," a "mission" chiefly of "self-denial" to "lay up treasures, not on earth, but in heaven." This employment she contrasts with the "toils" of Man, to whom was "appointed the out-door labor—to till the earth, dig the mines, toil in the foundries, traverse the ocean, transport the merchandise, labor in manufactories, construct houses ... and all the heavy work. ..."[30]

Beecher's apparently self-defeating endorsement of a view that ultimately discounted the value of women's labor arose from many sources, not the least of which was her own identification with the larger middle-class interests served by the ideology of spheres. Beecher enjoyed the new standing afforded middle-class women by their roles as moral guardians to their families and to societies, and based much of her own claim to status as a woman on the presumed differences between herself and immigrant and laboring-class women. For example, she ended an extended discussion of "the care of Servants" in *The American Woman's Home* with the resigned conclusion that "[t]he mistresses of American families, whether they like it or not, have the duties of missionaries imposed upon them by that class from which our supply of domestic servants is drawn."[31]

But, also like many women in antebellum America, Catharine Beecher was sharply aware of the power difference between males and females. It was a theme to which she constantly returned in her writings, especially in her discussions of women's rights.... In her *Essay on Slavery and Abolitionism*, Beecher was quite explicit about the reasons why a woman might cloak herself and her positions in the language of dependency and subordination:

> [T]he moment woman begins to feel the promptings of ambition, or the thirst for power, her aegis of defence is gone. All the sacred protection of religion, all the generous promptings of chivalry, all the poetry of romantic gallantry, depend upon woman's retaining her place as dependent and defenceless, and making no claims. ...

It was much the same point that Elizabeth Ellet would later make in her *The Practical Housekeeper*: since men had many more alternatives than women, the smart woman made it her "policy" to create an appearance of domestic serenity.[32]

But it would be a mistake to read women's endorsement of the pastoralization of housework purely as a protective strategy. Women were not immune from the values of their communities, and many wives appear to have shared the perception of the larger society that their work had separated from the economic life of the community and that it was, in fact, not really work at all.

Those misgivings were nowhere more evident than in the letter that Harriet Beecher Stowe wrote to her sister-in-law, Sarah Beecher, in 1850. It was the first opportunity Harriet had had to write since the Stowes had moved to Brunswick, Maine, the spring before. Since her arrival with the children, she explained, she had "made two sofas—or lounges—a barrel chair—divers bedspreads—pillowcases—pillows—bolsters—matresses ... painted rooms ... [and] revarnished furniture." She had also laid a month-long siege at the landlord's door, lobbying him to install a new sink. Meanwhile, she had given birth to her eighth child, made her way through the novels of Sir Walter Scott, and tried to meet the obligations of her increasingly active career as an author—all of this while also attending to the more mundane work of running a household: dealing with tradespeople, cooking, and taking care of the children. From delivery bed to delivery cart, downstairs to the kitchen, upstairs to the baby, out to a neighbor's, home to stir the stew, the image of Stowe flies through these pages like the specter of the sorcerer's apprentice.

Halfway through the letter, Stowe paused. "And yet," she confided to her sister-in-law, "I am constantly pursued and haunted by the idea that I don't do anything."[33] It is a jarring note in a letter—and a life—so shaped by the demands of housework. That a skilled and loving mother could impart dignity and a sense of humane purpose to a family otherwise vulnerable to the degradations of the marketplace, Stowe had no doubt. But was that really "work"? She was less certain. In that uncertainty, to borrow Daniel Eddy's words, lay "a world of domestic meaning"—for housewives of the antebellum era, and for women since.

Notes

1. See Luisella Goldschmidt-Clermont, *Unpaid Work in the Household: A Review of Economic Evaluation Methods* (Geneva, 1982).

2. See Edgar Martin, *The Standard of Living in 1860: American Consumption Levels on the Eve of the Civil War* (Chicago, 1942), p. 177; and Faye Dudden, *Serving Women: Household Service in Nineteenth-Century America* (Middletown, Conn., 1983), p. 149.

3. This is calculated on the basis of an average weekly budget for a working-class family of five, as itemized in the New York *Daily Tribune*, May 27, 1851. See also Martin, *Standard of Living*, p. 122.

4. New York *Daily Tribune*, May 27, 1851.

5. Martin, *Standard of Living*, p. 168.

6. Grant Thorburn, *Sketches from the Note-book of Lurie Todd* (New York, 1847), p. 12.

7. See Alice Kessler-Harris and Karen Brodlin Sacks, "The Demise of Domesticity in America," *Women, Households, and the Economy*, eds. Lourdes Beneria and Catherine R. Stimpson (New Brunswick, N.J., 1987), p. 67.

8. Quoted in Norman Ware, *The Industrial Worker, 1840–1860: The Reaction of American Industrial Society to the Advance of the Industrial Revolution* (New York, 1924; reprinted Gloucester, Mass., 1959), p. 77.

9. Jesse T. Peck, *The True Woman; or, Life and Happiness at Home and Abroad* (New York, 1857), p. 245.

10. *The Ladies Museum*, July 16, 1825, p. 3; Henry Ward Beecher, *Lectures to Young Men, on Various Important Subjects* (Boston, 1846), pp. 87, 91.

11. Peck, *The True Woman*, pp. 242–43.

12. *The Mother's Rule: or, The Right Way and the Wrong Way*, ed. T. S. Arthur (Philadelphia, 1856), p. 261; William A. Alcott, *The Young Wife, or, Duties of Woman in the Marriage Relation* (Boston, 1837), p. 149.

13. Daniel C. Eddy, *The Young Woman's Friend; or the Duties, Trials, Loves, and Hopes of Woman* (Boston, 1857), p. 23.

14. Alcott, *The Young Wife*, pp. 84–85.

15. For an excellent discussion of the concept of female "influence," see Lori D. Ginzburg, *Women and the Work of Benevolence: Morality and Politics in the Northeastern United States, 1820–1885* (New Haven, Conn., 1990).

16. J. H. Agnew, "Women's Offices and Influence," *Harper's New Monthly Magazine* 17: no. 3 (Oct. 1851):654–57, quote on p. 657.

17. Washington Irving, "The Wife," *Ladies Literary Cabinet*, July 4, 1819, pp. 82–84. Quotations are from Washington Irving, *The Sketch Book of Geoffrey Crayon, Gent.* (New York, 1961), pp. 34–36.

18. "Pastoral Letter of the Massachusetts Congregationalist Clergy" (1837) in *Up From the Pedestal: Selected Writings in the History of American Feminism*, ed. Aileen S. Kraditor (Chicago, 1968), pp. 51–52; Reverend Hubbard Winslow, *A Discourse Delivered in the Bowdoin Street Church* (Boston, 1837), p. 8.

19. *The Man*, May 13, 1835; *Life, Speeches, Labors, and Essays of William H. Sylvis*, ed. James C. Sylvis (Philadelphia, 1872), p. 120.

20. *The Rights of All*, June 12, 1829; *The Northern Star and Freeman's Advocate*, Dec. 8, 1842, and Jan. 2, 1843.

21. Moore is quoted in Sean Wilentz, *Chants Democratic: New York City and the Rise of the American Working Class, 1788–1850* (New York, 1986), p. 239. The "Cordwainers' Song" is printed in Alan Dawley, *Class and Community: The Industrial Revolution in Lynn* (Cambridge, Mass., 1976), pp. 82–83.

22. "A Mechanic," *Elements of Social Disorder: A Plea for the Working Classes in the United States* (Providence, R.I., 1844), p. 96.

23. Quoted in John Andrews and W. D. P. Bliss, *A History of Women in Trade Unions*, vol. 10 of *Report on Condition of Woman and Child Earners in the United States*, Senate Doc. 645, 61st Cong., 2d Sess. (Washington, D.C., 1911; reprint ed. New York, 1974), p. 48; "Mechanic," *Elements of Social Disorder*, p. 45; *Working Man's Advocate*, June 11, 1831.

24. Martha May, "Bread Before Roses: American Workingmen, Labor Unions and the Family Wage," in *Women, Work, and Protest: A Century of U.S. Women's Labor History*, ed. Ruth Milkman (Boston, 1985), p. 4; vol. 6 of *A Documentary History of American Industrial Society*, eds. John R. Commons et al. (New York, 1958), p. 281; "Mechanic," *Elements of Social Disorder*, p. 42.

25. Caroline Dall, *"Woman's Right to Labor"; or, Low Wages and Hard Work* (Boston, 1860), p. 57.

26. Christine Stansell, *City of Women: Sex and Class in New York, 1789–1860* (New York, 1986), pp. 193–216.

27. The phrase is from the title of Judith McGaw's study, *Most Wonderful Machine: Mechanization and Social Change in Berkshire Papermaking, 1801–1885* (Princeton, 1987).

28. See Wilentz, *Chants Democratic*; and Dawley, *Class and Community*, cited in n. 21 above.

29. Mrs. A. J. Garves, *Woman in America: Being an Examination into the Morals and Intellectual Condition of American Female Society* (New York, 1841), p. 156.

30. Catharine E. Beecher, *A Treatise on Domestic Economy, for the Use of Young Ladies at Home, and at School* (Boston, 1841), p. 26; Beecher, *An Essay on Slavery and Abolitionism, with Reference to the Duty of American Females* (Philadelphia, 1837), p. 128; Catharine E. Beecher and Harriet Beecher Stowe, *The American Woman's Home, or Principles of Domestic Science* (Hartford, Conn., 1975), p. 19.

31. Beecher and Stowe, *The American Woman's Home*, p. 327.

32. Beecher, *Essay on Slavery and Abolitionism*, pp. 101–2; *The Practical Housekeeper; a Cyclopaedia of Domestic Economy*, ed. Mrs. [Elizabeth] Ellet (New York, 1857), p. 17.

33. Harriet Beecher Stowe to Sarah Buckingham Beecher, Dec. 17 [1850], The Schlesinger Library, Radcliffe College, Cambridge, Mass.

STEPHANIE JONES-ROGERS
Mistresses in the Making

When masters spoke of their "family" they meant something very different than the meaning we now give that word. They meant an extended web of relations—not only their wives and children, brothers and sisters, nieces and nephews and cousins, but also apprentices bound to the household head for a term of years, and enslaved people bound for life. The buildings in which slaveowners lived were homes to the members of the masters' families but sites of oppression and often violence to the enslaved people who spent their lives there.

Families groom children for the lives that they are expected to lead. Slaveholding parents started to prepare their children early for an adulthood that involved the control of other people. In her careful reading of the correspondence of slaveowners and interviews with formerly enslaved people, Stephanie Jones-Rogers has found evidence of how girls were shaped for the roles that they were expected to play. The preparation of girls to be mistresses who demanded deference from the enslaved and were educated in a variety of punishments was as forceful as the preparation of boys to be masters. How does reading this essay alter your perception of the ways we tell stories about and histories of childhoods?

In 1847, Lizzie Anna Burwell was growing up in a slaveholding household in Lynesville, North Carolina. She, like many other girls in the region, loved flowers, and she often strolled through her parents' garden with Fanny, the enslaved female charged with her care. After spending so much time with Fanny, Lizzie Anna developed an intense bond with her, but one day something changed. Lizzie Anna became "vexed" with Fanny, so much so that she went to her father and demanded that he "cut Fanny's ears off and get her a new maid from Clarksville."[1]

During those walks through the garden, and perhaps while observing her parents interact with the enslaved people around them, Lizzie Anna learned how to be a slaveowner. She came to understand the obscene logic that made it perfectly acceptable to stroll through her family's garden enjoying the company of her enslaved caretaker in one moment, and threaten to mutilate her and buy another slave

Prepared especially for *Women's America*. Drawn from *Lady Flesh Stealers, Female Soul Drivers, and She-Merchants: White Women and the Economy of American Slavery*, by Stephanie Jones-Rogers, book manuscript in-progress, esp. chap. 1. Copyright 2014 by Stephanie Jones-Rogers.

to take her place in the next. In the comfort of her home, she recognized that she possessed the power to command others to do so, and her father did little to discourage her from believing that she did. In fact, he relayed the incident to his sister with an air of conviviality and amusement, which suggests that Lizzie Anna's aunt also accepted the logic underpinning her niece's behavior. All in all, Lizzie Anna was a mistress in the making, and the people around her were crucial to her development as such.

White southern girls like Lizzie Anna learned how to be mistresses and slaveowners through a learning process that spanned the years of their childhood and adolescence. During this time, white females practiced techniques of slave discipline and management, and decided what kind of slaveowners they wanted to become. Many of them decided that they wanted to be effective ones.

Slaveowning parents were critical to this learning process in two ways. Slaveowning parents gave enslaved men, women, and children to their young daughters as gifts on special occasions like birthdays and Christmas, and upon marriage—or for no reason at all.[2] They also bequeathed enslaved people to their daughters in their wills. And when they did so, their daughters came to value the crucial ties between slaveownership and autonomous and stable financial futures. Coupled with this, parents offered their daughters vicarious lessons on how to own and control enslaved people through their words and deeds. As young girls watched their parents interact with the enslaved people around them, they observed different models of slave mastery, and through a process of trial and error, they were able to develop styles of their own.

White southern girls grew up alongside the slaves their parents gave to them. They developed relationships of power with enslaved people. And through all of this, slaveownership became an important element of their identities, a fact that would shape their relationships with their husbands and communities once they reached adulthood.

Slave inheritances were essential aspects of white girls' development as slaveowners; these most frequently came from parents. Slaveowning parents thought very carefully about the kinds of property they would give to their daughters and one of their most critical considerations in this matter was the amount of control their daughters would have over the gift once married. Rosalie Calvert, for example, wrote to her father who lived in Belgium about her daughter's future inheritance. In her correspondence, Rosalie indicated that she and her husband were "presently thinking about giving her what is called here 'real property,' which is to say, lands or houses over which a husband has no power."[3] After the Revolutionary era, when primogeniture, or the practice of giving all property to a family's eldest son, fell out of favor, parents tended to give their daughters equal amounts of property; but they also gave them more slaves than land.[4] Young white girls came to expect these inheritances, and enslaved people anticipated these transfers of wealth too.

Enslaved people often knew that their owners would give them to their daughters well before the transfer of property took place. Bacchus White recalled that his owners "alwa's sed dat I wus to belon' to Miss Kathie." Agnes James's master had already chosen her as a gift to his daughter Janie Little, because, as Agnes remembered, "he give all his daughters one of us to have a care for dem." Cornelia Winfield "always knowed [she] wuz to belong to one of marster's daughters." But, for these enslaved girls born shortly before the Civil War broke out, freedom came before that transfer of ownership could take place.[5] Just as enslaved people came to anticipate the transition from one household to the next, young white girls did too.

As they planned out their daughters' futures, some slaveowning parents preferred to give their daughters female slaves, and they began doing so when they were only infants. Filmore Hancock's grandmother "was given to missus, as her own de day she was born." Remarkably, Filmore recalled, "old missus was only a year old den." Formerly enslaved people told of how a master "had women he gave to his daughters and men he give to his sons." Charity Bowery's first mistress "made it a point to give one of [her] mother's children to each of hers." Charity eventually belonged to her mistress's second daughter Elizabeth. An unnamed formerly enslaved woman told historian Frederic Bancroft that her owners gave her to their "daughter fer a present. Dey make *presunts* o' niggahs in *doze* days, dey did *dat*."[6]

Slaveowners often adhered to this inheritance practice over multiple generations too. Mrs. William Keller owned Sarah Thompson

Chavis, and she and Sarah gave birth to daughters around the same time. When Mrs. Keller's daughter Julia was still a young girl, she gave her Sarah's daughter Amy as a "daily gift."[7]

Slaveowners occasionally gave their female descendants human property in ritualized affairs, which shaped the young women's development as slaveowners. When these future slaveowners were just girls, elders would join the hands of their young heirs together with those of the slaves they were giving to them. After doing so, they would tell them that the enslaved people in question were their property forever.[8] "Drawing" ceremonies were sometimes held after the death of a slaveowner who wished to divide enslaved people equally among his or her heirs but had not stipulated who would receive whom by will. During these affairs, the potential legatees gathered to draw straws. Whichever straws they pulled determined which slaves (and sometimes other property) they received from their deceased loved one's estate. This is how Ora M. Flagg came to belong to her mistress, Julia Taylor: "[T]he old heads died. . . . Their children when they died drawed for the slaves. . . . The Taylors were relatives of the Scurlocks, and were allowed to draw, and Julia Taylor drawed my mother."[9] Another formerly enslaved person recalled a similar kind of drawing ceremony: "When my old mistress died she had four children. . . . When Christmas come we had to be divided out, and straws were drawn with our names on them. The first straw was drawn, you would get that darkey. . . . Miss Betsey drawed mother and drawed me. Everyone drawed two darkeis [sic] and so much money."[10] Occasionally, these kinds of estate divisions occurred when a slaveowner was still alive. Sallie Crane did not understand why her master's property was divided because "he wasn't dead nor nothin'," but she "fell to Miss Evelyn," his daughter.[11]

These affairs were not simply for show; the property transfers and acquisitions that took place became significant events in white girls' lives and these young women assumed partial responsibility for managing the enslaved people their parents and kinfolks gave them. Immediately upon transferal, enslaved men, women, and children took care of their new owners in whatever ways necessary. When Jennie Fitts was just a young person, her owner gave her to his daughter Annie: "Ise can membah whens de Marster takes me to Missy Annie and sez, 'Ise gibin you to Missy, You jest

do what she tells you to.'" Taking her master's charge very seriously, Jennie attended to her young mistress's every need and want: "Ise wid Missy Annie alls de time and 'tend to her. Ise wid her night and day, Ise sleeps at de foot ob her bed. Ise keeps de flies off her wid de fan, gets her drink and sich, goes places fo' to get things fo' her. When she am ready to go to sleep, eber night, Ise rub her feet." From Annie's head to her toes, Jennie "sho tend to Missy." Jennie undoubtedly had to learn how to perform many of the tasks that her mistress asked her to perform. Conversely, her mistress had to develop some important skills too. Above all, Annie had to learn how to be a mistress and she thought very self-consciously about what kind of slaveowner she would be. Jennie often heard her young mistress say "Ise sho an goin' to take care ob my nigger." And by Jennie's measure, "She sho did."[12]

For white girls newly inducted into slaveowning communities, "the plantation was a school" where they learned how to be propertied women. Ownership and control went hand-in-hand within the context of slavery such that developing adeptness in techniques of management and discipline was an important aspect of white girls' development as slaveowning mistresses. Their parents taught them about the principles of slaveownership and they learned vicariously through their parents' continued engagement with enslaved people in their midst. Slaveowning parents also allowed their daughters to assume the roles of instructors and disciplinarians very early on.[13]

One of the most significant, yet seemingly innocuous, methods that white parents used to teach their daughters how to be slaveowners began when they compelled enslaved people to recognize them as such. Immediately upon the birth of their children, slaveowning parents forced enslaved people to use the salutations "master" and "mistress." Enslaved children began to learn this lesson very early and the process continued over the course of their childhoods. A formerly enslaved woman remembered such a lesson which took place shortly after she was purchased at auction and brought to her new owners' home as a little girl: "When we got to the house, my mistress came out with a baby in her arm and said, 'Well, here's my little nigger. Shake hands with me.' Then he [her master] come up and said, 'Speak to your young mistress,' and I said, 'Where she at?'

He said, 'Right there,' and I said, 'No, I don't see no young mistress, that's a baby.'"[14] Savilla Burell's owners taught her "to call chillum three years old Young Marster, and say Missie." Another formerly enslaved person recalled that "[w]hen your marster had a baby born in his family they would call all the niggers and tell them to come in and 'see your new marster.' We had to call them babies 'Mr.' and 'Miss,' too."[15]

Slaveowners' objective in requiring this kind of deference was simple. They wanted enslaved people to recognize the power their children possessed over them, even at the time of their birth. Enslaved people understood this too. George Womble asserted that his owner wanted the slaves he owned to hold "him and his family in awe" and at the birth of new members of his family, enslaved people were compelled to "go and pay their respects to the newly born white children on the day after their birth. At such time they were required to get in line outside of the door and then one by one they went through the room and bowed their heads as they passed the bed and uttered 'Young Marster' or if the baby was a girl they said: 'Young Mistress'."[16]

Enslaved people paid a high cost if they failed to use the required salutations. Rebecca Jane Grant either could not or would not call her mistress's young son "Marster." One day, Rebecca's mistress wrote a note and asked her to deliver it to the clerk employed at the shop of a local storekeeper. The clerk prepared a package in accordance with the note's instructions and gave it to Rebecca to deliver to her mistress. When she returned, she quickly learned what was inside: "a cowhide strap about two feet long." Her mistress immediately pulled the whip out of the package and began to beat Rebecca. She did not know why her mistress was beating her until she exclaimed: "You can't say 'Marster Henry.' Miss?" Needless to say, Rebecca quickly responded: "Yes'm. Yes'm. I can say 'Marster Henry!'" She bitterly remarked to her interviewer: "Marster Henry was just a little boy about three or four years old. . . . [She] [w]anted me to say 'Marster' to him—a baby!"[17] When another formerly enslaved woman forgot to refer her mistress's eight- or nine-month-old daughter as "miss," her mistress put her "in a stock and beat" her. While she was in the stocks, the woman twisted her leg so that it broke. In spite of the excruciating pain that would likely come as a result of such an injury, her mistress continued to beat her until she was satisfied.[18] Teaching enslaved children to call their owner's offspring "master" or "mistress" also served to educate white slaveowning children in two significant ways; it taught them about the deference that all African-Americans, regardless of age, must show them, and it served to underscore their own superiority.

Slaveowners' daughters often grew up alongside enslaved children as playmates and companions; but these future slaveowners eventually came to realize that the African-American children they shared their days with were far more than that.[19] They came to know that these African-American children were their property and they treated them as such. White girls and the enslaved people around them underwent a mutual process of training, and both groups acquired knowledge about the differences between them. When Betty Cofer was born, her master's daughter Ella was only a little girl, but she nevertheless understood that this enslaved infant would live a life that was very different from her own. Ella "claimed" Betty as her slave shortly after her birth, and afterward they "played together an' grew up together." Betty became Ella's personal servant, waiting on her, standing behind her chair during meal times, and sleeping beside her on the bedroom floor.[20]

At age three, newly arrived in Georgia after having spent her earlier years in Britain, Sarah Kemble quickly grasped the distinction between slavery and freedom and some of the privileges accorded to those who were not in bondage. Sarah was the daughter of Pierce Mease Butler, scion of a wealthy Georgia white family, and famed actress-turned-writer Frances Anne Kemble. Kemble recorded an exchange between the young Sarah and Mary, an enslaved chambermaid who was charged with her care, in which Sarah told Mary that "some persons are free and some are not." She established her unbound status by saying, "I am a free person." She paused and waited for a reply. When she did not get one, she repeated her assertion: "I say, I am a free person, Mary—do you know that?" Finally, her chambermaid responded, "Yes, missis." And the little girl continued, "Some persons are free and some are not—do you know that, Mary?" And again Mary replied, but this time with her own understanding of the subject: "Yes, missis, *here* . . . I know it is so here, in this world." New to the plantation setting, Butler's and Kemble's daughter was discovering and understanding a fundamental distinction between herself and the woman her father owned, and she sought to communicate and reinforce that difference to her enslaved chambermaid. In this brief conversation, she drew the line between free and unfree; between the powerful and the disempowered. She placed herself on one side of it, ensured that Mary knew she was on the other, and implied that Mary must cross it.[21]

Slaveowning girls also made their ability to claim other human beings as their own property thoroughly clear in their conversations with the enslaved people they owned. Sylvia Watkins said that her "young missis . . . allus called me her little nig." Neal Upson's mistress similarly referred to him as her "little nigger."[22] A formerly enslaved woman named Melinda recalled that her young mistress would frequently tell her "when I get big and get married to a prince, you come with me and 'tend all my chilens." When her young mistress grew up and later married Honoré Dufour, she did indeed take Melinda with her as she and her husband established their new household.[23] As little girls, privileged southerners imagined how enslaved people would fit into their lives, not as playmates or companions, but as property. And when they were old enough, they made those fantasies real.

Young white girls began to practice different management and disciplinary strategies and techniques with the enslaved people they owned, and this helped them develop and refine the skills of slave mastery they would need once they became mistresses of their own households. Most white slaveowning women were also mothers, and many of them taught their children about different strategies for slave management and discipline. Tines Kendrick's mistress owned all of the slaves and the land, and she was determined to manage her estate as she saw fit without her husband's interference. As a consequence, Tines said that her mistress's husband Arch, "didn't have much to say 'bout de runnin' of de place or de' handlin' of de niggers." Tines's mistress enlisted her son's help instead, and she taught him everything he knew about effectively operating a large estate and cruelly managing the slaves who worked it. Tines recalled that he "got all he meanness from old mis' an' he sure got plenty of it too."[24]

Lewis Cartwright refused to be whipped without a fight, and in a bizarre role reversal,

his master asked his own mother to whip Lewis. Every time he tried to whip Lewis, he would fight him so much that he would have to stop. Constantly defeated, he began to have his mother whip Lewis because he knew that Lewis would not dare hit a white woman.[25] This may have been so, but it is quite possible that she was a more effective master, and her ability to command obedience from Lewis and other slaves reflected that.

On occasion, slaveowning mothers and daughters disciplined enslaved people together, bringing about trauma and disfigurement when they did. This is what happened to Henrietta King when she stole and ate a piece of her mistress's candy because she was hungry. Her mistress kept the people who labored in her home in a constant state of near starvation. When Henrietta was about eight or nine years of age, she was responsible for emptying her owners' chamberpots, and when she went to collect the pot in her mistress's room each morning she began to notice a piece of candy on the washstand. She knew her mistress left it there as a test to see if she would take it, and at first she resisted. But after several days Henrietta could no longer resist. One day, her mistress noticed that the candy was gone and questioned Henrietta about taking it. When she denied stealing it, her mistress commenced whipping her. Henrietta refused to remain still, so her mistress grabbed her by the legs and pinned her head under the rocker of her chair while her young daughter whipped Henrietta. For approximately an hour, her mistress rocked back and forth on Henrietta's head while her daughter beat her with a cowhide.

The beating crushed the bones in the left side of Henrietta's jaw, so much so that she could not open her mouth. The left side of her mouth constantly slid to the right side. Her mistress called a doctor in to examine her, and he determined that nothing could be done. Her face was irreparably damaged. After her mistress reckoned with what she had done, she would sit around and stare at Henrietta while she completed her tasks about the house. She never brutalized her again. But Henrietta and her disfigurement were disquieting, and so the decision was made to give her to a female cousin, who treated her kindly.

This one act of brutality profoundly affected Henrietta for the rest of her life. Because she could not chew, she was forced to consume "liquid, stews, an' soup." The teeth on the left side of her face never grew back. When children saw her disfigured face, they either laughed or cried. Adults would stare at her "wonderin' what debbil got in an' made [her] born dis way." Henrietta also had to contend with encounters with her mistress's descendants who apparently knew what happened to her. On one occasion, when she saw her former mistress's granddaughter in town, the young woman was so ashamed that she crossed the street and pretended that she did not see her.[26]

Not all slaveowning women endorsed the use of brutality against their slaves. As young girls practiced disciplinary and management techniques upon their slaves, slaveowning mothers might correct their children when they used tactics that displeased them. When Elsie Cottrell saw her daughter Martha abusing an enslaved adolescent, she interrupted her and said "Don't you know you will never have a nigger with any sense if you bump der heads against de wall?" Looking back on these events, her former slave Henry Gibbs believed that his mistress's daughter engaged in this practice because "[s]he was young and didn't know no better." But her mother wanted her to hone her methods of slave mastery in ways that preserved enslaved people's usefulness in the long run. As she acquired and refined this skill set, her mother molded and shaped her, making sure that she was equipped to manage, control and retain her human property for as long as possible and keep them in functional condition to labor for her, over her lifetime.[27]

Many women found their children to be agreeable pupils who easily absorbed their lessons in slave mastery; but others clashed with them over proper strategies for management and discipline. Mary Armstrong's mother belonged to a couple that she described as "the meanest two white folks what ever lived"; but in Mary's estimation, her mother's mistress was particularly cruel. "Old Polly" was the "devil if there ever was one," a woman who beat Mary's nine-month-old sister to death because she would not stop crying. Polly's daughter Olivia eventually came to own Mary. During one visit to Olivia's marital home, Polly tried to beat ten-year-old Mary. The enslaved woman retaliated by picking up "a rock 'bout as big as half your fist an' hit[ting] her right in the eye." Mary "busted the eyeball an' told her that was for whippin' my baby sister to death." When Mary told her young mistress what she had done to her mother, her mistress said,

"Well, I guess mamma has learnt her lesson at last." After years of watching her mother abuse and, in at least one case, murder the family's slaves, Olivia chose a different approach to managing the people she came to own as an adult. Although Mary described Olivia's parents as mean and cruel, she characterized Olivia in a starkly different way: "she was kind to everyone, an' everyone jes' love her." More profoundly, Olivia allowed Mary to defend herself against her own mother, something that may have created tension between them and altered their relationship thereafter.[28]

Of course, not all young slaveowning women diverged so significantly from the systems of management and discipline their mothers used. Some employed the same tactics, only milder in intensity. As Jennie Brown prepared for her upcoming marriage, her parents gave her a pick of their slaves. Elizabeth Sparks was among the ones she chose. Elizabeth was deeply relieved when Jennie selected her because she was "a good woman" who would "slap an' beat yer once in a while but she warn't no woman fur fighting fussin' an' beatin' yer all day." Jennie's mother was far more severe in the forms of punishment she used, beating slaves "with a broom or a leather strap or anythin' she'd git her hands on," without legitimate cause. Mistress Brown would also make Elizabeth's Aunt Caroline knit all day and well into the night, and if she dozed or if her body became limp as she drifted off into sleep, Jennie's mother would "come down across her haid [head] with a switch." Although Elizabeth clearly thought she could withstand her young mistress's disciplinary tactics, she suggested that it was only because she was still young and would have to learn how to be as brutal as her mother, something that would happen with age.[29]

As they learned how to be mistresses, white girls also trained enslaved people how to be the kind of servants that they would need later on. When Ellen Thomas and her mistress Cornelia Kimball were just young girls, Cornelia taught Ellen "the arts of good housekeeping, including fine sewing." Her training also involved being "blindfolded and then told to go through the motions of serving" so that she could "learn to do so without disturbing anything on the table."[30] Nancy Thomas recalled that she "was de special little girl fo' Mistress Harriett's daughter. Her name was Palonia. Even durin' dem days I would sew and knit. I had a little three-legged stool and I'd set it between Palony's legs, while she was settin' down. Den she'd watch me when I knitted. If I done somethin' wrong, she'd pinch my ear a little and say, 'Yo' dropped a stitch, Nannie.'"[31] As Nancy Thomas's testimony shows, Palonia was a mistress-in-the-making, responsible for overseeing Nancy's production and disciplining her when it diminished in quality. Palonia learned that Nancy was under her command and that as her "special little girl" she possessed the power to have Nancy do whatever she desired.

To be sure, enslaved people sometimes developed caring and loving relationships with their young owners. But no matter how amicable relations between young white girls and enslaved people may have been, these young slaveowners frequently articulated and exercised their power over them as mistresses-in-the-making. Some of these young girls and women enthusiastically assumed their roles as mistresses early in life, and some exhibited signs that they might evolve into brutal ones. When an unidentified woman spoke of the cruelties she suffered at the hands of her adult mistress, she included a telling account of similar suffering meted out by her mistress's daughter: "When we was little, she used to whip us and then make us kiss the switch. She was the meanest of the daughters."[32] As she interacted with the enslaved people around her, this young white girl was following her mother's footsteps of cruelty very closely.

What did it mean to young white girls to be given human beings as their own property or to expect to receive them during the course of their lives? How did witnessing slave punishments or hearing conversations about the value of enslaved human beings affect the relationships they cultivated with these individuals and to the institution as they matured? As the recollections and accounts above suggest, young white girls came to realize very early on that they could own and control other human beings. The ability to do so was integral to their identities as young white women in the slaveholding South.

Through wealth transfers from parents to daughters, white girls throughout the South became transformed. They were no longer just children who lived in southern households and communities filled with enslaved people who made a certain kind of lifestyle possible.

When their parents gave them enslaved people, they became slaveowners. Over the course of their lives, they grew up alongside the slaves they owned. In the process, they learned valuable lessons about the importance of owning property, how to be effective slaveowners, and when, if and how others would be involved with any aspect of their wealth in slaves.

When young slaveowning women married their husbands, they brought their slaves, and their ideas about how to control and manage them, into their new households with them. Yet few historians who explore the lives of married white women in the South focus on those who owned slaves. This tendency has much to do with prevailing assumptions about the ways that laws pertaining to marriage and property created legal and economic disabilities for married women. Coverture, for example, was a doctrine which stated that married women's legal and economic identities were subsumed into their husbands' upon marriage. During the period of coverture, married women's property and wages fell within the purview of their husbands' control. Furthermore, married women could not conduct legal or financial business in their own names, or without their husbands' consent. While coverture adversely impacted many women's lives, scholars discount the ways that kinship and communal networks, as well as the lifetime socialization of white girls in mastery and principles of slaveownership shaped the adult lives of others, their relationships with their spouses, and their decisions to circumvent the disabilities that coverture imposed.[33]

White parents raised their daughters with particular expectations related to owning slaves and, as a consequence, many of these women did not feel compelled to relinquish control over their slaves to spouses and male kin once they married. Instead, marriage marked a point at which their identities as slaveowners were fully realized, and many of them sought to manage and "master" their slaves, too. More profoundly, white slaveowning women's propertied status often formed the seed of marital conflicts, and their economic ties to slavery frequently influenced the internal order of their households and shaped their interactions with individuals beyond them.

In spite of the constraints of formal property laws, slaveowning women cultivated relationships of power with their slaves and found legal and extra-legal ways to protect their property from those who jeopardized their ability to control it. Women used various legal mechanisms such as separate estates, marital settlements, and separations in property to maintain control of their slaves before and after they married. But even slaveowning women who didn't secure control over their property with these mechanisms conducted themselves in ways that challenge scholars' assumptions about the sanctity of southern legal institutions and laws. The knowledge and skills that white females acquired as young people prepared them for these kinds of negotiations, challenges and conflicts. They valiantly fought to preserve their investments in slavery, and their former slaves tell us that in many cases, they were victorious. What is more, individuals in their communities routinely recognized and respected these women's choices.

NOTES

1. John A. Burwell ALS to Elizabeth T. Guy, Lynesville, N.C., April 30, 1847, Burwell-Guy Family Papers, William L. Clements Library, University of Michigan, Ann Arbor.

2. Jane Censer Turner, *North Carolina Planters and Their Children, 1800–1860* (Baton Rouge: Louisiana University Press, 1984), 105.

3. Rosalie Calvert to Henri J. Stier, November 9, 1817, in *Mistress of Riversdale: The Plantation Letters of Rosalie Stier Calvert, 1795–1821* (Baltimore: Johns Hopkins University Press, 1991), 325. Discussion of George Calvert's demand that his daughter Eugenia devise a marriage contract prior to receiving her inheritance appears on page 378.

4. Marylynn Salmon, *Women and the Law of Property in Early America* (Chapel Hill: University of North Carolina Press, 1986), 142, 158; Cara Anzilotti, *In the Affairs of the World: Women, Patriarchy, and Power in Colonial South Carolina* (Westport, Conn.: Greenwood Press, 2002), 74, 143; Turner, *North Carolina Planters and Their Children*, 107; Carole Shammas, *The History of Household Government in America* (Charlottesville: University of Virginia Press, 2002), 72.

5. Interviews with Bacchus White, in Charles L. Purdue, Thomas E. Barden, and Robert K. Phillips, eds., *Weevils in the Wheat: Interviews With Virginia Ex-Slaves* (Charlottesville: University of Virginia Press, 1976), 303; Interview with Agnes James, WPA Slave Narrative Project, South Carolina Narratives, Vol. XIV, Part 3, 8, *Born in Slavery: Slave Narratives from the Federal Writers' Project, 1936–1938*, http://memory.loc.gov/ammem/snhtml [hereafter cited as *Born in Slavery*]; Interview with Cornelia Winfield, WPA Slave Narrative Project, Georgia Narratives, Vol. IV, Part 4, 177, ibid.

6. Interview with "Uncle" Fil Hancock, WPA Slave Narrative Project, Missouri Narratives, Vol. 10, 148, *Born in Slavery*; Interview with Charity Bowery, in *Slave Testimony: Two Centuries of Letters, Speeches, Interview, and Autobiographies*, ed. John Blassingame (Baton Rouge: Louisiana State University Press,

1977), 261–67; Frederic Bancroft, *Slave Trading in the Old South* (Columbia: University of South Carolina Press, 1996; orig. pub. 1931), 292 (emphasis in original).

7. Interview with Amy Perry, WPA Slave Narrative Project, South Carolina Narratives, Vol. XIV, Part 3, *Born in Slavery*. I find that the phrase "daily gift" was peculiar to those raised in South Carolina and was used to refer to the gifting of slaves from a slaveowning parent to a child. For other examples, see interviews with Amos Gadsden and Jane Hollins, WPA Slave Narrative Project, South Carolina Narratives, Vol. XIV, Part 9, 291, *Born in Slavery*.

8. This method of property transferal was not legally binding without more formal documentation to support it, and some women learned this the hard way. See for example, *Goodwin v. Morgan*, 1 Stewart 278, January 1828, Ala.; *Irwin v. Morell*, Dudl. Ga. 72, July 1831; and *Carter v. Buchannon*, 3 Ga. 513, November 1847, in Helen Tunnicliff Catterall, ed., *Judicial Cases Concerning American Slavery and the Negro*, Vol. 3: *Cases from the Courts of Georgia, Florida, Alabama, Mississippi, and Louisiana* (New York: Octagon Books, 1968; orig. pub. 1932), 14, 18.

9. Interview with Ora M. Flagg, WPA Slave Narrative Project, North Carolina Narratives, Vol. XI, Part 1, 308, *Born in Slavery*.

10. Interview with unidentified enslaved person, *Unwritten History of Slavery: Autobiographical Accounts of Negro Ex-Slaves* (Nashville: Fisk University Social Science Institute, 1945), 117.

11. Interview with Sallie Crane, WPA Slave Narrative Project, Arkansas Narratives, Vol. II, Part 2, *Born in Slavery*.

12. Interview with Jennie Fitts, in *The American Slave: A Composite Autobiography, Supplement, Series 2*, Vol. 4: *Texas Narratives, Part 3*, ed. George P. Rawick (Westport, Conn.: Greenwood Press, 1979), 1351–2, digitized in *The African American Experience* (Greenwood Publishing Group). http://aae.greenwood.com/doc.aspx?fileID=RSW1&chapterID=RSW1-007-042&path=/primarydocenc/greenwood//.); this series is hereafter cited as *The American Slave*.

13. Ulrich B. Phillips, *Life and Labor in the Old South* (Boston: Little, Brown, 1929), 198–99.

14. Interview with unidentified formerly enslaved woman, in *Unwritten History*, 263.

15. Interviews with unidentified formerly enslaved person, *Unwritten History*, 150; and Savilla Burrell, *Before Freedom When I Just Can Remember*, ed. Belinda Hurmence (Winston-Salem: John F. Blair, 1989), 133.

16. Interview with George Womble, WPA Slave Narrative Project, Georgia Narratives, Volume IV, Part 4, 191, *Born in Slavery*.

17. Interview with Rebecca Jane Grant, in *Before Freedom When I Just Can Remember*, 57.

18. Interview with unidentified former slave, "Mistreatment of Slaves," WPA Slave Narrative Project, Georgia Narratives, Volume IV, Part 4, 303, *Born in Slavery*.

19. Nell Irvin Painter argues that white children often found themselves in situations under which they had to identify with either the enslaved or the enslaver. Furthermore, she argues that young girls often identified with slaves while young boys identified with slaveowners. See Painter, "Soul Murder and Slavery: Toward a Full Loaded Cost

Accounting," in *Southern History Across the Color Line* (Chapel Hill: University of North Carolina Press, 2002), 34–35. In my own research, while I found some cases that support Painter's assertion, many white slaveowning women did not identify with the slaves they owned.

20. Interview with Betty Cofer, WPA Slave Narrative Project, North Carolina Narratives, Volume XI, Part 1, 168, *Born in Slavery*.

21. Frances Anne Kemble, *Journal of a Residence on a Georgian Plantation, 1838–1839* (New York: Harper and Brothers, 1864), 22. Kemble was an actress, writer, and abolitionist whose publication of letters she wrote to Elizabeth Sedgwick caused an uproar in the United States and abroad. She deplored the institution of slavery and hoped that she could persuade her slaveowning husband that the system was wrong. He, on the other hand, hoped that Fanny's time on his plantation in Georgia would change her mind about slavery's injustice. With Kemble on one side of the slavery issue and Butler on the other, the couple soon separated and divorced. Butler retained custody of his two daughters until they reached twenty-one years old. Fanny and Pierce's youngest daughter, Frances Butler Leigh, became a staunch supporter of the Confederacy while their eldest Sarah supported the Union. One can only wonder whether Sarah's encounter with Mary shaped her stance on slavery in any way.

22. Interview with Sylvia Watkins, WPA Slave Narrative Project, Tennessee Narratives, Vol. XV, 76; interview with Neal Upson, Georgia Narratives, Vol. IV, Part 4, 55, *Born in Slavery*.

23. Interview with Melinda, *Mother Wit: The Ex-Slave Narratives of the Louisiana Writer's Project*, ed.

Ronnie Clayton (New York: Peter Lang, 1990), 167–68.

24. Interview with Tines Kendricks, WPA Slave Narrative Project, Arkansas Narratives, Vol. II, Part 4, 178–79, *Born in Slavery*.

25. Interview with J. L. Smith, WPA Slave Narrative Project, Arkansas Narratives, Vol, II, Part 6, 199, *Born in Slavery*.

26. Interview with Henrietta King, in *Weevils in the Wheat*, 190–92.

27. Interview with Henry Gibbs, *The American Slave, Supplement, Series 1*, vol. 8: *Mississippi Narratives*, 815.

28. Interview with Mary Armstrong, WPA Slave Narrative Project, Texas Narratives, vol. 16, Part 1, 25–27, *Born in Slavery*.

29. Interview with Elizabeth Sparks, WPA Slave Narrative Project, Virginia Narratives, Vol. XVII, 50–52, *Born in Slavery*.

30. Interview with Ellen Thomas, WPA Slave Narrative Project, Alabama Narratives, Vol. I, 376–77, *Born in Slavery*.

31. Interview with Nancy Thomas, in *The American Slave, Supplement, Series 2,* Vol. 9: *Texas Narratives, Part 8*, 3810.

32. Interview with unidentified formerly enslaved woman, in *Unwritten History of Slavery*, 279–80.

33. I explore these aspects of white slaveowning women's mastery in my forthcoming book manuscript, *Lady Flesh Stealers, Female Soul Drivers, and She-Merchants: White Women and the Economy of American Slavery*.

THAVOLIA GLYMPH

Women in Slavery: The Gender of Violence

The stereotypes of the gentle southern lady and the nurturing black "mammy" have long been a part of American stories and folklore. They figured in "Gone With the Wind," the epic film of 1939 which won ten academy awards, among them Best Supporting Actress to Hattie McDaniel, the first African American to win an Oscar. (McDaniel disapproved of the script but famously observed that she would "rather make seven hundred dollars a week playing a maid than seven dollars a week being one.") These stubborn stereotypes live on in our culture: where do you see them?*

*Molly Haskell, *Frankly, My Dear: Gone With the Wind Revisited* (New Haven, Conn.: Yale University Press, 2010), pp. 213–14. For the persistence of the mammy figure, see Michele McElya, *Clinging to Mammy: The Faithful Slave in Twentieth-Century America* (Cambridge, Mass.: Harvard University Press, 2007).

Excerpted from introduction and chs. 1 and 2 of *Out of the House of Bondage: The Transformation of the Plantation Household* by Thavolia Glymph (New York: Cambridge University Press, 2008). Reprinted by permission of the author and publisher. Notes have been edited and renumbered.

The lived experience of mistresses and their enslaved servants rarely matched the stereotype. Thavolia Glymph examines the oral histories of formerly enslaved men and women, court records, and the correspondence of slaveholders to document a society soaked in a culture of terror. She insists that we acknowledge what even many feminist historians have failed to see: privileged, white women were perpetrators of violence in routine fashion. In her essay in this volume, Jones-Rogers has shown how girls in slaveholding families learned to be powerful mistresses, whose untrammeled exercise of power, Glymph argues, "helped define their place in the world of slavery."

What are your responses to Glymph's question: "What did it mean to be a southern woman?"

"The word *home* has died upon my lips." Writing to her son late June 1865, Mary Jones summed up one outcome of the Civil War. Decades later, Katie Rowe remembered another. "It was de fourth day of June in 1865 I begins to live."[1] Without slaves to do the work of her home, Jones's world, her home, was dead. In that death, Katie Rowe saw life and a future to claim as her own. As a former mistress and a former slave, Jones and Rowe stood opposite each other in 1865. Once connected by the institution of slavery, they now faced a common task: to build new lives on the ground of freedom. Both were transformed. . . .

The story properly begins before the war, when enslaved and slaveholding women related to each other on the ground of slavery. For Mrs. Jones, the home that died was, whatever else, a workplace. Enslaved women mopped its floors, dusted its mahogany tables, made its beds, ironed, wet-nursed, and bathed and powdered their owners. In its yard and outbuildings—from kitchens, smokehouses, loom and weaving houses to spring and ice houses, wood sheds, dairies, and chicken houses—enslaved women scoured dishes, made biscuits and pies from scratch, churned butter, turned vegetables cultivated in gardens they worked and freshly-killed chickens into breakfast, supper, and evening meals, and fruits into jams and jellies. They washed damask tablecloths and every piece of clothing their owners wore, raised and fattened the poultry, and fetched wood.[2] They were expected to do these things in silence and reverence, barefooted and ill-clothed.[3] These expectations formed part of the legitimized violence to which they were subjected. The story ends with a transformed plantation household and the emergence of free black and white homes. In the transformed plantation household, former mistresses could no longer command labor or deference. In the new black homes, black women found some privacy and the space to live fuller lives. . . .

Historians have noticed and taken account of violence against slaves in the cotton, rice, sugar, and tobacco fields. Here it is easier to "see" because it took place in a "public" arena where cash crops were produced and came principally from the hands of men—masters, overseers, and slave drivers. Violence and power in the great house, the female side of domination, have not received nearly the commensurate attention. This neglect stems in part from the fact that violence in the household took place within a supposed private domain and came from the hands of women. We must remember that the plantation household was also a workplace, not a haven from the economic world, that it was not private or made so by the nature of the labor performed within it or the sex of the managers.

Home as a political figure and space comes into focus only when a key misconception is set aside: that the household is a private space. Once the public character of the plantation household comes into full view, so, too, does . . . a second misconception, that plantation mistresses wielded little or no power. Nothing could be further from the truth, which comes into focus when we notice that male dominance was not the controlling force within the plantation household. A third misconception interprets the aspirations and actions of black women on the basis of assumptions and questions that have framed the writing of the history of white women. Distinctions between modes of power are diminished. The fact that black and white women experienced different, and particular, modes of power within the plantation household becomes less visible. Just as plantation mistresses can be misconceived as more different than masters than the evidence shows, slave women can be misconceived as more like mistresses than the evidence shows.

If the authority of planter women is defined by the restrictions, legal and customary, imposed by white male authority, their power and violence disappear. On this view, the plantation household held freedom only for its male "white head."[4] Nothing bars the absurd conclusion that Mary Jones and Katie Rowe were equals by virtue of their femaleness. Indeed some scholars have challenged the idea of the southern lady that animated post–Civil War reminiscences, Lost Cause propaganda, and most historical studies prior to the mid-twentieth century. But their portrait generally depicts planter women as a silent abolitionist constituency and still, thus, as potent allies of slaves, and slave women in particular. Here were hardworking women so handicapped by patriarchy and paternalism that their lives more closely resembled those of enslaved women than the white men who were their fathers, husbands, and brothers; here were women who found in their own subjection the basis for an alliance with enslaved women.[5] Slaves rarely thought this. . . .

White women . . . owned slaves and managed households in which they held the power of . . . life and death, and the importance of those facts for southern women's identity—black and white—[was] enormous. In the antebellum period, white women were clearly subordinate in fundamental ways to white men, but far from being victims of the slave system, they dominated slaves.[6] . . . [My focus is] the female face of slave owners' power. . . . Once we acknowledge that white women wielded the power of slave ownership, then our culture's fascination with slavery's and mistresses' seeming elegance and "veneer of manners" becomes visible as a dodge and can be cleared away. Not only did white women's violence, and their ownership and management of slaves make it impossible for black people to see them as ideal models of a "kind and gentle womanhood," but they resulted in specific practices of resistance. . . . Contrary to most interpretations, violence on the part of white women was integral to the making of slavery, crucial to shaping black and white women's understanding of what it meant to be female, and no more defensible than masters'

violence. At the same time, white women's violence contradicted prevailing conceptions of white womanhood—and still does.

. . . [This work explores] the interplay of notions of domesticity and ideologies of race and slavery within the plantation household. Slaveholding women were called on to make their homes and themselves models of domestic virtue but depended on the work of slave women to accomplish these objectives. Southern prescriptive ideals asked them to "play the lady" *and* to be "domestic manager," and judged them according to both yardsticks. Accomplishing this required that they be both submissive and dominant. Their manners had to be perfect and their households had to demonstrate attention to order, punctuality, and economy. Failure threatened their status as ladies and the institution of slavery.

Success, in turn, depended on the cooperation of black women who notoriously refused to play their part. The ideology of domesticity required enslaved women to work for the plantation household as if their own interests were involved. Their failure to do so made it hard for mistresses to meet the emerging standards of domesticity. Mistresses couched black women's noncooperation as a refusal to be "better girls," in terms that suggested innate backwardness. This, not discontent under slavery, made them unalterably inefficient, slothful, and dirty. This was the source of their "misbehavior" and could be used to explain mistresses's violent responses and their inability to create the ideal domestic home, to be "better girls" themselves. Violence against enslaved women was thus justified. The disjuncture between these views and the fact that beds got made, meals cooked, clothes washed and ironing done, floors scrubbed, babies nursed, beds turned back, jams made, flies swatted, and much more is glaring but not unexplainable. In the end, black women's noncooperation defined and marked the failure of southern domesticity and simultaneously the defeat of its accomplice, the ideology of a gentle and noble white womanhood. . . .

Now, Missus Hodges studied 'bout meanness more'n [her husband] Wash [Hodges] done. She was mean to anybody she could lay her hands to, but special mean to me. She beat me and used to tie my hands and make me lie flat on the floor and she put snuff in my eyes. I ain't lyin' 'fore Gawd when I say I know that's why I went blind.[7]

. . . [Lulu] Wilson's description of [Mrs. Hodges] is the virtual antithesis of the paradigmatic good mistress with whom we have become so familiar. The "good" mistress dedicated her life to the never-ending task of managing her household and caring for her family and slaves in sickness and in health. Her comeliness was due in no small measure to her ability to satisfy all who depended on her, to manage a household rent by inequalities of race and gender with seeming equanimity. This ability was taught, of course, but it was also believed to be inherent in the very nature of white women, "racially naturalized," in today's shorthand. According to Kathleen Boone Samuels, "We were taught to speak very low and to be delicate in our ways." The mistress, as Maria Bryan put it, was a lady of delicacy and unmatched "gracefulness," as compared to the not-to-be envied "precision and primness of a northern fine lady, erect and stiff."[8]

. . . There have been other powerful and influential ideals of American womanhood but, arguably, none as coveted and admired.[9] Juxtaposing the claims of this ideal against the violence to which Wilson . . . [and others] testified brings to fuller view the literal as well as grammatical antagonism in the conjoined usage of the adjectives "delicate" and "slaveholding." The power of the plantation mistress is exposed . . . when we realize that in the American South, as elsewhere, the "domestic realm [w]as a site of power for women." It was also and therefore a site of struggle *between* women. For in the American South, no less than in more traditionally hierarchical societies, "rank could overcome the handicap of gender."[10] . . .

The testimony of former slaves is replete with bitter memories of violent acts committed by mistresses. As [historian] Norrece T. Jones writes, slaveholding women were "depicted frequently [by slaves and ex-slaves] as the most stringent and sadistic of the manor born." He describes the plantation household as a "war zone" where "spilling milk, breaking dishes, and a variety of other kitchen peccadilloes could and often did trigger barbaric responses from slaveholders throughout South Carolina."[11] . . .

In the enduring story of the Old South, mistresses gently ran households and nurtured their families, black and white. That they nonetheless engaged in violent behavior has confronted many historians with the vexing problem of what to call mistresses' violence, and how to explain it.[12] . . .

Mistresses were not masters, true. But when women slaveholders acted in the affairs of the household, a great deal of evidence says that they acted on their own authority, and not simply as their husbands' representatives. A great deal of evidence suggests that when black women resisted the plantation household, they resisted the authority that mistresses exercised.[13] . . .

In general, a silence surrounds white women's contributions to the basic nature of slavery, its maintenance, and especially, one of its central tendencies, the maiming and destruction of black life. With the silence goes an apparent reticence to probe mistresses' participation in the abuse of power even though slave ownership conferred that power. . . . The great house, whether a six-columned mansion or a rude house of four rooms, was a space of slavery and, thus, of domination and subordination. . . .

. . . If, "in the heat of the moment a mistress might strike out with whatever was handy," she nonetheless had to be preconditioned to this kind of response. She lived in a world in which actions of this kind were accepted as understandable if not laudatory "slips." She also lived in a world that denied to her witnesses, particularly the slaves among them, the recourse to restrain or retaliate. And finally, she lived in a world that did not construe her actions as damaging to her reputation as *compos mentis*.

All societies recognize a continuum of violence and advocate distinctions between legitimate and illegitimate violence, criminal homicide and justifiable homicide, random violence and coordinated violence. The slave South was no different. . . . The ruling classes of slave societies resorted to large-scale violence and brutality only in the last analysis. Their day-to-day domination depended more on their slaves' knowledge that their mistresses and masters *could* kill them but also subject them to the constant experience of "normal" violence. Ria Sorrell's memory of the pretty cruelties to which she was subjected haunted her long after emancipation. Her mistress "would hide her baby's cap an' tell me to find it. If I couldn't fin' it, she whipped me."[14] This kind of gratuitously perverse mental cruelty, with physical violence, reveals normative behavior in slave societies. . . . Such occasional or spontaneous acts of violence can be said to be "premeditated" in the important sense that their randomness and, sometimes, unpredictability were far more effective reminders of what could happen than sustained predictable assaults would be, not least because it left, more often than not, valuable labor power standing, if subdued.

In the end, white women's agency has been profoundly underestimated.[15] While conceding that slaveholding women internalized the social values of the Old South and reaped the rewards of slave labor, historians have been less clear about the role mistresses played in the construction of these values and in disciplining slaves. By the outbreak of the Civil War, slaveholding women had become, in fact if not in law, central partners in slavery's maintenance and management, more solidly members of the ruling class in their own right despite whatever civil and social disabilities they suffered because they were not men. . . .

Slavery, Delia Garlic concluded, "wuz hell." And it was as much hell in the plantation household, where mistresses were principal perpetrators of violence, as it was in the cotton, tobacco, sugar, and rice fields. Violence permeated the plantation household, where the control and management of slaves required white women's active participation and authorized the exercise of brute or sadistic force. Mistresses became expert in the use of psychological and physical violence and, from their perch in the household, influenced the construction of antebellum slave society in its gender and racial dimensions.[16]

Hellish punishment did not require large transgressions. The young female slave whose mistress beat her like a dog also suffered for her inability to go up and down a wooden staircase noiselessly. Her mistress called her a "black bitch" and threatened to kill her for going up the stairs "like a horse." On another occasion, her mistress called her a "nappy-head bitch" and, though sick, mustered enough strength to "try to hit me." Maria White's mistress beat the slaves in her household whenever their work displeased her. Austin Steward's mistress was "continually finding fault" and "frequently punished slave children herself by striking them over the head with a heavy iron key, until the blood ran." And even when not doing violence, she threatened violence. She "always kept by her side when sitting in her room," a cowhide whip, expecting, one imagines, to always find occasion to use it.[17]

Sometimes the punishments of hell required no transgressions at all on the slaves'

part. One mistress used the occasion of instructing her children in spelling to beat a female slave. "At every word them chillum missed," Harriet Robinson remembered, "she gived me a lick 'cross the head for it." Sarah Carpenter Colbert told her interviewer that her former mistress whipped slaves on a regular every-morning schedule; Hannah Plummer told how Caroline Manly, the daughter-in-law of North Carolina Governor Charles Manly, whipped her mother "most every day, and about anything, sometimes stripping her to her waist before beating her with a carriage whip." Jacob Branch's mother received a whipping every wash day.[18] . . .

Mistresses' violence against slave women in the plantation household ran along a continuum: Bible-thumping threats of hell for disobedience, verbal abuse, pinches and slaps, severe beatings, burnings, and murder. Frederick Douglass described one victim as "pinched, kicked, cut and pecked to pieces," with "scars and blotches on her neck, head and shoulders." The weapons mistresses took up against slaves ran the gamut from brooms, tongs, irons, shovels, and their hands to whatever was most readily available. Some mistresses did not leave the matter of choice of weapons to chance. The cowhide whip is ubiquitous in the slave narratives. It sat beside mistresses as they read to their children, knitted, or as they sat and rocked in their chairs doing nothing, as Frederick Douglass observed of "the psalm-singing Mrs. Hamilton," whose mistreatment of two slave women was common knowledge in the white community:

> She used to sit in a large rocking chair near the middle of the room, with a heavy cowskin . . . and I speak within the truth when I say, that those girls seldom passed that chair, during the day, without a blow from that cowskin, either upon their bare arms or upon their shoulders. As they passed her, she would draw that cowskin and give them a blow, saying, *"Move faster, you black jip!"* and, again, *"Take that, you black jip!"* continuing, *"If you don't move faster, I will give you more."* Then the lady would go on, singing her sweet hymns, as though her *righteous* soul were singing for the holy realms of paradise.

The cowhide whip, usually about three feet long, made from dried, untanned oxhide, was a weapon designed to cut the flesh and draw blood. Douglass described it "as hard as a piece of well-seasoned live oak" and "elastic and springy." The latter characteristic drew from its design: The whip was tapered from the part held by the hand to a point at the end. Douglass thought it was a more fearsome weapon than the more legendary cat-'o-nine tails.[19] . . .

Mistresses sometimes coupled physical violence with psychological violence. Slave children in the white household were introduced to these practices from an early age. The same hands, tongs, and shovels used in violence against adults were applied to children. Madison Jefferson said that his mistress pulled his hair so hard it came out and pinched his ears so hard that they bled. In addition to abusing enslaved children herself, she forced them to abuse each other. She had them "get a basin of water, and scrub each others faces with a corn cob . . . they bled under the affliction." He thought she looked for excuses to find fault with their work and to beat them, and that she took voyeuristic pleasure in observing their pain. Some evidence also suggests that slave-holding women who beat their slaves and/or were beaten by their husbands, in turn, abused their own children. . . .[20]

A kind of warring intimacy characterized many of the conflicts between mistresses and slave women in the household. The vision of a mistress dragging a slave woman into her house, or of a mistress and a household slave coming to blows in the mistress's kitchen, suggests one of the reasons we need not only to rethink relations between mistresses and slaves in the white household (and the image of mistresses as "ladies"), but also the very notion of that household as a space of domesticity apart from the public world of labor and labor disputes. . . .

Some mistresses, of course, neither beat their slaves nor delegated the task to others, rejecting the use of physical violence, sometimes using psychological tactics instead, or whipping, "as de las thing." A Wake County, North Carolina, mistress punished slaves variously by sending them to bed without supper, working them at night, or forcing them to memorize scripture and poems. But in the end, even if "once in a coon's moon," she used the whip.[21]

Overall, in narratives where slaves make explicit comparisons, mistresses are depicted as harder and crueler than masters. Mistresses emerge from these narratives not only as the principal actors in the violence that took place in the household, but as instigators inciting masters to violence. John Rudd was certain his mistress pressed his master to cruelties, always "rilin' him up." Lucretia Heyward said that her master never whipped her but her mistress "cut my back w'en I don't do to suit her."[22]

Other slaves drew no such contrast between cruel masters and mistresses. According to Armaci Adams, they "was both hell cats." Yet, even in these mixed accounts, mistresses are named the more brutal and sadistic. Ria Sorrell's master whipped slaves, but Sorrell noted that he seemed to take no joy in it. Her mistress, on the other hand, was a "bad" person, "de pure debil," a woman who fed slaves as little as possible and "jist joyed whuppin' Negroes," especially when her husband was away. At such times, she "raised ole scratch wid de slaves."[23] . . .

Slavery gave mistresses the power to be hard and cruel in punishing and humiliating slaves, and the prerogative to be indifferent. It was the cruelty of indifference that Lucinda Hall Shaw specifically recalled. Hall knew neither where she was born nor who her parents were. As a child she lived on a small farm belonging to Reuben and Sara Humphries Hall along with three other slaves. Here she witnessed the fatal beating of a slave woman and the woman's burial on the spot where she had been tied to a post. She was then "jus' rolled" into a grave that "wuzn't nuthin but a hole in de groun." Decades later, the memory still gnawed at Shaw, for what happened next was, to her mind, as heinous as the beating. She recalled seeing something "shoveled in . . . dat I tho't I saw move." She immediately told her mistress who "tend lak she did't see nuthin' . . . she tol' me atterwards, dat de overseer whipped her so hard she birfed a baby."[24] . . .

Slave resistance sometimes arose in direct response to white women's abuse and in particular to the "nasty forms" it took.[25] The 1861 slave conspiracy at Second Creek, Mississippi, the record suggests, matured from just such circumstances. The testimony of the slaves called to explain why they had conspired to kill their owners is striking in this regard. The rebels had many grievances. The "whipping colored people would stop," for example. But one grievance stood out. The slave men stressed the abuse that their sisters, daughters, and wives had suffered at the hands of white women. The rebellion would rid their community of white women who "whips our children." They referred repeatedly to the water torture of a young female slave who was beaten and had water thrown on her by a group of young white women. For "drowning and beating Wesley's sister," they testified, the young women deserved to be punished. This, the slaves offered, explained the decision of Wesley and his father to join the conspiracy to overthrow slavery. . . .[26]

. . . Despite proslavery ideology, which held that slaves were members, albeit inferior ones, of one family, black and white, this notion could not be sustained where relations of slavery existed. Mistresses's management of household slaves made the distinction clear. . . .

Like slaveholding men, slaveholding women acknowledged the integral role of violence in the mediation and maintenance of slavery. . . . It is a record of the extraordinary recorded as ordinary, the ordinary language of power where "[e]xtreme acts of violence are depicted matter-of-factly because of their regularity." Lucille McCorckle penned just such an account: "Business negligently done & much altogether neglected, some disobedience, much idleness, sullenness, slovenliness. . . Used the rod."[27] Lizzie Neblett's account of how she handled a slave stands out for its banality. "I haven't even dressed Kate [a teenager] but once since you left," she informed her husband in a letter during the Civil War, "& then only a few cuts." One finds no sense of equivocation in either account, no suggestion of anything unusual. Nor does either account suggest that the women found punishing slaves particularly disagreeable or necessarily viewed it as men's work.[28] . . . There was a quality of ordinariness and a certain quality of casualness in the way mistresses talked about and meted out punishment. . . .

In admonishing daughters on proper etiquette, parents often used the occasion to provide instruction on the demeanor expected of slaveholding women in their relationships to slaves. The colonial Virginia patriarch, Colonel Daniel Parke, gave this advice to his daughter Lucy Parke: "Mind your writing and everything else you have learnt, and do not learn to romp, but behave yourself soberly and like a gentlewoman. Mind reading, and carry yourself so that everybody may respect you. Be calm and obliging to all the servants, and when you speak, do it mildly, even to the poorest slave." When she became the mistress of her own household, Lucy Parke ignored the advice.[29]

Upon her marriage to William Byrd II, Lucy Parke Byrd dominated her household in the ways her father had cautioned against. She used the lash (and other instruments) frequently and brutally. Her husband's objections ultimately carried no more weight than her father's admonitions. He, like her father, objected to the more brutal punishments she inflicted on slaves, especially women. He chastised her for burning a slave with a hot iron and beating her with tongs. . . . [Byrd] condemned his wife's brutality and her use of the lash when he thought she acted out of mean spiritedness, or when she exercised her authority in the presence of guests, just as he would have condemned a man of his class for like behavior. He did not, however, deny "her authority" to beat slaves in the absence of guests when he thought she was justified. Her determination "to show her authority before company" breached prevailing conventions and undermined "her authority" among the slaves. . . .[30]

Prescriptive literature that directly targeted mistresses sanctioned punishment from their hands but urged restraint. An article in the *Southern Planter* gave this advice to mistresses: "Never scold when a servant neglects his duty, but *always punish* him, no matter how mildly, for mild treatment is the best; severity hardens them. Be firm in this, that no neglect go unpunished. Never let a servant say to you, '*I forgot it.*' That sentence, so often used, is no excuse at all."[31] . . .

. . . Observing the systems of management available to their husbands and fathers, mistresses might easily have thought they were more vulnerable to clashes with slaves [that they could not win without help]. All but the smallest slaveholders used systems of management for crop production—overseers or slave drivers—which allowed them to get cash crops produced, and maintain a certain distance from their slaves. Charles Manigault had one of the most insulating systems. Manigault's factor, for example, oversaw the purchase and sale of slaves and supplies, and hired, fired, and oversaw the overseers, thereby providing Manigault with several layers of protection and distance from slaves. For elite men, the work of managing slaves was divided, parceled out to factors, overseers, drivers, and sons. This gave them an important advantage over mistresses. Slaveholding men might stroll, or invade, the slave quarters when they felt so inclined or ride out to check their fields, but those who had overseers and drivers were not required to so every day.[32] . . .

The distance that separated planters from intimate contact with their slaves was in other ways more often literal in comparison to that between mistresses and household slaves. Planters often spent months away from their plantations, and often from their town homes as well; their wives were much less mobile.[33] ... Unlike European aristocrats, to whom they often compared themselves, slaveholders generally did not hire butlers or white female managers, or use slaves as household managers. ...

By contrast, the work of mistresses was done at close quarters, on a daily and intimate basis. ... Mistresses could and often did call upon and rely on the authority of their husbands, brothers, and fathers for assistance in managing slaves, to help settle scores, real and imagined. Yet this resort to masculine authority carried its own drawbacks. It undercut their own claims to authority over slaves within the household, marking them as poor and inefficient managers of the domestic space.[34] ...

Memories of the injuries of enslavement stayed with black women, and their husbands and children into the twentieth century. Children born after emancipation were certainly not unaffected. Dave Lawson was born long after emancipation—his mother was only six months old herself in 1865. He grew up, however, with the knowledge of slavery passed on to him by others who had been enslaved. From them he learned, when he was "ole enough to lissn," about Luzanne, whipped "kaze she burnt de biscuits," and from Aunt Becky, why his grandmother and grandfather were hanged, both at the "same time an' from de same lim'" of an oak tree on a North Carolina plantation. The first time he heard the story he was unable to sleep for a week.[35]

Mandy Cooper left her story with her children. Like many parents, she found talking to her children about slavery difficult and put off doing so until they saw her back one day as she was bathing. She began to explain but the children "thought she was tellin' a big story," and made fun of her. Angry and pained, Mandy Cooper taught her children a lesson both unorthodox and painful. She had them strip to the waist, and struck each with a whip severe enough to draw blood. She finished her story and her son conveyed it to posterity in the 1930s.[36] ...

The narratives of ex-slaves (and slaveholders) are "evidence" of the process by which terror was created and sustained on southern plantations and mistresses' role in its production. Slaveholding women's exercise of power over slaves helped define their place in the world of slavery. And this was not contradicted by their own vulnerability to violent acts committed by slaveholding fathers or husbands.

The scandal caused when Eliza Bird's husband "struck her down in the street," meaning to kill her, doubtless escaped neither the ears nor eyes of slaves nor, likely, the attempt of a drunken Georgia planter to "split" his wife's "head open" and kill her. Lewis Wallace's master was an alcoholic. When intoxicated, Wallace recalled, he would "grab old Missus by de hair of her head an' drag her up an' down de long front gallery." A slave named Peggy witnessed Thomas Powell beat his wife with a horsewhip and tried to intervene. Slaves talked about the mistress who died in childbirth along with her unborn child following a beating at the hands of her husband and noted that it was not the first time he had assaulted her and done so *publicly*, before their eyes. The last time, he had chased her around the house as he beat her with a whip.[37] ...

A commonplace among slaveholders was that slaves saw and heard too much, about which they "talk too much." In these overheard conversations, and by way of neighborhood gossip and their own witness, slaves indeed saw, heard, and talked about masters who, forgetful of patriarchal standards, neglected their families, and committed adultery and other forms of spousal abuse.[38] ...

Ultimately, mistresses found no shelter behind the curtains of the great house, not from slaves, not from the larger white public of which they were a part. Mary Culbreath was raped by the husband of one of her friends. The incident, remarkably, went to court, publicizing Culbreath's plight far beyond her home and neighborhood, where it had already caused great "excitement." Among those who took special notice were other white women in her community. Gertrude Thomas worried that the court might free the accused "to desolate the life of some other woman." Thomas's concern addressed the vulnerability of white women under supposed patriarchal protection. Culbreath's "insulted virtue," Thomas argued, required the defense of chivalrous men. The accused rapist, however, skipped town to avoid jail, leaving his wife and her friend, the rape victim, to face the consequences of his actions: the shame he had brought to two families and the embarrassed financial circumstance in which he left his wife and three children. A court levy against his already heavily mortgaged property left them further embarrassed and homeless.[39]

Mistresses turned out of their homes due to the fecklessness of their husbands, or who were victims of abuse, indeed may have kindled the greatest sympathy from slaves. But slaves also would have observed that they were not, as slaves were, without all protection or bereft of all civic capacity or rights. Despite the rule of patriarchy—and importantly because of it—white women found a judicial system that offered them some protection from errant husbands and, often enough, sympathetic judges willing to grant it. "A wife ill used, beaten and driven from her home by her husband, is entitled to the protection of the court, and will be allowed alimony, or the income of a settled property, for her maintenance until her husband received her home and treats kindly," the Court of Chancery ruled in a case.[40] . . .

Even though white women were generally required to make a clear case of "ill usage" on the part of their husbands, and "correct conduct" on their own part, in order to obtain alimony or access to their homes, the courts sought to ensure women's financial security even when they could not provide this kind of definitive evidence. This was especially true in cases involving the planter elite. But magistrates made it clear that they were not happy to see cases arising from the elites come before them. They were not above lecturing elite litigants on the impropriety of public airings of their domestic disputes. The court's position reflected its concern for the potential damage such cases could have on the stability of class and race relations. Unsavory behavior undermined elite power and authority, so the courts urged the elite to adjudicate in private charges of incontinence, adultery, or battery. Chancellor James emphasized in one case "how important it is for married persons to control their tempers." The significance of the case before him, extended, he wrote, to the "respectability of the parties litigant," and "the example it is to offer to the community."[41] In the community of slaves, the damage was most often already

done. Patriarchy stood exposed in new ways. Yet sympathy for the plight of white women among slaves could still only be limited.

In the end, mistresses's use of violence manifested the regular demands and challenges of slaveholding. It drew upon the certain knowledge that they acted on their own rights. Although there might be rules about when, and before whom, they could exercise their power, not all mistresses felt obliged to follow them. The violence and humiliation that marked white women's treatment of enslaved women raised implacable barriers between them and tempered the very meaning of womanhood in the South. What did it mean to be a southern woman? How, out of the bramble of hate and terror, subjection and fear, did white and black women of the South construct and reconstruct their identities, their notions of what it meant to be female, their ideas about citizenship and freedom? For these endeavors, what did it mean that mistresses might have limited legal rights to divorce and could be beaten by masters, but that they could own slaves whom they could beat? Or, that enslaved women had hand-sawed-up backs or backs that looked like chokeberry trees? The antebellum South was a world, ultimately, that neither white nor black women could easily abide. Enslaved women, [historian Elizabeth] Fox-Genovese writes, understood "that power was no abstraction: It wore a white male face." Yet, it was also the case that the antebellum South was a place where power could wear a white female face. And that made the common vulnerability of black and white women to white male power distinctly different in operation and meaning. Slaves interpreted the abuse mistresses meted out as deliberate and calculated. But even if they thought it unpremeditated or "petulant," it is hard to imagine how they would come to the conclusion that white women were their allies or women to be emulated. A sobering verdict came in the case of *State v. Montgomery*. A husband and wife, master and mistress, were tried "for killing a slave by undue correction. The husband was acquitted, but the wife was convicted, and sentenced to pay the fine . . . \$214.28." As Frederick Douglass, who experienced violent and nonphysically violent mistresses, wrote: "To talk of *kindness* entering into the relation of slave and slaveholder is most absurd, wicked, and preposterous."[42]

Notes

1. Mary Jones to Charles C. Jones Jr., June 26, 1985 in *Children of Pride: A True Story of Georgia and the Civil War*, ed. Robert Manson Myers (New Haven, Conn.: Yale University Press, 1972), p. 1275. Katie Rowe in *The American Slave: A Composite Autobiography, Oklahoma and Mississippi Narratives*, vol. 7 (Westport, Conn.: Greenwood, 1972), p. 284. Series hereafter cited by name of interviewee.

2. Elizabeth Fox-Genovese, *Within the Plantation Household: Black and White Women of the Old South* (Chapel Hill: University of North Carolina Press, 1988), pp. 137–138; John Michael Vlach, *Back of the Big House: The Architecture of Plantation Slavery* (Chapel Hill: University of North Carolina Press, 1993); Deborah Gray White, *Ar'n't I a Woman: Female Slaves in the Plantation South* (rev. ed., New York: W.W. Norton, 1999).

3. See, for example, Jacob Manson, *North Carolina Narratives*, vol. 15, pt. 2, p. 97.

4. Lee Ann Whites, *The Civil War as a Crisis in Gender: Augusta, Georgia, 1860–1890* (Athens: University of Georgia Press, 1995), p. 18.

5. This historiography has its modern roots in Anne Firor Scott's pioneering *The Southern Lady: From Pedestal to Politics* (1970; reprint, Charlottesville: University of Virginia Press, 1995) and Catherine Clinton's *The Plantation Mistress: Woman's World in the Old South* (New York: Pantheon Books, 1982). For more recent elaborations of the thesis, see, for example, Leslie A. Schwalm, *A Hard Fight for We: Women's Transition from Slavery to Freedom in South Carolina* (Urbana: University of Illinois Press, 1997); Brenda E. Stevenson, *Life in Black and White: Family and Community in the Slave South* (New York: Oxford University Press, 1996); and Marli F. Weiner, *Mistresses and Slaves, Mistresses and Slaves: Plantation Women in South Carolina, 1830–80* (Urbana: University of Illinois Press, 1998), pp. 123–24.

6. For an important corrective on this point, see White, *Ar'n't I a Woman?*, rev. ed., pp. 6–7.

7. Lulu Wilson in *The American Slave: A Composite Autobiography*, ed. George P. Rawick, *Texas Narratives*, Supplement Series 2, vol. 10, pt. 9 (Westport, Conn.: Greenwood, 1979), p. 4194.

8. Elizabeth R. Baer, ed., *Shadows on My Heart: The Civil War Diary of Lucy Rebecca Buck* (Athens: University of Georgia Press, 1997), p. xvii; Carol Bleser, ed., *Tokens of Affection: The Letters of a Planter's Daughter in the Old South* (Athens: University of Georgia, 1996), p. 20.

9. The most oft-cited example of this entrancement is Margaret Mitchell's *Gone With the Wind* (New York: Macmillan, 1936).

10. Quotes are from Ingrid H. Tague, *Women of Quality: Accepting and Contesting Ideals of Femininity in England, 1690–1760* (Suffolk, UK: Boydell Press, 2002), p. 97. My thinking about this question has benefited greatly from Amanda Vickery, *The Gentleman's Daughter: Women's Lives in Georgian England* (New Haven, Conn.: Yale University Press, 1998); Leonore Davidoff and Catherine Hall, *Family Fortunes: Men and Women of the English Middle Class, 1780–1850* (Chicago: University of Chicago Press, 2002); and Achille Mbembe, *On the Postcolony* (Berkeley: University of California Press, 2001), 26–27.

11. Jones, *Born a Child of Freedom Yet a Slave: Mechanisms of Control and Strategies of Resistance in Antebellum South Carolina* (Hanover, N.H.: University Press of New England, 1990), p. 116.

12. For mistresses, there were no equivalents to the publicly sanctioned outlets for violent impulses that existed for white men—such as duels, patrols, militia, and war. For a comparative perspective, see Hilary McD. Beckles, "Taking Liberties: Enslaved Women and Anti-Slavery in the Caribbean," in *Gender and Imperialism*, ed. Clare Midgley (Manchester: Manchester University Press, 1998), pp. 137–57; Beckles, "White Women and Slavery in the Caribbean," *History Workshop Journal* 36 (1993): 66–82.

13. Fox-Genovese draws the opposite conclusion that "the vast majority" of mistresses acted as "delegates of the master, or male authority" and that slave women's resistance in the household was a protest of the master's authority (*Within the Plantation Household*, pp. 102, 110, 135; note quote at p. 110).

14. Ria Sorrell, *North Carolina Narratives*, vol. 15, pt. 2, pp. 300–302, quote is at p. 302; Genovese, *Roll, Jordan, Roll*, pp. 333–34. See Joel Best, *Random Violence: How We Talk about New Crimes and New Violence* (Berkeley: University of California Press, 1999); Melanie Perrault, "'To Fear and to Love Us': Intercultural Violence in the English Atlantic," *Journal of World History* 17 (March 2006): 71–93.

15. As two studies of slave punishment that do not mention white women at all demonstrate, some scholars do not see white female power at all. See, for example, Stephen C. Crawford, "Punishments and Rewards," in *Without Consent or Contract, The Rise and Fall of American Slavery: Conditions of Slave Life and the Transition to Freedom: Technical Papers*, vol. 2, ed. Robert William Fogel and Stanley L. Engerman (New York: W.W. Norton, 1992), pp. 536–50; Charles Kahn, "An Agency Theory Approach to Slave Punishments and Rewards," in ibid., pp. 551–65.

16. Delia Garlic, *Alabama Narratives*, vol. 6, p. 129. On the need for studies of the psychological costs of slavery, see Deborah Gray White, *Ar'n't I a Woman? Female Slaves in the Plantation South* (1985; rev. ed., New York: Norton, 1999), pp. 9–10, and Nell Irvin Painter, "Soul Murder: Toward a Fully Loaded Cost Accounting," in *Southern History Across the Color Line* (Chapel Hill: University of North Carolina Press, 2002), pp. 15–39.

17. Clifton H. Johnson, ed., *God Struck Me Dead: Religious Conversion Experiences and Autobiographies of Ex-Slaves* (Philadelphia: Pilgrim Press, 1969), p. 154; see also pp. 155, 161. Maria White, *Mississippi Narratives*, Supplement Series I, vol. 10, pt. 5, p. 2277; Austin Stewart, *Twenty-Two Years a Slave, and Forty Years a Freeman* (1856; reprint, New York: Negro Universities Press, 1968), p. 17.

18. Harriet Robinson, *Oklahoma and Mississippi Narratives*, vol. 7, p. 271; Sarah Carpenter Colbert, *Alabama and Indiana Narratives*, vol. 6, p. 57; Lucretia Heyward, *South Carolina Narratives*, vol. 2, pt. 2, p. 279; Hannah Plummer, ibid., p. 180; Jacob Branch, *Texas Narratives*, vol. 4, pt. 1, p. 139.

19. Frederick Douglass, *My Bondage and My Freedom* (1855; reprint, New York: Negro Universities Press, 1969), pp. 103, 149–50, 150; White, *Ar'n't I a Woman?*, p. 50.

20. John W. Blassingame, ed., *Slave Testimony: Two Centuries of Letters, Speeches, Interviews, and Autobiographies* (Baton Rouge: Louisiana State University Press, 1977), p. 218; Carol Bleser, ed., *Tokens of Affection: The Letters of a Planter's Daughter in the Old South* (Athens: University of Georgia Press, 1996), p. 108. Mistresses' abuse of enslaved children tempers the view that they played a central and positive role in the socialization of enslaved children. For the latter view, see White, *Ar'n't I a Woman?*, pp. 52–53, and Weiner, *Mistresses and Slaves*, p. 82. On the abuse of slave children, see also Painter, "Soul Murder," pp. 22–25.

21. Valley Perry, *North Carolina Narratives*, vol. 15, pt. 2, p. 170.

22. John Rudd, *Indiana Narratives*, vol. 6, pt. 2, p. 169; Lucretia Heyward, *South Carolina Narratives*, vol. 2, pt. 2, pp. 279–81.

23. Charles L. Perdue, Jr., Thomas E. Barden, and Robert K. Phillips, eds., *Weevils in the Wheat: Interviews with Virginia Ex-Slaves* (Charlottesville: University Press of Virginia, 1976), p. 1; Ria Sorrell, *North Carolina Narratives*, vol. 15, pt. 2, pp. 300–301. On the brutality of masters, see, for example, Dave Lawson, *North Carolina Narratives*, vol. 15, p. 45.

24. Lucinda Hall Shaw, *Mississippi Narratives*, Supplement Series 1, vol. 10, pt. 5, p. 1927.

25. Quote is from Fox-Genovese, "To Be Worthy of God's Favor: Southern Women's Defense and Critique of Slavery," 32d Annual Fortenbaugh Memorial Lecture, Gettysburg College, 1993, p. 12.

26. Winthrop D. Jordan, *Tumult and Silence at Second Creek: An Inquiry into a Civil War Slave Conspiracy* (Baton Rouge: Louisiana State University Press, 1993), pp. 164–65, 167, 201–2, 276, 279, 281, 294, 298; quotes at pp. 165, 281, and 295, respectively. An end to beatings as a determinant of freedom struggles appears frequently in the slaves narratives. See, for example, William Moore Narrative, *Texas Narratives*, vol. 7, pt. 6, Supplement Series 2, p. 2770.

27. Saidiya V. Hartman, *Scenes of Subjection: Terror, Slavery, and Self-Making in Nineteenth-Century America* (New York: Oxford, 1997). Used the rod: quoted in Scott, *Southern Lady*, p. 37; see also Fox-Genovese, *Within the Plantation Household*, p. 136.

28. Neblett quoted in Drew Gilpin Faust, "'Trying to Do a Man's Business': Gender, Violence, and Slave Management in Civil War Texas," in Faust, *Southern Stories: Slaveholders in War and Peace* (Columbia: University of Missouri Press, 1992), p. 185. See also Drew Gilpin Faust, *Mothers of Invention: Women of the Slaveholding South in the American Civil War* (Chapel Hill: University of North Carolina Press, 1996), pp. 64–70.

29. Parke, quoted in David Hackett Fischer, *Albion's Seed: Four British Folkways in America* (New York: Oxford University Press, 1989), p. 320. See Clinton, *Plantation Mistress*, pp. 96–97; Scott, *Southern Lady*, pp. 4–21.

30. William Byrd, *The Secret Diary of William Byrd of Westover, 1709–1712*, eds. Louis B. Wright and Marion Tinling (Richmond, VA: Dietz Press, 1941), pp. 34–35, 205, 494.

31. Ulrich B. Phillips, *American Negro Slavery: A Survey of the Supply, Employment and Control of Negro Labor as Determined by the Plantation Regime* (Baton Rouge: Louisiana State University Press, 1966), pp. 276–77; Cecelia, "Management of Servants," *Southern Planter*, III (August 1843), p. 175, as quoted in Eugene D. Genovese, *Roll, Jordan, Roll: The World the Slaves Made* (New York: Vintage Books, 1974), pp. 334–35.

32. Douglass, *My Bondage and My Freedom*, p. 83.

33. See, for example, Drew Gilpin Faust, "Culture, Conflict and Community: The Meaning of Power on an Antebellum Plantation," *Journal of Social History* 14 (Autumn, 1980): 84.

34. For an extended discussion of domestic space and southern domesticity, see Thavolia Glymph, *Out of the House of Bondage: The Transformation of the Plantation Household* (New York: Cambridge University Press, 2008), ch. 3.

35. Jones, *Born a Child of Freedom Yet a Slave*, 7, 57. Dave Lawson, *North Carolina Narratives*, vol. 15, pt. 2, pp. 44–50.

36. Fred Cooper, *Indiana Narratives*, vol. 6, p. 61.

37. Bird: Bleser, ed., *Tokens of Affection*, pp. 131, 282; Mary Ellison, "Resistance to Oppression: Black Women's Response to Slavery in the United States." *Slavery and Abolition*, vol. 1 (May 1983): 57–59. Lewis Wallace, *Mississippi Narratives*, Supplement Series 1, vol. 10, pt. 5, pp. 2165–66. Peggy: Joan E. Cashin, ed., *Our Common Affairs: Texts from Women in the Old South* (Baltimore: Johns Hopkins Press, 1996), p. 208. Mistress beaten: Dave Lawson, *North Carolina Narratives*, vol. 15, pt. 2, pp. 44–48.

38. Talk too much: Augustin L. Taveau to [Delpine Taveau], 7 October 1863, Augustine Louis Taveau Papers, Duke University. For additional examples, see Virginia Ingraham Burr, ed., *The Secret Eye: The Journal of Ella Gertrude Thomas, 1848–1899*, Introduction by Nell Irwin Painter (Chapel Hill: University of North Carolina Press, 1990), February 9, 1958, p. 160.

39. Burr, ed., *The Secret Eye*, July 23, 1852, p. 111; March 30, 1856, p. 145 (quotation). See also, February 9, 1858, p. 160.

40. *Harriet Devall, by her next friend, v. Michael Devall and others*, Cases Argued and Determined in the Court of Chancery of South Carolina (June 1809), pp. 78–81.

41. See, for example, Anonymous, Court of Chancery Cases, pp. 94–95. In this case, the social status of the plaintiff and defendant was specifically raised.

42. The chokeberry tree reference is from Toni Morrison, *Beloved* (New York: Signet, 1991), pp. 20–21. Fox-Genovese, *Within the Plantation Household*, p. 190; *State v. Montgomery*, Cheves 120, February 1840, in Helen Tunnicliff Catterall, ed., *Judicial Cases Concerning American Slavery and the Negro, 1926–1937* (1926; reprint, New York: Negro Universities Press, 1968), p. 377; Douglass, *My Bondage and My Freedom*, p. 436.

Eliza R. Hemmingway and Sarah Bagley, Testimony on Working Conditions in Early Factories, 1845

The textile factories of the first wave of industrialization might not have been built at all had their owners not believed they could count on a steady supply of cheap female labor. The history of industrialization as it affected both men and women needs to be understood in the context of the segmented labor market that women entered. Women were a major part of the first new workforce that was shaped into "modern" work patterns: long, uninterrupted hours of labor in a mechanized factory with little or no room for individual initiative.

One of the earliest mill towns was Lowell, Massachusetts, where factory owners began recruiting young, unmarried women to work in six textile mills in 1823. Rural young women already toiled at home at farm labor and also at "out-work," making goods that could be sold for cash. Compared to the work they had done at home, mill work at first seemed to pay well and to offer new opportunities. The Lowell mills developed a system of boardinghouses, which assured families that girls would live in wholesome surroundings. Letters sent home and fiction published by young women in the first wave of employment often testified to their pride in the financial independence that their new work brought.

Work in the mills was strictly segregated by sex: men were supervisors and skilled mechanics; women attended the spinning and weaving machinery. The daily earnings of almost all female workers depended on piece rates—the number of pieces or the output of the particular machine they tended. Their wages ranged from one-third to one-half that of men; the highest-paid woman generally earned less than the lowest-paid man. Employers responded to economic downturns in the 1830s either by lowering wages or by requiring more pieces per day. Mills established stricter discipline: workers who were insubordinate were fired; those who did not fulfill their yearlong contracts were blacklisted. But boardinghouse life meant that the factory women developed strong support networks; when their wages were cut and work hours lengthened in the 1830s, those who lived together came together in opposition to the owners and staged some of the earliest industrial strikes in American history. In 1836, 1,500 women walked out in protest, claiming their inheritance as "Daughters of the Revolution." One manifesto stated: "As our fathers resisted unto blood the lordly avarice of the British ministry, so we, their daughters, never will wear the yoke which has been prepared for us."*

*Thomas Dublin, *Women at Work: The Transformation of Work and Community in Lowell, Massachusetts, 1826–1860* (New York: Columbia University Press, 1979), p. 98.

Excerpted from "The First Official Investigation of Labor Conditions in Massachusetts," in *A Documentary History of American Industrial Society*, vol. 8, eds. John R. Commons, Ulrich B. Phillips, Eugene A. Gilmore, Helen L. Sumner, and John B. Andrews (Cleveland, 1910), pp. 133–42.

Women at textile machinery in a New England mill, photograph, ca. 1850.
Note the poor lighting and the absence of anything to sit on during the long hours at the machines.
(Courtesy of George Eastman House.)

In January 1845, led by the indomitable worker Sarah Bagley, the Female Labor Reform Association organized a petition drive throughout the region, which forced the Massachusetts legislature to hold the first public hearings on industrial working conditions ever held in the United States. On February 13, 1845, Eliza Hemmingway and Sarah Bagley had their chance to testify. What did they think it was important for the legislators to know?

. . . The first petitioner who testified was Eliza R. Hemmingway. She had worked 2 years and 9 months in the Lowell Factories . . . Her employment is weaving—works by the piece . . . and attends one loom. Her wages average from $16 to $23 a month exclusive of board. She complained of the hours for labor being too many, and the time for meals too limited. In the summer season, the work is commenced at 5 o'clock, a.m., and continued till 7 o'clock, p.m., with half an hour for breakfast and three quarters of an hour for dinner. During eight months of the year, but half an hour is allowed for dinner. The air in the room she considered not to be wholesome. There were 293 small [oil] lamps and 61 large lamps lighted in the room in which she worked, when evening work is required. These lamps are also lighted sometimes in the morning. About 130 females, 11 men, and 12 children (between the ages of 11 and 14) work in the room with her. . . . The children work but 9 months out of 12. The other 3 months they must attend school. Thinks that there is no day when there are less than six of the females out of the mill from sickness. Has known as many as thirty. She herself, is out quite often, on account of sickness. . . .

She thought there was a general desire among the females to work but ten hours, regardless of pay. . . . She knew of one girl who last winter went into the mill at half past 4 o'clock, a.m. and worked till half past 7 o'clock, p.m. She did so to make more money. She earned from $25 to $30 per month. There is always a large number of girls at the gate wishing to get in before the bell rings. . . . They do this to make more wages. A large number come to Lowell to make money to aid their parents who are poor. She knew of many cases where married women came to Lowell and worked in the mills to assist their husbands to pay for their farms. . . .

Miss Sarah G. Bagley said she had worked in the Lowell Mills eight years and a half . . . She is a weaver, and works by the piece. . . . She thinks the health of the operatives is not so good as the health of females who do housework or millinery business. The chief evil, so far as health is concerned, is the shortness of time allowed for meals. The next evil is the length of time employed—not giving them time to cultivate their minds. . . . She had presented a petition, same as the one before the Committee, to 132 girls, most of whom said that they would prefer to work but ten hours. In a pecuniary point of view, it would be better, as their health would be improved. They would have more time for sewing. Their intellectual, moral and religious habits would also be benefited by the change. . . .

On Saturday the 1st of March, a portion of the Committee went to Lowell to examine the mills, and to observe the general appearance of the operatives. . . . [The Committee concluded:] Not only is the interior of the mills kept in the best order, but great regard has been paid by many of the agents to the arrangement of the enclosed grounds. Grass plats have been laid out, trees have been planted . . . everything in and about the mills, and the boarding houses appeared, to have for its end, health and comfort. . . . The [average hours of work per day throughout the year was 11½; the workday was longest in April, when it reached 13½ hours].

Maria Perkins Writes to Her Husband on the Eve of Being Sold, 1854

Because masters understood the connection between literacy and rebelliousness, slaves were rarely taught to read and write. This anguished letter from Maria Perkins is unusual because it was written by an enslaved woman. We do not know whether Perkins's husband Richard managed to persuade his master to buy her and keep the family together. If a trader did buy Maria Perkins or her child, the likelihood of permanent separation was great. Scottsville, mentioned in the letter, is a small town near Charlottesville; Staunton is some forty miles away.

Charlottesville, Oct. 8th, 1852
Dear Husband I write you a letter to let you know my distress my master has sold albert to a trader on Monday court day and myself and other child is for sale also and I want you to let [me] hear from you very soon before next cort if you can I don't know when I don't want you to wait till Christmas I want you to tell dr Hamelton and your master if either will buy me they can attend to it know and then I can go afterwards. I don't want a trader to get me they asked me if I had got any person to buy me and I told them no they took me to the court houste too they never put me up a man buy the name of brady bought albert and is gone I don't know where they say he lives in Scottesville my things is in several places some is in staunton and if I should be sold I don't know what will become of them I don't expect to meet with the luck to get that way till I am quite heartsick nothing more I am and ever will be your kind wife Maria Perkins.

Maria Perkins to Richard Perkins, October 8, 1852, Ulrich B. Phillips Collection, Yale University Library, New Haven.

BETWEEN NATIONS AND ON THE BORDERS

LUCY ELDERSVELD MURPHY

Public Mothers: Creole Mediators in the Northern Borderlands

What did "westward expansion" look like for the people and their communities who were being expanded upon? Lucy Eldersveld Murphy's essay reminds us that the Midwest in what is now the United States was a borderland. In other words, it was a region in which multiple cultures, nations, and peoples met and coexisted. She highlights in particular the role of indigenous and Métis (mixed-race) women in navigating these migration streams and diverse cultures. Murphy argues that these women played important roles as what she calls "public mothers" in these multicultural and multiracial communities. In fact, these public mothers were crucial in fostering a Creole or local culture.

As you read this essay, think about how the portrayal of public mothers changes the ways in which we think about conquest and about Anglo-Franco-Indian relations. Why were some women better able to bridge cultural and racial divides? Is the evidence for this convincing? Why is it important to make the distinction between Métis and Creole? How might you rewrite the history of westward expansion by focusing on the roles of indigenous and Métis women?

On the northwestern shore of Lake Michigan's Green Bay, where the Menominee River flows into the lake along an old fur trade route, there is a city straddling the border of Wisconsin and Michigan. This city, and the county that surrounds it, are named for a woman of color: she was Marinette Chevalier, and the place name is Marinette. A Menominee, Ojibwe, and French Métisse (mixed-race woman) related to a prominent Ojibwe family, she married one fur trader, separated from him and then married another according to "the custom of the country," working side-by-side with each husband at the mouth of the Menominee River, a region in which many Indians spent part of their year.[1] She eventually separated from her

second husband, took over the management of the trading post with the help of her children, and became extremely successful in business and in cultivating warm relationships with the Indian people living in the area, many of whom were her kin.

When she was in her twenties, the War of 1812 clamped U.S. sovereignty onto this northern borderland region, and the Native people and fur-trade families were colonized by the United States. The conquering army built new forts and fortified older ones, enforcing control to be administered by a new judicial and legislative system. Although Marinette Chevalier and most of the other residents spoke French and/or Indian languages, the United States

Excerpted from "Public Mothers: Native American and Métis Women as Creole Mediators in the Nineteenth-Century Midwest," by Lucy Eldersveld Murphy, *Journal of Women's History* 14, no. 4 (Winter 2003): 142–65. Reprinted by permission of the author and publisher. Notes have been edited and renumbered.

imposed English as a new court language. Waves of immigrants from the eastern United States and even some from Europe swarmed into the Midwest, bringing different ideas about race, class, and gender. Before long, such people as Marinette Chevalier were minorities in their own communities. Yet when English-speaking immigrants began to move into the Menominee River area, they, like the local Indians and Métis people, became her customers, neighbors, and friends.

An essay in the Michigan Pioneer Society's 1877 yearbook recounting the history of Menominee County praised Marinette Chevalier. The Anglophone author chose not to dwell on her entrepreneurial experiences, but focused instead on another of her roles. According to the article, "Marinette died in 1863, highly honored by all the residents about the river. She was 72 years old when she died, and had been looked to as a mother by all the early settlers and Indians, for she had always been ready to assist the needy and comfort the distressed." Not only are her experiences remarkable, but also is the fact that the Anglo writer for the pioneer society noted and even celebrated this Métis woman, and that a city and county (now in Wisconsin) were named in her honor.[2]

While Marinette Chevalier's experiences were notable, they were not unique. Many other women whose lives spanned the transition to U.S. control of the Midwest worked to mediate between cultural groups, as did some of their brothers, sons, and husbands. During the nineteenth century, as the newcomers were changing the region's economy, landscape, and government to the detriment of many Creole people, some of these women both created connections and even transcended the prejudices of the Anglo "pioneers" to gain the praise of their neighbors.

Although many members of the old fur-trade families were what Canadians would call "Métis," that is, people of mixed Indian and white ancestry, others were not. Residents of these communities such as Green Bay and Mackinac also included Indians, whites, and people with African backgrounds. Rather than having an identical *ancestry*, they had in common a *culture* born in the Midwest, one that was in place before the United States took control of the region. For this reason, the word "Creole" is used here as a general term to describe the culture and the people who created

it, with the understanding that it may refer to any of the long-time residents connected to the old fur-trade culture who were Métis, Indian, Euro-, or African American. This article will discuss the roles of Creole women in multiethnic and changing communities. Some of them, I argue, found ways to mediate between cultural groups, by negotiating overlapping ideals of womanhood common to both Anglos and Native-descended people, serving their communities in roles as "public mothers."

In many ways, Creole women's experiences in the American Midwest mirrored those of women facing colonization in other parts of the world. For example, during the eighteenth and nineteenth centuries, West African coastal women, often operating as traders, served as social and cultural intermediaries, helped to create networks linking people of different ethnic groups, and facilitated cultural fusion in changing communities. In Senegal, African women traders married European men and helped to create a hybrid society in Saint-Louis and Gorée; their Euro-African daughters might be political as well as economic and social mediators. In Sierra Leone, women traders facilitated cross-cultural contact both as travelers and as vendors in the great markets. Their roles and activities, however, were frequently overlooked or misunderstood by foreign observers.[3]

Creole families in the American Midwest were initially formed when, during the seventeenth and eighteenth centuries, French Canadian and French fur traders traveled into the Great Lakes region in increasing numbers and married into Indian customers' families and communities. These mixed couples raised biracial children in bicultural households. Many of these mixed families eventually moved from the Indian villages into their own fur-trade towns and developed hybrid societies. Over fifty Creole communities were founded during the eighteenth century in the western Great Lakes and upper Mississippi Valley by Francophone men who married Indian women and raised Métis children. At least ten to fifteen thousand people called these communities home by the late 1820s. . . .[4]

Marinette Chevalier usually spent part of each year in the fur-trade town of Green Bay, known in French as LaBaye. Like her, thousands of people lived in culturally mixed communities and shared a syncretic culture. These people spoke French and various Indian languages, dressed, farmed, traveled, and celebrated in unique ways, and were not particularly loyal to the United States of America. People who had been born in the Great Lakes region, residents of towns such as Green Bay, Prairie du Chien, St. Louis, Vincennes, Detroit, and Mackinac, included French and Anglo-American fur traders and related workers, Indian wives, and some of their kin, and a wide variety of young and old Métis people, with a few African Americans.

It is important to understand these people in the context of colonization, as residents who lived in this part of the Midwest before it was annexed by the United States. During the eighteenth century, they had created communities with a regional culture that was a distinctive mix of their varied cultural heritages. Although they were not indigenous in the same sense that Indian peoples were, they were residents with a culture that was specific to the region, and strongly related to Indian culture. Their history parallels that of the Spanish-speaking Californios, Tejanos, and Hispanos of the nineteenth-century Southwest, people who were also colonized by the United States in the nineteenth century.[5] The people of midwestern fur-trade communities thought of themselves in cultural rather than racial terms, and they were keenly aware that they were being invaded and dominated by the culturally different Anglos of the United States. Both they and the Anglos understood them to be an ethnic group that pre-dated U.S. hegemony. In the early nineteenth century, the word "Creole" was used in the Mississippi Valley to convey this sense of a culture group created in the previous colonial era (although the word had other meanings in other contexts).[6] Other somewhat misleading terms such as "Canadians," "French" people, or "half-breeds" were sometimes used.

Creole culture combined Native American and Euro-American elements as mixed families negotiated lifeways and selected ideas and practices from their collective traditions. Wives' Indian-kin connections linked traders to friends and customers during the fur-trade era. Children tended to speak both French and at least one Native language. Native wives, who had grown up in societies that regarded farming as women's work, often continued to be very active in growing food, while white or Métis husbands might raise livestock, a practice

that was not customary in Indian communities. Dairying might be unpopular with Creole wives, but Indian maple sugaring expeditions became part of their Lenten season.[7]

Creole culture was complex and variable: the people who lived and created it were often bi- (or even tri-) cultural; they might be Ojibwe, Dakota, Potawatomi, Sauk, Pawnee, or members of other Native tribes, French, Scottish, English, African American, or any combination of the above. Practices and beliefs varied from one community or family or individual to another; there was change over time, presenting a real challenge to historians. . . .

The colonization of the Midwest by the United States and the immigration of large numbers of Anglo-Americans chiefly from New England and the Mid-Atlantic states caused profound social change. Such people as Marinette Chevalier faced a new political reality that altered membership of society's elite class, imposed new ruling families, and worked to demote many previously elite Creoles.

The transition to Anglo hegemony had the potential to constrict women's rights, and to stigmatize and marginalize Creoles. . . . The newly dominant society not only brought different gender ideals, but also tried to enforce those values with a legal system that constricted the rights of wives and rigidified the concept of marriage. While the *coutume de Paris* [a customary law code] as applied in New France (including the Midwest) had allowed wives to be co-owners of a couple's property and guaranteed widows at least half of the estate, U.S. hegemony imposed coverture on wives and did not protect widows from [the claims of their husbands'] creditors. Local norms recognized marriages that had been contracted "according to the custom of the country," but under the new regime these marriages were sometimes considered illegitimate. . . . Marinette Chevalier's second husband was one of thirty-six men charged with fornication by a new judge in nearby Green Bay because the couple had not formalized their union according to the legal system of the United States.[8]

In addition, Creoles experienced both cultural prejudice and racism on the part of the colonizers. Anglophone immigrants referred to themselves as "settlers," and, later, . . . "pioneers." They arrived intending to build farms, towns, and businesses, bringing with them cultural baggage that included ethnocentrism and devotion to a social hierarchy based upon race. Most wanted to believe that they were creating a new society where none had existed before, so they wrote essays for their "pioneer societies" congratulating themselves for having brought "civilization" to the "wilderness." In their letters and memoirs, they often felt the need to denigrate the established populations of Indians and Creoles.

"The Americans generally consider the Canadians as ignorant," remarked an Italian traveler in the region in 1828. For example, Henry Schoolcraft, an Indian agent and folklorist, wrote, "it is but repeating a common observation to say, that in morality and intelligence they are far inferior to the American population." Caleb Atwater, an agent sent to Wisconsin for an 1827 treaty, wrote that the Creoles of Prairie du Chien were "without even one redeeming virtue." Claiming exclusive ownership on the nationality "American," constructed in ethnic terms, said it all.[9]

For other newcomers, the striking and unsettling thing about the Creoles was their skin color. For example, J. H. Lamotte wrote to a friend in 1836 that the elite fur traders were "as fat, ragged and black as their great-grandfathers were (if they ever had any)." James Lockwood remembered noticing a bothersome disjunction of color and status, race and class, and being amazed at finding "nut-brown" Indian wives and biracial children among the elites of the community.[10] From the Anglos' point of view, the Creoles were people of color, neither Negro nor Indian, but also not white, a reason—added to their cultural "otherness"—that the new social system so often worked to marginalize them.... This same prejudice also presents a challenge to historians, because it caused Anglo writers to disparage, ignore, or minimize the experiences of Creoles.

Prejudicial attitudes also affected the literary traditions that neglected the activities and contributions of women. "Pioneer" writers recording their region's history, of course, usually assumed that women's experiences and efforts were unimportant, often to an absurd degree. When they were mentioned at all, women were frequently identified by their relationships to men, often not even by their names, a pattern even more pronounced in the representations of women of color. For example, a typical article about "James Allen Reed: First Permanent Settler in Trempealeau County and Founder of Trempealeau [Wisconsin]"

written in 1914 by a Dr. Eben D. Price stated: "During his army life Reed married a Potawatomi woman, by whom he had five children, Elizabeth, Joseph, Mary, Madeline, and James. Upon her death in 1830 he was married a second time to a Menominee mixed blood, widow of the trader, Russell Farnham. Two children, Margaret and John, resulted from this union. He later married the widow of Amable Grignon, whose son Antoine was the chief source of this biography."

Several pages later, the article states that "the widow Grignon ... was a relative of the Sioux chief Wabashaw. Her relationship with the noted chief gave Reed great prestige among this band of Sioux." That Reed alone was considered to be the "first permanent settler" rather than, with one of his unnamed wives, as the first couple or the first family is equally typical. (For the record, the wives were Marguerite Oskache, Agathe Wood, and Archange Barret.)[11]

And yet biased Anglo writers praised such women of color as Marinette Chevalier.... [Why? I argue here that Creole women like Chevalier] did not act like ideal Anglo women. Anglo northeasterners might find them lacking in purity and submissiveness, and their religious participation did not always strictly conform to Protestant concepts of piety (partly because they were usually Catholic). They seemed, however, to possess many of the virtues of domesticity [and neighborliness that the Anglos associated nostalgically with] colonial-era hospitality [and] communalism.[12] [Simply put,] the pioneers were comforted by women of color who looked after their neighbors.

... Anglos' accounts are [often] our only written sources for Creole women.... [The accounts allow us to see,] in particular, elite Creole women—that is, those who were prominent, wealthy, and/or well-connected ... [taking] on activities related to charity, hospitality, healing, and midwifery. They nurtured their neighbors, newcomers, travelers, kin, and fellow clan and tribal members. They came from Native and Creole traditions in which women's roles ... could be at once public and private, social and political. Although political and economic roles for Creoles under the new regime were being constricted and the Anglo gender system being imposed was more restrictive than the systems of Creoles and Native Americans, some Creole women maintained quasi-public roles in transitional communities, because they were perceived by the newcomers as praiseworthy females doing motherly work. Although there are many instances of elite Creole men making connections and laboring to smooth intercultural relations, the role of Creole mediator [as reported by Anglos] is most evident in the actions of women.

Some Creole women reached out to their communities as healers—roles women could hold in Native communities—and as midwives, a trade women monopolized among Indians. Native and Métis women brought their knowledge of medicine, midwifery, and nurturing to the service of their neighbors. It is likely that bicultural women drew upon multiple medical traditions, making their range of treatment options greater than those available to people with access to only a single medical tradition. . . . Their efforts frequently brought them into the homes of neighbors who were culturally different, creating ties of respect and affection, and sometimes enhancing the healers' status and authority.

One such woman was Marianne LaBuche Menard, Prairie du Chien's midwife and healer, "a person of consequence," according to an 1856 pioneer writer who knew her in the early nineteenth century. She was a woman of French and African descent, a native of New Orleans who had thirteen children by three husbands. "She was sent for by the sick, and attended them as regularly as a physician, and charged fees therefor[e], giving them . . . 'device and yarb drink' [advice and herb drink] . . . she took her pay in the produce of the country, but was not very modest in her charges." After the U.S. army brought in a physician who would attend to civilians, many still preferred "Aunt Mary Ann," as she was called, and she sometimes cured people despaired of by the army doctor.[13]

During the mid-nineteenth century, an Ojibwe Métisse from Detroit came with her husband Louis Demarie to Chippewa Falls, Wisconsin. An Anglo neighbor wrote about Madame Demarie in 1875: "She was a woman of uncommon natural abilities, and with education and culture would have graced a high social position in any community. She was a born physician, and for many years the only one in the valley; and in making a diagnosis of disease, and her knowledge of the healing properties and proper application of many of the remedies used in the Materia Medica, exhibited extraordinary insight and skill in her practice. She was frequently called to attend upon myself and family, and her prescriptions were simple, natural, and always efficacious."[14]

Similarly, Josette DeRosier Duvernay Moon Robinson, another Ojibwe Métisse, cared for the sick and pregnant of Oceana County, Michigan, during the second half of the nineteenth century and delivered hundreds of babies. At the time of her death in 1904, an obituary in the Hart *Journal* stated, "Perhaps no other woman of Indian blood has been more respected and generally beloved than was Mrs. Robinson. . . . A woman of no literary education, yet she possessed much wisdom. . . . The sick and suffering always desired 'Grandma' Robinson as nurse, and she was never known to refuse aid whenever it was possible for her to render it. Every home in the township of Elbridge has welcomed her at their firesides and her death has caused more than usual mourning." Josette's daughter, Sarah Moon, also continued as a midwife.[15]

. . . Creoles expected prominent families to offer hospitality to travelers, particularly their own, but also to miscellaneous strangers. In doing so, they became the strangers' patrons but also served their communities by supervising the outsiders' behavior.

Marguerite LePage LeClaire, for example, was a Métisse related to a prominent Mesquakie (Fox) family and married to Potawatomi Métis interpreter Antoine LeClaire who was stationed for many years at Rock Island. She received a substantial land grant at the request of her Indian relatives at the time of the removal treaty of 1832, a grant which helped her family to become wealthy and prominent as founders of the city of Davenport, Iowa. Afterwards, according to a local historian in 1910, "delegations of the Sac and Fox Indians visited her place every year, where they were always made welcome, entertained as long as they wished to remain, and when leaving, always carried away as a free gift what necessaries they required—corn, flour, etc."[16] Anglo uneasiness about having Indians in town might be calmed by knowing that they were associates and relatives of Marguerite LePage LeClaire and that she was keeping an eye on them. Many other Creole women remained in touch with distant Indian communities, and welcomed, fed, and sheltered visitors. . . .

Creoles frequently offered hospitality not only to Native but also to non-Indian travelers and newcomers. Elizabeth Baird was one of Green Bay's hospitable Métisses six years after moving to Green Bay. . . . When Juliette Kinzie and her husband visited the town in 1830, . . . a party was thrown for them. "Everybody will remember that dance at Mrs. Baird's. All the people, young and old . . . were assembled. . . . Everybody was bound to do honor to the strangers by appearing in their very best [clothing]. It was to be an entertainment unequalled by any given before."[17] It is interesting that Kinzie remembered this party as being at *Mrs.* Baird's rather than as at the Baird home, or Mr. Baird's. . . .

In addition to gifts of lodging and food for sojourners, Creole giving benefited their neighbors as well, following Native tradition. Midwestern Indians valued generosity highly and expected elites to be the most giving of all. Reciprocity here was mixed with a heavy dose of communalism. Native people viewed wealth, in fact, as a sign of selfishness, a viewpoint that frustrated missionaries and agents trying to teach Native people acquisitiveness.[18]

Creoles adopted the Native sense of elite obligation, extending to neighbors the generosity they showed visitors. . . . Hononegah Mack [a HoChunk Winnebago] was known in northern Illinois for her hospitality and charity to everyone. When she died in 1847, her Anglo husband wrote: "In her the hungry and naked have lost a benefactor, the sick a nurse, and I have lost a friend who taught me to reverence God by doing good to his creatures. . . . Her funeral proved that I am not the only sufferer by her loss. My house is large but it was filled to overflowing by mourning friends who assembled to pay the last sad duties to her who had set them the example how to Live and how to Die." After her funeral, one Anglo man remarked to his neighbors, "The best woman in Winnebago County died last night." In later years, a forest preserve was named for her.[19]

A Trempealeau County, Wisconsin, pioneer in 1886 recalled a woman who, during the 1850s, epitomized for him the "twin traits [of] generosity and hospitality," one of James Reed's three invisible wives (probably Archange Barret). "Squaw though she was, she was an angel of mercy to the residents of Reed's Landing and Montoville. How distinctly I recall her commanding figure—going from house to house—not with words, for few could understand her broken French and native tongue—but with

well filled basket, and ready hand—tender as only a woman's is—to cheer the sick."[20] Although this Anglo writer racialized her as a "squaw," he viewed Archange Barret Reed's actions as appropriate, gendered behavior.

It is noteworthy that all kinds of people apparently referred to these women in kinship terms, as "Aunt," "Grandma," and "mother," and as elder relatives. . . . Métis people seem to have been traditionally viewed as kin by Indians ("all Indians called me sister," Elizabeth Baird recalled, looking back on herself as a young woman). Anglos did not necessarily think of Creoles in kinship terms, however, nor did Anglos consider their formally trained doctors as father, uncle, or grandfather figures. This sense of kinship that Anglos, Creoles, and Indians felt for such women as Menard, Chevalier, and DeRosier resulted from networks the women created in the community, demonstrating one way they successfully mediated among many groups. [I]t is also significant that people thought of them as older relatives. . . . "Mother," "Aunt," and "Grandma" are terms of deference, suggesting that these women of color likely derived some status and authority in their communities based not only on age but also from their ministrations to their neighbors.[21] . . .

. . . Creoles valued women and men who were community-minded, [and] they appreciated that public mothers did more than create personal links between themselves and other individuals. These women's actions had specific meaning for the community as a whole: their efforts served social welfare and educational functions, facilitated social control, provided inter-group diplomacy, promoted peace, and served to acculturate and assimilate newcomers into the community. . . .

. . . [Public mothers' roles in facilitating] diplomatic alliances [is vividly illustrated in the account of] a traveling Englishman who published under the pseudonym "A Merry Briton." [Ironically,] he did not understand what he was seeing. . . . [I]n 1841 [he] happened upon the home of Nancy McCrea and her husband Augustin Grignon, at a fur-trade center on Wisconsin's Wolf River consisting of a house and garden (including several acres of corn), with a number of Indian lodges nearby. The traveler entered the house uninvited, and observed "sundry pigeon-toed squaws, and mild-looking, half-breed girls, were busy preparing victuals about an immense fire-place."

Meanwhile, Augustin Grignon and another Creole man sat by a window working on account books, while "several Indians and half-breeds lounged about in various attitudes . . . smoking their tomahawk pipes." The Briton was greeted by Grignon, who made him welcome.[22]

At dusk, the Menominee chief Oshkosh, a kinsman of the Métis hostess Nancy McCrea, arrived with a number of companions and was warmly greeted by the family and other guests. After a meal consisting of "wild-duck stew, tea, and cakes," Oshkosh stood before the fireplace to make a long and formal speech in the Menominee language to the sizeable crowd. A member of the Grignon family translated the half-hour long presentation for the Briton. "The speech, from first to last, was in the declamatory style, and against whisky," he wrote. Another speech was clearly called for, and Nancy McCrea Grignon spoke up in the Menominee language. "Anon, old mother Grignon, a squaw of high and ancient family, with a crucifix round her neck, replied, in a nasal, whining voice: her speech was listened to with great attention." Unfortunately, we do not know what she said, as the Briton dozed off during the oration.[23]

McCrea . . . , the fur trader's wife, was clearly a person who connected people of different worlds. The daughter of a woman from an elite Menominee family and a Scottish fur trader, she spoke French and Menominee, and probably several other Indian languages.[24] Her role as public speaker in the simultaneously public and private arena of her home and the rapt attention of her family and guests testify to her significance in smoothing relations between the fur traders and Indian customers, between Creoles and Menominees, and between the extended Grignon family and the clan of Oshkosh. . . .

. . . [By the time of the Briton's visit, one longstanding arena of cross-cultural interaction was on the decline—marriage.] A look at 330 recorded marriages in Crawford County, Wisconsin, where Prairie du Chien is located, shows that exogamy—marriage to someone of another ethnic group—was declining as a proportion of all marriages. Exogamous marriages as a proportion of all marriages declined from 32 percent in the 1820s, to 24 percent in the 1830s, to 14 percent in the 1840s.[25] The relative decline in exogamy reduced opportunities for people to gain linguistic and cultural tools

needed to create alliances. Even so, many Creoles [as we have seen] responded to colonization by continuing to mediate, not only between Indians and Creoles, but also between these two groups and the immigrants. Indeed, the decrease in intermarriage in the face of surging Anglo immigration created a greater need for informal mediation within . . . [communities—mediation which public mothers provided. These women] had been reared observing negotiation and mediation, hearing [these approaches] praised, [and] perhaps even trained in [them].

No doubt Creole people attempted a variety of forms of negotiation, public mothering being only one of them. Probably there were some efforts that failed and others that succeeded but were not publicly lauded. Racism could cause failure. Rebecca Kugel has found, for example, that Creole women in Protestant mission schools aspired to leadership that could have allowed them to serve as intermediaries as teachers, missionaries, and interpreters, but the white Anglo missionaries tried to channel women of color into positions as domestic servants.[26] . . .

The behaviors of Creole public mothers, and the extent to which their efforts were appreciated and even valorized, teach us that they actively reached out to their communities, and that in doing so, they had found a middle ground among the various ideals of womanhood held by the region's people. . . . Their actions were in the best traditions of Native American, African American, Euro-American, and Creole women's activism. Although Creoles were frequently scorned for their cultural, ethnic, racial, and economic differences, some Creole women succeeded in reaching across the barriers by navigating the intersections of cultural ideals.

NOTES

1. The terms "Native American," "Native," and "Indian" are used interchangeably in this article, following American Indian Studies' conventional usage.

2. "Menominee County," Report of the Pioneer Society of the State of Michigan vol. 1 (1877), 266; Beverly Hayward Johnson, *Queen Marinette: Spirit of Survival on the Great Lakes Frontier* (Amasa, Michigan: White Water Associates, 1995).

3. George E. Brookes Jr., "The *Signares* of Saint-Louis and Gorée: Women Entrepreneurs in Eighteenth-Century Senegal," in Nancy J. Hafkin

and Edna G. Bay, eds., *Women in Africa: Studies in Social and Economic Change* (Stanford: Stanford University Press, 1976), 19–44; and E. Frances White, *Sierra Leone's Settler Women Traders* (Ann Arbor: University of Michigan Press, 1987).

4. Jacqueline Peterson, "The People In Between: Indian-White Marriage and the Genesis of a Métis Society and Culture in the Great Lakes Region, 1680–1830" (Ph.D. diss., University of Illinois at Chicago, 1981), 133, 136. On intermarriage see Clara Sue Kidwell, "Indian Women as Cultural Mediators," *Ethnohistory* 39 (1992), 97–107; Sylvia Van Kirk, *Many Tender Ties: Women in Fur-Trade Society, 1670* (Norman: University of Oklahoma Press, 1980); Jennifer S. H. Brown, *Strangers in Blood: Fur Trade Company Families in Indian Country* (Vancouver, 1980); Tanis Chapman Thorne, *The Many Hands of My Relations; French and Indians on the Lower Missouri* (Columbia: University of Missouri Press, 1996); Susan Sleeper-Smith, *Native Women and French Men: Rethinking Cultural Encounter in the Western Great Lakes* (Amherst: University of Massachusetts Press, 2001); and Lucy Eldersveld Murphy, *A Gathering of Rivers: Indians, Métis, and Mining in the Western Great Lakes, 1737–1832* (Lincoln: University of Nebraska Press, 2000).

5. Rodolfo Acuña, *Occupied America: A History of Chicanos* (New York: Harper and Row, 1988); Antonia Castañeda, "Presidarias y pobladoras: Spanish-Mexican Women in Frontier Monterey, Alta California, 1770–1821" (Ph.D. diss., Stanford University, 1990); and Douglas Monroy, *Thrown Among Strangers; The Making of Mexican Culture in Frontier California* (Berkeley: University of California Press, 1990).

6. Les and Jeanne Rentmeester, *The Wisconsin Creoles* (Melbourne, Fla.: privately published, 1987), v–iii; Mary Gehman, *Women and New Orleans, A History* (New Orleans: Margaret Media, 1988), 10; "Creoles," *The Iowa Patriot*, 6 June 1839.

7. Peterson, "People In Between"; Murphy, *Gathering of Rivers*, 45–76.

8. Johnson, *Queen Marinette*, 32–33. Allan Greer, *The People of New France* (Toronto: University of Toronto Press, 1997), 69–71; James H. Lockwood, "Early Times and Events in Wisconsin," *Collections of the State Historical Society of Wisconsin* 2 (1856), 121–122, 176; Jacqueline Peterson, "People In-Between," 1; and Ebenezer Childs, "Recollections of Wisconsin since 1820," *Collections of the State Historical Society of Wisconsin*, 4:167.

9. Giacomo Constantino Beltrami, *A Pilgrimage in Europe and America* (London: Hunt & Clarke, 1828), 2:174; Henry R. Schoolcraft, *A View of the Lead Mines of Missouri* (New York: Charles Wiley, 1819), 39; Caleb Atwater, *Remarks made on a tour to Prairie du Chien in 1829* (Columbus, Ohio: Isaac Whiting, 1831), 180.

10. J. H. LaMotte to William Beaumont, 2 September 1836, Beaumont Papers, Missouri Historical Society; Lockwood, "Early Times," 110.

11. Wisconsin Historical Society, *Proceedings* 1914, 108, 112. Wives' names: Hansen, "Crawford County, Wisconsin Marriages, 1816–1848," *Minnesota Genealogical Journal*, vol. 1 (May 1984), 48, 54, 55; and Hansen, "Prairie du Chien and Galena Church Records, 1827–29," *Minnesota Genealogical Journal* 5 (May 1986), 18. Oskache may have been Ojibwe, according to the marriage record.

12. Laurel Thatcher Ulrich, *Good Wives: Image and Reality in the Lives of Women in Northern New England, 1650–1750* (New York: Alfred A. Knopf, 1982), 59–65; Barbara Welter, "The Cult of True Womanhood, 1820–1860," *American Quarterly* 18 (1966), 151–74; Mary P. Ryan, *Cradle of the Middle Class: The Family in Oneida County, New York, 1790–1865* (New York: Cambridge University Press, 1981), 210–18. Community studies of mid-western Anglo settlements emphasize the ways in which "pioneers" idealized "good neighborship." See John Mack Faragher, *Sugar Creek: Life on the Illinois Prairie* (New Haven: Yale University Press, 1979), 15–20; and Merle Curti, *The Making of an American Community* (Stanford, Calif.: Stanford University Press, 1959), 114–16.

13. Lockwood, "Early Times," 125–26.

14. Thomas E. Randall, *History of the Chippewa Valley* (Eau Claire, Wisc.: Free Press Print, 1875), 17–18.

15. *Oceana County History*, 1880–1990, vol. 1. (Hart, Mich.: Oceana County Historical Society, 1991), 425; and Paula Stofer, "Angels of Mercy, Michigan's Midwives," *Michigan History*, 73:5 (1989), 46. "Mrs. H. L. Robinson Dead," *The Journal* (Hart, Michigan), 22 April 1904, 1. Typescript copy in the possession of Susan Russick.

16. "Memoir of Antoine LeClaire, Esquire, of Davenport, Iowa," *Annals of Iowa*, v. 1 (1863), 144–47; and Harry E. Downer, *History of Davenport and Scott County, Iowa* (Chicago: S.J. Clarke, 1910), 394–405 (quotation, 400).

17. Juliette M. Kinzie, *Wau-Bun: The "Early Day" in the North-West* [1856] (Urbana: University of Illinois Press, 1992), 19.

18. Richard White, *The Middle Ground: Indians, Empires, and Republics in the Great Lakes Region, 1650–1815* (Cambridge: Cambridge University Press, 1991), 38, 97–104.

19. Stephen Mack to H. M. Whittmore, Pecatoni, Oct. 6, 1847, quoted in David Bishop and Craig G. Campbell, *History of the Forest Preserves of Winnebago County, Illinois* (Rockford: Winnebago County Forest Preserve Commission, 1979), 35.

20. John McGilvray to B. F. Heuston, June 18, 1886, Heuston Collection, Murphy Library, University of Wisconsin–La Crosse, Wisconsin State Historical Society, LaCrosse.

21. Elizabeth T. Baird, "O-De-Jit-Wa-Win-Wing; Comptes du Temps Passe," Henry S. Baird Collection, Box 4, folder 9, State Historical Society of Wisconsin, Madison, chap. 17.

22. Anonymous, *A Merry Briton in Pioneer Wisconsin* [1842] (Chicago: State Historical Society of Wisconsin, 1950), 69.

23. Ibid., 71–72.

24. Virginia G. Crane, "A Métis Woman of the Fox River Frontier: The Two Cultures of Sophia Grignon Porlier," paper presented at the "Women of the Midwest: History and Sources; A Women's History Outreach Conference," Madison, Wisconsin, 13 June 1997.

25. Hansen, "Crawford County, Wisconsin Marriages," 39–58.

26. Rebecca Kugel, "Reworking Ethnicity: Gender, Work Roles, and Contending Redefinition of the Great Lakes Métis," in R. David Edmunds, ed., *Enduring Nations: Native Americans in the Midwest* (Urbana: University of Illinois Press, 2008), 160–81.

MAUREEN FITZGERALD
Habits of Compassion: Irish American Nuns in New York City

Even before the potato famine of 1845, the population of Ireland was declining, pressed by harsh British policies and the attraction of American opportunity. In the 1840s alone, death and immigration decreased the Irish population by more than 20 percent, and nearly half of all immigrants to the United States in that decade were Irish. And more than half of Irish immigrants were women. They were "the only significant group of foreign-born women who outnumbered men," writes historian Hasia Diner, and "the only significant group of women who chose to migrate in primarily female cliques."*

In the following essay, Maureen Fitzgerald examines the distinctive shape of Irish women's migration and the creative work of the institutions they built. How does Fitzgerald describe the desirability of convent life for Irish American women? How did Irish American nuns "change the nature of convent life even as they embraced it"? How did nuns respond to urban poverty? In what ways did they claim power in the public sphere? How were these ways different from the ways claimed by Protestant women of the same generation?

On Monday morning, August 17, 1896, a simple black hearse pulled by a single horse traveled through the streets of New York City. The hearse carried the body of Sister Mary Irene Fitzgibbon and was followed by four hundred of the three thousand Catholic nuns active in the city.[1] Like Sister Irene, most of the sisters hailed from Irish backgrounds, the children of Irish famine refugees. Thousands of mourners, including Protestants and Jews as well as Catholics, watched from the sidewalks and followed the hearse as it passed by their workplaces and through their neighborhoods, until the procession was estimated at twenty thousand. Secular and Catholic newspapers alike marked her death with prominent articles; the *New York Times'* headline read simply "Sister Mary Irene Is Dead." The *Times* called her "the most remarkable woman of her age in her sphere of philanthropy," and other non-Catholic newspapers agreed. The *Herald* characterized the massive yet simple procession that marked her death as unprecedented: "Never in the history of New York has such a tribute been paid."[2]

Over the weekend before 3,500 mourners paid their respects at the Foundling Asylum, Sister Irene's crowning achievement, an institution she had founded and then supervised for twenty-seven years. The Foundling Asylum housed an average of six hundred women and 1,800 infants at a time and also provided day care for working mothers, a maternity hospital for poor women, a children's hospital, and a shelter for unwed mothers. With an annual budget of $250,000 derived from *city taxes*, secured initially through Irish Catholic men's control of Tammany Hall, the Foundling Asylum was the largest institution of its kind in the country and the only one in New York City to guarantee care for all children and women who came to its doors, regardless of religion, race or ethnicity, marital status, or ability to pay for care.

*Hasia Diner, *Erin's Daughters in America: Irish Immigrant Women in the Nineteenth Century* (Baltimore: Johns Hopkins University Press, 1983), p. xiv.

Excerpted from the introduction and ch. 1 of *Habits of Compassion: Irish Catholic Nuns and the Origins of New York's Welfare System, 1830–1920*, by Maureen Fitzgerald (Urbana: University of Illinois Press, 2006). Reprinted by permission of the author and publisher. Notes have been edited and renumbered.

The tribute paid to Sister Irene, although remarkable in itself, becomes more so when we consider that Sister Irene Fitzgibbon is virtually unknown to historians of women in the United States. She was but one of approximately two thousand Catholic nuns then active in New York City charities and whose charitable work was dependent primarily or exclusively on public funding. . . .

In the United States between 1830 and 1900, Catholic women established 106 new foundations of women religious and grew to a collective workforce of approximately fifty thousand. In New York City alone, the number of women religious rose from eighty-two in 1848 to 2,846 in 1898, not only increasing their own numbers exponentially but also composing the majority of the church workforce. While men and women joined the church in New York City in relatively equal numbers at mid century, the number of nuns grew to almost triple that of the combined number of priests and brothers by 1898.[3]

Irish and Irish American women, moreover, changed the nature of convent life even as they embraced it. . . . They transform[ed] convents from institutions run by elite women to those composed of and administered by women who had been poor or were from the working class. Convents thus became a primary means through which working class Irish Catholic women gained public power [although not a public voice]. Moreover, convents provided the Irish Catholic working class with the means to articulate and make manifest its political agendas and social vision.

Irish Catholic nuns considered protecting women and children in their group from the ravages of poverty, dislocation, and racial oppression to be central to their work, and they often did so through direct confrontation with Protestant middle-class women. The most derided and vulnerable of Irish Catholic women in nineteenth-century America was the destitute mother with children; she became the archetypal image of a woman whose mothering in poverty necessitated drastic societal intervention. Because they viewed poverty in the nineteenth century, as [many do] today, as a moral problem with roots in particular cultures, Protestant reformers believed that the best strategy for eradicating it was to intervene in motherhood so as to alter the reproduction of moral traits associated with poverty. According to the logic of Protestant reformers,

Catholicism either exacerbated or was wholly responsible for the tendency toward dependency, and even alcoholism, evident in the behavioral patterns of the Irish Catholic poor. The sooner children could be removed from the influence of such a mother, community, and religion, the better. . . .

From the early 1850s through the mid-1870s, Protestant elite reformers removed tens of thousands of poor immigrant children from New York City streets and homes and sent them to Protestant homes in the Midwest. . . . The practice of taking urban poor children away from their natural parents rested on the normative belief that the American Protestant nuclear family, guided by the maternal devotion of the American woman, was the only proper setting for child-rearing in the American republic. . . .

A large workforce of Irish Catholic nuns in concert with a city political machine dominated by Irish Catholic men was able in the 1870s and 1880s to construct Catholic institutions that directly offset such programs. Sisters funded these institutions, moreover, through city taxes. In the name of the "parental rights" of the poor, nuns housed tens of thousands of children. . . . By 1885 they directly controlled most of New York City's public child-care system, rearing more than 80 percent of its dependent children while Jews and Protestants controlled 10 percent each. Nuns alone housed fifteen thousand children at a time; perhaps most important, they constructed a "revolving door" policy. They took children into their institutions at the initiation of poor parents, and on a temporary basis only, to be returned when parents themselves thought they were financially able to provide for them.[4] . . .

. . . After the Council of Trent in the early sixteenth century, all Catholic nuns were required to make solemn, lifelong vows and observe papal cloister or enclosure, thereby severely restricting their mobility, rights to property, and ability to transact business or interact directly with the larger populace. These contemplative orders, distinguished from "active" orders by enclosed status and a focus on prayer and meditation, were more likely to exist when and where wealthy women could bring sufficient dowries to convents to fund lifelong seclusion.[5]

In the late eighteenth century . . . Catholic women in Ireland and the United States began to form active "religious institutes" sanctioned by the pope but not regulated by the Vatican until the turn of the twentieth century. Because the women did not call themselves nuns but rather "sisters" or "women religious" and made annual, or what they termed "simple," vows, they were not subject to the same regulation of convent life that governed contemplative orders.[6] Catholic women transformed this opening into a cultural and political mechanism for collective organization and public authority. . . .

Irish Catholic women religious of the early nineteenth century were above all at the center of a nation that existed only in the imaginations of those committed to an Ireland free of British rule. . . . [T]hrough the Penal Laws instituted after Oliver Cromwell's conquest of the island in the seventeenth century, . . . Catholics in Ireland were legally barred from worship in Catholic churches, voting, holding public office, or passing on property to heirs. By 1750 Catholics owned only 5 percent of all the land in Ireland. The . . . [British], moreover, developed ideological rationales for colonization and Protestant rule that linked race to religion. The Irish were judged an inferior race over which dominion was justified because of the strength of Catholic "barbarism" among its people.[7] Although individual Irish people could avoid the worst effects of the Penal Laws by converting to Protestantism, few did. . . .

. . . Consider, for instance, Mother Mary Augustine, born Ellen McKenna, who joined the Sisters of Mercy in New York in 1849, approximately three years after a small contingent of the order had set off from their motherhouse in Dublin to establish themselves in the city. From the earliest days of her childhood McKenna was encouraged by her family to support the development of Catholicism as a gesture of solidarity with other Irish and against British colonialism.[8] . . .

Unlike most of the Irish peasantry who remained Gaelic-speaking, illiterate, and only nominally tied to the institutional church, for instance, Ellen McKenna was sent to school in Waterford at an early age. . . . Ellen McKenna's desire to enter a Catholic sisterhood was not an attempt to leave the world and its strife but rather an effort to play a leading role in shaping nationalist institutional Catholicism. The rise of institutional Catholicism in nineteenth-century Ireland was, perhaps above all, a cultural project in which Irish Catholic nationalists attempted to supplant the institutional structures of British colonialism with institutions of their own. Education and charities, because they decreased dependence on British National Schools and the British Poor Laws, were as central to that [catholic] nationalist vision as the building of parishes. By 1840, although having a workforce of only 1,600 sisters (in a population of eight million), 81 percent of Irish Catholic convents had instituted facilities and programs for the poor, including sick and prisoner visitation, free schools, meal and clothing distribution, houses of industry, and visitation of workhouses among other activities. Of the convents in Ireland, 84 percent ran schools by 1864.[9] . . . Some men in religious orders oversaw the education and care of boys, especially older boys, but charities, as in New York, were to become the almost exclusive province of nuns.

Although from a prosperous family, Ellen McKenna nonetheless experienced the trauma and catastrophe of famine by the mid-1840s, and emigration proved her greatest burden and constant inspiration. When the famine struck just after her father died, she aided the impoverished until the McKennas' own poverty became so great that they were forced to emigrate. Ellen deemed that experience a political "exile" as coerced as a political deportation. And yet she "offered it up" as penance, invoking the forced exile of St. Columba from Ireland:

> Dear St. MacCartin, fearful was the sorrow
>   I offered at thy shrine as penance dread
> Upon this day, long, long ago, for Willville
>   And home, and hope, to seek strange lands instead
> God, merciful and patient, oh! accept it—
>   This hard Columban penance—thus away
> From our sweet motherland, our native country,
>   To wear out life. Oh! aid me still, I pray.[10]

Ellen was no longer in Ireland but neither was she about to "wear out life." When her mother died in New York City in 1849, Ellen and her sister, Julia, both joined the Mercy Sisters in New York.

Called Sister Mary Augustine in religious life, Ellen worked immediately in the House of Mercy, the shelter for female famine migrants, where she interacted with thousands of starving Gaelic-speaking women who had fled peasant areas in western Ireland. At every point in her life thereafter she helped move the order into uncharted areas of charitable work, including the establishment of a home for destitute girls in 1860.

As mother superior of the order after the Civil War she also aggressively sought, and won, public funding through Tammany Hall, thereby enabling the order to branch out into work with children on an unprecedented scale. Ireland, however, was never far from her mind, nor were the British, whom she struggled to "forgive" as an act of charity. The continuing migration of the Irish to North America was for her a constant reminder of the deprivation and cultural losses the Irish were forced to endure and the responsibility she felt for re-producing that culture. As she characteristi-cally observed to another Sister of Mercy in 1878, "It grieves me when the children we bring up know little about [St. Patrick] and about St. Brigid, the glory of Irishwomen.[11] . . .

. . . By 1860 the Irish accounted for 1.6 of the 2.2 million Catholics throughout the United States, thereby dwarfing the French, German, and Anglo Catholic communities. The strength of Irish cultural and ecclesiastic power in New York City was premised in part on the proportion of the church's workforce that was Irish. Fifty-nine (55 percent) of 107 male clergy in 1845 were born in Ireland. By 1865, twenty-three of the thirty-two Catholic parishes in New York City were Irish, distin-guished from the rest by the English language spoken by priests.[12] The organization of the city's women religious also reflected Irish dominance as the Sisters of Charity, the Sisters of Mercy, and the Sisters of the Good Shep-herd, established in New York City in 1817, 1846, and 1859, respectively, became more Irish over time. Each existed outside parish struc-tures, in contrast to others such as the French Holy Cross Sisters and the German Sisters of Notre Dame that were attached, respectively, to French and German parishes. . . .

. . . Without a substantial middle class to foot the bill for churches, charities, and educa-tion, and with an ever-growing number of des-titute people from peasant backgrounds constituting the laity, the church was poor and resources were scarce. Prioritizing how best to use the resources of the community, especially its labor and funding, was a constant and un-resolved tension, and Catholic sisters were often at the center of such battles. . . .

Irish Catholic sisters had to contend with anti-Catholicism of all types, but anti-nun lit-erature and Protestant assumptions about nuns' victimization certainly framed their struggles through the century. . . . [T]he belief that convents were brothels for the use of priests, in which women were tortured and raped, was not limited to a fringe of nativist fanatics. The most popular American version of the immorality of convent life, that contrib-uted by Maria Monk in her *Awful Disclosures of the Hotel Dieu Nunnery of Montreal*, was pub-lished originally in 1836 and sold more than three hundred thousand copies by the Civil War, making it second only to *Uncle Tom's Cabin* in antebellum book sales.[13] . . .

Burning convents, avenging "escaped" nuns, and demanding convent inspection laws throughout the United States during the 1850s were all premised on an abhorrence of wom-en's public space, free from male control. . . . Irish Catholic sisters were . . . at the very least inscrutable. Their daily lives, dress, behavior, and value systems did not reflect a "true wom-anhood" in which domesticity and mother-hood rhetorically defined duties to family and nation. Nuns' "delusions" [e]voked . . . pity be-cause their commitment to Catholicism, through which they established independence from individual men, made them literally in-comprehensible as women.

Why then would Ellen McKenna choose life in a convent? When asked that question on applications for the Sisters of Mercy in New York, McKenna's cohorts were likely to state that they aspired to life in a sisterhood "for the greater Glory of God."[14] Yet such an assertion reveals relatively little about the reasons for the growth of convent life in nineteenth-century Ireland or why so many Irish women chose that life compared, for instance, to women in other Catholic cultures. . . . They, like Ellen McKenna, were likely to see opportunities and possibilities in the life of a religious that ren-dered other options less desirable.

At the heart of the choice was a willing-ness to make vows of chastity, poverty, and obedience. Making such vows seems a simple ritual on its surface, but each was made in the context of larger cultural shifts, and none was ever simple. . . . In the experience of women committed to life in a sisterhood the vows were not discrete but often in conflict. Negoti-ating their relative weight and balance in any situation or circumstance was at the heart of convent politics. . . .

Catholic women made vows of chastity in direct renunciation of the familial roles as wives, mothers, and daughters. The vows ena-bled nuns to cast themselves as special women sanctioned by the social and religious culture to live apart from the familial obligations most women were expected to honor. Nuns did not derive status because they were women but because they denied themselves the pleasures and fruits of the female body, especially sex and motherhood. And yet the vows were not only experienced as renunciation but also [paradoxically] as liberation. As Rose-Mary Reuther has [observed,] . . . "Women dedicated to asceticism could count on the support of the Church in making decisions against their family's demands that they marry and bear children."[15] . . .

Church leaders encouraged Irish Catholics to believe that a son or daughter's entrance into the church was a great honor for the family in general, yet Catholic parental resistance was often overt. When the founder of the New York convent of the Sisters of Mercy, thirty-year-old Mary O'Connor, decided to leave Dublin for New York in 1846, her mother beseeched the Dublin male hierarchy to interfere with her daughter's and the Mercy order's decision and convince her to stay in Ireland instead. . . . [From the convent nun's point of view,] conflicts between parents and postulants were expected. . . . [A]pplications for admission to orders asked explicitly if there was parental resistance to the women's entrance. . . . [Convents often denied] entrance to a novice if they believed that aged parents were dependent on that woman's wages or relied on her caretaking for their health. . . .

Among the most important reasons that so many Irish women chose to become women religious was that committing to a life of celibacy was not a radical break from the sexual patterns evident in much of Ireland. . . . The rising rural middling classes increasingly . . . plac[ed] enormous emphasis on consolidating land holdings. Instead of the rampant subdivision characteristic of peasants, only one daughter and one son in each family would be dowered or receive land. . . . Few women in this class could marry in Ireland. . . . Those deemed superfluous, moreover, such as a second or third daughter, understood from an early age that they would not be given a dowry and therefore had few options for marriage. As this pattern accelerated in the aftermath of the famine the proportion of people who remained unmarried in Ireland through most or all of their lives became very high by international standards despite high levels of emigration.[16]

Depopulation, not reproduction, was the organizing principle in gender and sexual relations in postfamine Ireland. One million deaths from starvation and disease and urgent emigration decreased Ireland's population from more than 8 million in 1841 to 5.8 million in 1861. By 1921 Ireland's population was at 4.3 million, roughly half the 1841 census. Subdivision and population growth were unthinkable, given their role in making the poor so vulnerable to the potato crop's failure and contributing to what all classes believed was the death of Ireland as they knew it.[17] For many, sex itself was the culprit in Ireland's ruin, and demonizing sexual behavior outside, or even inside, marriage became a critical foundation for Irish Catholic sexual culture.

Thus as the nineteenth century wore on the respectability of all Irish Catholic women was contingent upon maintaining a sexually chaste lifestyle. Unlike American Protestant middle-class culture, however, Irish Catholic dependence on Catholic ascetic tradition worked in tandem with cultural shifts to position mothers and wives on relatively low rungs of a hierarchy of sexual respectability. In the Irish Catholic schema, "virgins" and nuns came first; widows, second; and wives, because of their continuing sexual experience, third. Once a woman lost her status as a virgin in Irish Catholic society, even within marriage, she would never regain it, nor would her position as mother offset the loss of status entailed by heterosexual experience. Protestant women, in contrast, continued to be labeled as sexually "pure" so long as their sexual experience was contained within the institution of marriage. . . .

For nuns, the vow of chastity was never only one of renouncing heterosexuality but always simultaneously a commitment to live in a community of women throughout one's lifetime and according to rules, and with cultural power, governing convent life. Women's ability, desire, and willingness to make a lifelong commitment to live and work with other women provided the social foundation of a sisterhood. Convent rules were often written with proscriptions against "particular friendships," meaning any attachment of particular nuns to each other that might interfere with the general harmony of community life, including exclusive attachments or favoritism, or friendships that led to sexual relations. . . .

Lifelong and very close friendships in convents were not just tolerated but assumed and encouraged. Sometimes two or three natural sisters would join the same sisterhood simultaneously. Women who could count favorite aunts or cousins as role models often followed them into convent life and sometimes into the same convent. Friends often entered convents together. . . . Sisters of Charity Irene Fitzgibbon and Teresa Vincent together founded and administered the Foundling Asylum, their partnership/friendship providing the core of continuity through nearly three decades of work and activism.[18] . . .

The vow of poverty was a complex and even paradoxical one. . . . At base, the vow of poverty was not intended to impoverish women religious but rather to encourage identification with "Christ's poor" in their work and spiritual lives. At times that meant suffering through very real poverty, but at other times women religious risked their work with the poor if they squandered or did not reproduce the wealth they had. Nor did all women religious embrace the same kind of commitment to poverty. Even within orders, poverty was often an unequal experience. . . .

. . . [E]ntrance into a convent allowed women the opportunity to collectivize wealth with other women and apart from men. Some who formed sisterhoods in pre-famine Ireland were very wealthy. . . . Their collectivization of women's wealth made sisterhoods perhaps the most powerful and rich female institutions in pre-famine Ireland. The act of joining a sisterhood moved an individual's wealth to the larger collective, and thus any individual lost their wealth as such. Yet through that action women also removed wealth from the control of men by placing it outside standard patriarchal inheritance structures. When those who dedicated their wealth to the sisterhood died, relatives could not claim an inheritance; the property remained in the hands of the present and future sisterhood.

The premise of sisterhoods' financial autonomy was augmented by the American legal system; nuns maintained feme sole legal status throughout their lifetimes. Married women of the period, who were defined [as] feme covert, or "covered" in marriage, generally did not hold property individually; the property was assumed to become their husbands'. . . .

Nuns, conversely, by virtue of their feme sole status, could and did collectivize wealth, incorporate institutions under exclusively female control, derive revenue from business transactions, sign contracts, and secure loans. No men in the church, furthermore, had either legal or cultural claims to such wealth. Their collective financial and legal power thereby enabled women religious to establish female-run and female-owned public institutions at a time when the most radical woman's rights activists in Protestant America rarely lived apart from marriage or owned property of their own. Catharine Beecher herself, the chief advocate of American marital domesticity, noted in 1843 that Catholic nuns had means to power that she did not. "The rich and noble have places provided as heads of great establishments," she wrote, "where in fact they have a power and station and influence which even ambition might seek." That Catholic nuns lived and worked in the public sphere in all-female enclaves long before such organization was perceived as a social or political possibility for Protestant middle-class women was for Beecher self-evident. As an ambitious unmarried woman who spent her adult lifetime with no clear channels through which to engage her talents and education, Beecher lamented that Protestant culture did not allow her to live and work together with other women in a women's community.[19]

Not all sisters shared equally in that wealth and power. European orders, including those of Irish origin, were divided into lay and choir sisters, the latter the more wealthy postulants. At mid-century, poor women who entered sisterhoods would most likely make vows as a "lay sister." Lay sisters were expected to perform the tasks of domestic servants in convents, thereby freeing the choir sisters for "higher" pursuits. In the American context, however, these distinctions quickly eroded, both because there were so few wealthy women with a requisite choir sister's dowry (approximately five hundred pounds) and because lay sisters actively protested against this caste system. . . .

. . . New York's Mercy lay sisters were successful in gradually winning the abolition of outward indications of class status. In 1878 they were no longer required to wear a distinctive apron that set them apart from choir, and by 1895 community records no longer referred to any single member as choir or lay, even if they were professed as such. Individual work schedules of the New York Mercy Sisters show that while some women worked consistently in high-status or low-status jobs, such as academy teaching or kitchen work, there was often considerable flexibility in work assignments for women over a lifetime. One sister worked alternatively as a first- and fourth-grade teacher in the select school, a kitchen worker, and sewing worker in the boys' home over a ten-year period. Others alternated between sewing, kitchen, teaching, and administrative duties throughout their lifetimes.[20]

Poverty was understood broadly as an ascetic life, denying pleasure and comfort. . . . And yet freedom *from* the world, rather than *in* the world, allowed women public legitimacy in offering a critique of society. . . . As the Irish poor swelled the prisons in New York City and the Sisters of Mercy and Sisters of Charity undertook daily prison visitations, they frequently befriended men and women characterized as irredeemable by native-born Protestants. Catherine Seton, . . . [one of] the Mercy Sisters, became attached to a young man who spent time variously at Sing Sing, the Tombs, and the city penitentiary. After his failed attempt at armed robbery, Mother Seton sent him $5 to aid in his escape and promised to care for his wife and children. When another of her protegés died, she inherited the tools he used for breaking and entering, including jimmies and pistols.[21] That such stories were included in the Mercy Sisters' published annals suggests an unwillingness to accept uncritically the notions of the native-born middle class about exactly what constituted criminality, respectability, or viciousness. In classic Irish fashion it also made for a good, funny story in the midst of tragedy.

For those orders committed to work with the poor in New York City and throughout the United States, financial pressures constantly vied with individual sisterhoods' efforts to keep their work and "mission" focused on those in poverty. . . . In the United States, all charitable sisterhoods had to devise a means of income capable of sustaining both the order itself and its charitable work. The most common strategy was to create an elite school in which tuition was charged and then use that tuition for the convent's upkeep and charities. . . .

Until the mid 1840s, women formed and joined convents in the United States and Ireland with the understanding that women's orders were parallel, separate entities that coexisted with but were not subordinate to local or national male ecclesiastical structures. Convents and monasteries were subordinate to the pope and maintained hierarchies within their respective orders, but most were not subject to the bishops in the dioceses in which they worked. Between their foundation in New York in 1817 and 1846, for instance, New York's Sisters of Charity, like other local convents of the Sisters of Charity, was accountable to their motherhouse at Emmitsburg, Maryland. The motherhouse retained ultimate control of sisters who worked in any specific diocese, and the wishes of local bishops, priests, and laity were considered secondary to the demands and needs of the order at large. Within the motherhouse, a mother general was considered the head officer, followed by assistant mother, bursar, mistress of novices, and various grades of sisters, including professed sisters, novices, and postulants. In each city in which the sisters worked, moreover, internal convent hierarchies were replicated.[22] when nuns established institutions in which they lived apart from the main local convent, particular sisters, usually called sisters superior or head sisters, would be given ultimate charge of the specific institutions. Although the rationalization of the order allowed nuns in localities distant from the motherhouse to govern their own lives and activism in ways responsive to local contexts, they remained ultimately responsible to the motherhouse.

Motherhouse rule was the linchpin in convent autonomy, and through it sisters were able to control the kinds of work they did, their religious lives, and, most important, their ability to make vows of obedience to other women, not to men. Until 1846 the Sisters of Charity did not make vows of obedience to the church at large, but rather to the order to which they belonged, specifically to the mother superior and other female leadership. Obedience, moreover, was interpreted more broadly than simple subordination to specific people. It included the utilization of individual conscience to determine if a superior's actions were in accordance with the larger "mission" or apostolate of each distinctive sisterhood. Dedicating the order and collective lives of nuns to charity, for instance, and to a particular group in poverty—whether orphans, prostitutes, or unwed mothers—meant that those who made vows of obedience were dedicating themselves simultaneously to a religious lifestyle and a lifetime of work. A postulant would learn about the "spirit" or "mission" of the order through intensive study and contemplation of the reasons for the order's foundation, especially through writing by and stories about the founding superior.

When individuals or groups in a community felt that the superiors of an order took action that pitted their obligations to the mission against those to the convent's leadership, community discord could be great enough to induce the majority of professed sisters in the community to impede the reelection or encourage resignation of convent officers. . . .

On an individual level, women religious who rejected the tenor or politics of convent life could simply leave. Despite the dramatic "escapes" so vivid in anti-nun literature, no active orders were "enclosed," and therefore no women within them were barred from leaving at will. Sisters in active orders took yearly "simple vows," not lifelong vows, and therefore could leave convents without a formal repudiation of those vows. In practice, however, the system of novitiate, postulancy, and final profession, which lasted anywhere from three to five years, was expected to weed out those who either did not want to commit to the order for a lifetime or were considered unacceptable by the professed sisters, who would have the final vote in chapter meeting to recommend continuance or expulsion.

On both an individual and collective level, obedience demanded a selflessness that required extraordinary ascetic discipline. As Mother McKenna advised young Sisters of Mercy about to make their vows in 1873, that sacrifice was intended to benefit both the soul and others in the world:

> . . . I pray God that your heart and soul may be devoted to the poor, sick, and that serving the Lord in His poor, He may make you rich in graces and blessings. . . . Inch by inch this sacrifice is exacted by little trials, more galling than great ones. To say nothing when we would naturally say something sharp; to do simply as we are told, without objection or remonstrance, . . . to seem cheerful when the heart aches, to be kind in return for unkindness, . . .—these efforts will be sacrifices.

Yet Mother Augustine McKenna was also supremely conscious of the need to balance obedience against ambition and assertiveness, particularly when that ambition was in the name of others who needed her help. As the chief architect of the order's work with children, then Sister McKenna wrote out a separate promise to herself and God in 1860 and placed it at the back of the book that held her original vows. She showed it to no one, but other Sisters of Mercy found it and buried it with her. Mother McKenna wrote [in part]:

> In the name of our Lord and Saviour, Jesus Christ, and under the protection of His Immaculate Mother, Mary ever Virgin, I, Sister Mary Augustine, for the love of his Sacred Heart, do resolve, but not vow, to suffer all the blame, shame, and humiliation, toil, trial, and trouble, that it may be God's will to permit, in order to establish a home for homeless children. I protest that, in all that concerns it, I rely solely on the assistance of God and the guidance of the Holy Spirit. . . . [23]

[When she wrote this, she knew that her proposal for moving into work with poor children would provoke the archbishop's anger.] As Mother McKenna's resolution suggests, obedience was hardly passivity. . . . Her obedience to the spiritual authorities above was constructed in such a way to ready herself for the worldly battles to come.

And yet few even in the Catholic community understood fully what either Mother McKenna or other sisters did and thought on a regular basis. Indeed, the single most salient political limitation affecting sisters' overall power in nineteenth-century America was their relative lack of public voice. Whereas white, Protestant, middle-class women increasingly legitimated their claims to public power through a set of rational discourses promoting their cause as women or as mothers, nuns were reluctant to promote their causes through public discourse.

The effect of that limitation was both far-reaching and paradoxical. The most powerful women in the church, including the founder of the Foundling Asylum, Sister Irene Fitzgibbon, demanded that they be treated, and nuns under their guidance should treat themselves, as "old shoe[s]."[24] Consistent with an ethic of ascetic selflessness, Sister Irene's pronouncements should not lead historians to assume that these ostensible "old shoes" lacked substantial power. And yet their reluctance to claim that power as such, especially in public and to the larger community, proved decisive in public arenas in which the Catholic hierarchy or Protestant native-borns contested that power. Women religious were thus most vulnerable when discussion of themselves or their work moved to public arenas. Nor did this limitation affect only nuns. Because they were the female leaders in the Irish Catholic community, their unwillingness to spar publicly with Catholic men or Protestant native-borns made the relative power of Irish Catholic women as a group, and the causes they championed, similarly vulnerable to their posture of collective selflessness.

Part of the reason that nuns nave remained virtually invisible in nineteenth-century women's history is that the measures, or signposts, of their public power do not fit the framework constructed for understanding the public power of Protestant middle-class and elite women during the same period. Nuns' strengths were centered in areas of Protestant female reformers' relative weakness. Both white and black Protestant middle-class women derived public power through associational organizations and claims to public voice, especially through their role as mothers. Nuns' effectiveness, however, was based on an ability to live together and organize themselves as large bodies of single women who lived apart from marriage and domesticity. Convents became powerful collectives for activist labor through the sisterhoods' combined labor power in educational and welfare institutions, their centuries-long apprenticeship traditions and systems in nursing, teaching, and charities, their feme sole legal status and accumulation of wealth under exclusively female control, and their freedom from mothering and the direct controls of husbands. It was a form of public organization for welfare work, moreover, that most Protestant women were unable to construct until the turn of the twentieth century.

Indeed, if we concentrate on the spectacular growth of Catholic convents in America through the late nineteenth century, the dominant narrative of Protestant women's work in social reform through the Progressive Era begins to take new shape. Although histories of "women's" constructions of nursing, teaching, and social work rarely acknowledge the influence of Catholic female traditions in these areas, the roots of these "professions" are nonetheless everywhere entwined with the work of nuns. Settlement work in particular is deemed an extraordinary departure from all tradition in that it allowed Protestant women to live together, apart from marriage and within immigrant neighborhoods, and from that base construct charitable programs. The parallels to convent life are so obvious that the compelling question is not whether the convent served as a model for settlement life but why this parallel goes unanalyzed. That such a connection is not thought conspicuously absent is made possible primarily by our construction of frameworks that render nuns historically invisible.

. . . The limits and threats to nuns' power, . . . , were also often distinct from those that threatened Protestant women. Over the course of [the 19th century] nuns' relative power to men in their group was threatened most directly by the rationalization of bishops' authority over religious orders in their dioceses. That process of rationalization, however, was uneven. . . . A critical factor determining whether or for how long nuns could deflect male control . . . was their ability to gain financial independence from the hierarchy. [T]he public funding of nuns' charitable work helped orders delay substantial loss of autonomy until the early twentieth century.

NOTES

1. Throughout this work I refer to Catholic women in religious institutes as "women religious," "sisters," and "nuns," thereby reflecting common usage but not canon law, which stipulated that only enclosed women religious be referred to as nuns.

2. *New York Times*, Aug. 17, 1896, 6; *New York Herald Tribune*, Aug. 18, 1896.

3. Mary Ewens, *The Role of the Nun in Nineteenth-Century America* (1971, repr. Salem, N.H.: Ayer, 1984), 86, 201, 252; *The Catholic Almanac for 1848* (Baltimore: F. Lucas, Jr., 1849), 180–81; *Hoffmann's Catholic Directory, Almanac and Clergy List* (Milwaukee: Hoffmann Brothers, 1898), 98–104.

4. A sizable literature on the availability of this option nationwide makes evident that poor parents used a variety of institutions to rear children temporarily through the Gilded Age period. See especially Patricia Kelleher, "Maternal Strategies: Irish Women's Headship of Families in Gilded Age Chicago," *Journal of Women's History* 13 (Summer 2001): 80; Timothy Hasci, *Second Home: Orphan Asylums and Poor Families in America* (Cambridge: Harvard University Press, 1997); Matthew Crenson, *Building the Invisible Orphanage: A Prehistory of the American Welfare System* (Cambridge: Harvard University Press, 1998).

5. Among the literature on Catholic sisters that has been critical to my understanding of their collective and distinctive histories are Carol K. Coburn and Martha Smith, *Spirited Lives: How Nuns Shaped Catholic Culture and American Life, 1836–1920* (Chapel Hill: University of North Carolina Press, 1999); JoAnn Kay McNamara, *Sisters in Arms: Catholic Nuns through Two Millennia* (Cambridge: Harvard University Press, 1996); and Diane Batts Morrow, *Persons of Color and Religious at the Same Time: The Oblate Sisters of Providence, 1828–1860* (Chapel Hill: University of North Carolina Press, 2002).

6. Two sophisticated studies of Catholic charities have put the development of Catholic charities in a national context and in relation to the larger welfare system: Mary J. Oates, *The Catholic Philanthropic Tradition in America* (Bloomington: Indiana University Press, 1995), and Dorothy M. Brown and Elizabeth McKeown, *The Poor Belong to Us: Catholic Charities and American Welfare* (Cambridge: Harvard University Press, 1997).

7. Kerby A. Miller, *Emigrants and Exiles: Ireland and the Irish Exodus to North America* (New York: Oxford University Press, 1985), 21–23; William V. Shannon, *The American Irish* (New York: Collier Books, 1963), 21.

8. [Mother Mary Teresa] Austin Carroll, *Leaves from the Annals of the Sisters of Mercy*, 4 vols. (New York: Catholic Publication Society, 1889), 3: 203–13.

9. Caitriona Clear, *Nuns in Nineteenth-Century Ireland* (Dublin: Gill and MacMillan, 1987), 101–105.

10. Carroll, *Leaves from the Annals*, 3:207.

11. Ibid., 3:216.

12. Carol Wittke, *The Irish in America* (Baton Rouge: Louisiana State University Press, 1956), 89; James Olson, *Catholic Immigrants in America* (Chicago: Nelson-Hall, 1987), 29; Jay Dolan, *The Immigrant Church: New York's Irish and German Catholics, 1815–1865* (Baltimore: Johns Hopkins University Press, 1975), 22.

13. Preface to Maria Monk, *Awful Disclosures of the Hotel Dieu Nunnery* (1836, repr. Hamden: Archon Books, 1962), 1.

14. Applications for the Sisters of Mercy of New York, Archives of the Sisters of Mercy, Dobbs Ferry, N.Y. (hereafter ASMNY).

15. Rosemary Ruether, "Mothers of the Church: Ascetic Women in the Late Patristic Age," in *Women of Spirit: Female Leadership in the Jewish and Christian Traditions*, edited by Rosemary Ruether and Eleanor McLaughlin (New York: Simon and Schuster, 1979), 72.

16. K. H. Connell, *The Population of Ireland, 1750–1845* (New York: Oxford University Press, 1950); Robert Kennedy, *The Irish: Emigration, Marriage and Fertility* (Berkeley: University of California Press, 1973); Hasia Diner, *Erin's Daughters in America: Irish Immigrant Women in the Nineteenth Century* (Baltimore: Johns Hopkins University Press, 1983), 6–29.

17. Miller, *Emigrants and Exiles*, 346.

18. Sister Marie De Lourdes Walsh, *The Sisters of Charity of New York, 1809–1959*, 3 vols. (New York: Fordham University Press, 1960), 3:64–88.

19. Catherine E. Beecher to Sarah Buckingham Beecher, Aug. 20, 1843, reprinted in *The Limits of Sisterhood: The Beecher Sisters on Women's Rights and Woman's Sphere*, edited by Jeanne Boydston, Mary Kelley, and Anne Margolis (Chapel Hill: University of North Carolina Press, 1988), 110, 239–40.

20. "Notes from the Annals of St. Catherine's Convent of Mercy," 1878, ASMNY; *Acts of Chapter, St. Catherine Convent, Madison Avenue, New York*, ASMNY; "Work Schedules," ASMNY.

21. Carroll, *Leaves from the Annals*, 171–72.

22. For the range of elective practices by convents in the United States, see Ewens, *The Role of the Nun*, passim.

23. Mother Mary Augustine McKenna to other Sisters of Mercy, 1873, reprinted in Carroll, *Leaves from the Annals*, 209, 215.

24. Sister Francis Cecilia Conway, "Notes on Foundling," Archives of the Sisters of Charity of New York at Mount St. Vincent. Sister Francis Conway worked with Sister Irene at the Foundling from 1890 to 1896.

INTIMACY AND DISCIPLINING BODIES

SHARON BLOCK
Lines of Color, Sex, and Service: Sexual Coercion in the Early Republic

A long tradition of describing northern society as "free" and southern society as "slave" has had the unfortunate effect of making distinctions seem far more clear in retrospect than they were in experience. Manumission was gradual and grudging in parts of the North where significant numbers of people were held as property. In Massachusetts, New Hampshire, and Vermont, many enslaved took their freedom by walking away from owners or bringing successful freedom suits based on the civil rights promised by the new state constitutions. However, other jurisdictions passed gradual emancipation laws that paid more attention to slave owners' property rights than to human rights. For example, by the 1780 Pennsylvania statute, all enslaved persons living at the time remained in bondage; all children born in the future to enslaved women were declared free but had to serve their mother's owner until the age of twenty-eight. This confusing legal landscape meant that African-descended people experienced a mixture of statuses—enslaved, indentured, free—throughout the first half of the nineteenth century.

Moreover, parental poverty, itinerancy, or perceived idleness could trigger laws allowing local officials to take children and place them in other households as indentured workers. Thus, in the early republic, youths of black, Indian, and white parents were regularly put out to bound labor. Burdened by their work, they were also vulnerable to the power and authority of their masters. This included, as we see in the essay that follows, vulnerability to sexual coercion—a term Sharon Block uses to mark a wider range of experience than is suggested by the simple term *rape*.[*] The essay that follows is based on a close reading of a Pennsylvania court record and on one of the great autobiographies of the nineteenth century, Harriet Jacobs's *Incidents in the Life of a Slave Girl*. Writing under a pseudonym after years as a fugitive, supported in her project by the abolitionist writer and editor Lydia Maria Child, Jacobs herself became invisible to historians. For many years her narrative was treated as fiction. Not until 1987, when historian Jean Fagan Yellin published an edition identifying virtually all the individuals and substantiating virtually all the

---

[*]Sharon Block explains that first names are used for all actors in incidents of sexual coercion because first names more easily distinguish men from women and eliminate confusion in identifying members of the same family.

Excerpted from "Lines of Color, Sex, and Service: Comparative Sexual Coercion in Early America" by Sharon Block in *Sex, Love, Race: Crossing Boundaries in North American History*, ed. Martha Hodes (New York: New York University Press, 1999). Reprinted by permission of the author and publisher. Notes have been edited and renumbered.

events, has it been possible to understand the narrative as nonfiction. It is compelling reading.[†]

    In what ways did Rachel Davis and Harriet Jacobs try to avoid the power of their masters? In whom did they find allies? In what ways were the experiences of these young women similar? What difference did slavery make?

Rachel Davis was born a free white child in the Pennsylvania mountains in 1790. She was fourteen years old when she became an indentured servant to William and Becky Cress in Philadelphia County. By the time Rachel was fifteen, William had begun making sexual overtures to her. After months of continuing sexual assaults, William's wife, Becky, suspected that her husband was having a sexual relationship with their servant. Ultimately, Becky demanded that Rachel be removed from the house. William continued to visit Rachel at her new home, again trying to have sex with her. In 1807, Rachel's father found out what had occurred and initiated a rape prosecution against William, who was found guilty and sentenced to ten years in prison.[1]

    Harriet Jacobs was born an enslaved black child in Edenton, North Carolina, in 1813. In 1825, she became a slave in James and Mary Norcom's household. By the time Harriet was sixteen, James had begun making sexual overtures toward her. After months of continuing sexual assaults, James's wife, Mary, suspected that her husband was having a sexual relationship with their slave. Ultimately, Mary demanded that Harriet be removed from the house. James continued to visit Harriet at her new home, again trying to have sex with her. In 1835, Harriet became a runaway slave, and spent the next seven years a fugitive, hiding in her free grandmother's attic crawl space.[2]

    If we were to focus on the conclusions to these stories, we would frame a picture of the contrasting consequences for masters who sexually coerced black and white women: the master of the white servant was sent to prison, while the black slave imprisoned herself to escape her abuser. But these opposing ends tell only part of the story. Until their conclusions, both women engaged in nearly parallel struggles with masters, mistresses, and unwanted sexual overtures. This contrast between the laborers' similar experiences and their stories' opposing conclusions suggests that the practice

of sexual coercion and the classification of the criminal act of rape were differently dependent on status and race.

    . . . Rachel had an opportunity for institutional intervention that was unequivocally denied to Harriet. Enslaved women in early America did not have access to legal redress against white men who raped them. While no colonial or early republic statute explicitly excluded enslaved women from being the victims of rape or attempted rape, many mid-Atlantic and Southern legislatures set harsh punishments for black men's sexual assaults on white women, thus implicitly privileging white women as victims of rape.[3] At the same time, enslaved people could only be witnesses against non-white defendants, so an enslaved woman could not testify against a white man who had raped her.[4] Accordingly, no historian has recorded a conviction of a white man for the rape of a slave at any point from 1700 to the Civil War, let alone a conviction of a master for raping his own slave. Rape in early America was a crime whose definition was structured by race.[5]

    Even though the early American legal system segregated Rachel Davis and Harriet Jacobs into incomparable categories, their own presentations told nearly parallel stories of sexual coercion. In both women's stories, their masters attempted to control the parameters and meanings of sexual acts. Thus, rape in these situations was not just an act of power, it was also the power to define an act. Servants and slaves could not only be forced to consent, but this force was refigured as consent. At the same time, neither Harriet Jacobs nor Rachel Davis presented herself as an abject victim of her master's will.

    Rather than a clear demarcation between the rape of slaves and the rape of servants, these narratives suggest that black and white laboring women interpreted and experienced a master's sexual coercion in strikingly similar ways. The parallels in these two stories, however, stopped at the courtroom door, where a racially

---

[†]Harriet A. Jacobs, *Incidents in the Life of a Slave Girl: Written by Herself,* ed. Jean Fagan Yellin (Cambridge, Mass.: Harvard University Press, 1987). Jean Fagan Yellin, *Harriet Jacobs: A Life* (New York: Basic Civitas Books, 2004).

based legal system ended the women's comparable negotiations of personal interactions.

CREATING MASTERY: THE PROCESS OF COERCION

How did a master sexually coerce a servant or slave in early America? A master did not have to rely on physical abilities to force his dependents into a sexual act. Instead, he might use the power of his position to create opportunities for sexual coercion, backing a woman into a corner where capitulation was her best option. A servant or enslaved woman often recognized this manipulation and tried to negotiate her way around her master's overtures rather than confront him with direct resistance. But that compromise came at a high price ... negotiation implied willingness, and a woman's willingness contrasted with the early American legal and social code that rape consisted of irresistible force. Despite its surface counterintuitiveness, it was precisely women's attempts to bargain their way out of sexual assaults that made these sexual encounters seem consensual.[6]

Both Harriet Jacobs and Rachel Davis drew direct links between their status and their masters' sexual assaults on them. Each explained how her master had forced her into situations where he could sexually coerce her without being discovered. Rachel described how William ordered her to hold the lantern for him one night in the stable, where he "tried to persuade me to something." In the most blatantly contrived incident, when they were reaping in the meadow, William "handed me his sickle & bad me to lay it down. He saw where I put it." Later that night, William asked Rachel,

> where I put them sickles. I asked if he did not see—he said no, I must come & show him. I told him I cd go with my sister, or by myself. he said that was not as he bad me. I went. Before we got quite to sickles, he bad me stop—I told him I was partly to the sickles—he bad me stop—I did—he came up & threw me down. . . . I hallowed—he put his hand over my mouth . . . he pulled up my cloathes, & got upon me . . . he did penetrate my body. I was dreadfully injured.

According to Rachel's statement, William had forced her to accompany him into a dark field on a contrived search for a purposefully lost farm implement so that he could rape her. William's authority to control where she went and what she did was integral to his ability to force Rachel to have sex with him.

Harriet Jacobs was even more explicit about the connections between James Norcum's mastery and his ability to force her into sexually vulnerable positions. It seemed to Harriet that he followed her everywhere—in her words, "my master met me at every turn"—trying to force her to have sex with him. As William did with Rachel, James structured Harriet's work so that she was often alone with him. He ordered Harriet to bring his meals to him so that while she watched him eat he could verbally torture her with the consequences of refusing his sexual overtures. Harriet further recalled that "when I succeeded in avoiding opportunities for him to talk to me at home, I was ordered to come to his office, to do some errand." Tiring of Harriet's continued resistance, James ordered his four-year-old daughter to sleep near him, thus requiring that Harriet also sleep in his room in case the child needed attention during the night. James repeatedly used his position as a master who controlled his slave's labor to manipulate Harriet into sexually vulnerable situations.[7] Controlling a woman's daily routine, her work requirements, and her physical presence—in other words, control over her labor and her body—gave men in positions of mastery access to a particular means of sexually coercive behavior.

Each woman also recalled how she had challenged her master's right to force her into a sexual relationship. Rachel recounted how she had "resisted" and "cried" when William tried to pull her into a darkened bedroom after sending the rest of the servants to bed, and how she threatened that she would tell his wife what he was doing. When these forms of resistance did not end his overtures, Rachel tried to carry out her master's orders in ways that might prevent her own sexual vulnerability. Rachel's description of being raped in the dark field began by recollecting that she had suggested that William could find the sickle himself, and then offered to find it on her own or with her sister. Ultimately, William resorted to his position as a master—"he said that was not as he bad me"—and issued a direct order for Rachel to accompany him. Rachel portrayed an interactive relationship with William: she may not have been able to override her master's orders, but she forced him to change their content. Rather than sex in the bedroom while the other children slept and his wife was away, Rachel forced William to order her into the dark field, thereby disrupting his original attempts at a seamless consensual interaction.

Harriet Jacobs's story contained similar efforts to avoid her master's sexual overtures that forced him to refigure his behavior. When Mary Norcum's suspicions made her husband revert to physical gestures instead of words to convey his sexual desires to Harriet, Harriet responded by letting "them pass, as if I did not understand what he meant." When James realized that Harriet could read, he wrote her notes that expressed his sexual intentions. But Harriet repeatedly pretended "I can't read them, sir." Overall, "by managing to keep within sight of people, as much as possible during the day time, I had hitherto succeeded in eluding my master." Harriet forced James into baldly claiming his right for sexual access as a privilege of mastery: according to Harriet, James began constantly "reminding me that I belonged to him, and swearing by heaven and earth that he would compel me to submit to him" because "I was his property; that I must be subject to his will in all things." Like Rachel Davis, Harriet Jacobs engaged in an exchange of maneuvers with her master where each tried to foil the other's plans and counterplans. Despite her master's legal property in her body, Harriet did not portray herself as utterly powerless. By playing into his image of her as too stupid to understand his signs and too illiterate to read his notes, Harriet used her own position as a slave to avoid her master's sexual overtures, forcing him to raise the stakes of his desires toward her.[8]

Because he did not receive unquestioned acquiescence from a servant or slave, a master had to create situations in which his laborers had little choice but to have sexual relations with him. Rachel's attempted refusal to go alone into a dark field with her master and Harriet's feigned ignorance of her master's intentions forced each man to modify his route to sexual interactions. By not consenting to a master's more subtle attempts at sexual relations, a servant or slave might force her master into more overtly coerced sexual acts. Ironically, this compelled a master to enact his laborer's interpretation of his overtures. Rather than the sexual offers that the masters first proposed, the men were forced to use coercion to carry out their sexual plans. Theoretically, a master could coerce through his physical prowess, but most masters did not have to rely exclusively on fists or whips to commit rape. Instead, they could rely on the strength of their mastery.

Beyond the unadorned physical power that could compel a woman into a sexual act, a master had an array of indirect means to force a dependent to have sex with him that simultaneously denied her resistance to him. . . . Harriet characterized her master as "a crafty man, [who] resorted to many means to accomplish his purposes. Sometimes he had stormy, terrific ways, that made his victims tremble; sometimes he assumed a gentleness that he thought must surely subdue." James promised Harriet that if she would give in to him sexually, "I would cherish you. I would make a lady of you." The possibility of a better life that transcended her racial and labor status was more than a bribe to induce Harriet's consent. It created a fiction that Harriet could voluntarily choose to have sexual relations with her master. By switching between the threats of physical harm and the gifts of courtship, James undercut the appearance of a forced sexual interaction. By theoretically allowing space for Harriet's consent to his sexual overtures, James was redefining coercion into consensual sexual relations.[9]

Similarly, William's verbal narration of consensual relations overlay his forceful attempts at sex. While he had Rachel trapped underneath his body, William told her that "he wd have the good will of me." William's modification of the classic legal description of rape as a man having carnal knowledge of a woman "against her will" verbally created a consensual act even as he used force to have sexual relations.[10] In the same incident, William called Rachel by her family nickname, telling her, "Nate you dear creature, I must fuck you." Even while forcing Rachel to have sex with him, William used terms of endearment toward her. William's presentation of an affectionate and therefore consensual sexual relationship with Rachel differentiated his actions from the brutality that early Americans would most easily recognize as rape.

Thus, the process of master–servant and master–slave sexual coercion was not exclusively tied to racial boundaries. Harriet Jacobs's and Rachel Davis's similarly recounted experiences suggest that their sexual interactions were more directly shaped by lines of status and dependency. These patterns would be repeated as masters and their servants or slaves struggled to control public perceptions of what had occurred.

CREATING MASTER NARRATIVES: THE PROCESS OF PUBLICITY

Given these different versions of events, how did families, other household members, and communities interpret evidence of a possibly coercive sexual interaction? How did assaulted women portray what had happened to them? Harriet Jacobs's and Rachel Davis's narratives show that the process of publicizing a master's sexual overtures was again structured by the woman's position as his personally dependent laborer. Words—the power to speak them and the power to construct their meaning—became the prize in a struggle among masters, mistresses, and the assaulted servant or slave.

After attempting sexual overtures toward their laborers, masters had to contend with the possibility that the women would tell others about their masters' behavior. Harriet Jacobs's and Rachel Davis's masters attempted to threaten their laborers into silence about their sexual interactions. Harriet wrote that her master "swore he would kill me, if I was not as silent as the grave."[11] Similarly, William told Rachel that if she told "any body, he wd be the death of me." When Rachel threatened to tell his wife what William had been doing, "he sd if I did, I shd repent." By demanding her silence, each master tried to dictate the parameters of his sexual interactions with his servant or slave without outside interference that might contradict his interpretation or stop his sexual pursuit.

But both women also believed that their masters were afraid of the damage that they could do by publicizing their sexual behavior. Besides his threats of physical violence, William promised Rachel a "gown if she would not tell" what he had done, and on another occasion, "begged [Rachel] not to tell" her new mistress because "it wd be the Ruin of him." Harriet similarly believed that her master "did not wish to have his villainy made public." Instead, he "deemed it prudent to keep up some outward show of decency." From each woman's vantage point, then, her master's concern about his public image again allowed her some room for negotiation: he needed his servant or slave to conceal their sexual interactions. But by not telling anyone about her master's sexual assaults, a woman increased the likelihood that their sexual relationship would not appear to be a rape. This double-edged sword made the servant or slave an unwilling accomplice in the masking of her own sexual coercion.[12]

If pressuring his servant or slave into silence through bribes or threats did not silence her, a master might try to control her description of their sexual interaction. William Cress enacted an elaborate punishment scene that forced Rachel Davis to claim responsibility for anything that may have passed between them. After Rachel's complaints to her mistress prompted Mary to confront her husband about Rachel's allegations, William immediately challenged Rachel. "Well Rachael," William accused, "what are this you have been scraping up about me?," denying even in his question the possibility of his own misdeeds. When Rachel could not present a satisfactory answer, William employed the power of physical correction allowed to him as her master to reform her story. According to Rachel, he "whipt me dreadfully & he said . . . that he never had such a name before. . . . I fell down—he damned me, & bad me beg his pardon. I said I did not know how—he bad me go on my knees . . . he bad me go to house & tell" his wife that she (Rachel) had lied. By whipping Rachel, William attempted to disprove her story of sexual assault: his wife had said that if Rachel's assertions of sexual relations between herself and William "was lies" as William claimed, "he ought to whip" Rachel for her dishonesty. This whipping was not just a punishment unfairly inflicted, it was a punishment that retroactively attempted to define the sexual interactions between a servant and a master. Once subjugated, Rachel was required to deny that William had forced her to have sex with him. Rachel's younger sister, also a servant to William, believed this new version of events: she admitted that "I do remember D[efendant] whipping my sister—it was for telling so many lies." William was using his position as master to rewrite the sexual act that had taken place between them.

Rachel ended her description of this incident by stating that after William had beaten her, "he went to church that day & I showed my back to [my] Sister." Those final words on her master's brutal punishment (a whipping that prevented Rachel from lying on her side for three weeks) revealed the irony of the situation: while William continued to appear as a publicly reverent and virtuous patriarch, Rachel secretly bore the signs of his sins, visible only to those most intimate with her. In the process of sexual coercion, force did not have a solely physical purpose: masters also used force to create an image of consent.

Harriet Jacobs also noted the discrepancy between her master's public image and private behavior, telling her readers how he had preserved his image at her expense. When Harriet's mistress confronted Harriet with suspicions of her husband's sexual improprieties, Harriet swore on a Bible that she had not had a sexual relationship with her master. When Mary questioned her husband, however, James contradicted Harriet's statements. And just like Rachel's mistress, Harriet's mistress "would gladly have had me flogged for my supposed false oath." But unlike William Cress, James Norcum did not allow Harriet to be whipped because "the old sinner was politic. The application of the lash might have led to remarks that would have exposed him" to his family and community.[13]

In Rachel's and Harriet's narratives, their mistresses—the wives of their abusers—played important roles in the categorization of the sexually abusive relationship. Each woman had to deal with a mistress who ultimately took her displeasure at her husband's sexual relationship out on her servant or slave. Each mistress also used her position of secondary mastery to create a temporary alliance with her servant or slave. Once this alliance outlived its usefulness, it became another tool with which the mistress could assist in redefining or denying the sexual relationship between the master and the slave or servant.

In both women's stories, the masters' wives did not immediately take their hostility at their sexually aggressive husbands out on the objects of their husbands' overtures. When Rachel and William came back from retrieving the "lost" sickle, his wife, Becky, asked "where he had been—he said, after the sickles, with nate (so they called me in family) she sd it was very extraordinary, no body else could go." Perhaps Becky suspected some sort of sexual liaison between her husband and their servant, and her pointed questions let her husband know of her suspicions. When Becky heard William trying to kiss Rachel in the cellar, she "said she had caught him & he wd deceive her no longer," but William denied any wrongdoing and Becky left in tears. These verbal confrontations apparently did not alter William's behavior; he continued to force himself sexually upon Rachel. Finally, Rachel's mistress "saw something was the matter with

me, & asked what it was. I told her." After questioning her husband had little visible effect, Becky turned to Rachel to find out about her husband's actions. This temporary alliance brought Rachel some protection from William's retribution, if not from his sexual overtures: when William heard that Rachel had told another relative some of what he had done to her, "he whipt me again, but not so bad—his wife wd not let him & said, he was in Fault."

Similarly, Harriet Jacobs believed that her mistress suspected James's illicit behavior: "She watched her husband with unceasing vigilance; but he was well practised in means to evade it." After Mary heard that her husband planned to have Harriet sleep in his room, she began questioning Harriet, who told her how James had been sexually harassing her. Harriet claimed that Mary, like most slave mistresses "had no compassion for the poor victim of her husband's perfidy. She pitied herself as a martyr." But Harriet also admitted that Mary "spoke kindly, and promised to protect me," ordering Harriet to sleep with her, rather than with James. This protective kindness also allowed Mary to try to obtain the "truth" of Harriet and James's relationship out of Harriet while Harriet slept: "she whispered in my ear, as though it was her husband who was speaking to me, and listened to hear what I would answer." When Harriet did not provide any self-incriminating information, Mary confronted her husband, but Mary's interventions did not end James's sexual overtures toward Harriet.[14]

If mistresses could not personally control their husbands' behavior, how could they stop the sexual relationship between master and laborer that was making a mockery of their marital vows? Theoretically, mistresses could turn to the legal system to petition for a divorce from their husbands. By the early nineteenth century, most states had divorce laws that allowed wives to apply for divorce on the grounds of their husbands' adultery, but women's petitions for divorce were more commonly based on charges of desertion.[15] Furthermore, proving adultery with a slave might be difficult without firsthand witnesses to the sexual interactions, since the slave was limited in her ability to testify against the white man. Married women also had a vested interest in their husbands' social and economic standing. Divorce or incarceration would most probably result in a woman's economic downturn from the loss of her husband's labor.

Ultimately, Rachel Davis's and Harriet Jacobs's mistresses concentrated their energies on removing their laborers from the household. Instead of bringing charges against her husband or applying for a divorce on the grounds of adultery, Becky Cress told Rachel Davis that she must "leave the house." Rachel recalled that "they then hired me out." Rachel's mistress may have ultimately recognized that her husband was (at best) complicit in his sexual relations with Rachel, but she also recognized that she, as his wife, was in a poor position to mandate a reform in his behavior. She could, however, as a mistress, remove the more disposable partner in the sexual relationship, and so she ordered Rachel to leave their home. Whether or not Becky believed Rachel's story of rape, she did not hold Rachel entirely innocent of wrongdoing. At the very least, she spread blame equally between her servant and her husband, with much of the resulting punishment falling on the more vulnerable of the two parties. As Rachel stated, "Before I was hired out, [my mistress] used me very bad & said she would knowck me down if I came to table to eat." Because William was a master—both of Rachel and of his household—his wife could enact only limited direct retribution against him. She could watch his behavior, confront him, and let him know her displeasure, but ultimately, it was easier to remove the object of his overtures than publicly to accuse him of wrongdoing.

Mary Norcum demanded that Harriet Jacobs leave the house once she learned that Harriet was pregnant, believing that conception was proof of their slave's sexual relationship with her husband. Harriet was not the only slave who was reputed to have been kicked out of her house because of a sexual relationship with the master. Recalling a story told to her by her grandmother about another slave, Harriet wrote that "her mistress had that day seen her baby for the first time, and in the lineaments of its fair face she saw a likeness to her husband. She turned the bondswoman and her child out of doors, and forbade her ever to return." In both of these examples, the mistress felt herself in sexual competition with the slave—even if the slave were not a willing competitor for the master's affections.[16]

Thus, while a wife's place in the household hierarchy may have proscribed her options, it did not leave her entirely at her husband's mercy. By forcing her husband to prove his marital loyalty by whipping the laborer for telling untruths about his sexual conduct, each mistress tried to create her own version of household sexual alliances. When mistresses could not force husbands to modify their behavior, these wives turned to regulating their servant's or slave's actions: first, by using them as the source of incriminating information, and later, as a problem that could be eliminated. Mistresses would not permanently join forces with slave or servant women to overthrow the household patriarch; they might want to change their husbands' behavior, but these wives did not wish publicly to condemn or disassociate themselves from their husbands through divorce or other legal action.

The silencing of sexual coercion was more profound in Harriet Jacobs's autobiography than it was in Rachel Davis's court-ordered testimony specifically about rape. Harriet's representation of her conflict with her master centered on the power to create a singular version of reality through the privilege of public speech. Throughout her narrative, Harriet insisted that her master sexually assaulted her only with words, never with his body. She wrote that he "tried his utmost to corrupt the pure principles my grandmother had instilled. He peopled my mind with unclean images." Harriet silenced her own description of her master's actions by calling the sexual degradation of slavery "more than I can describe." Harriet's versions of her master's verbal actions may have stood in for the literally unspeakable physical sexual abuse she suffered at his hands. By describing only James's speech, Harriet turned his possibly physical assaults on her into verbal assaults that no reader could expect her to control.[17]

In a personal letter written a few years before the publication of *Incidents in the Life of a Slave Girl* in 1861, Harriet hinted that she had indeed concealed the extent of James's actions. While she had tried to give a "true and just" account of her life in slavery, she admitted that "there are somethings I might have made plainer I know—Woman can whisper—her cruel wrongs into the ear of a very dear friend—much easier than she can record them for the world to read." In this passage, Jacobs drew a distinction between the private version of her pain and the version she chose to present for public consumption. Victorian womanhood's emphasis on modesty and respectability as well as the established genre of sexual euphemism popularized in sentimental novels probably encouraged Harriet Jacobs to present a sanitized version of her master's assaults on her. But her decision may also have reflected a personal need to distance herself from painful events, and a difficulty in telling others about her suffering that was shared by other victims—black and white—of a master's sexual harassment.[18]

Both Harriet and Rachel first told those closest to them about their masters' unwelcome sexual overtures. Harriet originally hesitated to tell Molly Horniblow, her grandmother and closest living relative, how James was treating her. Harriet "would have given the world to have laid my head on my grandmother's faithful bosom, and told her all my troubles," but James's threats and her own fear of her grandmother's reaction made her stay silent. When Harriet eventually did talk to her grandmother, she told her only some of her difficulties: "I talked with my grandmother about it, and partly told her my fears. I did not dare to tell her the worst." Harriet also told her uncle about some of her suffering. He told another relative that "you don't know what a life they lead her. She has told me something about it, and I wish [her master] was dead, or a better man." Harriet's recollection of interactions with her grandmother and her uncle emphasized that neither relative knew the entire story of her master's abuses. Just as the reader was given a sanitized version in the public transcript of Harriet's life, her hesitancy to confess the full extent of sexual coercion was reiterated in Harriet's personal interactions. Her inability to confess "the worst" of her experiences may have maintained Harriet's image of sexual purity and self-identity, but it was at the cost of denying the full spectrum of her master's assaults on her.[19]

Similarly, Rachel eventually told people close to her—one of her sisters (a servant in another household), her aunt, and her new mistress—about what William was doing to her. She recounted that she was hesitant to tell the whole story even to them. Rachel told her new mistress "something of what passed in the meadow, but not the worst of it. I told my sister Becky . . . the whole of it." Like Harriet's claim that it was easier to tell a close friend than to proclaim one's victimization publicly, Rachel had an easier time confessing her problems to her sister than to her new mistress. When Rachel spoke with her aunt, Elizabeth

Ashton, she again refrained from disclosing the full extent of William's coercion. Elizabeth told the court that Rachel had explained how William had isolated her in the cellar, had told her to go to bed with him when his wife was away, had cornered her in the barn, and had forced her to go with him to retrieve the sickle in the meadow. But Rachel stopped short of telling her aunt that William had succeeded in raping her, that his manipulative maneuvers had led to forced sexual intercourse. Elizabeth specified under cross-examination that "I did not understand from her that he had fully effected his purpose in the meadow."[20] By minimizing the extent of her master's abuse of her, Rachel created a public version of her master's actions that denied that she had been raped.

The victims of sexual coercion were not the only people who purposefully avoided discussions of sexual assaults. Elizabeth Ashton did not know that William had raped Rachel partly because, as she told the court, "I did not enquire whether he obtained his will in the meadow." When Rachel's sister told her own mistress that "Mr Cress wanted to be gret [great] with her sister Rachael," the mistress replied, "I wanted to hear no more." When this sister eventually told their father what had happened, Jacob Davis recalled that she "did not tell me directly, she did not tell me the worst—I did not think it was so bad." A voluntary conspiracy of silence—from the servant who had difficulty discussing what had happened, to the other women who wanted neither to hear nor tell the full extent of William's abuse of Rachel—worked to deny the sexual coercion that William committed on his servant.

Similarly, Harriet Jacobs's fellow slaves were hesitant to volunteer verbal or physical assistance. Harriet believed that while her friends and relatives knew that she was being sexually abused, they were unable to speak of it. Harriet recalled that "the other slaves in my master's house noticed" her changed behavior as a result of her master's treatment, but "none dared to ask the cause. . . . They knew too well the guilty practices under that roof; and they were aware that to speak of them was an offence that never went unpunished." Harriet's fellow slaves' silence, necessary for their own self-preservation, limited their ability to help Harriet resist their master's overtures. By controlling potential allies, a master enmeshed his original acts of sexual coercion in an ever-widening coercive web that structured his victim's possibilities for support or redress.[21]

By not telling others what had happened to her, Harriet was at the mercy of other people's versions of events. James's wife, Mary, went to the house of Harriet's free grandmother to tell her that Harriet was pregnant with James's baby. Molly Horniblow then turned on Harriet, apparently believing Mary's story that Harriet had consented to the relationship: "I had rather see you dead than to see you as you now are," she told her granddaughter. "You are a disgrace to your dead mother. . . . Go away . . . and never come to my house, again." Because Harriet had consistently denied or downplayed her master's sexual attempts on her, her grandmother believed Mary's story that Harriet had voluntarily had sexual relations with James. Later, Harriet's grandmother learned that Harriet had chosen to become pregnant with another man's baby to try to force her sexually abusive master to leave her alone or sell her. Once her grandmother understood "the real state of the case, and all I had been bearing for years. . . . She laid her old hand gently on my head, and murmured, 'Poor child! Poor child!'" Harriet's inability to speak about her master's sexual coercion temporarily isolated Harriet from the woman who was most able to support her. When Harriet ultimately received her grandmother's forgiveness, she also gained an ally in her fight against her master's sexual demands.[22]

Both Harriet and Rachel believed that an independently powerful figure outside of the household could counterbalance their masters' attempts at dominance. When Rachel's aunt questioned "why she did not go to a Squire to complain" about her master's sexual assaults, Rachel replied "she did not dare—she a bound girl & her father absent." After telling her sister what had happened, her sister "advised her to stay there & be a good girl. . . . I thought nothing could be done, as my father was away." Rachel herself told the court that "I did not know if I went to a Justice, he wd take notice of it. Enough people knew it, but waited till my Father came back." Without a patriarchal figure beside her, Rachel would not directly confront her master, and did not believe herself entitled to legal justice, a belief encouraged (or at least not contradicted) by the women in whom she confided. For Rachel, her father's support was crucial to her ability to receive public redress for her master's sexual assaults on her.

Enslaved women ordinarily did not have access to the protection offered by a patriarchal figure. Harriet Jacobs observed that enslaved men "strive to protect wives and daughters from the insults of their masters. . . . [but] Some poor creatures have been so brutalized by the lash that they will sneak out of the way to give their masters free access to their wives and daughters." Although Harriet Jacobs did not have a waiting patriarchal figure to whom she could turn for protection, supporters outside of the household were still crucial to her limited redress. Harriet repeatedly spoke of her free grandmother's respect in the community, of how James "dreaded" this woman's "scorching rebuke," so that "her presence in the neighborhood was some protection to me." Ultimately, her grandmother's home became a partial refuge from James's pursuit. Harriet also spoke of her white lover's assistance in combating her master's "persecutions" of her through his "wish to aid me." Harriet partly justified her decision to have sexual relations with this man (pseudonymously referred to as "Mr. Sands") because she was "sure my friend, Mr. Sands, would buy me . . . and I thought my freedom could be easily obtained from him." While Harriet could not hope for institutional retribution against her master, she could hope that her new lover would help provide freedom from her master.[23]

Both Harriet Jacobs and Rachel Davis fought similar battles against the veil of silence surrounding their masters' treatment of them. Both were confronted by relatives and neighbors who had limited authority over another household's problems. Both women turned to another powerful figure—father or free grandmother and elite white lover, respectively—to rescue them from their masters' sexual abuse. When Rachel finally told her father about her master's sexual assaults, Jacob Davis successfully encouraged the local legal system to begin a criminal prosecution. But neither Harriet Jacobs's ultimate confession to her grandmother nor her involvement with a white lover could lead to legal intervention. The legal system marked an irreversible disjuncture in the two women's experiences.

EPILOGUE: CREATING RAPE: THE LEGAL PROCESS

Following the process of sexual coercion has led us back to this essay's opening, as Harriet Jacobs's and Rachel Davis's parallel stories reach diametrically opposed conclusions: while Rachel's master was convicted of rape and served a substantial jail sentence, there is no evidence that Harriet's master was ever subject to legal repercussions for his behavior. When a master tried to define coercive sex as consensual sex, both servants and slaves could negotiate with his terms and battle against his actions. But when the legal system defined enslaved women outside the judicial parameters of rape, there was little room for negotiation. The parallels in Harriet Jacobs's and Rachel Davis's stories ended with the legal distinction of criminal behavior. Rachel Davis may not have had easy access to criminal justice—her master was convicted of rape several years after he had first assaulted her. Yet she ultimately received legal protections that were denied to Harriet Jacobs.

We need to understand not only the legal history of rape, but the social history of sexual coercion. By taking seriously the possibility that white and black women in early America could have some experiences in common, we can begin to reassemble the complicated interactions of race, gender, and social and economic status in American history. Certainly the comparative possibilities are not exhausted with these two stories. Historians could compare the sexual experiences of free and enslaved African American women or white and black free servants. Were similar strategies used outside of households, in any relationship between a powerful man and a less powerful woman? In all of these comparisons, we should think carefully about how sex was coerced and how the crime of rape was defined. If we frame our investigations using solely the legal judgment of rape, we not only miss much of the story, we again replace women's experiences—much as their coercers had tried to do—with external categorizations. Instead, by interrogating the multiple and contested meanings of sexual coercion, we can better understand the historical relationships of social and sexual power.

Notes

1. "Commonwealth v. William Cress, Feb. 1808," Pennsylvania Court Papers, 1807–1809, Historical Society of Pennsylvania, Philadelphia, Pa. Unless otherwise noted, all quotations regarding Rachel Davis are from these documents. For the criminal prosecution of William Cress, see "Commonwealth v. William Cress, Philadelphia, Feb. 15, 1808," Pennsylvania Oyer and Terminer Docket, 1778–1827, 261, 262, 263, 265, Pennsylvania Historic and Museum Commission, Harrisburg, Pa.

2. Harriet Jacobs, *Incidents in the Life of a Slave Girl Written by Herself,* ed. Jean Fagan Yellin (1861; reprint, Cambridge, Mass.: Harvard University Press, 1987).

3. For examples of statutes specifying the crime of black-on-white rape, see John D. Cushing, ed., *The Earliest Printed Laws of Pennsylvania, 1681–1713* (Wilmington, Del.: Michael Glazier, 1978), 69; B. W. Leigh, ed., *The Revised Code of the Laws of Virginia* (n.p., 1819), 585–86. See also Peter Bardalgio, "Rape and the Law in the Old South: 'Calculated to Excite Indignation in Every Heart,'" *Journal of Southern History* 60 (1994): 756–58.

4. See Thomas D. Morris, "Slaves and the Rules of Evidence in Criminal Trials," *Chicago-Kent Law Review* 68 (1993): 1209–39.

5. For further discussion of the cultural definitions of rape in early America, see Sharon Block, *Rape and Sexual Power in Early America* (Chapel Hill: Omohundro Institute of Early American History and Culture with University of North Carolina Press, 2006).

6. Much of the following discussion about resistance's reformulation into consent was inspired by Ellen Rooney, "'A Little More than Persuading': Tess and the Subject of Sexual Violence," in *Rape and Representation,* eds. Lynn A. Higgins and Brenda R. Silver (New York: Columbia University Press, 1991), 87–114, and the fictional exploration of twentieth-century household sexual coercion in J. M. Redmann's three-book series culminating in *The Intersection of Law and Desire* (New York: W. W. Norton, 1995).

7. Jacobs, *Incidents,* 27, 28, 31–32. See also p. 41.

8. Ibid., 27, 28, 31, 32.

9. Ibid., 27, 35.

10. Italics added.

11. Jacobs, *Incidents,* 28. See also 32.

12. Ibid., 29.

13. Ibid., 34, 35.

14. Ibid., 31, 33, 34.

15. On divorce in the antebellum South, see Jane Turner Censer, "'Smiling Through Her Tears': Antebellum Southern Women and Divorce," *American Journal of Legal History* 25 (1981): 24–47; for Pennsylvania, see Merril D. Smith, *Breaking the Bonds: Marital Discord in Pennsylvania, 1730–1830* (New York: New York University Press, 1991); Thomas Meehan, "'Not Made out of Levity': Evolution of Divorce in Early Pennsylvania," *Pennsylvania Magazine of History and Biography* 92 (1968): 441–64.

16. Jacobs, Incidents, 59, 122.

17. Ibid., 27–28.

18. Harriet Jacobs to Amy Post, June 21, 1857, in Jacobs, *Incidents,* 242. For a discussion of African American women's psychological reactions to systemic sexual exploitation, see Darlene Clark Hine, "Rape and the Inner Lives of Black Women in the Middle West: Preliminary Thoughts on the Culture of Dissemblance," *Signs* 14 (1989), 265–277.

19. Jacobs, *Incidents,* 25, 28, 38.

20. Underlining in original.

21. Jacobs, *Incidents,* 28.

22. Ibid., 56, 57.

23. Ibid., 29, 54–55.

CARROLL SMITH-ROSENBERG

The Female World of Love and Ritual: Relations between Women in Nineteenth-Century America

Carroll Smith-Rosenberg's close reading of middle-class girls' and women's diaries and letters to explore the nature of their intense friendships represented a radically new approach when it was published in 1975. It was pioneering in several areas of inquiry that have since become familiar—not just women's and gender history, but the histories of sexuality, family life, and emotions. Note that the essay was published in the pathbreaking, multidisciplinary, community-building women's studies journal *Signs*—and as the opening article in its first issue. As you read it, think about why the essay would have been disconcerting and challenging to many, if not most, members of the historical profession in the 1970s.

The author's work reflected the reinvigorated practices of women's history in the early 1970s, part of the transformation of scholarship and academia wrought by second-wave feminism. But new historical research on gender and sexuality took years to reach publication and constitute a critical mass. College teachers compiling syllabi for courses on women's history coped with a dramatic scarcity of secondary material that they could assign. Unlike the rich resources at our fingertips today, there were no women's history textbooks, syntheses, journals, or websites to consult.

Today, Smith-Rosenberg's nuanced analysis remains a touchstone for scholars' continuing investigation and vigorous debate on the historical existence and meanings of women's same-sex friendships, partnerships, and loves globally.*

The female friendship of the nineteenth century, the long-lived, intimate, loving friendship between two women, is an excellent example of the type of historical phenomena which most historians know something about, which few have thought much about, and which virtually no one has written about.[1] It is one aspect of the female experience which consciously or unconsciously we have chosen to ignore. Yet an abundance of manuscript evidence suggests that eighteenth- and nineteenth-century women routinely formed emotional ties with other women. Such deeply felt, same-sex friendships were casually accepted in American society. Indeed, from at least the late eighteenth through the mid-nineteenth century, a female world of varied and yet highly structured relationships appears to have been an essential aspect of American society. These relationships ranged from the supportive love of sisters, through the

*Leila Rupp, *Sapphistries: A Global History of Love between Women* (New York: New York University Press, 2009; Judith M. Bennett, "'Lesbian-like' and the Social History of Lesbianisms," *Journal of the History of Sexuality* 9 (2000): 1–24. For another pioneering integration of sexuality and social history, see Blanche Wiesen Cook, "Female Support Networks and Political Activism: Lillian Wald, Crystal Eastman, Emma Goldman," *Chrysalis* 3 (1977): 43–61.

enthusiasms of adolescent girls, to sensual avowals of love by mature women. It was a world in which men made but a shadowy appearance.[2] . . .

. . . Intimate friendships between men and men and women and women existed in a larger world of social relations and social values. To interpret such friendships more fully they must be related to the structure of the American family and to the nature of sex-role divisions and of male-female relations both within the family and in society generally. . . . The ties between mothers and daughters, sisters, female cousins and friends, at all stages of the female life cycle constitute the most suggestive framework for the historian to begin an analysis of intimacy and affection between women. Such an analysis would emphasize general cultural patterns rather than the internal dynamics of a particular family or childhood. . . .

This analysis . . . [is] based upon the correspondence and diaries of women and men in thirty-five families between the 1760s and the 1880s. These families, though limited in number, represented a broad range of the American middle class, from hard-pressed pioneer families and orphaned girls to daughters of the intellectual and social elite. It includes families from most geographic regions, rural and urban, and a spectrum of Protestant denominations ranging from Mormon to orthodox Quaker. Although scarcely a comprehensive sample of America's increasingly heterogeneous population, it does, I believe, reflect accurately the literate middle class to which the historian working with letters and diaries is necessarily bound. It has involved an analysis of many thousands of letters written to women friends, kin, husbands, brothers, and children at every period of life from adolescence to old age. Some collections encompass virtually entire life spans; one contains over 100,000 letters as well as diaries and account books. It is my contention that an analysis of women's private letters and diaries which were never intended to be published permits the historian to explore a very private world of emotional realities central both to women's lives and to the middle-class family in nineteenth-century America.[3]

The question of female friendships is peculiarly elusive; we know so little or perhaps have forgotten so much. . . . Before attempting to reconstruct their social setting, therefore, it might be best first to describe two not atypical friendships. These two friendships, intense, loving, and openly avowed, began during the women's adolescence and, despite subsequent marriages and geographic separation, continued throughout their lives. For nearly half a century these women played a central emotional role in each other's lives, writing time and again of their love and of the pain of separation. Paradoxically to twentieth-century minds, their love appears to have been both sensual and platonic.

Sarah Butler Wister first met Jeannie Field Musgrove while vacationing with her family at Stockbridge, Massachusetts, in the summer of 1849. Jeannie was then sixteen, Sarah fourteen. During two subsequent years spent together in boarding school, they formed a deep and intimate friendship. Sarah began to keep a bouquet of flowers before Jeannie's portrait and wrote complaining of the intensity and anguish of her affection. Both young women assumed nom de plumes, Jeannie a female name, Sarah a male one; they would use these secret names into old age. They frequently commented on the nature of their affection: "If the day should come," Sarah wrote Jeannie in the spring of 1861, "when you failed me either through your fault or my own, I would forswear all human friendship, thenceforth." A few months later Jeannie commented: "Gratitude is a word I should never use toward you. It is perhaps a misfortune of such intimacy and love that it makes one regard all kindness as a matter of course, as one has always found it, as natural as the embrace in meeting."[4]

Sarah's marriage altered neither the frequency of their correspondence nor their desire to be together. In 1864, when twenty-nine, married, and a mother, Sarah wrote to Jeannie: "I shall be entirely alone [this coming week]. I can give you no idea how desperately I shall want you. . . ." After one such visit Jeannie, then a spinster in New York, echoed Sarah's longing: "Dear darling Sarah! How I love you & how happy I have been! You are the joy of my life. . . . I cannot tell you how much happiness you gave me, nor how constantly it is all in my thoughts. . . . My darling how I long for the time when I shall see you. . . ." After another visit Jeannie wrote: "I want you to tell me in your next letter, to assure me, that I am your dearest. . . . I do not doubt you, & I am not jealous but I long to hear you say it once more & it seems already a long time since your voice fell on my ear. So just fill a quarter page with caresses & expressions of endearment. Your silly Angelina." Jeannie ended one letter: "Goodbye my dearest, dearest lover—ever your own Angelina." And another, "I will go to bed ... [though] I could write all night—A thousand kisses—I love you with my whole soul—your Angelina."

When Jeannie finally married in 1870 at the age of thirty-seven, Sarah underwent a period of extreme anxiety. Two days before Jeannie's marriage Sarah, then in London, wrote desperately: "Dearest darling—How incessantly have I thought of you these eight days—all today—the entire uncertainty, the distance, the long silence—are all new features in my separation from you, grevious to be borne. . . . Oh Jeannie. I have thought & thought & yearned over you these two days. Are you married I wonder? My dearest love to you wherever and whoever you are." Like many other women in this collection of thirty-five families, marriage brought Sarah and Jeannie physical separation; it did not cause emotional distance. Although at first they may have wondered how marriage would affect their relationship, their affection remained unabated throughout their lives, underscored by their loneliness and their desire to be together.[5]

During the same years that Jeannie and Sarah wrote of their love and need for each other, two slightly younger women began a similar odyssey of love, dependence and—ultimately—physical, though not emotional, separation. Molly and Helena met in 1868 while both attended the Cooper Institute School of Design for Women in New York City. For several years these young women studied and explored the city together, visited each other's families, and formed part of a social network of other artistic young women. Gradually, over the years, their initial friendship deepened into a close intimate bond which continued throughout their lives. The tone in the letters which Molly wrote to Helena changed over these years from "My dear Helena," and signed "your attached friend," to "My dearest Helena," "My Dearest," "My Beloved," and signed "Thine always" or "thine Molly."[6]

The letters they wrote to each other during these first five years permit us to reconstruct something of their relationship together. As Molly wrote in one early letter:

> I have not said to you in so many or so few words that I was happy with you during those few so incredibly short weeks but surely you do not need words to tell you what you must know. Those two or three days so dark without, so bright with firelight and contentment within I shall always remember as proof that, for a time, at least—I fancy for quite a long time—we might be sufficient for each other. We know that we can amuse each other for many idle hours together and now we know that we can also work together. And that means much, don't you think so?

She ended: "I shall return in a few days. Imagine yourself kissed many times by one who loved you so dearly."

The intensity and even physical nature of Molly's love was echoed in many of the letters she wrote during the next few years, as, for instance in this short thank-you note for a small present: "Imagine yourself kissed a dozen times my darling. Perhaps it is well for you that we are far apart. You might find my thanks so expressed rather overpowering. I have that delightful feeling that it doesn't matter much what I say or how I say it, since we shall meet so soon and forget in that moment that we were ever separated. . . . I shall see you soon and be content."[7]

At the end of the fifth year, however, several crises occurred. The relationship, at least in its intense form, ended, though Molly and Helena continued an intimate and complex relationship for the next half-century. The exact nature of these crises is not completely clear, but it seems to have involved Molly's decision not to live with Helena, as they had originally planned, but to remain at home because of parental insistence. Molly was now in her late twenties. Helena responded with anger and Molly became frantic at the thought that Helena would break off their relationship. Though she wrote distraught letters and made despairing attempts to see Helena, the relationship never regained its former ardor—possibly because Molly had a male suitor. Within six months Helena had decided to marry a man who was, coincidentally, Molly's friend and publisher. Two years later Molly herself finally married. The letters toward the end of this period discuss the transition both women made to having male lovers—Molly spending much time reassuring Helena, who seemed depressed about the end of their relationship and with her forthcoming marriage.[8]

It is clearly difficult from a distance of 100 years and from a post-Freudian cultural perspective to decipher the complexities of Molly and Helena's relationship. Certainly Molly and

Helena were lovers—emotionally if not physically. The emotional intensity and pathos of their love becomes apparent in several letters Molly wrote Helena during their crisis: "I wanted so to put my arms round my girl of all the girls in the world and tell her . . . I love her as wives do love their husbands, as *friends* who have taken each other for life—and believe in her, as I believe in my God. . . . If I didn't love you do you suppose I'd care about anything or have ridiculous notions and panics and behave like an old fool who ought to know better. I'm going to hang on to your skirts. . . . You can't get away from [my] love." Or as she wrote after Helena's decision to marry: "You know dear Helena, I really was in love with you. It was a passion such as I had never known until I saw you. I don't think it was the noblest way to love you." The theme of intense female love was one Molly again expressed in a letter she wrote to the man Helena was to marry: "Do you know sir, that until you came along I believe that she loved me almost as girls love their lovers. *I know I loved her so.* Don't you wonder that I can stand the sight of you." This was in a letter congratulating them on their forthcoming marriage.[9]

The essential question is not whether these women had genital contact and can therefore be defined as heterosexual or homosexual. The twentieth-century tendency to view human love and sexuality within a dichotomized universe of deviance and normality, genitality and platonic love, is alien to the emotions and attitudes of the nineteenth century and fundamentally distorts the nature of these women's emotional interaction. These letters are significant because they force us to place such female love in a particular historical context. There is every indication that these four women, their husbands and families—all eminently respectable and socially conservative—considered such love both socially acceptable and fully compatible with heterosexual marriage. Emotionally and cognitively, their heterosocial and their homosocial worlds were complementary.

One could argue, on the other hand, that these letters were but an example of the romantic rhetoric with which the nineteenth century surrounded the concept of friendship. Yet they possess an emotional intensity and a sensual and physical explicitness that is difficult to dismiss. Jeannie longed to hold Sarah in her arms; Molly mourned her physical isolation from Helena. Molly's love and devotion to Helena, the emotions that bound Jeannie and Sarah together, while perhaps a phenomenon of nineteenth-century society, were not the less real for their Victorian origins. A survey of the correspondence and diaries of eighteenth- and nineteenth-century women indicates that Molly, Jeannie, and Sarah represented one very real behavioral and emotional option socially available to nineteenth-century women.

This is not to argue that individual needs, personalities, and family dynamics did not have a significant role in determining the nature of particular relationships. But the scholar must ask if it is historically possible and, if possible, important, to study the intensely individual aspects of psychosexual dynamics. Is it not the historian's first task to explore the social structure and the worldview which made intense and sometimes sensual female love both a possible and an acceptable emotional option? From such a social perspective a new and quite different series of questions suggests itself. What emotional function did such female love serve? What was its place within the hetero- and homosocial worlds which women jointly inhabited? Did a spectrum of love-object choices exist in the nineteenth century across which some individuals, at least, were capable of moving? Without attempting to answer these questions it will be difficult to understand either nineteenth-century sexuality or the nineteenth-century family.

Several factors in American society between the mid-eighteenth and the mid-nineteenth centuries may well have permitted women to form a variety of close emotional relationships with other women. American society was characterized in large part by rigid gender-role differentiation within the family and within society as a whole, leading to the emotional segregation of women and men. The roles of daughter and mother shaded imperceptibly and ineluctably into each other, while the biological realities of frequent pregnancies, childbirth, nursing, and menopause bound women together in physical and emotional intimacy. It was within just such a social framework, I would argue, that a specifically female world did indeed develop, a world built around a generic and unself-conscious pattern of single-sex or homosocial networks. These supportive networks were institutionalized in social conventions or rituals which accompanied virtually every important event in a woman's life, from birth to death. Such female relationships were frequently supported and paralleled by severe social restrictions on intimacy between young men and women. Within such a world of emotional richness and complexity devotion to and love of other women became a plausible and socially accepted form of human interaction.

An abundance of printed and manuscript sources exists to support such a hypothesis. Etiquette books, advice books on child rearing, religious sermons, guides to young men and young women, medical texts, and school curricula all suggest that late eighteenth- and most nineteenth-century Americans assumed the existence of a world composed of distinctly male and female spheres, spheres determined by the immutable laws of God and nature.[10] The unpublished letters and diaries of Americans during this same period concur, detailing the existence of sexually segregated worlds inhabited by human beings with different values, expectations, and personalities. Contacts between men and women frequently partook of a formality and stiffness quite alien to twentieth-century America and which today we tend to define as "Victorian." Women, however, did not form an isolated and oppressed subcategory in male society. Their letters and diaries indicate that women's sphere had an essential integrity and dignity that grew out of women's shared experiences and mutual affection and that, despite the profound changes which affected American social structure and institutions between the 1760s and the 1870s, retained a constancy and predictability. The ways in which women thought of and interacted with each other remained unchanged. Continuity, not discontinuity, characterized this female world. Molly Hallock's and Jeannie Field's words, emotions, and experiences have direct parallels in the 1760s and the 1790s. There are indications in contemporary sociological and psychological literature that female closeness and support networks have continued into the twentieth century—not only among ethnic and working-class groups but even among the middle class.[11]

Most eighteenth- and nineteenth-century women lived within a world bounded by home, church, and the institution of visiting—that endless trooping of women to each other's homes for social purposes. It was a world inhabited by children and by other women. Women helped each other with domestic chores

and in times of sickness, sorrow, or trouble. Entire days, even weeks, might be spent almost exclusively with other women. Urban and town women could devote virtually every day to visits, teas, or shopping trips with other women. Rural women developed a pattern of more extended visits that lasted weeks and sometimes months, at times even dislodging husbands from their beds and bedrooms so that dear friends might spend every hour of every day together. When husbands traveled, wives routinely moved in with other women, invited women friends to teas and suppers, sat together sharing and comparing the letters they had received from other close women friends. Secrets were exchanged and cherished, and the husband's return at times viewed with some ambivalence.[12]

Summer vacations were frequently organized to permit old friends to meet at water spas or share a country home. In 1848, for example, a young matron wrote cheerfully to her husband about the delightful time she was having with five close women friends whom she had invited to spend the summer with her; he remained at home alone to face the heat of Philadelphia and a cholera epidemic. Some ninety years earlier, two young Quaker girls commented upon the vacation their aunt had taken alone with another woman; their remarks were openly envious and tell us something of the emotional quality of these friendships: "I hear Aunt is gone with the Friend and wont be back for two weeks, fine times indeed I think the old friends had, taking their pleasure about the country . . . and have the advantage of that fine woman's conversation and instruction, while we poor young girls must spend all spring at home. . . . What a disappointment that we are not together. . . ."[13]

Friends did not form isolated dyads but were normally part of highly integrated networks. Knowing each other, perhaps related to each other, they played a central role in holding communities and kin systems together. Especially when families became geographically mobile women's long visits to each other and their frequent letters filled with discussions of marriages and births, illness and deaths, descriptions of growing children, and reminiscences of times and people past provided an important sense of continuity in a rapidly changing society.[14] Central to this female world was an inner core of kin. The ties between sisters, first cousins, aunts, and nieces provided the underlying structure upon which groups of friends and their network of female relatives clustered. Although most of the women within this sample would appear to be living within isolated nuclear families, the emotional ties between nonresidential kin were deep and binding and provided one of the fundamental existential realities of women's lives. Twenty years after Parke Lewis Butler moved with her husband to Louisiana, she sent her two daughters back to Virginia to attend school, live with their grandmother and aunt, and be integrated back into Virginia society. The constant letters between Maria Inskeep and Fanny Hampton, sisters separated in their early twenties when Maria moved with her husband from New Jersey to Louisiana, held their families together, making it possible for their daughters to feel a part of their cousins' network of friends and interests. The Ripley daughters, growing up in western Massachusetts in the early 1800s, spent months each year with their mother's sister and her family in distant Boston; these female cousins and their network of friends exchanged gossip-filled letters and gradually formed deeply loving and dependent ties.[15]

Women frequently spent their days within the social confines of such extended families. Sisters-in-law visited each other and, in some families, seemed to spend more time with each other than with their husbands. First cousins cared for each other's babies—for weeks or even months in times of sickness or childbirth. Sisters helped each other with housework, shopped and sewed for each other. Geographic separation was borne with difficulty. A sister's absence for even a week or two could cause loneliness and depression and would be bridged by frequent letters. Sibling rivalry was hardly unknown, but with separation or illness the theme of deep affection and dependency reemerged.[16]

Sisterly bonds continued across a lifetime. In her old age a rural Quaker matron, Martha Jefferis, wrote to her daughter Anne concerning her own half-sister, Phoebe: "In sister Phoebe I have a real friend—she studies my comfort and waits on me like a child. . . . She is exceedingly kind and this to all other homes (set aside yours) I would prefer—it is next to being with a daughter." Phoebe's own letters confirmed Martha's evaluation of her feelings. "Thou knowest my dear sister," Phoebe wrote, "there is no one . . . that exactly feels [for] thee as I do, for I think without boasting I can truly say that my desire is for thee."[17]

Such women, whether friends or relatives, assumed an emotional centrality in each other's lives. In their diaries and letters they wrote of the joy and contentment they felt in each other's company, their sense of isolation and despair when apart. The regularity of their correspondence underlies the sincerity of their words. Women named their daughters after one another and sought to integrate dear friends into their lives after marriage.[18] As one young bride wrote to an old friend shortly after her marriage: "I want to see you and talk with you and feel that we are united by the same bonds of sympathy and congeniality as ever." After years of friendship one aging woman wrote of another: "Time cannot destroy the fascination of her manner . . . her voice is music to the ear. . . ." Women made elaborate presents for each other, ranging from the Quakers' frugal pies and breads to painted velvet bags and phantom bouquets.[19] When a friend died, their grief was deeply felt. Martha Jefferis was unable to write to her daughter for three weeks because of the sorrow she felt at the death of a dear friend. Such distress was not unusual. A generation earlier a young Massachusetts farm woman filled pages of her diary with her grief at the death of her "dearest friend" and transcribed the letters of condolence other women sent her. She marked the anniversary of Rachel's death each year in her diary, contrasting her faithfulness with that of Rachel's husband who had soon remarried.[20]

These female friendships served a number of emotional functions. Within this secure and empathetic world women could share sorrows, anxieties, and joys, confident that other women had experienced similar emotions. One mid-nineteenth-century rural matron in a letter to her daughter discussed this particular aspect of women's friendships: "To have such a friend as thyself to look to and sympathize with her—and enter into all her little needs and in whose bosom she could with freedom pour forth her joys and sorrows—such a friend would very much relieve the tedium of many a wearisome hour. . . ." A generation later Molly more informally underscored the importance of this same function in a letter to Helena: "Suppose I come down . . . [and] spend Sunday with you quietly," she wrote Helena ". . . that means talking all the time until you are relieved of all your latest troubles, and I of mine. . . ." These were frequently troubles that apparently no man could understand. When Anne Jefferis Sheppard was first married, she and her older sister Edith (who then lived with Anne) wrote in detail to their mother of the severe depression and anxiety which they experienced. Moses Sheppard, Anne's husband, added cheerful postscripts to the sisters' letters—which he had clearly not read—remarking on Anne's and Edith's contentment. Theirs was an emotional world to which he had little access.[21]

This was, as well, a female world in which hostility and criticism of other women were discouraged, and thus a milieu in which women could develop a sense of inner security and self-esteem. As one young woman wrote to her mother's longtime friend: "I cannot sufficiently thank you for the kind unvaried affection & indulgence you have ever shown and expressed both by words and actions for me. . . . Happy would it be did all the world view me as you do, through the medium of kindness and forbearance." They valued each other. Women, who had little status or power in the larger world of male concerns, possessed status and power in the lives and worlds of other women.[22]

An intimate mother-daughter relationship lay at the heart of this female world. The diaries and letters of both mothers and daughters attest to their closeness and mutual emotional dependency. Daughters routinely discussed their mother's health and activities with their own friends, expressed anxiety in cases of their mother's ill health and concern for her cares.[23] Expressions of hostility which we would today consider routine on the part of both mothers and daughters seem to have been uncommon indeed. On the contrary, this sample of families indicates that the normal relationship between mother and daughter was one of sympathy and understanding.[24] Only sickness or great geographic distance was allowed to cause extended separation. When marriage did result in such separation, both viewed the distance between them with distress.[25] Something of this sympathy and love between mothers and daughters is evident in a letter Sarah Alden Ripley, at age sixty-nine, wrote her youngest and recently married daughter: "You do not know how much I miss you, not only when I struggle in and out of my mortal envelop and pump my nightly potation and no longer pour into your sympathizing ear my senile gossip, but all the day I muse away, since the sound of your voice no longer rouses me to sympathy with your joys or sorrows. . . .

You cannot know how much I miss your affectionate demonstrations."[26] A dozen aging mothers in this sample of over thirty families echoed her sentiments.

Central to these mother-daughter relations is what might be described as an apprenticeship system. In those families where the daughter followed the mother into a life of traditional domesticity, mothers and other older women carefully trained daughters in the arts of housewifery and motherhood. Such training undoubtedly occurred throughout a girl's childhood but became more systematized, almost ritualistic, in the years following the end of her formal education and before her marriage. At this time a girl either returned home from boarding school or no longer divided her time between home and school. Rather, she devoted her energies on two tasks: mastering new domestic skills and participating in the visiting and social activities necessary to finding a husband. Under the careful supervision of their mothers and of older female relatives, such late-adolescent girls temporarily took over the household management from their mothers, tended their young nieces and nephews, and helped in childbirth, nursing, and weaning. Such experiences tied the generations together in shared skills and emotional interaction.[27]

Daughters were born into a female world. Their mother's life expectations and sympathetic network of friends and relations were among the first realities in the life of the developing child. As long as the mother's domestic role remained relatively stable and few viable alternatives competed with it, daughters tended to accept their mother's world and to turn automatically to other women for support and intimacy. It was within this closed and intimate female world that the young girl grew toward womanhood. . . .

At some point in adolescence, the young girl began to move outside the matrix of her mother's support group to develop a network of her own. Among the middle class, at least, this transition toward what was at the same time both a limited autonomy and a repetition of her mother's life seemed to have most frequently coincided with a girl's going to school. Indeed education appears to have played a crucial role in the lives of most of the families in this study. Attending school for a few months, for a year, or longer, was common even among daughters of relatively poor families, while middle-class girls routinely spent at least a year in boarding school. These school years ordinarily marked a girl's first separation from home. They served to wean the daughter from her home, to train her in the essential social graces, and, ultimately, to help introduce her into the marriage market. It was not infrequently a trying emotional experience for both mother and daughter.[28]

In this process of leaving one home and adjusting to another, the mother's friends and relatives played a key transitional role. Such older women routinely accepted the role of foster mother; they supervised the young girl's deportment, monitored her health and introduced her to their own network of female friends and kin. Not infrequently women, friends from their own school years, arranged to send their daughters to the same school so that the girls might form bonds paralleling those their mothers had made. For years Molly and Helena wrote of their daughters' meeting and worried over each other's children. When Molly finally brought her daughter east to school, their first act on reaching New York was to meet Helena and her daughters. Elizabeth Bordley Gibson virtually adopted the daughters of her school chum, Eleanor Custis Lewis. The Lewis daughters soon began to write Elizabeth Gibson letters with the salutation "Dearest Mama." . . .[29]

Even more important to this process of maturation than their mother's friends were the female friends young women made at school. Young girls helped each other overcome homesickness and endure the crises of adolescence. They gossiped about beaux, incorporated each other into their own kinship systems, and attended and gave teas and balls together. Older girls in boarding school "adopted" younger ones, who called them "Mother."[30] Dear friends might indeed continue this pattern of adoption and mothering throughout their lives; one woman might routinely assume the nurturing role of pseudomother, the other the dependency role of daughter. The pseudomother performed for the other woman all the services which we normally associate with mothers; she went to absurd lengths to purchase items her "daughter" could have obtained from other sources, gave advice and functioned as an idealized figure in her "daughter's" imagination. Helena played such a role for Molly, as did Sarah for Jeannie. Elizabeth Bordley Gibson bought almost all Eleanor Parke Custis Lewis's

necessities—from shoes and corset covers to bedding and harp strings—and sent them from Philadelphia to Virginia, a procedure that sometimes took months. Eleanor frequently asked Elizabeth to take back her purchases, have them redone, and argue with shopkeepers about prices. These were favors automatically asked and complied with. . . .[31]

A comparison of the references to men and women in these young women's letters is striking. Boys were obviously indispensable to the elaborate courtship ritual girls engaged in. In these teenage letters and diaries, however, boys appear distant and warded off—an effect produced both by the girl's sense of bonding and by a highly developed and deprecatory whimsy. Girls joked among themselves about the conceit, poor looks or affectations of suitors. Rarely, especially in the eighteenth and early nineteenth centuries, were favorable remarks exchanged. Indeed, while hostility and criticism of other women were so rare as to seem almost tabooed, young women permitted themselves to express a great deal of hostility toward peer-group men. . . .[32]

Even if young men were acceptable suitors, girls referred to them formally and obliquely: "The last week I received the unexpected intelligence of the arrival of a friend in Boston," Sarah Ripley wrote in her diary of the young man to whom she had been engaged for years and whom she would shortly marry. Harriet Manigault assiduously kept a lively and gossipy diary during the three years preceding her marriage, yet did not once comment upon her own engagement nor indeed make any personal references to her fiancé— who was never identified as such but always referred to as Mr. Wilcox.[33] The point is not that these young women were hostile to young men. Far from it; they sought marriage and domesticity. Yet in these letters and diaries men appear as an other or out group, segregated into different schools, supported by their own male network of friends and kin, socialized to different behavior, and coached to a proper formality in courtship behavior. As a consequence, relations between young women and men frequently lacked the spontaneity and emotional intimacy that characterized the young girls' ties to each other.

Indeed, in sharp contrast to their distant relations with boys, young women's relations with each other were close, often frolicsome, and surprisingly long lasting and devoted. They wrote secret missives to each other, spent long solitary days with each other, curled up together in bed at night to whisper fantasies and secrets.... Elizabeth Bordley and Nelly Parke Custis, teenagers in Philadelphia in the 1790s, routinely secreted themselves until late each night in Nelly's attic, where they each wrote a novel about the other.[34] Quite a few young women kept diaries, and it was a sign of special friendship to show their diaries to each other. The emotional quality of such exchanges emerges from the comments of one young girl who grew up along the Ohio frontier:

> Sisters CW and RT keep diaries & allow me the inestimable pleasure of reading them and in turn they see mine—but O shame covers my face when I think of it; theirs is so much better than mine, that every time. Then I think well now I *will* burn mine but upon second thought it would deprive me the pleasure of reading theirs, for I esteem it a very great privilege indeed, as well as very improving, as we lay our hearts open to each other, it heightens our love & helps to cherish & keep alive that sweet soothing friendship and endears us to each other by that soft attraction.

Girls routinely slept together, kissed and hugged each other. Indeed, while waltzing with young men scandalized the otherwise flighty and highly fashionable Harriet Manigault, she considered waltzing with other young women not only acceptable but pleasant.[35]

Marriage followed adolescence. With increasing frequency in the nineteenth century, marriage involved a girl's traumatic removal from her mother and her mother's network. It involved, as well, adjustment to a husband, who, because he was male came to marriage with both a different worldview and vastly different experiences. Not surprisingly, marriage was an event surrounded with supportive, almost ritualistic, practices. (Weddings are one of the last female rituals remaining in twentieth-century America.) Young women routinely spent the months preceding their marriage almost exclusively with other women—at neighborhood sewing bees and quilting parties or in a round of visits to geographically distant friends and relatives. Ostensibly they went to receive assistance in the practical preparations for their new home—sewing and quilting a trousseau and linen—but of equal importance, they appear to have gained emotional support and reassurance. Sarah Ripley spent over a month with friends and relatives in Boston and Hingham before her wedding; Parke Custis Lewis exchanged visits with her aunts and first cousins throughout Virginia. Anne Jefferis,

who married with some hesitation, spent virtually half a year in endless visiting with cousins, aunts, and friends. Despite their reassurance and support, however, she would not marry Moses Sheppard until her sister Edith and her cousin Rebecca moved into the groom's home, met his friends, and explored his personality. The wedding did not take place until Edith wrote to Anne: "I can say in truth I am entirely willing thou shouldst follow him even away in the Jersey sands believing if thou are not happy in thy future home it will not be any fault on his part...."[36]

Sisters, cousins, and friends frequently accompanied newlyweds on their wedding night and wedding trip, which often involved additional family visiting. Such extensive visits presumably served to wean the daughter from her family of origin. As such they often contained a note of ambivalence. Nelly Custis, for example, reported homesickness and loneliness on her wedding trip. "I left my Beloved and revered Grandmamma with sincere regret," she wrote Elizabeth Bordley. "It was sometime before I could feel reconciled to traveling without her." Perhaps they also functioned to reassure the young woman herself, and her friends and kin, that though marriage might alter it would not destroy old bonds of intimacy and familiarity.[37]

Married life, too, was structured about a host of female rituals. Childbirth, especially the birth of the first child, became virtually a *rite de passage,* with a lengthy seclusion of the woman before and after delivery, severe restrictions on her activities, and finally a dramatic reemergence. This seclusion was supervised by mothers, sisters, and loving friends. Nursing and weaning involved the advice and assistance of female friends and relatives. So did miscarriage.[38] Death, like birth, was structured around elaborate unisexed rituals. When Nelly Parke Custis Lewis rushed to nurse her daughter who was critically ill while away at school, Nelly received support, not from her husband, who remained on their plantation, but from her old school friend, Elizabeth Bordley. Elizabeth aided Nelly in caring for her dying daughter, cared for Nelly's other children, played a major role in the elaborate funeral arrangements (which the father did not attend), and frequently visited the girl's grave at the mother's request. For years Elizabeth continued to be the confidante of Nelly's anguished recollections of her lost daughter. These memories, Nelly's letters make clear, were for Elizabeth alone. "Mr. L. knows nothing of this," was a frequent comment.[39] Virtually every collection of letters and diaries in my sample contained evidence of women turning to each other for comfort when facing the frequent and unavoidable deaths of the eighteenth and nineteenth centuries. While mourning for her father's death, Sophie DuPont received elaborate letters and visits of condolence—all from women. No man wrote or visited Sophie to offer sympathy at her father's death. Among rural Pennsylvania Quakers, death and mourning rituals assumed an even more extreme same-sex form, with men or women largely barred from the deathbeds of the other sex. Women relatives and friends slept with the dying woman, nursed her, and prepared her body for burial.[40]

Eighteenth- and nineteenth-century women thus lived in emotional proximity to each other. Friendships and intimacies followed the biological ebb and flow of women's lives. Marriage and pregnancy, childbirth and weaning, sickness and death involved physical and psychic trauma which comfort and sympathy made easier to bear. Intense bonds of love and intimacy bound together those women who, offering each other aid and sympathy, shared such stressful moments.

These bonds were often physical as well as emotional. An undeniably romantic and even sensual note frequently marked female relationships. This theme, significant throughout the stages of a woman's life, surfaced first during adolescence. As one teenager from a struggling pioneer family in the Ohio Valley wrote in her diary in 1808: "I laid with my dear R[ebecca] and a glorious good talk we had until about 4[A.M.]—O how hard I do *love* her. . . ." Only a few years later Bostonian Eunice Callender carved her initials and Sarah Ripley's into a favorite tree, along with a pledge of eternal love, and then waited breathlessly for Sarah to discover and respond to her declaration of affection. The response appears to have been affirmative. A half-century later urbane and sophisticated Katherine Wharton commented upon meeting an old school chum: "She was a great pet of mine at school & I thought as I watched her light figure how often I had held her in my arms—how dear she had once been to me." Katie maintained a long intimate friendship with another girl. When a young man began to court this friend seriously, Katie commented in her diary that she had never realized "how deeply I loved Eng and how fully."

She wrote over and over again in that entry: "Indeed I love her!" and only with great reluctance left the city that summer since it meant also leaving Eng with Eng's new suitor.[41]

Peggy Emlen, a Quaker adolescent in Philadelphia in the 1760s, expressed similar feelings about her first cousin, Sally Logan. The girls sent love poems to each other . . . , took long solitary walks together, and even haunted the empty house of the other when one was out of town. Indeed Sally's absences from Philadelphia caused Peggy acute unhappiness. So strong were Peggy's feelings that her brothers began to tease about her affection for Sally and threatened to steal Sally's letters, much to both girls' alarm. In one letter that Peggy wrote the absent Sally she elaborately described the depth and nature of her feelings: "I have not words to express my impatience to see My Dear Cousin, what would I not give just now for an hours sweet conversation with her, it seems as if I had a thousand things to say to thee, yet when I see thee, everything will be forgot thro' joy. . . . I have a very great friendship for several Girls yet it dont give me so much uneasiness at being absent from them as from thee. . . . [Let us] go and spend a day down at our place together and there unmolested enjoy each others company."[42]

Sarah Alden Ripley, a young, highly educated woman, formed a similar intense relationship, in this instance with a woman somewhat older than herself. The immediate bond of friendship rested on their atypically intense scholarly interests, but it soon involved strong emotions, at least on Sarah's part. "Friendship," she wrote Mary Emerson, "is fast twining about her willing captive the silken hands of dependence, a dependence so sweet who would renounce it for the apathy of self-sufficiency?" Subsequent letters became far more emotional, almost conspiratorial. Mary visited Sarah secretly in her room, or the two women crept away from family and friends to meet in a nearby woods. Sarah became jealous of Mary's other young friends. Mary's trips away from Boston also thrust Sarah into periods of anguished depression. Interestingly, the letters detailing their love were not destroyed but were preserved and even reprinted in a eulogistic biography of Sarah Alden Ripley.[43]

Tender letters between adolescent women, confessions of loneliness and emotional dependency, were not peculiar to Sarah Alden, Peggy Emlen, or Katie Wharton. They are found throughout the letters of the thirty-five families studied. They have, of course, their parallel today in the musings of many female adolescents. Yet these eighteenth- and nineteenth-century friendships lasted with undiminished, indeed often increased, intensity throughout the women's lives. Sarah Alden Ripley's first child was named after Mary Emerson. . . . Eunice Callender remained enamored of her cousin Sarah Ripley for years and rejected as impossible the suggestion by another woman that their love might some day fade away. Sophie DuPont and her childhood friend, Clementina Smith, exchanged letters filled with love and dependency for forty years while another dear friend, Mary Black Couper, wrote of dreaming that she, Sophie, and her husband were all united in one marriage. Mary's letters to Sophie are filled with avowals of love and indications of ambivalence toward her own husband. Eliza Schlatter, another of Sophie's intimate friends, wrote to her at a time of crisis: "I wish I could be with you present in the body as well as the mind & heart—I would turn your *good husband out of bed*—and snuggle into you and we would have a long talk like old times in Pine St.—I want to tell you so many things that are not *writable*. . . ."[44]

Such mutual dependency and deep affection is a central existential reality coloring the world of supportive networks and rituals. In the case of Katie, Sophie, or Eunice—as with Molly, Jeannie, and Sarah—their need for closeness and support merged with more intense demands for a love which was at the same time both emotional and sensual. Perhaps the most explicit statement concerning women's lifelong friendships appeared in the letter abolitionist and reformer Mary Grew wrote about the same time, referring to her own love for her dear friend and lifelong companion, Margaret Burleigh. Grew wrote, in response to a letter of condolence from another woman on Burleigh's death: "Your words respecting my beloved friend touch me deeply. Evidently . . . you comprehend and appreciate, as few persons do . . . the nature of the relation which existed, which exists, between her and myself. Her only surviving niece . . . also does. To me it seems to have been a closer union than that of most marriages. We know there have been other such between two men and also between two women. And why should

there not be. Love is spiritual, only passion is sexual."[45]

How then can we ultimately interpret these long-lived intimate female relationships and integrate them into our understanding of Victorian sexuality? Their ambivalent and romantic rhetoric presents us with an ultimate puzzle: the relationship along the spectrum of human emotions between love, sensuality, and sexuality. . . .

It is possible to speculate that in the twentieth century a number of cultural taboos evolved to cut short the homosocial ties of girlhood and to impel the emerging women of thirteen or fourteen toward heterosexual relationships. In contrast, nineteenth-century American society did not taboo close female relationships but rather recognized them as a socially viable form of human contact—and, as such, acceptable throughout a woman's life. Indeed it was not these homosocial ties that were inhibited but rather heterosexual leanings. While closeness, freedom of emotional expression, and uninhibited physical contact characterized women's relationships with each other, the opposite was frequently true of male-female relationships. One could thus argue that within such a world of female support, intimacy, and ritual it was only to be expected that adult women would turn trustingly and lovingly to each other. It was a behavior they had observed and learned since childhood. A different type of emotional landscape existed in the nineteenth century, one in which Molly and Helena's love became a natural development.

Of perhaps equal significance are the implications we can garner from this framework for the understanding of heterosexual marriages in the nineteenth century. If men and women grew up as they did in relatively homogeneous and segregated sexual groups, then marriage represented a major problem in adjustment. From this perspective we could interpret much of the emotional stiffness and distance that we associate with Victorian marriage as a structural consequence of contemporary sex-role differentiation and gender-role socialization. With marriage both women and men had to adjust to life with a person who was, in essence, a member of an alien group. . . .

. . . Based on my research into this nineteenth-century world of female intimacy, I suggest that . . . we view sexual and emotional impulses as part of a continuum or spectrum of affect gradations strongly affected by cultural norms and arrangements, a continuum influenced in part by observed and thus learned behavior. At one end of the continuum lies committed heterosexuality, at the other uncompromising homosexuality; between, a wide latitude of emotions and sexual feelings. Certain cultures and environments permit individuals a great deal of freedom in moving across this spectrum. I would like to suggest that the nineteenth century was such a cultural environment. That is, the supposedly repressive and destructive Victorian sexual ethos may have been more flexible and responsive to the needs of particular individuals than those of mid-twentieth century.

NOTES

1. An exception to this rule is William R. Taylor and Christopher Lasch, "Two 'Kindred Spirits': Sorority and Family in New England, 1839–1846," *New England Quarterly* 36 (1963): 25–41. I do not accept the Taylor-Lasch thesis that female friendships developed in the mid-nineteenth century because of geographic mobility and the breakup of the colonial family. I have found these friendships as frequently in the eighteenth century as in the nineteenth and would hypothesize that the geographic mobility of the mid-nineteenth century eroded them as it did so many other traditional social institutions. . . .

2. I do not wish to deny the importance of women's relations with particular men. Obviously, women were close to brothers, husbands, fathers, and sons. However, there is evidence that despite such closeness relationships between men and women differed in both emotional texture and frequency from those between women. See my articles: "Puberty to Menopause: The Cycle of Femininity in Nineteenth-Century America," *Feminist Studies* 1 (1973):58–72, and, with Charles Rosenberg, "The Female Animal: Medical and Biological Views of Women in 19th Century America," *Journal of American History* 59 (1973):331–56.

3. See, e.g., the letters of Peggy Emlen to Sally Logan, 1768–72, Wells Morris Collection, Box 1, Historical Society of Pennsylvania, Philadelphia (hereafter, HSP); and the Eleanor Parke Custis Lewis Letters, HSP.

4. Sarah Butler Wister was the daughter of Fanny Kemble and Pierce Butler. In 1859 she married a Philadelphia physician, Owen Wister. (The novelist Owen Wister was her son.) Jeannie Field Musgrove was the half-orphaned daughter of constitutional lawyer and New York Republican politician David Dudley Field. Their correspondence (1855–98) is in the Sarah Butler Wister Papers, Wister Family Papers, HSP. Sarah Butler, Butler Place, S.C., to Jeannie Field, New York, Sept. 14, 1855; Sarah Butler Wister, Germantown, Pa., to Jeannie Field, New York, Sept. 25, 1862, Oct. 21, 1863; Jeannie Field, New York, to Sarah Butler Wister, Germantown, July 3, 1861, Jan. 23 and July 12, 1863; Sarah Butler Wister, Germantown,

to Jeannie Field, New York, June 5, 1861, Feb. 29, 1864; Jeannie Field to Sarah Butler Wister, Nov. 22, 1861, Jan. 4 and June 14, 1863.

5. Sarah Butler Wister, London, to Jeannie Field Musgrove, New York, June 18 and Aug. 3, 1870; for post-marriage, see two of Sarah's letters to Jeannie: Dec. 21, 1873, July 16, 1878.

6. This is the 1868–1920 correspondence between Mary Hallock Foote and Helena, a New York friend (the Mary Hallock Foote Papers are in the Manuscript Division, Stanford University). Like Molly and Helena, women frequently began letters to each other with salutations such as "Dearest," "My Most Beloved," "You Darling Girl," and signed them "tenderly" or "to my dear dear sweet friend, good-bye."

7. Mary Hallock [Foote] to Helena, n.d. [1869–70], n.d. [1871–72], Folder 1, Mary Hallock Foote Letters.

8. Mary Hallock [Foote] to Helena, Sept. 15 and 23, 1873, n.d. [Oct. 1873], Oct. 12, 1873; n.d. [Jan. 1874], n.d. [Spring 1874].

9. Mary Hallock [Foote] to Helena, Sept. 23, 1873; Mary Hallock [Foote] to Richard, Dec. 13, 1873. Molly's and Helena's relationship continued for the rest of their lives.

10. See Barbara Welter, "The Cult of True Womanhood: 1820–1860," *American Quarterly* 18 (Summer 1966):151–74; Anne Firor Scott, *The Southern Lady: From Pedestal to Politics, 1830–1930* (Chicago: University of Chicago Press, 1970), chaps. 1–2; Smith-Rosenberg and Rosenberg, "The Female Animal."

11. See, e.g., the letters of Peggy Emlen to Sally Logan, 1768–72. Elizabeth Botts, *Family and Social Network* (London: Tavistock Publications, 1957).

12. Harriet Manigault Wilcox Diary, June 28, 1814, and passim, HSP; Ann Sterling Biddle Family Papers, passim, Friends Historical Society, Swarthmore College; Phoebe Bradford Diary, Jan. 13, Nov. 16–19, 1832, Apr. 26 and May 7, 1833, HSP.

13. Lisa Mitchell Diary, 1860s, passim, Manuscript Division, Tulane University; Jeannie McCall, Cedar Park, to Peter McCall, Philadelphia, June 30, 1849, McCall Section, Cadwalader Collection, HSP; Peggy Emlen to Sally Logan, May 3, 1769.

14. For a prime example of this type of letter, see Eleanor Parke Custis Lewis to Elizabeth Bordley Gibson, passim.

15. Eleanor Parke Custis Lewis to Elizabeth Bordley Gibson, Apr. 20 and Sept. 25, 1848; Maria Inskeep to Fanny Hampton Correspondence, 1823–60, Inskeep Collection, Tulane University Library; Eunice Callender, Boston, to Sarah Ripley [Stearns], Sept. 24 and Oct. 29, 1803, Feb. 16, 1805, Apr. 29 and Oct. 9, 1806, May 26, 1810, Sarah Alden Ripley Correspondence, Schlesinger Library, Radcliffe College.

16. Sophie DuPont to her younger brother Henry, e.g., Dec. 13, 1827, Jan. 10 and Mar. 9, 1828, Feb. 4 and Mar. 10, 1832, Samuel Francis DuPont Papers, Eleutherian Mills Foundation, Wilmington, Del.; Mary B. Ashew Diary, July 11 and 13, Aug. 17, Summer and Oct. 1858.

17. Martha Jefferis to Anne Jefferis Sheppard, Jan. 12, 1845; Phoebe Middleton to Martha Jefferis, Feb. 22, 1848, Jefferis Family Correspondence, Chester County Historical Society, West Chester, Penna.

18. Rebecca Biddle to Martha Jefferis, 1838–49, passim; Martha Jefferis to Anne Jefferis Sheppard,

July 6, 1846; Anne Jefferis Sheppard to Rachael Jefferis, Jan. 16, 1865; Sarah Foulke Farquhar [Emlen] Diary, Sept. 22, 1813, Friends Historical Library, Swarthmore College.

19. Sarah Alden Ripley to Abba Allyn, n.d.; Phoebe Bradford Diary, July 13, 1832; Mary Hallock [Foote] to Helena, Dec. 23 [1868 or 1869]; Phoebe Bradford Diary, Dec. 8, 1832; Martha Jefferis and Anne Jefferis Sheppard letters, passim.

20. Martha Jefferis to Anne Jefferis Sheppard, Aug. 3, 1849; Sarah Ripley [Stearns] Diary, Nov. 12, 1808, Jan. 8, 1811.

21. Martha Jefferis to Edith Jefferis, Mar. 15, 1841; Mary Hallock Foote to Helena, n.d. [1874–75?]; Anne Jefferis Sheppard to Martha Jefferis, Sept. 29, 1841.

22. Frances Parke Lewis to Elizabeth Bordley Gibson, Apr. 29, 1821; Mary Jane Burleigh, Mount Pleasant, S.C., to Emily Howland, Sherwood N.Y., Mar. 27, 1872, Howland Family Papers.

23. See, e.g., Harriet Manigault Diary, Aug. 15, 21, and 23, 1814.

24. Mrs. S. S. Dalton, "Autobiography" (Circle Valley, Utah, 1876), pp. 21–22, Bancroft Library, University of California, Berkeley; Sarah Foulke Emlen Diary, Apr. 1809; Louisa G. Van Vleck, Appleton, Wis., to Charlena Van Vleck Anderson, Göttingen, n.d. [1875].

25. Abigail Brackett Lyman, Boston, to Mrs. Abigail Brackett (daughter to mother), n.d. [1797], June 3, 1800; Sarah Alden Ripley wrote weekly to her daughter, Sophy Ripley Fisher, after the latter's marriage (Sarah Alden Ripley Correspondence, passim). Daughters evidently frequently slept with their mothers—into adulthood (Harriet Manigault [Wilcox] Diary, Feb. 19, 1815; Eleanor Parke Custis Lewis to Elizabeth Bordley Gibson, Oct. 10, 1832). Daughters also frequently asked mothers to live with them and professed delight when they did so. . . . We did find a few exceptions to this mother-daughter felicity (M. B. Ashew Diary, Nov. 19, 1857, Apr. 10 and May 17, 1858). Sarah Foulke Emlen was at first very hostile to her step-mother (Sarah Foulke Emlen Diary, Aug. 9, 1807), but they later developed a warm supportive relationship.

26. Sarah Alden Ripley to Sophy Thayer, n.d. [1861].

27. See, e.g., Mary Hallock Foote to Helena [Winter 1873] (no. 52); Jossie, Stevens Point, Wis., to Charlena Van Vleck [Anderson], Appleton, Wis., Oct. 24, 1870, Anderson Family Papers, Manuscript Division, Stanford University; Pollie Chandler, Green Bay, Wis., to Charlena Van Vleck [Anderson], Appleton, n.d. [1870]; Eleuthera DuPont to Sophie DuPont, Sept. 5, 1829.

28. Sarah Foulke Emlen Journal, Sarah Ripley Stearns Diary, Mrs. S. S. Dalton, "Autobiography"; Maria Revere to her mother [Mrs. Paul Revere], June 13, 1801, Paul Revere Papers, Massachusetts Historical Society, Boston.

29. Frances Parke Lewis, Woodlawn, Va., to Elizabeth Bordley Gibson, Philadelphia, Apr. 11, 1821, Lewis Correspondence.

30. See, e.g., Sarah Ripley Stearns Diary, Mar. 9 and 25, 1810; Peggy Emlen to Sally Logan, Mar. and July 4, 1769; Deborah Cope, West Town School, to Rest Cope, Philadelphia, July 9, 1828, Chester County Historical Society, West Chester, Pa.

31. Anne Jefferis Sheppard to Martha Jefferis, Mar. 17, 1841.

32. See, e.g., Peggy Emlen to Sally Logan, Mar. 1769, Mount Vernon, Va. Sophie M. DuPont and Eleuthera DuPont, Brandywine, to Victorine DuPont Bauday, Philadelphia, Jan. 25, 1832.

33. Sarah Ripley [Stearns] Diary and Harriet Manigault Diary, passim.

34. Elizabeth Bordley Gibson, introductory statement to the Eleanor Parke Custis Lewis Letters [1850s], HSP. See also, e.g., Sophie Madeleine DuPont to Eleuthera DuPont, Dec. 1827; Clementina Beach Smith to Sophie Madeleine DuPont, Dec. 26, 1828; Sarah Faulke Emlen Diary, July 21, 1808, Mar. 30, 1809; Jeannie Field, New York, to Sarah Butler Wister, Germantown, Apr. 6, 1862.

35. Sarah Foulke [Emlen] Diary, Mar. 30, 1809; Harriet Manigault Diary, May 26, 1815.

36. Sarah Ripley [Stearns] Diary, May 17 and Oct. 2, 1812; Eleanor Parke Custis Lewis to Elizabeth Bordley Gibson, Apr. 23, 1826; Anne Jefferis to Martha Jefferis, Nov. 22 and 27, 1840, Jan. 13 and Mar. 17, 1841; Edith Jefferis, Greenwich, N.J., to Anne Jefferis, Philadelphia, Jan. 31, Feb. 6, and Feb. 1841.

37. Eleanor Parke Custis Lewis to Elizabeth Bordley, Nov. 4, 1799.

38. See, e.g., Mary Hallock to Helena DeKay Gilder [1876] (no. 81); n.d. (no. 83), Mar. 3, 1884; Mary Ashew Diary, vol. 2, Sept.–Jan. 1860; Fanny Ferris to Anne Biddle, Nov. 19, 1811; Eleanor Parke Custis Lewis to Elizabeth Bordley Gibson, Nov. 4, 1799, Apr. 27, 1827.

39. Eleanor Parke Custis Lewis to Elizabeth Bordley Gibson, Oct.–Nov. 1820, passim.

40. See, e.g., Emily Howland to Hannah, Sept. 30, 1866; Emily Howland Diary, Feb. 8, 11, and 27, 1880; Phoebe Bradford Diary, Apr. 12 and 13, and Aug. 4, 1833; Mary Black [Couper] to Sophie Madeleine DuPont, Feb. 1827 [Nov. 1, 1834], Nov. 12, 1834, two letters [late Nov. 1834]; Eliza Schlatter to Sophie Madeleine DuPont, Nov. 2, 1834; Martha Jefferis to Anne Jefferis Sheppard, Sept. 28, 1843, Aug. 21 and Sept. 25, 1844, Jan. 11, 1846, Summer 1848, passim.

41. Sarah Foulke [Emlen] Diary, Dec. 29, 1808; Eunice Callender, Boston, to Sarah Ripley [Stearns], Greenfield, Mass., May 24, 1803; Katherine Johnstone Brinley [Wharton] Journal, Apr. 26, May 30, and May 29, 1856, HSP.

42. A series of roughly fourteen letters written by Peggy Emlen to Sally Logan (1768–71) has been preserved in the Wells Morris Collection, Box 1, HSP (see esp. Jan. 8, 1768, May 3 and July 4, 1769).

43. The eulogistic biographical sketch appeared in Mrs. O. J. Wister and Miss Agnes Irwin, eds., *Worthy Women of Our First Century* (Philadelphia: J. B. Lippincott & Co., 1877).

44. See Sarah Alden Ripley to Mary Emerson, Nov. 19, 1823. Mary Black Couper to Sophie M. DuPont, Mar. 5, 1832. The Clementina Smith–Sophie DuPont correspondence is in the Sophie DuPont Correspondence. The quotation is from Eliza Schlatter, Mount Holly, N.J., to Sophie DuPont, Brandywine, Aug. 24, 1834.

45. Mary Grew, Providence, R.I., to Isabel Howland, Sherwood, N.Y., Apr. 27, 1892, Howland Correspondence, Sophia Smith Collection, Smith College.

JAMES C. MOHR
Abortion in America, 1800–1880

If we observe nineteenth-century society through women's eyes, surely no experience was as widely shared as the experience of childbirth. The biological act of maternity created powerful bonds among women as they coped with the experience of childbirth. Until the twentieth century, most births took place at home, where the birthing mother was likely to be surrounded by her mother, sisters, and cousins, a midwife and other experienced women, and her woman friends. The "female world of love and ritual" that Carroll Smith-Rosenberg describes "formed across the childbirth bed," writes historian Judith Walzer Leavitt. "When women had suffered the agonies of watching their friends die, when they had helped a friend recover from a difficult delivery, or when they had participated in a successful birthing they developed a closeness that lasted a lifetime." Leavitt finds that these circles of friendly support made significant choices. "The collectivity of women gathered around the birthing bed made sure that birth attendants were responsive to their wishes. They made decisions about when and if to call physicians to births that midwives were attending; they gave or withheld permission for physicians' procedures; and they created the atmosphere of female support in a room that might have contained both women and men." Leavitt argues that when in the twentieth century birthing moved to hospitals, much of this support evaporated; the reforms in hospital practices demanded by feminists since the 1970s have been an effort to reclaim what had been lost.*

During the centuries before reliable fertility control measures made it possible for women to set limits on reproduction, most married women and many unmarried women felt considerable physical and psychological burdens from repeated pregnancies, childbirths, and postpartum recoveries. The cost in terms of time, energy, dreams, and bodies was high. If we observe nineteenth-century society through women's eyes, surely no statistic was as significant as the one that marked the decline in the average number of children borne by each woman. Childbirth was a time of terror.

It is therefore notable that in the early nineteenth century, a sharp decline took place in the birth rates; the decline was particularly marked in urban areas. No innovations in birth control technology appeared in this period; the decline was the result of choices—later age at marriage, abstinence from sexual intercourse—that

---

*Judith Walzer Leavitt, "Under the Shadow of Maternity: American Women's Responses to Death and Debility Fears in Nineteenth-Century Childbirth," *Feminist Studies* 12 (1986): 129–54. Maine midwife Martha Ballard, who practiced up until her death in 1812 at age seventy-seven, left an extraordinary diary that reveals not only the community of women who gathered for births, but also Ballard's skill. She delivered some 900 women without losing a mother in childbirth. See Laurel Thatcher Ulrich, *A Midwife's Tale: The Life of Martha Ballard Based on Her Diary, 1785–1812* (New York: Alfred A. Knopf, 1990), esp. ch. 5; also the 90-minute film of the same name (produced by Laurie Kahn-Leavitt and directed by Richard P. Rogers for PBS's *American Experience* series, 1997). The diary is reproduced in its entirety on www.dohistory.org, a website with features that invite interactive analysis and exploration.

Excerpted from chs. 1 and 4 of *Abortion in America: The Origins and Evolution of National Policy* by James C. Mohr (New York: Oxford University Press, 1978). Used by permission of the author and publisher. Notes have been renumbered and edited.

functioned to limit the number of times women faced childbirth. In the mid-eighteenth century, the average rural woman of free status could expect to face childbirth eight or nine times; by the early nineteenth century, that number had dropped to six and in some urban areas to four. Except for occasional "baby booms," birth rates in the United States have fallen steadily and continue to stabilize in our own time.

When unsuccessful in avoiding pregnancies, many women attempted to abort them. The methods of the times were dangerous, but until the 1840s, the women were rarely censured by the community if fetal movement had not been felt (this was called quickening). It was not until the 1820s that states began to pass laws criminalizing certain methods of abortion performed after quickening; penalties fell on the medical practitioner not the pregnant woman. Legislators in this period were concerned that "rash" or "irregular" doctors were prescribing toxic potions or performing risky operations and thus endangering women's lives.* As these two sections from James Mohr's comprehensive study suggest, the vigorous attack on abortion after 1840 may well have been a response to the growing willingness of married women to attempt it.

What does the debate on abortion policy reveal about public attitudes toward women and their place in the family and in society?

ABORTION IN AMERICA, 1800–1825

In the absence of any legislation whatsoever on the subject of abortion in the United States in 1800, the legal status of the practice was governed by the traditional British common law as interpreted by the local courts of the new American states. For centuries prior to 1800 the key to the common law's attitude toward abortion had been a phenomenon associated with normal gestation known as quickening. Quickening was the first perception of fetal movement by the pregnant woman herself. Quickening generally occurred near the midpoint of gestation, late in the fourth or early in the fifth month, though it could and still does vary a good deal from one woman to another. The common law did not formally recognize the existence of a fetus in criminal cases until it had quickened. After quickening, the expulsion and destruction of a fetus without due cause was considered a crime, because the fetus itself had manifested some semblance of a separate existence: the ability to move. The crime was qualitatively different from the destruction of a human being, however, and punished less harshly. Before quickening, actions that had the effect of terminating what turned

out to have been an early pregnancy were not considered criminal under the common law in effect in England and the United States in 1800.[1]

Both practical and moral arguments lay behind the quickening distinction. Practically, because no reliable tests for pregnancy existed in the early nineteenth century, quickening alone could confirm with absolute certainty that a woman really was pregnant. Prior to quickening, each of the telltale signs of pregnancy could, at least in theory, be explained in alternative ways by physicians of the day. Hence, either a doctor or a woman herself could take actions designed to restore menstrual flow after one or more missed periods on the assumption that something might be unnaturally "blocking" or "obstructing" her normal cycles, and if left untreated the obstruction would wreak real harm upon the woman. Medically, the procedures for removing a blockage were the same as those for inducing an early abortion. Not until the obstruction moved could either a physician or a woman, regardless of their suspicions, be completely certain that it was a "natural" blockage—a pregnancy—rather than a potentially dangerous situation. Morally, the question of whether

---

*Chapters 2, 5, and 8 in Mohr, *Abortion in America*, address three distinct stages of legislation. For an examination of an abortion that led to a young women's death and a series of prosecutions in 1740s Connecticut, see Cornelia Hughes Dayton, "Taking the Trade: Abortion and Gender Relations in an Eighteenth-Century New England Village," *William and Mary Quarterly*, 3rd ser., 48 (Jan. 1991): 19–49.

or not a fetus was "alive" had been the subject of philosophical and religious debate among honest people for at least 5000 years. The quickening doctrine itself appears to have entered the British common law tradition by way of the tangled disputes of medieval theologians over whether or not an impregnated ovum possessed a soul.[2] The upshot was that American women in 1800 were legally free to attempt to terminate a condition that might turn out to have been a pregnancy until the existence of that pregnancy was incontrovertibly confirmed by the perception of fetal movement.

An ability to suspend one's modern preconceptions and to accept the early nineteenth century on its own terms regarding the distinction between quick and unquick is absolutely crucial to an understanding of the evolution of abortion policy in the United States. However doubtful the notion appears to modern readers, the distinction was virtually universal in America during the early decades of the nineteenth century and accepted in good faith. Perhaps the strongest evidence of the tenacity and universality of the doctrine in the United States was the fact that American courts pointedly sustained the most lenient implications of the quickening doctrine even after the British themselves had abandoned them. . . .

Because women believed themselves to be carrying inert non-beings prior to quickening, a potential for life rather than life itself, and because the common law permitted them to attempt to rid themselves of suspected and unwanted pregnancies up to the point when the potential for life gave a sure sign that it was developing into something actually alive, some American women did practice abortion in the early decades of the nineteenth century. One piece of evidence for this conclusion was the ready access American women had to abortifacient information from 1800 onward. A chief source of such information was the home medical literature of the era.

Home medical manuals characteristically contained abortifacient information in two different sections. One listed in explicit detail a number of procedures that might release "obstructed menses" and the other identified a number of specific things to be avoided in a suspected pregnancy because they were thought to bring on abortion. Americans probably consulted William Buchan's *Domestic* *Medicine* more frequently than any other home medical guide during the first decades of the nineteenth century.[3] Buchan suggested several courses of action designed to restore menstrual flow if a period was missed. These included bloodletting, bathing, iron and quinine concoctions, and if those failed, "a tea-spoonful of the tincture of black hellebore [a violent purgative] . . . twice a day in a cup of warm water." Four pages later he listed among "the common causes" of abortion "great evacuations [and] vomiting," exactly as would be produced by the treatment he urged for suppressed menses. Later in pregnancy a venturesome, or desperate, woman could try some of the other abortion inducers he ticked off: "violent exercise; raising great weights; reaching too high; jumping, or stepping from an eminence; strokes [strong blows] on the belly; [and] falls."[4] . . .

Like most early abortion material, Buchan's . . . advice harked back to almost primordial or instinctual methods of ending a pregnancy. Bloodletting, for example, was evidently thought to serve as a surrogate period; it was hoped that bleeding from any part of the body might have the same flushing effect upon the womb that menstrual bleeding was known to have. This primitive folk belief lingered long into the nineteenth century, well after bleeding was abandoned as medical therapy in other kinds of cases, and it was common for abortionists as late as the 1870s to pull a tooth as part of their routine.[5] . . .

In addition to home medical guides and health manuals addressed to women, abortions and abortifacient information were also available in the United States from midwives and midwifery texts.[6] . . .

Herbal healers, the so-called Indian doctors, and various other irregular practitioners also helped spread abortifacient information in the United States during the early decades of the nineteenth century. Their surviving pamphlets, of which Peter Smith's 1813 brochure entitled "The Indian Doctor's Dispensary" is an example, contained abortifacient recipes that typically combined the better-known cathartics with native North American ingredients thought to have emmenagogic properties. For "obstructed menses" Smith recommended a concoction he called "Dr. Reeder's chalybeate." The key ingredients were myrrh and aloes, combined with liquor, sugar, vinegar, iron dust, ivy, and Virginia or seneca snakeroot.[7]

A sweet-and-sour cocktail like that may or may not have induced abortion, but must certainly have jolted the system of any woman who tried one. . . .

Finally, and most importantly, America's regular physicians, those who had formal medical training either in the United States or in Great Britain or had been apprenticed under a regular doctor, clearly possessed the physiological knowledge and the surgical techniques necessary to terminate a pregnancy by mechanical means. They knew that dilation of the cervix at virtually any stage of gestation would generally bring on uterine contractions that would in turn lead to the expulsion of the contents of the uterus. They knew that any irritation introduced into the uterus would have the same effect. They knew that rupturing the amniotic sac, especially in the middle and later months of pregnancy, would usually also induce contractions and expulsion, regardless of whether the fetus was viable. Indeed, they were taught in their lecture courses and in their textbooks various procedures much more complex than a simple abortion, such as in utero decapitation and fetal pulverization, processes they were instructed to employ in lieu of the even more horribly dangerous Caesarean section. Like the general public, they knew the drugs and herbs most commonly used as abortifacients and emmenagogues, and also like the general public, they believed such preparations to have been frequently effective.[8] . . .

This placed great pressure on physicians to provide what amounted to abortion services early in pregnancy. An unmarried girl who feared herself pregnant, for example, could approach her family doctor and ask to be treated for menstrual blockage. If he hoped to retain the girl and her family as future patients, the physician would have little choice but to accept the girl's assessment of the situation, even if he suspected otherwise. He realized that every member of his profession would testify to the fact that he had no totally reliable means of distinguishing between an early pregnancy, on the one hand, and the amenorrhea that the girl claimed, on the other. Consequently, he treated for obstruction, which involved exactly the same procedures he would have used to induce an early abortion, and wittingly or unwittingly terminated the pregnancy. Regular physicians were also asked to bring to a safe conclusion abortions that irregulars or women themselves

had initiated. . . . And through all of this the physician might bear in mind that he could never be held legally guilty of wrongdoing. No statutes existed anywhere in the United States on the subject of abortion, and the common law . . . considered abortion actionable only after a pregnancy had quickened. No wonder then that Heber C. Kimball, recalling his courtship with a woman he married in 1822, claimed that she had been "taught . . . in our young days, when she got into the family way, to send for a doctor and get rid of the child"; a course that she followed.[9]

In summary, then, the practice of aborting unwanted pregnancies was, if not common, almost certainly not rare in the United States during the first decades of the nineteenth century. A knowledge of various drugs, potions, and techniques was available from home medical guides, from health books for women, from midwives and irregular practitioners, and from trained physicians. Substantial evidence suggests that many American women sought abortions, tried the standard techniques of the day, and no doubt succeeded some proportion of the time in terminating unwanted pregnancies. Moreover, this practice was neither morally nor legally wrong in the eyes of the vast majority of Americans, provided it was accomplished before quickening.

The actual number of abortions in the United States prior to the advent of any statutes regulating its practice simply cannot be known. But an equally significant piece of information about those abortions can be gleaned from the historical record. It concerns the women who were having them. Virtually every observer through the middle of the 1830s believed that an overwhelming percentage of the American women who sought and succeeded in having abortions did so because they feared the social consequences of an illegitimate pregnancy, not because they wanted to limit their fertility per se. The doctor who uncovered the use of snake root as an abortifacient, for example, related that in all of the many instances he heard about "it was taken by women who had indulged in illegitimate love. . . ."[10]

In short, abortion was not thought to be a means of family limitation in the United States, at least on any significant scale, through the first third of the nineteenth century. This was hardly surprising in a largely rural and essentially preindustrial society, whose birth-rates were exceeding any ever recorded in a European nation.[11] One could, along with medical student [Thomas] Massie, be less than enthusiastic about such an "unnatural" prac-tice as abortion, yet tolerate it as the "recourse . . . of the victim of passion . . . the child of nature" who was driven by "an unrelenting world" unable to forgive any "deviation from what they have termed virtue."[12] Conse-quently, Americans in the early nineteenth century could and did look the other way when they encountered abortion. Nothing in their medical knowledge or in the rulings of their courts compelled them to do otherwise, and, as Massie indicated, there was considera-ble compassion for the women involved. It would be nearly midcentury before the per-ception of who was having abortions for what reasons would begin to shift in the United States, and that shift would prove to be one of the critical developments in the evolution of American abortion policy.

A final point remains to be made about abortion in the United States during the first decades of the nineteenth century. Most ob-servers appeared to consider it relatively safe, at least by the medical standards of the day, rather than extremely dangerous. . . . This too must have reassured women who decided to risk an abortion before quickening. According to the lecture notes of one of his best students, Walter Channing told his Harvard classes that abortion could be troublesome when produced by external blows, because severe internal hemorrhage would be likely, but that generally considered, "abortion [was] not so dangerous as commonly supposed."[13]

The significance of these opinions lay less in whether or not they were accurate than in the fact that writers on abortion, including physicians, saw no reason to stress the dangers attendant to the process. Far from it. They were skeptical about poisons and purgatives, but appear to have assessed physically induced abortions as medically acceptable risks by the standards of the day, especially if brought on during the period of pregnancy when both popular belief and the public courts condoned them anyhow. Here again was a significant early perception that would later change. That change, like the shift in the perception of who was having abortions for what purposes, would also have an impact on the evolution of American abortion policy. . . .

THE SOCIAL CHARACTER OF ABORTION IN AMERICA, 1840–1880

Before 1840 abortion was perceived in the United States primarily as a recourse of the des-perate, especially of the young woman in trouble who feared the wrath of an overexacting society. After 1840, however, evidence began to accu-mulate that the social character of the practice had changed. A high proportion of the women whose abortions contributed to the soaring in-cidence of that practice in the United States be-tween 1840 and 1880 appeared to be married, native-born, Protestant women, frequently of middle- or upper-class status. The data came from disparate sources, some biased and some not, but in the end proved compelling.

Even before the availability of reliable evi-dence confirmed that the nation's birthrates were starting to plummet, observers noticed that abortion more and more frequently in-volved married women rather than single women in trouble. Professor Hugh L. Hodge of the University of Pennsylvania, one of the first physicians in the United States to speak out about abortion in anything approaching a public forum, lectured his introductory obstet-rics students in 1839 that abortion was fast be-coming a prominent feature of American life. Hodge still considered women trying "to de-stroy the fruit of illicit pleasure" to be the ones most often seeking abortions, but he alerted his students to the fact that "married women, also, from the fear of labor, from indisposition to have the care, the expense, or the trouble of children, or some other motive" were more and more frequently requesting "that the embryo be destroyed by their medical attendant." Hodge attributed a good deal of this activity to the quickening doctrine, which allowed "women whose moral character is, in other re-spects, without reproach; mothers who are de-voted, with an ardent and self-denying affection, to the children who already constitute[d] their family [to be] perfectly indifferent respecting the foetus in the utero."[14] . . .

Opinion was divided regarding the social status of the women who accounted for the great upsurge of abortion during the middle period of the nineteenth century. While most observers agreed "all classes of society, rich and poor" were involved to some extent, many thought that the middle and upper classes practiced abortion more extensively than the lower classes.[15] The Michigan State Medical So-ciety in 1859 declared that abortion "pervade[d] all ranks" in that state.[16] The Medical Society of Buffalo pointed out that same year "now we have ladies, yes, *educated and refined ladies*" involved as well.[17] On the other hand, court cases revealed at least a sprinkling of lower-class women, servant girls, and the like. . . .

Although the going price for an abortion varied tremendously according to place, time, practitioner, and patient, abortions appear to have been generally quite expensive. Regular physicians testified repeatedly throughout the period that the abortion business was enormously lucrative. Those doctors pledged not to perform abortions bitterly resented men like the Boston botanic indicted for manslaughter in an abortion case in 1851, who posted $8000 bond and returned to his offices, at a time when the average university professor in the United States earned under $2000 per year.[18] . . .

When women turned from regulars to the commercial abortionists, the prices were still not cheap. Itinerants and irregulars generally tried to charge whatever they judged the traffic would bear, which could vary anywhere from $5 to $500. During the 1840s, for example, Madame Restell charged $5 for an initial visit and diagnosis, then negotiated the price of the operation "according to the wealth and liberality of the parties." In a case for which she was indicted in 1846 she asked a young woman about "her beau's circumstances" before quoting a figure, and then tried to get $100 when she found out the man was a reasonably successful manufacturer's representative. The man thought that was too costly, and only after extensive haggling among go-betweens was a $75 fee agreed upon.[19] . . .

Despite the apparent gradual leveling of prices, however, the abortion business remained a profitable commercial venture well into the 1870s. Anthony Comstock, the single-minded leader of a massive anti-obscenity campaign launched in the United States during the 1870s, kept meticulous and extensive records of all of the people he helped arrest while operating as a special agent of the Post Office Department. Between 1872 and 1880 Comstock and his associates aided in the indictment of 55 persons whom Comstock identified as abortionists. The vast majority were very wealthy and posted large bonds with ease. . . .

. . . [A]bortion entered the mainstream of American life during the middle decades of the nineteenth century. While the unmarried and the socially desperate continued to have recourse to it as they had earlier in the century, abortion also became highly visible, much more frequently practiced, and quite common as a means of family limitation among white, Protestant, native-born wives of middle- and upper-class standing. These dramatic changes, in turn, evoked sharp comment from two ideologically opposed groups in American society, each of which either directly or indirectly blamed the other for the shift in abortion patterns. On one side of the debate were the antifeminists, led by regular physicians, and on the other side were the nation's feminists. Both groups agreed that abortion had become a large-scale and socially significant phenomenon in American life, but they disagreed over the reasons why.

Before examining the two chief explanations put forward by contemporaries for the striking shifts in the incidence and the character of abortion in the United States after 1840, two observations may be worth making. First, it is never easy to understand why people do what they do even in the most straightforward of situations; it is nearly impossible to know with certainty the different reasons, rational and irrational, why people in the past might have taken such a psychologically loaded action as the termination of a suspected pregnancy. Second, most participants on both sides of the contemporary debate over why so many American women began to practice abortion after 1840 actually devoted most of their attention to the question of why American women wanted to limit their fertility. This confirmed that abortion was important between 1840 and 1880 primarily as a means of family limitation, but such discussions offer only marginal help in understanding why so many American women turned to abortion itself as a means toward that end.

Cultural anthropologists argue that abortion has been practiced widely and frequently in preindustrial societies at least in part because "it is a woman's method [of limiting fertility] and can be practiced without the man's knowledge."[20] This implies a sort of women's conspiracy to limit population, which would be difficult to demonstrate in the context of nineteenth-century America. Nonetheless, there is some evidence, though it must be considered carefully, to suggest that an American variant of this proposition may have been at least one of the reasons why abortion became such a common form of family limitation in the United States during the period. A number of physicians, as will become evident, certainly believed that one of the keys to the upsurge of abortion was the fact that it was a uniquely female practice, which men could neither control nor prevent. . . .

Earlier in the century observers had alleged that the tract literature and lectures of the women's rights movement advocated family planning and disseminated abortifacient information.[21] In 1859 Harvard professor Walter Channing reported the opinion that "women for whom this office of foeticide, unborn-child-killing, is committed, are strong-minded," and no later writer ever accused them of being weak-minded.[22] . . .

The most common variant of the view that abortion was a manifestation of the women's rights movement hinged upon the word "fashion." Over and over men claimed that women who aborted did so because they cared more about scratching for a better perch in society than they did about raising children. They dared not waste time on the latter lest they fall behind in the former. Women, in short, were accused of being aggressively self-indulgent. Some women, for example, had "the effrontery to say boldly, that they have neither the time nor inclination to nurse babies"; others exhibited "self-indulgence in most disgusting forms"; and many of the women practicing abortion were described as more interested in "selfish and personal ends" or "fast living" than in the maternity for which God had supposedly created them.[23] . . . For this reason, some doctors urged that feticide be made a legal ground for divorce.[24] A substantial number of writers between 1840 and 1880, in other words, were willing to portray women who had abortions as domestic subversives. . . .

Notwithstanding the possibility that recourse to abortion sometimes reflected the rising consciousness of the women who had them, and notwithstanding the fact that some males, especially regular physicians, were distinctly uneasy about the practice because of what its ultimate effects upon the social position of women might be, the relationship between abortion and feminism in the nineteenth century nevertheless remained indirect and ironical. This becomes evident when the arguments of the feminists themselves are analyzed. One of the most forceful early statements of what subsequently became the feminist position on abortion was made in the 1850s in a

volume entitled *The Unwelcome Child*.[25] The author, Henry C. Wright, asserted that women alone had the right to say when they would become pregnant and blamed the tremendous outburst of abortion in America on selfishly sensual husbands. Wright's volume was more interesting than other similar tracts, however, because he published a large number of letters from women detailing the circumstances under which they had sought abortions.

One of Wright's letters was from a woman who had her first abortion in 1841, because her one-year-old firstborn was sick and her husband was earning almost nothing. She "consulted a lady friend, and by her persuasion and assistance, killed" the fetus she was carrying. When she found herself pregnant again shortly thereafter she "consulted a physician. . . . He was ready with his logic, his medicines and instruments, and told me how to destroy it. After experimenting on myself three months, I was successful. I killed my child about five months after conception." She steeled herself to go full term with her next pregnancy and to "endure" an addition to her impoverished and unhappy household. When pregnant again she "employed a doctor, to kill my child, and in the destruction of it . . . ended my power to be a mother." The woman's point throughout, however, was that abortion "was most repulsive" to her and her recourse to it "rendered [her] an object of loathing to [her]self." Abortion was not a purposeful female conspiracy, but an undesirable necessity forced by thoughtless men. As this woman put it: "I was the veriest slave alive."[26] . . .

The attitudes expressed by Wright's correspondents in the 1840s and 1850s became the basis of the official position of American feminists toward abortion after the Civil War. As Elizabeth Cady Stanton phrased it, the practice was one more result of "the degradation of woman" in the nineteenth century, not of woman's rising consciousness or expanding opportunities outside the home.[27] . . . The remedy to the problem of abortion in the United States, in their view, was not legalized abortion open to all but "the education and enfranchisement of women" which would make abortion unnecessary in a future world of egalitarian respect and sexual discretion.[28] In short, most feminists, though they agreed completely with other observers that abortion was endemic in America by midcentury, did not blame the increase on the rising ambitions of women but asserted with Matilda E. J. Gage "that this crime of 'child murder,' 'abortion,' 'infanticide,' lies at the door of the male sex."[29] The *Woman's Advocate* of Dayton, Ohio, put it even more forcefully in 1869: "Till men learn to check their sensualism, and leave their wives free to choose their periods of maternity, let us hear no more invectives against women for the destruction of prospective unwelcome children, whose dispositions, made miserable by unhappy ante-natal conditions, would only make their lives a curse to themselves and others."[30] . . .

Despite the blame and recrimination evoked by the great upsurge of abortion in the United States in the nineteenth century, some of which was directed at women and some at men, it appears likely that most decisions to use abortion probably involved couples conferring together, not just men imposing their wills or women acting unilaterally, and that abortion was the result of diffuse pressures, not merely the rising consciousness of women or the tyrannical aggressions of men. American men and women wanted to express their sexuality and mutual affections, on the one hand, and to limit their fertility, on the other. Abortion was neither desirable nor undesirable in itself, but rather one of the few available means of reconciling and realizing those two higher priorities. And it seems likely that the man and woman agreed to both of those higher priorities in most instances, thus somewhat mooting in advance the question of which one was more responsible for the decisions that made abortion a common phenomenon in mid-nineteenth-century America.[31]

Court records provide one source of evidence for the mutuality of most abortion decisions. Almost every nineteenth-century abortion case that was written up, whether in the popular press, in medical journals, or in the official proceedings of state supreme courts, involved the agreement of both the man and the woman. There is no record of any man ever having sued any woman for aborting his child. . . .

Perhaps the best evidence for the likely mutuality of most abortion decisions is contained in the diary that Lester Frank Ward, who later became one of America's most famous sociologists, kept as a newlywed in the 1860s. Though Ward was unique in writing down the intimate decisions that he and his wife had to make, the couple seemed otherwise typical young Americans, almost

as Tocqueville might have described them, anxious for further education and ambitious to get ahead quickly. Both Ward and his wife understood that a child would overburden their limited resources and reduce the probability of ever realizing either their individual goals of self-improvement or their mutual goals as a couple. They avoided pregnancy in pre-marital intercourse, then continued to avoid it after their marriage in August 1862. Not until early in 1864 did Lizzie Ward become pregnant. In March, without consulting her husband, she obtained "an effective remedy" from a local woman, which made her very sick for two days but helped her to terminate her pregnancy. She probably took this action after missing three or four periods; it was still early enough in gestation that her husband did not realize she was pregnant but late enough that lactation had begun. Ward noted in his diary that "the proof" she had been pregnant was "the milk" that appeared after the abortion.[32]

Anti-feminists might have portrayed Lizzie Ward's action as diabolical, a betrayal of duty. Feminists might have viewed it as the only recourse open to a female who wanted both to further her own education and to remain on good terms with an ambitious spouse who would certainly have sacrificed his wife's goals to child-rearing, while he pursued his own. But the decision was really the result of a pre-existing consensus between the two of them. Though Ward had not been party to the process in a legal or direct sense, which may go some distance toward confirming the role of abortion as a more uniquely female method of family limitation than contraception, he was clearly delighted that his wife was "out of danger" and would not be having a child. After this brush with family responsibility, the Wards tried a number of new methods of contraception, which they presumably hoped would be more effective than whatever they had been using to avoid pregnancy before Lizzie had to resort to abortion. These included both "pills" and "instruments." Not until the summer of 1865, after Ward had obtained a decent job in Washington, did the couple have a baby.[33]

Abortion had been for the Wards what it apparently also was for many other American couples: an acceptable means toward a mutually desirable end, one of the only ways they had to allow themselves both to express their sexuality and affection toward each other with some degree of frequency and to postpone family responsibilities until they thought they were better prepared to raise children. The line of acceptability for most Americans trying to reconcile these twin priorities ran just about where Lizzie Ward had drawn it. Infanticide, the destruction of a baby after its birth, was clearly unacceptable, and so was abortion after quickening, though that was a much grayer area than infanticide. But abortion before quickening, like contraception itself, was an appropriate and legally permissible method of avoiding unwanted children. And it had one great advantage, as the Wards learned, over contraception: it worked. As more and more women began to practice abortion, however, and as the practice changed from being invisible to being visible, from being quantitatively insignificant to being a systematic practice that terminated a substantial number of pregnancies after 1840, and from being almost entirely a recourse of the desperate and the socially marginal to being a commonly employed procedure among the middle and upper classes of American society, state legislators decided to reassess their policies toward the practice. Between 1840 and 1860 law-makers in several states began to respond to the increase of abortion in American life.

Notes

1. The quickening doctrine went back to the thirteenth century in England. . . . On quickening in the common law see Cyril C. Means, Jr., "The Law of New York concerning Abortion and the Status of the Foetus, 1664–1968: A Case of Cessation of Constitutionality," *New York Law Forum* XIV, no. 3 (Fall 1968): 419–26.

2. Ibid., pp. 411–19, and John T. Noonan, Jr., "An Almost Absolute Value in History," in John T. Noonan, Jr., ed., *The Morality of Abortion* (Cambridge, Mass., 1970), pp. 1–59. . . .

3. . . . Buchan's volume was published in Philadelphia as early as 1782, where it went through many editions. . . . This remarkably successful book continued to be reprinted in America through 1850.

4. Buchan, *Domestic Medicine*, pp. 400, 403–4.

5. See, for example, Frederick Hollick, *Diseases of Women, Their Causes and Cure Familiarly Explained: With Practical Hints for Their Prevention, and for the Preservation of Female Health: For Every Female's Private Use* (New York, 1849), p. 150. . . .

6. . . . [See] George Ellington, *The Women of New York, or the Under-World of the Great City* (New York, 1869), pp. 399–400.

7. Peter Smith, "The Indian Doctor's Dispensary, Being Father Peter Smith's Advice Respecting Diseases and Their Cure; Consisting of Prescriptions for Many Complaints: And a Description of Medicines, Simple and Compound, Showing Their Virtues and How to Apply Them," [1813] reproduced in

J. U. Lloyd, ed., *Bulletin of the Lloyd Library of Botany, Pharmacy and Materia Medica* (1901), Bull. #2, Reproduction Series #2, pp. 46–47.

8. John Burns, *Observations on Abortion: Containing an Account of the Manner in Which It Takes Place, the Causes Which Produce It, and the Method of Preventing or Treating It* (Troy, N.Y., 1808), pp. 73–81. . . .

9. Heber C. Kimball in the *Journal of Discourses*, 26 vols. (Liverpool, 1857), V:91–92.

10. Thomas Massie, "An Experimental Inquiry into the Properties of the Polygala Senega," in Charles Caldwell, ed., *Medical Theses*, . . . (Philadelphia, 1806), p. 203.

11. . . . William Petersen's widely used *Population* (New York, 3rd ed., 1975), p. 15, labels [the U.S. population from 1800 to 1830 as] the "underdeveloped" type and identifies its characteristics as a mixed economy, high fertility rates, falling mortality rates, and very high rates of population growth.

12. Massie, "Polygala Senega," p. 204.

13. John G. Metcalf, student notebooks written while attending Dr. Walter Channing's lectures of midwifery at Harvard Medical School, 1825–1826 (Countway Library, Harvard Medical School), entry for Dec. 27, 1825. . . .

14. Hugh L. Hodge in Francis Wharton and Moreton Stillé, *Treatise on Medical Jurisprudence* (Philadelphia, 1855), p. 270.

15. "Report on Criminal Abortion," *Transactions of the American Medical Association* XII (1859):75.

16. E. P. Christian, "Report to the State Medical Society on Criminal Abortions," *Peninsular & Independent Medical Journal* II:135.

17. "Criminal Abortions," *Buffalo Medical Journal and Monthly Review* XIV (1859):249.

18. *Boston Medical and Surgical Journal* XLIV, no. 14 (May 7, 1851):288. . . . Worthington Hooker, *Physician and Patient* . . . (New York, 1849), passim, and especially pp. 405–8. The estimate on income is from Colin B. Burke, "The Quiet Influence" (Ph.D. diss, Washington University of St. Louis, 1973):69, Table 2.19.

19. A Physician of New-York, *Trial of Madame Restell, For Producing Abortion on the Person of Maria Bodine,* . . . (New York, 1847), pp. 3–4, 10.

20. Kingsley Davis and Judith Blake, "Social Structure and Fertility: An Analytical Framework," *Economic Development and Cultural Change* IV, no. 3 (April 1956):230.

21. Hooker, *Physician and Patient*, p. 93; James Reed, *From Private Vice to Public Virtue: The Birth Control Movement and American Society since 1830* (New York, 1978), chaps. 1–5.

22. Walter Channing, "Effects of Criminal Abortion," *Boston Medical and Surgical Journal* LX (Mar. 17, 1859):135.

23. E. M. Buckingham, "Criminal Abortion," *Cincinnati Lancet & Observer* X (Mar. 1867):141; Channing, "Effects of Criminal Abortion," p. 135; J. C. Stone, "Report on the Subject of Criminal Abortion," *Transactions of the Iowa State Medical Society* I (1867):29; J. Miller, "Criminal Abortion," *The Kansas City Medical Record* I (Aug. 1884):296.

24. [See] H. Gibbons, Sr., "On Feticide," *Pacific Medical and Surgical Journal* (San Francisco) XXI, no. 3 (Aug. 1879):97–111; . . .

25. Henry C. Wright, *The Unwelcome Child; or, the Crime of an Undesigned and Undesired Maternity* (Boston, 1860). The volume was copyrighted in 1858.

26. Ibid., pp. 65–69.

27. E[lizabeth] C[ady] S[tanton], "Infanticide and Prostitution," *Revolution* I, no. 5 (Feb. 5, 1868):65.

28. Ibid. For the same point reiterated see "Child Murder," in ibid. I, no. 10 (Mar. 12, 1868): 146–47. . . .

29. Ibid. I, no. 14 (Apr. 9, 1868):215–16.

30. E. V. B., "Restellism, and the N.Y. Medical Gazette," *Woman's Advocate* (Dayton, Ohio) I, no. 20 (Apr. 8, 1869):16. . . .

31. Carl N. Degler is one of those who have argued persuasively that nineteenth-century American women were very much aware of their own sexuality and desirous, morality books notwithstanding, of expressing it: "What Ought To Be and What Was: Women's Sexuality in the Nineteenth Century," *American Historial Review* LXXIX, no. 5 (Dec. 1974):1467–90.

32. Lester Ward, *Young Ward's Diary*, Bernhard J. Stern, ed. (New York, 1935), p. 140.

33. Ibid., pp. 150, 152–53, 174.

Comstock Act, 1873

This "Act for the Suppression of Trade in, and Circulation of Obscene Literature and Articles of Immoral Use" was passed at the urging of Anthony Comstock, the head of the New York Society for the Suppression of Vice. The first section prohibited the sale of the described materials in the District of Columbia and the territories; subsequent sections prohibited the sending of these materials through the mails or their importation into the United States. Enforcement, as historian Helen Horowitz has explained, was placed in the hands of a newly created "special agent in the United States Post Office with power to confiscate immoral matter in the mails and arrest those sending it." In the 1870s, many states passed their own versions of the federal law.

The link of "obscene literature and articles of immoral use" reflected contemporary practice. Erotic literature and pornography were often sold in the same shops that sold condoms and other birth control devices; these devices, and substances offering to induce abortion, were often advertised in the pages of pornographic literature. Anthony Comstock included in this category writings on sexual reform and free love. The law reflected a belief that both contraception and abortion were acts of interference with the natural order and with God's intentions. No distinction was made between drugs used for abortion and materials used for contraception, or, indeed, pornographic pictures that encouraged masturbation; all were treated in the same terms. The law may have begun "as a measure to protect children against erotica," but it included "contraceptive information and materials and advertisements for abortion. . . . it was possible to construe this law as banning printed advocacy of free love."* Note the heavy penalties provided.

Be it enacted . . . That whoever, within the District of Columbia or any of the Territories of the United States . . . shall sell . . . or shall offer to sell, or to lend, or to give away, or in any manner to exhibit, or shall otherwise publish or offer to publish in any manner, or shall have in his possession, for any such purpose or purposes, any obscene book, pamphlet, paper, writing, advertisement, circular, print, picture, drawing or other representation, figure, or image on or of paper or other material, or any cast, instrument, or other article of an immoral nature, or any drug or medicine, or any article whatever, for the prevention of conception, or for causing unlawful abortion, or shall advertize the same for sale, or shall write or print, or cause to be written or printed, any card, circular, book, pamphlet, advertisement, or notice of any kind, stating when, where, how, or of whom, or by what means, any of the articles in this section . . . can be purchased or obtained, or shall manufacture, draw, or print, or in any wise make any of such articles, shall be deemed guilty of a misdemeanor, and on conviction thereof in any court of the United States . . . he shall be imprisoned at hard labor in the penitentiary for not less than six months nor more than five years for each offense, or fined not less than one hundred dollars nor more than two thousand dollars, with costs of court. . . .

*Helen Lefkowitz Horowitz, *Rereading Sex: Battles over Sexual Knowledge and Suppression in Nineteenth-Century America* (New York: Alfred A. Knopf, 2002), pp. 381, 385.

Public Laws of the United States of America, Passed at the Third Session of the Forty-Second Congress (Boston, 1873), p. 598.

REFORMING SOCIETY

SUSAN ZAESKE
Signatures of Citizenship: Debating Women's Antislavery Petitions

As women's activities during the Revolution demonstrate, women participated in politics and public life despite not having the vote. Petitioning legislatures, governors, and town governments had long been a strategy of women who wished to articulate a grievance or ask for relief, often on behalf not directly of themselves but of their family. In the decades before the Civil War, activist women working together presented the U.S. Congress with a radically innovative document: the large-scale collective petition.

The mass petition effort was motivated by the fervent desire some women felt to end slavery. In demanding that Congress hear their voices, abolitionist women had to have thick skins. Petitioning women often found other women hesitant and fearful, and found men scornful, even those political men who were supposed to take such good care of women's interests that they should be content not to have the vote.

The act of petitioning involved more than the silent scribbling of a signature, Susan Zaeske reports. To make a collective petition, someone had to carry it to potential signers and then convince a friend or neighbor or stranger to sign. The person who circulated the petition, who walked house to house in her neighborhood or brought it to church or market, had to be an articulate debater, prepared to meet contempt with patience and reason. As citizens who participate in political campaigns in our own time continually find, seeking political change is itself a politicizing experience.

What criticisms were leveled at women's efforts to petition for antislavery causes? Whose interests—besides those of slaveholders—were undermined by women's political participation? How did women—and their allies, like John Quincy Adams—defend their activities? How is it possible to have a political impact without the vote? (In our own time, young people involved in the environmental movement use some of the strategies that antislavery women devised.) What do you think is the relationship between the women's antislavery petition campaign and subsequent movements for women's rights and for the vote?

Early in February 1834 Louisa, Maria, Abigail, Rosey, and Caroline Dickinson signed their names to a petition addressed to the Senate and House of Representatives of the United States. They were joined by . . . scores of other Ohio women who together prayed Congress to abolish slavery in the District of Columbia. These westerners were among the first women

Excerpted from the introduction and chs. 5 and 6 of *Signatures of Citizenship: Petitioning, Antislavery, and Women's Political Identity* by Susan Zaeske (Chapel Hill: University of North Carolina Press, 2003). Reprinted by permission of the author and publisher. Notes have been edited and renumbered.

in the United States to collectively petition Congress on a political issue. In so doing they defied the long-standing custom of females limiting their petitioning of Congress to individual prayers regarding personal grievances. During the coming years hundreds of thousands of women from throughout the North would join the petition campaign and risk association with the unpopular cause of immediate abolitionism. Maria Weston Chapman, a leader of the petitioning effort, recalled that when antislavery women began to petition Congress, many Americans—male and female alike—were not "wont to witness the appeals kindly." Time and again female petitioners were assailed for leaving their "proper" sphere of the home and abandoning benevolent charitable causes to engage in petitioning and political action in the public arena. Yet antislavery women persevered, . . . seizing the radical potential of one of the few civil rights they were understood to possess—the right of petition— to assert substantial political authority.[1] . . . Large numbers of white and free black American women engaged in collective petitioning of Congress in an attempt to reshape public opinion and influence national policy. . . . [A]bsent the right of suffrage, petitioning provided a conduit for women to assert a modified form of citizenship. Although at the beginning of their involvement in the campaign in 1835 women tended to disavow the political nature of their petitioning, by the 1840s they routinely asserted the right of women to make political demands of their representatives. This change in the rhetoric of female antislavery petitions and appeals, from a tone of humility to a tone of insistence, reflected an ongoing transformation of the political identity of signers from that of subjects to that of citizens. Having encouraged women's involvement in national politics, women's antislavery petitioning created an appetite for further political participation and more rights. After female abolitionists established the right of women to petition Congress collectively on political issues, countless women employed that right to lobby their representatives and agitate public opinion to promote causes such as temperance, antilynching, and ultimately, woman suffrage.

From 1831 to 1863 women publicly expressed their opinion about slavery by affixing approximately 3 million signatures to petitions aimed at Congress. Women's efforts enabled abolitionists to send enough petitions to Congress to provoke debate over the question of slavery, a feat petitioning by men alone had failed to accomplish. . . . Deluged with petitions, in June 1836 the House of Representatives passed a rule immediately tabling all memorials on the subject of slavery. The [gag] rule proved a "godsend" to the struggling antislavery movement, for it linked the popular right of petition with the unpopular cause of immediate abolitionism. Petitioning was intended not only to pressure congressmen but also to rectify public opinion with regard to the sinfulness of slavery. By gathering signatures in family and female social networks as well as through soliciting door-to-door, women discussed the issue of slavery with people who would never go to hear an abolitionist lecturer and who could not read abolitionist tracts. . . .

Although women's petitioning soon became highly controversial, at the outset the philosophy of moral suasion and the tool of petitioning seemed to offer an especially suitable means for women to participate in the abolition movement. Women could use the right of petition—a right that, unlike the ballot, they were generally understood to possess—to apply the force of their supposedly superior morality to reform public opinion with regard to the sin of slavery. Although petitioning was less direct than voting, in the 1830s at least, it was not necessarily considered less powerful. Petitioning was seen as a pure expression of individual moral conscience, as opposed to the vote, which was viewed as tainted with personal interest and party spirit.

Central to comprehending the history of women's antislavery petitioning and its effect on women's political status is an understanding of the nature of the right of petition. At its core a petition is a request for redress of grievances sent from a subordinate (whether an individual or a group) to a superior (whether a ruler or a representative). As a genre of political communication, the petition is characterized by a humble tone and an acknowledgment of the superior status of the recipient.[2]

The supplicatory nature of the right of petition held radical potential for women, for natural law assumed that all subjects (and later all citizens) possessed the right of petition and that rulers (and later representatives) were obliged to receive and respond to petitions regardless of the subject of their prayer. Abolition women relied on the first assumption in order to claim and defend their right to petition amidst an environment in which their political status, like that of free blacks, was undergoing constant renegotiation. In fact, so labile was the political status of certain groups of inhabitants of the republic that state constitutional reform conventions of the 1820s and 1830s revoked free black men's voting rights, rights they had previously possessed and exercised. In 1837 the House of Representatives decided that slaves were not citizens and passed a resolution stating that they had no right of petition. For women, also a group whose political rights were vulnerable, petitioning amounted to an assertion that they possessed the right of petition and that they were citizens, though a type of citizen different from enfranchised men. By assuming the status of petitioners, women, though they lacked the vote, forced a hearing of their requests, for their representatives were obligated, in principle at least, to receive and respond to their grievances. Even when the House repeatedly passed gag rules that immediately tabled all antislavery petitions, through their continued petitioning, women kept alive the slavery question in public discourse. They added to congressional and general public debate, moreover, discussion of women's rights and the nature of female citizenship. . . .

. . . Sarah Grimké, an experienced signature gatherer, complained, "I have sometimes been astonished and grieved at the servitude of women, and at the little idea many of them have of their own moral existence and responsibilities. A woman who is asked to sign a petition for the abolition of slavery in the District of Columbia . . . not infrequently replies, 'My husband does not approve of it.'"[3] . . .

When women affixed their signatures to petitions, making a mark that authorized petitions as statements of their opinions, they threw off the cover of their husbands or fathers and asserted their existence as political individuals. For some women, lending their signature to a petition may have involved rejecting the notion that the signature of their husband, father, or brother adequately represented their opinion. For other women, signing a petition was an act of defiance against the wishes of male protectors, who might have opposed abolitionism or opposed women petitioning or both. It is worth noting, moreover, that throughout the campaign the vast majority of women eschewed the use of marital titles and signed petitions as, for example, Chloe F. Metcalf, Lydia W. Fairbanks, and even Philomela Johnson Jr. rather than Mrs. Metcalf, Mrs. Fairbanks, and Mrs. Johnson. Given that in 1890

Frances E. Willard was still urging women to write their names as individuals rather than as the wives of someone else, the petitioners' decision to drop "Mrs." during the 1830s appears to radically defy gendered signature norms.[4] . . .

Not only signing but also circulating petitions effected a transformation in women's political identities, for it provided practical experience in carrying out a campaign to influence public opinion. Female canvassers developed strategies specially suited to win women's signatures by incorporating women's daily routines and the spaces they inhabited into patterns of circulating petitions. Upper-class antislavery women, for instance, adapted the rituals associated with social visiting to the political activity of circulating antislavery petitions. . . . Middle-class women relied on family and religious networks in addition to other female associations, such as sewing circles, in order to circulate petitions. Hundreds of women of varying class and religious backgrounds went door-to-door seeking signatures from strangers.[5] . . .

Petition circulators also gained experience in practicing their skills of interpersonal persuasion, which involved internalizing arguments they read and heard as well as sharpening their skills of oral argumentation. Such skills are evident in a female signature gatherer's account of her interaction with an older woman who was reluctant to sign a petition. "My *darter* [daughter] says that you want the niggers and whites to marry together," the elder woman reportedly said. Yet when pressed by the petition circulator, the woman admitted that she did not understand abolitionists to condone amalgamation and asked if indeed they did. "Why, no—that's no business of ours," the abolitionist assured her. "We leave all to do as they please with regard to it." The canvasser then explained that the petition simply asked Congress to free slaves in the District of Columbia. After making clear the goal of the petition, the circulator stated, "I suppose you know that the colored people in the District are held as property, bought and sold like beasts, and treated very cruelly. Now what we ask is, that Congress, which 'possesses exclusive jurisdiction' there, should give all those slaves their freedom and place them under the protection of law." The older woman responded in agreement and lamented the fact that her daughter was so mistaken.[6]

Although signature gathering "engendered self-confidence and assertiveness" . . . the resistance they encountered understandably led female abolitionists to regard circulating petitions as an unpleasant duty.... Several members of the Providence Rhode Island Female Anti-Slavery Society reported that although they had won many signatures, they found petitioning to be a "self-denying, and unpleasant task."[7] ...

The burden of petitioning was worsened by denunciations from the press and the pulpit. Clergy and other traditionalists anxious about male political dominance were alarmed to see women encouraging one another to express publicly their opinions separate from those of their husbands. The *Boston Religious Magazine,* the *New York Commercial Advertiser,* and the *Providence Journal* all "sharpened their pens and brightened up their wits" to attack the idea of women circulating and signing petitions to Congress. These newspapers ... questioned whether women knew anything about slavery and despised the idea that women should meddle with politics. They scolded "female petitioners" for the "impertinence" of "undertaking to teach Congress their duty."[8]

As bad as the editorial condemnations were, they were nowhere near as punitive as those issued by clergymen such as Pastor Albert A. Folsom of the Universal Church in Hingham, Massachusetts.... Folsom spelled out the unfortunate consequences that would befall a woman who petitioned with the "clamorous" abolitionists. Such a woman, he said, would begin by seeking "relaxation too often from her domestic obligations." Then she would leave her children and become a slave to her "appetites and passions" while she interested herself "with wonderful zeal in the cause of the Southern negro." Besides suggesting that women petitioners were sexually involved with male slaves for whom they advocated, Folsom predicted that abolition petitioning would poison women's souls, embitter their affections, and exasperate their feelings. "She, who is naturally amiable and modest, ... is imperceptively transformed into a bigoted, rash, and morose being.... Self-sufficiency, arrogance and masculating boldness follow naturally in the train."[9] ...

Male editors and clergy were not alone in condemning the political activism of antislavery women generated by the petition campaign. Early in 1837 the well-known reformer and female educator Catharine E. Beecher launched her attack on abolitionists and female activism through publication of *An Essay on Slavery and Abolitionism with Reference to the Duty of American Females,* which she wrote in response to Angelina Grimké's *Appeal to the Christian Women of the South.* In the process of encouraging women to petition and take action to abolish slavery, Grimké's *Appeal* advocated a radical expansion of women's role in reform work. Particularly alarming to Beecher was the fact that in carving out a role for women in the abolitionist movement, Grimké had described a model woman as deeply interested in political issues, critical of the clergy, resistant to social norms, confident of her authority to interpret the Bible, unwilling to subordinate herself to men, and defiant of the law. Beecher responded in her *Essay* that the plan of "arraying females" in the abolition movement was "unwise and inexpedient." Engaging in antislavery activity, she feared, would draw women "forth from their appropriate retirement" and thrust them into the "arena of political collision." Once woman entered the political sphere, Beecher predicted, she would be corrupted by power and would lose her "aegis of defence": her moral purity. Consequently she would forfeit "all the sacred protection of religion, all the generous promptings of chivalry, all the poetry of romantic gallantry." Rather than embracing Grimké's model of the active woman, Beecher pleaded with readers to preserve the status of woman by retaining "her place as dependent and defenceless, and making no claims, and maintaining no right but what are the gifts of honour, rectitude and love."[10]

Especially upsetting to Beecher were Grimké's entreaties for women to petition. "Petitions to congress, in reference to the official duties of legislators, seem, IN ALL CASES, to fall entirely without the sphere of female duty," Beecher retorted. The only proper persons to make appeals to rulers, she maintained, were those who appointed rulers: men. Women's role was not to petition legislators but to influence male friends and relatives to address legislators. "But if females cannot influence their nearest friends, to urge forward a public measure in this way, they surely are out of their place, in attempting to do it themselves...."[11]

On one hand, defenders of women's right of petition clung to the argument that female moral superiority rendered women uniquely suited to petition. On the other hand, advocates employed bolder arguments that women possessed a natural and constitutional right of petition and that they were endowed with equal responsibilities and therefore equal rights with man. Angelina Grimké went so far as to argue that the fact that women were denied the right to vote provided no reason to deny them the right of petition. Republican principles demanded that women be heard in some way, she maintained, or Congress would be guilty of taxation without representation. The same reasoning, she implied, also led to the conclusion that women possessed the right to vote. Grimké was not alone in defending women's right to petition and connecting it to the franchise. In the course of defending the right of women to petition against slavery, John Quincy Adams would question, on the floor of the U.S. House of Representatives, the practice of denying women the right to vote.

Although the flood of antislavery petitions that swept into Congress when it convened on December 7, 1837, was sandbagged by a gag [rule,] those pertaining to the annexation of Texas continued to seep onto the floor of the House of Representatives. On March 5, 1838, the House referred all memorials relating to the Texas question to the Committee on Foreign Affairs, which was charged with composing a report about the content of the petitions and the expediency of granting their requests. On June 14 the report was presented by the committee's chairman, Benjamin Howard of Maryland. Annoyed by the preponderance of petitions from females, Howard expressed his "regret" that so many of the memorials were signed by women. It was inappropriate for women to petition their legislators, he said, because females were afforded ample opportunity for the exercise of their influence by approaching their fathers, husbands, and children in the domestic circle and by "shedding over it the mild radiance of the social virtues, instead of rushing into the fierce struggles of political life." By leaving their proper sphere, Howard charged, women were "discreditable, not only to their own particular section of the country, but also to the national character."[12]

Although few northern representatives during the 1830s defended abolitionists' right of petition, especially that of abolitionist women, John Quincy Adams rose to the occasion. "Sir, was it from a son—was it from a father—was it from a husband, that I heard these words?" demanded the former president. "Does this gentleman consider that women, by petitioning this House in favor of suffering and distress, perform an office 'discreditable' to themselves, to the section of the country where they reside, and to the nation?" Adams offered Howard a chance to retract his assertion: "I have a right to make this call upon him. It is to the wives and to the daughters of my constituents that he applies this language." Howard stood his ground. Adams retorted with a four-day harangue defending the propriety of women involving themselves in political matters and of exercising their constitutional right of petition....

... John Dickson of New York and Caleb Cushing and Levi Lincoln of Massachusetts, followed Adams's lead in answering attacks on female petitioners.... [P]resenting the petition from the 800 ladies of New York, Dickson emphasized the benevolent nature of women's memorializing. "In the Jewish, Greek, and Roman histories," he recalled, "female remonstrance" heard in public councils "were the cause of 'enlargement and deliverance,' of 'light, and gladness, and joy, and honor,' to a despised and an oppressed people." They were, he said, "all-powerful in expanding and extending the principles of charity, humanity, and benevolence, and in breaking the chains of oppression." ... Dickson characterized female antislavery petitions as motivated not by political gain but by benevolence. "Surely," he hoped more than believed, "the chivalry of this House will never permit it to turn a deaf ear to the remonstrance of ladies, pleading, as they believe, for the wronged and oppressed."[13]

Given the obstreperous attacks southerners leveled against female petitioners, it was necessary for northern members to do much more than deny that antislavery women harbored political motivations. They had to defend the character of female petitioners. As Adams complained, the petitions had been treated with contempt, and "foul and infamous imputations" had been "poured upon a class of citizens as pure and virtuous as the inhabitants of any section of the Union": females. Likewise, Lincoln represented petitioners from his district as "pure, elevated, and [of as high] intellectual character as any in the world, men and women, kind and generous, and of tenderest sympathies, who would no sooner do an injury or an act of injustice to any human being than the most chivalrous or true-hearted of the sons or daughters of the South."[14]

Yet at issue in the arguments over the character of female antislavery petitioners was more than their reputations as women. At issue was their status as citizens. Adams readily apprehended that attacks on the character of female petitioners effectively denied women's right of petition, and he took [Benjamin] Howard to task for representing the exercise of the right of petition as disgraceful to women as well as to their section of the Union and the nation as a whole. "Now to say, respecting women, that any action of theirs was disgraceful, was more than merely contesting their legal right so to act," Adams averred; "it was contesting the right of the mind, of the soul, and the conscience." This was no "light question," no mere quarrel over the honor of a few women, he emphasized. It concerned "the very utmost depths of the Constitution of the country" and affected "the political rights of one half of the People of the nation."[15]

Throughout the debates . . . , Adams maintained vehemently that there was no legal or constitutional principle linking the right of petition with the character of petitioners. When Adams presented a petition purportedly signed by nine ladies of Fredericksburg, Virginia, Representative Patton, who had lived in that city, assailed Adams for bringing before the House a petition from "mulatto" women of "infamous character." . . . Patton's insinuation that the petition emanated from prostitutes, disclosed Adams, influenced him not a wit in deciding whether or not to present the paper. Rather than worrying over the character of the petitioners, Adams said that he "adhered to the right of petition."

> Where is your law which says that the mean, and the low, and the degraded, shall be deprived of the right of petition, if their moral characters is not good? Where, in the land of freemen, was the right of petition ever placed on the exclusive basis of morality and virtue? Petition is supplication— it is entreaty—it is prayer! And where is the degree of vice or immorality which shall deprive the citizen of the right to supplicate for a boon, or to pray for mercy?[16]

. . . Adams grasped the opportunity . . . to turn the table and question the character of opponents of women's petitions. When in the course of debate Patton disclaimed actually "knowing" the "bad" women who had signed the petition but stated that he "knew of them," Adams said he was glad to hear it, for otherwise he would ask "if they were infamous women, then who was it that had made them infamous?" Not their own color, he judged, but their masters. Adams said he was inclined to

believe this because "there existed great resemblances in the South between the progeny of the colored people and the white men who claimed the possession of them. Thus, perhaps, the charge of being infamous might be retorted upon those who made it, as originating from themselves."

Adams's comments threw the House into great agitation, for he had stabbed brutally at the honor of southern gentlemen. Despite the fact that in February 1837 he faced formal censure for casting character aspersions on southerners in return for the imputations against the Fredericksburg women, he persisted in the strategy of questioning the character of representatives who opposed female petitions. Adams shamed representatives who would turn a deaf ear to women's petitions, asking each member to suppose that his own mother was one of the petitioners: "Would you reject and turn the petition out of doors, and say that you would not even hear it read?" "Every member of the House has, or had, a mother," he observed, adding that "in the whole class of human affections, was there one sentiment more honorable, or more divested of earthly alloy, than that which every man must entertain for his mother.". . .[17]

. . . [I]n his 1838 speech Adams focused on extending the reach of women's duties to include political affairs. . . . In response to Howard's claim that women had no right to petition Congress on political subjects, Adams asked rhetorically, "What does the gentleman understand by 'political subjects'?" Adams answered that "every thing which relates to peace and relates to war, or to any other of the great interests of society, is a political subject. Are women to have no opinions or action on subjects relating to the general welfare?" Fellow Massachusetts representative Caleb Cushing bolstered Adams's statements, maintaining that "it seems to me a strange idea to uphold, in this enlightened age, that woman, refined and educated, intellectual woman, is to have no opinion, or no right to express that opinion.". . .[18]

Hoping to take advantage of patriotic sentiments, Adams also invoked heroines of the American Revolution. . . . He called up the example of Deborah [Sampson] Gannett, who had adorned herself in men's clothes, joined the patriot army, and fought for three years until she was wounded. Members of the House were aware of Gannett's feats because within recent memory they had voted to give her husband a military pension based on the services of his wife and had praised her on the grounds that she had "fought and bled for human liberty." After commending Gannett's actions, which involved rushing physically into "the vortex of politics," Adams asked how Howard could conceivably think it wrong for women to petition on a matter of politics. . . .[19]

Although Adams redefined politics to include all subjects relating to the general welfare and adduced numerous historical examples of women's involvement in politics, . . . he recommended a three-pronged test by which one could determine whether it was proper for women to deviate from the custom of remaining distant from politics. When presented with such a circumstance, prescribed Adams, one must inquire "into the motive which actuated them, the means they employ, and the end they have in view." Adams then applied this test to the case at hand, the petitions against annexation of Texas. As for the motive, he said, it was of the "highest order" of purity: "They petition under a conviction that the consequence of the annexation would be the advancement of that which is sin in the sight of God, viz: slavery." The means were appropriate, Adams said, because it was Congress who must decide the question, and it was Congress to whom the women must petition. Echoing a justification offered by the female petitioners themselves, he stated, "It is a petition—it is a prayer—a supplication—that which you address to the Almighty Being above you. And what can be more appropriate to their sex?" As for the end sought by female petitioners, it, too, was virtuous, pure, and of the most exalted character: "to prevent the perpetuation and spread of slavery through America." . . . Adams concluded, "the correct principle is, that women are not only justified, but exhibit the most exalted virtue when they do depart from the domestic circle, and enter on the concerns of their country, of humanity and of their God." Thus Adams repeated the argument employed in the women's appeals, addresses, circulars, and petitions that it was the moral duty of women to speak for those who could not speak for themselves and to help those who could not help themselves. In fact, Adams believed that benevolent activity was a particularly feminine trait: "I say that woman, by the discharge of her duties; has manifested a virtue which is even above the virtues of mankind, and approaches to a superior nature."[20] . . .

. . . Adams characterized Howard as denying women the right of petition because they had no right to vote. Then he asked, "Is it so clear that they have no such right as this last? And if not, who shall say that this argument of the gentleman's is not adding one injustice to another?" In a few short breaths Adams, son of the woman who in 1776 threatened that "the ladies . . . will not hold ourselves bound by any laws in which we have no voice, or representation," went so far as to suggest that women did, in fact, possess the right to vote and that it was an injustice that they were denied the practice of that right. In so doing he embraced a position more radical than that of many women's rights advocates of his time. On the floor of the House of Representatives he questioned the assumption that the Constitution denied women the right to vote. He suggested that the reason women did not vote was custom rather than lack of a right to the franchise. . . . It would be another eight years before the women of New York petitioned their legislature for the vote, a decade before the National Woman's Rights Convention would assert that women possessed the right of suffrage, and eight decades before an organized movement of women persuaded Congress and the public to adopt the position Adams began to articulate on Friday, June 29, 1838.[21]

Women who had signed petitions were particularly pleased to read Adams's defense of their actions and showered praises upon him. When he returned to Massachusetts after Congress had adjourned, Adams was greeted by expressions of approbation in the form of several celebratory events hosted by women in towns of his congressional district. On September 4, 1838, the ladies of Quincy hosted a formal picnic and ball to honor him for defending their rights. . . . When Adams addressed the group, he thanked the women for their kind celebration and acknowledged the large number of petitions he had received from females of the district. Reviewing scenes from the two most recent sessions of Congress, he recalled that Howard had committed a "violent outrage . . . upon the [female] petitioners, and [an] insult upon the sex." . . . Adams said that he believed questions about the duty of women to participate in public affairs should be left to women's own discretion, and he felt assured "there was not the least danger of their obtruding their wishes upon any of the ordinary subjects of legislation," such as banks, tariffs, and public lands, "all which so profoundly agitate the men of this country." Women, he trusted, were concerned with other kinds of matters. In fact, he believed that "far from being debarred by any rule of delicacy" from petitioning, by the "law of their nature," which rendered them kind, benevolent, and compassionate, women were "fitted above all others" for the exercise of this right.[22] Adams could not bring himself to endorse unlimited exercise by women of the absolute right of petition. Instead he trusted—or perhaps urged—that they would act only on public matters related to woman's moral duty and would take no interest in purely political matters such as banks and tariffs. In other words, Adams expected female moral duty to guide the exercise of women's natural rights.

... At the core of the southern case against receiving female petitions was the indictment that the petitions constituted not good works resulting from women's Christian duty but, rather, politically motivated machinations controlled by fanatical ministers and wholly improper actions for women. Conflating notions of female duty with political rights, southerners argued that the women's petitions should be ignored because, having transgressed beyond their proper duties, these women were not respectable, and the House was not obligated to accept petitions from people of questionable character.

Adams remained steadfast in his conviction that women possessed a natural right of petition and perhaps a natural right to vote, yet he linked the exercise of women's civil rights to their duties as women. . . . [He was not] willing to abandon the notion that men and women possessed different natures and therefore different duties. But Adams did attempt to use political philosophies associated with women's rights to expand significantly the entailments of women's duty into what many considered the male political realm. . . .

Notwithstanding the decline of organized abolition at the state and national levels in 1839, women continued to petition throughout the 1840s, 1850s, and 1860s, sending massive abolition petitions to Congress on the most pressing political issues of the day. . . . By the 1840s they had begun to mix their signatures with those of men; no longer did women accept the notion that men's names should be allowed to stand out because their opinions meant more to representatives. Moreover, the language of women's petitions during this later period dropped deferential overtures characteristic of the memorials of the 1830s and took on a bolder tone. By the 1850s female petitioning had grown so much

more acceptable and abolitionist sentiment so much more popular that even its most outspoken critic of the 1830s—Catharine E. Beecher—signed her name at the top of a petition. Acceptance of the propriety of women exercising their right to petition was crucial to the success of the petition campaign to win passage of the Thirteenth Amendment. Finally, after three decades of petitioning and due in large part to the ongoing efforts of women who signed and circulated petitions, abolitionists secured their ultimate goal of emancipating the slaves. In the process of petitioning to end slavery, many women transformed their political identity from humble subjects to national citizens.

NOTES

1. Maria Weston Chapman, *Right and Wrong in Massachusetts* (Boston: Henry L. Deveraux, 1840), pp. 11–13.
2. This definition of petitioning is drawn from the *Oxford English Dictionary*.
3. Sarah Grimké, *Letters on the Equality of the Sexes* (1837), in Larry Ceplair, ed., *The Public Years of Sarah and Angelina Grimké: Selected Writings* (New York: Columbia University Press, 1989), p. 239.
4. Frances E. Willard, "A White Life for Two" (1890), in Karlyn Kohrs Campbell, ed. *Man Cannot Speak for Her: Key Texts of the Early Feminists,* Vol. 2 (New York: Praeger, 1989), pp. 335–36.
5. Gerda Lerner, "The Political Activities of Antislavery Women," in *The Majority Finds Its Past: Placing Women in History* (New York: Oxford University Press, 1979), pp. 120–21.
6. *Liberator*, Aug. 4, 1837.
7. Lerner, "Political Activities of Antislavery Women," p. 125.
8. *Emancipator*, Aug. 17, 1837.
9. "A Lecture, Delivered Sunday Evening, by Albert A. Folsom, Pastor of the Universal Church, Hingham, Massachusetts," extracted in *Liberator*, Sept. 22, 1837.
10. Catharine E. Beecher, *An Essay on Slavery and Abolitionism, with Reference to the Duty of American Females* (Philadelphia: Henry Perkins, 1837), pp. 3–6, 97, 101.
11. Ibid., pp. 103–104.
12. John Quincy Adams, *Speech on the Right of the People, Men and Women, to Petition; on the Freedom of Speech and Debate in the House of Representatives of the United States; on the Resolutions of Seven State Legislatures and the Petitions of More than One Hundred Thousand Petitioners, Relating to the Annexation of Texas to this Union. Delivered in the House of Representatives of the United States, in fragments in the morning hour, from the 16th of June to the 7th of July, 1838, inclusive* (Washington, D.C.: Gales and Seaton, 1838), pp. 76–77.
13. *Gales and Seaton's Register of Debates in Congress*, 24th Cong., 1st sess., Feb. 2, 1835, pp. 1131–1132.
14. Ibid., 2d sess., Jan. 9 and Feb. 7, 1837, pp. 1315, 1624.
15. Adams, *Speech on the Right of the People to Petition*, pp. 74, 77–78.

16. *Gales and Seaton's Register of Debates*, 24th Cong., 2d sess., Feb. 6, 1837, pp. 1589, 1596.

17. Ibid., 2d sess., Feb. 9, 1837, p. 1675 and Jan. 9, 1837, p. 1315.

18. Adams, *Speech on the Right of the People to Petition*, pp. 65–66, 69; *Gales and Seaton's Register of Debates*, 24th Cong., 2d sess., Feb. 7, 1837, p. 1645.

19. Adams, *Speech on the Right of the People to Petition*, pp. 70–75.

20. Ibid., pp. 68, 81.

21. Ibid., pp. 65, 77. On the petitions for suffrage directed at the New York legislature, see Jacob Katz Cogan and Lori D. Ginzberg, "1846 Petition for Woman's Suffrage," *Signs* 22 (Winter 1997), pp. 427–439.

22. John Quincy Adams, *Memoirs of John Quincy Adams, Comprising Portions of his Diary from 1795 to 1848*, vol. 10, Charles Francis Adams, ed. (Philadelphia: J.B. Lippincott, 1874–77), pp. 35–37.

GERDA LERNER
The Meanings of Seneca Falls, 1848–1998

In the 1830s and 1840s, individual voices criticizing the way American law and custom defined gender relations began to be heard. The 1848 Declaration of Sentiments (see pp. 247–250) gathered these complaints into a manifesto and offered an agenda for change that would shape a women's rights movement deep into our own time. But the Declaration itself has its own history, emerging out of the specific social conditions in western New York State, out of political and religious arguments, and out of the personal experiences of the women and men who wrote its words and signed their names to it.

The meticulous research of Judith Wellman has enabled us to know the class position, religious affiliation, kin relations, and political sympathies of many of the signers at Seneca Falls. Two-thirds of the signers were women; the signers' ages stretched from fourteen-year-old Susan Quinn to sixty-eight-year-old George Pryor. Most came with another family member: wives with husbands, mothers with daughters, sisters with brothers. (Daniel Anthony was there, but his daughter Susan would not meet Stanton for another three years.) Seventy percent came from the immediate locality of Seneca Falls and neighboring Waterloo, an area that had seen substantial dislocation from a farm region to a manufacturing town, where a substantial group of men had broken with the Democratic and Whig parties to join the abolitionist Free Soilers, and where dissidents from the Quaker Genesee Yearly Meeting formed their own society of Friends devoted to egalitarian gender relations and abolition. Legislative battles over married women's property acts made women's rights especially visible in New York.*

The Declaration of Sentiments, Stanton's indictment of the relations between men and women in her own society, is still stunning in its energy, its precision, and its foresight. In the essay that follows, written for the quincentenary of the Seneca Falls convention, the distinguished historian Gerda Lerner reflects on the meaning of the Declaration for its time and for our own.

*Judith Wellman, "The Seneca Falls Woman's Rights Convention: A Study of Social Networks," *Journal of Women's History* 3 (1991): 9–37; and Wellman, *The Road To Seneca Falls: Elizabeth Cady Stanton and the First Woman's Rights Convention* (Urbana: University of Illinois Press, 2004).

Originally published in *Dissent* (Fall 1998): 35–41. Copyright © Gerda Lerner, 1998. All rights reserved. We mourn Gerda Lerner's death at age 92 on January 2, 2013. See the profile of her by historian Kathryn Kish Sklar at http://jwa.org/encyclopedia/article/lerner-gerda.

Elizabeth Cady Stanton at age 33.
In the most commonly-reproduced photographs of her, Elizabeth Cady Stanton comes to us as she appeared in her fifties and older—a plump, matronly woman with graying hair and a kindly face. But in 1848, when she wrote the great manifesto that set the agenda for the American women's movement for 150 years, she was thirty-three years old, and the one photograph we have of her from that time shows her to be slight and thin, her dark hair hanging in limp ringlets. She is pictured here with Daniel and Henry; the smallest, Gerrit, was a toddler. Did she look tired because she was the mother of three boys under six? Her future—and ours—lay before her. (Courtesy of Elizabeth Cady Stanton Trust/Coline Jenkins–Sahlin.)

In 1848, according to Karl Marx and Frederick Engels, "a specter [was] haunting Europe—the specter of communism." In that same year, the upstate New York village of Seneca Falls hosted a gathering of fewer than three hundred people, earnestly debating a Declaration of Sentiments to be spread by newsprint and oratory. The Seneca Falls Woman's Rights Convention marked the beginning of the woman's rights movement.

The specter that haunted Europe developed into a mighty movement, embracing the globe, causing revolutions, wars, tyrannies and counterrevolutions. Having gained state power in Russia, China and Eastern Europe, twentieth-century communism, in 1948, seemed more threatening a specter than ever before. Yet, after a bitter period of "cold war," which pitted nuclear nations against one another in a futile stalemate, it fell of its own weight in almost all its major centers.

The small spark figuratively ignited at Seneca Falls never produced revolutions, usurpation of power or wars. Yet it led to a transformation of consciousness and a movement of empowerment on behalf of half the human race, which hardly has its equal in human history.

Until very recently, the Seneca Falls convention of 1848 was not recognized as significant by historians, was not included in history textbooks, not celebrated as an important event in public schools, never mentioned in the media or the press. In the 1950s, the building where it was held, formerly the Wesleyan chapel, was used as a filling station. In the 1960s, it housed a laundromat. It was only due to the resurgence of modern feminism and the advances of the field of Women's History that the convention has entered the nation's consciousness. The establishment of Women's History Month as a national event during the Carter administration and its continuance through every administration since then has helped educate the nation to the significance of women's role in history. Still, it took decades of struggle by women's organizations, feminist historians and preservationists to rescue the building at Seneca Falls and finally to persuade the National Park Service to turn it into a historic site. . . . This history of "long forgetting and short remembering" has been an important aspect of women's historic past, the significance of which we only understood as we began to study women's history in depth.

Elizabeth Cady Stanton, the great communicator and propagandist of nineteenth-century feminism, has left a detailed account of the origins of the Seneca Falls convention both in her autobiography and in the monumental *History of Woman Suffrage*. The idea for such a meeting originated with her and with Lucretia Mott, when they both attended the 1840 World Antislavery Convention in London, at which representatives of female antislavery societies were denied seating and voting rights. Outraged by this humiliating experience, Stanton and Mott decided in London that they would convene a meeting of women in the United States to discuss their grievances as soon as possible. But her responsibilities as mother of a growing family intervened, and Stanton could not implement her plan until 1848, when Lucretia Mott visited her sister Martha Wright in Waterloo, a town near Seneca Falls. There, Stanton met with her, her hostess Jane Hunt and their friend Mary Ann McClintock. Stanton wrote: "I poured out that day the torrent of my long accumulating discontent with such vehemence and indignation that I stirred myself, as well as the rest of the party, to do or dare anything." The five drafted an announcement for a "Woman's Rights Convention" to be held at Seneca Falls on the nineteenth and twentieth of July, and placed the notice in the local paper and the abolitionist press.

The five women who issued the call to the Seneca Falls convention were hardly as naive and inexperienced as later, somewhat mythical versions of the events would lead one to believe. Lucretia Mott was an experienced and highly acclaimed public speaker, a Quaker minister and longtime abolitionist. She had attended the founding meeting of the American Antislavery Society in 1833, which admitted women only as observers. She was a founder of the Philadelphia Female Anti-Slavery Society and its longterm president. The fact that she was announced as the principal speaker at the Seneca Falls convention was a distinct drawing card.

Elizabeth Cady Stanton's "long accumulating discontent" had to do with her struggle to raise her three children (she would later have four more) and run a large household in the frequent absences of her husband Henry, a budding lawyer and Free Soil politican. Still, she found time to be involved in the campaign for reform of women's property rights in New York state, where a reform bill was passed just prior to the convention, and she had spoken before the state legislature.

Martha Wright, Jane Hunt and Mary Ann McClintock were all separatist Quakers, long active in working to improve the position of women within their church. All of them were veterans of reform and women's organizations and had worked on antislavery fairs.

The [region] where they held their convention . . . had for more than two decades been the center of reform and utopian movements, largely due to the economic upheavals brought by the opening of the Erie Canal and the ensuing competition with western agriculture, which brought many farmers to bankruptcy. Economic uncertainty led many to embrace utopian schemes for salvation. The region was known as the "burned-over" district, because so many schemes for reforms had swept over it in rapid succession, from the evangelical revivalism of Charles Grandison Finney, to temperance, abolition, church reform, Mormonism and the chiliastic movement of William Miller, who predicted the second coming of Christ with precision for October 12, 1843 at three A.M. The nearly one million followers of Miller had survived the uneventful passing of that night and the similarly uneventful revised dates of March or October 1844, but their zeal for reform had not lessened.

The men and women who gathered in the Seneca Falls Wesleyan chapel were not a national audience; they all came from upstate New York and represented a relatively narrow spectrum of reform activists. Their local background predisposed them to accept radical pronouncements and challenging proposals. Most of them were abolitionists, the women having been active for nearly ten years in charitable, reform, and antislavery societies. They were experienced in running petition campaigns and many had organized antislavery fund-raising fairs. Historian[s] Nancy Isenberg [and Judith Wellman] who [have] analyzed the origins and affiliations of those attending the convention, showed that many were religious dissidents, Quakers, who just two months prior had separated from their more traditional church and would shortly form their own group, New York Congregationalist Friends. Another dissident group were Wesleyan Methodists who had been involved in a struggle within their church about the role of women and of the laity in church governance. Yet another group came from the ranks of the temperance movement. Among the men in attendance several were local lawyers with Liberty Party or Free Soil affiliations. Also present and taking a prominent part in the deliberations was Frederick Douglass, the former slave and celebrated abolitionist speaker, now editor of the *North Star*.

Far from representing a group of inexperienced housewives running their first public meeting, the majority of the convention participants were reformers with considerable organizational experience. For example, Amy Post and six other women from Rochester who came to Seneca Falls were able to organize a similar woman's rights convention in Rochester just two weeks later. One of the significant aspects of the Seneca Falls convention is that it was grounded in several organizational networks that had already existed for some time and could mobilize the energies of seasoned reform activists.

Most of the reformers attending had family, church and political affiliations in other areas of the North and Midwest. It was through them that the message of Seneca Falls spread quickly and led to the formation of a national movement. The first truly national convention on Woman's Rights was held in Worcester, Massachusetts in 1850. By 1860 ten national and many local woman's rights conventions had been organized.

THE DECLARATION OF SENTIMENTS

The first day of the Seneca Falls meeting was reserved to women, who occupied themselves with debating, paragraph by paragraph, the Declaration of Sentiments prepared by Elizabeth Cady Stanton. Resolutions were offered, debated and adopted. At the end of the second day, sixty-eight women and thirty-two men signed their names to a Declaration of Sentiments, which embodied the program of the nascent movement and provided a model for future woman's rights conventions. The number of signers represented only one third of those present, which probably was due to the radical nature of the statement. . . .

By selecting the Declaration of Independence for their formal model and following its preamble almost verbatim, except for the insertion of gender-neutral language, the organizers of the convention sought to base their main appeal on the democratic rights embodied in the nation's founding document. They also put the weight and symbolism of this revered text behind what was in their time a radical assertion: "We hold these truths to be self-evident: that all men and women are created equal."

The feminist appeal to natural rights and the social contract had long antecedents on the European continent, the most important advocate of it being Mary Wollstonecraft. Her work was well known in the United States, where the same argument had been well made by Judith Sargent Murray, Frances Wright, Emma Willard, Sarah Grimké and Margaret Fuller.

The second fundamental argument for the equality of woman was religious. As stated in the Declaration:

> Resolved, That woman is man's equal—was intended to be so by the Creator, and the highest good of the race demands that she should be recognized as such.

And one of the "grievances" is:

> He [man] has usurped the prerogative of Jehovah himself, claiming it as his right to assign to her a sphere of action, when that belongs to her conscience and her God.

The feminist argument based on biblical grounds can be traced back for seven hundred years prior to 1848, but the women assembled at Seneca Falls were unaware of that fact, because of the nonexistence of anything like Women's History. They did know the Quaker argument, especially as made in her public lectures by Lucretia Mott. They had read Sarah Grimke's *Letters on the Equality of the Sexes*, and several of the resolutions in fact followed her text. They knew the biblical argument by Ann Lee of the Shakers and they echoed the anti-slavery biblical argument, applying it to women.

The Declaration departed from precedent in its most radical statement:

> The history of mankind is a history of repeated injuries and usurpations on the part of man toward woman, having in direct object the establishment of an absolute tyranny over her.

The naming of "man" as the culprit, thereby identifying patriarchy as a system of "tyranny," was highly original, but it may have been dictated more by the rhetorical flourishes of the Declaration of Independence than by an actual analysis of woman's situation. When it came to the list of grievances, the authors departed from the text and became quite specific.

Woman had been denied "her inalienable right to the elective franchise"; she had no voice in the making of laws; she was deprived of other rights of citizenship; she was declared civilly dead upon marriage; deprived of her property and wages; discriminated against in case of divorce, and in payment for work. Women were denied equal access to education and were kept out of the professions, held in a subordinate position in Church and State and assigned by man to the domestic sphere. Man has endeavored to destroy woman's self-respect and keep her dependent.

They concluded that in view of the disfranchisement of one-half the people of this country

> ... we insist that [women] have immediate admission to all the rights and privileges which belong to them as citizens of these United States.

It has been claimed by historians, and by herself, that Stanton's controversial resolution advocating voting rights for women—the only resolution not approved unanimously at the convention—was her most important original contribution. In fact, Sarah and Angelina Grimké had advocated woman's right to vote and hold office in 1838, and Frances Wright had done so in the 1830s. It was not so much the originality, as the inclusiveness of the listed grievances that was important.

The Declaration claimed universality, even though it never mentioned differences among women. Future woman's rights conferences before the Civil War would rectify this omission and pay particular attention to the needs of lower class and slave women.

While grievances pertaining to woman's sexual oppression were not explicitly included in the Declaration of Sentiments, they were very much alive in the consciousness of the leading participants. Elizabeth Cady Stanton had already in 1848 begun to include allusions to what we now call "marital rape" in her letters and soon after the Seneca Falls convention made such references explicit, calling on legislatures to forbid marriage to "drunkards." She soon became an open advocate of divorce and of the right of women to leave abusive marriages. Later woman's rights conventions would include some of these issues among their demands, although they used carefully guarded language and focused on abuses by "drunkards." This was a hidden feminist theme of the mainstream woman's temperance movement in the 1880s and caused many temperance women to embrace woman suffrage. What we now call "a woman's right to her body" was already on the agenda of the nineteenth-century woman's rights movement.

It was the confluence of a broad-ranging programmatic declaration with a format familiar and accessible to reformers that gave the event its historical significance. The Seneca Falls convention was the first forum in which women gathered together to publicly air their own grievances, not those of the needy, the enslaved, orphans or widows. The achievement of a public voice for women and the recognition that women could not win their rights unless they organized, made Seneca Falls a major event in history.

RIGHTS AND EMANCIPATION

... It is useful to think of women's demands as encompassing two sets of needs: women's rights and women's emancipation.

Women's rights essentially are civil rights—to vote, to hold office, to have access to education and to economic and political power at every level of society on an equal basis with men.... These rights are demanded on the basis of a claim to *equality:* as citizens, as members of society, women are by rights equal and must therefore be treated equally. All of the rights here listed are based on the acceptance of the status quo; ... These are essentially reformist demands.

Women's emancipation is freedom from oppressive restrictions imposed by reason of sex; self-determination and autonomy. Oppressive restrictions are biological restrictions due to sex, as well as socially imposed ones. Thus, women's bearing and nursing children is a biological given, but the assignment to women of the major responsibility for the rearing of children and for housework is socially imposed.

Self-determination means being free to decide one's own destiny, to define one's own social role. Autonomy means earning one's status, not being born into it or marrying it. . . . It means freedom to define issues, roles, laws and cultural norms on an equality with men. The demands for emancipation are based on stressing women's difference from men, but also on stressing women's difference from other women. They are radical demands, which can only be achieved by transforming society for men and women, equalizing gender definitions for both sexes, assigning the reproductive work of raising the next generation to both men and women, and reorganizing social institutions so as to make such arrangements possible.

Women, just like men, are placed in society as individuals *and* as citizens. They are both equal *and* different. The demand for women's emancipation always includes the demand for women's rights, but the reverse is not true. Generally speaking, women's rights have been won or improved upon in many parts of the world in the past 150 years. Women's emancipation has not yet been won anywhere.

The movement started at Seneca Falls . . . from the start embraced both [concepts]—by demanding legal, property, civil rights; and by demanding changes in gender-role definition and in woman's rights to her own body. As the nineteenth-century movement matured, there developed some tension between advocates of these two different sets of demands, with the mainstream focusing more and more on legal and property rights, while radicals and outsiders, like sex reformers, birth control advocates, and socialist feminists, demanded more profound social changes.

. . . But the same distinctions and tensions . . . have appeared in . . . [the twentieth-century women's movement]. One wing focused mainly on women's rights—adoption of ERA, legal/political rights and representation and civil rights for women of different classes, races and sexual orientations. The other wing began as "radical women's liberation" and later branched off into many more specialized groups working

on abortion rights; protection of women against violence and sexual harassment; the opening up to women of nontraditional occupations: self-empowerment and the creation of women cultural institutions, ranging from lesbian groupings to women's music festivals and pop culture. The two informally defined wings of the movement often overlapped, sometimes collaborated on specific narrow issues, and recently have worked more and more on bridge-building. The Women's Studies movement has struggled long and hard to bridge the two wings and encompass them educationally. Further, new forms of feminism by women of color or women who define themselves as "different" from the majority in various ways have sprung up and served their own constituencies. Their existence has not weakened the movement, as its critics like to claim, but has strengthened it immensely by grounding it more firmly in different constituencies.

Let us not forget, ever, that when we talk about women's rights we talk about the rights of half the human race. No one expects all men to have the same interests, issues or demands. We should therefore never expect women to have one agenda, one set of issues or demands.

The women's rights demands first raised at Seneca Falls have in the United States been generally achieved for middle-class white women. They have been partially achieved for working-class women and women of color, but progress has been very uneven. . . .

The feminization of poverty and the increasing income gap between the rich and the poor have turned many legal gains won by women into empty shells. An example is the way in which legal restrictions on women's right to choose abortion have fallen more heavily on poor women than on the well-to-do. The uneven availability of child care for working mothers is another example.

The cultural transformation on which demands for woman's emancipation build, has been enormous. Many demands that seemed outrageous 150 years ago are now commonly accepted, such as a woman's right to equal guardianship of her children, to divorce, to jury duty, to acceptance in nontraditional occupations. Female police and fire officers and female military personnel are accepted everywhere without question. Women's participation in competitive sports is another area in which progress has been great, though it is far from complete. Many other feminist demands that seemed outrageously radical thirty years ago have become commonplace today—the acceptance of lesbians as "normal" members of the community; single motherhood; the criminal character of sexual harassment and marital rape. The acceptance of such ideas is still uneven and different in different places, but generally, the feminist program has been accepted by millions of people who refuse to identify themselves as "feminists." What critics decry as the splintering and diffusion of the movement is actually its greatest strength today.

It should also be recognized that the aims of feminism are transformative, but its methods have been peaceful reform, persuasion and education. For 150 years feminists have organized, lobbied, marched, petitioned, put their bodies on the line in demonstrations, and have overcome ancient prejudices by heroic acts of self-help. Whatever gains were won, had to be won step by step, over and over again. Nothing "was given" to women; whatever gains we made we have had to earn. And perhaps the most precious "right" we have won in these two centuries, is the right to know our own history, to draw on the knowledge and experience of the women before us, to celebrate and emulate our heroines and finally to know that "greatness" is not a sexual attribute.

WHAT MEANING DOES SENECA FALLS HOLD TODAY?

- It shows that a small group of people, armed with a persuasive analysis of grievances and an argument based on generally held moral and religious beliefs, can, if they are willing and able to work hard at organizing, create a transformative mass movement. . . . The women who launched a small movement in 1848 had to . . . build, county by county, state by state, the largest grassroots movement of the nineteenth century and then build it again in the twentieth century to transform the right to vote into the right to equal representation. . . .

- Seneca Falls and the movement it spawned show that legal changes . . . can be reversed, unless social and cultural transformations sustain them. . . . Over the past 150 years all of the grievances listed at Seneca Falls have been resolved or at least dealt with, though new inequities and grievances arise in each generation. The "specter that haunted Europe" left some gains, but mostly bloodshed, terror and devastation in its wake, and most of the inequities it sought to adjust are still with us. Feminism has behind it a record of solid gains without the costs of bloody war and revolution.

Although the media and many politicians with monotonous frequency declare feminism to be dead, many of its goals have been accomplished and its momentum, worldwide, is steadily rising. [The worldwide movement of women for their emancipation is irreversible.] It will continue to live and grow, as long as women anywhere have "grievances" they can proclaim and as long as they are willing and able to organize to rectify them.

ROSE STREMLAU
"I Know What an Indian Woman Can Do": Sarah Winnemucca Writes about Rape on the Northern Paiute Frontier

The Comstock Lode—a rich vein of silver ore—was discovered by European Americans in the late 1850s in western Nevada, just east of Lake Tahoe and south of Pyramid Lake. Thousands of men trekked to the spot, coming westward over the Oregon Trail and eastward from California. As a consequence, the population of the nearest town, Virginia City, exploded, reaching 30,000 when extraction peaked in 1877. Anglos understood themselves to be seizing opportunity in the rugged wilderness. But far from being "virgin land," the forested mountains and river valleys of the surrounding landscape were the home territory of the Northern Paiutes. As had occurred in so many places in the Americas since 1492, a gender frontier—and a social flashpoint—was created as white settlers quickly outnumbered the locals who had different understandings of gender roles, manliness, and womanliness.

As Rose Stremlau's essay reveals, we know about the reactions of Northern Paiute women to the new dangers and survival challenges they faced because of the writings of one of them, Sarah Winnemucca (1844?–91). Active in lobbying military officers, territorial legislatures, the Interior Department in Washington, and President Hayes to improve conditions for her tribe and to compel governments to keep their promises, Winnemucca was an ardent reformer, a traveling lecturer, and an educator akin to the Grimké sisters. She befriended influential women in the East, securing their help in getting her autobiography published in Boston in 1883. Her biographer, Sally Zanjani, claims it to be "the first book written by an American Indian woman, the first by a Native American west of the Rockies, and the first to describe Paiute culture."* But Sarah Winnemucca died discouraged, with her people relegated to woefully inadequate reservation land, and the school she had established in her later years lacking sufficient external funding. If her vision of several such schools flourishing throughout the West had come to pass, the outcomes for many Indian children would have been very different (see Zitkala-Ša, pp. 345–349). Her statue now represents the state of Nevada in the U.S. Capitol Statuary Hall in Washington, D.C.

As you read the essay, ask yourself what skills and systems of knowledge Northern Paiute women needed for everyday living both before and after white settlers infiltrated their homelands. Compare to those of the white colonial goodwives described by Laurel Thatcher Ulrich (pp. 45–53). Given that Sarah Winnemucca's autobiography is 240 pages long, what insights do we gain by focusing on its stories of sexual violence and intimidation? Is Stremlau's evocation of a rape culture helpful in understanding other places and moments in U.S. history?

In April 1860, while Northern Paiute elders and leaders met in council at Pyramid Lake to determine how best to respond to the non-Indian invasion of their homeland and the destruction of their resource base, Northern Paiute families carried on their day-to-day subsistence work as best they could. Searching for one of their most important food sources, two young Northern Paiute women gathered roots near Williams's Station, a settlers' trading post. Several white men seized the girls, dragged them into a barn, and repeatedly gang raped them. The men . . . held the young women captive, and when the girls' families came searching for them, the men denied having seen them and threatened to shoot whoever continued to scout around their homestead for evidence of the girls. Their posturing was ineffective, however; the Northern Paiute men heard their women's screaming, and they would retaliate.[1]

*Online Nevada Encyclopedia, a project of Nevada Humanities, "Sarah Winnemucca," http://www.onlinenevada.org/sarah_winnemucca (accessed Mar. 20, 2009).

Excerpted from Rose Stremlau, "Rape Narratives on the Northern Paiute Frontier: Sarah Winnemucca, Sexual Sovereignty, and Economic Autonomy, 1844–1891," in Portraits of Women in the American West, ed. Dee Garceau-Hagen (New York: Routledge, 2005). Reprinted by permission of the author and publisher. Notes have been edited and renumbered.

In Sarah Winnemucca's autobiography, such stories of sexual victimization are as much a part of the Northern Paiute experience as their seasonal hunting and gathering cycle. In particular, Winnemucca described how sexual violence characterized many white men's relations with the Native American women and girls whom they considered racially and culturally inferior and economically marginal. But Winnemucca's life story should not be read as a police blotter detailing individual crimes. Her vivid descriptions of sexual violence suggest how Native people experienced and responded to interracial rape, and her stories of rape point to larger themes in Northern Paiute adaptation. Winnemucca posited that the Northern Paiutes' best chance at survival lay not in assimilation to white culture but in the restoration of their economic autonomy, symbolized by women's ability to work without fear of sexual assault.

Born in approximately 1844 near the Humboldt River in what is today western Nevada, Sarah Winnemucca grew to adulthood in a world turned upside down by rapid, unprecedented change. [Although] the Northern Paiutes had never met an American until the late 1840s, by 1859, non-Indians outnumbered her people in their own homeland. Winnemucca lived her life at an interchange of power relations that would confound even the brightest of us. As a young girl, she keenly perceived that gender roles functioned differently in white society than in her own. From her earliest contacts with Americans, she described a culture infused with masculinity and violence and in which the combination of the two equated to power. As an American Indian woman, Winnemucca had no claim to power in the rough West of non-Indian miners, soldiers, and settlers. But in her culture, she did have power, in part because Northern Paiutes valued the work that women did.

Prior to the non-Indian settlement of the Great Basin, the Northern Paiutes practiced an extremely flexible gendered division of labor that enabled them to adapt rapidly to changes in their environment. Their homeland covered over 70,000 square miles in present-day southeastern Oregon, southwestern Idaho, northwestern Nevada, and northeastern California. Microclimatic variation caused environmental diversity, and across the Great Basin, arid, desert landscapes blended into fertile, lush valleys and waterfronts. These Great Basin hunters and gatherers adapted to their environment by diversifying their sources of food and establishing extended kin relations, which enabled communication and cooperation among groups in times of abundance and need. While lean periods were common, starvation was not, because Native people utilized such a wide variety of natural resources.[2]

The Northern Paiutes migrated from food source to food source in small families and family groups or clusters. Depending on the availability of resources, a married couple or a set of married siblings and their children composed the core of groups that expanded to include a handful of families and then contracted back to the immediate family group. Households joined together for particular communal subsistence activities, especially the pine nut harvest and rabbit drives, or in particularly rich areas, such as near fisheries. Due to the limited food supplies throughout much of the Great Basin, however, the collective labor of larger groups usually proved a disadvantage over that of an individual or couple. Throughout most of the year, then, families functioned as self-contained units, and the gendered division of labor within families enabled the efficient exploitation of their environment.

Married couples comprised the basic unit of production and social reproduction. Among the Northern Paiutes, marriage was not a private concern between a man and a woman. Instead, married couples produced food and children, and the relationships between husbands and wives also bound kin groups together. Marriage among the Northern Paiutes was a mutually beneficial process rather than an event. When a man visited a woman's home at night and eventually moved his belongings into her home with her consent, the family recognized the couple as married and integrated them into the gendered, adult world of production and reproduction. Marriages ended as informally as they began when husbands moved out of, or were removed from, their wives' homes. . . . [W]hile Great Basin societies lacked the economic, social, political, or religious institutions that bound wives to husbands and ensured the permanence of marital unions, these societies valued the economic and social complementarity that husbands and wives provided each other.[3] . . .

. . . In her autobiography, Winnemucca emphasized the bonds of affection between husbands and wives; reciprocity, it seems, was emotional and physical as well as economic. Many relationships lasted for a lifetime. She explained, "They not only take care of their children together, but they do everything together; and when they grow blind, which I am sorry say is very common, for the smoke they live in destroys their eyes at last, they take sweet care of one another. Marriage is a sweet thing when people love each other."[4]

Married couples divided some tasks and shared others in order to maximize their utilization of local resources. Both spouses' labor was essential to a family's survival, and families formed self-sufficient economic units. Men usually hunted, trapped, and fished, but men also worked alongside their female relatives gathering when the needs of the family demanded it. Individually or in small groups, men stalked large game including deer, pronghorn, and bighorn sheep. Alternately, several hunters sometimes worked together to corral a herd of animals and to net rabbits and other small mammals and fish. Northern Paiute men developed a variety of ways to kill: they shot game with poisoned arrows; tracked them with dogs; prayed and sacrificed for them; ambushed them; enchanted them with spiritual power; netted them; snared them; charged at them in disguises; tricked them into entering traps with noises; and set out fishing lines with specified hooks. Winnemucca explained that because they avoided warfare, Northern Paiute conceptions of masculinity were bound up solely with the skills of hunting and fishing, which provided food for their families.

Women typically gathered plants, roots, and nuts, but they also hunted small animals and fished. Their selective utilization of natural resources and development of many specific subsistence technologies for procuring and processing food suggest that Northern Paiute women were skilled laborers. They developed, transmitted, and continuously perfected systems of knowledge that made edible and palatable piñon nuts, acorns, cattails, rice grass, many species of seeds, camas, swamp onion, biscuit roots, bitterroots, other types of roots, buckberries, wolfberries, other fruits and berries, leaves, stalks, and greens. Women also prepared meat and fish for consumption through a variety of techniques, including roasting and making pemmican. Northern Paiute women did not simply harvest the resources in their environment, however; they manipulated it to produce more abundant harvests in the future. They burned unwanted vegetation, pruned and plucked plants, and broadcast seeds. Just as importantly, they prayed and gave offerings to the spirits of the plants and animals that they consumed to ensure plentiful seasons in the future.[5]

Northern Paiute women may have provided . . . over half of their families' livelihood and perhaps the most important part. Plants provided a significant percentage of nutrients, and nuts provided valuable fat and protein in a diet otherwise prone to deficiencies. Women were accustomed to spending a significant amount of their time gathering away from men's supervision and protection. These women were independent workers unaccustomed to being sexually harassed.

Northern Paiute women's economic contributions accorded them high status as they wielded both spiritual and political power often seen as interrelated. Because of their ability to provide food, women had a political voice. Female and male leaders attained spiritual power in one of three ways: through dreams, through inheritance from a powerful, deceased relative, and through visiting foreign, unknown places. Male and female elders made decisions for family groups, and as Winnemucca explained, "The women know as much as the men do, and their advice is often asked. We have a republic as well as you. The council-tent is our Congress, and anybody can speak who has anything to say, women and all." . . . Notably, Winnemucca went on to explain that women and men sat in different circles in council, but she did not consider this a sign of inferiority. Rather, it was a sign of complementarily and social order.[6]

. . . [M]otherhood also accorded Northern Paiute women status. Whether from the earth or their bodies, women brought forth life, and they were valued for it. Beginning with their first menstruation, young Northern Paiute women underwent a period of seclusion involving fasting, laboring, and bathing in preparation for the roles of wife and mother. Once pregnant, both men and women followed specific taboos intended to insure the well-being of mothers and babies. For men, according to Winnemucca, this included assuming much of women's domestic labor. She wrote: "If he does not do his part in the care of the child, he is considered an outcast. . . . The young mothers often get together and exchange experiences about the attentions of their husbands; and inquire of each other if the fathers did their duty to their children, and were careful of their wives' health." . . . Such complementarity fostered a culture of respect between Northern Paiute men and women, one in which violence had no place.[7]

The sudden, unexpected influx of non-Indians into their homeland compromised the Northern Paiutes' natural resources and rendered their seasonal rounds impossible. While they had obtained horses and European goods by the mid to late eighteenth century, Northern Paiutes did not directly contact Europeans or non-Indian Americans until the early nineteenth century. They paid these trappers and traders little mind until the opening of the Oregon Trail and the discovery of gold in California during the 1840s brought thousands of migrants through the heart of their territory. . . . [I]n 1859, the discovery of gold and silver in Northern Paiute territory along the Virginia Range and the Owyhee Basin attracted thousands of settlers to the area. The Comstock Lode shifted the demographics of their territory within a few months as a minority population of a few hundred whites exploded into a majority of many thousands. As ethnohistorians Martha C. Knack and Omer C. Stewart explain, "Despite the initial trickle of transients, this onslaught of white domination was sudden, complete, and irreversible. The opportunity for natives to respond and resist was nearly gone before they could even comprehend the threat." Seeking rapid profits, these non-Indians destroyed Native hunting and gathering lands; miners cut down groves of piñon trees for shoring and building mine shafts and diverted streams for flumes; ranchers seized grasslands and water; and town dwellers seized timber and the choicest land.[8]

Women's contributions to the family pot may have taken on increasing importance as non-Indians consumed the natural resources most familiar to them, particularly game, and limited the Northern Paiutes' access to other resources, such as fisheries, by locating their settlements near the rivers and lakes. In response, women's skilled gathering of resources with which non-Indians were unfamiliar became vital to Northern Paiute survival. . . .

Northern Paiutes responded to the invasion by trying to maintain their seasonal hunting and gathering cycle, but they did so in different ways; some fled away from non-Indians and

onto reservations where they tried to survive by supplementing their traditional food sources with rations and agriculture. Others relocated to the margins of non-Indian communities and combined the seasonal cycle with wage labor. Neither response enabled women to adequately gather, fish, or trap to feed their families. Regardless of their choices and however well they adapted to the new extractive, market-oriented economy of the Great Basin, many Northern Paiutes suffered from a new social ill—chronic starvation.

Most Northern Paiutes could not get far enough away from the newcomers. As early as the 1830s, the Northern Paiutes altered their hunting and gathering cycle by going to the mountains in the summer instead of the valleys where they usually gathered . . . In 1859, as miners flooded into the Great Basin, Northern Paiutes began relocating onto reservations. The Pyramid Lake reservation was established in 1859 and the Malheur in 1873, but poverty stalked the reservations, too. Even under the best of circumstances reservations wanted for funding and capable leadership. Sarah Winnemucca, like her father and many other Great Basin leaders, considered reservations no better than death camps. Unable to continue their seasonal hunting and gathering cycle with the necessary regularity, unprepared to farm, often swindled by the agents charged to care for them, and unsupplied with the rations promised in treaties, Great Basin Indians starved on reservations. Winnemucca wrote her autobiography as a condemnation of the corrupt reservation system, and she recalled a heated exchange between Chief Egan and Agent William Reinhart. Egan begged for the food locked in the agency storehouse: "My children are dying with hunger. I want what I and my people have worked for, that is, we want the wheat." Reinhart replied, "Nothing here is yours. It is all the government's." Like prison camps, reservations condemned Native people, even those who wanted to work to feed their families, to dependency on the government for food. According to Winnemucca, this dependency was emotionally, spiritually, physically, and mentally intolerable to men and women who had been self-sufficient adults just a few years earlier.[9]

Northern Paiutes who settled among non-Indians struggled, too. Forced to adapt and utilize non-Indians as another available resource, Northern Paiutes balanced their seasonal cycle with barter or wage labor in menial jobs. Men cut trees, hauled goods, and tended livestock. Because of the shortage of white women, Indian women easily found domestic work as housekeepers, seamstresses, and laundresses. . . . In the Indian shantytown that bordered Virginia City, Northern Paiute women with their gathering baskets rose early to pick rotting food from non-Indian trash piles. Others waited outside the mines for workers to empty the leftovers from their lunch pails into their baskets. Despite their meager resources. Northern Paiute women continued to provide a significant portion of their families' livelihoods through their adaptation of the subsistence round. Still, whether they lived on the reservations or in towns, Northern Paiute women were vulnerable to poverty and exploitation.[10]

Winnemucca exemplifies how Northern Paiute women put traditional skills to use at non-traditional work as they adapted to survive in the new Great Basin economy. During her early childhood, Winnemucca learned Northern Paiute women's customary domestic and subsistence tasks; she came to understand a woman's role by helping her mother care for her siblings and their household. For example, she prepared food like cattail pollen cakes and practiced crafts like weaving cattails and sagebrush into baskets for gathering and mats for clothing and shelter. As a teenager, her skill at handiwork enabled her to live by selling needlework door-to-door in Virginia City. In her early twenties, she worked as a laundress on the reservation. By her thirties, she had saved enough money to purchase a wagon and team, and when not working as a maid, she hired herself out as a teamster, not an unlikely job for a woman who grew up migrating and moving her home among campsites. In the 1870s, as the speaker of five languages; English, Paiute, Shoshone, Spanish, and Washoe; she translated and taught on the reservation. In the late 1870s, having gained familiarity with the territory through the seasonal round, she scouted for the United States Army. Beginning in the 1870s and through the rest of her life, Winnemucca, member of a chiefly family who had attained power in her own right, served as an ambassador and spokeswoman for her people: she wrote letters, visited American political leaders, gave lectures, and wrote her autobiography to obtain provisions and ensure safe communities for the Northern Paiutes. In the late 1880s, she established and ran a school that educated Northern Paiute children in their own and Anglo-American culture.[11] . . .

Poverty was not the only challenge that Northern Paiute women faced; their work as providers for their families also made them vulnerable to sexual assault. Hunting, gathering, and wage work took women beyond the protection of brothers, fathers, and husbands. In this new world following the non-Indian invasion, women's work became particularly unsafe. The influx of whites brought a disproportionate number of non-Indian men without families to Northern Paiute territory. The mining industry created several new types of communities: only corporations had the assets to transport the equipment necessary to procure minerals from bedrock, and these large mines sparked the establishment of towns, such as Virginia City. Other miners worked alone or in small groups and migrated from base camp to base camp. Mining also attracted supporting industries, such as trading and ranching. Bandits and outlaws roamed the basin looking for easy targets to plunder. Soldiers manned military posts established throughout the territory to protect mining interests and keep the peace between Indians and non-Indians. Many of these new non-Indian communities lacked permanent female residents. Northern Paiutes, who had no standing army or labor system that kept men away from women for long periods of time, noted the preponderance of men without women and families with disapproval.[12] . . .

Newcomers to the Great Basin did not appreciate the Northern Paiutes' egalitarian gender roles, and, often without women of their own, they considered Native women to be subject, sexual resources. While they had never seen a Northern Paiute woman before, many white male newcomers to the Great Basin believed that they were experts on the subject of Indian women. Since the colonial era, Anglo-American culture had adopted the image of the "Indian princess" to symbolize virtue, but Americans associated overt, primitive sexuality with her "darker twin," the "squaw." . . . According to the stereotype, Native women worked like slaves and had sex like animals. Moreover, like their European forebears, Americans claimed sexual access to women, along with other forms of property, as a right of conquest. These beliefs were not limited to men of low status. While recognizing that not all Indian women were "wanton,"

General Oliver O. Howard, under whom Winnemucca served as a scout and with whom she developed a mutually respectful friendship, commented that he understood why "squaw men" took Indian wives: allegedly the women were compliant and sexually eager.[13]

Some Northern Paiute women utilized their sexuality as another resource that enabled them to survive during this tumultuous period. Many Northern Paiute women, including Sarah Winnemucca and her sister, married white men, perhaps in an effort to broaden their resource base through extending kin ties as Northern Paiutes had always done. Others worked in a nontraditional industry—sex work. Indian women worked as prostitutes in frontier towns across the West during the Gold Rush. Regardless of whether or not particular Indian women actually were working as prostitutes, the predominance of stereotypes about Indian women's sexuality enabled whites to come to the conclusion that they were.[14] . . .

The discovery of Comstock Lode sparked a frenzied competition for resources in the Great Basin and created an environment particularly conducive to violence against American Indian women. Historians of rape have argued that sexual violence often occurs at societal flashpoints, places where diverging groups struggle over power and status. In particular, historians have suggested that men rape women whom they consider racially or culturally inferior and economically dependent. In the Humboldt Sink in the 1850s and 1860s, white men looked down on Northern Paiute women, and their economic vulnerability made them more readily accessible. Dismissed by the American legal system, Northern Paiute women were also not likely to bring charges against rapists.

. . . As whites became increasingly land-hungry, Native people became more defensive and vocal in demanding protection from the army and the federal government. Each resented the other's claim to the land and what grew on it or lay below the surface. Northern Paiute women could not gather roots in the same land that white men mined for silver. When they occupied the land and raped women who came near their camps and posts, these newcomers discouraged women from continuing their subsistence gathering cycle. White men did not simply rape to satisfy sexual urges; they raped Northern Paiute and other Great Basin Indian women to assert their dominance over them and the kinsmen unable to protect them. It worked. The Northern Paiutes were intimidated. Winnemucca explained, "My people have been so unhappy for a long time they now wish to disincrease, instead of multiply. The mothers are afraid to have more children, for fear they shall have daughters, who are not safe even in their mother's presence."[15]

It is historically and morally important to acknowledge that non-Indian men raped Indian women as part of the conquest of the American West. The Anglo-American West bred a *rape culture*, or a "complex of beliefs that encourages male sexual aggression and supports violence against women." Rape cultures equate domination and violence with sexuality, and in rape cultures women experience sexual violence along a continuum of behavior from economic marginalization to rape and murder. Perpetrators in a rape culture assume their behavior is a normal, inevitable aspect of life. While coined by activists working to end rape in contemporary culture, the term *rape culture* is useful to historians because it reminds us that sexual violence is culturally constructed: not all men across time and place have raped women, and when and where men have raped women, they have not committed rape for the same reasons. Likewise, while they may endure similar physical acts, women experience rape differently in cultures that provide for alternative frameworks for understanding rape other than victimization.[16] That we remember the role of rape in conquest is important, but it is just as important to understand the extent and meaning of Native women's resistance if we want to understand how Native people and their cultures adapted and survived. . . .

. . . While they adopted some aspects of American culture, Northern Paiutes rejected non-Indian redefinitions of sexually appropriate behavior, such as female economic dependence and male sexual aggression. They disapproved of sexually aggressive behavior and labeled men who raped as deviant. Northern Paiutes distinguished among non-Indians based, in part, on their treatment of Native women, and many white men behaved quite badly according to Northern Paiute conceptions of masculinity. Throughout her autobiography, Winnemucca alluded to the ever-present threat posed by "bad white men who might harm us" and noted that she and other Northern Paiute leaders complained about the frequency of sexual assaults to American leaders in the hopes that they would take steps to prevent them.

But Winnemucca and the Northern Paiutes did more than plead to outsiders for assistance; they adapted their own lifestyles to prevent sexual attacks on Northern Paiute women and girls. Because they often experienced sexual violence together as family groups, Northern Paiutes rearranged their domestic relationships to better ensure the safety of female family members. Winnemucca described in detail how her family prevented the gang rape of her sister. During her early childhood, her grandfather, Truckee, moved part of her family cluster to California where he and several of her brothers worked for a rancher. Several white ranch hands repeatedly tried to gang rape Winnemucca's older sister, a young teenager. Each night the family fled their camp as the men came for her sister. Fearing violent retaliation themselves, her kinsmen felt that they could not physically defend the girl. One evening, five men came into their camp, and two entered their darkened tent and closed off the exit behind them. Winnemucca's uncles and brothers attacked the men and scared them off, and the family then boarded with their employers away from the rest of the workers. Finally, after the men asked Truckee for the girl outright—a request he scornfully refused—the family decided the terrified girl would no longer work alongside her mother but would spend her days under the direct supervision of her grandmother in camp and away from the dangers women faced as they worked away from the safety of their base camp.... Northern Paiute families experienced sexual violence as a process and a persistent threat instead of as single events.

... Northern Paiute families looked to established and newly formed social networks for protection from violence. Above all, ... Northern Paiute women relied on kin for protection. In her autobiography, Winnemucca offered several examples of Northern Paiute men ensuring the safety of their female relatives. ... But women also took care of each other. Winnemucca only left her sister-in-law, Mattie, at a military post because she knew her brother would arrive shortly. ...

Northern Paiutes also relied on some newcomers for protection from others. When traveling, Winnemucca took every opportunity to stay in homes occupied by white women, although this was not always possible because of the gender imbalance of the non-Indian community.... [she] also recognized that some white men posed no threat. When traveling, she commented, "No white women on all the places where we stopped—all men—yet we were treated kindly by all of them, so far."[17]

While fearing common soldiers, the Northern Paiutes sought protection from army officers against miners, settlers, and soldiers. Winnemucca and other Northern Paiute leaders developed close relationships with officers whom they identified as friendly and powerful allies. While scouting for them, Winnemucca accepted the escorts of officers who worried for her safety, but she was more proactive than that: she demanded protection when she felt vulnerable. Perhaps playing into her readers' expectations of feminine vulnerability, she recalled having once pleaded: "Colonel, I am all alone with so many men, I am afraid. I want your protection. I want you to protect me against your soldiers, and I want you to protect my people also."[18]

Unable to always prevent attacks, Northern Paiute women resisted sexual assaults the best they could with the options posed by their cultural worldview. Winnemucca's Anglo-American readers expected women to avoid rape by maintaining a virtuous appearance and reputation, a process that included keeping their bodies fully covered in clothing, appearing in public with appropriate male escorts, and not working outside their homes. While adapting some aspects of their dress, Northern Paiute women did not embrace constrictive gendered expectations of Anglo-American women concerning sexual violence. They continued to work alone or in small groups with other women and without male escort. They continued to gather outside their camps; they had to in order to eat. For Northern Paiute women, to do otherwise, such as send men to gather, made no sense.[19]

When threatened, Northern Paiute women attempted to outrun rapists. Winnemucca recalled an incident that occurred ... when [she was] traveling with her sister. [N]on-Indian men followed the women.... [They] resolved to go down fighting if overtaken:

> Away we went, and they after us like wild men. We rode on till our horses seemed to drop from under us. At last we stopped, and I told sister what to do if the whole three of them overtook us. We could not do very much, but we must die fighting. If there were only two we were all right,—we could kill them; if one we would see

what he would do. If he lassoed me she was to jump off her horse and cut the rope, and if he lassoed her I was to do the same. If he got off his horse and came at me she was to cut him, and I would do the same for her. Now we were ready for our work.[20]

In the end, Winnemucca and her sister escaped their would-be rapists. . . .

When unable to outrun perpetrators, . . . Northern Paiute women attacked them or outsmarted them, proving that successful resistance did not necessarily correspond with physical strength. Winnemucca suggested that Northern Paiute women verbally threatened would-be rapists with physical violence and implied that Northern Paiute women were often armed, and thus, that retaliation could hurt. Winnemucca bragged of breaking an offender's nose. The man, a fellow traveler bunked down near her, suggestively laid his hand on her in the middle of the night, and with one straight punch to his face, Winnemucca shunned his proposition. She bloodied his nose and sent him running for the door while she shouted, "Go away, or I will cut you to pieces, you mean man!" Winnemucca sliced another attempted rapist's face with a knife. On a March evening in 1875, Julius Argasse, a white man, either approached Winnemucca on the street or, according to another account, entered her home. Either way Winnemucca refused him with her knife. She was subsequently arrested, but the judge dismissed the charges against her.[21]

When other options for prevention and redress failed, Northern Paiutes and other Great Basin Natives killed rapists. Military doctor George M. Kober recalled a conversation he had with Winnemucca's father in which the chief blamed the ongoing violence on miners and Prospectors who "had no regard for the chastity of Indian women."[22] Winnemucca explained that the rapes of Native women and girls prompted the outbreak of the two Indian wars that she experienced. The Paiute War of 1860 began when the tribe retaliated against the men who kidnapped and raped the two young women who had been gathering roots. Outraged at the treatment of the young women and the men's initial denial of having seen them, the Northern Paiutes killed the four men. Some local whites considered the men upstanding citizens and led a campaign against the Northern Paiutes that resulted in their confinement at Pyramid Lake reservation by the end of the summer. Others, such as settler

Richard N. Allen, believed that the Northern Paiutes' retaliation was justified and clearly in response to a wrong committed by these brothers since nearby settlers were unharmed by the Northern Paiutes.[23] . . .

. . . [F]or many Northern Paiutes, distance from non-Indians provided the best protection from violence. The Northern Paiutes' rapid acceptance of reservations must be considered in this context. As Leggins and Egan, two chiefs, explained when the government threatened to open part of their reservation land to non-Indian settlement, "And another thing, we do not want to have white people near us. We know what they are, and what they do to our women and daughters."[24]

While accounts of and allusions to rape permeate her autobiography, Winnemucca revealed little information about the victims. The details she provided suggest that sexual violence threatened all Northern Paiute women. Victims were old and young. Some were women that she did not know while others were family. Winnemucca herself survived sexual violence. Notably, nearly all victims were working, somehow trying to provide food for their families, or in Winnemucca's case, for her people. While she appealed to her readers' belief in women's vulnerability, Winnemucca never questioned the chastity or moral character of victims, and she refused to engage in non-Indian culture's debate over Native sexuality or pander to their stereotypes of Native women. Winnemucca's accounts of rape suggest what experts on contemporary sexual violence confirm: rape is not an act of sexual pleasure reflective of the victim's sexual appeal according to societal standards of beauty; rather it is an act of power, domination, and conquest inseparable from its social, economic, racial, cultural, and gendered context. In other words, sexual violence was intertwined with racial and economic oppression. . . .

. . . While other members of her tribe took up arms against invaders, Winnemucca waged a war of words in defense of Northern Paiute lifeways. Beginning in 1870 with a letter that ended up in the hands of the commissioner of the Bureau of Indian Affairs, Winnemucca repeatedly brought the Northern Paiutes' suffering to the attention of outsiders and demanded redress. . . . At her people's request, Winnemuca wrote letters to influential military and civilian leaders, and then traveled to San Francisco to lecture and to Nevada to lobby politicians. She continued her letter and speaking campaigns following their removal to Malheur and subsequent removals and relocations. Always she pleaded with her readers and listeners for food and land for the Northern Paiutes. In 1880, Winnemucca led a Northern Paiute delegation to Washington, D.C. to meet with Secretary of the Interior Carl Schurz, who directed Indian affairs, in order to obtain the Northern Paiutes' release from their reservations and to secure the allotment of their land into 160-acre plots for each family. Once she returned west and was no longer the subject of stories in eastern newspapers, Schurz failed to deliver on his promises to her. So Winnemucca turned to western newspapers to attack the Bureau of Indian Affairs. In 1883, with the support of Protestant reformers, Winnemucca moved East where she lectured and wrote her autobiography.

Expecting to hear and read titillating accounts of indigenous cultural practices, audiences instead felt their heartstrings pulled by Winnemucca's account of the abuse of Northern Paiute women and girls. By recounting the Northern Paiutes' story, including stories about rape, she generated an enormous amount of sympathy for the Northern Paiutes and aroused anger against the Bureau. Instead of responding to her criticism, the Bureau of Indian Affairs countered with attacks on her character, particularly her chastity. Winnemucca responded by including character references in the conclusion of her autobiography.

Winnemucca's stories of rape did not just generate public sympathy for the Northern Paiutes; they posited solutions to the Northern Paiutes' problems. Historian Miranda Chaytor argues that women's accounts of rape reveal more than the details of their violation because in them, women name the violence, contain it, and identify the people and things that will enable their recovery. When describing rape in the Great Basin, Winnemucca emphasized the vulnerability of women at work. . . . For these women, labor ordered their lives and accorded them status by enabling them to sustain their families. Winnemucca's accounts of rape, therefore, point to what she felt her people had lost that made them so sexually vulnerable—their economic self-sufficiency and autonomy.[25]

. . . During the late nineteenth century, reformers endorsed allotment, or the subdivision of communal land and resources among individual male heads of households, as a means to rapidly assimilate Native Americans into Anglo-American culture. They . . . believed that private land ownership would destroy the extended families that characterized most Native cultures and replace them with patriarchal, nuclear families, complete with a husband in the fields and a wife in the home. . . . Winnemucca lobbied for allotments, . . . not to enable the Northern Paiutes to assimilate but to facilitate the restoration of their economic self-sufficiency. Though she recognized that their seasonal cycle was destroyed, Winnemucca did not believe that it was irreplaceable, and she looked to allotment to restore the economic autonomy of Northern Paiute families through ranching and farming. On allotments, Northern Paiute husbands and wives could work sometimes together and other times apart as they had always done in order to maintain their families in the Northern Paiute way.

Winnemucca spent her final years attempting to prove that Northern Paiute families could survive and even thrive on their own small farms. In 1885, her brother, Natches, purchased a 160-acre ranch, and while Natches farmed, Winnemucca established a school. She taught Northern Paiute children reading, writing, and arithmetic, and the children helped Natches with the farming, and domestic chores. Most importantly, she treated the children kindly according to Northern Paiute custom and schooled them in Northern Paiute culture. The Peabody Institute, named after an eastern donor, was enormously popular with Northern Paiute students and parents, who abhorred the militarized boarding schools that the government forced Indian children to attend. Natches and Winnemucca's ranch and school blossomed for several years until their financial burden and poor health forced them to close in the summer of 1889. Financially and emotionally exhausted, Winnemucca moved to her sister Elma's ranch where she died in 1891.

During her life and since her death, Winnemucca has been the subject of much controversy. Literary and academic audiences honor Winnemucca as the first Native American woman to write her autobiography, *Life among the Paiutes*, but many Native people criticize her for her more ambiguous accomplishments, such as scouting for the United States Army and endorsing assimilationist federal policies, particularly allotment. Some Northern Paiutes disown her for her inability to force the federal government to keep its promises to them, and pointing to her notoriety, they dismiss her as a self-serving opportunist. But other Northern Paiutes emphasize her devotion to their sovereignty and culture, generations before whites recognized the value of indigenous ways of life.

Perhaps Winnemucca remains so controversial because she was a leader ahead of her time. In the 1880s, she denounced the disproportionately high incidence of sexual violence against Native American women, and worked to ease their poverty and dramatize the relationship between sexual and economic oppression. Over a century later, the percentage of Native Americans living below the poverty line is over twice that of other Americans, and Native American women still experience sexual abuse in disproportionately high numbers—3.5 times that of other American racial groups. Moreover, unlike other racial groups, someone of another race assaults 90 percent of American Indian rape victims.[26] But Winnemucca also remains controversial because she defied stereotypes of Native American women as sexually lax and available. She personified their power, rooted in cultures that have not totally adopted American culture's attitudes toward women and their sexuality. Through her autobiography, she made Northern Paiute women's power intelligible to white readers during an era when Anglo-Americans were struggling with the question of women's rights themselves; she provided them with an alternative model of gender relations other than male dominance. Winnemucca proclaimed: "I know what an Indian woman can do. . . . My dear reader, I have not lived in this world for over thirty or forty years for nothing, and I know what I am talking bout."[27]

NOTES

Hopkins was Winnemucca's married name; we've silently changed it to Winnemucca.

1. Richard N. Allen, *The Tennessee Letters: From Carson Valley, 1857–1869*, David Thompson, compiler (Reno: Grace Dangberg Foundation, 1983), 137–141, 157, 159–160; Myron Angel, *History of Nevada* (Oakland, CA: Thompson and West, 1881; New York: Arno Press, 1973), 150–158.

2. For a description of the Northern Paiute seasonal cycle, see Catherine S. Fowler and Sven Liljeblad, "Northern Paiute," in *The Handbook of North American Indians, Great Basin*, vol. 11, ed. Warren L. D'Azevedo (Washington, DC: Smithsonian Institution, 1986), 435–465; Martha C. Knack and Omer C. Stewart, *As Long as the River Shall Run: An Ethnohistory of the Pyramid Lake Indian Reservation* (Berkeley: University of California Press, 1984), chapter 1.

3. Judith Shapiro, "Kinship," in *The Handbook of North American Indians*, 620–629.

4. Sarah Winnemucca Hopkins, *Life Among the Piutes: Their Wrongs and Claims*, ed. Mrs. Horace Mann (New York: G. P. Putnam and Sons of New York, 1883; reprint, Reno: University of Nevada Press, 1994), 53 (hereafter cited as Winnemucca). Most scholars believe that Winnemucca wrote her autobiography with minimal editing by Mrs. Horace Mann. Sally Zanjani, *Sarah Winnemucca* (Lincoln: University of Nebraska Press, 2001).

5. Fowler, "Subsistence," in *The Handbook of North American Indians*, 64–97; Winnemucca, 50–51.

6 Fowler and Liljeblad, 450–452; Knack and Stewart, 230; and Winnemucca, 52–54.

7. Winnemucca, 45–51.

8. Fowler and Liljeblad; Knack and Stewart, chapter 2.

9. Winnemucca, chapters 5–8; Knack and Stewart, chapters 1–4.

10. Eugene M. Hattori, "'And Some of Them Swear Like Pirates': Acculturation of American Indian Women in Nineteenth Century Virginia City," in *Comstock Women: The Making of a Mining Community*, ed. Ronald M. James and C. Elizabeth Raymond (Reno: University of Nevada Press, 1998), 229–245; Knack and Stewart, chapter 2; Dorothy Nafus Morrison, *Chief Sarah: Sarah Winnemucca's Fight for Indian Rights* (New York: Atheneum, 1980), chapter 6.

11. For detailed accounts of all of Winnemucca's various jobs, see Winnemucca, Morrison, and Zanjani.

12. Winnemucca, 58–59, 231; Knack and Stewart, chapter 2.

13. Rayna Green, "The Pocahontas Perplex: The Images of Indian Women in American Culture," in *Unequal Sisters: A Multicultural Reader in U.S. Women's History*, ed. Ellen Carol DuBois (New York: Routledge, 1990), 15–21; Oliver O. Howard, *My Life and Experiences among Our Hostile Indians* (New York: Da Capo Press, 1972), 214, 222–223, 524–533.

14. Knack and Stewart, 47.

15. Winnemucca, 3–4; Knack and Stewart, chapters 2–8. For accounts of the rape of Indian women during the California Gold Rush, see Albert L. Hurtado, *Indian Survival on the California Frontier* (New Haven: Yale University Press, 1988), chapter 9.

16. Emilie Buchwald, Pamela Fletcher, and Martha Roth, preamble to *Transforming a Rape Culture* (Minneapolis, MN: Milkweed, 1993).

17. Winnemucca, 228.

18. Ibid., 100–104, 167, 178, 188, 231.

19. Hattori, 233–235; Knack and Stewart, chapters 4–5.

20. Winnemucca, 180–182, 228–230.

21. Winnemucca, 231; *Nevada State Journal*, 28 March 1875; *Silver State*, 27 March 1875; Zanjani, 126.

22. George M. Kober, *Reminiscences of George Martin Kober, M.D., LL. D.* (Washington, DC: Kober Foundation of Georgetown University, 1930), 280.

23. Fowler and Liljeblad, 457; Winnemucca, 70–73.

24. Winnemucca, 116.

25. "Husband(ry): Narratives of Rape in the Seventeenth Century," *Gender and History* 7 (1995): 378–407.

26. U.S. Department of Justice, Bureau of Justice Statistics, February 1999 for the period 1992–1996, http://www/vday.org/ie/index2cfm?articleID +864. U.S. Department of Commerce, *We the First Americans* (Washington, DC: Government Printing Office, 1993).

27. Winnemucca, 228.

The Grimké Sisters, Sarah and Angelina, Talk Truth to Power

Sarah and Angelina Grimké were the first, and it seems likely the only, women of a slaveholding family to speak and write publicly as abolitionists. They were the first women agents of the American Anti-Slavery Society to tour widely and to speak to audiences of men and women. They were the first women who, from within the abolitionist movement, defended their rights *as women* to free speech. They were sustained in their work by a deep religious devotion, and their writings are examples of the spirit in which many women's rights advocates developed a wide-ranging critique of the relationship between the state, churches, and families.

The Grimké sisters grew up in Charleston, South Carolina. Their father was a distinguished legislator and judge; although he gave his daughters a traditional female education (lacking Greek, Latin, and philosophy), when he trained his sons for the law he included his daughters in the exercises. Both young women were sensitive to the injustices of slavery; as a young woman Sarah broke the law against teaching slaves to read and Angelina held prayer meetings for the family's slaves. When she was twenty-four years old, Sarah accompanied her father to Philadelphia, where he sought medical treatment; after his death she returned there in 1821 to live among Quakers, who impressed her by their piety, simplicity, and refusal to hold slaves. In 1829 Angelina joined her; both became members of a Quaker meeting. Sarah committed herself to boycott products made in slavery; Angelina joined the Philadelphia Female Antislavery Society. When reformers faced violence from proslavery mobs in the summer of 1835, William Lloyd Garrison wrote strong editorials in the *Liberator* denouncing what he called a "reign of terror." Angelina Grimké responded with a letter complimenting him on his fortitude: "The ground on which you stand is holy ground," she wrote, "never— never surrender it."

Garrison surprised her by printing her letter; thus encouraged to write for a wide audience, Angelina went on to write *An Appeal to the Christian Women of the South*, part of which follows. The pamphlet sold widely in the North and made her reputation, but it was burned in Charleston.

When the American Anti-Slavery Society organized a group of "Agents" to travel and speak on slavery, Angelina and Sarah Grimké were among them. They began in late 1836, speaking to women in private parlors in New York City; by the turn of the year, no private room was big enough and they held their sessions in a Baptist church. They involved themselves in founding women's antislavery societies and organizing women's antislavery petitions to Congress; they published their speeches as pamphlets. In mid-1837 they moved on to Boston, where an

From *The Public Years of Sarah and Angelina Grimké: Selected Writings, 1835–1839*, ed. Larry Ceplair. Copyright © 1989 by Columbia University Press. Reprinted with permission of the publisher. The selections that follow are taken from pp. 37–38, 54–56, 211, 216, 220–23, 268–69.

intense debate among factions of abolitionists was already under way. Sarah wrote a series of essays that appeared first in newspapers and then as a pamphlet, *Letters on the Equality of the Sexes and the Condition of Women*. Here, we reprint excerpts from two of her letters.

In the summer of 1837, the Congregational ministers of Massachusetts published a "Pastoral Letter" attacking the Grimkés as unwomanly (partly reprinted here, with Sarah Grimké's response). In the past, the two reformers had offered their criticism of slavery in the context of religious faith; now they claimed that as moral individuals, women had as much right to take political positions as men. Though even some of their allies—including Theodore Dwight Weld, whom Angelina would soon marry—sought to dissuade them, they were forthright, as you can see, in their response to the clergymen. The term *feminist* had not yet been invented—it would be devised in the 1910s—but the ingredients of the concept were already present in the ideas of the Grimké sisters.*

ANGELINA GRIMKÉ, APPEAL TO THE CHRISTIAN WOMEN OF THE SOUTH (1836)

. . . Sisters in Christ I feel an interest in *you*, and often has the secret prayer arisen on your behalf, Lord "open thou their eyes that they may see wondrous things out of thy Law"—It is then, because I *do feel* and *do pray* for you, that I thus address you upon a subject about which of all others, perhaps you would rather not hear any thing; but, "would to God ye could bear with me a little in my folly, and indeed bear with me, for I am jealous over you with godly jealousy." Be not afraid then to read my appeal; it is *not* written in the heat of passion or prejudice, but in that solemn calmness which is the result of conviction and duty. It is true, I am going to tell you unwelcome truths, but I mean to speak those *truths in love*, and remember Solomon says, "faithful are the *wounds* of a friend." I do not believe the time has yet come when *Christian women* "will not endure sound doctrine," even on the subject of slavery, if it is spoken to them in tenderness and love, therefore I now address you. . . .

We must come back to the good old doctrine of our forefathers who declared to the world, "this self evident truth that *all* men are created equal, and that they have certain *inalienable* rights among which are life, *liberty*, and the pursuit of happiness." It is even a greater absurdity to suppose a man can be legally born a slave under *our free Republican* Government, than under the petty despotisms of barbarian Africa. If then, we have no right to enslave an African, surely we can have none to enslave an American; if it is a self evident truth that *all* men, every where and of every color are born equal, and have an *inalienable right to liberty*, then it is equally true that *no* man can be born a slave, and no man can ever *rightfully* be reduced to *involuntary* bondage and held as a slave, however fair may be the claim of his master or mistress through will and title-deeds. . . .

But perhaps you will be ready to query, why appeal to *women* on this subject? *We* do not make the laws which perpetuate slavery. No legislative power is vested in *us*; *We* can do nothing to overthrow the system, even if we wished to do so. To this I reply, I know you do not make the laws, but I also know that *you are the wives and mothers, the sisters and daughters of those who do*; and if you really suppose *you* can do nothing to overthrow slavery, you are greatly mistaken. You can do much in every way: four things I will name. 1st. You can read on this subject. 2d. You can pray over this subject. 3d. You can speak on this subject. 4th. You can *act* on this subject. I have not placed reading before praying because I regard it more important, but because, in order to pray aright, we must understand what we are praying for; it is only then we can "pray with the understanding and the spirit also."

1. Read then on the subject of slavery. Search the Scriptures daily, whether the things I have told you are true. Other books and papers might be a great help to you in this investigation, but they are not necessary. . . .

2. Pray over this subject. When you have entered into your closets, and shut to the doors,

then pray to your father, who seeth in secret, that he would open your eyes to see whether slavery is *sinful*, and if it is, that he would enable you to bear a faithful, open and unshrinking testimony against it, and to do whatsoever your hands find to do . . .

3. Speak on this subject. It is through the tongue, the pen, and the press, that truth is principally propagated. Speak then to your relatives, your friends, your acquaintances on the subject of slavery; be not afraid if you are conscientiously convinced it is *sinful*, to say so openly, but calmly, and to let your sentiments be known. If you are served by the slaves of others, try to ameliorate their condition as much as possible; never aggravate their faults, and thus add fuel to the fire of anger already kindled in a master and mistress's bosom. . . .

4. Act on this subject. Some of you *own* slaves yourselves. If you believe slavery is *Sinful*, set them at liberty, "undo the heavy burdens and let the oppressed go free." If they wish to remain with you, pay them wages, if not let them leave you. Should they remain teach them, and have them taught the common branches of an English education; they have minds and those minds, *ought to be improved*. So precious a talent as intellect, never was given to be wrapt in a napkin and buried in the earth. It is the *duty* of all, as far as they can, to improve their own mental faculties, because we are commanded to love God with *all our minds*, as well as with all our hearts, and we commit a great sin, if we *forbid or prevent* that cultivation of the mind in others, which would enable them to perform this duty. Teach your servants then to read & c, and encourage them to believe it is their *duty* to learn, if it were only that they might read the Bible.

But some of you will say, we can neither free our slaves nor teach them to read, for the laws of our state forbid it. Be not surprised when I say such wicked laws *ought to be no barrier* in the way of your duty, and I appeal to the Bible to prove this position. What was the conduct of Shiphrah and Puah, when the king of Egypt issued his cruel mandate, with regard to the Hebrew children? *"They feared God*, and did *not* as the King of Egypt commanded them, but saved the men children alive." Did these *women* do right in disobeying that monarch? *"Therefore* (says the sacred text,) God *dealt well* with them, and made them houses."

SARAH M. GRIMKÉ, LETTERS ON THE EQUALITY OF THE SEXES AND THE CONDITION OF WOMEN (1837)

LETTER VIII: "ON THE CONDITION OF WOMEN IN THE UNITED STATES"

During the early part of my life, my lot was cast among the butterflies of the *fashionable* world; and of this class of women, I am constrained to say, both from experience and observation, that their education is miserably deficient; that they are taught to regard marriage as the one thing needful, the only avenue to distinction; hence to attract the notice and win the attentions of men, by their external charms, is the chief business of fashionable girls. They seldom think that men will be allured by intellectual acquirements, because they find, that where any mental superiority exists, a woman is generally shunned and regarded as stepping out of her "appropriate sphere," which, in their view, is to dress, to dance, to set out to the best possible advantage her person, to read the novels which inundate the press, and which do more to destroy her character as a rational creature, than any thing else. . . .

There is another and much more numerous class in this country, who are withdrawn by education or circumstances from the circle of fashionable amusements, but who are brought up with the dangerous and absurd idea, that *marriage* is a kind of preferment; and that to be able to keep their husband's house, and render his situation comfortable, is the end of her being. Much that she does and says and thinks is done in reference to this situation; and to be married is too often held up to the view of girls as the sine qua non of human happiness and human existence. . . . I do long to see the time, when it will no longer be necessary for women to expend so many precious hours in furnishing "a well spread table," but that their husbands will forego some of the accustomed indulgences in this way, and encourage their wives to devote some portion of their time to mental cultivation, even at the expense of having to dine sometimes on baked potatoes, or bread and butter. . . .

There is another way in which the general opinion, that women are inferior to men, is manifested, that bears with tremendous effect on the laboring class, and indeed on almost all who are obliged to earn a subsistence, whether it be by mental or physical exertion—I allude to the disproportionate value set on the time and labor of men and of women. A man who is engaged in teaching, can always, I believe, command a higher price for tuition than a woman—even when he teaches the same branches, and is not in any respect superior to the woman. This I know is the case in boarding and other schools with which I have been acquainted, and it is so in every occupation in which the sexes engaged indiscriminately. As for example, in tailoring, a man has twice, or three times as much for making a waistcoat or pantaloons as a woman, although the work done by each may be equally good. In those employments which are peculiar to women, their time is estimated at only half the value of that of men. A woman who goes out to wash, works as hard in proportion as a wood sawyer, or a coal heaver, but she is not generally able to make more than half as much by a day's work. . . .

There is another class of women in this country, to whom I cannot refer, without feelings of the deepest shame and sorrow. I allude to our female slaves. Our southern cities are whelmed beneath a tide of pollution; the virtue of female slaves is wholly at the mercy of irresponsible tyrants, and women are bought and sold in our slave markets, to gratify the brutal lust of those who bear the name of Christians. In our slave States, if amid all her degradation and ignorance, a women desires to preserve her virtue unsullied, she is either bribed or whipped into compliance, or if she dares resist her seducer, her life by the laws of some of the slave States may be, and has actually been sacrificed to the fury of disappointed passion. Where such laws do not exist, the power which is necessarily vested in the master over his property, leaves the defenceless slave entirely at his mercy, and the sufferings of some females on this account, both physical and mental, are intense.

LETTER XV: MAN EQUALLY GUILTY WITH WOMAN IN THE FALL

. . . In contemplating the great moral reformations of the day, and the part which they are bound to take in them, instead of puzzling themselves with the harassing, because unnecessary inquiry, how far they may go without overstepping the bounds of propriety, which separate male and female duties, they will only inquire, "Lord, what wilt thou have us do?" They will be enabled to see the simple truth, that God has made no distinction between men and women as moral beings; that the distinction now so much insisted upon between male and female virtues is as absurd as it is unscriptural, and has been the fruitful source of much mischief—granting to man a license for the exhibition of brute force and conflict on the battlefield; for sternness, selfishness, and the exercise of irresponsible power in the circle of home—and to woman a permit to rest on an arm of flesh, and to regard modesty and delicacy, and all the kindred virtues, as peculiarly appropriate to her. Now to me it is perfectly clear, that WHATSOEVER IT IS MORALLY RIGHT FOR A MAN TO DO, IT IS MORALLY RIGHT FOR A WOMAN TO DO; and that confusion must exist in the moral world, until woman takes her stand on the same platform with man, and feels that she is clothed by her Maker with the *same rights*, and, of course, that upon her devolve the *same duties*.

PASTORAL LETTER: THE GENERAL ASSOCIATION OF MASSACHUSETTS TO THE CHURCHES UNDER THEIR CARE

III.—We invite your attention to the dangers which at present seem to threaten the female character with wide spread and permanent injury.

The appropriate duties and influence of women are clearly stated in the New Testament. Those duties and that influence are unobtrusive and private, but the sources of mighty power. When the mild, dependant [sic], softening influence of woman upon the sternness of man's opinion is fully exercised, society feels the effects of it in a thousand forms. The power of woman is in her dependence, flowing from the consciousness of that weakness which God has given her for her protection, and which keeps her in those departments of life that form the character of individuals and of the nation. There are social influences which females use in promoting piety and the great objects of Christian benevolence which we cannot too highly commend. We appreciate the unostentatious prayers and efforts of woman in advancing the cause of religion at home and abroad; in Sabbath schools; in leading religious inquirers to the pastors for instruction; and in all such associated effort as becomes the modesty of her sex; and earnestly hope that she may abound more and more in these labors of piety and love.

But when she assumes the place and tone of man as a public reformer, our care and protection of her seem unnecessary; we put ourselves in self-defence against her; she yields the power which God has given her for protection, and her character becomes unnatural. If the vine, whose strength and beauty is to lean upon the trellis and half conceal its clusters, thinks to assume the independence and the overshading nature of the elm, it will not only cease to bear fruit, but fall in shame and dishonor into the dust. We cannot, therefore, but regret the mistaken conduct of those who encourage females to bear an obtrusive and ostentatious part in measures of reform, and countenance any of that sex who so far forget themselves as to itinerate in the character of public lecturers and teachers. We especially deplore the intimate acquaintance and promiscuous conversation of females with regard to things "which ought not to be named"; by which that modesty and delicacy which is the charm of domestic life, and which constitutes the true influence of woman in society is consumed, and the way opened, as we apprehend, for degeneracy and ruin. . . .

SARAH M. GRIMKÉ, RESPONSE TO "THE PASTORAL LETTER . . ."

The motto of woman, when she is engaged in the great work of public reformation should be,—"The Lord is my light and my salvation; whom shall I fear? The Lord is the strength of my life; of whom shall I be afraid?" She must feel, if she feels rightly, that she is fulfilling one of the important duties laid upon her as an accountable being, and that her character, instead of being "unnatural," is in exact accordance with the will of Him to whom, and to no other, she is responsible for the talents and the gifts confided to her. As to the pretty simile, introduced into the "Pastoral Letter," "If the vine whose strength and beauty is to lean upon the trellis work, and half conceal its clusters, thinks to assume the independence and the overshadowing nature of the elm," & c. I shall only remark that it might well suit the poet's fancy, who sings of sparkling eyes and coral lips, and knights in armor clad; but it seems to me utterly inconsistent with the dignity of a Christian body, to endeavor to draw such an anti-scriptural distinction between men and women. Ah! how many of my sex feel in the dominion, thus unrighteously exercised over them, under the gentle appellation of *protection*, that what they have leaned upon has proved a broken reed at best, and oft a spear.

Thine in the bonds of womanhood,

Sarah M. Grimké

Keziah Kendall Protests Coverture

We know nothing more about "Keziah Kendall" than what she revealed in this letter, which historians Dianne Avery and Alfred S. Konefsky discovered among the papers of Simon Greenleaf, a prominent Harvard law professor. It has not been possible to locate the author in the usual places—tax lists, land records, church lists. Keziah and her sisters carry the names of Job's daughters; whether the names are real or fictional, the writer assumed that her readers would remember the biblical reference: ". . . in all the land there were no women so fair as Job's daughters; and their father gave them inheritance among their brothers."

Kendall had been dismayed by what she heard at a public lyceum lecture on women's rights given by Greenleaf in early 1839. At a time when the legal disabilities of inherited common law were increasingly being questioned—in Massachusetts, the abolitionists Sarah and Angelina Grimké had only recently delivered a

Letter from Keziah Kendall to Simon Greenleaf (undated), Box 3, Folder 10, Simon Greenleaf Papers, Harvard Law School Library. Excerpted from Diane Avery and Alfred S. Konefsky, "The Daughters of Job: Property Rights and Women's Lives in Mid-Nineteenth-Century Massachusetts," *Law and History Review* 10 (Fall 1992): 323–56. Notes have been renumbered and edited.

forthright series of lectures on the rights of women—Greenleaf devoted his lecture to the claim that American women were well protected by American law as it stood. He argued that excluding women from politics saved society from "uproar" and impropriety, and that constraints on married women's use of their property was merely a technicality because in a happy marriage all property became part of "a common fund . . . it can make but little difference . . . by whose name it is called." And he insisted that except for "restriction in *political matters*" there were no significant "distinctions between the legal rights of unmarried women, and of men."

Keziah Kendall was unpersuaded, and wrote to demand that Greenleaf offer another lecture, acknowledging the "legal wrongs" of women. What are Kendall's objections to the law as she experienced it? What connections does she draw between paying taxes, voting, and officeholding? Why does she blame Massachusetts property law for her fiancé's death? Why is she worried about her sister's forthcoming marriage?

Keziah Kendall to Simon Greenleaf [1839?] I take the liberty to write to you on the subject of the Lyceum lecture you delivered last Feb but as you are not acquainted with me I think I will introduce myself. My name is Keziah Kendall. I live not many miles from Cambridge, on a farm with two sisters, one older, one younger than myself. I am thirty two. Our parents and only brother are dead—we have a good estate—comfortable house—nice barn, garden, orchard & c and money in the bank besides. Jemima is a very good manager in the house, keeps everything comfortable—sees that the milk is nicely prepared for market— looks after everything herself, and rises before day, winter and summer,—but she never had any head for figures, and always expects me to keep all accounts, and attend to all business concerns. Keranhappuck, (who is called Kerry) is quite young, only nineteen, and as she was a little girl when mother died, we've always petted her, and let her do as she pleased, and now she's courted. Under these circumstances the whole responsibility of our property, not less than twenty five thousand dollars rests upon me. I am not over fond of money, but I have worked hard ever since I was a little girl, and tried to do all in my power to help earn, and help save, and it would be strange if I did not think more of it than those who never earned anything, and never saved anything they could get to spend, and you know Sir, there are many such girls nowadays. Well—our milkman brought word when he came from market that you were a going to lecture on the legal rights of women, and so I thought I would go and learn. Now I hope you wont think me bold when I say, I did not like that lecture much. I dont speak of the

manner, it was pretty spoken enough, but there was nothing in it but what every body knows. We all know about a widow's thirds,[1] and we all know that a man must maintain his wife, and we all know that he must pay her debts, if she has any—but I never heard of a yankee woman marrying in debt. What I wanted to know, was good reasons for some of those laws that I cant account for. I do hope if you are ever to lecture at the Lyceum again, that you will give us some. I must tell my story to make you understand what I mean. One Lyceum lecture that I heard in C. stated that the Americans went to war with the British, because they were taxed without being represented in Parliament. Now we are taxed every year to the full amount of every dollar we possess—town, county, state taxes—taxes for land, for movables, for money and all. Now I dont want to go representative or any thing else, any more than I do to be a "constable or a sheriff," but I have no voice about public improvements, and I dont see the justice of being taxed any more than the "revolutionary heroes" did. You mention that woman here, are not treated like heathen and Indian women—we know that—nor do I think we are treated as Christian women ought to be, according to the Bible rule of doing to others as you would others should do unto you. I am told (not by you) that if a woman dies a week after she's married that her husband takes all her personal property and the use of her real estate as long as he lives[2]—if a man dies his wife can have her thirds—this does not come up to the Gospel rule. Now the young fellow that is engaged to our Kerry, is a pleasant clever fellow, but he is not quite one and twenty, and I dont s'pouse he ever earned a coat in his life. Uncle told me there was a way for a woman to have her property trustee'd,[3] and I told it to Kerry—but she, poor girl has romantic notions owing to reading too many novels,[4] and when I told her of it, she would not hear of such a thing—"What take the law to keep my property away from James before I marry him—if it was a million of dollars he should have it all." So you see I think the law is in fault here—to tell you the truth I do not think young men are near so careful about getting in debt as girls, and I have known more than one that used their wife's money to pay off old scores. . . . I had rather go to my mantua maker[5] to borrow twenty dollars if I needed it, than to the richest married woman I know.

Another thing I have to tell you—when I was young I had a lover, Jos. Thompson, he went into business in a neighboring town, and after a year or two while I was getting the wedding things—Joe failed, he met with misfortunes that he did not expect,—he could have concealed it from me and married, but he did not—he was honorable, and so we delayed. He lived along here two or three years, and tried all he could to settle with his creditors, but some were stiff and held out, and thought by and by we would marry, and they should get my property. Uncle said he knew if we were married, there were those who would take my cattle and the improvement of my land. Joseph used to visit me often those years, but he lost his spirits and he could not get into business again, and he thought he must go to sea. I begged him not to, and told him we should be able to manage things in time, but he said no—he must try his luck, and at least get enough to settle off old scores, and then he would come here and live and we would make the best of what I had. We parted—but it pleased God he should be lost at sea. What I have suffered, I cannot tell you. Now Joe was no sailor when I engaged with him, and if it had been a thing known that I should always have a right to keep possession of my own, he need never have gone to sea, and we might have lived happily together, and in time with industry and economy, he might have paid off all. I am one that cant be convinced without better reasons than I have heard of, that woman are dealt with by the "gospel rule." There is more might than right in such laws as far as I can see—

if you see differently, do tell us next time you lecture. Another thing—you made some reflections upon women following the Anti's. . . . Women have joined the Antislavery societies, and why? Women are kept for slaves as well as men—it is a common cause, deny the justice of it, who can! To be sure I do not wish to go about lecturing like the Misses Grimkie, but I have not the knowledge they have, and I verily believe that if I had been brought up among slaves as they were, and knew all that they know, and felt a call from humanity to speak, I should run the venture of your displeasure, and that of a good many others like you.[6] I told Uncle that I thought your lecture was a one-sided thing—and he said, "why Keziah, Squire Greenleaf is an advocate, not a judge, you must get him to take t'other side next time." Now I have taken this opportunity to ask you to give us a remedy for the "legal wrongs" of women, whenever you have a chance. The fathers of the land should look to these things—who knows but your daughter may be placed in the sad situation I am in, or the dangerous one Kerry is in. I hear you are a good man, to make it certain—do all the good you can, and justify no wrong thing.

Yours with regard
Keziah Kendall

Notes

1. She is, of course, referring to a widow's dower rights. (See pp. 85–86.)
2. "Kendall" was correct in her understanding of a husband's rights in his wife's personal property if she should die as early as "a week after she's married." But under the common law he would not inherit a life interest in her real estate unless they were parents of a child.
3. This is a reference to the equitable device of placing the woman's property in a trust before marriage for the purpose of avoiding the husband's common law rights in her property as well as protecting it from the husband's creditors. Under the trust agreement, the trustee would be obligated to manage the property for the benefit of the married woman.
4. "Kendall" shared a widely held distrust of romantic novels.
5. In the early republic, mantua makers [i.e., skilled dressmakers] were often economically independent women.
6. "Kendall" is probably referring here to the "Pastoral Letter" issued by the Congregationalist ministers in the summer of 1837 denouncing the public lecturing of the Grimké sisters. (see pp. 241–242).

Ellen F. Watkins Goes on the Lecture Circuit

At age twenty-nine, Frances Ellen Watkins (later Harper) set out to follow Sarah and Angelina Grimké's risk-strewn path, lecturing widely and publishing in protest of slavery and racial discrimination. In these decades, the vast majority of white Americans disdained and feared abolitionists as outrageous radicals. A prolific poet and essayist, and, later, novelist, Harper emerged over time as a revered literary figure. After the Civil War, she was an active reformer for decades on behalf of African American rights, temperance, peace, and women's rights; she died in 1911. Notably, she was one of a small number of black women to hold "positions of leadership in the national organizations controlled by white female reformers," such as the Women's Christian Temperance Union, the American Woman Suffrage Association, and the International Council of Women. Born in Baltimore in 1825, Harper was orphaned at age three when her mother, a free woman of color, died. She grew up in the household of her learned uncle, William J. Watkins, Sr., a United Methodist minister and founder of the Watkins Academy, which offered "one of the best educations" then available to African Americans and where his niece was a pupil. In the documents below, we hear her narrate her successes and troubles as a public activist early in her career, prior to her marriage in 1860 to Fenton Harper of Ohio.* Witness how her response to an urban streetcar operator marks her as an ally of Emma Coger, Ida B. Wells, Rosa Parks, and countless other women who refused to acquiesce to unequal treatment in public accommodations (see pp. 290–291, 323).

Chronicling her very first lecture in the summer of 1854 and on through the decade, Harper's letters serve as a journal of her travels and public lecturing as an employee of antislavery societies. Like other reformers on the lecture circuit, Harper's schedule could be grueling: for example, between September 5 and October 20, 1854, she spoke in twenty-one towns in Maine, and two to four times in some of them. When she was the featured speaker (not sharing the stage with another), she often spoke for an hour and a half. A former schoolteacher and seamstress, Harper (then Watkins) quickly acquired the reputation among abolitionists as being among the most effective female orators on circuit. Her friend, Philadelphia-based William Still, noted that "perhaps few speakers surpass her in using language and arguments, more potently, in impressing and charming her audiences." Fellow activist, African American newspaper editor Mary Ann Shadd Cary, wrote of a moment

*Bettye Collier-Thomas, "Frances Ellen Watkins Harper: Abolitionist and Feminist Reformer, 1825–1911," in *African American Women and the Vote, 1837–1965*, ed. Ann D. Gordon (Amherst: University of Massachusetts Press, 1997), 42, 44, 49. See also Frances Smith Foster, ed., *A Brighter Coming Day: A Frances Ellen Watkins Harper Reader* (New York: Feminist Press at the City University of New York, 1990), 3–47.

The following letters, except for the one dated April 1858, are excerpted from William Still, *The Underground Rail Road: A Record of Facts, Authentic Narratives, Letters, &c., Narrating the Hardships, Hair-breadth Escapes, and Death Struggles of the Slaves in their Efforts for Freedom, as Related by Themselves and Others, or Witnessed by the Author* ... (Philadelphia: Porter and Coates, 1872), pp. 758–760. (Note: the book has been digitized by hathitrust.org.) The April 1858 letter from Watkins "to a friend" was published in William Lloyd Garrison's abolitionist newspaper, *The Liberator*, April 23, 1858, p. 3.

when they were both in Detroit: "why the whites & colored people here are just going crazy with excitement about her. She is the greatest female speaker ever was here, so wisdom obliges me to keep out of the way [e.g., not offer to lecture] as . . . there would just be no chance of favorable comparison."[†] In your experience, what qualities and strategies help a relatively young person be a successful public speaker—without amplification aids like a microphone?

Some of the most militant and determined abolitionists in Britain and the United States embraced the Free Produce movement, which Harper mentions approvingly. But committing oneself to purchase and use only commodities not produced by enslaved workers was logistically hard to pull off. The handful of Quaker shopkeepers in the nation who ran "free produce stores," such as Lydia White of Philadelphia, had difficulty keeping their shelves adequately stocked. Customers complained that the sugar they bought at these stores had "a very disagreeable taste and odor" and that the rice was "very poor, dark and dirty." One solution in terms of clothing was to avoid cotton altogether. Yet, ready-made "free labor" gowns often failed to sell, deemed either too ugly or not plain enough by abolitionist shoppers. While this early initiative to label ethical goods presaged many later episodes in what we now call consumer politics, by the 1850s most North American antislavery activists had given up on the exhausting and frustrating free produce endeavor, convinced that their energies were better channeled into direct political action.[**] One wonders how often the outspoken women reformers featured in this set of documents believed they were wearing free labor garments and at what point in their careers they decided other expressions of long-distance solidarity with oppressed workers were more effective.

Aug. 1854: Well, I am out lecturing. I have lectured every night this week; [and] besides [I] addressed a Sunday-school, and I shall speak, if nothing prevent it, to-night. My lectures have met with success. Last night I lectured in a white church in Providence. Mr. Gardener was present, and made the estimate of about six hundred persons. Never, perhaps, was a speaker, old or young favored with a more attentive audience. . . . My voice is not wanting in strength, as I am aware of, to reach pretty well over the house. . . . My maiden lecture was Monday night in New Bedford on the Elevation and Education of our People.

Sept. 28, 1854, from Buckstown Centre, Maine: I spoke in Boston on Monday night. . . . Well, I am but one, but can do something, and, God helping me, I will try. . . . [Since then,] the agent of the State Anti-Slavery Society of Maine travels with me, and she is a pleasant, dear, sweet lady.

I do like her so. We travel together, eat together, and sleep together. (She is a white woman.) In fact I have not been in one colored person's house since I left Massachusetts; but I have a pleasant time. . . . I have met with some of the kindest treatment up here that I have ever received. . . . I have lectured three times this week.

Thursday, Oct. 20, 1854, from Temple, Maine: [At the annual meeting of the Maine Anti-Slavery Society,] I spoke on Free Produce, and now by the way I believe in that kind of Abolition. Oh, it does seem to strike at one of the principal roots of the matter. I have commenced since I read Solomon Northrup. Oh, if Mrs. Stowe [Harriet Beecher Stowe, the novelist] has clothed American slavery in the graceful garb of fiction, Solomon Northrup comes up from the dark habitation of Southern cruelty where slavery fattens and feasts on human blood with such mournful revelations that one

[†] Still, *The Underground Rail Road*, 760; Still, in *Provincial Freeman* [Chatham, Ontario], March 7, 1857; Cary, quoted in Shirley J. Yee, *Black Women Abolitionists: A Study in Activism, 1828–1860* (Knoxville: University of Tennessee Press, 1992), 117.

[**] Lawrence B. Glickman, "'Buy for the Sake of the Slave': Abolitionism and the Origins of American Consumer Activism," *American Quarterly* 56 (Dec. 2004), 889–912, esp. 891 (quotation), 900.

might almost wish for the sake of humanity that the tales of horror which he reveals were not so.[††] Oh, how can we pamper our appetites upon luxuries [such as sugar] drawn from reluctant fingers? Oh, could slavery exist long if it did not sit on a commercial throne? . . . I have reason to be thankful that I am able to give [e.g., pay] a little more for a Free Labor dress, [even] if it is coarser. I can thank God that upon its warp and woof I see no stain of blood and tears [of enslaved cotton pickers]; that to procure a little finer muslin for my limbs no crushed and broken heart went out in sighs; and that from the field where it was raised went up no wild and startling cry unto the throne of God to witness there in language deep and strong, that in demanding that cotton I was nerving oppression's hand for deeds of guilt and crime. If the liberation of the slave demanded it, I could consent to part with a portion of the blood from my own veins if that would do him any good.

April 1858: Now let me tell you about Pennsylvania. I have been travelling nearly four years,

and have been in every New England State, in New York, Canada and Ohio: but of all these places, this is about the meanest . . . as far as the treatment of colored people is concerned. I have been insulted in several railroad cars. The other day, in attempting to ride in one of the city cars, after I had entered, the conductor came to me, and wanted me to go out on the platform. Now, was not that brave and noble? As a matter of course, I did not. Some one interfered, and asked or requested that I might be permitted to sit in a corner. I did not move, but kept the same seat. When I was about to leave, he [the conductor] refused my money, and I threw it down on the car floor, and got out, after I had ridden as far as I wished. Such impudence!

On the Carlisle Road [west of Philadelphia and Lancaster], I was interrupted and insulted several times. Two men came after me in one day.

I have met, of course, with kindness among individuals and families; all is not dark in Pennsylvania; but the shadow of slavery, oh how drearily it hangs!

Declaration of Sentiments, 1848

The Declaration of Sentiments, Stanton's indictment of the relations between men and women in her own society, is still stunning in its energy, its precision, and its foresight. It challenged many elements of American law and social practice which—thanks to five generations of political activism—no longer exist.

But the Declaration was only the beginning. Out of their vision of a community of equals, out of their discomfort with a social environment that privileged men and undermined women, the men and women at Seneca Falls dedicated themselves to Herculean political work. In one seventeen-day period in 1855 they held sixteen political meetings in fourteen different counties in upstate New York. In 1864, when it seemed possible that an end to slavery might also mean universal equal citizenship, they sent petitions with 100,000 signatures to the Senate and dreamed of getting a million.

[††] Here, Harper refers to Harriet Beecher Stowe's best-selling novel, *Uncle Tom's Cabin; or, Life Among the Lowly*, published in March 1852, and to Northup's memoir, *Twelve Years a Slave: Narrative of Solomon Northup, a Citizen of New-York, Kidnapped in Washington City in 1841, and Rescued in 1853*, published in 1853. The latter was the basis of a 2013 feature film, *Twelve Years a Slave* (dir. Steve McQueen).

Declaration of Sentiments, in *History of Woman Suffrage*, vol. 1, ed. Elizabeth Cady Stanton, Susan B. Anthony, and Matilda Joslyn Gage (New York: Fowler & Wells, 1881), pp. 70–71. The Declaration and many related documents can be found at the website of the Papers of Elizabeth Cady Stanton and Susan B. Anthony, http://ecssba.rutgers.edu.

They denounced the exclusion of women from learned professions and "nearly all the profitable employments." Male teachers earned $700 a year; women teachers earned $250. Susan B. Anthony would soon be demanding "equal pay for equal work," but there would be no federal equal pay act until 1963.

If Stanton and her Seneca Falls colleagues were to reappear in our own time, what changes would please them? What elements of their agenda would they believe are still alive?

Seneca Falls, New York,
July 19–20, 1848

When, in the course of human events, it becomes necessary for one portion of the family of man to assume among the people of the earth a position different from that which they have hitherto occupied, but one to which the laws of nature and of nature's God entitle them, a decent respect to the opinions of mankind requires that they should declare the causes that impel them to such a course.

We hold these truths to be self-evident: that all men and women are created equal; that they are endowed by their Creator with certain inalienable rights; that among these are life, liberty, and the pursuit of happiness; that to secure these rights governments are instituted, deriving their just powers from the consent of the governed. Whenever any form of government becomes destructive of these ends, it is the right of those who suffer from it to refuse allegiance to it, and to insist upon the institution of a new government, laying its foundation on such principles, and organizing its powers in such form, as to them shall seem most likely to effect their safety and happiness. Prudence, indeed, will dictate that governments long established should not be changed for light and transient causes; and accordingly all experience hath shown that mankind are more disposed to suffer, while evils are sufferable, than to right themselves by abolishing the forms to which they were accustomed. But when a long train of abuses and usurpations, pursuing invariably the same object evinces a design to reduce them under absolute despotism, it is their duty to throw off such government, and to provide new guards for their future security. Such has been the patient sufferance of the women under this government, and such is now the necessity which constrains them to demand the equal station to which they are entitled.

The history of mankind is a history of repeated injuries and usurpations on the part of man toward woman, having in direct object the establishment of an absolute tyranny over her. To prove this, let facts be submitted to a candid world.

He has never permitted her to exercise her inalienable right to the elective franchise.

He has compelled her to submit to laws, in the formation of which she had no voice.

He has withheld from her rights which are given to the most ignorant and degraded men—both native and foreigners.

Having deprived her of this first right of a citizen, the elective franchise, thereby leaving her without representation in the halls of legislation, he has oppressed her on all sides.

He has made her, if married, in the eye of the law, civilly dead.

He has taken from her all right in property, even to the wages she earns.

He has made her, morally, an irresponsible being, as she can commit many crimes with impunity, provided they be done in the presence of her husband. In the covenant of marriage, she is compelled to promise obedience to her husband, he becoming, to all intents and purposes, her master—the law giving him power to deprive her of her liberty, and to administer chastisement.

He has so framed the laws of divorce, as to what shall be the proper causes, and in case of separation, to whom the guardianship of the children shall be given, as to be wholly regardless of the happiness of women—the law, in all cases, going upon a false supposition of the supremacy of man, and giving all power into his hands.

After depriving her of all rights as a married woman, if single, and the owner of property, he has taxed her to support a government which recognizes her only when her property can be made profitable to it.

He has monopolized nearly all the profitable employments, and from those she is permitted to follow, she receives but a scanty remuneration. He closes against her all the avenues to wealth and distinction which he considers most honorable to himself. As a teacher of theology, medicine, or law, she is not known.

He has denied her the facilities for obtaining a thorough education, all colleges being closed against her.

He allows her in Church, as well as State, but a subordinate position, claiming Apostolic authority for her exclusion from the ministry, and, with some exceptions, from any public participation in the affairs of the Church.

He has created a false public sentiment by giving to the world a different code of morals for men and women, by which moral delinquencies which exclude women from society, are not only tolerated, but deemed of little account in man.

He has usurped the prerogative of Jehovah himself, claiming it as his right to assign for her a sphere of action, when that belongs to her conscience and to her God.

He has endeavored, in every way that he could, to destroy her confidence in her own powers, to lessen her self-respect, and to make her willing to lead a dependent and abject life.

Now, in view of this entire disfranchisement of one-half the people of this country, their social and religious degradation—in view of the unjust laws above mentioned, and because women do feel themselves aggrieved, oppressed, and fraudulently deprived of their most sacred rights, we insist that they have immediate admission to all the rights and privileges which belong to them as citizens of the United States.

In entering upon the great work before us, we anticipate no small amount of misconception, misrepresentation, and ridicule; but we shall use every instrumentality within our power to effect our object. We shall employ agents, circulate tracts, petition the State and National legislatures, and endeavor to enlist the pulpit and the press in our behalf. We hope this Convention will be followed by a series of Conventions embracing every part of the country.

The following resolutions were discussed by Lucretia Mott, Thomas and Mary Ann McClintock, Amy Post, Catharine A. F. Stebbins, and others, and were adopted:

WHEREAS, The great precept of nature is conceded to be, that "man shall pursue his own true and substantial happiness." Blackstone in his Commentaries remarks, that this law of Nature being coeval with mankind, and dictated by God himself, is of course superior in obligation to any other. It is binding over all the globe, in all countries, and at all times; no human laws are of any validity if contrary to this, and such of them as are valid, derive all their force, and all their validity, and all their authority, mediately and immediately, from this original; therefore;

Resolved, That such laws as conflict, in any way, with the true and substantial happiness of woman, are contrary to the great precept of nature and of no validity, for this is "superior in obligation to any other."

Resolved, That all laws which prevent woman from occupying such a station in society as her conscience shall dictate, or which place her in a position inferior to that of man, are contrary to the great precept of nature, and therefore of no force or authority.

Resolved, That woman is man's equal—was intended to be so by the Creator, and the highest good of the race demands that she should be recognized as such.

Resolved, That the women of this country ought to be enlightened in regard to the laws under which they live, that they may no longer publish their degradation by declaring themselves satisfied with their present position, nor their ignorance by asserting that they have all the rights they want.

Resolved, That inasmuch as man, while claiming for himself intellectual superiority, does accord to woman moral superiority, it is preeminently his duty to encourage her to speak and teach, as she has an opportunity, in all religious assemblies.

Resolved, That the same amount of virtue, delicacy, and refinement of behavior that is required of woman in the social state, should also be required of man, and the same transgressions should be visited with equal severity on both man and woman.

Resolved, That the objection of indelicacy and impropriety, which is so often brought against woman when she addresses a public audience, comes with a very ill-grace from those who encourage, by their attendance, her appearance on the stage, in the concert, or in feats of the circus.

Resolved, That woman has too long rested satisfied in the circumscribed limits which corrupt customs and a perverted application of the Scriptures have marked out for her, and that it is time she should move in the enlarged sphere which her great Creator has assigned her.

Resolved, That it is the duty of the women of this country to secure to themselves their sacred right to the elective franchise.

Resolved, That the equality of human rights results necessarily from the fact of the identity of the race in capabilities and responsibilities.

Resolved, therefore, That, being invested by the Creator with the same capabilities, and the same consciousness of responsibility for their exercise, it is demonstrably the right and duty of woman, equally with man, to promote every righteous cause by every righteous means; and especially in regard to the great subjects of morals and religion, it is self-evidently her right to participate with her brother in teaching them, both in private and in public, by writing and by speaking, by any instrumentalities proper to be used, and in any assemblies proper to be held; and this being a self-evident

truth growing out of the divinely implanted principles of human nature, any custom or authority adverse to it, whether modern or wearing the hoary sanction of antiquity, is to be regarded as a self-evident falsehood, and at war with mankind.

At the last session Lucretia Mott offered and spoke to the following resolution:

Resolved, That the speedy success of our cause depends upon the zealous and untiring efforts of both men and women, for the overthrow of the monopoly of the pulpit, and for the securing to woman an equal participation with men in the various trades, professions, and commerce.

Married Women's Property Acts, New York State, 1848 and 1860

I ronically, the first married women's property acts, passed in Mississippi in 1839 and in New York in 1848, were supported by many male legislators out of a desire to preserve the estates of married daughters against spendthrift sons-in-law. Four out of the five sections of the Mississippi act broadened the rights of married women over their own slaves.

Note the limits of the 1848 New York law, and the ways in which women's rights were extended by the 1860 revision. This pattern—of an initial statute that offered married women very modest control over property, followed by subsequent revisions that slowly and very gradually extended their claims—was typical of virtually all states. Under coverture, husbands had property rights in their wives' services, and state legislatures were reluctant to erase these rights. These "services" included the right of "consortium"—understood as including not only housekeeping but also love, affection, companionship, and sexual relations. If a married woman were injured by the negligence of another person, her husband could sue for damages, which included a monetary estimate of the worth of his loss of consortium. A married woman had a right to financial support from her husband but no right to consortium, and if he were injured she had no claim for the loss of his companionship and sexual relations. This imbalance between the sexes in marriage was rarely tested, but when it was—in the case of major accidents—the impact was severe. Not until the early 1950s was a married woman successful in making such a claim (in Washington, D.C., in 1950; in Iowa in 1951) and the states were very slow to recognize it. Feminist lawyers, men and women, pressed the claim throughout the 1970s and 1980s, but not until the 1990s could it be said that all states recognized it.

Laws of the State of New-York, Passed at the Seventy-First Session of the Legislature . . . (Albany, 1848), pp. 307–8; *Laws of the State of New York, Passed at the Eighty-Third Session of the Legislature* . . . (Albany, 1860), pp. 157–59.

The nineteenth-century Married Women's Property Acts were narrowly interpreted. For example, although married women were authorized to "carry on any trade or business, and perform any labor or services on her sole or separate account," that authorization was regularly interpreted as applying only when her work was not done on family property. When Mary Ann Brooks, a married woman with a part-time job outside the home, was injured when hit by Adolphus Schwerin's horse and wagon in the early 1870s, she brought suit in her own name for damages. The New York court approved her suit to the limits of her lost wages, but she did not have the right to sue for her inability to perform housework in her own home. For that, Mr. Brooks would have to sue. In some states, when a woman purchased property with her own earnings, she would have to register it in the county courthouse if she wished to assert control over it; if she neglected to register, it could be seized for the payment of her husband's debts, as one Mrs. Odell of Davenport, Iowa, discovered when the piano she had bought with her own money and had shipped at great expense from Chicago was seized when her husband's business went bankrupt.* A married woman could rarely make claims for her earnings within the family; deep into the twentieth century, farm women had no legal claim to the "butter and egg money" that custom encouraged them to talk about as theirs because they did the hard work of the barn and the chicken coop.

1848

The real and personal property of any female [now married and] who may hereafter marry, and which she shall own at the time of marriage, and the rents issues and profits thereof shall not be subject to the disposal of her husband, nor be liable for his debts, and shall continue her sole and separate property, as if she were a single female. . . .

It shall be lawful for any married female to receive, by gift, grant, devise or bequest, from any person other than her husband and hold to her sole and separate use, as if she were a single female, real and personal property, and the rents, issues and profits thereof, and the same shall not be subject to the disposal of her husband, nor be liable for his debts. . . .

1860

[The provisions of the law of 1848 were retained, and others were added:]
A married woman may bargain, sell, assign, and transfer her separate personal property, and carry on any trade or business, and perform any labor or services on her sole and separate account, and the earnings of any married woman from her trade . . . shall be her sole and separate property, and may be used or invested by her in her own name. . . .

Any married woman may, while married, sue and be sued in all matters having relation to her . . . sole and separate property . . . in the same manner as if she were sole. And any married woman may bring and maintain an action in her own name, for damages, against any person or body corporate, for any injury to her person or character, the same as if she were sole; and the money received upon the settlement . . . shall be her sole and separate property.

No bargain or contract made by any married woman, in respect to her sole and separate property . . . shall be binding upon her husband, or render him or his property in any way liable therefor.

Every married woman is hereby constituted and declared to be the joint guardian of her children, with her husband, with equal powers, rights, and duties in regard to them, with the husband. . . .

*Brooks v. Schwerin, 54 N.Y. 343 (1873); Odell & Updegraff v. Lee & Kinnard et al., 14 Iowa 411 (1868).

Sojourner Truth's Visiting Card, 1864

Sojourner Truth (ca. 1797–1883) is better known in the twentieth century for words she did not utter—"ar'n't I a woman?"—than for her fierce and exemplary insistence on asserting her rights to express her religious convictions and to speak and act publicly. This portrait, made in a photographer's studio around 1864, depicts the reformer standing, with her hat, shawl, walking stick, and traveling bag, as if on the brink of departing for yet another speaking engagement. It is in the genre of *cartes de visite* (visiting cards), which were very popular in the mid-nineteenth century, both among middle-class women making social calls and as forms of publicity used by politicians, writers, and fund-raisers. As the card's inscription explains, Sojourner Truth sold copies of the card to support herself; her biographer Nell Irvin Painter reports that she charged the common market price of thirty-three cents per card.

I SELL THE SHADOW TO SUPPORT THE SUBSTANCE.
SOJOURNER TRUTH.

Entered according to Act of Congress, in the year 1864, by S. T. in the clerk's office of the U.S. District court, for Eastern District of Michigan. (Courtesy Sophia Smith Collection, Smith College, Northhampton, Mass.)

She was born into slavery as Isabella in the region north of New York City and south of Albany; her first language was Dutch, and in later life her fluent English would have a Dutch accent. As a child she had four different masters; when she married it was under an 1809 New York State law that recognized slave marriages and the legitimacy of children born to married couples, but Isabella's owner chose her husband for her. When Isabella achieved her freedom six months before New York's gradual emancipation law went into effect on July 4, 1827, she owed no further service, but her five children, born after 1799, remained bound—boys until they reached the age of twenty-eight, girls until they reached twenty-five. As indentured servants, her son would not be free until 1849, her daughters not until 1850 and 1851. Around the time Isabella became free, her owner sold her five-year-old son, Peter, to his brother, who resold the boy to another brother, who resold him yet again to a brother-in-law who took him to Alabama where slavery was permanent and legal. Newly freed, Isabella had the confidence to take the matter to court; with financial and legal support from prominent Quakers and Dutch men for whom she worked, she won her suit and his freedom. Her seven-year-old son returned covered with scars from violent whippings. His sisters remained bound to service.

In 1828 Isabella moved to New York City where she found work as a domestic servant. She joined an unorthodox Methodist church and then a radical religious commune; she made a reputation as a preacher at camp meetings. In 1843 divine inspiration directed her to take the name Sojourner Truth and become an itinerant preacher; she made her way up the Connecticut River Valley to Massachusetts, where she joined the Utopian Northampton Association, an abolitionist commune that had recently been founded by William Lloyd Garrison's sister and brother-in-law, Sarah and George Benson. Garrison himself was a frequent visitor; Frederick Douglass, a former slave and articulate abolitionist, was another. They drew her into abolitionist lecture tours and women's rights meetings. Indeed, she spoke at the first national women's rights convention, in Worcester, Massachusetts, held little more than a year after Seneca Falls and featuring some of the same leading participants, including Elizabeth Cady Stanton.

In 1850 Sojourner Truth dictated her life history to Olive Gilbert, a close friend of Sarah Benson; she paid for its publication and supported herself by selling copies of *The Narrative of Sojourner Truth* wherever she traveled, updating it throughout her long life.

Sojourner Truth spoke the words that would make her famous at a women's rights convention attended by hundreds of women and men in Akron, Ohio, in the summer of 1851. Contemporary newspapers reported various versions of what they agreed was powerful oratory: "I have heard much about the sexes being equal: I can carry as much as any man, and can eat as much too, if I can get it. . . . As for intellect, all I can say is, if a woman have a pint and a man a quart—why cant she have her little pint full? You need not be afraid to give us our rights for fear we will take too much,—for we cant take more than our pint'll hold. . . . I cant read, but I can hear. I have heard the bible and have learned that Eve caused man to sin. Well if woman upset the world, do give her a chance to set it right side up again."

But no contemporary witness noted her speaking the refrain "Ar'n't I a woman?" Historians agree that was added a dozen years later by Frances Dana Gage, a women's rights activist who had been at the Akron meeting, and who wrote a highly dramatized and elaborated version of the event, which underscored

Truth's strength and authority. Gage's version was reprinted by Elizabeth Cady Stanton and Susan B. Anthony in the first volume of *The History of Woman Suffrage* (1881) and from there found its way into widespread use.

Sojourner Truth would live until her mid-eighties. She embraced the Union cause during the Civil War, even before Lincoln embraced emancipation. She went door-to-door in Battle Creek, Michigan (where she had moved in the 1850s), to raise money to support the local African American regiment (in which her grandson was enlisted). She traveled from Michigan to Washington, D.C., making campaign speeches for Lincoln's reelection; she met Abraham Lincoln; she worked to help freedpeople find jobs, and she worked for projects to give former enslaved people free land in Kansas. With all this public activity, Sojourner Truth became famous—the "celebrated colored woman"—and visitors made their way to Battle Creek especially to meet her. Cared for by her children and grandchildren, who lived nearby, she died in Battle Creek in 1883.*

Consider how Sojourner Truth presents herself in the photograph here. What does she hope viewers—in her own time and in ours—will conclude about her?

*Nell Irvin Painter, *Sojourner Truth: A Life, A Symbol* (New York: W. W. Norton, 1996), chs. 18, 26; on speaking Dutch, see p. 7; on the *cartes de visite*, see ch. 20; on the ambivalence of the meeting with Lincoln, see ch. 21. See also Carlton Mabee, *Sojourner Truth: Slave, Prophet, Legend* (New York: New York University Press, 1993), and Margaret Washington, *Sojourner Truth's America* (Urbana: University of Illinois Press, 2009).

1. This English print, made between 1785 and 1805, was available for purchase. Anglo-Americans often displayed such prints as we would posters by preserving them in a scrapbook or affixing them to a wall. The multiple architectural features and banners of text were mnemonic (memory-aiding) devices, sending messages of caution and restraint. See how many you can identify! The central figure, whose upper-class status is given away by her fine apparel, is knotting or tatting even as she walks. In the upper left corner, a story unfolds about how indulging in a single vice (drinking) leads to other vices; where is the female protagonist in the final scene? What is the ultimate purpose of women, according to this item of prescriptive literature? (*Keep within Compass*, ca. 1785–1805. Courtesy of the Henry Francis du Pont Winterthur Museum.)

The banner text reads:
THE HERO WHO DEFENDED THE MOTHERS
WILL PROTECT THE DAUGHTERS
DECEM 26 1776

2. This engraving depicts George Washington with the First Regiment of the United States on his way to be inaugurated for his first term as president. Have the women, who fill the public space surrounding Washington and his aides, left the narrow bounds of the compass? They have brought their daughters with them; together they strew his path with flowers. Does the message on the banner acknowledge new political roles for women? (*George Washington on the Bridge at Trenton, New Jersey, 1789.* Courtesy of the Maine Historical Society.)

3. In the antebellum decades, many women embraced reform and benevolence activities, whether through their churches, all-female secular organizations, or ladies' auxiliaries of organizations run by men. They met on planning boards composed of women only, and when they spoke to large gatherings the audience was usually composed of women. By limiting their colleagues to women, they did not compete directly with men, and escaped some—but not all—severe criticism for stepping out of their appropriate sphere of activity. Only a minority of radical women, fiercely devoted to abolishing slavery, resolutely stepped outside the boundaries of the compass to agitate and speak in what critics derided as "promiscuous assemblies," meaning public gatherings that included women and men. (For women's antislavery petitions to Congress, see pp. 213–221.)

A year after its founding in 1837, the Pennsylvania Anti-Slavery Society opened its membership to women. Thereafter, women were integrated into the organization's leadership, as this image of the Executive Committee in 1850 or 1851 makes clear. Many on the committee, including the Motts and Sarah Pugh, were deeply involved in woman's suffrage, as well as belonging to multiple abolition groups. Those standing in the rear, from left to right, are Mary Grew, E. M. Davis, Haworth Wetherfield, Abby Kimber, J. Miller McKim, and Sarah Pugh; those seated, from left to right, are Oliver Johnson, Margaret Jones Burleigh, Benjamin C. Bacon, Robert Purvis, Lucretia Mott, and James Mott. (Phototype reproduction by Frederick F. Gutekunst, Jr. Courtesy of the Sophia Smith Collection, Smith College. For more on the image and its subjects, see "An Anti-Slavery Group of 1850," *Friends' Intelligencer,* Oct, 24, 1896, p. 732. We thank Sherrill Redmon of the Sophia Smith Collection and Christopher Densmore of the Friends Historical Library for their counsel and assistance in finding and identifying this image.)

WASHINGTON, D. C.—THE JUDICIARY COMMITTEE OF THE HOUSE OF REPRESENTATIVES RECEIVING A DEPUTATION OF FEMALE SUFFRAGISTS, JANUARY 11TH—A LADY DELEGATE READING HER ARGUMENT IN FAVOR OF WOMAN'S VOTING, ON THE BASIS OF THE FOURTEENTH AND FIFTEENTH CONSTITUTIONAL AMENDMENTS.—SEE PAGE 242.

4. Printing technology improved markedly, and costs were lowered in the nineteenth century. Daily newspapers proliferated, as did magazines. Including illustrations became an important marketing strategy. Here, in the wake of the Civil War, a "female delegation" appears before the House Judiciary Committee to argue that the Fourteenth and Fifteenth amendments provided the constitutional basis for women to vote.

A few decades earlier, women's petitions to Congress were often tabled; women's bodies were allowed only in the spectator galleries. Women had to go to great lengths to have their voices reach male legislators. For example, in the 1850s, Susan B. Anthony repackaged an 1854 speech that Elizabeth Cady Stanton had given at the New York State Women's Rights Convention as a pamphlet retitled "Address . . . to the Legislature of New York." Copies were placed on the legislators' desks. But not until 1860 did Stanton actually speak in person to the legislature, and it was not until after the Civil War that a standing committee of the U.S. Congress took women's testimony.

This illustration shows Victoria Woodhull reading a statement on January 11, 1871, to members of the House Judiciary Committee. The room is filled by other women who spoke—Susan B. Anthony and Isabella Beecher Hooker (Harriet Beecher Stowe's sister)—and other women who had come to support them. Elizabeth Cady Stanton is sitting behind Woodhull's left elbow; would you recognize her from the photograph on page 222, taken more than twenty years before? The men in the room included some who supported woman suffrage, among them Albert Gallatin Riddle, a former congressman and leading Washington lawyer. The occasion was timed to coordinate with a national convention, which drew dozens of woman suffrage activists to Washington.

The journalist who reported the occasion used a patronizing tone typical of the era and a wide range of metaphors: "Miss Victoria C. Woodhull led her women-at-arms into the committee-room. . . . Among the warriors present were . . . Mrs. Stanton . . . [and] lesser lights. Shortly after ten o'clock Miss Victoria C. Woodhull opened the ball . . . Miss Woodhull . . .laid aside her alpine hat [and] pulled out a paper. . . . in which she took far higher ground than has usually been assumed by her coadjutors. Her sex's right of suffrage [already exists,] she claims, . . . without [the need for an additional] Amendment."

During the days that followed, women delegates to the convention lobbied members of Congress "with a ferocity never known before." They tallied their supporters carefully, counted approximately sixty votes on their side from the 243–member House of Representatives, and predicted victory in five years. ("The Feminine Invasion of the Capitol," *Frank Leslie's Illustrated Newspaper* 31, no. 801 (Feb. 4, 1871): 347, 349.)

5. Elizabeth Cady Stanton's daughter Harriot Stanton Blatch led New York City suffragists to adopt the tactic of annual parades as a way of making support for the vote visible. In 1910 some 400 women marched to Union Square, where 10,000 people gathered to hear the speakers; by 1912 it was estimated that there were 10,000 *marchers*. This was a time of transition for the movement from community organizing on a small scale to raising substantial amounts of money for more visible activities such as renting large halls for meetings, publishing and distributing newspapers, and hiring lobbyists and organizers who would make politics their profession. The ability to organize a major parade—which involved building speakers' platforms and hiring bands—was a mark of the maturity and newfound power of the movement. On October 23, 1915, a week before a state referendum on women's suffrage (and almost the 100th anniversary of Elizabeth Cady Stanton's birth), New York suffragists sponsored the parade shown in this dramatic photograph. Well over 25,000 women and 2,500 men marched; at least four times that many watched from sidewalks.

Women had won the right to serve as poll watchers for this special election, to guard against corruption by observing the counting of the ballots. The New York amendment was defeated by the relatively narrow margin of 250,000 votes. ("Suffrage Parade, New York City, October 23, 1915." Courtesy of George Grantham Bain Collection, LT 11052-4, Library of Congress, Prints and Photographs Division Washington, D.C.)

6. In his second successful campaign for the presidency, Woodrow Wilson promised—vaguely—to support woman suffrage. In January 1917, Alice Paul and the National Woman's Party undertook a permanent demonstration—a picket line—in front of the White House, near the gates, to hold the president to his promise. Their silent protest was modeled on the campaigns of British suffragists and may have been the first use of this political strategy in the United States. To provoke continued press attention and to represent the widespread support for the cause, Paul ingeniously arranged for themed days. First came State days—Maryland was first—in which the pickets came exclusively from the given state. On College Day, the one represented in this photograph, thirteen women wore sashes announcing their alma maters. On the afternoon of Wilson's second inaugural, March 4, 1,000 women, in a freezing rain, encircled the White house in one long, marching line, with the pictures and story generating unprecedented press coverage.

In April, with Congress about to declare war and the pickets' banners offering sharp political jibes, the strategy proved divisive among women's rights advocates. Some called the tactic indecorous, insulting to the president, and close to treasonous. Press commentary grew shrill, and the crowds gathered to heckle the "silent sentinels" grew violent; banners were torn to shreds. Arrests followed, in April and on into the fall—not of the attackers but of the pickets for "obstructing sidewalk traffic." These women accepted jail or workhouse terms rather than pay the $25 fine; and on release, they returned defiantly to the picket line.

The cycle of peaceful protest and violent response intensified in August, when the picketers provocatively carried banners mocking "Kaiser Wilson" and highlighting the contradiction between the U.S. policies of criticizing the kaiser for denying democracy in Germany and denying the vote to the half of the U.S. population. In the fall, jailed picketers, including Alice Paul, went on hunger strikes because they had asked for and been denied political prisoner status. Like British suffragists, they were force-fed—an intrusive act that was painful and medically dangerous. All were released in late November, when local officials anticipated (rightly) that the arrests and detentions would be ruled unconstitutional on appeal.

Meanwhile, the pickets of 1917, the private letters that Wilson received from feminists such as Jane Addams and Carrie Chapman Catt, and the exigencies of war led to a presidential change of mind: in early January 1918, Wilson announced his support for the federal woman suffrage amendment then making its way through Congress. In September, he went to the Senate to urge passage there, presenting the matter as critical to the war effort. However, it would take new elections and a newly constituted Senate for the bill to pass, and another year until ratification (see pp. 416–417). ("College Day in the Picket Line, Feb. 1917," National Women's Party Records, Library of Congress, Washington, D.C., LC-USZ62-31799. See Katherine H. Adams and Michael L. Keene, *Alice Paul and the American Suffrage Campaign* [Urbana: University of Illinois Press, 2007], and the documentary film by Ruth Pollak for the *American Experience* and WGBH, *One Woman, One Vote* [PBS Home Video, 1995; reissued on DVD, 2006], especially the closing episodes.)

7. Women used their vote for a wide range of political expression. The Ku Klux Klan began to recruit women in 1923, not long after the founding of the Klan itself. Many women found the Klan's claims of moral purity appealing; in some localities, Klansmen made themselves useful to white Protestant women by intimidating husbands who engaged in domestic violence. Klanswomen joined in opposing interracial marriage and in linking Catholics, Jews, and African Americans to degeneracy. Believing that immigrants were likely to undermine morality, they supported the exclusion of Asians and the restriction of immigration to Western Europeans. They energetically boycotted anti-Klan business owners and ran for positions on school boards, where they used their influence to fire Catholic and Jewish teachers and distribute Bibles in classes. Within a year of its founding, the Women's Ku Klux Klan claimed more than 250,000 members in each of the forty–eight states. Here they parade proudly down Pennsylvania Avenue in 1928; the U.S. Capitol looms in the background. (Courtesy of the Library of Congress, Prints and Photographs Division, Washington, D.C.)

8. In this photograph, taken sometime between 1935 and 1940, probably in New York City, laundry workers of the International Union, Local 135, strike for better working conditions. The scene reminds us that laundering and domestic service were often the only jobs open to African American women. Rain or no rain, the picture gives us a sense of workers' standards of how to dress when out in public. Look especially at their feet and heads. (Courtesy of the Library of Congress, Prints and Photographs Division, Washington, D.C.)

9. Young Elizabeth Eckford faces the gauntlet of racial heckling and hatred at the Court-ordered integration of schools in Little Rock, Arkansas, in 1957. When the Arkansas governor defied the Supreme Court order, President Dwight Eisenhower reluctantly sent in federal troops to enforce it. Even with military protection, the young people who actually integrated public schools had to put up with racist slurs, harassment, and intimidation that required of them daily displays of uncommon courage and self-possession. Summoning up such courage became commonplace for thousands of rank-and-file African Americans, many of them girls and women. Indeed, it was women who carried the civil rights struggle at the grassroots level, often at considerable risk to their physical safety and even their lives. As this picture makes clear, white women were prominent among the harassers. Other white women worked for integration in practice by keeping the schools open. (Photograph by Will Counts.)

10. This antidraft poster features singer and activist Joan Baez (*far left*) with her sisters, Pauline and Mimi. Proceeds from the poster sales went toward draft resistance for the Vietnam War. At a performance at Madison Square Garden in 1965, Baez told the crowd, "If you feel that to go to war is wrong, then you must say no to the draft. And if young ladies feel it's wrong to kill, then you can say yes to the young men that say no to the draft." In what senses do you think Baez meant women should say yes? Unidentified poster maker, "Girls Say Yes to Boys Who Say No," ca. 1968. Photomechanical lithograph, photograph by Larry Gates. Gift of William Mears. (Courtesy of the National Museum of American History, Smithsonian Institution.)

11. This famous photograph records the ceremonial last mile of the Torch Relay, a feat that ushered in the National Women's Conference in Houston in 1977. The United Nations had declared 1977 International Women's Year (later extending it to a decade), and President Ford had earlier signed legislation spearheaded by Congresswoman Bella Abzug authorizing the expenditure of $5 million to hold a national women's conference as part of the nation's bicentennial observance. Delegates were elected in all fifty states; three First Ladies attended (guess which three); and Maya Angelou read a poem composed for the occasion (one line reads: "We recognize . . . those unknown and unsung women whose strength gave birth to our strength"). The torch, which you see above runner Peggy Kokernot's head, had been carried by a sequence of over 2,000 women runners from Seneca Falls to Texas to symbolize the link between those early feminists who drafted the Declaration of Sentiments and their contemporary counterparts. The complex logistical work behind the relay was undertaken chiefly by the 13,000-member National Association of Girls and Women in Sports. All torchbearers wore bright blue T-shirts with the conference's logo and the relay-inspired slogan, Women on the Move.

The professional photographer who snapped the picture, Diana Mara Henry, recalls: "I was rushing backward as fast as I could in order to get the shot of these proud and happy women energetically marching" to the conference opening.* The mix of women in this front row—by age, ethnic heritage, and national/local prominence—sent a deliberate message about the appeal of feminist principles. Linked arm-in-arm from right to left are Billie Jean King, Susan B. Anthony II (namesake of her great aunt), and Bella Abzug. Next are Houston runners, Sylvia Ortiz, then a college senior, marathon runner Kokernot, and Mechele Cearcy, a high school track star. Next to Cearcy you may recognize Betty Friedan. Rather than an inclusive picture like Henry's, *TIME* chose for its cover a portrait of Peggy Kokernot applauding the proceedings. Why would the magazine editors choose that particular framing?

The Houston conference was a major milestone in feminist organizing and nationwide mobilization. The 20,000 persons at the gathering cheered or jeered the 2,000-plus delegates who, plank by plank, voted on a detailed plan of action geared toward achieving the elusive goal of gender equality. Twenty percent of delegates represented the conservative end of the political spectrum, and although they voted in favor of economic rights planks, they vigorously debated and mostly voted against planks on the equal rights amendment, lesbian rights, and abortion. A bipartisan effort mandated and funded by the U.S. Congress to address issues of concern to ordinary women, this sort of conference has never been repeated.

By the late 1970s, there were no longer strict dress codes for women in public; or, if some groups still believed in them, feminists deliberately flouted them. What range of choices in dress, accoutrements, and symbolic items were these women making? (Photograph copyright © 1978 by Diana Mara Henry.)

---

*Jewish Women's Archive, https://jwa.org/feminism/_html/JWA035.htm.

12. On November 12, 2002, a new woman-initiated grassroots group, CODEPINK, began a four-month vigil in front of the White House as a "pre-emptive strike for peace." Since the days of Alice Paul's radical, extended maneuver to post silent sentinels with banners at Woodrow Wilson's gates, protests at the White House fence had become a familiar part of the political scene. But in fall 1995, after the Oklahoma City bombing, this particular stretch—the block with the front of the White House on one side and Lafayette Park on the other—was closed to vehicular traffic as an antiterrorist precaution. Thus, White House picketers lost their ability to interact with the random public represented by drivers and riders in cars. The women who rotated on vigil duty in the winter before the official start of the war in Iraq chose to wear pink jackets and sport pink umbrellas. Ponder what messages they were sending in making that visually arresting choice, and what scenes in U.S. history they may have been conscious of echoing. The vigil culminated on March 8, 2003, International Women's Day, when over 10,000 activists marched in Washington, D.C., to protest U.S. militarism. In an echo of 1917, 25 women, including the feminist writers Alice Walker, Maxine Hong Kingston, and Susan Griffin, and CODEPINK cofounder Medea Benjamin, were arrested for protesting too close to the White House gates. Compare the details of CODEPINK's staged protest with that of the suffragists in the sixth image of this photo essay. ("Women for Peace." CODEPINK Demonstration at the White House, ca. 2002. Courtesy of CODEPINK.)

CIVIL WAR AND AFTERMATH

STEPHANIE MCCURRY
Women Numerous and Armed: Politics and Policy on the Confederate Home Front

The Civil War profoundly disrupted and reshaped American society; more people died in it than in all America's subsequent wars put together. It tested the stability of the Union and the meaning of democracy. Confederates insisted that their vision of a republic, which rested on racial hierarchy and the subordination of blacks, sustained the same claims to self-determination that had been central to the principles of the Revolution of 1776. The war would involve civilians in novel ways.

Because soldiers were recruited as companies from the same locality, it was not impossible for women to dress as men and enlist; buddies kept their secrets. A conservative estimate is that some 400 women joined in this way. A handful of women crossed military lines as spies, some disguising their race or their gender in the process. Thousands more women were recruited as hospital workers in both North and South; late in the war the Union recruited hundreds of freedwomen for this service. The bureaucracy of the federal government was vastly expanded during the war, and the personnel shortage was solved by hiring, for the first time in U.S. history, women to work in the same offices as men doing similar work.

Throughout the nation, familiar patterns of gender relations were disrupted as in the Revolutionary War, but on a far greater and more frightening scale. In the South, as Stephanie McCurry explains, the departure of white men for war meant that white women of all classes came into a more direct relationship with the government than ever before. Reading the letters and petitions that poured into the Confederate States of America (CSA) offices in Richmond, McCurry argues that a new political class, soldier's wives, suddenly became very visible.

Would you have joined the food riots described here? Create a historically based, imaginary biographical profile for yourself as food rioter and explain your motivations.

What types of southern, white women did not join these crowd actions? Does McCurry convince you that these women's actions changed Confederate policy in fundamental ways? What are examples from other wars around the globe where women's vigorous actions on the home front have had major political impacts?

Excerpted and slightly revised by the author from "Women Numerous and Armed: The Confederate Food Riots in Historical Perspective" by Stephanie McCurry, *OAH Magazine of History* 27, no. 2 (2009), 35–39, and *Confederate Reckoning: Power and Politics in the Civil War South* by Stephanie McCurry (Cambridge, Mass.: Harvard University Press, 2010), 154–55, 167, 192–96, 198–201, 209, 214–17.

The Confederate war ripped like an earthquake through the foundation of Southern life. Its impact registered in every domain from the high reaches of the central state to the intimate recesses of the household. Transformation is the essential characteristic of war because the calling in of obligations fundamentally changes the citizen's relationship to, and expectations of, the state. In the Confederate States of America, the government reached far past the ranks of those white men called upon to serve, to their dependents—the women, children, and slaves who made up the massive unfranchised Southern population. It is not too much to say that the war forged a new understanding of the relationship between citizens and their government, a renegotiation of the social contract. For white women who were not parties to the original contract—as citizens governed in the household state—the impositions and openings the war created were especially historic. When the conflict ended neither the idea of the people nor of the government was the same.

One consequence of war was the reconfiguration of Southern political life, particularly the way power on the home front shifted along gender lines, as white women emerged into authority and even leadership on a range of issues at the heart of popular politics in the Civil War South. The thousands of women's letters to government officials in archives testify to a fundamental shift in the very terms and practices of political representation in the war: the penetration of the state into their household business and also the rearrangement of household relations, local political networks, and modes of communication. Indeed, what these letters convey is the development of new, war-borne individual and collective political identities: chief among them, the "soldier's wife." There were new issues in Civil War politics, and there were also new players.

These developments are not easy to place historically. The key actors are Southern white women, most from yeoman, poor white, or urban laborer households. Their actions had nothing to do with feminism or the women's rights movement, and they were not part of an organized political movement in the institutional sense. They do not fit the usual interpretive categories of women's history or Civil War history, and they cannot be placed in the history of suffrage or Confederate nationalism. These women did not really speak a language of rights or of nationalism. But they made

themselves part of political life nonetheless, reshaping its organization, circuits of power and authority, and discourses of qualification and entitlement, thus redefining the relationship between the state in its various forms and the citizens and subjects it claimed to represent and rule. This was something new and, in the Confederacy at least, it made a difference.

If there had ever been a sense that women were outside politics that kind of thinking was obliterated by the shocking events of 1863. Then, in a wave of food riots, Confederate soldiers' wives impressed their politics on a shocked nation. The riots were spectacular and numerous: at least a dozen violent attacks (there are rumors of more) on stores, government warehouses, army convoys, salt works, railroad depots, and granaries by mobs of women, numbering between twelve and three hundred, armed with navy revolvers, pistols, repeaters, bowie knives, and hatchets. The attacks were carried out in broad daylight in the space of one month between the middle of March and the middle of April 1863: a Confederate spring of soldiers' wives' discontent.

The events were stunning: in their boldness, organization, violence, and in the shrewdness of the rioters' management of public opinion. For whatever mayors and editors said, the public simply assumed that the mobs were composed of soldiers' wives—as if prior developments had prepared them for the actions on the streets—as indeed they had. This was no simple expression of desperation. These were manifestly political events—a highly public expression of soldiers' wives' mass politics of subsistence—events in a women's political history we are just beginning to write.

The wave of riots in 1863 riveted public attention on soldiers' wives and their claims for justice for the Confederate poor, but the riots have a deep backstory, one not often told. It consists of a multitude of attempts by poor women to alert their leaders to the consequences of a conscription policy that eviscerated their livelihoods and violated the pledge made to soldiers that their families would be protected. The South was an agrarian society, whole regions of it populated by yeoman and poor white families. No one had ever imagined that women could make subsistence on those farms without the labor of men. And indeed they could not. By 1863, with husbands and sons in the service, the countryside was stripped of

"Sowing and Reaping: Southern Women Hounding Their Men on to Rebellion . . . South-ern Women Feeling the Effects of Rebellion, and Creating Bread Riots," engraving, 1863. Stephanie McCurry explains that "this illustration, published in Frank Leslie's Illustrated Newspaper *on May 23, 1863, depicts the emerging political power of women on the home front during the Civil War. The left half credits women with helping fill the ranks of the Confederate army, while the right half pictures the epitome of a politically empowered woman, standing defiantly in the midst of a bread riot with one hand clenched into a fist and the other holding a revolver." (Image courtesy of the Library of Congress, Prints and Photographs Division, Washington, D.C.)*

men and the food crisis in the Confederacy would reach starvation proportions.

1862 had seen a bad harvest, and in the following spring the prospect of another bore down on the Confederate States of America (C.S.A.), with public officials, journalists, and citizens alike warning that the situation was dire. In the Mississippi Valley, the drumbeat of battles was near. The Confederacy was still reeling from a series of military disasters in the winter and spring of 1862, the fall of Forts Donelson and Henry at the head of the Tennessee river system and the towns of Nashville, Corinth, and Memphis. Union armies marched steadily southward. As early as May 1862, the governor of Alabama, John Gill Shorter, had pleaded with the secretary of war to delay conscription of yeoman soldiers in northern Alabama, concerned about the suffering of women and children if their men were taken before the grain and provision crops were harvested. Shorter was reacting to a series of letters he had received from soldiers, soldiers' wives, and military commanders describing dire conditions.[1]

Even in the east where General Robert E. Lee continued to hold off far larger Union armies, it is clear that 1863 was a moment in which most civilian and military men alike acknowledged that the war had entered a phase that tested the people and not just the armies. Few denied that home front and military conditions were inextricable. A debate about the equity of conscription had already erupted in the Confederate Congress in August 1862. But in that moment, with Union navies and armies penetrating by river into the very heart of the black belt South, concern for the Confederate poor was overridden by concern about how to maintain control of slaves. Congressmen, overwhelmingly slaveholders themselves, yielded to the demands of planters and the plaintive letters of planter women claiming protection and passed the notorious "twenty-negro law" [by which households owning twenty slaves or more could exempt one adult, white male from conscription]. Defended as a measure that would free up planters and their slaves to grow food for the armies and destitute civilians, the exemption was resisted from the outset as class legislation reflecting the government's blatant preference for the rich and its abandonment of the poor left to fight their wars. "Why not let the poor men stay at home to protect his own family against the slaves of the rich men," Mississippi senator James Phelan raged during the debate. "If we are to have class legislation . . . let's legislate in favor of the poor." But they did not. By December of 1862 public outrage over the law threatened to spill over into civil disobedience and mass desertion. The "twenty-negro law" spoke directly to the dilemma of the slave regime at war: how to protect the property of slaveholders without putting undue service burdens on backcountry yeomen—and on their women, left at home to shoulder the plow.[2]

As the food crisis mounted, yeoman and poor white women inundated politicians with petitions and letters, announcing in the process the formation of a new collective identity in Southern political life: soldiers' wives. "We soldier's wives as sign thare name," or more poignantly, as in another, "Mary Tisinger with 6 chilrin, soldier wife," "Mary Stilwell, soldiers widow 6 children," and so on down the list of signatures. Every woman who signed—there were twenty-three in this particular petition to the secretary of war—specified her identity in terms of the family relation to men in military service and the sacrifice made to the cause. For women identified as "soldier's wife," or sometimes just "sw," so obvious was the shorthand, sacrifice was grounds for entitlement, with the soldier's wife a critical new identity in relation to the state. At first, in 1862, the letters just begged for individual relief such as the release of a husband from the army. But by 1863 the correspondence had grown increasingly threatening, demanding a change

in government policies and justice for the Confederate poor. What emerges from the archives is a portrait of a political class coming into being.[3]

By 1863 soldiers' wives were legion in the Confederate states, as much a product of the draft as their soldier husbands. As a social group they were an index to the rapid process of state formation underway in the C.S.A. and to the problems faced by a slave regime at war. With 40 percent of its adult male population enslaved and unavailable for military service, the Davis administration had no choice but to dig ever deeper into the ranks of the male citizenry, mobilizing an estimated 75 to 85 percent of adult white men (in contrast to the Union's 50 percent).[4] In addition to conscription, the C.S.A. adopted a highly centralized taxation policy to feed and clothe the army. In April 1863 the Congress passed the infamous one-tenth tax or tithe, as it was called, which required citizens to surrender one-tenth of everything grown and raised on their farms and plantations beyond what was required for subsistence. The tax was to be paid in-kind, which required tax collectors, TIK men as they were called, to go into each household, farm, workshop, and plantation and remove part of everything produced there. It was not only onerous, it was highly intrusive, forcing ordinary men and, more often, women into regular confrontations with government agents. To poor soldiers' wives, the 10 percent tax was, quite literally, an impossible burden, the very difference between an eked-out subsistence and starvation. "They are gathering everything they can of the poor soldiers' wives and children," C. W. Walker protested to her governor about the TIK men in her community. "They are as grate enemys as the yankies."[5] Along with a stringent tax collection policy, conscription thickened the network of extraction and bureaucracy within which ordinary citizens, including women, became enmeshed. Tax and conscription agents were everywhere.

Left at home, women suffered under, and protested, the onslaught. The particular conditions were evident in the content of the politics they forged. The nexus of issues women agitated against—from the government's manpower policies, soldiers' wages, government prices for women's work, federal taxes, monetary policy, to inadequacy of relief—were as comprehensive as the struggle to sustain life itself. Together these issues constituted what we might call "a politics of subsistence." It took shape on the farms and in households of the rural and urban South, as poor white women struggled to scrape out subsistence absent the labor or wages of husbands and grown sons.

Up from the farmsteads, workshops, settlements, country towns, and cities came a tidal wave of protest and resistance, much of it from women in their newly useful identity as soldiers' wives. "As gustic [justice] belongs to the people," one woman memorably put it, "let us have it." Political danger loomed, not least in the easy way poor white women came to speak in the collective voice—for soldiers' wives, for nonslaveholders, or, more generally, for the poor. Clerks in government offices confronted with documents signed by large numbers of women must have wondered about the political backstory. How was the petition organized? Did someone carry it around the neighborhood? Was it written at a mass meeting? We do not know. We do know that there was no political institution or national or state organization behind them, and there were no preprinted forms as in Union women's antislavery petition drive. But in the winter and spring of 1863, as internal correspondence in the War Department confirmed the looming food crisis, the content of the mail bags made it clear that women were coming together to demand action.[6]

Nowhere was that more clear than in North Carolina, where the Gov. Zebulon Vance, was perceived as a sympathetic figure. He had already received threatening letters, including one that concluded a typical account of how women cannot "make support for ther familys" by warning that "the women talk of Making up Companys going to try to make peace." And then there was an anonymous letter that landed on Vance's desk exactly six weeks before the wave of food riots broke out in nearby Salisbury; the letter came from "a company" of women in Bladen County who called themselves "Reglators." The term was calculated to place the authors in the state's long (formerly male) tradition of rural justice and direct action. They would have corn at two dollars a bushel or they would seize it, the women informed Vance matter-of-factly in the opening line: "the time has come that we the comon people has to hav bread or blood and we are bound boath men and women to hav it or die in the attempt." The letter bore all the hallmarks of rural soldiers' wives' protests expressed in hundreds, maybe thousands, of other letters written in the Southern states by the end of the war. Even so, the cry of bread or blood—which would echo across the C.S.A. a few weeks later—was new. The Reglators laid out the crisis of subsistence that soldiers' wives faced: the erosion of household independence with the conscription of their men; the impossible equation between privates' pay and the prices planter speculators demanded for food; the need for the state to set prices in the interest of the poor. To that list the Reglators added a far more radical view of the war as a species of class warfare. This group was prepared to take matters into their own hands. "Sir," they told Vance, "we has sons, brothers an husbands now fighting for the big mans negro and we are determined to have bread out of their barns or we will slaughter as we go." Violence, or so they said, was part of the soldiers' wives' political repertoire.[7]

The food riots did not come out of nowhere. They were, rather, the most dramatic manifestation of poor white women's mass politics of subsistence. So while there is a long tradition of rough justice in which they might be seen, there is also a more immediate and local context: a mass movement of Confederate women, empowered as soldiers' wives, largely confined to nonviolent protest—and an emboldened minority who crossed the line from threats to violent direct action.

The food riot in Richmond was the biggest but not the first. The first was Atlanta, on March 16, 1863, then in Salisbury, North Carolina, then on the next day in Mobile, Alabama, and Petersburg, Virginia, and Richmond on April 2. "Bread or blood," the Richmond women notoriously shouted—a trademark cry already seen in Reglators' written threats and on the banners of Mobile's army of women (as one participant described them).[8]

Everything about the riots in Atlanta and elsewhere shows the connections between violent new developments and the local political culture of Confederate soldiers' wives. In Atlanta, the fifteen or twenty women who collected "in a body" and proceeded to sack provisions stores began and finished with speeches to the merchant and the public about the "impossibility of females in their condition" paying the asking price for the necessities of life. In Salisbury, the next day, when another mob of forty or fifty women mounted armed attacks on about seven merchant establishments, they justified their actions in the same language soldiers' wives used in their petitions. "We Governor are all soldiers' wives or mothers," Mary Moore, a member of the mob petitioned the governor for leniency, appealing "for protection and a remedy of these evils." Though criminal, the women's actions were effective. Moore admitted that they had stolen food and money at gun point—twenty-three barrels of flour, two sacks of salt, half a barrel of molasses, and twenty dollars in cash—but cast the riot as the seizure only of what was rightly owed to the people whose claims the women had decided to enforce. "Now Sir, this is all we have done" she finished. Moore's defense of the Salisbury women's mob action confidently tapped an idea about the social contract with soldiers and their wives that went deep in popular political culture and expressed a sense of entitlement that was clearly historic. What was owed to soldiers' wives? As in Salisbury, few argued with the women's view.[9]

After the actions in Atlanta and Salisbury came riots in Mobile, Petersburg, and Macon, Georgia—five or more in the space of two weeks. Then activity in Richmond and beyond. It was a strikingly coherent series of events, each organized and pulled off locally (as far as we know), yet so closely spaced, so similar in pattern that there was wild speculation about the connections. By the time the wave crested in Richmond, conspiracy theories abounded. "That they are the emissaries of the Federal Government it is ... difficult to doubt" ventured the *Richmond Daily Examiner*. Such seemingly connected and highly organized events were far beyond the capacity of mere women. This had to be the work of professionals: Yankee operatives.[10]

In its respect for the level of organization achieved, the conspiracy theory, in fact, speaks powerfully to the political capacity of women. As the evidence accrued—a result of the Richmond city government's decision to pursue criminal charges—the Confederate public learned just how the riot was organized and pulled off. In other riots there are suggestions of prior organization—the way women (whether twelve or fifty) just materialized "in a body" at a particular, apparently predesignated time and place with banners, slogans, and speeches at the ready. In Richmond the sheer numbers—an estimated three hundred women followed by a crowd of about one thousand—confirm there was a plan.

Richmond puts to rest all questions about Confederate women's political ability. As shocking as it surely was to many, what came out in court testimony was indisputable evidence that the riot on April 2 was a highly organized event, planned for at least ten days and, despite widespread assertions that it was instigated by men, that it was, in fact, the work of Mary Jackson, soldier's mother, farm wife, and huckster in meat in Richmond's Second Market. Mary Jackson and about three hundred women planned and pulled off the biggest civilian riot in Confederate history.[11]

The Richmond riot offers a stunning portrait of poor white women's mass political mobilization. Recruiting apparently began around March 22, 1863, with Jackson organizing "a meeting of the women in relation to the high prices." Jackson's networks were rural as well as urban. Witnesses reported a stream of women coming in from the country the day before, joining women in the market where Jackson worked and at government clothing factories in town. More than three hundred women turned up for the planning in the Belvidere Baptist Church on Oregon Hill on April 1. "All were women there except two boys," one witness explained. By all accounts it was a rowdy meeting. Jackson was clearly in command. In a stunning assumption of male authority she "went up into the pulpit" to address the meeting and to issue instructions. "She didn't want the women to go along the streets like a parcel of heathens," one woman testified later, "but to go quietly to the stores and demand goods at government prices and if the merchants didn't grant their demand to break open the stores and take the goods." Jackson told the women to meet the next morning at nine a.m., to leave their children at home, and to come armed.[12]

As unusual and violent as the riot was, Jackson and the women who planned it were products of the same politics of subsistence as the mass of Confederate soldiers' wives. Jackson literally so. John Jones, a clerk in the War Department, knew her from her "frequent application at the war office for the discharge of her son." Before Jackson took to the streets, in other words, she had been one of the mass of ordinary petitioning Confederate women. Her strategy for the riot also suggests as much. In insisting that rioters first make an offer of government price for the goods they planned to seize and in first seeking an audience with the governor to air their grievances (an inspired bit of political choreography)—she showed the group's deep investment in the ideas and practices of white women's wartime political culture. The women had guns, but they also had a public relations strategy.[13]

Still, violence was planned for from the beginning. Jackson was seen with a bowie knife and six-barreled pistol as she left the market on the morning of the riot. When the mob surged out of Capitol Square, marching silently as Jackson had instructed, the women were heavily armed with domestic implements and the rejected contents of an old armory, as one witness described. For a good two hours they wreaked havoc on the streets of Richmond, targeting known speculators, smashing their way into stores with hatchets and axes, looting at gunpoint, and loading stolen goods onto wagons they impressed on the street. At least twelve stores were looted before the public guard was called out and, threatening to fire on the rioters, managed to quell the activity. Among those caught in the subsequent dragnet were otherwise unknown women such as Mary Duke, a soldiers' wife, left at home with four children and her husband in Robert E. Lee's army. The ringleaders, including Mary Jackson, were also caught; she was picked up around noon in a mob of women trying to break into a store, still unbowed, brandishing a bowie knife, saying "bread or blood."[14]

There would be more riots in 1863—six at least—and they also played out in violent form the politics of subsistence that soldiers' wives had forged. In all of them, women's anger was turned as much against government officials as against merchants and planters and had as much to do with the inadequacy of welfare as with speculation. That was one of the critical policy implications of the women's riots and is the chief measure of their efficacy in Confederate politics and policy. It was really only after—and in response to—the riots that local, state, and (to a lesser extent) federal officials undertook a systematic reform and extension of the traditional antebellum system of delivering relief.

In many places city officials promised aid even as rioters ran in the streets. In Atlanta, a group of gentlemen expressed a deep sympathy for the ladies by raising a fund for their relief. In Richmond, Governor John Letcher appeared in the midst of the action promising to distribute food. All of the city councils and Southern legislatures—even the Confederate Congress, which had long regarded social provision as the domain of the states—quickly took it up as a matter of public policy.[15]

The quantities of money involved varied from the local and small to the state and significant in terms of budget share. All the governments in the C.S.A. were highly strapped. Carving out significant chunks of money for welfare thus had to be a huge political priority. In the cities the aid poured in and took numerous forms. In Mobile the city council appropriated $15,000, created a Citizen Relief Committee to scour the countryside for food, and thereafter attended carefully to ensuring the provision of food at reasonable prices to the poor. In Richmond, the mayor formed a citywide committee to investigate the needs of soldiers' dependents. By April 13 the city council had written and passed new laws establishing a free market in food for the poor.[16]

On the level of the states, the response was also direct, nowhere with more urgency than in Georgia, where governor Joseph Brown jumped into action. Just nine days after the Atlanta food riot, he called the legislature back into session early and delivered the blunt message that in whole sections of the state where land was cultivated almost entirely by white labor, "the women and children are destitute of bread." Action was imperative: "the great question in this revolution is now a question of *bread*," he bellowed. Brown delivered property tax exemptions, free salt, free corn, and so much aid in money to the counties that, as a share of the state budget, it almost equaled that expended on wartime military costs. The legislature appropriated $2.5 million in 1863, $6 million in 1864, and $8 million in 1865 to "assist soldiers' families, the children and widows of deceased soldiers and disabled veterans," although it was never enough.[17]

In North Carolina a new law passed in 1863 was titled "Act for the Relief of the Wives and Families of Soldiers in the Army." The state funded that act to the tune of $1 million a year, although the treasurer often struggled to meet the fiscal obligations. At the local level, a considerable number of people and amounts of money passed through the system. In Orange County, 508 women and 735 children were on the rolls in late 1863; by 1865 more than 600 women and 800 children, 20 percent of the adult female population of the county and a whopping 35 percent of the white children. In

Duplin County even more white women met the official criterion of indigence, meaning "not enough food to sustain life." In the terrible year that spanned November 1863 to November 1864, agents in Randolph County collected and disbursed roughly $55,000, most of it distributed in small amounts. Local committeemen received detailed instructions: "the allowance for each *woman* shall not exceed three dollars per month, children under eight years of age, one dollar and fifty cents," one set read. "Needy fathers" and widows and children of deceased soldiers were to "receive the same as a lone woman." Indeed, as the court instructions assumed, women constituted the vast bulk of recipients of relief and received most of the welfare dollars. Clearly, the unprecedented expansion of state welfare was a political response to the mobilization of the yeoman and poor white women of the Confederacy. And that new welfare system was made in the image of the soldier's wife.[18]

Poor white Southern women kept themselves on the political agenda through local activism until the last days of the war, mobilizing to secure the entitlements already established. Whether they liked it or not—and most didn't—local officials were accountable to the women, forced to treat them as significant members of the political constituency they had been elected or appointed to serve. Poor white women, for their part, had learned how to hold the men accountable, how to make the system respond to their needs to some extent, to insist on a measure of self-representation. All of which is to say that they had entered fully into the practice of politics in the Civil War South.

In 1857 Supreme Court Justice Roger Taney had been able to define citizenship without any reference to women.[19] The architects of the Confederacy had been able to effect secession and declare war without their consent. But war had expanded the terms of consent and legitimacy, created new political identities, expanded the concept of the body politic, widened the conception of citizenship, rerouted the paths of power and patronage, and engendered new political subjects and constituencies. This war, the Confederate war, had its own unexpected developments, the significance of which intensifies in light of the original Confederate vision. Far from perfecting the republic of white men, fixing forever the exclusion of black and female dependents, the war had proved its undoing,

most unpredictably, perhaps, in the way it brought white women—especially poor white women—to a position of unquestionable salience in Confederate politics.

That much was strangely confirmed in 1866 when the North Carolina legislature (like a lot of other states) wiped the docket clean of all political crimes left over from the war by passing a blanket amnesty law that initially covered the political acts of soldiers. Three months later, with a docket still stacked with cases of women who had made "raids upon any county, state or Confederate States Commissaries or Quartermasters, or other person or persons," they extended the amnesty to include women, writing into law an explicit recognition of women's "crimes" as political acts. In doing so they offered an official acknowledgment of women as political subjects.[20]

It would be tempting to cast this history of Confederate women as an episode in the history of citizenship in the United States, to slot it into the dominant liberal framework of American political history by which disfranchised people progressively claimed citizenship and its attendant rights. But there is evidence supporting a less predictable interpretive approach. "Citizen" was a term rarely used by soldiers' wives. Unlike the masses of female petitioners who sought the abolition of slavery in the Union (see pp. 213–221, Zaeske's essay), Confederate soldiers' wives did not move to make their claims based on perceived rights as citizens of the nation. As an explicitly proslavery nation in conception and design, the C.S.A. had a deep investment in limiting democracy, and it was committed, as a matter of ideology, to the exclusion of free women and enslaved men and women from political life. White women occupied a peculiar position in that, unlike slaves, they did have civil standing as citizens. But not only did they lack the attendant political rights; most of the legal and civil rights of the married majority were vitiated by coverture. Fundamentally shaped by this state of affairs, Confederate soldiers' wives, in entering the political arena, did not—could not—advance a universal claim to the equal rights of citizens. That lay entirely outside the politics of the possible.[21]

But if Confederate soldiers' wives cannot simply be cast as a chapter in American political history as we usually tell it, they might prompt us to rethink the story outside national boundaries. For the mobilization of poor, mostly rural women in the Confederate South during the Civil War bears resemblance far more to the way politics was practiced by poor rural and urban people in the modern world: what one historian has called the politics of the governed. Indeed, in some respects Confederate women's behavior is so like that of the poor in twentieth-century India that it reminds us that the strategies of the governed (including violence) are needful and practiced—perhaps particularly by women—not just in non-Western, postcolonial societies but also in modern Western nation-states as well, long after the formal introduction of so-called universal suffrage, which meant, of course, suffrage only for men.[22]

Seen in this broad context, the situation as it unfolded in Confederate political life was strikingly like that in other modern, formally democratic societies in which the mass of people are "not proper members of civil society," have no right of representation or to hold office, but manage nonetheless to mobilize as particular communities to influence government policy in their favor. Unable to participate in political life as equal citizens, they instead take categories the state uses to govern the population—refugees, the poor, or "soldiers' wives"—and infuse them with moral content. In doing so, they effectively invest those categories with the imaginative possibilities of community and produce a new rhetoric of political claims. Although not advanced on the terrain of nation and citizenship, these claims are irreducibly political and constitute a separate and critical arena of political society.[23] It is hardly likely that Confederate state actors would have conceded that point of view, but it can hardly be denied that in their own creative, instrumental, if limited way one female part of the Confederate governed had managed to widen the field of popular democratic practice and had rendered suspect the practicality of the strictly delimited Confederate vision of the people.

NOTES

1. Armstead Robinson, *Bitter Fruits of Bondage: The Demise of Slavery and the Collapse of the Confederacy, 1861–1865* (Charlottesville, 2005), 118–31, 202–205, 215–216; John Gill Shorter to Randolph (Secretary of War), May 30, 1862, Letters Received by the Confederate Secretary of War, National Archives, Washington, D.C., roll 71.

2. Robinson, *Bitter Fruits of Bondage*, 184–187.

3. Mary C. Tisinger and others to Gov. Brown, Aug. 15, 1864, Upson County, Ga, Box 3, Executive Department, Petitions, RG1–1, Georgia Department of Archives and History.

4. By 1864 military age was defined as ages 17–50. For the enlistment figures, see Gary Gallagher, *The Confederate War: How Popular Will, Nationalism, and Military Strategy Could Not Stave Off Defeat* (New York, 1997), 28–29, 16–18.

5. C. W. Walker to Gov. Vance, May 8, 1863, box 165, Zebulon B. Vance, Governors Papers, North Carolina Department of Archives and History (hereafter ZBV).

6. Sarah Halford and others to Governor Vance, Dec. 23, 1863, Rutherford County, NC, Box 172, ZBV.

7. Anonymous ["Reglators"] to Governor Vance, Feb. 18, 1863, Bladen County, NC, Box 162, ZBV.

8. Harriet E. Amos, "All Absorbing Topics: Food and Clothing in Confederate Mobile," *Atlanta Historical Journal*, 22 (Fall/Winter 1978), 23; *Richmond Daily Examiner*, April 4, April 24, 1863.

9. *Atlanta Intelligencer*, March 19, 20, 23, 1863. Mary C. Moore to Governor Vance, March 21, 1863, Salisbury, NC, Box 163, ZBV.

10. *Richmond Daily Examiner*, April 4, 1863.

11. Ibid.; Louis H. Manarin, ed., *Richmond at War: The Minutes of the City Council, 1861–1865* (Chapel Hill, 1966).

12. *Richmond Daily Examiner*, April 4, 24, 1863; Michael V. Chesson, "Harlots or Heroines? A New Look at the Richmond Bread Riot," *Virginia Magazine of History and Biography* 92, no.2 (Apr. 1984), 161.

13. Jones's testimony reported in *Richmond Daily Examiner*, April 6, 1863.

14. *Richmond Daily Examiner*, April 4, 6, 7, 8, 13, 24, Oct. 12, 1863. On Mary Duke, see Chesson, "Harlots or Heroines?" 165.

15. *Atlanta Intelligencer*, Mar. 19, 1863; Chesson, "Harlots or Heroines?" 149. On the upsurge of activity around welfare, see Drew Gilpin Faust, *The Creation of Confederate Nationalism: Ideology and Identity in the Civil War South* (Baton Rouge, 1988); Paul Escott, "The Moral Economy of the Crowd in Confederate North Carolina," *Maryland Historian* 13 (Spring/Summer, 1982), 1–18; and Robinson, *Bitter Fruits of Bondage*.

16. Amos, "All Absorbing Topics," 23–26; Manarin, *Richmond at War*, 312, 314–15, 317, 320; *Richmond Daily Examiner*, April 23, 1863.

17. Governor Joseph Brown, Message of March 25, 1863, in Allen Daniel Candler, ed., *Confederate Records of the State of Georgia*, 6 vols. (1909–1911; New York, 1972), 2:369–370; *Atlanta Intelligencer*, Mar. 24, 1863. See also Peter Wallenstein, *From Slave South to New South: Public Policy in Nineteenth-Century Georgia* (Chapel Hill, 1987), 105; and Paul Escott, "Joseph E. Brown, Jefferson Davis, and the Problem of Poverty in the Confederacy," *Georgia Historical Quarterly* 61 (Spring 1977), 65, 69.

18. *Public Laws of the State of North Carolina Passed by the General Assembly at Its Session of 1862–63* (Raleigh, 1863), 33–35. The evolution of welfare policy in Mississippi followed much the same pattern. For the Orange and Duplin County numbers (1863), see Paul Escott, "Poverty and Governmental Aid for the Poor in Confederate North Carolina," *North Carolina Historical Review* 61 (Oct. 1984), 477–480. For 1865: J. W. Norwood, Report of the County Corn Agent, Jan. 4, 1865, folder 3, Orange County, Misc. Records; Randolph County financing in Report

of the Committee on Finance, folder 3, Randolph County, Misc. Records (Civil War Records), both at the State Archives, Division of Archives and History, Raleigh, North Carolina. For the instructions to the agent, see Provisions for Families of Soldiers, folder 1, Orange County Court, Feb. term, Mar. 3, 1863 Orange County, Misc. Records, ibid.

19. Dred Scott v. Sandford, 60 U.S. (19 How.) 393 (1857). See Don E. Fehrenbacher, *The Dred Scott Case: Its Significance in American Law and Politics* (New York, 1978).

20. *Public Laws of the State of North Carolina Passed by the General Assembly at the Sessions of 1866–67* (Raleigh, 1867), 8–9.

21. Social citizenship is another rubric we might apply; see T. H. Marshall and Tom Bottomore, *Citizenship and Social Class* (London, 1992), 3–51; Judith N. Shklar, *American Citizenship: The Quest for*

Inclusion (Cambridge, UK, 1991); and Rogers M. Smith, *Civic Ideals: Conflicting Visions of Citizenship in the United States* (New Haven, 1997). For antebellum women antislavery petitioners, see Susan Zaeske, *Signatures of Citizenship: Petitioning, Antislavery, and Women's Political Identity* (Chapel Hill, 2003).

22. Partha Chatterjee, *The Politics of the Governed: Reflections on Popular Politics in Most of the World* (New York, 2004); on gender, see 76. See also Ranajit Guha, *Elementary Aspects of Peasant Insurgency in Colonial India* (Durham, 1999), and a very moving short essay by Guha, "The Small Voice of History," in *Subaltern Studies IX*, ed. Shahid Amin and Dipesh Chakrabarty (Oxford, 1966), 1–12; James Scott, *Domination and the Arts of Resistance: Hidden Transcripts* (New Haven, 1990).

23. Chatterjee, *Politics of the Governed*, 47, 35, 59–60, 46, 69.

TERA W. HUNTER

Reconstruction and the Meanings of Freedom

When the Civil War was ended at Appomattox, a long and complex struggle over its meaning had just begun. The Thirteenth Amendment technically ended slavery, but it left much room for interpretation about the meaning of servitude. It said nothing about equality, leaving resentful southerners to conclude that the North would condone systems of racial hierarchy. Even after the 1868 passage of the Fourteenth Amendment, which provided that "[a]ll persons born or naturalized in the United States . . . are citizens of the United States and of the State wherein they reside," the meanings of "citizenship" remained to be defined.

The aftermath of defeat is an internationally shared phenomenon. How did white southerners understand their defeat? What tensions marked postwar society? What would it mean to "reconstruct" the former Confederacy? Tera Hunter examines the experiences of freedpeople in the city of Atlanta, Georgia—Roda Ann Childs lived not far away. She finds that the process of rebuilding their lives could be quite different for men than for women. What opportunities did African American men have that African American women did not? What strategies might freedwomen use to stabilize their lives? In what ways did freedwomen participate in political life?

The Union victory at Appomattox in the spring of 1865 marked the official end of the war and inspired somber reflection, foot-stomping church meetings, and joyous street parades among the newly free. African Americans eagerly rushed into Atlanta in even greater numbers than before. Between 1860 and 1870, blacks in Atlanta increased from a mere nineteen hundred to ten

Excerpted from "Reconstruction and the Meanings of Freedom," ch. 2 of *To 'Joy My Freedom: Black Women's Lives and Labors after the Civil War* by Tera W. Hunter (Cambridge, Mass.: Harvard University Press, 1997). Reprinted by permission of the author and publisher. Notes have been numbered and edited.

thousand, more than doubling their proportion in the city's population, from 20 to 46 percent. Women made up the majority of this burgeoning population.[1] . . .

Wherever they came from, virtually all black women were compelled to find jobs as household workers once they arrived in the city. Some had acquired experience in such jobs as house slaves; others had worked in the fields or combined field and domestic chores. Whether or not they were working as domestics for the first time, black women had to struggle to assert new terms for their labor. The Civil War had exposed the parallel contests occurring in white households as the conflict on the battlefield, in the marketplace, and in the political arena unfolded. The war continued on the home front during Reconstruction after the Confederacy's military defeat. . . .

Just as black women and men in Atlanta had to reconstitute their lives as free people and build from the ground up, the city was faced with similar challenges. The legacy of physical desecration left by Sherman's invasion was everywhere. Tons of debris, twisted rails, dislodged roofs, crumbled chimneys, discharged cannon balls, and charred frame dwellings cluttered the streets.[2] Visitors to the city swapped remarks on the distinctive spirit of industry exemplified in the repair and rebuilding. . . . Atlanta aspired to construct a city in the New South in the image of established cities above the Mason-Dixon line.[3]

The capitalist zeal that impressed outsiders offered few benefits to the average person, however. Overwhelmed contractors could not keep up with demands, which added to housing shortages that sent prices for rents soaring beyond the means of most residents.[4] . . . Some builders took advantage of the shortage to offer makeshift huts and shanties to freedpeople at exorbitant prices.[5] Ex-slaves in more dire straits assembled scanty lodging that consisted of tents, cabins, and shanties made of tin, line, and cloth on rented parcels of land.[6] . . . The cost of food and other consumer goods likewise followed the pattern of scarcity, poor quality, and deliberate price gouging.[7]

The abrupt population growth and the inability of private charities or public coffers to relieve the migrants of want exacerbated postwar privation. Almost everyone in the city, regardless of race, shared the status of newcomer. It was not just African Americans who were migrating to the city in large numbers; so did many whites. In 1860, there were 7,600 whites living in Atlanta, ten years later there were 11,900.[8] White yeoman farmers fled to the city to find wage labor in the wake of the elimination of their rural self-sufficiency. White Northern and foreign industrial workers followed the prosperity promised by the railroad and construction boom.

Women and children, black and white, were particularly noticeable among the destitute sprawled over the desolate urban landscape. The indigent included elderly, single women, widows of soldiers, and wives of unemployed or underemployed men. White women seamstresses who numbered in the thousands during the war were reduced to poverty with the collapse of military uniform manufacturers.[9] Labor agents egregiously contributed to the disproportionate sex ratio among urban blacks by taking away men to distant agricultural fields, leaving the women and children deserted.[10] Those abandoned wandered the streets and scavenged for food, often walking between ten and forty miles per day. "Sometimes I gits along tolerable," stated a widow washerwoman with six children. "Sometimes right slim; but dat's de way wid everybody—times is powerful hard right now."[11]

The municipal government showed neither the capability nor the ambition to meet the needs of the poor. It allocated few resources for basic human services. Yet the Freedmen's Bureau, which was established by the federal government in 1865 to distribute rations and relief to ex-slaves, to monitor the transition to a free labor system, and to protect black rights, proved inadequate also. The bureau was preoccupied with stemming migration, establishing order, and restoring the economy, which led it to force blacks into accepting contracts without sufficient regard for the fairness of the terms. The federals evicted ex-slaves from contraband camps or pushed them further from the center of town to the edges—out of sight and out of mind.[12] Bureau officials urged their agents: "You must not issue rations or afford shelter to any person who can, and will not labor for his or her own support."[13] . . .

Ex-slaves who were evicted from the camps by the end of 1865 were more fortunate than they could appreciate initially. They escaped a smallpox epidemic in the city that devastated the enclaves. One missionary reported a horrifying scene she witnessed in the camps: "Men, women, and children lying on the damp ground suffering in every degree from the mildest symptoms to the most violent. The tents crowded, no fire to make them comfortable, and worse all the poor creatures were almost destitute of wearing apparel."[14] The dead who lay around the sick and suffering were buried in the ground half-naked or without clothes at all. . . .

African-American women and men were willing to endure the adversities of food shortages, natural disasters, dilapidated housing, and inadequate clothing in postwar Atlanta because what they left behind in the countryside, by comparison, was much worse. In the city at least there were reasons to be optimistic that their strength in numbers and their collective strategies of empowerment could be effective. In rural areas, however, their dispersion and separation by miles of uninhabited backwoods left them more vulnerable to elements intent on depriving them of life, liberty, and happiness. Abram Colby, a Republican legislator from Greene County, summed up the motivations for migration by stating that blacks went to Atlanta "for protection." He explained further: "The military is here and nobody interferes with us here . . . we cannot stop anywhere else so safely."[15]

African Americans moved to the city not only in search of safety, but also in search of economic self-sufficiency. Though most ex-slaves held dreams of owning farm land, many preferred to set up households in a city with a more diverse urban economy. In Atlanta they encountered an economy that was quickly recovering from the war and continuing to grow in the direction propelled by military demands and the promise of modernization.[16] . . .

Though the kaleidoscope of industry appeared to offer vast possibilities for workers, African Americans were slotted into unskilled and service labor. Black men filled positions with the railroads; as day workers, they groomed roads, distributed ballast, and shoveled snow off the tracks. As brakemen, they coupled and uncoupled stationary cars and ran along the roof of moving trains to apply the brakes, risking life and limb. Many others worked in rolling and lumber mills, mostly in the lowest-paid positions as helpers to white men. Hotels employed black men as cooks, waiters, porters, bellhops, and barroom workers. A few ex-slaves worked in bakeries, small foundries, the paper mill, and candy factories. Slave artisans were high in number in the antebellum South, but in the postbellum era black

men were rarely hired in skilled positions. They were able to benefit from the aggressive physical rebuilding of Atlanta, however, in the construction trades, as painters, carpenters, and brickmasons. Between 1870 and 1880, the proportion of black male shoemakers tripled to constitute the majority of the entire trade. A select few owned small businesses such as barber shops and grocery stores or worked in the professions as teachers and ministers.[17]

The range of job opportunities for black women was more narrow than for men. Black women were excluded from small manufacturing plants that hired white women, such as those that made candy, clothing, textiles, paper boxes, bookbinding, and straw goods. They were confined primarily to domestic labor in private homes as cooks, maids, and child-nurses. A few black women found related jobs in local hotels—a step above the same work performed in private households. Large numbers worked in their own homes in a relatively autonomous craft as laundresses, which had the advantage of accommodating family and community obligations. More desirable, yet less accessible, were skilled jobs outside domestic service as seamstresses or dressmakers. . . . Only a few black women were able to escape common labor and enter the professions as teachers.[18]

Reconstruction of the post-slavery South occurred on many levels. Just as the city's infrastructure had to be rebuilt for daily life to reach a new normalcy, so blacks had to rebuild their lives as free people by earning an independent living. Women's success or frustrations in influencing the character of domestic labor would define how meaningful freedom would be. Slave women had already demonstrated fundamental disagreements with masters over the principles and practices of free labor during the war. This conflict continued as workers and employers negotiated new terms. Even the most mundane and minute details of organizing a free labor system required rethinking assumptions about work that had previously relied on physical coercion. An employer acknowledged the trial-and-error nature of this process: "I had no idea what was considered a task in washing so I gave her all the small things belonging to the children taking out all the table cloths sheets counterpanes & c." The novice employer then decided in the same haphazard manner to pay the laundry worker 30 cents a day. But the laborer asserted her own understanding of fair work.

"She was through by dinner time [and] appeared to work steady. I gave her dinner and afterwards told her that I had a few more clothes I wished washed out," the employer explained. "Her reply was that she was tired." The worker and employer held different expectations about the length of the work day and the quantity of the output of labor.[19]

African Americans labored according to their own sense of equity, with the guiding assumption that wage labor should not emulate slavery—especially in the arbitrariness of time and tasks. The experience of an ex-slave named Nancy illustrates this point. As some ex-slaves departed from their former masters' households, the burden of the work shifted to those who remained. Consequently, when the regular cook departed, Nancy's employer added cooking and washing to her previous child-care job, without her consent. Nancy faked illness on ironing days and eventually quit in protest against the extra encumbrance.[20] If workers and employers disagreed on the assignment of specific tasks, they also disagreed on how to execute them. Workers held to their own methods and preferences; employers held to theirs. . . .

If [a worker's] frustrations reached an intolerable level, she could exercise a new privilege as a free worker to register the ultimate complaint: she could quit and seek better terms for her work. Ex-slaves committed themselves to this precept of free labor with a firmness that vexed employers. "We daily hear of people who are in want of servants, and who have had in their employ in the last three or four months, a dozen different ones," stated a familiar news report. "The common experience of all is that the servants of the 'African-persuasion' can't be retained," it continued. "They are fond of change and since it is their privilege to come and go at pleasure, they make full use of the large liberty they enjoy."[21] . . .

African-American women decided to quit work over such grievances as low wages, long hours, ill treatment, and unpleasant tasks. Quitting could not guarantee a higher standard of living or a more pleasant work environment for workers, but it was an effective strategy to deprive employers of complete power over their labor. . . .

Employers did not share the same interpretations of labor mobility, however. They blamed the subversive influence of Yankees and "pernicious" Negroes for inciting "bad" work habits, or they explained quitting as a scientifically proven racial deficiency.[22] Whereas recently freed slaves often worked as much as they needed to survive and no more, white Southerners believed that if they refused to work as hard as slaves driven by fear they were mendicants and vagrants. "When a wench gets very hungry and ragged, she is ready to do the cooking for any sized family," a news report exclaimed. "But after she gets her belly well filled with provender, she begins to don't see the use of working all day and every day, and goes out to enjoy her freedom."[23]

Although many white Southerners resented the presence of the Freedmen's Bureau as the Northern overseer of Reconstruction, they readily sought its assistance to stem the revolving door of domestic workers. "What are persons to do when a 'freedman' that you hire as a nurse goes out at any time & against your direct orders?" one former master queried the bureau. "What must be done when they are hired and do only just what they please? orders being disregarded in every instance," he asked further. A bureau agent responded with an answer to alleviate the employer's frustrations and to teach him a lesson about the precepts of free labor. "Discharge her and tell her she dont suit you," the agent stated simply. "If you have a written contract with them and they quit you without good and sufficient cause—I will use all my power to have them comply," he reassured. But if these words provided comfort, the bureau agent made clear that the operative words were "without good and sufficient cause." He reiterated the employers' obligations and responsibilities to respect the liberties of workers: "You are expected to deal with them as Freemen and Freewomen. Individual exceptions there may be but as a whole where they are well treated they are faithful and work well."[24]

The federal government refused to return to white employers unilateral power to prohibit the mobility of black workers, leading employers to elicit the support of local laws. Quitting work became defined as "idleness" and "vagrancy"—prosecutable offenses. Southern state legislatures began passing repressive Black Codes in 1865 to obstruct black laborers' full participation in the marketplace and political arena. In 1866, the Atlanta City Council responded in a similar vein to stop the movement of household workers: it passed a law requiring employers to solicit recommendations from previous jobs in order to distinguish "worthy" from "worthless" laborers and to make it more difficult for workers to change jobs. Complaints continued long after the law took effect, which suggests its ineffectiveness.[25] . . .

Black women used the marginal leverage they could exercise in the face of conflict between employers to enhance their wages and to improve the conditions of work. When Hannah, "a cook & washer of the first character," was approached by Virginia Shelton in search of domestic help, she bargained for an agreement to match her needs. Hannah wanted to bring along her husband, a general laborer, and expected good wages for both of them. Shelton made an initial offer of $5 per month to Hannah and $10 per month to her husband. But the couple demanded $8 and $15, to which Shelton acceded. Shelton realized that it was worth making compromises with a servant she had traveled a long distance to recruit.[26]

Not all negotiations ended so pleasantly or in the workers' favor, however. . . . Domestic workers often complained of physical abuse by employers following disputes about wages, hours of work, or other work-related matters. . . . Samuel Ellison explained the argument that led to the death of his wife, Eliza Jane. Mrs. Ellison had argued with her employer, Mrs. L. B. Walton, about washing clothes. According to Ellison's husband, "My wife asked Mrs. Walton who would pay her for her washing extra clothes and which she was not bound to do by her contract." Walton's husband intervened and "abused" the laundress for "insulting" his wife. He left the house, returned and began another argument, insisting to Ellison, "shut up you God damn bitch." The fight ended when Walton shot Eliza Jane Ellison to death.[27]

African-American women like Ellison undoubtedly paid a high price for the simple desire to be treated like human beings. Incidents like this one made it apparent that freedom could not be secured through wage labor alone. The material survival of African Americans was critical, but they also needed to exercise their political rights to safeguard it. The political system had to undergo dramatic transformation to advance their interests, but here too they faced many obstacles.

The Ku Klux Klan, an anti-black terrorist organization founded by former Confederate soldiers in 1866, mounted the most bitter opposition to black rights. The KKK quickly became dominated by Democratic Party officials bent on preempting black participation in the electoral arena. The Klan sought to wrest economic and political power from the governing Republicans in order to restore it to the antebellum planter elite and to the Democrats. KKK members victimized Republican politicians like Abram Colby, whom they stripped and beat for hours in the woods. They harassed registered voters and independent landholders, ransacked churches and schools, intimidated common laborers who refused to bow obsequiously to planters, and tormented white Republicans sympathetic to any or all of the foregoing.[28]

African Americans' recalcitrance in commonplace disagreements with employers routinely provoked the vigilantes. Alfred Richardson, a legislator from Clarke County, suggested how labor relations continued to have strong political ramifications. The KKK assisted employers in securing the upper hand in conflicts with wage household workers. "Many times, you know, a white lady has a colored lady for cook or waiting in the house, or something of that sort," Richardson explained. "They have some quarrel, and sometimes probably the colored woman gives the lady a little jaw. In a night or two a crowd will come in and take her out and whip her." The Klan stripped and beat African Americans with sticks, straps, or pistol barrels when all else failed to elicit their compliance.[29]

If the KKK was determined to halt the reconstruction of a free labor system, it was most insistent about eliminating black political power. Though women were denied the right to vote in the dominant political system, they actively engaged in a grass-roots political culture that valued the participation of the entire community. Black women and children attended parades, rallies, and conventions; they voiced their opinions and cast their votes on resolutions passed at mass meetings. In the 1860s and 1870s, women organized their own political organizations, such as the Rising Daughters of Liberty Society, and stood guard at political meetings organized by men to allow them to meet without fear of enemy raids. They boldly tacked buttons on the clothing they wore to work in support of favorite candidates. They took time off from work to attend to their political duties, such as traveling to the polls to make sure men cast the right ballots. White housekeepers were as troubled by the dramatic absences of domestic workers on election day or during political conventions as were the planters and urban employers of men.[30] During an election riot in nearby Macon, a newspaper reported: "The Negro women, if possible, were wilder than the men. They were seen everywhere, talking in an excited manner, and urging the men on. Some of them were almost furious, showing it to be part of their religion to keep their husbands and brothers straight in politics."[31]

Whether they gave political advice and support to the men in their families and communities or carried out more directly subversive activities, black women showed courage in the face of political violence. Hannah Flournoy, a cook and laundress, ran a boardinghouse in Columbus well known as a gathering place for Republicans. When George Ashburn, a white party leader stalked by the KKK, looked to her for shelter she complied, unlike his other supporters in the town. Flournoy promised him, "You are a republican, and I am willing to die for you. I am a republican, tooth and toe-nail."[32] But neither Flournoy nor Ashburn could stop the Klan in its determination to take the life of freedom fighters. After Klansmen killed Ashburn, Flournoy escaped to Atlanta, leaving behind valuable property.

Republican activists like Ashburn and Flournoy were not the only victims of KKK violence. The Klan also targeted bystanders who happened to witness their misdeeds. In White County, Joe Brown's entire family was subjected to sadistic and brutal harassment because Brown had observed a murder committed by the Klan. "They just stripped me stark naked, and fell to beating us," Brown reported later. "They got a great big trace-chain, swung me up from the ground, and swung [my wife] up until she fainted; and they beat us all over the yard with great big sticks." The Klan continued its torture against his mother-in-law and sister-in-law. "They made all the women show their nakedness; they made them lie down, and they jabbed them with sticks." Indiscriminate in violating adults and children, the KKK lined up Brown's young daughters and sons "and went to playing with their backsides with a piece of fishing-pole."[33] . . .

Migrating to Atlanta certainly improved the personal safety of ex-slaves escaping the KKK and sexual assaults, but it did not ensure foolproof protection against bodily harm. Black women risked sexual abuse no matter where they lived. Domestics in white homes were the most susceptible to attacks. A year after the war ended, Henry McNeal Turner and other black men mounted the podium and wrote petitions

to demand the cessation of sexual assaults upon black women. Freedom, they insisted, was meaningless without ownership and control over one's own body. Black men took great offense at the fact that while they were falsely accused of raping white women, white men granted themselves total immunity in the exploitation of black women. *"All we ask of the white man is to let our ladies alone,* and they need not fear us," Turner warned. "The difficulty has heretofore been *our ladies were not always at our disposal."*[34] In Savannah, black men mobilized the Sons of Benevolence "for the protection of female virtue" in 1865.[35] In Richmond, African Americans complained to military authorities that women were being "gobbled up" off the streets, thrown into the jail, and ravished by the guards. In Mobile, black men organized the National Lincoln Association and petitioned the Alabama State Constitutional Convention to enact laws to protect black women from assault by white civilians and the police.[36]

Most whites refused to acknowledge the culpability of white men in abusing black women. "Rape" and "black women" were words that were never uttered in the same breath by white Southerners. Any sexual relations that developed between black women and white men were considered consensual, even coerced by the seductions of black women's lascivious nature. Rape was a crime defined exclusively, in theory and in practice, as perceived or actual threats against white female virtue by black men, which resulted in lynchings and castrations of numbers of innocent black men. But Z. B. Hargrove, a white attorney, admitted with rare candor that the obsession with black men raping white women was misplaced. "It is all on the other foot," as he put it. The "colored women have a great deal more to fear from white men."[37]

Black Atlantans during Reconstruction were subjected to other kinds of physical violence, especially at the hands of white civilians and police. . . . When Mary Price objected to being called a "damned bitch" by a white neighbor, Mr. Hoyt, he brought police officer C. M. Barry to her door to reprimand her. Price's mother, Barbara, pregnant at the time, intervened and spoke to the police: "I replied that I would protect my daughter in my own house, whereupon he pulled me out of the house into the street. Here he called another man and the two jerked and pulled me along [the street] to the guard house and threw me in there." When a Freedmen's Bureau agent complained to the mayor and city council on the Prices' behalf, the complaint was rebuffed by a unanimous vote acquitting the policeman of all charges against him. Meanwhile, mother and daughter were arrested, convicted for using profane language, and forced to pay $350 each in fines and court costs. Only after it became clear that the Bureau would persist in its efforts to get justice for the Price women did the mayor have a change of heart and fine the offending policeman. Barry was one of the worst officers on the force, and the Freedmen's Bureau eventually forced the city council to fire him, though he was rehired a year later.[38]

African Americans not only had to ward off physical threats; they were also challenged by the existence of perfectly legal abuses that diminished the meaning of freedom. Ex-slaves defined the reconstruction of their families torn asunder by slavery and war as an important aspect of the realization of the full exercise of their civil rights. But former masters seized upon the misery of African Americans, with the assistance of the law, to prolong the conditions of slavery and deny them the prerogative of reuniting their families. The Georgia legislature passed an Apprentice Act in 1866, ostensibly to protect black orphans by providing them with guardianship and "good" homes until they reached the age of consent at twenty-one. Planters used the law to reinstate bondage through uncompensated child labor.[39] Aunts, uncles, parents, and grandparents inundated the Freedmen's Bureau with requests for assistance in rescuing their children, though this same agency also assisted in apprenticing black minors. Martin Lee, for example, a former slave living in Florence, Alabama, wrote to the chief of the Georgia bureau for help in releasing his nephew from bondage. He had successfully reunited part of his extended family, but could not gain the release of his nephew despite the fact that he and the child's mother, Lee's sister, were both willing and able to take custody.[40]

If admitted enemies of black freedom recklessly disregarded the unity of black families through apprenticeships, some of their friends operated just as wantonly. The American Missionary Association (AMA) sometimes impeded parents and relatives who wished to reclaim their children. In 1866, the AMA started an orphanage that operated out of a tent. Soon afterward they opened the Washburn Orphanage in a building to accommodate the large number of homeless black children who were surviving on the streets on scant diets of saltpork and hardtack. But the asylum functioned as a temporary way station for children before apprenticing them out as domestic help to white sponsors. "I succeeded in getting a little girl from the orphans asylum by the name of Mary Jane Peirce," one eager patron of the orphanage exclaimed. "Her father and mother are both dead. She has a step mother and a little step brother." Peirce's new guardian minced no words in disclosing reckless disregard for the reunion of the child's family. "I am glad she will have no outside influence exherted upon her," the guardian admitted.[41] . . .

African Americans persisted in pursuing the reconstitution of family ties, despite the obstacles put in their way. [Rebeca] Craighead [the matron of the asylum,] recognized the persistence of these ex-slaves, yet she showed neither respect nor sensitivity toward the virtues of their ambition. "Somehow these black people have the faculty of finding out where their children are," she acknowledged.[42] Both the uncle, Martin Lee, who used official channels to retrieve his nephew, and the anonymous aunt, who relied on her own resources to "steal" her niece, displayed no small measure of resourcefulness in achieving their aims. Men no less than women, non-kin as well as kin, sought to recreate the family bonds that had been strained or severed by slavery and the Civil War.

Not all missionaries were as insensitive as Craighead; there were others, like Frederick Ayers, who fully appreciated the significance of family to ex-slaves. "The idea of 'freedom' of independence, of calling their wives and their children, and little hut their *own*, was a soul animating one, that buoyed up their spirits," he observed.[43] . . .

Broad understandings of kinship encouraged black women to assume responsibility for needy children other than their natural offspring. Silvey, for example, could hardly survive on the minimal subsistence she earned, yet she extended compassion to the youngsters lost or deserted by other ex-slaves. "She was hard put to it, to work for them all," observed her former owner, Emma Prescott. But "of course, as our means were all limited, we could not supply her enough to feed them. Her life, was anything but ease & it was a pitiful sight."[44] . . .

The most complicated family issues involved romantic relationships between women and men. For generations slaves had married one another and passed on the importance of conjugal obligations, despite the absence of legal protection. Marriages between slaves were long-term commitments, usually only disrupted by forcible separation or the death of a spouse. Emancipation offered new opportunities to reaffirm marital vows and to reunite couples who had previously lived "abroad" in the households of different masters. Even before the last shots of gunfire ending the Civil War, thousands of husbands and wives sought the help of Union officers and Northern missionaries to register their nuptials and to conduct wedding ceremonies.[45] The significance of formalizing these ties was articulated by a black soldier: "*I praise God for this day! The Marriage Covenant is at the foundation of all our rights.*"[46] Putting marriages on a legal footing bolstered the ability of ex-slaves to keep their families together, to make decisions about labor and education, and to stay out of the unscrupulous grasp of erstwhile masters.

The hardships of slavery and war that disrupted families, however, meant that in the postwar period spouses were not always reunited without problems and tensions. Slaves traveled long distances to reunite with spouses from whom they had been separated for years. They wrote love letters and mailed them to churches and to the Freedmen's Bureau, and retraced the routes of labor agents who had taken their partners away.[47] Emotional bonds were sometimes so intense that spouses would choose to suffer indefinitely if they could not be reunited with their lost loved ones. But affections undernourished by hundreds of miles and many years might be supplanted by other relationships. Many ex-slaves faced awkward dilemmas when spouses presumed to be dead or long-lost suddenly reappeared. Ex-slaves created novel solutions for the vexing moral, legal, and practical concerns in resolving marital relations disrupted by forces beyond their control. One woman lived with each of her two husbands for a two-week trial before making a decision. Some men felt obligated to two wives and stayed married to one wife while providing support to the other. In one case, perhaps unique, a wife resumed her relationship with her first husband, while the second husband, a much older man, was brought into the family as a "poor relation."[48]

The presence of children complicated marriages even further. Some spouses registered their marriages with the Freedmen's Bureau or local courts even when their spouses were dead or missing, in order to give legal recognition to their children. When both parents were present and unable to reconcile their differences, child custody became a point of contention. Madison Day and Maria Richardson reached a mutual agreement to separate after emancipation. The love between husband and wife may have changed, but the love that each displayed for their children did not. The Richardsons put the Freedmen's Bureau agent in a quandary in determining who should receive custody. "Neither husband nor wife seem to be in a condition to provide for the children in a manner better than is usual with the freedpeople," the agent noted. "Still both appear to have an affectionate regard for the children and each loudly demands them."[49] . . .

Sheer survival and the reconstruction of family, despite all the difficulties, were the highest priorities of ex-slaves in the postwar period. But the desire for literacy and education was closely related to their strategies for achieving economic self-sufficiency, political autonomy, and personal enrichment. By 1860, 5 percent of the slave population had defied the laws and learned to read and write. Some were taught by their masters, but many learned to read in clandestine sessions taught by other blacks. African Americans all over the South organized secret schools long before the arrival of Northern missionaries. When a New England teacher arrived in Atlanta in 1865, he discovered an ex-slave already running a school in a church basement.[50]

African Americans welcomed the support of New England teachers and the federal government in their education movement. But centuries of slavery had stirred the longing for self-reliance in operating schools and filling teaching staffs, with assistance, but without white control. Ex-slaves enthusiastically raised funds and donated in-kind labor for building, repairing, and maintaining school houses. They opened their spartan quarters to house teachers and shared vegetables from their gardens to feed them. Ex-slaves in Georgia ranked highest in the South in the amount of financial assistance donated to their own education.[51]

The education movement among African Americans in Georgia went hand in hand with the demand for political rights. In January 1865, black ministers formed the Savannah Education Association, which operated schools staffed entirely with black teachers. Despite the efforts of General Davis Tillson, the conservative head of the Freedmen's Bureau, to keep politics out of the organization, African Americans and more

liberal white allies infused the group with political objectives. The name was changed to the
Georgia Equal Rights and Education Association, explicitly linking equal rights in the political arena with the pursuit of education. The
organization became an important training
ground for black politicians and laypersons at
the grass-roots level and functioned as the
state's predecessor to the Republican Party.[52] . . .

African Americans' advocacy of universal
public education did not fare well at the city
level, because the municipal government was
firmly controlled by Democrats and businessmen. William Finch, elected in 1870 as one of
Atlanta's first black city councilmen, made
universal education a hallmark of his election
campaign. Finch attempted, but failed, to gal-
vanize the support of the white working class
on this issue. City Hall's cold reception shifted
the burden of basic education for blacks to private foundations. Finch did succeed in getting
the council to absorb two primary schools run
by the AMA. After his short term in office and
unsuccessful bid for reelection in December
1871, he continued to be a strong advocate of
public education and helped negotiate a deal
in 1872 whereby the city would pay nominal
costs for some blacks to receive secondary
training at Atlanta University. No publicly
funded high school for blacks would be created until a half-century later, however.[53]

Former slaves of all ages were undeterred
in their goals to achieve literacy, regardless of
the obstacles imposed by municipal and state
governments. "It is quite amusing to see little
girls eight or ten years old lead up full-grown
women, as well as children, to have their
names enrolled," remarked a missionary.
"Men, women, and children are daily inquir-
ing when the 'Free School' is to commence,
and whether all can come[.] There is a large
class of married women who wish to attend, if
the schools are not too crowded."[54] Household
workers figured prominently among this
group of older, eager scholars. Their eagerness
to learn was not diminished, although often
interrupted, by the pressing demands of gain-
ful labor. In fact, these obstacles may have increased the value of education in the eyes of
the ex-slaves. Sabbath schools operated by
black churches and evening classes sponsored
by the Freedmen's Bureau and Northern missionaries afforded alternatives for those who
could not sacrifice time during the day. But
black women also inventively stole time away

from work by carrying their books along and
studying during spare moments—even fasten-
ing textbooks to backyard fences to glimpse
their lessons as they washed clothes.[55]

As parents, working-class adults were especially committed to the education of their
children. The story of Sarah J. Thomas, a young
woman from Macon, whose mother was a cook
and washerwoman, is a poignant illustration.
Thomas wrote Edmund Asa Ware, president of
Atlanta University, to gain his support in her
plans to enroll in the secondary school. "I ex-
spected to come to Atlanta to morrow but I am
dissappointed. The reason I can not come to
morrow is this. You know how mothers are! I
guess about their youngest children *girls* especially," she wrote. Mother Thomas was protective of her daughter and reluctant to send her
away alone. "In order that I may *come* Mr. Ware!
mother says can she get a place to work there in
the family?" she asked. The younger Thomas
boasted of her mother's fine skills and reputation and slipped in her salary history. She assured the president, surely swamped by
requests for financial aid, that her matricula-
tion depended upon parental supervision, not
the need for money. "Mother says she dont
mean not the least to work to pay for *my schooling?* father pays for that him self she dont have
any thing to do with it she only want to be
where she can see me."[56] The young scholar's
astute strategizing swayed both her mother
and the school's president; she entered Atlanta
University and achieved a successful teaching
career after graduation in 1875.

Clandestine antebellum activities and
values had bolstered the exemplary efforts of
African Americans to seek literacy and to
build and sustain educational institutions
after the war. Ex-slaves took mutual obligations seriously. Their belief in personal development was aided rather than hampered by
ideals that emphasized broad definitions of
kinship and community. Freedom meant the
reestablishment of lost family connections, the
achievement of literacy, the exercise of political
rights, and the security of a decent livelihood
without the sacrifice of human dignity or self-
determination. Ex-slave women migrated to
Atlanta, where they hoped they would have a
better chance of fulfilling these expectations.
They were faced with many challenges; uppermost among them were the white residents
who were resentful of the abolition of slavery
and persisted in thwarting the realization of

the true meaning of freedom. Black women continued to struggle, resilient and creative, in pursuing their goals for dignity and autonomy. The character of the contest had already been cast, but the many guises of domination and resistance had yet to be exhausted as life in the New South unfolded.

NOTES

1. . . . Franklin M. Garrett, *Yesterday's Atlanta* (Miami: E. A. Seeman, 1974), p. 38; Eric Foner, *Reconstruction: America's Unfinished Revolution, 1863–1877* (New York: Harper & Row, 1988), pp. 81–82; Leon F. Litwack, *Been in the Storm So Long: The Aftermath of Slavery* (New York: Knopf, 1979), pp. 310–316; U.S. Department of the Treasury, Register of Signatures of Depositors in the Branches of the Freedman's Savings and Trust Company, Atlanta Branch, 1870–1874 (Microfilm Publication, M-544), National Archives (hereafter cited as Freedman's Bank Records). Frederick Ayer to George Whipple, 15 February 1866 (Georgia microfilm reels), American Missionary Association Archives, Amistad Research Center, Tulane University (hereafter cited as AMA Papers).

2. John Richard Dennett, *The South As It Is: 1865–1866*, ed. Henry M. Christman (New York: Viking, 1965), pp. 267–271; Sidney Andrews, *The South Since the War: As Shown by Fourteen Weeks of Travel and Observation in Georgia and the Carolinas* (Boston, 1866; reprint ed., New York: Arno, 1970), pp. 339–340; Don H. Doyle, *New Men, New Cities, New South: Atlanta, Nashville, Charleston, Mobile, 1860–1910* (Chapel Hill: University of North Carolina Press, 1990), p. 31.

3. Rebecca Craighead to [Samuel] Grant, 15 January 1866, Georgia, AMA Papers; Andrews, *South Since the War*, p. 340; Whitelaw Reid, *After the War: A Tour of the Southern States, 1865–1866* (London, 1866; reprint ed., New York: Harper & Row, 1965), p. 355; Doyle, *New Men*, pp. 34–35; Howard N. Rabinowitz, *Race Relations in the Urban South 1865–1890* (New York: Oxford University Press, 1978), pp. 5–17.

4. See James Michael Russell, *Atlanta, 1847–1890: City Building in the Old South and the New* (Baton Rouge: Louisiana State University Press, 1988), pp. 117–128.

5. Frederick Ayers to Rev. George Whipple, 15 February 1866, Georgia, AMA Papers.

6. See Rebecca Craighead to Rev. Samuel Hunt, 30 April 1866, Georgia, AMA Papers; E. T. Ayer to Rev. Samuel Grant, 3 February 1866, Georgia, AMA Papers; Harriet M. Phillips to Rev. Samuel Grant, 15 January 1866, Georgia, AMA Papers; *American Missionary* 13 (January 1869): 4; John T. Trowbridge, *The South: A Tour of Its Battlefields and Ruined Cities* (Hartford, 1866; reprint ed., New York: Arno, 1969), p. 453.

7. Frederick Ayers to Rev. George Whipple, 15 February 1866, Georgia, AMA Papers.

8. *Ninth Census: Population* (1872), vol. 1, p. 102; *Tenth Census: Population* (1883), vol. 1, p. 417.

9. Gretchen Ehrmann Maclachlan, "Women's Work: Atlanta's Industrialization and Urbanization, 1879–1929" (Ph.D. diss., Emory University, 1992), p. 29.

10. H. A. Buck to General [Davis Tillson], 2 October 1865, Letters Recd., ser. 732, Atlanta, Ga. Subasst. Comr., Record Group 105: Bureau of Refugees, Freedmen, and Abandoned Lands (hereafter cited as BRFAL), National Archives (hereafter cited as NA), [FSSP A-5153]; Franklin Brown to Gen. Tillson, 30 July 1866, Unregistered Letters Recd., ser. 632, Ga. Asst. Comr., BRFAL, NA, [FSSP A-5327]; clipping from *Augusta Constitutionalist*, 16 February 1866, filed with Lt. Col. D. O. Poole to Brig. Gen. Davis Tillson, 19 February 1866, Unregistered Letters Recd., ser. 632, Ga. Asst. Comr., BRFAL, NA, [FSSP A-5447]. Citations for photocopied documents from the National Archives that were consulted at the Freedmen and Southern Society Project, University of Maryland, conclude with the designation "FSSP" and the project's document control number in square brackets: for example, [FSSP A-5447].

11. Quoted in Trowbridge, *South Tour*, pp. 453–454.

12. Jerry Thornbery, "The Development of Black Atlanta, 1865–1885" (Ph.D. diss., University of Maryland, 1977), pp. 48–53; Edmund L. Drago, *Black Politicians and Reconstruction in Georgia: A Splendid Failure* (Baton Rouge: Louisiana State University Press, 1982), pp. 113–116.

13. Brig. Genl. Davis Tillson to Captain George R. Walbridge, 12 March 1866, Letters Recd., ser. 732, Ga. Subasst. Comr., BRFAL, NA, [FSSP A-5153].

14. Rebecca Craighead to Rev. Samuel Hunt, 15 February 1866, Georgia, AMA Papers; see also F. Ayers to Rev. George Whipple, 15 February 1866, Georgia, AMA Papers.

15. Testimony of Abram Colby, 28 October 1871, in 42nd Congress, 2nd Session, House Report no. 22, pt. 6, *Testimony Taken by the Joint Select Committee to Inquire into the Condition of Affairs in the Late Insurrectionary States* (Washington, D.C., 1872), vol. 2, p. 700 (hereafter cited as KKK Hearings). See also testimony of Alfred Richardson, 7 July 1871, KKK Hearings, vol. 1, p. 12.

16. Doyle, *New Men*, pp. 38–48, 151; Jonathan W. McLeod, *Workers and Workplace Dynamics in Reconstruction Era Atlanta* (Los Angeles: Center for Afro-American Studies, University of California), pp. 10–16.

17. McLeod, *Workers and Workplace*, pp. 24–31, 45, 61, 75, 81, 91, 94.

18. Ibid., pp. 77–92, 100–103; Thornbery, "Black Atlanta," pp. 191–225.

19. Entry of 27 May 1865, Ella Gertrude Clanton Thomas Journal, William R. Perkins Library, Duke University (hereafter cited as DU).

20. See entries for May 1865, Thomas Journal, DU.

21. Atlanta *Daily Intelligencer*, 25 October 1865.

22. Emma J. S. Prescott, "Reminiscences of the War," typescript, pp. 49–50, 55, Atlanta History Center (hereafter cited as AHC).

23. Atlanta *Daily New Era*, 27 February 1868.

24. Mr. J. T. Ball to Maj. Knox, 19 March 1866, Unregistered Letters Recd., ser. 2250, Meridian, Miss. Subasst. Comr., BRFAL, NA, [FSSP A-9423].

25. Alexa Wynell Benson, "Race Relations in Atlanta, As Seen in a Critical Analysis of the City Council Proceedings and Other Related Works, 1865–1877" (M.A. thesis, Atlanta University, 1966), pp. 43–44; Foner, *Reconstruction*, pp. 199–202; Theodore Brantner Wilson, *The Black Codes of the South*

(University, Ala.: University of Alabama Press, 1965); Rabinowitz, *Race Relations,* pp. 34–35; Atlanta *Daily New Era,* 27 February 1868.

26. Virginia Shelton to William Shelton, 20 August 1866, Campbell Family Papers, DU. See also Ellen Chisholm to Laura Perry, 27 July 1867, Perry Family Papers, AHC.

27. Affidavit of Samuel Ellison, 16 Jan 1867 BRFAL, NA.

28. Foner, *Reconstruction,* pp. 425–444; see testimony of Abram Colby, 28 October 1871, KKK Hearings, vol. 2, pp. 699–702.

29. Testimony of Alfred Richardson, 7 July 1871, KKK Hearings, vol. 1, pp. 12, 18.

30. Foner, *Reconstruction,* pp. 87, 290–291; Elsa Barkley Brown, "Negotiating and Transforming the Public Sphere: African American Political Life in the Transition from Slavery to Freedom," *Public Culture* 7 (Fall 1994): 107–126; Thomas C. Holt, *Black Over White: Negro Political Leadership in South Carolina during Reconstruction* (Urbana: University of Illinois Press, 1977), pp. 34–35.

31. Macon *Georgia Weekly Telegraph,* 8 October 1872, as quoted in Edmund L. Drago, "Militancy and Black Women in Reconstruction Georgia," *Journal of American Culture* 1 (Winter 1978): 841.

32. Testimony of Hannah Flournoy, 24 October 1871, KKK Hearings, vol. 1, p. 533. On Ashburn's death see Drago, *Black Politicians,* pp. 145, 153.

33. Testimony of Joe Brown, 24 October 1871, KKK Hearings, vol. 1, p. 502.

34. Henry McNeal Turner's emancipation speech, 1 January 1866, Augusta, as quoted in Herbert G. Gutman, *The Black Family in Slavery and Freedom, 1750–1925* (New York: Pantheon Books, 1977), p. 388. See also Catherine Clinton, "Bloody Terrain: Freedwomen, Sexuality and Violence During Reconstruction," *Georgia Historical Quarterly* 76 (Summer 1992): 318; Atlanta *Weekly Defiance,* 24 February 1883.

35. Eliza Frances Andrews, *The War-Time Journal of a Georgia Girl, 1864–1865,* ed. Spencer Bidwell King, Jr. (Macon, Ga.: Arvidian Press, 1960), p. 349.

36. Gutman, *Black Family,* pp. 387–388.

37. Testimony of Z. B. Hargrove, 13 July 1871, KKK Hearings, vol. 1, p. 83. See also testimony of George B. Burnett, 2 November 1871, KKK Hearings, vol. 2, p. 949. See Jacquelyn Dowd Hall, *Revolt Against Chivalry: Jesse Daniel Ames and the Women's Campaign Against Lynching* (New York: Columbia University Press, 1974).

38. Affidavit of Barbara Price, 15 May 1867, Misc. Court Records, ser. 737, Atlanta, Ga. Subasst. Comr., BRFAL; Bvt. Maj. Fred. Mosebach to Mayor and City Council of Atlanta, 15 May 1867, and Bvt. Maj. Fred. Mosebach to Col. C. C. Sibley, 21 May 1867, vol. 99, pp. 49 and 53–54, Letters Sent, ser. 729, Atlanta, Ga. Subasst. Comr., BRFAL, NA, [FSSP A-5709]. See also James M. Russell and Jerry Thornbery, "William Finch of Atlanta: The Black Politician as Civic Leader," in Howard N. Rabinowitz, ed. *Southern Black Leaders of the Reconstruction Era* (Urbana: University of Illinois Press, 1982), pp. 317, 332.

39. The apprenticeship system was not entirely limited to the conscription of minors; young adults actively providing for themselves were also apprenticed. For example, a turpentine worker with a wife

and child was defined as an orphan in North Carolina. See Foner, *Reconstruction,* p. 201.

40. Martin Lee to Mr. Tillson, 7 December 1866, in Ira Berlin et al., "Afro-American Families in the Transition from Slavery to Freedom," *Radical History Review* 42 (Fall 1988): 102–103.

41. Entry of 27 May 1865, Thomas Journal, DU. Evidence from ex-slave narratives suggests a pattern of exploitation of child laborers; they received little or no cash wages. See testimony of Nancy Smith, in George P. Rawick, ed., *The American Slave: A Composite Autobiography* (Westport, Conn.: Greenwood Press, 1941; 1972), *Georgia Narratives,* vol. 13, pt. 3, p. 302 (hereafter cited as WPA Ga. Narr.); testimony of Georgia Telfair, WPA Ga. Narr., vol. 13, pt. 4, p. 5.

42. Rebecca M. Craighead to Bvt. Brig. Gen. J. H. Lewis, 11 May 1866, Ga. Asst. Comr., C-69, 1867, Letters Recd., ser. 631, Ga. Asst. Comr., BRFAL, NA, [FSSP A-415].

43. F. Ayers to Rev. George Whipple, 15 February 1866, Georgia, AMA Papers.

44. Prescott, "Reminiscences of the War," p. 56, AHC. Prescott goes on to reveal that Silvey died penniless, without the help of former owners.

45. Gutman, *Black Family,* pp. 9–23; Berlin et al., "Afro-American Families," pp. 92–93.

46. Corporal Murray, as quoted in J. R. Johnson to Col. S. Lee, 1 June 1866, in Berlin et al., "Afro-American Families," p. 97.

47. For examples of these efforts see Wm. H. Sinclair to Freedmen's Bureau agent at Savannah, Ga., 12 September 1866, Unregistered Letters, ser. 1013, Savannah, Ga. Subasst. Comr., BRFAL, NA, [FSSP A-5762]; R. F. Patterson to Col. D. C. Poole, Letters Recd., ser. 732, Atlanta, Ga. Subasst. Comr., BRFAL, NA, [FSSP A-5704].

48. Gutman, *Black Family,* pp. 418–425.

49. 1st Lt. F. E. Grossmann to the Acting Assistant Adjutant General, 1 October 1866, in Berlin et al., "Afro-American Families," pp. 97–98. Gutman, *Black Family,* pp. 418–425.

50. James D. Anderson, *The Education of Blacks in the South, 1860–1935* (Chapel Hill: University of North Carolina Press, 1988), pp. 4–9, 16; Herbert G. Gutman, "Schools for Freedom: The Post-Emancipation Origins of Afro-American Education," in Herbert G. Gutman, *Power and Culture: Essays on the American Working-Class,* ed. Ira Berlin (New York: Pantheon, 1987), p. 294; Jacqueline Jones, *Soldiers of Light and Love: Northern Teachers and Georgia Blacks 1865–1873* (Chapel Hill: University of North Carolina Press, 1980), p. 59.

51. Gutman, "Schools for Freedom," pp. 286, 294; Jones, *Soldiers of Light and Love,* p. 62; Anderson, *Education of Blacks in the South,* pp. 4–32.

52. Drago, *Black Politicians,* pp. 27–28.

53. Russell and Thornbery, "William Finch of Atlanta," pp. 319, 322; Russell, *Atlanta,* p. 181.

54. Mrs. E. T. Ayers to Rev. Samuel Hunt, 1 September 1866, Georgia, AMA Papers.

55. Jennies Barium to Rev. Samuel Grant, 27 January 1866, Georgia, AMA Papers; Andrews, *South Since the War,* p. 338.

56. Sarah J. Thomas to Mr. [Edmund A.] Ware, 11 October 1869, Edmund A. Ware Papers, Robert W. Woodruff Library, Clarke Atlanta University.

A. S. Hitchcock, "Young women particularly flock back & forth . . ."

Early in the Civil War, before the Emancipation Proclamation, the Union Army occupied the Sea Islands off the coasts of South Carolina and Georgia; plantation owners fled and the army established base camps there. Although the Union forces expected former slaves to continue to work on their old plantations as contract laborers, freedpeople believed that the end of slavery should mean that they could travel freely and that they could choose other ways of supporting themselves.

How did Union officials interpret the movement of women around the islands (which included Beaufort and Hilton Head)? What limited types of work did they posit as appropriate for African American women and men? Note the ways in which black people's efforts at family reunion were criminalized.

A. S. HITCHCOCK, ACTING GENERAL SUPERINTENDENT OF CONTRABANDS, TO PROVOST MARSHAL GENERAL OF THE DEPARTMENT OF THE SOUTH, AUGUST 25, 1864

In accordance with a request made by you at this office . . . concerning measures to be instituted to lessen the number of idle & dissolute persons hanging about the central Posts of the Department & traveling to & from between them . . . I write this note. . . .

Had I the control of the negroes the first thing I would endeavor to do, & the thing I think of most importance to be done, is to Keep all the people possible on the farms or plantations at *honest steady* labor. As one great means to this end, I would make it as difficult as possible for them to get to the centres of population.—Young women particularly flock back & forth by scores to Hilton Head, to Beaufort, to the country simply to while away their time, or constantly to seek some new excitement, or what is worse to live by lasciviousness. . . . I would allow no peddling around camps whatsoever. . . . All rationing I would stop utterly, & introduce the poor house system, feeding none on any pretense who would not go to the place provided for all

paupers to live. . . . All persons out of the poor house running from place to place to beg a living I would treat as vagabonds, & also all persons, whether in town or on plantations, white or black, who lived without occupation should either go to the poor house or be put in a place where they *must work*—a work house or chain gang, & if women where they could wash iron & scrub for the benefit of the public. . . .

SEPTEMBER 6, 1864
GENERAL ORDERS NO. 130

Hilton Head, S.C. . . . The practice of allowing negro women to wander about from one plantation to another, and from one Post or District to another, on Government transports, for no other purpose than to while away their time, or visit their husbands serving in the ranks of the Army, is not only objectionable in every point of view, both to the soldiers and to themselves, but is generally subversive of moral restraint, and must be discontinued at once. All negro women, in future found wandering in this manner, will be immediately arrested, and compelled to work at some steady employment on the Plantations.

Excerpted from *Freedom: A Documentary History of Emancipation, 1861–1867*, ser. 1, vol. 3, ed. Ira Berlin, Joseph P. Reidy, and Leslie S. Rowland, pp. 316–19. Reprinted with the permission of Cambridge University Press.

Roda Ann Childs, "I was more dead than alive"

In January 1865, before the Civil War was over, Congress and the states in the Union ratified the Thirteenth Amendment, putting an end to slavery and "involuntary servitude, except as punishment for crime whereof the party shall have been duly convicted." Once peace was established, it became clear that the states of the former Confederacy were quite creative in devising systems that maintained racial subordination (for example, broad definitions of what counted as "vagrancy" which, as crimes, could be punished by involuntary servitude). The Civil Rights Act of 1866 was designed to protect freedpeople; it promised "citizens of every race and color . . . full and equal benefit of all laws and proceedings for the security of person and property, as is enjoyed by white citizens. . . ." But the statute had been passed only over the veto of President Andrew Johnson, who denied that the states of the Confederacy had forfeited all civil rights and privileges by their rebellion. The Freedmen's Bureau was charged with protecting the rights of former slaves and assisting their transition to a market economy; it accomplished much, but it was always underfunded and understaffed, and many of its staff members were themselves deeply skeptical of freedpeople.

In a political climate marked by struggle between Congress and the President, the Ku Klux Klan and other vigilantes who wanted to intimidate freedpeople and take vengeance for their own defeat in war seized their opportunity. Not until 1871 did Congress pass the Ku Klux Klan Act, prescribing fines and imprisonment for those who went in disguise to terrorize others. The congressional committee that conducted a traveling inquiry into "the Condition of Affairs in the Late Insurrectionary States" filed a twelve-volume report. Its testimony of violence and intimidation, in excruciating detail, makes it clear that Roda Ann Childs's experience was replicated throughout the South.

Roda Ann Childs made her way to a Freedmen's Bureau agent in Griffin, Georgia, to swear this affidavit; she signed it with her mark. There is no evidence that her case was pursued. What clue does she offer for why she was a target for mob violence?

[*Griffin, GA*] Sept. 25, 1866 Roda Ann Childs came into this office and made the following statement:

Myself and husband were under contract with Mrs. Amelia Childs of Henry County, and worked from Jan. 1, 1866, until the crops were laid by, or in other words until the main work of the year was done, without difficulty. Then, (the fashion being prevalent among the planters) we were called upon one night, and my husband was demanded; I Said he was not there. They then asked where he was. I Said he was gone to the water mellon patch. They then Seized me and took me Some distance from the house, where they 'bucked' me down across a log, Stripped my clothes over my head, one of the men Standing astride my neck, and beat me across my posterior, two men holding my legs. In this manner I was beaten until they were tired. Then they turned me parallel with the log, laying my neck on a limb which projected from the log, and one man placing his foot upon my neck, beat me again on my hip and thigh. Then I was thrown upon the ground on my back, one

Excerpted from *Freedom: A Documentary History of Emancipation, 1861–1876*, ser. 2, ed. Ira Berlin, Joseph P. Reidy, and Leslie S. Rowland, p. 807. Reprinted with the permission of Cambridge University Press.

of the men Stood upon my breast, while two others took hold of my feet and stretched My limbs as far apart as they could, while the man Standing upon my breast applied the Strap to my private parts until fatigued into stopping, and I was more dead than alive. Then a man, Supposed to be an ex-confederate Soldier, as he was on crutches, fell upon me and ravished me. During the whipping one of the men ran his pistol into me, and Said he had a hell of a mind to pull the trigger, and Swore they ought to Shoot me, as my husband had been in the 'God damned Yankee Army,' and Swore they meant to kill every black Son-of-a-bitch they could find that had ever fought against them. They then went back to the house, Seized my two daughters and beat them, demanding their father's pistol, and upon failure to get that, they entered the house and took Such articles of clothing as Suited their fancy, and decamped. There were concerned in this affair eight men, none of which could be recognized for certain.

her
Roda Ann × Childs
mark

Reconstruction Amendments, 1868, 1870

Until 1868, the U.S. Constitution made no explicit distinctions on the basis of gender. Of qualifications for voters, it said only that "the electors in each State shall have the qualifications requisite for electors of the most numerous branch of the State legislature" (art. 1, sec. 2). Reformers merely needed to persuade each state legislature to change its own rules in order to enfranchise women in national elections.

The word *male* was introduced into the Constitution in section 2 of the Fourteenth Amendment, as part of a complex provision—never enforced—intended to constrain former Confederates from interfering with the civil rights of newly freed slaves. Suffragists were bitterly disappointed at the failure to include sex as a category in the Fifteenth Amendment. But until the test case of *Minor v. Happersett* (pp. 294–295), they clung to the hope that the first article of the Fourteenth Amendment would be interpreted broadly enough to admit women to the polls.

FOURTEENTH AMENDMENT, 1868

1. All persons born or naturalized in the United States, and subject to the jurisdiction thereof, are citizens of the United States and of the State wherein they reside. No State shall make or enforce any law which shall abridge the privileges or immunities of citizens of the United States; nor shall any State deprive any person of life, liberty, or property, without due process of law; nor deny to any person within its jurisdiction the equal protection of the laws.

2. Representatives shall be apportioned among the several States according to their respective numbers, counting the whole number of persons in each State, excluding Indians not taxed. But when the right to vote at any election for the choice of electors for President and Vice-President of the United States, Representatives in Congress, the executive and judicial officers of a State, or the members of the legislature thereof, is denied to any of the male inhabitants of such State, being twenty-one years of age and citizens of the United States, or in any way abridged, except for participation in rebellion, or other crime, the basis of representation therein shall be reduced in the proportion which the number of such male citizens shall bear to the whole number of male citizens twenty-one years of age in such State. . . .

FIFTEENTH AMENDMENT, 1870

The right of citizens of the United States to vote shall not be denied or abridged by the United States or by any State on account of race, color, or previous condition of servitude. . . .

Win Some, Lose Some: Women in Court: **Coger v. The North Western Union Packet Company,** *Supreme Court of Iowa, 1873;* **Bradwell v. Illinois,** *1873;* **Minor v. Happersett,** *1874*

COGER V. THE NORTH WESTERN UNION PACKET COMPANY, SUPREME COURT OF IOWA, 1873

A long-established rule of Anglo-American common law is that transportation services licensed by the state are "legally bound to carry all passengers or freight as long as there is enough space, the fee is paid, and no reasonable grounds to refuse to do so exist."* What counts as "reasonable grounds" is open to interpretation. One popular way to evade universal common carrier rules has been to charge different fees for first- and second-class accommodations—thus segregating by economic class—and make only second-class accommodations available to all people of color. The "ladies' car" in railroads or the "ladies' table" on steamships was a popular subterfuge for racial segregation. Throughout the post–Civil War years, African American women challenged their exclusion from ladies' accommodations—often at real physical risk to themselves. (Being thrown off a moving train was the worst of these risks.)

In 1873, Emma Coger, a schoolteacher of mixed race, tried to buy a first-class ticket on a steamboat that crossed the Mississippi from Keokuk, Iowa, to her hometown of Quincy, Illinois. She refused the clerk's offer of a ticket that did not entitle her to meals at the first-class table reserved for ladies traveling alone; she found another passenger, a white man, who purchased a first-class meal ticket on her behalf. When she took a seat at the ladies' table in the cabin, the guard told her to move to the deck or to the pantry, where people of color were to eat. She refused. The captain of the boat appeared, making the same demand; she again refused, and, as the subsequent court record describes it, "he proceeded by force to remove her from the table and the cabin of the boat."

The feisty Emma Coger did not go quietly. As one witness testified, "She swore and abused the captain, saying 'I told you I'd get even with you, you white-livered sons of bitches.' . . . Her conduct was very bad and her language worse. In the struggle, the covering of the table was torn off, dishes broke, and the officer received a slight injury."† Coger was defiant; she sued the steamship company for assault and battery.

Emma Coger hedged her bets. She claimed "she was as white as anybody." A jury trial was held in the Lee District Court. The judge instructed the jury that if Coger's "rights to first-class accommodations were denied her, simply because she has African or negro blood in her veins . . . then the court charges you that the plaintiff is entitled to recover" damages.

Coger won. The steamship company appealed to the Iowa Supreme Court, claiming that the well-known custom on all their boats was that "colored persons could not receive . . . first class privileges. . . . [Coger] purchased a ticket which entitled her to the rights of a colored person . . . and gave her no right to meals. . . .

---

*West Encyclopedia of American Law, 2008, http://legal-dictionary.thefreedictionary.com/Common+carrier.

†Record quoted in Barbara Young Welke, *Recasting American Liberty: Gender, Race, Law, and the Railroad Revolution, 1865–1920* (New York: Cambridge University Press, 2001), pp. 292–93.

Afterward, by fraud, she purchased such a ticket for meals as were sold to white persons. . . . [N]o greater force was used than was necessary to take her, against her resistance, from the table."

Earlier that year, dealing with Myra Bradwell's claim that the Fourteenth Amendment's promise of equal protection should sustain her right to practice law, the U.S. Supreme Court had interpreted the amendment very narrowly. But Iowa Chief Justice Joseph M. Beck had participated in the deliberations of his court when, only a few years before, it had ruled that racially segregated schools were a denial of equal protection of the laws—interpreting the Fourteenth Amendment broadly. Now he wrote the opinion for a unanimous court.

Iowa was unusual. Ten years later, in Tennessee, Ida B. Wells (see pp. 323–325) would have experiences similar to Emma Coger's, but with the opposite result. In 1883, Wells physically resisted her removal from a ladies' car, biting the conductor's hand as he forced her off the train. She sued the railroad company for discrimination; she won in the trial court but lost when the railroad appealed to the Tennessee Supreme Court. (The court offered the opinion that it was Wells who had, by her lawsuit, harassed the railroad.)

The lawsuits courageously brought by Emma Coger, Ida B. Wells, and dozens of other individual African American women in the years after the Civil War tested the claim that the common carriers (railroads, streetcars, steamboats) provided "separate but equal" accommodations to black and white people. Their lawsuits laid the ground for the famous test case challenging separate streetcars for whites and blacks, brought—at no physical risk to themselves—by Homer Plessy and a group of African American professional men in New Orleans at the end of the nineteenth century. In *Plessy v. Ferguson*, the U.S. Supreme Court ruled that laws requiring the separation of the races merely reflect social custom and do not label one race as inferior. *Plessy* would not be overturned until the Supreme Court's 1954 decision in *Brown v. Board of Education*.

How did the Iowa Supreme Court describe the issues on which it had to decide? On what grounds did they hold for Emma Coger? Contrast this interpretation of the meaning of the Fourteenth Amendment with the U.S. Supreme Court's decision in *Bradwell* and *Minor* rulings excerpted in this document cluster.

CHIEF JUSTICE JOSEPH BECK,
FOR A UNANIMOUS COURT:

[I]n our opinion, the doctrines and authorities involved in the argument [that Coger is white] are obsolete, and have no longer existence and authority, anywhere within the jurisdiction of the federal constitution, and most certainly not in Iowa. The ground upon which we base this conclusion will be discovered, in the progress of this opinion, to be the absolute equality of all men. We will . . . accept the statement of fact as made by the counsel of [the steamship company], namely, that plaintiff is a woman of color.

In our opinion the plaintiff was entitled to the same rights and privileges while upon defendant's boat, notwithstanding the negro blood, be it more or less, admitted to flow in her veins, which were possessed and exercised by white passengers.

These rights and privileges rest upon the equality of all before the law, the very foundation principle of our government. If the negro must submit to different treatment, to accommodations inferior to those given to the white man, when transported by public carriers, he is deprived of the benefits of this very principle of equality. . . . It may be claimed that as he does not get accommodations equal to the white man he is not charged as great a price. But this does not modify the. . . absurdity and gross injustice of the rule—nay, its positive wickedness. . . .

Coger v. The North Western Packet Union Company, 37 Iowa 145 (1873).

The decision is planted on the broad and just ground of the equality of all men before the law, which is not limited by color, nationality, religion or condition in life. This principle of equality is announced and secured by the very first words of our State constitution which relate to the rights of the people, in language most comprehensive, and incapable of misconstruction, namely: "All men are, by nature, free and equal." . . . But the doctrine of equality and its application to the rights of [Emma Coger] . . . depend . . . not alone upon the constitution of this State [but also] . . . are recognized and secured by the recent constitutional amendments and legislation of the United States. . . . The persons contemplated by the [Fourteenth] amendment [see p. 309] are: 1. All persons born or naturalized in the United States. . . . These . . . are secured the right of citizenship of the United States, and protected against abridgment of their privileges and immunities. 2. All persons within the jurisdiction of the States . . . are protected and secured the equal protection of the laws. [Coger] belongs to both classes of persons, to whom rights are secured and protection extended. . . .

Her money would not purchase for her that which the same sum would entitle a white passenger to receive. . . . [S]he claimed no social privilege, but substantial privileges pertaining to her property and the protection of her person. It cannot be doubted that she was excluded from the table and cabin . . . because of prejudice entertained against her race, growing out of its former condition of servitude—a prejudice, be it proclaimed to the honor of our people, that is fast giving way to nobler sentiments, and, it is hoped, will soon be entombed with its parent, slavery. . . .

[A] common carrier cannot refuse to transport all persons without distinctions based upon color or nationality. . . . Her dinner ticket gave her a right to dine in the cabin on an equality with other passengers. . . .

BRADWELL V. ILLINOIS, 1873

Although she could not practice in the courts until the end of her career, Myra Bradwell was perhaps the most notable female lawyer of the nineteenth century. She read law in the office of her husband, a prominent Chicago attorney and county judge. In 1868 she began to publish the *Chicago Legal News*, a weekly newspaper covering developments in courts and legislatures throughout the country. Because she had received a special charter from the state legislature under which she was permitted to act without the usual legal disabilities of a married woman, she ran the *News* as her own business. She wrote vigorous editorials, evaluating legal opinions and new laws, assessing proposed state legislation, and supporting progressive developments like prison reform, the establishment of law schools, and women's rights. She drafted bills improving married women's rights to child custody and to property, including the Illinois Married Woman's Property Act of 1869. Thanks in part to her own lobbying efforts, Illinois permitted women to own property and to control their own earnings.

It was only logical that Myra Bradwell should seek admission to the bar. Although she passed the entrance tests in 1869, although the Illinois Married Woman's Property Act permitted her to own property, and although the law that gave the state supreme court the power to license attorneys did not explicitly exclude women, her application was rejected by the Illinois Supreme Court on the grounds that she was a married woman, and therefore not a truly free agent. Appealing to the United States Supreme Court, her attorney argued that among the "privileges and immunities" guaranteed to each citizen by the Fourteenth Amendment was the right to pursue any honorable profession. "Intelligence, integrity and honor are the only qualifications that can be prescribed . . . the broad shield of the Constitution is over all, and protects each in that measure of success which his or her individual merits may secure."

Bradwell v. Illinois, 83 U.S. 130 (1873).

The Court's decision came in two parts. Speaking for the majority and citing the most recent decision of the Supreme Court in the slaughterhouse cases, Justice Samuel F. Miller held that the right to practice law in the courts of any particular state was a right that had to be granted by the individual state; it was not one of the "privileges and immunities" of national citizenship. This judgment was supplemented by a concurring opinion, in which Justice Joseph P. Bradley offered an ideological justification for the Court's decision that was based on inherent differences between men and women and that was to be widely used thereafter to defend the exclusion of women from professional careers.

While her case was pending before the U.S. Supreme Court, Bradwell and Alta M. Hulett, another woman who had been refused admission to the bar even though she was otherwise qualified, successfully lobbied for a law that granted freedom of occupational choice to all Illinois citizens, both male and female. The bill was passed in 1872; a year later Alta Hulett was sworn in before the Illinois Bar. Bradwell did not think she should have to beg for admission, and she never formally applied for a license to practice law under the new statute. In the *Chicago Legal News* she observed that "having once complied with the rules and regulations of the court . . . [I] declined to . . . again ask for admission." In 1890, twenty years after her initial application, the Illinois Supreme Court admitted Bradwell to the bar. Two years before her death in 1894 she was admitted to practice before the U.S. Supreme Court, but she never did argue a case there.*

MR. JUSTICE JOSEPH P. BRADLEY:

The claim of the plaintiff, who is a married woman, to be admitted to practice as an attorney and counselor at law, is based upon the supposed right of every person, man or woman, to engage in any lawful employment for a livelihood. The supreme court of Illinois denied the application on the ground that, by the common law, which is the basis of the laws of Illinois, only men were admitted to the bar, and the legislature had not made any change in this respect. . . .

The claim that, under the 14th Amendment of the Constitution, which declares that no state shall make or enforce any law which shall abridge the privileges and immunities of citizens of the United States, and the statute law of Illinois, or the common law prevailing in that state, can no longer be set up as a barrier against the right of females to pursue any lawful employment . . . assumes that it is one of the privileges and immunities of women as citizens to engage in any and every profession, occupation or employment in civil life.

It certainly cannot be affirmed, as a historical fact, that this has ever been established as one of the fundamental privileges and immunities of the sex. On the contrary, the civil law, as well as nature herself, has always recognized a wide difference in the respective spheres and destinies of man and woman. Man is, or should be, woman's protector and defender. The natural and proper timidity and delicacy which belongs to the female sex evidently unfits it for many of the occupations of civil life. The constitution of the family organization, which is founded in the divine ordinance, as well as in the nature of things, indicates the domestic sphere as that which properly belongs to the domain and functions of womanhood. The harmony, not to say identity, of interests and views which belong or should belong to the family institution, is repugnant to the idea of a woman adopting a distinct and independent career from that of her husband. So firmly fixed was this sentiment in the founders of the common law that it became a maxim of that system of jurisprudence that a woman had no legal existence separate from her husband, who was regarded as her head and representative in the social state; and, notwithstanding some recent modifications of this civil status, many of the special rules of law flowing from and dependent

---

*See also Frances Olsen, "From False Paternalism to False Equality: Judicial Assaults on Feminist Community, Illinois, 1869–1895," *Michigan Law Review* 84 (1986): 1518–43.

upon this cardinal principle still exist in full force in most states. One of these is, that a married woman is incapable, without her husband's consent, of making contracts which shall be binding on her or him. This very incapacity was one circumstance which the supreme court of Illinois deemed important in rendering a married woman incompetent fully to perform the duties and trusts that belong to the office of an attorney and counselor.

It is true that many women are unmarried and not affected by any of the duties, complications, and incapacities arising out of the married state, but these are exceptions to the general rule. The paramount destiny and mission of woman are to fulfill the noble and benign offices of wife and mother. This is the law of the Creator. And the rules of civil society must be adapted to the general constitution of things, and cannot be based upon exceptional cases. . . .

MINOR V. HAPPERSETT, 1874

In 1872 suffragists in a number of places attempted to test the possibilities of the first section of the Fourteenth Amendment. "The power to regulate is one thing, the power to prevent is an entirely different thing," observed Virginia Minor, president of the Woman Suffrage Association of Missouri, and she presented herself at the polls in St. Louis in 1872. When the registrar refused to permit her to register to vote, she and her husband sued him for denying her one of the "privileges and immunities of citizenship"; when they lost the case they appealed to the Supreme Court.

In a unanimous opinion the justices held that if the authors of the Constitution had intended that women should vote, they would have said so explicitly. The decision of the Court meant that woman suffrage could not be developed by way of a quiet reinterpretation of the Constitution but would require an explicit amendment to the Constitution or a series of revisions in the laws of the states.

MR. CHIEF JUSTICE MORRISON R. WAITE DELIVERED THE OPINION OF THE COURT:

The question is presented in this case, whether, since the adoption of the fourteenth amendment, a woman, who is a citizen of the United States and of the State of Missouri, is a voter in that State, notwithstanding the provision of the constitution and laws of the State, which confine the right of suffrage to men alone. . . . The argument is, that as a woman, born or naturalized in the United States and subject to the jurisdiction thereof, is a citizen of the United States and of the State in which she resides, she has the right of suffrage as one of the privileges and immunities of her citizenship, which the State cannot by its laws or constitution abridge.

There is no doubt that women may be citizens. They are persons, and by the fourteenth amendment "all persons born or naturalized in the United States and subject to the jurisdiction thereof" are expressly declared to be "citizens of the United States and of the State wherein they reside." But, in our opinion, it did

not need this amendment to give them that position . . . sex has never been made one of the elements of citizenship in the United States. In this respect men have never had an advantage over women. The same laws precisely apply to both. The fourteenth amendment did not affect the citizenship of women any more than it did of men. . . . Mrs. Minor . . . has always been a citizen from her birth, and entitled to all the privileges and immunities of citizenship.

If the right of suffrage is one of the necessary privileges of a citizen of the United States, then the constitution and laws of Missouri confining it to men are in violation of the Constitution of the United States, as amended, and consequently void. The direct question is, therefore, presented whether all citizens are necessarily voters.

The Constitution does not define the privileges and immunities of citizens. For that definition we must look elsewhere. In this case we need not determine what they are, but only whether suffrage is necessarily one of them.

Minor v. Happersett, 88 U.S. 162 (1874).

It certainly is nowhere made so in express terms. The United States has no voters in the States of its own creation. The elective officers of the United States are all elected directly or indirectly by state voters ... it cannot for a moment be doubted that if it had been intended to make all citizens of the United States voters, the framers of the Constitution would not have left it to implication. . . .

It is true that the United States guarantees to every State a republican form of government. . . . No particular government is designated as republican, neither is the exact form to be guaranteed, in any manner especially designated. . . . When the Constitution was adopted . . . all the citizens of the States were not invested with the right of suffrage. In all, save perhaps New Jersey, this right was only bestowed upon men and not upon all of them. . . . Under these circumstances it is certainly now too late to contend that a government is not republican,

within the meaning of this guaranty in the Constitution, because women are not made voters. . . . If suffrage was intended to be included within its obligations, language better adapted to express that intent would most certainly have been employed. . . .

. . . For nearly ninety years the people have acted upon the idea that the Constitution, when it conferred citizenship, did not necessarily confer the right of suffrage. If uniform practice long continued can settle the construction of so important an instrument as the Constitution of the United States confessedly is, most certainly it has been done here. Our province is to decide what the law is, not to declare what it should be.

We have given this case the careful consideration its importance demands. If the law is wrong, it ought to be changed; but the power for that is not with us. . . . No argument as to woman's need of suffrage can be considered. We can only act upon her rights as they exist. . . .

The Women's Centennial Agenda, 1876

The capstone of the celebration of the Centennial was a public reading of the Declaration of Independence in Independence Square, Philadelphia, by a descendant of a signer, Richard Henry Lee. Elizabeth Cady Stanton, who was then president of the National Woman Suffrage Association, asked permission to silently present a women's protest and a written Declaration of Rights. The request was denied. "Tomorrow we propose to celebrate what we have done the last hundred years," replied the president of the official ceremonies, "not what we have failed to do."

Led by suffragist Susan B. Anthony, five women appeared at the official reading, distributing copies of their declaration. After this mildly disruptive gesture, they withdrew to the other side of Independence Hall, where they staged a counter-Centennial and Anthony read the following address. Compare it to the Declaration of Sentiments (pp. 247–250) of twenty-eight years before. Note the splendid oratorical flourish of the final paragraph.

July 4, 1876
While the nation is buoyant with patriotism, and all hearts are attuned to praise, it is with sorrow we come to strike the one discordant note, on this one-hundredth anniversary of our country's birth. When subjects of kings, emperors, and czars, from the old world join in our

national jubilee, shall the women of the republic refuse to lay their hands with benedictions on the nation's head? Surveying America's exposition, surpassing in magnificence those of London, Paris, and Vienna, shall we not rejoice at the success of the youngest rival among the nations of the earth? May not our hearts, in

Excerpted from Susan B. Anthony, Declaration of Rights for Women by the National Woman Suffrage Association, in *History of Suffrage, vol. 3, ed.* Elizabeth Cady Stanton, Susan B. Anthony, and Matilda Joselyn Gage (Rochester, N.Y.: Susan B. Anthony, 1886), pp. 31–34.

unison with all, swell with pride at our great achievements as a people; our free speech, free press, free schools, free church, and the rapid progress we have made in material wealth, trade, commerce and the inventive arts? And we do rejoice in the success, thus far, of our experiment of self-government. Our faith is firm and unwavering in the broad principles of human rights proclaimed in 1776, not only as abstract truths, but as the corner stones of a republic. Yet we cannot forget, even in this glad hour, that while all men of every race, and clime, and condition, have been invested with the full rights of citizenship under our hospitable flag, all women still suffer the degradation of disfranchisement.

The history of our country the past hundred years has been a series of assumptions and usurpations of power over woman, in direct opposition to the principles of just government, acknowledged by the United States as its foundation. . . .

And for the violation of these fundamental principles of our government, we arraign our rulers on this Fourth day of July, 1876,— and these are our articles of impeachment:

Bills of attainder have been passed by the introduction of the word "male" into all the State constitutions, denying to women the right of suffrage, and thereby making sex a crime—an exercise of power clearly forbidden in article 1, sections 9, 10, of the United States constitution. . . .

The right of trial by a jury of one's peers was so jealously guarded that States refused to ratify the original constitution until it was guaranteed by the sixth amendment. And yet the women of this nation have never been allowed a jury of their peers—being tried in all cases by men, native, and foreign, educated and ignorant, virtuous and vicious. Young girls have been arraigned in our courts for the crime of infanticide; tried, convicted, hanged—victims, per chance, of judge, jurors, advocates—while no woman's voice could be heard in their defense. . . .

Taxation without representation, the immediate cause of the rebellion of the colonies against Great Britain, is one of the grievous wrongs the women of this country have suffered during the century. Deploring war, with all the demoralization that follows in its train, we have been taxed to support standing armies, with their waste of life and wealth. Believing in temperance, we have been taxed to support the vice, crime and pauperism of the liquor traffic. While we suffer its wrongs and abuses infinitely more than man, we have no power to protect our sons against this giant evil. . . .

Unequal codes for men and women. Held by law a perpetual minor, deemed incapable of self-protection, even in the industries of the world, woman is denied equality of rights. The fact of sex, not the quantity or quality of work, in most cases, decides the pay and position; and because of this injustice thousands of fatherless girls are compelled to choose between a life of shame and starvation. Laws catering to man's vices have created two codes of morals in which penalties are graded according to the political status of the offender. Under such laws, women are fined and imprisoned if found alone in the streets, or in public places of resort, at certain hours. Under the pretense of regulating public morals, police officers seizing the occupants of disreputable houses, march the women in platoons to prison, while the men, partners in their guilt, go free. . . .

Representation of woman has had no place in the nation's thought. Since the incorporation of the thirteen original States, twenty-four have been admitted to the Union, not one of which has recognized woman's right of self-government. On this birthday of our national liberties, July Fourth, 1876, Colorado, like all her elder sisters, comes into the Union with the invidious word "male" in her constitution. . . .

The judiciary above the nation has proved itself but the echo of the party in power, by upholding and enforcing laws that are opposed to the spirit and letter of the constitution. When the slave power was dominant, the Supreme Court decided that a black man was not a citizen, because he had not the right to vote; and when the constitution was so amended as to make all persons citizens, the same high tribunal decided that a woman, though a citizen, had not the right to vote. Such vacillating interpretations of constitutional law unsettle our faith in judicial authority, and undermine the liberties of the whole people.

These articles of impeachment against our rulers we now submit to the impartial judgment of the people. To all these wrongs and oppressions woman has not submitted in silence and resignation. From the beginning of the century, when Abigail Adams, the wife of one president and mother of another, said, "We will not hold ourselves bound to obey laws in which we have no voice or representation," until now, woman's discontent has been steadily increasing, culminating nearly thirty years ago in a simultaneous movement among the women of the nation, demanding the right of suffrage. In making our just demands, a higher motive than the pride of sex inspires us; we feel that national safety and stability depend on the complete recognition of the broad principles of our government. Woman's degraded, helpless position is the weak point in our institutions today; a disturbing force everywhere, severing family ties, filling our asylums with the deaf, the dumb, the blind; our prisons with criminals, our cities with drunkenness and prostitution; our homes with disease and death. It was the boast of the founders of the republic, that the rights for which they contended were the rights of human nature. If these rights are ignored in the case of one-half the people, the nation is surely preparing for its downfall. Governments try themselves. The recognition of a governing and a governed class is incompatible with the first principles of freedom. Woman has not been a heedless spectator of the events of this century, nor a dull listener to the grand arguments for the equal rights of humanity. From the earliest history of our country woman has shown equal devotion with man to the cause of freedom, and has stood firmly by his side in its defense. Together they have made this country what it is. Woman's wealth, thought and labor have cemented the stones of every monument man has reared to liberty.

And now, at the close of a hundred years, as the hour-hand of the great clock that marks the centuries points to 1876, we declare our faith in the principles of self-government; our full equality with man in natural rights; that woman was made first for her own happiness, with the absolute right to herself—to all the opportunities and advantages life affords for her complete development; and we deny that dogma of the centuries, incorporated in the codes of all nations—that woman was made for man—her best interests, in all cases, to be sacrificed to his will. We ask of our rulers, at this hour, no special privileges, no special legislation. We ask justice, we ask equality, we ask that all the civil and political rights that belong to citizens of the United States, be guaranteed to us and our daughters forever.

III

MODERN AMERICA EMERGES

1880–1920

GENDER AND THE
JIM CROW SOUTH

GLENDA GILMORE
Forging Interracial Links
in the Jim Crow South

Anna Julia Cooper—an extraordinary woman in her own right—wrote in 1892, "the colored woman of today . . . is confronted by a woman question and a race problem."* Equality of the sexes, Cooper insisted, would mean that black women should not be passive and subordinate in their relationships with black men; and black men should not criticize women's efforts to obtain equal rights. Equality of the sexes, Cooper continued, meant sharing the leadership burden in the struggle against racism. A remarkable group of African American women did just that.

Part of a small but growing black middle class in the South, they were prepared by education, professional training, and voluntary work to be the vanguard of their race. Following the disfranchisement of black men in the 1890s, they emerged not only as community activists but also as ambassadors to the white community and astute political strategists. Their political skills were put to the test when, during the most racist era in U.S. history, these black women attempted to forge links with elite white women in an interracial movement. At the forefront of the effort was a remarkable North Carolinian, Charlotte Hawkins Brown.

With sensitivity and insight, Glenda Gilmore illuminates Brown's search for fault lines in the system of white supremacy. She also demonstrates just how Brown manipulated class, gender, and even her own identity in the interests of racial justice. In the end, Brown's generation fell short of their goal of racial and sexual equality. The odds against them were overwhelming. In the process, however, they created and nourished a tradition of activism that would emerge with new force and greater success in the 1960s.

Consider Brown's strategy. What were her options? What were the personal costs? Do you agree with Gilmore's characterization of her as a "political genius"?

---

*Anna Julia Cooper, *A Voice from the South by a Black Woman of the South* (Xenia, Ohio: Aldine, 1892), p. 135.

Excerpted from "Forging Interracial Links," ch. 7 of *Gender and Jim Crow: Women and the Politics of White Supremacy in North Carolina, 1896–1920,* by Glenda Elizabeth Gilmore (Chapel Hill: University of North Carolina Press, 1996). Reprinted by permission of the author and publisher. The author has supplied new paragraphs, and renumbered and edited the notes.

In the segregated world of the Jim Crow South, laws told black and white people where to eat and where to sit. Undergirding those laws lay a complex web of custom. Its strands separated the races in places beyond the reach of legislation. Custom dictated, for example, which part of the sidewalk belonged to whites and which to blacks. When whites and blacks sometimes occupied the same space, custom demanded that African Americans behave in a subservient manner. Any breach of these codes by a black person could bring an instant response from a white person: a reprimand, a beating, a jail sentence, or even death at the end of a lyncher's rope.

Whites held two unshakable beliefs that gave them the courage and energy to structure such a complicated society, making good on its rules with violence and even murder. First, whites thought that they acted to protect white women from black men's sexual desires. Second, they firmly believed that African Americans should be excluded from the American democratic system. They spoke freely and acted openly against any extension of political rights to blacks. After the turn of the century, restrictive legislation prevented most southern black men from voting and segregation laws crowded the books. White men considered their work done. Henceforth, they thought, African Americans would be a permanent lower caste in southern society: physically separated and politically powerless.

But the white supremacists did not reckon with black women. From behind the borders of segregation and disfranchisement, African American women became diplomats to the white community. They built social service and civic structures that wrested some recognition and meager services from the expanding welfare state. Ironically, as black men were forced from the political sphere, the functions of government expanded, opening a new space for black women to approach officials as good citizens intent on civic betterment.

One of their political strategies was to build contacts with white women. Meager and unequal as they were, these interracial connections often provided black women access to resources for their families, students, and neighbors. Charlotte Hawkins Brown personified such black women across the South who forged invisible careers in interracial politics.

As president of the North Carolina Association of Colored Women's Clubs, Charlotte Hawkins Brown began to direct African American women's formal civic experiences in the state in 1912 and continued to do so for twenty-five years.... No black man could claim prominence to equal hers in . . . the state during the period. Brown's work and racialist ideologies illustrate that the decade before woman suffrage constituted a critical period in defining the boundaries of race relations that would remain in place until the post–World War II era.

Charlotte Hawkins Brown's life also provides a parable of the possibilities and the personal costs of interracial cooperation. Her story is so interwoven with myth—fiction that she fashioned to outmaneuver racism—that it is difficult to separate the reality of her experience from the result of her self-creation. The difference between her lived life and her public persona reveals a great deal about her perception of southern whites' racial ideologies and the points at which she saw possibility. Charlotte Hawkins Brown invented herself, repeatedly and with brilliance, but at great personal cost.[1]

According to her account, she was born in Henderson, North Carolina, in 1883 to Caroline Frances Hawkins, the daughter of Rebecca and Mingo Hawkins. Her father was Edmund H. Hight, from "whom fate separated me at birth" and who "belonged to a family that had grown up on the adjoining plantation."[2] Brown characterized her grandmother, Rebecca Hawkins, as a "fair" woman "with blue eyes," the African American sister of her white master, "a great railroad captain whose vision and foresight built up the great Southern Railroad." Brown cast the white master as the Hawkins family's "protector."[3] About the time of my birth, colored people in large numbers were leaving for parts north," she remembered. Charlotte moved with her mother and brother to Cambridge, Massachusetts, where her mother married and the family lived in a large, handsome house near Harvard University.[4] Caroline Hawkins managed a hand laundry in the basement, and Charlotte attended the public schools of Cambridge. Whisked away from the South at an early age, Charlotte was "not conscious of the difference in color and took part in all the activities of my class."[5] She acquired a New England accent, which she kept all of her life.

Charlotte Hawkins's family insisted that she get a practical education and sent her to

Massachusetts State Normal School in Salem. Alice Freeman Palmer, the wife of a Harvard professor and the first female president of Wellesley College, was a member of the state board of education that oversaw the school. One day a few months before she entered the normal school, as Charlotte Hawkins was pushing a baby carriage while reading a high school Latin textbook, she chanced to meet Palmer on the street. Hawkins was babysitting to raise money for a silk slip to wear under her new organdy graduation dress, but Palmer assumed that she was an impoverished student, overcoming all odds to get an education. Palmer mentioned Hawkins favorably to the principal of her high school when they next met, and the incident ended. Now, when Hawkins realized that Palmer was an overseer of her normal school, she wrote to her and reminded her of their chance meeting. Palmer responded by paying Hawkins's tuition.[6]

Several months before graduation, Charlotte Hawkins met a supervisor from the American Missionary Association (AMA) on a train. The AMA representative impressed upon Hawkins the needs of the South, and Hawkins left school to accept a position at a one-teacher school in Sedalia, North Carolina, near Greensboro in 1901.[7] The AMA funded the school for two years, then withdrew support. For a year, Hawkins drew no salary, and she and the students survived on what they grew, the produce their parents donated, and a $100 county appropriation. Charlotte Hawkins returned to Cambridge and approached Alice Freeman Palmer for financial help, which Palmer promised to consider when she returned from Europe some months later. Palmer died in Europe, however, and Hawkins decided to name the school in her memory. With continuing county support and private contributions, Palmer Memorial Institute taught practical vocational skills to its students, and Hawkins became active in the North Carolina Teachers Association and in women's club work. In 1911, Hawkins married Edward S. Brown. But the marriage lasted only a few months since Edward said he could not remain in Sedalia and be "Miss Hawkins's husband."[8]

In the South, Brown tells us, she demanded the respect of whites and received it from the "quality people." She insisted upon being addressed as "Miss," "Mrs.," or, after she gained honorary degrees, "Doctor."[9] She refused to be Jim Crowed and reported that several times she was "put out of Pullman berths and seats during all hours of the night." . . . By 1920, with the support of prominent Greensboro whites, Brown built Palmer Memorial Institute into a sprawling complex. She was proud that the most powerful whites in Greensboro served on the Palmer board, including Lula McIver and Julius Cone, head of the huge Cone Mills.[10]

As Brown rendered it, the theme of her life story is challenge met through interracial cooperation. Brown shaped the narrative in two critical ways: she minimized the restrictions of race in her daily life and exaggerated whites' helpfulness at every critical juncture. She obscured the fact that she was illegitimate by making it seem as if her father, Edmund Hight, was separated from the family by slavery. Brown was born in 1883 and had an older brother, demonstrating that her mother had a long-term relationship with Hight. The Hight family continued to live near Henderson throughout the twentieth century. Brown's grandmother, Rebecca Hawkins, may have been the sister of railroad magnate Captain John Hawkins, Jr., but, far from acting as the family's protector, he retained no contact with his black relatives and was a Democrat of the white supremacist persuasion.[11]

Brown mythologized her birth to remind southern whites of slavery's legacy: their shared kinship with African Americans. At the same time, she drew whites as sympathetic figures, the "protectors" of their African American relatives. Such circumstances did exist in the South; they just did not happen to exist within Charlotte's immediate family. As whites created the fictional "good darky" who treasured the interpersonal relationships that sprang from the close association of whites and blacks during slavery, Brown created a fictional "good master" who realized the responsibilities of miscegenation and loved his family, white and black. She used this good master to assuage whites' guilt about slavery and to argue that even slaves and masters achieved interracial understanding. She did not have to fight whites who melded ancestral ties to romantic class mythologies; she could simply join them. She shared their aristocratic roots.

Brown had moved to Cambridge not "about the time of my birth" but at the age of six. Yet she claimed to have no memory of her early life in North Carolina, no first-hand recollection of discrimination against blacks in the South, indeed no racial consciousness while growing up, even though she spent a great deal of time in the South during her childhood, even entire summers. Brown remade herself as a New Englander. When asked how her name should appear on her high school diploma, she instantly dropped her North Carolina name—Lottie Hawkins—for the more genteel sounding "Charlotte Eugenia Hawkins," which she made up on the spot. She spoke in a manner that "combine[d] the mellow tones of the southern Negro and the quick clipped qualities of New England—people turn[ed] around to see who [was] speaking."[12]

By casting herself as a New Englander, Brown attempted to remain above the southern racial structure. In Greensboro, she occupied a place much like that of African diplomats to the United States—she was an exotic but North Carolina's own exotic. If whites accused her of being an outside agitator, Brown could fall back on her North Carolina roots. Then she presented herself as native stock, a female, black Ulysses who fought her way back to the South and to her own people, where she belonged.

The story of the AMA's dispatch of Charlotte Hawkins to the South to save her people competes with another, more complicated parable that Brown merely hinted at and may have consciously avoided dwelling upon. Rather than seeing herself as a New England missionary to a foreign place, Brown may have construed her return to North Carolina as coming to terms with the realities of race in her own life. One night at a Cambridge meeting, she watched magic lantern slides of the race work being done by African Americans in the South. She was particularly struck by two educators, Joseph Price, the founder of Livingstone College, and Lucy Laney, the founder of Haines Institute in Augusta, Georgia. She noted that both Price and Laney were, like herself, very dark skinned. Price and Laney were also brilliant, and their faces on the screen moved Brown to feel that there was a place where she might belong: the South.[13] Brown never acknowledged publicly that she had any personal reason for wanting to leave New England, choosing rather to emphasize the missionary aspect of her return.

As the years passed, accounts of the relationship between Alice Freeman Palmer and Brown made it seem as if Palmer had sent Brown to the South to found the school and that they had enjoyed a close friendship. . . . Contemporary newspaper accounts, which relied on Brown's own promotional material, reported that Palmer's "efforts" had made the school possible and "until her death she was an ardent supporter of her namesake."[14]

Although Brown did not actually lie about Palmer's interest in her and the school, she embroidered the truth. Brown and Palmer spent less than fifteen minutes together in their lifetimes, and Palmer never promised that she would personally contribute to the school. Instead, Palmer had told Brown upon their second meeting that she was too busy at the moment but that after her return from Europe she would contact friends in Boston to encourage them to support the school. Why, then, when Palmer never returned, did Brown name the school Palmer Memorial Institute? Actually, Brown originally named the school Alice Freeman Palmer Settlement in order to gain support from Palmer's friends in Boston.[15] Palmer, after a brilliant career, had died at a young age and was mourned by her friends, and a memorial to her could prompt contributions. . . .

Around 1910, Brown cannily began to play southern pride against northern dollars when she inspired white leaders in Greensboro to challenge their community to take over the financial support of Palmer.[16] In soliciting southern white support, Brown . . . most often called the school Sedalia rather than Palmer. For example, Brown named the group of students who sang African American spirituals the Sedalia Singers.[17] She understood the white southerners' sense of place, and since her school was the only thing in the crossroads of Sedalia, she did not encroach upon white territory in appropriating the name. The location of Palmer at Sedalia facilitated support from Greensboro whites. It was ten miles outside of the city, surrounded by sparsely populated farmland. Brown never permitted Palmer students to travel alone to Greensboro but instead brought them as a group, with the boys clad in coats and ties and the girls wearing hats and white gloves. Once in the city, they did not mingle with Greensboro's African Americans; rather, Brown negotiated special seating sections for her students at public events.[18]

Although Brown cloaked the curriculum at Palmer in vocational disguises and portrayed it to the press as an industrial school until the late 1930s, the institute offered mostly academic courses from its inception.[19] Booker T. Washington met Brown on a trip to Boston while she was still a student there and pronounced her "the only convert that he made in New England." If he believed her to be a convert, she outfoxed the Wizard himself.[20] . . . Brown never embraced Washington's vocational philosophy past the point of providing for the school's basic needs, but she portrayed the school as industrial, detailing "farm yields" in fund-raising letters.[21] An unidentified Palmer teacher explained the ruse this way: "[Brown] always had a college preparatory class . . . a cultural academic school. All the Negroes had to have that in order to get along in the South." Even though this teacher believed, along with Brown, that African Americans profited most from classical knowledge coupled with reinforcement of middle-class values, support for that sort of training did not exist. So Brown and her teachers positioned Palmer as a "vocational" school. Funding for industrial education "could always get through," the teacher recalled. Despite the vocational exterior, she continued, "you could teach anything you wanted when you got in your school. You came inside your class room and you taught them Latin and French and all the things you knew."[22] Although initially Brown's students were the poor children of the neighborhood, by 1920, Palmer functioned as an academic boarding school that drew students from counties across the state and included secondary grades.[23]

Notwithstanding her vocal cover, at times Brown argued that her approach to "cultural" instruction benefited whites as well as African Americans. She explained, "Recognizing the need of a cultural approach to life, believing absolutely in education through racial contacts, I have devoted my whole life to establish for Negro youth something superior to Jim Crowism." She tried to accomplish this "by bringing the two races together under the highest cultural environment that will increase race pride, mutual respect, confidence, sympathetic understanding, and interracial goodwill."[24]

Why did Brown repeatedly overdraw white understanding and support and minimize the restrictions that her color placed on her? Throughout her life, she operated by a simple rule: it is better to overestimate possibility than to underestimate it. Charlotte Hawkins Brown created a fictional mirror of civility in race relations and held it up to whites as a reflection of their better selves. From slavery, she drew compassion; from the loneliness of Cambridge, racial liberality among her schoolmates; from Alice Freeman Palmer's deferral, a legacy; and from frightened, pinched southern whites, chivalry of a sort. Brown was a political genius, especially suited for interracial work. Her renderings served her own purposes, but she did not . . . delude herself into thinking that they were true. Immune to her own romantic stories, Brown was the consummate pragmatist. So convinced was she of her mission and of her opponent's rigid character, that she could risk the heartbreak of gilding the lily. She expected nothing, received little, and turned that pittance into bounty.

But Charlotte Hawkins Brown was a double agent. When she refused to turn her head toward the "colored" waiting room, she must have felt the stares of its patrons burn into her consciousness. In the decade preceding 1920, Brown immersed herself in social welfare projects and political activity that she kept hidden from whites. After 1920, Brown acquired a national reputation for her interracial work and landed official positions in interracial organizations, success that brought her activities under public scrutiny. Until then, and thereafter when she could, Brown generally said one thing to whites and then did another if it suited her purposes.

Brown's double life left its mark on her. . . . Living her life as a diplomat to the white community, Brown could never be just Lottie Hawkins. African American women who chose to take up interracial work walked a tightrope that required them to be forever careful, tense, and calculating. One slip would end their careers; they worked without nets.

In Lula Martin McIver, Brown found an exception to her belief that the southern white woman stood at the center of the race "problem." Their first meeting represents a classic case of the Brown treatment. Constantly seeking funds for Palmer Memorial Institute, Brown decided in the spring of 1905 that she must approach prominent white men in Greensboro for support. In Greensboro, Brown had no magic key such as Alice Freeman Palmer's name. Sedalia was a crossroads, Palmer Institute tiny, and Brown unknown. She had no historic connections to white North Carolinians there, no reputation in the black community, no denominational bridge since she had converted to Congregationalism, a faith rare in the South among either African Americans or whites. She had only herself—the New England persona she so carefully cultivated—and courage.

In 1904, she had written a poignant letter to Charles McIver, president of the white women's normal college in Greensboro. It began, "This letter may come to you from a strange source, but it comes from one whose heart is in the educational and moral uplift of our people." It concluded by begging McIver to come to Palmer for a visit. A year later, Brown was still imploring him to the same end, touting the ease of the train ride and signing herself "Very Anxiously Yours."[25] Still McIver did not come. One morning Brown dressed carefully in her customary ankle-length dress, hat, and white gloves and set out to call on him in Greensboro. She had no appointment. Most often Brown did not write or telephone ahead and risk refusal from those she wished to meet but simply appeared on their doorstep. That morning she knocked on the front door of the president's residence and found that he was away. His wife, Lula Martin McIver, invited Brown in, an unusual act in itself. Lula McIver was stunned by Brown's appearance at the door. "Her daring, her enthusiasm, her faith intrigued me," McIver recalled. The two women talked for over an hour and warmed toward each other. Soon, McIver was advising Brown on "the best way to win friends" and on how to raise money among the Greensboro elite for the school.[26]

When Lula McIver opened the door, Brown chanced upon a valuable connection that would prove enduring. Brown sat in the parlor of the state's foremost white female educational advocate. Graduated from the Moravian academy in Salem, Lula Martin had longed to become a doctor like her father. After she learned that the profession was virtually closed to women, she became an outspoken feminist. As an adolescent, she abandoned the Moravians for the Methodists upon reading that the early Moravian settlers chose wives by lottery. In 1885, strong-willed Lula Martin met Charles Duncan McIver, a dedicated young teacher, who supported her feminist ideas and called her a "most sensible" woman. They married in a ceremony that omitted the word "obey," and Lula refused a wedding ring, which she regarded as a "badge of slavery."[27]

The McIvers worked to build North Carolina's white public educational system one school at a time. While Charles traveled throughout the state promoting grade school education, Lula served as his advance team, preceding him to scrub courthouse venues speckled with tobacco juice, to set up chairs, to post flyers, and to raise a crowd. She was delighted when Charles became first president of the state-supported normal school for white women since both felt that educating women would be the key to building an effective public school system. She helped to found the Woman's Association for the Betterment of Public School Houses, and after Charles's death, she accepted a paying position as its field secretary.[28]

The subtleties of Lula McIver's racial ideology are elusive, but at the center of her thinking about race lay the strongly held belief that African Americans deserved a good education. For nearly a half century after they met, McIver continually raised money for Palmer Memorial Institute. Lula McIver attended meetings of black women's clubs in Greensboro. After the early death of Charles McIver in 1909, and to the eternal perplexity of Greensboro whites, each semester Lula McIver invited a male African American student from nearby North Carolina Agricultural and Technical College to board in the president's residence where she lived until her death. There, surrounded by young white women students, Lula McIver offered an object lesson in race relations.[29]

Both Brown and McIver realized the restrictions on their relationship in the Jim Crow South. For starters, McIver was a woman and thus not powerful in her own right. Moreover, as the normal school's maternal figurehead, she had to act circumspectly since all of her actions reflected upon the school, which was still in the minds of some a dangerous experiment that wasted state money to educate women. Given these restrictions, McIver could do three concrete things for Brown: influence prominent white Greensboro men to support her, introduce leading club women to Palmer's mission, and raise money. She did another intangible and invaluable thing for Brown: Lula McIver publicly referred to Charlotte Hawkins Brown as her friend.[30]

It appears that Lula McIver realized that her husband's influence would be more valuable than her own, and she urged Charles to write an "open letter of endorsement" for Palmer Memorial Institute shortly after she met Brown. Since Charles McIver served on the Southern Education Board, his vote of confidence carried weight in the North as well as the South. The letter went out in June 1905, but Charles McIver admitted in it that he had never been to Palmer.[31] He died four years later. Long after that, Brown named Charles D. McIver as her "first friend" in North Carolina.[32] There is no record that McIver ever made the trip to Sedalia or that Brown ever met him. With Lula McIver's help, Brown appropriated the memory of Charles McIver as she had that of Alice Freeman Palmer.

Local support of Palmer flowered around 1914 when Lula McIver brought a delegation of white women from across the state to visit the school. A member of the delegation wrote an account of the visit that appeared in the *Greensboro Daily Record* and encouraged white women to take an interest in Brown's work. Brown struck just the right note in her solicitation letter: Palmer, she said, "has conducted its work for the past 13 years without seeking very much help from our southern friends." She claimed friendship and a debt come due in the same breath.[33] The 1914 campaign was the beginning of a steady stream of white visitors to the school and financial support from white North Carolinians.[34] In 1917, Lula McIver conducted some of Greensboro's leading white businessmen on a tour of the school. Many of the men who had ignored Brown's previous appeals converted after that visit. E. P. Wharton recalled that Charlotte Brown had called on him around 1903 to obtain support for Palmer and that he was "ashamed of [him]self for losing sight" of Brown's work. He subsequently served for decades as a Palmer trustee. By 1920, the board of Palmer Memorial Institute included a Greensboro attorney, a banker, and an industrial magnate.[35] McIver sought no publicity for a trip she made to Boston with Charlotte Hawkins Brown two years later. There McIver called upon prominent white women, vouched for Brown's success, and asked for contributions to Palmer. When northern white women visited Palmer, they would not spend the night at the black school but stayed instead with Lula McIver.[36]

In 1919, Charlotte Hawkins Brown, with the endorsement of Lula McIver, published a remarkable novel, *Mammy*. On its face, the appearance of *Mammy* places Brown squarely in the accommodationist camp of African Americans, currying favor from whites by invoking the ties of slavery. The story tells of a loving black woman who nurses a white family and raises its children. Then, when the woman becomes old and ill, the family provides no help beyond an occasional visit to her drafty log cabin. Ultimately, they stand by as Mammy goes to the county home. Brown dedicated the book to "my good friend, Mrs. Charles Duncan McIver." She continued, "It is with gratitude I acknowledge her personal interest in the colored members of her household."[37]

What could Brown have hoped to accomplish by the publication of *Mammy*? At the time, she served as president of the statewide Association of Colored Women's Clubs, refused Jim Crow seating, and was secretly organizing a campaign to interest the state's black women in woman suffrage. She had spent almost twenty years building her dignity in North Carolina. It was amazing that she would play the *Mammy* card now. A close reading of Brown's introduction and McIver's response to the dedication indicates that both saw *Mammy* as a tool to promote their agenda: interracial cooperation among women. Mammies represented the one point of contact between southern black and white women, and white women continually bragged about their love for their Mammies. But Brown's *Mammy* is not a tale of love rewarded; it is an indictment of white neglect of African Americans. Brown calls upon white women to remember their duty to black women and redefines that duty in new ways. It is no longer enough to be fond of ol' Mammy; white women must act on that affection.

McIver framed her endorsement of *Mammy* carefully. She said that today's white woman was not the person her mother was, for in her mother's day, there was "understanding and sympathy" between the races. The problem was the separation of the races since there could be no racial harmony without "knowledge of each other's problems and an active interest in solving them." McIver endorsed the concept of "racial integrity" but reminded white southerners that their "task [was the] training of the uncivilized African." Brown must have winced at that remark, but it preceded McIver's most important statement: "I verily believe that to the most intelligent southern white women we must look for leadership in keeping our 'ship of state' off the rocks of racial antagonism." She signed the piece, "Your friend, Lula Martin McIver."[38]

Interracial cooperation, association among black and white women to solve mutual problems, was the solution that *Mammy* endorsed. McIver did not propose that white women individually care for their mammies but that they enter the public sphere and provide leadership. Male sailors had steered the ship of state onto rocky racial shores. It was time for women to man the lifeboats and rescue government from the oppressive racial politics of the white supremacists. In the same month that *Mammy* appeared, the state's white and black women began to do just that by traveling to Memphis, Tennessee, for a formal interracial summit. The state associations of women's clubs and the YWCAs sent forth those first intrepid female navigators.

Most of the black women who traveled to the Memphis interracial summit learned leadership skills in the National Association of Colored Women, but their experience in working with white women had come from two other sources as well: heretofore racially segregated groups that came together on the homefront in World War I and the interracial work of the Young Women's Christian Association (YWCA). During World War I organizational lines between women's groups of both races blurred when the Council of National Defense chose white women from each southern state to head committees to coordinate work on the homefront. In North Carolina, white women set up integrated county councils that included African American and white women, carefully chosen to represent clubs, YWCAs, and denominational social service programs.[39]

The work of the black YWCA centered on another upheaval of the time: African American migration from farm to town. Southern black women believed strongly in the YWCA's ability to reach poor young women who had moved to the city to find work. The national YWCA board determined that any southern African American branch must be supervised by an existing "central" YWCA. "Central" meant white. Once founded, the black YWCA must be overseen by a management committee of three white women and two black women. The rules mandated interracial "cooperation" of a sort. Despite these humiliating restrictions, two southern black women, Mary McCrorey of Charlotte, North Carolina, and Lugenia Burns Hope of Atlanta, founded Ys in their cities.[40]

On the train to Memphis, a group of white men pulled Brown out of the Pullman car and marched her past "southern white women passing for Christians" who were on their way to the Memphis meeting. The white women sat silent as the men forced Brown to the Jim Crow car.[41] Brown probably recognized among the fellow Memphis delegates North Carolina white women whom she had come to know over the past decade. Among them was the wife of the governor, Fanny Bickett. . . .

When Brown rose to address the white women, the frustration of a decade of interracial work erupted, and she shared the humiliation of being ousted from the Pullman car two nights before. She exhorted white women to fight lynching, to recognize the dignity of the African American woman, and to help black women. Brown ended on an ominous note: "You are going to reach out for the same hand that I am reaching out for but I know that the dear Lord will not receive it if you are crushing me beneath your feet."[42] Most of the white women were profoundly moved.

As it happened, the women's Memphis interracial meeting foundered on the spot that Lula McIver had warned of in *Mammy*: the shoal of politics. Two months before the meeting, a federal amendment had mandated woman suffrage and a month after the meeting women would vote for the first time. Just before Brown left for Tennessee, she had been secretly organizing black women in North Carolina to register to vote. One faction of black women would not budge on the issue of suffrage at the Memphis meeting. A full year later, the white and black women still had not agreed on a statement of goals for an interracial movement. Brown, McCrorey, and Hope favored a version that included the controversial demand for protection of African American voting rights. Their language was blunt: "We believe that the ballot is the safe-guard of the Nation and that every citizen in the Nation should have the right to use it. We believe that if there is ever to be any justice before the law, the Negro must have the right to exercise the vote."[43] But the white women balked at the suffrage statement and the condemnation of lynching, both points "which the Negro women dared not leave out."[44] Whites suggested the wording, "We believe that the ballot is the safe-guard of the Nation, and that every *qualified* citizen in the Nation should have the right to use it."[45]

Interracial cooperation led straight into politics. As black and white women inched toward cooperation on a grass roots level, they came face-to-face with larger political forces. With a decade of women's interracial experience behind them, many African American women believed that the time had come to take a firm stand on suffrage. Black women looked to their white allies to support their right to vote, a gesture that underscores the success of interracial cooperation. Yet white women's confusion over black women's suffrage reveals the limits of voluntary interracial work. Upon the passage of woman suffrage, white women involved with interracial social service projects had to chose between gender and race. They could support black women's right to vote as women, or oppose their right to vote as *black* women. Charlotte Hawkins Brown called the question when she used the NACW to organize black women's voter registration drives in urban areas in the fall of 1920. Across the South, other black women did the same thing, reporting back to the National Association for the Advancement of Colored People (NAACP).

In Mobile, Alabama, registrars told black women that they must own property to vote, and when the black juvenile court officer challenged them, court officials fired her.[46] From Birmingham came the news that when a black teacher attempted to register, the registrar "called her an ugly name and ordered her out." Another teacher "answered every question asked her—ex post facto law, habeas corpus proceedings, etc." The frustrated registrar still would not yield and "tore up her card and threw it in her face."[47] Ultimately, in Birmingham, 225 black women succeeded in registering, although 4,500 made the attempt.[48]

It is impossible to judge Charlotte Hawkins Brown's success in the North Carolina registration campaign. Most registration books failed to survive, but those that exist show not only that black women succeeded in urban areas, but that voter registration increased for black men as well. Probably less than 1,000 black women registered in North Carolina that fall.[49] To judge the results of black women's drive for suffrage, however, one must look not just at the few thousand who managed to register in 1920, but at the heritage of interracial work upon which they built and at the example they set for those who followed. The number of black women who voted in 1920 may have

been small, but their significance in the South's racial politics was large. For the first time since the nineteenth century in the South, black voters approached the registrars en masse. They assembled as the result of a coordinated, subversive campaign that crossed over the boundaries of voluntary interracial work to reintroduce black civil rights in electoral politics. By their presence at the polls, black women dared whites to use violence and won the dare. In 1921, white supremacy still stood, but black women had found faultlines in its foundations.

NOTES

1. Ceci Jenkins, incomplete notes for "The Twig Bender of Sedalia" ([1946]), unpublished biography of Charlotte Hawkins Brown, reel 1, #12, Brown Collection, Manuscript Collection, Schlesinger Library (SL). See also Stephen Birmingham, *Certain People: America's Black Elite* (Boston: Little, Brown, 1977).

2. "A Biography," reel 1, and "Some Incidents in the Life and Career of Charlotte Hawkins Brown Growing out of Racial Situations, at the Request of Dr. Ralph Bunche," reel 1, #2, both in Brown Collection, SL.

3. "Some Incidents," 1–2, reel 1, #2, ibid.

4. "A Biography," reel 1, ibid. The language of "A Biography" is closely echoed in Sadie L. Daniel, *Women Builders* (Washington, D.C.: Associated Publishers, 1970), 133–63.

5. "A Biography," 13, reel 1, Brown Collection, SL.

6. On Palmer, see Ruth B. Bordin, *Alice Freeman Palmer: The Evolution of a New Woman* (Ann Arbor: University of Michigan Press, 1993). On the Brown/Palmer relationship, see "A Biography," 16–18, reel 1, and Jenkins, "Twig Bender of Sedalia," reel 1, #7, both in Brown Collection, SL.

7. Daniel, *Women Builders*, 139; "A Biography," 19, reel 1, Brown Collection, SL.

8. Charlotte E. Hawkins to Dr. Buttrick, 31 Aug. 1904, folder 1005, box 111, series 1, subseries 1, General Education Board Collection, RAC. Mary Grinnell to Charlotte Hawkins Brown, 4 Oct. 1910, 8 Feb. 1911; H. F. Kimball to Charlotte Hawkins Brown, 12 June 1911; and J. G. Bright to Charlotte Hawkins Brown, 1 Aug. 1911, all on reel 2, #33; Mary T. Grinnell to Charlotte Hawkins Brown, 6 Aug. 1912, 17 Feb. 1913, reel 2, #34; and Charlotte Hawkins Brown Ebony Questionnaire, 16, reel 1, #11, all in Brown Collection, SL.

9. Brown wrote that it was a "big surprise" that the white people in the South refused to "use the term 'Miss'" when they addressed black women. She continued, "Naturally I was constantly being insulting and insulted which merited for me the name 'Yankee Huzzy.'" See "Some Incidents," 5, reel 1, #2, Brown Collection, SL. Leading whites in Greensboro referred to her as "Dr. Brown" after she received honorary degrees from Wilberforce, Lincoln, and Howard universities. See Junius Scales to Glenda Gilmore, 4 Jan. 1990, in author's possession.

10. Letterhead, Palmer Memorial Institute, C. Hawkins Brown to W. E. B. Dubois [*sic*], to June 1930, W. E. B. Du Bois Papers, reel 33, University of Massachusetts, Amherst.

11. Ruth Anita Hawkins Hughes, *Contributions of Vance County People of Color* (Raleigh: Sparks Press, 1988).

12. Jenkins, "Twig Bender of Sedalia," 1, reel 1, #7, Brown Collection, SL.

13. Ibid., insert B; "Some Incidents," 9, reel 1, #2, Brown Collection, SL.

14. Eva M. Young, "Palmer Memorial Institute Unique," *Charlotte Observer*, 10 Mar. 1940, folder 51, box 94–3, ibid.

15. Jenkins, "Twig Bender of Sedalia," E.F. 16, reel 1, #7, Brown Collection, SL.

16. Ibid., E.F. 16, E.F. 17; "Some Incidents," reel 1, #2, Brown Collection, SL.

17. For an example of the conflation of Sedalia and Palmer Institute, see *Palmer Memorial Institute: The Mission and the Legacy* (Greensboro: Women of Greensboro, [1981]).

18. The description here is from interviews and conversations with Dawn Gilmore, Brooks Gilmore, and Lois MacKenzie, the author's aunt, uncle, and mother, respectively. The author's grandfather, Clyde Manly Gilmore, was Brown's physician, and the author's mother, MacKenzie, was her attorney's secretary in the 1950s.

19. Brown transformed the institute in the late 1930s into a preparatory school for upper-class African Americans. By 1940, the school letterhead read: "The Charm School Idea of the Palmer Memorial Institute, Charlotte Hawkins Brown, President and Promoter." See C. Hawkins Brown to My Dear Friend, 20 Mar. 1940, folder 124, box 112–4, Washington Conservatory of Music Records, Moorland-Spingarn Research Center, Howard University (MRSC).

20. Jenkins, "Twig Bender of Sedalia," insert G, reel 1, #7, Brown Collection, SL.

21. Charlotte Hawkins Brown to Wallace Buttrick, 19 Dec. 1912, folder 1005, box 111, series 1, subseries 1, General Education Board Collection, Rockefeller Archive Center (RAC).

22. "Charlotte Hawkins Brown," Dannett Collection, uncataloged, LC. See also Sylvia G. L. Dannett, *Profiles of Negro Womanhood* (New York: M. W. Lads, 1964–66), 59–63. The notes for Dannett's biographical sketches often do not identify the interviewee and are fragmentary.

23. Map, "Palmer Memorial Institute—Sedalia—Enrol[l]ment—1920–1921," folder 1006, box 111, series 1, subseries 1, General Education Board Collection, RAC.

24. "Some Incidents," reel 1, #2, Brown Collection, SL.

25. Board, 1904, Correspondence G-M, box 14, and C. E. Hawkins to Dr. McIver, 13 Apr. 1905, file Southern Education Board, 1905, Correspondence, E-L, box 15, both in Charles D. McIver Collection, University Archives, Walter Clinton Jackson Library, University of North Carolina, Greensboro (WCJL).

26. Mrs. Charles D. McIver to editor of *Greensboro Daily News*, [ca. 1940], reel 1, #13, and Jenkins, "Twig Bender of Sedalia," reel 1, #7, both in Brown Collection, SL.

27. Rose Howell Holder, *McIver of North Carolina* (Chapel Hill: University of North Carolina Press, 1917), 63–67. See also Virginia T. Lathrop, "Mrs. McIver Believes Greatness of the Past Holds State's Hope for Present and Future," *News and Observer*, 6 Oct. 1940, Clipping File, vol. 94, reel 24, 371–72, North Carolina Collection, University of North Carolina, Chapel Hill (NCC).

28. James Leloudis, "'A More Certain Means of Grace': Pedagogy, Self, and Society in North Carolina, 1880–1920" (Ph.D. diss., University of North Carolina at Chapel Hill, 1989), and Pamela Dean, "Covert Curriculum: Class and Gender in a New South Women's College" (Ph.D. diss., University of North Carolina at Chapel Hill, 1995). On the association, see James Leloudis, "School Reform in the New South: The Woman's Association for the Betterment of Public School Houses in North Carolina, 1902–1919," *Journal of American History* 69 (March 1983): 886–909. See also Lula Martin McIver to Charles L. Coon, 4 Feb. 1909, folder 28, box 2, and Lula Martin McIver to Charles L. Coon, 25 Jan. 1910, folder 29, box 2, both in Coon Papers, Southern Historical Collection, University of North Carolina, Chapel Hill (SHC).

29. Sallie Waugh McBryan to Mrs. McIver, 22 Nov. 1913, file Correspondence, 1909–44, box 141, Lula Martin McIver Collection, WCJL; "Famous Landmark at WCUNC Razed," *Durham Morning Herald*, 26 Oct. 1952, Clipping File, vol. 94, reel 24, 343–44, NCC.

30. Lula Martin McIver to Charlotte Hawkins Brown, 6 Apr. 1920, reel 2, #41, Brown Collection, SL.

31. Charles D. McIver letter, 5 June 1905, reel 2, #30, Correspondence, 1902–6, ibid.

32. "Award Will Go to Dr. Brown," *Greensboro Daily News*, 10 Apr. 1947, Clipping File, vol. 18, reel 5, 239, NCC.

33. C. Hawkins Brown to My dear Sir [Professor Julius I. Foust], 25 May 1914, file General Correspondence, 1913–15, box 57, Foust Collection, WCJL.

34. Jenkins, "Twig Bender of Sedalia," 77, reel 1, #12, Brown Collection, SL.

35. E. P. Wharton to Charlotte Hawkins Brown, 12 Jan. 1917, reel 2, #37, Jan.–Apr. 1917; Mrs. Charles D. McIver to editor of *Greensboro Daily News*, n.d., reel 1 #13; and Jenkins, "Twig Bender of Sedalia," 78, reel 1, #12, all in Brown Collection, SL.

36. H. F. Kimball to Charlotte Hawkins Brown, 6 Nov. 1916, reel 2, #36, 1916, and "Notes," copy of notebook maintained by Charlotte Hawkins Brown, reel 1, #8, both in Brown Collection, SL; Annie L. Vickery to My Dear Mrs. McIver, 7 Mar. 1917, file Correspondence, 1909–44, box 141, Lula Martin McIver Collection, WCJL.

37. Charlotte Hawkins Brown, *Mammy* (Boston: Pilgrim Press, 1919).

38. Lula Martin McIver to Charlotte Hawkins Brown, 6 Apr. 1920, reel 2, #41, Brown Collection, SL.

39. Laura Holmes Reilley to D. H. Hill, 18 Oct. 1917, file Women's Committee, box 30, North Carolina Council of Defense, World War I Papers, 1903–33, pt. 2, Military Collection, North Carolina Department of Archives and History.

40. Mary J. McCrorey to Mrs. Hope, 7 May 1920; "Mrs. Hope of the Cleveland Meeting, 1920," 29 May 1920; "What the Colored Women Are Asking of the

Y.W.C.A."; "To the National Board of the Young Women's Christian Association"; Minutes of the Cleveland Meeting, 1920; "Minutes of the meeting held in the offices of the South Atlantic Field Committee, Richmond, Virginia, 3 July 1920"; and Mary J. McCrorey to Mrs. Hope, 27 Jan. 1921, all in box 5, NU 14-C-5, Y.W.C.A., Neighborhood Union Papers, Special Collections, Robert Woodruff Library, Atlanta University, Atlanta, Georgia. Mary J. McCrorey to Charlotte Hawkins Brown, 2 Apr. 1920, reel 2, #41, Brown Collection, SL.

41. Jacquelyn Dowd Hall, *Revolt against Chivalry: Jessie Daniel Ames and the Women's Campaign against Lynching*, rev. ed. (New York: Columbia University Press, 1987), 93; "Some Incidents," reel 1, #2, Brown Collection, SL.

42. Brown address, folder 1, box 1, ibid.; Hall, *Revolt against Chivalry*, 93–94.

43. "First Draft," section 2, folder 1, box 1, ibid.

44. "Statement of Negro Women in Session, Mar. 26, 1921," folder 1, box 1.

45. Folder 1, box 1, ibid. (emphasis added).

46. W. E. Morton to NAACP, file Voting, 10–30 Nov. 1920, C284, National Association for the Advancement of Colored People Papers, Library of Congress.

47. H. M. Kingsley to NAACP, 9 Nov. 1920, file Voting, 1–9 Nov. 1920, C284, NAACP Papers.

48. Charles McPerson to NAACP, file Voting, 1–9 Nov. 1920, C284, NAACP Papers. For a summary of reports from across the South, see "Disfranchisement of Colored Americans in the Presidential Election of 1920" ([1920]), file Voting, Dec. 1920, C284, NAACP Papers.

49. Glenda E. Gilmore, *Gender and Jim Crow: Women and the Politics of White Supremacy in North Carolina, 1896–1920* (Chapel Hill: University of North Carolina Press, 1996), 219–224.

KIM E. NIELSEN
The Southern Identity of Helen Keller

Although Helen Keller is widely regarded as a "national icon representing the triumphs of the disabled," Kim E. Nielsen urges us to understand Keller in a more complex way by acknowledging that her regional background and racial identity shaped her life. In other words, Nielsen offers an intersectional analysis, analyzing how being white, southern, middle-class, and gendered female affected Keller's experience with disability. The author keeps in play many dimensions of Keller's life: her spirituality, her relationships with her parents, her activism (national and international), her geographic comings and goings, and her reading. Nielsen also helps us imagine what it might have been like for a displaced southerner like Keller to read *Gone with the Wind* the year it came out. Compare this with your own encounters with Margaret Mitchell's novel and the movie based on it.

Does Nielsen's portrayal of Keller change the ways you think about her? What do you see as the significance of her southern background? Why is Keller's whiteness important to understanding her identity?

Though Helen Keller left her parents' home in Tuscumbia, Alabama, at the young age of eight, the culture, people, and sensory adventures of her native state were essential to her outlook throughout her life. The deaf-blind activist, author, and world traveler, born in 1880, considered Ivy Green, her family's Tuscumbia home, as her own. Beginning in her lifetime and continuing today, Tuscumbia and Alabama have similarly regarded her as their own—even featuring her on the 2003 state quarter. Keller was also a child of the broader South. Though after her initial departure she always lived outside the region, her southern childhood and

Excerpted from "The Southern Ties of Helen Keller," *Journal of Southern History* 73:4 (November 2007): 783–806, by Kim E. Nielsen. Reprinted by permission of the author and publisher. Notes have been edited and renumbered.

family ties formed and constituted vital elements of her public and private identity. She claimed this identity fondly but frequently labeled as shameful the dominant southern racial ideologies and practices.

Paradoxically, it was perhaps Keller's disability that provided the opportunities that most frequently caused her to question southern gender and racial traditions. Her disability took her physically away from the South, as she and her family turned to northern educational institutions with historical ties to abolitionism. Her disability and her politics as an adult separated her from her family ideologically and geographically. Once she became world famous and increasingly active politically, those commenting upon or questioning her political ideas used her southern identity to either praise or deride her and her principles. As she traveled more, claiming global citizenship and analyzing national and world politics, she naturally did so from a base of knowledge and culture built on her southern background. Today, however, Keller is embraced as a national icon representing the triumphs of the disabled. Her image is now divorced from her southern identity. She is viewed as an American, devoid of regional affiliations or associations. In contrast, this essay positions Keller as a southerner of a Confederate family whose background and beliefs helped shape her worldview and her life as a white, southern woman with a disability.[1]

Keller and her family embraced an esteemed southern heritage, which they perhaps regarded as being more illustrious than it really had been. When Keller wrote her autobiography, *The Story of My Life,* in 1903, she described her lineage according to both geography and the Civil War. In this narrative the men served and the women sired. Helen's father, Arthur H. Keller, served as a captain and her maternal grandfather as a brigadier general for the Confederacy. Her paternal grandmother, she noted, was second cousin to Robert E. Lee. Captain Keller edited the Tuscumbia *North Alabamian* for many years and served in the mid-1880s as U.S. marshal for the northern district of Alabama. Through him, the young Helen claimed Alexander Spotswood, a lieutenant governor (and de facto governor) in early-eighteenth-century Virginia, as her great-great-grandfather.[2]

Captain Arthur Keller considered his family to be part of the deserving upper-class white elite. . . . Like many other southern land-holding and formerly slaveholding whites, they had lost much of their wealth between 1860 and 1880. At the time of Helen Keller's birth, her family lived on the homestead her grandfather had built and named Ivy Green decades earlier due to the "beautiful English ivy" covering trees and fences. The Kellers were, however, no longer the wealthy family they once were. Moreover, the daily physical labor demanded to sustain the household, even with the aid of the formerly enslaved and their descendants, had surprised and exhausted Helen's young mother, Kate, after she became the second wife of the much older man whom all called Captain Keller.[3]

The young toddler Helen, Kate's first child, became blind and deaf due to an illness at the age of nineteen months. From Ivy Green, Arthur and Kate Keller sought assistance with the child whom they loved but, as she grew older, felt increasingly incapable of parenting. Family members encouraged placing the girl in an asylum or institution.

Talladega, only about 170 miles away from Tuscumbia, hosted both the Alabama School for the Deaf (founded in 1858) and the Alabama School for the Blind (founded in 1867). While technically separate, the schools had at one point shared a campus and were only blocks apart. Keller would not have been the first deaf-blind student, for another had enrolled as early as 1867. Neither school admitted African Americans.[4] Apparently neither Keller parent considered sending Helen to either of these schools, likely because both institutions had few resources and floundering reputations, having emerged from the Civil War damaged and inadequately funded.

Kate Keller initially refused to send her young child away from home. Like most Americans at that time, she doubted that a deaf-blind child could be educated. As a parent, however, she clearly had hopes for her daughter's life. In the mid-1880s the obviously literate Mrs. Keller read Charles Dickens's *American Notes* (1842) and in it his reference to Laura Bridgman and abolitionist Samuel Gridley Howe, the founder of Boston's Perkins Institution. Bridgman also had lost her sight and hearing at a fairly young age due to illness. Howe's successful effort to teach Bridgman to use the manual alphabet to communicate and perhaps his even greater success at publicizing her had made Howe, Perkins, and Bridgman nearly world famous.[5] Mrs. Keller reasoned that if Bridgman had learned such communication, so might Helen.

Kate Keller's first effort ended after she learned that Howe had died in 1876, but the mother of the young deaf-blind girl persisted. She and her husband tried again, contacting Baltimore oculist Dr. Julian Chisholm. He encouraged them to contact Alexander Graham Bell. . . . Captain Keller traveled by train first to Baltimore and then to Washington, D.C., with the six-year-old and apparently very unruly Helen in order to consult with both doctors personally. Bell recommended that the Kellers seek assistance for their daughter from the Perkins Institution, . . . [then directed by Howe's] son-in-law, Michael Anagnos. For Bell the school where the by-then-elderly Laura Bridgman still lived was the only logical place to seek an education for Helen.[6]

Southerners often looked at educational institutions for deaf and blind children with suspicion because of the linkage between educational reformers and abolitionism. Despite this source of doubt, Keller's parents were not alone as they turned to northern educational institutions. Southern whites with resources tended to send deaf or blind children to schools in the North. Northern educational institutions had stronger reputations, greater fiscal resources, enhanced international ties, and more highly educated teachers than did those in the South.[7]

In July 1886 Arthur Keller allowed his concern for his daughter to trump his hesitancy about northern educational institutions, and he wrote to Perkins's director. . . . Keller sought a skilled teacher willing to travel to Tuscumbia in order to care for young Helen. Anagnos said his thoughts "almost instinctively turned towards Miss Annie M. Sullivan," who was then summering in Brewster, Massachusetts. He recommended her "most highly and without any reservation." After exchanges of letters in numerous directions, Captain Keller agreed to Sullivan as an appropriate teacher and assured Anagnos that she would be treated "as one of our immediate family." He would pay her twenty-five dollars per month, a significant salary.[8]

The Keller family knew relatively little about Anne Sullivan. As the 1886 valedictorian of Perkins, she had given an address described . . . as "a beautiful original production, teeming with felicitous thoughts clothed in a graceful style."[10] Anagnos likely thought of her as a teaching candidate because of her intellectual skills, but he also considered her because she needed employment direly. Sullivan had arrived at Perkins via the almshouse. After the death of her mother and subsequently being deserted by her father, the blind, ten-year-old child of poor Irish immigrants had entered the almshouse of the Massachusetts State Infirmary at Tewksbury. Only by begging an education from touring philanthropists was the child able to enroll at Perkins. Numerous eye operations temporarily improved her eyesight; but her eyes frequently caused her pain, and her vision fluctuated. Despite graduating from Perkins, few respectable or viable employment opportunities existed for the twenty-year-old woman. . . .[9]

In March 1887 Anne Sullivan entered the gardens of Ivy Green with a northern viewpoint as firm as the Keller family's southern identity. . . . Sullivan grew up valorizing several sworn enemies of slavery and the Confederacy. Both Franklin B. Sanborn, who as general state inspector of charities in Massachusetts had enabled her escape from the Tewksbury almshouse, and Samuel Gridley Howe, founder of the Perkins Institution, had conspired as part of John Brown's so-called secret six [Bostonians who funded Brown's plan to start a slave insurrection in Virginia]. In the almshouse and at Perkins she had pored over the Boston *Pilot* (a weekly Irish American newspaper), particularly drawn to its coverage of abolitionist and orator Wendell Phillips. And to what must have been the horror of Captain Keller if he ever found out, Sullivan most favored Major General Benjamin Butler—the (in)famous Union "Beast" of New Orleans, supporter of black military regiments in the Civil War, female suffragist, punisher of the Confederacy, and Massachusetts advocate for the poor. As governor of Massachusetts from 1882 to 1886, he had rigorously investigated the ill treatment of residents at Tewksbury, and Sullivan adored him for it. Though many northerners increasingly "overlooked the history of American slavery" by the 1880s, Sullivan did not do so.[10] . . .

Sullivan purportedly hesitated to even accept employment in the Keller household for fear (correctly) that the family had once owned slaves. Friends warned her that she should "hold my peace while [in the] south, that any reference to conditions before or during the

Civil War would cause my instant dismissal." . . . As Sullivan later put it, she "did not like the idea of going south to live in a family that had probably been slave-holders."[11]

The arrival at the segregated Tuscumbia train station of the twenty-one-year-old Boston girl with a lingering Irish accent was novel enough for it to be a community event. A crowd gathered alongside Kate Keller, eagerly awaiting a glimpse of "the Yankee girl who was going to teach the Keller child." And just as the Tuscumbia community had never before encountered anyone like Anne Sullivan, she in turn had never before been to a place like Tuscumbia.[12]

Sullivan's descriptions of her life in Tuscumbia focus almost exclusively either on Helen or on the characteristics that made the region both southern and disagreeable (in her opinion). Her criticisms ranged widely, including the "untidy, shiftless manner of keeping house," "the shabbiness of the grounds and out-houses," and the muddy state of country roads. "Finding it very difficult not to air my righteous indignation," she ignored the advice of her friends and argued the war vigorously with Keller family members, particularly Captain Keller's brother Frank. After one bitter argument with "Uncle Frank"—in which "all the torrents of my wrath broke restraint, and I opened fire, and I did not cease until I had my say out to the last bitter word"—she temporarily packed her carpetbag to leave.[13]

The household in which young Helen grew up and in which Sullivan struggled held a strong Confederate identity. By the time of Keller's birth in 1880, white Alabamians had brutally silenced the discussions of racial equality and freedom formulated during the Civil War. As Sullivan arrived in 1887, white Alabamians were building and observing Lost Cause mythology via memoirs, memorials, parades, the glorification of veterans such as Keller's father, and a widely celebrated statewide public tour by Jefferson Davis. In the words of historian David W. Blight, it was the "diehard era" of the Lost Cause, in which Civil War remembrance became "a lucrative industry."[14] . . .

Keller thus grew up embedded in stories of the Old South and shared in the privileges of the Jim Crow "New" South. The household's daily schedule, labor divisions, and balances of power maintained the privileges of whiteness and patriarchy. Like other family members,

Helen Keller, young and disabled though she was, benefited from the system of racial inequalities.

Though deaf-blind and young, by 1887 the seven-year-old girl had already learned how to reinforce racial hierarchies. For example, the child Helen expected her nurse Viny and the household's cook, both African American servants, to serve her. This expectation is reflected unquestioningly in Keller's 1903 autobiography, The Story of My Life. Many of her childhood memories centered [on] Martha Washington, "a little coloured girl . . . the child of our cook," who accompanied, entertained, and monitored the difficult child. . . . As Keller put it unself-consciously, "I seldom had any difficulty in making her do just as I wished. It pleased me to domineer over her, and she generally submitted to my tyranny rather than risk a hand-to-hand encounter." In 1903 Keller attributed her successful dominance to the fact that she was "strong, active, indifferent to consequences," and willing "to fight tooth and nail"—not to her whiteness. Her biographers have generally attributed her violent behavior as a child to her frustration at being unable to communicate. Clearly, however, the young Keller directed her "tyranny" most often at Washington, for whom responding with physical violence held great consequence. Most likely Washington, two or three years older than Keller, respected the violence that the young white child could and did frequently accomplish. Yet Washington also undoubtedly knew that most African American boys and girls like herself were expected to serve white children. For whites, it was a way to care for their own children while indoctrinating black children in service and racial obsequiousness. Keller maintained her tyranny with the threat of personal violence, [an] . . . aggression [that] was a part of and enabled by the much larger racial realities of post-Redemption Alabama.[15]

As Keller's knowledge of the world rapidly expanded after Sullivan arrived in 1887, the child also learned more about race and southern racial mores. Early in the educational process Sullivan explained to Keller, in a lesson the teacher considered to be about colors, that Keller was white and the servants black. Keller quickly "concluded that all who occupied a similar menial position were of the same hue." Race determined status. It humored Sullivan that Keller hesitantly replied "blue" when questioned about the "colour of some one whose occupation she did not know."[16]

The contradictory, changing, and sometimes uneasy nature of the lessons of race provided challenges to all involved. By Christmas 1892 the then-twelve-year-old had received substantial monetary gifts and publishing earnings from an article in the magazine *Youth's Companion*. She desired, at least according to Sullivan, to spend some of that money on Christmas presents for "two darkey namesakes." Her father prohibited it. Sullivan, apparently considering herself more racially enlightened (despite the "darkey" language she used), defied Mr. Keller and used her own funds to buy the presents. Sullivan proudly believed that "The servants, and indeed the Negroes generally, are devoted to Helen. Several of them have learned to talk to her and it is touching to see how patient and gentle she is with them always—ever ready with an excuse in explanation of their faults."[17] . . .

Keller's education included not only race but also the more formalized topics of literature, history, science, and religion. Everyone assumed that as a child Helen should learn of God in some way. . . . Sullivan, an alienated and angry Catholic, had little but scorn for religiosity during her early years with Helen in Tuscumbia, but Sullivan felt a . . . responsibility toward responding to Helen's questions truthfully.[18] . . . Keller's parents held other priorities.

Thus, though the daughter of a Presbyterian father and an Episcopalian mother, as a child Keller learned of religion primarily through Sullivan. The overwhelming cultural presence of religion and religiosity made it a topic impossible to avoid. In 1888 a group of Presbyterian clergy, meeting in Tuscumbia, encountered the increasingly famous child. When asked "What do ministers do?" Keller knew enough about organized religion to reply, "They read and talk loud for people to be good." Sullivan wrote privately of the ministers, presumably reflecting her larger attitudes and beliefs about religion, "And thirty such stupid and homely men I have never met before. If they had only been moderately good looking one might excuse the length, logic and nonsense of their fire and brimstone sermons. But being as ugly as it was possible for them to be one felt like saying very disagreeable things about them."[19]

The teacher did her best, but the literature and history she and Helen read, the discussions they had of creation and science, and the people around Keller prompted question after question from the inquisitive child. By early 1890 Sullivan found Keller's questions too much to handle and turned to the assistance of a major Bostonian religious figure, the Reverend Phillips Brooks, the rector of Trinity Church and an Episcopalian preacher at Harvard. . . . Keller and Brooks began a lengthy correspondence, and while in Boston she often met with him. Her parents left no record of their thoughts on their young child's religious inquiry, though it tied her to Boston and New England religiosity. Helen grew extremely fond and appreciative of Brooks. Her parents approved enough of the relationship to bend to eleven-year-old Helen's desire in 1891 to name her new baby brother Phillips Brooks Keller—likely one of the few white Alabamians of the late nineteenth century named after a Boston preacher.[20]

Within a year of her arrival in Tuscumbia, the forceful Sullivan persuaded Keller's reluctant parents to allow the pair to visit Boston and the Perkins Institution. She insisted to them that Keller needed to be removed from her overly protective family circle and that Perkins was the sensible educational choice. Privately she acknowledged her personal, almost desperate wish to return to Boston.[21] For the rest of the 1880s and 1890s Keller and Sullivan moved back and forth between Boston, Tuscumbia, and New York, though nearly always summering in Tuscumbia. After 1900, however, except for periods in the summers of 1916, 1919, and 1922, Keller spent little time in either Tuscumbia or the larger South. Anne Sullivan became the dominant and most consistent guide in her life. After her initial breakthrough in comprehending finger spelling, Keller also learned to write, to read lips by touch, and to speak. As an adolescent and adult, Keller reveled in the cultural and intellectual life of Boston—Harvard University and Radcliffe College specifically—and then New York.

Keller's conversion to the Christian faith tradition of Swedenborgianism further removed her from southern culture and society. . . . As a teenager, she had been unable to find all the answers she desired in the teachings and Christianity of Phillips Brooks. Guided by John Hitz, the secretary of Alexander Graham Bell who provided Emanuel Swedenborg's writings in Braille, she embraced Swedenborgianism in 1896 and followed it for the rest of her life. Many New England reformers, radicals, and spiritualists adopted the belief system, which was built on the eighteenth-century Christian mysticism of the Swedish Lutheran Swedenborg. He argued for the permeability of the veil between the physical and spiritual worlds. His writings taught Keller that her blindness and deafness mattered nil; her spiritual senses, her internal life, enabled her to access God. The faith also resonated with Keller's growing dedication toward action and service. Swedenborg equated love with service, but he believed that living a "life of the spirit" exemplified active service. Whatever form Keller's service took, again regardless of her disability, when done in a "life of the spirit" it qualified as vital and genuine Christian service.[22]

As an adult, Keller consistently sought a life of active public citizenship synonymous with her theological and political conceptualization of service. She first became familiar with radical and progressive analyses of hierarchy, oppression, and exploitation while a student at Boston's Radcliffe College (1900–1904), the prestigious female counterpart to Harvard. There she read, argued, listened, and was thrilled by the intellectual debates. Perhaps she attended services at the Swedenborgian congregation not far from Harvard Square. For the first time she testified before a state legislature. She began to realize that political efficacy was possible, even for a woman deaf, blind, and from Alabama.

Keller thus embraced a wide-ranging, enduring, and intensely active public life based on a commitment to compassion, justice, and equality. Like her mother, she embraced female suffrage (though Kate Keller likely did not endorse Alice Paul's National Woman's Party, as her daughter did). Helen went on to endorse birth control, the radical Industrial Workers of the World, racial equality, and the causes of striking workers, and she joined the Socialist Party of America in 1909. She advocated for people with disabilities but blamed the inequalities of capitalism for causing disability among a disproportionately high number of working-class people. She criticized World War I as a profit-making venture and later condemned the U.S. use of atomic weapons in World War II. For the American Foundation for the Blind she became an incredibly effective fund-raiser and lobbyist. International politics fascinated her, as did world travel and other cultures, and she became one of the nation's

most successful unofficial ambassadors in the cold war era.[23]

Despite the intellectual life of her mother, as an adult Keller seems to have fallen prey to the stereotypical belief that all southern white women were apolitical and subservient. All evidence indicates that throughout her life she remained largely unaware of the various streams of reform and progressive activism percolating among some southern white women. Keller was simply one of a number of white women, liberals and radicals, who in varying ways sought to remake southern white womanhood throughout the decades of the twentieth century. . . . [Yet] throughout her lifetime Keller had very little contact with those engaged in similar efforts. Perhaps her disability, the viciousness of antiradical attacks on activists for racial equality, or simply her northern residency deterred this contact.[24]

Keller had become a displaced southerner. Her regional background, however, constituted a widely known part of her even more widely known personal story. She was a deaf-blind woman from a region frequently considered inferior: economically, socially, politically disabled. Northerners taught her oral language, while the South lacked the institutions and faculty to do so.[25] She became an uprooted southerner reconstructed by the North, but still always southern.

Throughout this transformation, what it meant to Keller and others for her to be southern was often unclear and contradictory. She left behind little reflective analysis of her southern identity, most likely because of her complicated uneasiness with that heritage. Some of her childhood memories brought her joy; southern racial inequalities made her "ashamed in my very soul." She knew that her own intellectual and personal renewal had come from northern reformers and their followers. She seemingly was unaware of home-grown efforts to refigure southern identity and cultural memories.[26] . . . Her most common acknowledgment of her southern identity was in superficial, and stereotypical, reflections on the beauty and sensuality of southern flowers and trees.

Keller's complicated relationship with her southern background often became entangled with another aspect of her identity—the essential question of her intellectual capacity and abilities, of her humanity. From childhood through old age, others frequently questioned whether she, as a person with a disability, had the capacity to genuinely know anything. As an adult attempting to shape an active political and intellectual life, she regularly encountered the belief that her disability disqualified her from such an undertaking. Because politics and political participation interested her intensely, this dismissal of her as unfit frustrated and enraged her.[27] Detractors made her battle for a public identity even more problematic when they voiced their criticisms in regional terms, as they frequently did.

For example, when as a young adult Keller expressed political opinions considered radical in the early 1900s, opponents from her home state of Alabama blamed it on the Yankee influence of her by-then-married teacher Anne Sullivan Macy and her husband John Macy. These criticisms became very explicit after Keller sent a hundred dollars and a statement of vigorous support—including an expression of shame in her southern heritage—to the National Association for the Advancement of Colored People (NAACP) in 1916. Her views became public after W. E. B. Du Bois printed the letter in the NAACP's newspaper, the *Crisis*. "I warmly endorse your efforts," she had written, "to bring before the country the facts about the unfair treatment of the colored people in some parts of the United States. What a comment upon our social justice is the need of an association like yours!" She felt that "It should bring the blush of shame to the face of every true American to know that ten millions of his countrymen are denied the equal protection of the laws." The Alabama daughter of a Confederate captain confessed, "Ashamed in my very soul I behold in my own beloved southland the tears of those who are oppressed, those who must bring up their sons and daughters in bondage, to be servants because others have their fields and vineyards, and on the side of the oppressor is power." She insisted, drawing on her own theological beliefs, that "The outrages against the colored people are a denial of Christ."[28]

Keller's sentiments did not go unnoticed. The Selma (Ala.) *Journal* reprinted the NAACP letter and accompanied it with an editorial that described the letter as "full of untruths, full of fawning and bootlicking phrases." Implying that Keller could not have generated such beliefs herself, the editorial blamed her teachers: "The people who did such wonderful work in training Miss Keller must have belonged to the old Abolition Gang for they seemed to have thoroughly poisoned her mind against her own people."[29] Her disability and resulting education supposedly left her politically pliable, especially vulnerable to northern educators and abolitionists, and incapable of intentional deliberation. It caused her to be a disloyal southerner.

Though her father was by then dead, Keller's family pressured her to retreat from her public stance in support of the NAACP. Her mother appealed for her to consider the reputations of extended family members living in Selma. Acquiescing, Keller wrote to the Selma *Times*, the competing newspaper of the Selma *Journal*, that the *Journal* had misinterpreted her letter to the NAACP. With unclear differentiation, she insisted that she had advocated "equality of all men before the law," rather than "the social equality of white people and Negroes."[30]

In early 1917 Keller's personal life fell into chaos that sent her southward into the fray. Perhaps this is one reason she resisted her family's pressure so halfheartedly. Anne Macy suffered ill health, tuberculosis, undoubtedly made worse by the deterioration of her marriage to John Macy and a relatively unsuccessful 1916 Chautauqua tour for the student and teacher duo. Doctors advised that Anne Macy have a rest, which she took, away from Keller, in Lake Placid and then Puerto Rico. Separated from her friend for one of the first times in decades, Keller planned to spend several months with her widowed mother in Alabama, perhaps smoothing over their relationship. Before leaving the North, however, she fell in love and made secret plans to marry a finger-spelling fellow socialist, Peter Fagan. The remaining members of Keller's nuclear family, already angry at Helen, drew the line. Purportedly sneaking her away on a forced midnight train trip and chasing Fagan away with a gun, they insisted to her that her disability rendered her ineligible for marriage and childbearing.[31]

Keller submitted and cut off contact with Fagan. . . . Presumably she grieved the close of her relationship with Fagan and the normality he represented in her life. She expressed constant concern to Anne Macy about the possibility of the war in Europe enveloping the United States. Keller complained that in Montgomery "[p]arties, dresses, babies, weddings—and obesity are the topics of conversation." In turn, Macy wrote with little cheer of her failed marriage to John and made preparations that assumed her death would come soon. She tried unconvincingly to reassure Helen. "Yes, it is true that most people you meet in Montgomery lack individuality," Macy wrote. "It is equally true of most places."[32]

As Keller understood and experienced her family relationships, both departure from the geographic South and her departure from the traditional gender and racial politics of the white South went hand in hand with emotional separation from her mother. Her fond but often uneasy adult relationship with her mother reflected these concerns. Contemplating their relationship eight years after her mother's death, she wrote in 1929, "My mother talked intelligently, brilliantly, about current events, and she had a Southerner's interest in politics. But after my mind took a radical turn she could never get over the feeling that we had drifted apart. It grieves me that I should have added to the sadness that weighed upon her."[33] To be a disloyal southerner, as her family understood it and as Keller often experienced it, meant geographical and familial exile.

Southerners sometimes questioned her southern identity, but people living in the North frequently defined Keller as inherently southern even though she lived most of her life in the northeastern United States. It was an identity she could not escape. In 1929 she spoke "as a representative of the South" at the monthly meeting of the group "Alabamians in New York." Along with a representative of the American Federation of Labor she there urged study of the working conditions of southern textile mill hands. . . . In 1938 publisher H. E. Maule approached her about writing a biography of Clara Barton. He picked her, he said, because "As a woman interested in social work and aid to the handicapped, and as a Southerner by birth, it occurred to me that you would be sympathetic to her great voice."[34] . . .

The 1937 publication of Margaret Mitchell's *Gone with the Wind* prompted Keller, like many other Americans, to reflect on the Old South, its meanings for United States race relations, and the implications for her personal identity. She read the twelve-volume Braille version . . . while sailing for Japan in April 1937. Anne Macy had died in October 1936. As an escape, and seeking new purpose, Keller seized the opportunity to advocate for blind people in other countries. Friends offered her the chance in Japan. She thus read the book while grieving

the loss of Macy, pondering her past and better times, and attempting to determine the future course of her life.[35]

In many ways Mitchell's work enchanted Keller. "How charmingly the book opens," she wrote, "with a placid life on a Georgia plantation!" It was a sensual delight that drew to her memories of home. "It stirs in me a nostalgia for the drowsy, sweet spring and early summer days in Tuscumbia, the red earth, the huge old magnolia trees and live oaks. Again I smell Mother's royal wealth of roses, the masses of tangled honeysuckle and paulownia blossoms heavy in the afternoon heat. Again the air about me vibrates with excitement as the men fulminate against some political group or refight the Civil War." It caused her to remember, in terms and imagery paralleling Mitchell's images of slavery, "the Negroes" who gathered water at the spring. "Picturesque in bright-colored bandanas, barefooted, always singing or dancing or performing a cakewalk, they warm my heart, and I long for the joyous pickaninnies who so good-naturedly played with the insatiate tomboy I was."[36]

Mitchell's romanticization of white supremacy and her mythic Old South captivated Keller, just as it did many other readers. By the book's completion, Keller had even adopted Mitchell's historical analysis of Reconstruction. "For the first time," Keller proclaimed, "I am beginning to form a clear picture of the dreadful Reconstruction Period in the South. . . . The criminally stupid descent of the North upon prostrate states with a deluge of carpetbaggers and scalawags turns into a mockery the bloody Civil War fought to emancipate the slaves." Perhaps her embrace of Mitchell's version of history reflected her own yearnings for a happier time. *Gone with the Wind* offered examples of men and women struggling valiantly against economic depression, just as many Americans were doing in the late 1930s. It also offered solace in a false but idyllic past while Keller's own future grew increasingly uncertain. She yearned for Macy. As she wrote in March 1937, "from the moment I wake in the morning until I lie down at night there is an ache at my heart which never stops."[37] Mitchell's myth offered personal comfort and reflection that tomorrow would always come. It offered female models who survived. And . . . it "offered a nostalgic depiction of the Old South but did not advocate its return."[38]

Keller uncomfortably recognized the contradictions between her personal memories, the cultural memories reinforced by *Gone with the Wind*, and the personal knowledge she had garnered over the previous decades. She clearly enjoyed the book, but that pleasure discomforted her: she variably exclaimed passionate opinions about the actions and characters of Rhett, Scarlett, and Melanie and then disavowed her interest with calmer political analyses. The contradictions increased her discomfort and guilt. Despite her fervor for the book, she wrote that "time's disillusioning searchlight" forced her to realize that all may not have been happy in the Old South. "Sadly I recall the degrading poverty, the ignorance and superstition into which those little ones were born and the bitterness of the Negro problem through which many of them are still living."[39] . . . Luckily for her, perhaps, the intoxicating effects of *Gone with the Wind* did not last long. Confronting her personal shame and identity could be once more avoided. After her initial read in 1937, she never mentioned the book again.

U.S. politics, however, forced Keller to pay increasing attention to racial inequalities in both North and South as civil rights campaigns developed in the post–World War II period. . . . In 1946 she attended and spoke at a Danbury, Connecticut, rally "to urge justice to negroes of Connecticut." There she met black and white activists, including opera singer Marian Anderson.[40] Events such as these allowed her to acknowledge racial inequalities and her own shame about them, but in a context that spread responsibility for racial inequalities and shame over both the North and the South. . . . As she became more open with herself and others about racial inequalities, she also grew to realize those inequities went far beyond the geography of the American South.

After the Danbury rally, enthused and contemplative, Keller wrote to a friend that she felt "unquenchable shame" over the social, political, and economic conditions of African Americans. "This revolt has never slumbered within me since I began to notice for myself how they are degraded, and with what cold-blooded deliberation the keys of knowledge, self-reliance and well paid employment are taken from them, so that they may not enter the gate of social competence." She detailed a long list of incidents large and small that infuriated her. She remembered when a "colored

teacher of high culture and noble dignity" visited her and was forced to take the southern hotel's freight elevator. Continued lynching and violence "augur[ed] ill for America's future." The blinding of an African American veteran by a police officer who acted in supposed self-defense was "another abyss of evil . . . moral infection by traitors to Christianity and to the whole democratic spirit in the best traditions of America." She compared her "concentrated horror and fury" to that she had felt when reading Shakespeare's *King Lear* for the first time.[41]

Keller also began to draw connections between racism, the discrimination faced by people with disabilities, and the additive discrimination confronted by African Americans with disabilities. In her 1944 testimony to the House Labor Committee urging expansion of the Social Security Act, she highlighted the circumstances of "the colored blind" and "the deaf-blind." These were, she said, "the hardest pressed and least cared-for" among her "blind fellows." After the 1946 Danbury rally she continued: "It stabs me to the soul to recall my visits to schools for the colored blind which were shockingly backward, and what a hard struggle it was for them to obtain worth while instruction and profitable work because of race prejudice." . . . Her disability activism and the opportunities created by her fame as a person with a disability provided her with the tools necessary to begin to analyze southern racial mores. It did not, however, provide her with instant answers.[42]

A 1951 trip to South Africa pushed Keller to a deeper examination of racial inequalities globally and of the relationship between racism and discrimination against people with disabilities. The journey thrilled the seventy-one-year-old global adventurer. She traveled with the blessings and assistance of the U.S. State Department and the American Foundation for the Blind (an international educational, lobbying, and research group she had worked for since 1921). The State Department found her global travels extremely beneficial because of the positive press and goodwill she elicited. An invitation from the Reverend Arthur Blaxall, a white member of the South African National Council for the Blind and an acquaintance of hers since 1931, initiated the visit. Again her analyses began with memories of her childhood in Alabama. She wrote that she "was the more ready to accept Mr. Blaxall's invitation because I remembered the earliest years when little Afroamericans were my playmates."[43]

Keller's preparations for the trip pushed her further into national and international racial politics and into closer contact with African American and African activists. She read Alan Paton's *Cry the Beloved Country* and Mohandas Gandhi's *Autobiography* to learn more about South Africa's racial apartheid. She gleaned all she could about South African people, plants, and animals from an acquaintance.... In Harlem, perhaps for the first time, she attended a "colored debutantes' cotillion" as a guest of the Reverend Dr. Adam Clayton Powell Sr., famed race man and minister at Harlem's Abyssinian Baptist Church. There she met guest of honor Ralph Bunche, from whom she learned "the historic point of view." Only months previously, Bunche had been awarded the Nobel Peace Prize (for which Keller would later be nominated) for his powerful advocacy of civil rights and decolonization. The eloquence, charisma, and dynamism with which he critiqued South African racial injustices appealed to her sense of service. Energized, she committed herself to confronting South African racism.[44]

Keller sought to do so directly but proceeded cautiously. She knew that disregard and lack of social support made the lives of many blind people across the world difficult, but racism compounded the problem for "the colored blind" in South Africa. Her goal, as she described it to her host Arthur Blaxall before departure, was to use "skill and tact as well as enthusiasm to obtain the right help for the colored blind, who, owing to their handicap are more subject to the arbitrary will of white society than their seeing fellows."[45] ...

Once in South Africa, Keller found the country's beauty contrasted sharply with its brutality and racial inequality. She could not deny her enjoyment at being covered with the spray of Victoria Falls or the awesomeness of Kruger National Park. Once, looking for hippopotami, she stood alone: "the tall grasses rustled against me, and I drank in the sweet, clean air and the sense of four hundred miles where wild animals were free to roam." And, as wherever she went when she traveled, she attracted immense attention. As her host described it, "for two months she was the center of interests, and a subject of conversation, eclipsing even the parliamentary news of the day."[46]

In spite of the warm welcome she and her companion Polly Thomson received at the twenty-eight schools and institutions she visited and the forty-eight meetings and receptions she addressed, "the bitter sense of racial discrimination and injustice" soured her visit. Racism even compounded her schedule, as the laws and attitudes of apartheid required separate assemblies for "the whites, the colored people, the natives and the Indians."[47]

Despite efforts to "keep watch over our mutinous lips" around powerful and wealthy donors, Keller did criticize apartheid publicly. She acknowledged, however, that it took "all the courage and fortitude Polly and I could command" to do so. Her insistence on addressing and visiting assemblies of nonwhites forced acknowledgment of their existence and needs. On at least one occasion her address to a white audience included "concern about the thousands of natives who were as yet untaught and unbefriended." She wrote to one dear friend, "Many times my heart sank as I observed how apathetic many of the public had been toward those unfortunates ["the natives blind or deaf"], and occasionally in my dreams I banged my head against an impenetrable wall trying to discover a break-through." ... Nothing, she wrote privately, "made me more ashamed of my own race" than the ideology of "Afrikaaners."[48] Just as in the United States, racism compounded the discrimination and limited options of people of African descent who had disabilities.

In the years following Keller's return from South Africa, ... the United States civil rights movement grew in activism and success. Evidence indicates that she followed and approved of its course, but she was never actively involved (perhaps partly due to her age). In response to Emmett Till's death in 1955 she sought to give financial assistance to the NAACP.[49] No evidence remains of ties to other white female dissidents [and advocates of racial equality] from the South, like Anne Braden or Katharine Lumpkin....

Examining Keller's southern identity reveals the important role of region in forming personal identity. Keller never questioned the region's uniqueness and its influence on her. Though geographically separated from the South and often in conflict with her family (which to her sometimes seems to have become synonymous with the region) because of her politics, she retained a personal identification as a southerner. Her southern roots also shaped how others defined her. For some, it caused pride, for others derision, and it led many to expect or demand political stances from her that reflected dominant southern hierarchies of race, gender, and class.

Keller both savored and resented this southern identification. At times it gave her pleasure, at other times discomfort. In either case, however, she could not shed the collective cultural memories and regional identity integral to forming her personal outlook. As an adult, she struggled to separate regional identity from acceptance of Lost Cause mythology.

Examining Keller as a southerner provides an example of the historical and personal evolution of white shame, the term she frequently used in the latter half of her life. As Tara McPherson has written, "guilt emerges as a central aspect of twentieth-century southern feeling, and a variety of approaches to managing guilt are tracked across the southern landscape."[50] Racial politics remained central to a southern white identity in the late-nineteenth- and twentieth-century United States, even for one who had moved far away from her Alabama childhood. Race and the South's regionally focused politics based on maintaining the color line lingered omnipresent in her analyses, her sense of home, and her exploration of world politics. While claiming her southern ties fondly, Keller tended to do so only by linking them with accompanying statements of shame and disavowal.

As an adult Keller increasingly drew connections between racism, the discrimination faced by people with disabilities, and the additive discrimination confronted by African Americans with disabilities. Examining her as a southerner provides clues as to how, unaided by other intellectual theorists, she grew to comprehend that systems of hierarchy—whether based upon race, class, gender, or the abilities of one's body—were inherently linked and intertwined. Like others, she struggled to clarify and articulate the connections between efforts to end discrimination and stereotyping. Keller did not, however, connect with the organizations and people of the rapidly growing disability rights movement, just as she failed to do so during her earlier years.[51] Even today, activists in the racial freedom movements, the disability rights movement, and the feminist movement seek to fully theorize these connections.

Finally, examining Helen Keller as a southerner expands the realization that southern womanhood is not monolithic. . . . Keller's experience of southern white womanhood—and her attempts to reformulate it—was influenced equally by factors as disparate as family tales of the glory days of the Old South, her disability, and her northern education. While Keller studied at Radcliffe and walked the streets of Cambridge, Massachusetts, between 1900 and 1904, she wrote, "Never have I found in the greenhouses of the North such heart-satisfying roses as the climbing roses of my southern home. They used to hang in long festoons from our porch, filling the whole air with their fragrance, untainted by any earthly smell; and in the early morning, washed in the dew, they felt so soft, so pure, I could not help wondering if they did not resemble the asphodels of God's garden."[52] To her, though she never again lived for a long period in the South, the region always remained an idyllic and sensual geography. The physicality of place became the easiest way, or perhaps simply the least complicated way, for her to feel southern.

Notes

1. For more on Helen Keller see Kim E. Nielsen, "Was Helen Keller Deaf? Blindness, Deafness, and Multiple Identities," in Brenda Jo Brueggemann and Susan Burch, eds., *Women and Deafness: Double Visions* (Washington, D.C., 2006); Kim E. Nielsen, ed., *Helen Keller: Selected Writings* (New York, 2005); Kim E. Nielsen, *The Radical Lives of Helen Keller* (New York, 2004); Joseph P. Lash, *Helen and Teacher: The Story of Helen Keller and Anne Sullivan Macy* (New York, 1980); and Dorothy Herrmann, *Helen Keller: A Life* (New York, 1998).

2. Helen Keller, *The Story of My Life: With Supplementary Accounts by Anne Sullivan and John Albert Macy*, edited by Roger Shattuck and Dorothy Herrmann (1903; new ed., New York, 2003), 12–13; Herrmann, *Helen Keller*, 8.

3. Keller, *Story of My Life*, 14.

4. In 1892 educators founded the Alabama School for the Negro Deaf and Blind, also in Talladega. See the website of the Alabama Institute for Deaf and Blind at http://www.aidb.org/aidb-story-overview/.

5. See Ernest Freeberg, *The Education of Laura Bridgman: First Deaf and Blind Person to Learn Language* (Cambridge, Mass., 2001); and Elisabeth Gitter, *The Imprisoned Guest: Samuel Howe and Laura Bridgman, the Original Deaf-Blind Girl* (New York, 2001).

6. Keller described this trip in *Story of My Life*, 23–24.

7. See Hannah Joyner, "'This Unnatural and Fratricidal Strife': A Family's Negotiation of the Civil War, Deafness, and Independence," in Paul K. Longmore and Lauri Umansky, eds., *The New Disability*

History: American Perspectives (New York, 2001), 83–106; Hannah Joyner, *From Pity to Pride: Growing Up Deaf in the Old South* (Washington, D.C., 2004); and Steven Noll, *Feeble-Minded in Our Midst: Institutions for the Mentally Retarded in the South, 1900–1940* (Chapel Hill, 1995).

8. *Fifty-Sixth Annual Report of the Trustees of the Perkins Institution*, 79, 81; Arthur Keller to Michael Anagnos, January 28, 1887 (Samuel P. Hayes Research Library, Perkins School for the Blind, Watertown, Mass.).

9. *Fifty-Sixth Annual Report of the Trustees of the Perkins Institution*, 79; Herrmann, *Helen Keller*, chap. 3.

10. "Teacher's Life, Tewksbury," undated and unnumbered notes by Anne Sullivan Macy, Notes of Nella Braddy Henney, Nella Braddy Henney Collection (Hayes Research Library, Perkins School for the Blind); Nella Braddy Henney, *Anne Sullivan Macy: The Story Behind Helen Keller* (Garden City, N.Y., 1933), 34; Nina Silber, *The Romance of Reunion: Northerners and the South, 1865–1900* (Chapel Hill, 1993), 124.

11. "The South," undated and unnumbered notes by Anne Sullivan Macy, Notes of Nella Braddy Henney, Henney Collection.

12. "Going to Tuscumbia," undated and unnumbered notes by Anne Sullivan Macy, ibid.

13. "The South," undated and unnumbered notes by Anne Sullivan Macy, ibid.

14. David W. Blight, *Race and Reunion: The Civil War in American Memory* (Cambridge, Mass., 2001), 171, 260. See also Gaines M. Foster, *Ghosts of the Confederacy: Defeat, the Lost Cause, and the Emergence of the New South, 1865 to 1913* (New York, 1987).

15. Keller, *Story of My Life*, 18, 163–64. The enslaved girl's name, Martha Washington, clearly begs for analysis. Whether the name Keller used in her autobiography was indeed the girl's name—or a pseudonym—is unclear.

16. Ibid., 174.

17. Anne Sullivan to Michael Anagnos, January 23, 1893, Annie Sullivan Letters (Manuscript Department, American Antiquarian Society, Worcester, Mass.).

18. Nielsen, *Radical Lives*, 20.

19. Ibid., 182; Anne Sullivan to Michael Anagnos, April 20, 1888, Sullivan Letters.

20. Anne Sullivan to Michael Anagnos, July 7, 1890, Sullivan Letters; Lash, *Helen and Teacher*, 780.

21. For example, see Annie M. Sullivan to Michael Anagnos, April 22, 1888, Sullivan Letters.

22. Helen Keller, "A Vision of Service," quoted in Keller, *Light in My Darkness*, edited by Ray Silverman (1994; 2nd ed., New York, 2000), 107. Keller's most lengthy explanation of her faith is in Keller, *My Religion* (New York, 1927).

23. Nielsen, *Radical Lives*.

24. On southern women's activism, see, for example, Elna C. Green, *Southern Strategies: Southern Women and the Woman Suffrage Question* (Chapel Hill, 1997); Anastatia Sims, *The Power of Femininity in the New South: Women's Organizations and Politics in North Carolina, 1880–1930* (Columbia, S.C., 1997); Elizabeth Hayes Turner, *Women, Culture, and Community: Religion and Reform in Galveston, 1880–1920* (New York, 1997); Jane Turner Censer, *The Reconstruction of White Southern Womanhood, 1865–1895* (Baton Rouge, 2003); Jacquelyn Dowd Hall, "Open

Secrets: Memory, Imagination, and the Refashioning of Southern Identity," *American Quarterly*, 50 (March 1998), 109–24; Catherine Fosl, *Subversive Southerner: Anne Braden and the Struggle for Racial Justice in the Cold War South* (New York, 2002); and Jacquelyn Dowd Hall, "Women Writers, the 'Southern Front,' and the Dialectical Imagination," *Journal of Southern History*, 69 (February 2003), 3–38.

25. Educators generally considered northern educational institutions for deaf people superior because of their post–Civil War switch to oralism rather than sign language. Southern institutions remained signing institutions largely because of funding shortages that made hiring and training new oralist teachers difficult. See Douglas C. Baynton, *Forbidden Signs: American Culture and the Campaign against Sign Language* (Chicago, 1996).

26. Nielsen, *Radical Lives*, 38–39 (quotation on p. 38), 42. After 1924 Keller primarily expressed her interest in radical politics privately, but her interest remained.

27. Kim Nielsen, "Helen Keller and the Politics of Civic Fitness," in Longmore and Umansky, eds., *New Disability History*, 268–90.

28. New York *Crisis*, April 1916, pp. 305–6; Nielsen, *Radical Lives*, 38–39, 42; Lash, *Helen and Teacher*, 454–56; Herrmann, *Helen Keller*, 204.

29. Lash, *Helen and Teacher*, 454; Herrmann, *Helen Keller*, 205.

30. Herrmann, *Helen Keller*, 205; Lash, *Helen and Teacher*, 454–55.

31. Nielsen, *Radical Lives*, 40–41. Keller's mother, Kate Keller, was particularly opposed to a possible marriage and any form of a sexual life for her daughter. Not only did Keller's family and Anne Sullivan Macy hold eugenic fears about Helen's possible reproduction and sexuality, but also many state laws prohibited women with disabilities from marriage and children. For information on eugenics and disability see Wendy Kline, *Building a Better Race: Gender, Sexuality, and Eugenics from the Turn of the Century to the Baby Boom* (Berkeley, 2001); Martin S. Pernick, *The Black Stork: Eugenics and the Death of "Defective" Babies in American Medicine and Motion Pictures Since 1915* (New York, 1996); and Steven Selden, "Eugenics and the Social Construction of Merit, Race and Disability," *Journal of Curriculum Studies*, 32 (March 2000), 235–52.

32. Lash, *Helen and Teacher*, 452; Anne Sullivan Macy to Helen Keller, undated letter from 1917, Folder 5, Box 69, Helen Keller Archives (American Foundation for the Blind, New York).

33. Helen Keller, *Midstream: My Later Life* (1929; reprint, New York, 1968), 220.

34. "Sees Much Poverty in Trade Centres," *New York Times*, November 13, 1929, p. 46; H. E. Maule to Helen Keller, June 16, 1938 (copy to Nella Braddy Henney), Henney Collection.

35. For more on Keller's travels to Japan, see Nielsen, *Radical Lives*, chaps. 3 and 4.

36. Helen Keller, *Helen Keller's Journal, 1936–1937* (Garden City, N.Y., 1938), 281, 298.

37. Ibid., 305; Keller, *Helen Keller's Journal*, 231.

38. However, the female models who survived [in the book] were white women whose survival became racially defined. On this point, see Tara

McPherson, *Reconstructing Dixie: Race, Gender, and Nostalgia in the Imagined South* (Durham, N.C., 2003), 47–64. Nostalgic depiction: Sarah E. Gardner, *Blood and Irony: Southern White Women's Narratives of the Civil War, 1861–1937* (Chapel Hill, 2004), 239. See also Marian J. Morton, "'My Dear, I Don't Give A Damn': Scarlett O'Hara and the Great Depression," *Frontiers* 5 (Autmun 1980), 52–56; Drew Gilpin Faust, "Clutching the Chains that Bind: Margaret Mitchell and *Gone with the Wind*," *Southern Cultures* 5 (Spring 1999), 6–20; Elizabeth Fox-Genovese, "Scarlett O'Hara: The Southern Lady as New Woman," *American Quarterly* 33 (Autumn 1981), 391–41.

39. Keller, *Helen Keller's Journal*, 298–99.

40. Helen Keller to Nella Braddy Henney, September 22, 1946, Henney Collection.

41. Ibid.

42. Helen Keller's speech before the House Labor Committee Investigating Aid to the Handicapped. October 3, 1944. Legislation-Federal Folder, Social Security Act—Title X, Folder 4, Box 36, Helen Keller Archives. See also "Helen Keller Urges More Help to Blind," *New York Times*, October 4, 1944, p. 25. Helen Keller to Nella Braddy Henney, September 22, 1946, Henney Collection.

43. Arthur William Blaxall, *Helen Keller Under the Southern Cross* (Cape Town, 1952), 32. For more on Keller's travels to South Africa see Nielsen, *Radical Lives*, 102–5.

44. Blaxall, *Helen Keller Under the Southern Cross*, 32; Nielsen, *Radical Lives*, 102–5; Helen Keller to Jo Davidson, January 24, 1951, Jo Davidson File, Folder 9, Box 52, Helen Keller Archives (quotations).

45. Lash, *Helen and Teacher*, 724.

46. Helen Keller to Jo Davidson, August 1, 1951, Box 11, Papers of Jo Davidson (Manuscript Division, Library of Congress, Washington, D.C.). Blaxall, *Helen Keller Under the Southern Cross*, 25.

47. Helen Keller to Jo Davidson, August 1, 1951, Box 11, Papers of Jo Davidson.

48. Undated newspaper clipping from 1951, Nella Braddy Henney Journal, Henney Collection; Blaxall, *Helen Keller Under the Southern Cross*, 36; Helen Keller to Jo Davidson, August 1, 1951, Box 11, Papers of Jo Davidson.

49. Nella Braddy Henney to Polly Thomson, October 23, 1955, Nella Braddy Henney File, Folder 7, Box 58, Helen Keller Archives.

50. McPherson, *Reconstructing Dixie*, 6.

51. For further information on the disability rights movement, see Joseph P. Shapiro, *No Pity: People with Disabilities Forging a New Civil Rights Movement* (New York, 1993); Paul K. Longmore and David Goldberger, "The League of the Physically Handicapped and the Great Depression: A Case Study in the New Disability History," *Journal of American History* 87 (December 2000), 888–922; and Doris Zames Fleischer and Frieda Zames, *The Disability Rights Movement: From Charity to Confrontation* (Philadelphia, 2001). For more on Keller's relationship with the disability rights movement, see Nielsen, *Radical Lives*, chap. 5.

52. Keller, *Story of My Life*, 14–15.

Ida B. Wells, *Southern Horrors* (with an introduction by Patricia A. Schechter)

Ida B. Wells's 1892 pamphlet *Southern Horrors: Lynch Law in All Its Phases* launched a critical phase of the African American struggle for civil rights. Its statistical refutation of the rape charge against black men that was used to justify lynching is a sociological breakthrough that has stood the test of time and study. Wells also demonstrates how the concepts of "race" and "rape" were tied to power relations in the administration of justice, in the media, and in everyday life. Finally, Wells expounds the racial and class dimensions of the sexual double standard in ways that connect to contemporary feminist concerns with violence against all women, communities of color, and the poor in the United States and globally.

The insights expressed in *Southern Horrors* reflect Wells's personal and community survival strategy in the New South. Her situation was shaped by both new opportunities and new oppressions facing the first generation of free African Americans who came of age after the Civil War. Wells's parents, who had been slaves in Mississippi, bequeathed to their children a legacy of strong religious faith, pride in wage-earning, and a commitment to education that echoes through the many projects their daughter undertook over her lifetime. Wells's father, James Wells, was a skilled carpenter and a member of the Masons who, after the war, served on the board of Holly Springs local American Missionary Association school, Rust College, which his daughter attended. Wells's mother, "Lizzie" Warrenton Wells, worked as a cook and was a devout Methodist who made sure her children attended church, where she herself learned to read the Bible. After James and Lizzie's untimely deaths in 1878 from a yellow fever epidemic that swept the Delta, sixteen-year-old Ida B. Wells was left to care for her five siblings, earning money by teaching school.

The prospect of better wages and the presence of extended family soon drew Wells to Memphis, Tennessee. There, her intellectual, social, and political horizons expanded in a burgeoning black community notable for its highly accomplished middle-class and elite members. Aspirations for equality nourished community institutions like schools, newspapers, social clubs, literary lyceums, and churches, especially the Baptist and African Methodist Episcopal denominations. In Memphis, Wells found encouragement to turn her intellectual talents into leadership by teaching Sunday school and by pursuing literary activities, especially journalism. Her first newspaper article appeared in 1883 in a Baptist weekly. It explained how Wells had been unfairly ejected from a first-class "ladies" railroad coach and how she fought racial discrimination by taking her case to court. While tens of thousands of educated women joined the paid labor force as

This introduction was written by the author expressly for *Women's America*. © by Patricia A. Schechter, published by permission of the author.

school "ma'ams," religious educators, and journalists in the late nineteenth century, these social roles had particular significance for African American women, whose personal, family, and community well-being was intimately bound up with their wage-earning, educational activities, and community-betterment work.

As *Southern Horrors* emphatically argues, a white racist backlash followed closely upon the achievements of African Americans after Reconstruction. The result of this backlash was "Jim Crow" segregation, a set of laws designed for the economic deprivation, social marginalization, and political disfranchisement of black people. Jim Crow was established and enforced through systematic violence and terror. Ida B. Wells's eight pamphlets, written between 1892 and 1920, painstakingly document the ways in which African Americans were deprived of their rights through mob and police violence, through negative propaganda campaigns in the media, and through the elimination of economic opportunity and political rights.* Few aspects of Jim Crow escaped Wells's sharp scrutiny in the press and eventually, while in Memphis, she caught the negative attention of critics. As the following excerpt explains, she was forced to leave the South as a kind of political exile, first traveling to New York, then to Great Britain, and finally settling in Chicago in 1895. There, she married lawyer and fellow activist Ferdinand L. Barnett (hyphenating her name to Wells-Barnett) and raised a family of four children.

Post-exile, Wells-Barnett's writing and activism were sustained through African American community networks and by organizations shared by black and white women reformers, such as the Woman's Christian Temperance Union. Her work with black women's church and club networks nurtured her into a powerful public speaker and political organizer. Between 1892 and 1895, Wells-Barnett organized scores of antilynching committees and women's clubs all over the United States and abroad, and helped inaugurate the National Association of Colored Women (NACW), a group that functioned as the preeminent civil rights organization up to World War I. In 1909, Wells-Barnett cofounded the National Association for the Advancement of Colored People (NAACP), which, in 1917, assumed principal leadership of the antilynching fight in the United States.

The trajectory of Wells-Barnett's civil rights agitation was neither simple nor smooth. Controversy followed her and her work, especially during its first decade. White supremacists in the North and South vilified her in the press, slandering her morals and threatening her with violence for speaking out against lynching. While most African American communities embraced Wells-Barnett as a heroine, there was little consensus about how, exactly, to end lynching or resist Jim Crow. Black leaders were a diverse group ideologically and generationally; regional considerations also came into play as black southerners found themselves more circumscribed than their northern peers. Women's roles were also fundamental to the building of black communities and to resistance work. Though black women's families and communities were dependent upon their contributions, any move on their part into official political and intellectual leadership—especially where interactions with whites were concerned—usually sparked controversy. Whether in

---

*Besides *Southern Horrors*, the pamphlets were *The Reason Why the Colored American Is Not in the World's Columbian Exposition: The Afro-American's Contribution to Columbian Literature* (Chicago: Ida B. Wells, 1893); *United States Atrocities: Lynch Law* (London: Lux Publishing, 1894); *A Red Record: Tabulated Statistics and Alleged Causes of Lynchings in the United States, 1892–1893–1894* (Chicago: Donahue & Henneberry, 1895); *Lynch Law in Georgia* (Chicago: Ida B. Wells-Barnett, 1899); *Mob Rule in New Orleans: Robert Charles and His Fight to the Death* (Chicago: Ida B. Wells-Barnett, 1900); *The East St. Louis Massacre: The Greatest Outrage of the Century* (Chicago: The Negro Fellowship Herald Press, 1917); *The Arkansas Race Riot* (Chicago: Ida B. Wells-Barnett, 1920).

journalism, public speaking, or institutional leadership—as with her Chicago social settlement, the Negro Fellowship League (1909–1919)—Wells-Barnett's initiatives were always double-edged, affording new spaces for community defense and activism while potentially exposing black men as somehow deficient in their protective or leadership roles. For every celebration of her hard work and successes, there were always powerful voices affirming the propriety of male ministers, business leaders, and elected officials leading the civil rights agenda for African Americans. Wells-Barnett remained staunchly committed to equality for black women, however, fighting hard for suffrage rights in Illinois and nationally. After the passage of the Nineteenth Amendment, she eventually ran for public office herself, in 1930.

Wells-Barnett's steadfast commitment to full equality not just for lynching victims but for "every citizen" rings through *Southern Horrors*, lending the text its prophetic, visionary quality; hers is a plea, to quote further from the pamphlet's preface, that "justice be done though the heavens fall." *Southern Horrors* draws on a number of powerful currents in American thought and style to make its case. As a graphic exposé, *Southern Horrors* shares kinship with muckraking journalism, a hallmark of the U.S. press at the turn of the century. Its empirical bent draws on statistical work to be found in the nascent academic field of sociology. *Southern Horrors* also stands in a tradition of radical pamphleteering in U.S. history that includes Tom Paine's *Common Sense* (1776) and David Walker's *Appeal to the Colored People of the Americas* (1829). Like these texts, *Southern Horrors* is peppered with wilting sarcasm and theatrical asides designed to provoke, starting with its title, a mocking send up of "southern honor." Instead of the neat closure of genteel fiction, *Southern Horrors* is full of questions and commands in a kind of call-and-response engagement with the reader, a pattern of expression at the heart of black worship traditions and one designed to work a deep transformation in participants. Finally, *Southern Horrors* ends with a practical list of strategies for "self-help," including education, boycotts, migration, agitation for protective legislation, suing through the courts, and even armed self-defense, to be "used to give that protection which the law refuses to give." Nearly five thousand Americans, almost three-fourths of them black, were lynched in Wells-Barnett's lifetime. Repeated efforts of African American activists to pass federal legislation making lynching a crime were defeated in Congress in 1922, 1937, and 1940.

What are the different kinds of violence or threats of violence that Wells documents in *Southern Horrors*? How is violence linked to issues of sexual, racial, and class privilege? How does Wells compare the social and sexual experiences of black and white women under Jim Crow? In what ways does class shape the social behavior and political strategies of the historical actors Wells describes?

CHAPTER I: THE OFFENSE

Wednesday evening May 24th, 1892, the city of Memphis was filled with excitement. Editorials in the daily papers of that date caused a meeting to be held in the Cotton Exchange Building; a committee was sent for the editors of the *Free Speech*, an Afro-American journal published in that city, and the only reason the open threats of lynching that were made were not carried out was because they could not be found. The cause of all this commotion was the following editorial published in the *Free Speech* May 21st, 1892, the Saturday previous.

Eight negroes lynched since last issue of the *Free Speech*, one at Little Rock, Ark., last Saturday morning where the citizens broke (?) into the

Excerpted from Ida B. Wells, *Southern Horrors: Lynch Law in All Its Phases* (New York: New York Age, 1892).

penitentiary and got their man; three near Anniston, Ala., one near New Orleans; and three at Clarksville, Ga., the last three for killing a white man, and five on the same old racket—the new alarm about raping white women. The same programme of hanging, then shooting bullets into the lifeless bodies was carried out to the letter.

Nobody in this section of the country believes the old threadbare lie that Negro men rape white women. If Southern white men are not careful, they will over-reach themselves and public sentiment will have a reaction; a conclusion will then be reached which will be very damaging to the moral reputation of their women.

The Daily Commercial of Wednesday following, May 25th, contained the following leader:

Those negroes who are attempting to make the lynching of individuals of their race a means for arousing the worst passions of their kind are playing with a dangerous sentiment. The negroes may as well understand that there is no mercy for the negro rapist and little patience with his defenders. A negro organ printed in this city, in a recent issue publishes the following atrocious paragraph: "Nobody in this section of the country believes the old thread-bare lie that negro men rape white women. If Southern white men are not careful they will over-reach themselves, and public sentiment will have a reaction; and a conclusion will be reached which will be very damaging to the moral reputation of their women."

The fact that a black scoundrel is allowed to live and utter such loathsome and repulsive calumnies is a volume of evidence as to the wonderful patience of Southern whites. But we have had enough of it.

There are some things that the Southern white man will not tolerate, and the obscene intimations of the foregoing have brought the writer to the very outermost limit of public patience. We hope we have said enough.

The *Evening Scimitar* of same date, copied the *Commercial's* editorial with these words of comment: "Patience under such circumstances is not a virtue. If the negroes themselves do not apply the remedy without delay it will be the duty of those whom he has attacked to tie the wretch who utters these calumnies to a stake at the intersection of Main and Madison Sts., brand him in the forehead with a hot iron and perform upon him a surgical operation with a pair of tailor's shears."

Acting upon this advice, the leading citizens met in the Cotton Exchange Building the same evening, and threats of lynching were freely indulged, not by the lawless element upon which the deviltry of the South is usually saddled—but by the leading business men, in their leading business centre. Mr. Fleming, the business manager and owning a half interest the *Free Speech*, had to leave town to escape the mob, and was afterwards ordered not to return; letters and telegrams sent me in New York where I was spending my vacation advised me that bodily harm awaited my return. Creditors took possession of the office and sold the outfit, and the *Free Speech* was as if it had never been.

The editorial in question was prompted by the many inhuman and fiendish lynchings of Afro-Americans which have recently taken place and was meant as a warning. Eight lynched in one week and five of them charged with rape! The thinking public will not easily believe freedom and education more brutalizing than slavery, and the world knows that the crime of rape was unknown during four years of civil war, when the white women of the South were at the mercy of the race which is all at once charged with being a bestial one.

Since my business has been destroyed and I am an exile from home because of that editorial, the issue has been forced, and as the writer of it I feel that the race and the public generally should have a statement of the facts as they exist. They will serve at the same time as a defense for the Afro-American Sampsons who suffer themselves to be betrayed by white Delilahs.

The whites of Montgomery, Ala., knew J. C. Duke sounded the keynote of the situation—which they would gladly hide from the world, when he said in his paper, *The Herald*, five years ago: "Why is it that white women attract negro men now more than in former days? There was a time when such a thing was unheard of. There is a secret to this thing, and we greatly suspect it is the growing appreciation of white Juliets for colored Romeos." Mr. Duke, like the *Free Speech* proprietors, was forced to leave the city for reflecting on the "honah" of white women and his paper suppressed; but the truth remains that Afro-American men do not always rape (?) white women without their consent.

Mr. Duke, before leaving Montgomery, signed a card disclaiming any intention of slandering Southern white women. The editor of the *Free Speech* has no disclaimer to enter, but asserts instead that there are many white women in the South who would marry colored men if such an act would not place them at once beyond the pale of society and within the clutches of the law. The miscegnation laws of the South only operate against the legitimate union of the races; they leave the white man free to seduce all the colored girls he can, but it is death to the colored man who yields to the force and advances of a similar attraction in white women. White men lynch the offending Afro-American, not because he is a de-spoiler of virtue, but because he succumbs to the smiles of white women.

CHAPTER II: THE BLACK AND WHITE OF IT

The *Cleveland Gazette* of January 16, 1892, publishes a case in point. *Mrs. J. S. Underwood*, the wife of a minister of Elyria, Ohio, accused an Afro-American of rape. She told her husband that during his absence in 1888, stumping the State for the Prohibition Party, the man came to the kitchen door, forced his way in the house and insulted her. She tried to drive him out with a heavy poker, but he overpowered and chloroformed her, and when she revived her clothing was torn and she was in a horrible condition. She did not know the man but could identify him. She pointed out William Offett, a married man, who was arrested and, being in Ohio, was granted a trial.

The prisoner vehemently denied the charge of rape, but confessed he went to Mrs. Underwood's residence at her invitation and was criminally intimate with her at her request. This availed him nothing against the sworn testimony of a minister's wife, a lady of the highest respectability. He was found guilty, and entered the penitentiary, December 14, 1888, for fifteen years. Some time afterwards the woman's remorse led her to confess to her husband that the man was innocent.

These are her words: "I met Offett at the Post Office. It was raining. He was polite to me, and as I had several bundles in my arms he offered to carry them home for me, which he did. He had a strange fascination for me, and I invited him to call on me. He called, bringing chestnuts and candy for the children. By this means we got them to leave us alone in the room. Then I sat on his lap. He made a proposal to me and I readily consented. Why I did so, I do not know, but that I did is true. He visited me several times after that and each time I was indiscreet. I did not care after the first

time. In fact I could not have resisted, and had no desire to resist."

When asked by her husband why she told him she had been outraged, she said: "I had several reasons for telling you. One was the neighbors saw the fellow here, another was, I was afraid I had contracted a loathsome disease, and still another was that I feared I might give birth to a Negro baby. I hoped to save my reputation by telling you a deliberate lie." Her husband horrified by the confession had Offett, who had already served four years, released and secured a divorce.

There are thousands of such cases throughout the South, with the difference that the Southern white men in insatiate fury wreak their vengeance without intervention of law upon the Afro-Americans who consort with their women. A few instances to substantiate the assertion that some white women love the company of the Afro-American will not be out of place. Most of these cases were reported by the daily papers of the South.

In the winter of 1885–6 the wife of a practicing physician in Memphis, in good social standing whose name has escaped me, left home, husband and children, and ran away with her black coachman. She was with him a month before her husband found and brought her home. The coachman could not be found. The doctor moved his family away from Memphis, and is living in another city under an assumed name. . . .

Sarah Clark of Memphis loved a black man and lived openly with him. When she was indicted last spring for miscegenation, she swore in court that she was *not* a white woman. This she did to escape the penitentiary and continued her illicit relation undisturbed. That she is of the lower class of whites, does not disturb the fact that she is a white woman. "The leading citizens" of Memphis are defending the "honor" of *all* white women, *demi-monde* included.

Since the manager of the *Free Speech* has been run away from Memphis by the guardians of the honor of Southern white women, a young girl living on Poplar St., who was discovered in intimate relations with a handsome mulatto young colored man, Will Morgan by name, stole her father's money to send the young fellow away from that father's wrath. She has since joined him in Chicago. . . .

The very week the "leading citizens" of Memphis were making a spectacle of themselves in defense of all white women of every kind, an Afro-American, M. Stricklin, was found in a white woman's room in that city. Although she made no outcry of rape, he was jailed and would have been lynched, but the woman stated she bought curtains of him (he was a furniture dealer) and his business in her room that night was to put them up. A white woman's word was taken as absolutely in this case as when the cry of rape is made, and he was freed.

What is true of Memphis is true of the entire South. . . . Frank Weems of Chattanooga who was not lynched in May only because the prominent citizens became his body guard until the doors of the penitentiary closed on him, had letters in his pocket from the white woman in the case, making the appointment with him. Edward Coy who was burned alive in Texarkana, January 1, 1892, died protesting his innocence. Investigation since as given by the Bystander in the *Chicago Inter-Ocean*, October 1, proves: . . . The woman who was paraded as a victim of violence was of bad character; her husband was a drunkard and a gambler. . . . She was compelled by threats, if not by violence, to make the charge against the victim. . . . When she came to apply the match Coy asked her if she would burn him after they had "been sweethearting" so long. . . .

Hundreds of such cases might be cited, but enough have been given to prove the assertion that there are white women in the South who love the Afro-American's company even as there are white men notorious for their preference for Afro-American women.

There is hardly a town in the South which has not an instance of the kind which is well-known, and hence the assertion is reiterated that "nobody in the South believes the old thread-bare lie that negro men rape white women." Hence there is a growing demand among Afro-Americans that the guilt or innocence of parties accused of rape be fully established. They know the men of the section of the country who refuse this are not so desirous of punishing rapists as they pretend. The utterances of the leading white men show that with them it is not the crime but the *class*, Bishop Fitzgerald has become apologist for lynchers of the rapists of *white* women only. . . . But when the victim is a colored woman it is different.

Last winter in Baltimore, Md., three white ruffians assaulted a Miss Camphor, a young Afro-American girl, while out walking with a young man of her own race. They held her

escort and outraged the girl. It was a deed dastardly enough to arouse Southern blood, which gives its horror of rape as excuse for lawlessness, but she was an Afro-American. The case went to the courts, an Afro-American lawyer defended the men and they were acquitted.

In Nashville, Tenn., there is a white man, Pat Hanifan, who outraged a little Afro-American girl, and, from the physical injuries received, she has been ruined for life. He was jailed for six months, discharged, and is now a detective in that city. . . . Only two weeks before Eph. Grizzard, who had only been *charged* with rape upon a white woman, had been taken from the jail, with Governor Buchanan and the police and militia standing by, dragged through the streets in broad daylight, knives plunged into him at every step, and with every fiendish cruelty a frenzied mob could devise, he was at last swung out on the bridge with hands cut to pieces as he tried to climb up the stanchions. . . .

At the very moment these civilized whites were announcing their determination "to protect their wives and daughters," by murdering Grizzard, a white man was in the same jail for raping eight-year-old Maggie Reese, an Afro-American girl. He was not harmed. The "honor" of grown women who were glad enough to be supported by the Grizzard boys and Ed Coy, as long as the liasion was not known, needed protection; they were white. The outrage upon helpless childhood needed no avenging in this case; she was black. . . .

CHAPTER III: THE NEW CRY

. . . Thoughtful Afro-Americans with the strong arm of the government withdrawn and with the hope to stop such wholesale massacres urged the race to sacrifice its political rights for the sake of peace. They honestly believed the race should fit itself for government, and when that should be done, the objection to race participation in politics would be removed.

But the sacrifice did not remove the trouble, nor move the South to justice. One by one the Southern States have legally (?) disfranchised the Afro-American, and since the repeal of the Civil Rights Bill nearly every Southern State has passed separate car laws with a penalty against their infringement. The race regardless of advancement is penned into filthy, stifling partitions cut off from smoking cars. . . . The dark and bloody record of the

South shows 728 Afro-Americans lynched during the past eight years; . . . and not less than 150 have been known to have met violent death at the hands of cruel bloodthirsty mobs during the past nine months.

To palliate this record (which grows worse as the Afro-American becomes intelligent) and excuse some of the most heinous crimes that ever stained the history of a country, the South is shielding itself behind the plausible screen of defending the honor of its women. This, too, in the face of the fact that only *one-third* of the 728 victims to mobs have been *charged* with rape, to say nothing of those of that one-third who were innocent of the charge. . . .

Even to the better class of Afro-Americans the crime of rape is so revolting they have too often taken the white man's word and given lynch law neither the investigation nor condemnation it deserved.

They forget that a concession of the right to lynch a man for a certain crime, not only concedes the right to lynch any person for any crime, but (so frequently is the cry of rape now raised) it is in a fair way to stamp us a race of rapists and desperadoes. They have gone on hoping and believing that general education and financial strength would solve the difficulty, and are devoting their energies to the accumulation of both. . . .

Mary McLeod Bethune,
"How the Bethune-Cookman College Campus Started"

Mary McLeod Bethune was one of the most distinguished educators of her generation. The daughter of slaves, she received her early education from missionary teachers. Like others of her race who saw education as a key to racial advancement at a time when the white South was indifferent if not hostile to the aspirations of African-Americans, Bethune faced extraordinary obstacles. When she began a little school at Daytona Beach, Florida, in 1904, America was entering an era of reform. Yet even most northern progressives—with the notable exception of women such as Mary White Ovington, one of the founders of the NAACP—shared the racist assumptions of that era, believing that the future of black women, like immigrant women, lay in domestic service. Bethune had larger dreams. Because of her courage, energy, and vision, she was able to keep her school afloat with her intrepid fund-raising, guiding its growth from grammar school to high school and to what finally became an accredited four-year college. President of the institution from its founding until her resignation in 1942, she remained a trustee of Bethune-Cookman College until her death in 1955. She was an activist and held many important posts within the black community, founding such organizations as the National Association of Colored Women's Clubs and the National Council of Negro Women. A national figure as well, she served in the Roosevelt administration during the 1930s, advising the president on minority affairs. She was also involved in early efforts on behalf of the United Nations. Her many offices and honors, however, never diverted her from her primary purpose—the pursuit of full citizenship rights for all black Americans.*

*See Joyce A. Hanson, *Mary McLeod Bethune and Black Women's Political Activism* (Columbia: University of Missouri Press, 2003).

Excerpted from "Faith That Moved a Dump Heap" by Mary McLeod Bethune, in *Who, The Magazine about People* 1, no. 3 (June 1941): 31–35, 54.

Soon after opening the Daytona Educational and Industrial Institute for Negro Girls, its founder, Mary McLeod Bethune, posed with pupils lining the road leading to its first Daytona Beach building—a four-room cottage. One of the fields nearby, nicknamed Hell's Hole, would soon be purchased by Bethune as the foundation of a genuine campus. At the time, Florida's handful of state-supported public "high" schools for blacks operated only five months a year, in contrast to nine for whites' schools. Bethune, a tireless fundraiser, chose Daytona Beach, despite the fact that it was home to a Ku Klux Klan chapter, because of two primary factors: it had a fast-growing black population attracted by relatively good jobs, and its wealthy whites, both year-round and summer residents, included some who supported her efforts. (Courtesy of the State Archives of Florida.)

On October 3, 1904, I opened the doors of my school, with an enrollment of five little girls, aged from eight to twelve, whose parents paid me fifty cents' weekly tuition. My own child was the only boy in the school. Though I hadn't a penny left, I considered cash money as the smallest part of my resources. I had faith in a living God, faith in myself, and a desire to serve. . . .

We burned logs and used the charred splinters as pencils, and mashed elderberries for ink. I begged strangers for a broom, a lamp, a bit of cretonne to put around the packing case which served as my desk. I haunted the city dump and the trash piles behind hotels, retrieving discarded linen and kitchenware, cracked dishes, broken chairs, pieces of old lumber. Everything was scoured and mended. This was part of the training to salvage, to reconstruct, to

make bricks without straw. As parents began gradually to leave their children overnight, I had to provide sleeping accommodations. I took corn sacks for mattresses. Then I picked Spanish moss from trees, dried and cured it, and used it as a substitute for mattress hair.

The school expanded fast. In less than two years I had 250 pupils. In desperation I hired a large hall next to my original little cottage, and used it as a combined dormitory and classroom. I concentrated more and more on girls, as I felt they especially were hampered by lack of educational opportunities. . . .

I had many volunteer workers and a few regular teachers, who were paid from fifteen to twenty-five dollars a month and board. I was supposed to keep the balance of the funds for my own pocket, but there was never any balance—only a yawning hole. I wore old clothes sent me by mission boards, recut and rede-signed for me in our dress-making classes. At last I saw that our only solution was to stop renting space, and to buy and build our own college.

Near by was a field, popularly called Hell's Hole, which was used as a dumping ground. I approached the owner, determined to buy it. The price was $250. In a daze, he fi-nally agreed to take five dollars down, and the balance in two years. I promised to be back in a few days with the initial payment. He never knew it, but I didn't have five dollars. I raised this sum selling ice cream and sweet-potato pies to the workmen on construction jobs, and I took the owner his money in small change wrapped in my handkerchief.

That's how the Bethune-Cookman college campus started. . . .

As the school expanded, whenever I saw a need for some training or service we did not supply, I schemed to add it to our curriculum. Sometimes that took years. When I came to Florida, there were no hospitals where a Negro could go. A student became critically ill with appendicitis, so I went to a local hospital and begged a white physician to take her in and operate. My pleas were so desperate he finally agreed. A few days after the operation, I vis-ited my pupil.

When I appeared at the front door of the hospital, the nurse ordered me around to the back way. I thrust her aside—and found my little girl segregated in a corner of the porch behind the kitchen. Even my toes clenched with rage.

That decided me. I called on three of my faithful friends, asking them to buy a little cot-tage behind our school as a hospital. They agreed, and we started with two beds.

From this humble start grew a fully equipped twenty-bed hospital—our college infirmary and a refuge for the needy through-out the state. It was staffed by white and black physicians and by our own student nurses. We ran this hospital for twenty years as part of our contribution to community life; but a short time ago, to ease our financial burden, the city took it over.

Gradually, as educational facilities ex-panded and there were other places where small children could go, we put the emphasis on high-school and junior-college training. In 1922, Cookman College, a men's school, the first in the state for the higher education of Negroes, amalgamated with us. The combined coeducational college, now run under the aus-pices of the Methodist Episcopal Church, is called Bethune-Cookman College. We have fourteen modern buildings, a beautiful campus of thirty-two acres, an enrollment in regular and summer sessions of 600 students, a faculty and staff of thirty-two, and 1,800 graduates. The college property, now valued at more than $800,000, is entirely unencumbered.

When I walk through the campus, with its stately palms and well-kept lawns, and think back to the dump-heap foundation, I rub my eyes and pinch myself. And I remember my childish visions in the cotton fields.

But values cannot be calculated in ledger figures and property. More than all else the college has fulfilled my ideals of distinctive training and service. Extending far beyond the immediate sphere of its graduates and stu-dents, it has already enriched the lives of 100,000 Negroes.

In 1934, President Franklin D. Roosevelt appointed me director of the division of Negro affairs of the National Youth Administration. My main task now is to supervise the training provided for 600,000 Negro children, and I have to run the college by remote control. Every few weeks, however, I snatch a day or so and return to my beloved home.

This is a strenuous program. The doctor shakes his head and says, "Mrs. Bethune, slow down a little. Relax! Take it just a little easier." I promise to reform, but in an hour the promise is forgotten.

For I am my mother's daughter, and the drums of Africa still beat in my heart. They will not let me rest while there is a single Negro boy or girl without a chance to prove his worth.

WOMEN IN THE WEST

PEGGY PASCOE

Ophelia Paquet, a Tillamook of Oregon, Challenges Miscegenation Laws

When Ophelia Paquet's husband died in 1919, the county court recognized her as his widow—the Paquets had been married for thirty years—and appointed Ophelia to administer his estate. As there were no children, Ophelia stood to inherit her late husband's property. It was a just arrangement inasmuch as it was her money that had been used to purchase the land and pay taxes on it. John Paquet, Fred's disreputable brother, thought otherwise. Ultimately the court awarded the estate to him, leaving the sixty-five-year-old widow destitute.

Ophelia's story is a complicated one. It illuminates many issues: the purpose of miscegenation laws, the role of marriage in the transmission of property, the "invisibility" of married women's economic contributions, and the way race can compound gender disadvantage.

In what respects does John Paquet's victory illuminate the convergence of race and class? What parallels does Pascoe draw between the Paquet case and contemporary debates over same-sex marriage? How is the failure to count Ophelia's economic contribution to the marriage related to the "pastoralization" of housework that Jeanne Boydston discusses on pages 128–139?

Although miscegenation laws are usually remembered (when they are remembered at all) as a Southern development aimed at African Americans, they were actually a much broader phenomenon. Adopted in both the North and the South in the colonial period and extended to western states in the nineteenth century, miscegenation laws grew up with slavery but became even more significant after the Civil War, for it was then that they came to form the crucial "bottom line" of the system of white supremacy embodied in segregation.

The earliest miscegenation laws, passed in the South, forbade whites to marry African Americans, but the list of groups prohibited from marrying whites was gradually expanded, especially in western states, by adding first American Indians, then Chinese and Japanese (both often referred to by the catchall term "Mongolians"), and then Malays (or Filipinos). And even this didn't exhaust the list. Oregon prohibited whites from marrying "Kanakas" (or native Hawaiians); South Dakota proscribed "Coreans"; Arizona singled out Hindus; and

From "On the Significance of Miscegenation Law in United State History," in *New Viewpoints in Women's History: Working Papers from the Schlesinger Library 50th Anniversary Conference, March 4–5, 1994*, ed. Susan Ware (Cambridge, Mass.: Arthur and Elizabeth Schlesinger Library on the History of Women in America, Radcliffe College, [1994]). Condensed and reprinted by permission of the author. Notes have been renumbered and edited. We mourn Peggy Pascoe's death on July 23, 2010. For Estelle Freedman's remembrance, see http://www.historians.org/publications-and-directories/perspectives-on-history/november-2010/in-memoriam-peggy-pascoe.

Georgia prohibited whites from marrying "West" and "Asiatic" Indians.

Many states packed their miscegenation laws with multiple categories and quasi-mathematical definitions of "race." Oregon, for example, declared that "it shall not be lawful within this state for any white person, male or female, to intermarry with any negro, Chinese, or any person having one fourth or more negro, Chinese, or Kanaka blood, or any person having more than one half Indian blood." Altogether, miscegenation laws covered forty-one states and colonies. They spanned three centuries of American history: the first ones were enacted in the 1660s, and the last ones were not declared unconstitutional until 1967.

Although it is their sexual taboos that have attracted most recent attention, the structure and function of miscegenation laws were . . . more fundamentally related to the institution of marriage than to sexual behavior itself. In sheer numbers, many more laws prohibited interracial marriage than interracial sex. And in an even deeper sense, all miscegenation laws were designed to privilege marriage as a social and economic unit. Couples who challenged the laws knew that the right to marry translated into social respectability and economic benefits, including inheritance rights and legitimacy for children, that were denied to sexual liaisons outside marriage. Miscegenation laws were designed to patrol this border by making so-called "miscegenous marriage" a legal impossibility. Thus criminal courts treated offenders as if they had never been married at all; that is, prosecutors charged interracial couples with the moral offense of fornication or other illicit sex crimes, then denied them the use of marriage as a defense.

Civil courts guarded the junction between marriage and economic privilege. From Reconstruction to the 1930s, most miscegenation cases heard in civil courts were ex post facto attempts to invalidate relationships that had already lasted for a long time. They were brought by relatives or, sometimes, by the state, after the death of one partner, almost always a white man. Many of them were specifically designed to take property or inheritances away from the surviving partner, almost always an African American or American Indian woman. By looking at civil law suits like these (which were, at least in appeals court records, more common than criminal cases), we can begin to trace the links between white

patriarchal privilege and property that sustained miscegenation laws.

Let me illustrate the point by describing [a] sample case, In re Paquet's Estate, decided by the Oregon Supreme Court in 1921.[1] The Paquet case, like most of the civil miscegenation cases of this period, was fought over the estate of a white man. The man in question, Fred Paquet, died in 1919, survived by his 63-year-old Tillamook Indian wife, named Ophelia. The Paquet estate included 22 acres of land, some farm animals, tools, and a buggy, altogether worth perhaps $2500.[2] Fred and Ophelia's relationship had a long history. In the 1880s, Fred had already begun to visit Ophelia frequently and openly enough that he had become one of many targets of a local grand jury which periodically threatened to indict white men who lived with Indian women.[3] Seeking to formalize the relationship—and, presumably, end this harrassment—Fred consulted a lawyer, who advised him to make sure to hold a ceremony which would meet the legal requirements for an "Indian custom" marriage. Accordingly, in 1889, Fred not only reached the customary agreement with Ophelia's Tillamook relatives, paying them $50 in gifts, but also sought the formal sanction of Tillamook tribal chief Betsy Fuller (who was herself married to a white man); Fuller arranged for a tribal council to consider and confirm the marriage.[4] Afterwards Fred and Ophelia lived together until his death, for more than thirty years. Fred clearly considered Ophelia his wife, and his neighbors, too, recognized their relationship, but because Fred died without leaving a formal will, administration of the estate was subject to state laws which provided for the distribution of property to surviving family members.

When Fred Paquet died, the county court recognized Ophelia as his widow and promptly appointed her administrator of the estate. Because the couple had no children, all the property, including the land, which Ophelia lived on and the Paquets had owned for more than two decades, would ordinarily have gone to her. Two days later, though, Fred's brother John came forward to contest Ophelia for control over the property.[5] John Paquet had little to recommend him to the court. Some of his neighbors accused him of raping native women, and he had such an unsavory reputation in the community that at one point the county judge declared him "a man of immoral habits ... incompetent to transact ordinary business affairs and generally untrustworthy."[6] He was, however, a "white" man, and under Oregon's miscegenation law, that was enough to ensure that he won his case against Ophelia, an Indian woman.

The case eventually ended up in the Oregon Supreme Court. In making its decision, the key issue for the court was whether or not to recognize Fred and Ophelia's marriage, which violated Oregon's miscegenation law.[7] The Court listened to—and then dismissed—Ophelia's argument that the marriage met the requirements for an Indian custom marriage and so should have been recognized as valid out of routine courtesy to the authority of another jurisdiction (that of the Tillamook tribe).[8] The Court also heard and dismissed Ophelia's claim that Oregon's miscegenation law discriminated against Indians and was therefore an unconstitutional denial of the Fourteenth Amendment guarantee of equal protection. The Court ingenuously explained its reasoning; it held that the Oregon miscegenation law did not discriminate because it "applied alike to all persons, either white, negroes, Chinese, Kanaka, or Indians."[9] Following this logic, the Court declared Fred and Ophelia's marriage void because it violated Oregon's miscegenation law; it ordered that the estate and all its property be transferred to "the only relative in the state," John Paquet, to be distributed among him, his siblings and their heirs.[10]

As the Paquet case demonstrates, miscegenation law did not always prevent the formation of interracial relationships, sexual or otherwise. Fred and Ophelia had, after all, lived together for more than thirty years and had apparently won recognition as a couple from many of those around them; their perseverance had even allowed them to elude grand jury crackdowns. They did not, however, manage to escape the really crucial power of miscegenation law: the role it played in connecting white supremacy to the transmission of property. In American law, marriage provided the glue which allowed for the transmission of property from husbands to wives and their children; miscegenation law kept property within racial boundaries by invalidating marriages between white men and women of color whenever ancillary white relatives like John Paquet contested them.[11] ... Property, so often described in legal sources as simple economic assets (like land and capital) was

actually a much more expansive phenomenon, one which took various forms and structured crucial relationships. ... Race is in and of itself a kind of property.[12] As [legal scholar] Derrick Bell ... explains, most whites did—and still do—"expect the society to recognize an unspoken but no less vested property right in their 'whiteness.'" "This right," Bell maintains, "is recognized and upheld by courts and the society like all property rights under a government created and sustained primarily for that purpose."[13]

As applied to the Paquet case, this theme is easy to trace, for, in a sense, the victorious John Paquet had turned his "whiteness" (the best—and perhaps the only—asset he had) into property, and did so at Ophelia's expense. This transformation happened not once but repeatedly. One instance occurred shortly after the county judge had branded John Paquet immoral and unreliable. Dismissing these charges as the opinions of "a few scalawags and Garibaldi Indians," John Paquet's lawyers rallied enough white witnesses who would speak in his defense to mount an appeal which convinced a circuit court judge to declare Paquet competent to administer the estate.[14] Another example of the transformation of "whiteness" into property came when the Oregon Supreme Court ruled that Ophelia Paquet's "Indianness" disqualified her from legal marriage to a white man; with Ophelia thus out of the way, John and his siblings won the right to inherit the property.

The second property relationship [is] illuminated by the etymological connection between the words "property" and "propriety." Miscegenation law played on this connection by drawing a sharp line between "legitimate marriage" on the one hand and "illicit sex" on the other, then defining all interracial relationships as illicit sex. The distinction was a crucial one, for husbands were legally obligated to provide for legitimate wives and children, but men owed nothing to "mere" sexual partners: neither inheritance rights nor the legitimacy of children accompanied illicit relationships.

By defining all interracial relationships as illicit, miscegenation law did not so much prohibit or punish illicit sex as it did create and reproduce it. Conditioned by stereotypes which associated women of color with hypersexuality, judges routinely branded long-term settled relationships as "mere" sex rather than marriage. Lawyers played to these assumptions by reducing interracial relationships to interracial sex, then distinguishing interracial sex from marriage by associating it with prostitution. Describing the relationship between Fred and Ophelia Paquet, for example, John Paquet's lawyers claimed that "the alleged 'marriage' was a mere commercial affair" that did not deserve legal recognition because "the relations were entirely meretricious from their inception."[15]

It was all but impossible for women of color to escape the legacy of these associations. Ophelia Paquet's lawyers tried to find a way out by changing the subject. Rather than refuting the association between women of color and illicit sexuality, they highlighted its flip side, the supposed connection between white women and legitimate marriage. Ophelia Paquet, they told the judge, "had been to the man as good a wife as any white woman could have been."[16] In its final decision, the Oregon Supreme Court came as close as any court of that time did to accepting this line of argument. Taking the unusual step of admitting that "the record is conclusive that [Ophelia] lived with [Fred] as a good and faithful wife for more than 30 years," the judges admitted that they felt some sympathy for Ophelia, enough to recommend—but not require—that John Paquet offer her what they called "a fair and reasonable settlement."[17] But in the Paquet case, as in other miscegenation cases, sexual morality, important as it was, was nonetheless still subordinate to channelling the transmission of property along racial . . . lines. Ophelia got a judicial pat on the head for good behavior, but John and his siblings got the property.

Which brings me to the third form of property relationship structured by miscegenation laws—and, for that matter, marriage laws in general—and that is women's economic dependence on men. Here the problems started long before the final decision gave John Paquet control of the Paquet estate. One of the most intriguing facts about the Paquet case is that everyone acted as if the estate in question belonged solely to Fred Paquet. In fact, however, throughout the Paquet marriage, Fred had whiled away most of his time; it was Ophelia's basket-making, fruit-picking, milk-selling, and wage work that had provided the income they needed to sustain themselves. And although the deed to their land was made out in Fred Paquet's name, the couple had used Ophelia's earnings, combined with her proceeds from

government payments to Tillamook tribal members, both to purchase the property and to pay the yearly taxes on it. It is significant . . . that, although lawyers on both sides of the case knew this, neither they nor the Oregon Supreme Court judges considered it a key issue at the trial in which Ophelia lost all legal right to what the courts considered "Fred's" estate.

Indeed, Ophelia's economic contribution might never have been taken into account if it were not for the fact that in the wake of the Oregon Supreme Court decision, United States Indian officials found themselves responsible for the care of the now impoverished Ophelia. Apparently hoping both to defend Ophelia and to relieve themselves of the burden of her support, they sued John Paquet on Ophelia's behalf. Working through the federal courts that covered Indian relations and equity claims, rather than the state courts that enforced miscegenation laws, they eventually won a partial settlement. Yet their argument, too, reflected the assumption that men were better suited than women to the ownership of what the legal system referred to as "real" property. Although their brief claimed that "Fred Paquet had practically no income aside from the income he received through the labor and efforts of the said Ophelia Paquet," they asked the Court to grant Ophelia the right to only half of the Paquet land.[18] In the end, the Court ordered that Ophelia should receive a cash settlement (the amount was figured at half the value of the land), but only if she agreed to make her award contingent on its sale.[19] To get any settlement at all, Ophelia Paquet had to relinquish all claims to actual ownership of the land, although such a claim might have given her legal grounds to prevent its sale and so allow her to spend her final years on the property.

It is not even clear that she received any payment on the settlement ordered by the court. As late as 1928, John Paquet's major creditor complained to a judge that Paquet had repeatedly turned down acceptable offers to sell the land; perhaps he had chosen to live on it himself.[20]

Like any single example, the Paquet case captures miscegenation law as it stood at one moment, and a very particular moment at that, one that might be considered the high water mark of American courts' determination to structure both family formation and property transmission along racial dividing lines.

Today, most Americans have trouble re-membering that miscegenation laws ever ex-isted . . . [and] are incredulous at the injustice and the arbitrariness of the racial classifica-tions that stand out in [such] . . . cases. [Yet] few . . . notice that one of the themes raised in the Paquet case—the significance of marriage in structuring property transmission—not only remains alive and well, but has, in fact, outlived both the erosion of traditional patriar-chy and the rise and fall of racial classifications in marriage law.

More than a generation after the demise of miscegenation laws . . . the drawing of exclu-sionary lines around marriage [continues]. . . . The most prominent—though hardly the only—victims are lesbian and gay couples, who point out that the sex classifications cur-rently embedded in marriage law operate in much the same way that the race classifications embedded in miscegenation laws once did: that is, they allow courts to categorize same-sex relationships as illicit sex rather than legiti-mate marriage and they allow courts to exclude same-sex couples from the property benefits of marriage, which now include everything from tax advantages to medical insurance coverage.

Both these modern legal battles and the earlier ones fought by couples like Fred and Ophelia Paquet suggest . . . that focusing on the connections between property and the po-litical economy of marriage . . . offer a reveal-ing vantage point from which to study both the form and power of analogies between race and sex classifications in American law and the relationships between race and gender hi-erarchies in American history.

NOTES

1. The Paquet case can be followed not only by reading the text of the appeals court decision, *In re Paquet's Estate*, 200 P 911 (Oregon 1921), but also in the following archival case files: *Paquet v. Paquet*, file No. 4268, Oregon Supreme Court, 1920; *Paquet v. Henkle*, file No. 4267, Oregon Supreme Court, 1920; and Tillamook County Probate file #605, all in the Oregon State Archives; and in *U.S. v. John B. Paquet*, Judgment Roll 11409, Register No. 8-8665, March 1925, National Archives and Records Administra-tion, Pacific Northwest Branch.

2. Initial estimates of the value of the estate were much higher, ranging from $4500 to $12,500. I have relied on the figure of $2528.50 provided by court-appointed assessors. See Tillamook Country Probate file #605, Inventory and Appraisement, June 15, 1920.

3. *Paquet v. Paquet*, Respondent's brief, November 1, 1920, pp. 2–5.

4. Tillamook County Probate file #605, Judge A.M. Hare, Findings of Facts and Conclusions of Law, February 3, 1920; *Paquet v. Paquet*, Appellants Abstract of Record, September 3, 1920, pp. 10–16.

5. *Paquet v. Paquet*, Appellants Abstract of Record, September 3, 1920, p. 3.

6. Tillamook County Probate file #605, Judge A. M. Hare, Findings of Fact and Conclusions of Law, February 3, 1920.

7. Court records identify Fred Paquet as being of French Canadian origin. Both sides agreed that Fred was a "pure" or "full-blooded" "white" man and Ophelia was a "pure" or "full-blooded" "Indian" woman. *Paquet* v. *Paquet*, Appellant's First Brief, Oc-tober 8, 1920, p. 1; *Paquet v. Paquet*; Respondent's brief, November 1, 1920, p. 2.

8. The question of legal jurisdiction over Indian tribes was—and is—a very thorny issue. Relations with Indians were generally a responsibility of the U.S. federal government, which, although it advo-cated assimilating Indian families into white mid-dle-class molds, had little practical choice but to grant general recognition to tribally-determined marriages performed according to Indian custom. In the U.S. legal system, however, jurisdiction over marriage rested with the states rather than the fed-eral government. States could, therefore, use their control over marriage as a wedge to exert some power over Indians by claiming that Indian-white marriages, especially those performed outside rec-ognized reservations, were subject to state jurisdic-tion. In the Paquet case, for example, the court insisted that, because the Tillamook had never been assigned to a reservation and because Fred and Ophelia lived in a mixed settlement, Ophelia could not be considered part of a recognized tribe nor a "ward" of the federal government. As events would later show, both contentions were inaccurate: Ophe-lia was an enrolled member of the Tillamook tribe, which was under the supervision of the Siletz Indian Agency; the federal government claimed her as "a ward of the United States." See *U.S. v. John B. Paquet*, Bill of Complaint in Equity, September 21, 1923, p. 3.

9. In re Paquet's Estate, 200 P 911 at 913 (Oregon 1921).

10. In re Paquet's Estate, 200 P 911 at 914 (Oregon 1921).

11. Although the issue did not come up in the Paquet case, . . . in miscegenation cases, not only the wife but also the children might lose their legal standing, for one effect of invalidating an interracial marriage was to make the children technically ille-gitimate. According to the law of most states, ille-gitimate children automatically inherited from their mothers, but they could inherit from their fathers only if their father had taken legal steps to formally recognize or adopt them. Since plaintiffs could rarely convince judges that fathers had done so, the children of interracial marriages were often disin-herited along with their mothers.

12. Derrick Bell, "Remembrances of Racism Past," in Hill and Jones, *Race in America: The Struggle for Equality* (Madison: University of Wisconsin Press, 1992), 78. See also Bell, "White Superiority in Amer-ica: Its Legal Legacy, Its Economic Costs," *Villanova Law Review* 33 (1988), 767–779.

13. *Paquet v. Henkle,* Respondent's brief, March 14, 1920, p. 6; *Paquet v. Henkle,* Index to Transcript, August 25, 1920, p. 3.

14. *Paquet v. Paquet,* Respondent's brief, November 1, 1920, p. 7. Using typical imagery, they added that the Paquet relationship was "a case where a white man and a full blooded Indian woman have chosen to cohabit together illictly [sic], to agree to a relation of concubinage, which is not only a violation of the law of Oregon, but a transgression against the law of morality and the law of nature" (p. 16).

15. *Paquet v. Paquet,* Appellant's First Brief, October 8, 1920, p. 2.

16. In re Paquet's Estate, 200 P 911 at 914 (Oregon 1921).

17. *U.S. v. John B. Paquet,* Bill of Complaint in Equity, September 21, 1923, pp. 4, 6–7.

18. *U.S. v. John B. Paquet,* Stipulation, June 2, 1924; *U.S. v. John B. Paquet,* Decree, June 2, 1924.

19. Tillamook County Probate file #605, J. S. Cole, Petition, June 7, 1928. Cole was president of the Tillamook-Lincoln County Credit Association.

20. For a particularly insightful analysis of the historical connections between concepts of "race" and "family," see Liu, "Teaching the Differences among Women in a Historical Perspective," *Women's Studies International Forum* 14 (1991): 265–276.

JUDY YUNG
Unbound Feet: From China to San Francisco's Chinatown

The imbalance of men and women in the largest Chinese community on the West Coast was a source of immense frustration, especially after the Immigration Act of 1924 effectively barred Chinese wives, even those married to U.S. citizens, from entering the country. Pany Lowe, an American-born Chinese man, expressed the feelings of men: "I think most Chinese in this country like have their son go to China get married. Under this new law . . . can't do this. No allowed marry white girl. Not enough American-born Chinese to go around. China only place to get wife. Not allowed to bring them back. For Chinaman, very unjust."* Although the act was amended in 1930 to allow the entry of women who had been married to U.S. citizens prior to May 26, 1924, the process of gaining entrance was lengthy, costly, and humiliating for most Chinese women. Many men, like Pany Lowe, chose to visit their wives in China rather than subject them to the ordeal of immigration.

Judy Yung's essay traces the experiences of three women from Guangdong Province who arrived in San Francisco in 1922. Two, Wong Ah So and Law Shee Low, came from impoverished villages to join their husbands in arranged marriages. Wong Ah So was in for a major surprise when she discovered her "marriage" was part of a system of enslaving women in forced prostitution to fill what was perceived to be a pressing need in a Chinese bachelor society. The third woman came from a different background with different expectations. Jane Kwong Lee was an urbanized, unmarried "new woman" who came to the

*Quoted in Judy Yung, *Unbound Feet: A Social History of Chinese Women in San Francisco* (Berkeley: University of California Press, 1995), p. 58.

United States to further her education. While she would endure many of the same gender and racial restrictions as the other two women, differences in her class and education made her experience—and the opportunities available to her—significantly different from that of other immigrant Chinese women in the 1920s.

Women's emancipation was heralded in San Francisco's Chinatown on the afternoon of November 2, 1902, when Sieh King King, an eighteen-year-old student from China and an ardent reformer, stood before a theater full of men and women and, according to newspaper accounts, "boldly condemned the slave girl system, raged at the horrors of footbinding and, with all the vehemence of aroused youth, declared that men and women were equal and should enjoy the privileges of equals."[1] Her talk and her views on women's rights were inextricably linked with Chinese nationalism and the 1898 Reform Movement, which advocated that China emulate the West and modernize in order to throw off the yoke of foreign domination. Elevating the status of women to the extent that they could become "new women"—educated mothers and productive citizens—was part of this nationalist effort to strengthen and defend China against further encroachment.

What Sieh King King advocated on behalf of Chinese women—unbound feet, education, equal rights, and public participation—remained at the heart of social change for Chinese women for the next three decades. This was due largely to the continuous influence of nationalism and women's emancipation in China, the reform work of Protestant missionary women in Chinatown, and Chinese women's entry into the urban economy. By 1929, immigrant women had made considerable progress toward freeing themselves of social restrictions and moving into the public arena. Footbinding was no longer practiced, prostitution had been eradicated, and a substantial number of women were working outside the home, educating themselves and their daughters, and playing a more visible role in community affairs. This discussion of the lives of Chinese immigrant women from 1902, when Sieh King King introduced her feminist views in San Francisco, to 1929, the beginnings of the Great Depression, will illustrate how socioeconomic developments in China and the United States

facilitated the unbinding of their feet and of their lives.

JOURNEY TO GOLD MOUNTAIN

At the time of Sieh King King's speech, China was still suffering under the stranglehold of Western imperialism and the inept rule of the Manchus. Life for the ordinary Chinese remained disrupted; survival was precarious. Consequently, many able-bodied peasants in Southeast China continued to emigrate overseas where kinfolk had already settled. Despite the Chinese Exclusion Acts and anti-Chinese hostilities, a good number went to California, the Gold Mountain. As increased numbers of Chinese sojourners became settlers, some found the economic means by which to get married or send for their wives and children from China. American immigration laws and the process of chain migration determined that most Chinese women would continue to come from the rural villages of Guangdong Province, where traditional gender roles still prevailed. Among these women were Wong Ah So and Law Shee Low, who both emigrated as obedient daughters in 1922 to escape poverty at home. Jane Kwong Lee, who also came the same year, was among the small number of urbanized "new women" who emigrated on their own for educational reasons. Together, these three women's stories provide insights into the gender roles and immigration experiences of Chinese women in the early twentieth century.

"I was born in Guangdong Province," begins Wong Ah So's story. "My father was sometimes a sailor and sometimes he worked on the docks, for we were very poor."[2] Patriarchal cultural values often put the daughter at risk when poverty strikes: From among the five children in the family, her mother chose to betroth her, the eldest daughter, to a Gold Mountain man in exchange for a bride price of 450 Mexican dollars.

> I was 19 when this man came to my mother and said that in America there was a great deal of gold. Even if I just peeled potatoes there, he told my

mother I would earn seven or eight dollars a day, and if I was willing to do any work at all I would earn lots of money. He was a laundryman, but said he earned plenty of money. He was very nice to me, and my mother liked him, so my mother was glad to have me go with him as his wife.

Out of filial duty and economic necessity, Ah So agreed to sail to the United States with this laundryman, Huey Yow. He had a marriage certificate prepared and told her to claim him as her husband to the immigration officials in San Francisco, although as she admitted later, "I claimed to be the wife of Huey Yow, but in truth had not at any time lived with him as his wife."

In Law Shee Low's case, her family succumbed to poverty after repeated raids by roving bandits in the Chungshan District of Guangdong Province. Conditions became so bad that the family had to sell their land and give up their three servants; all four daughters had to quit school and help at home. Speaking of her arranged marriage to a Gold Mountain man, she said, "I had no choice; we were so poor. We had no food to go with rice, not even soy sauce or black bean paste. Some of our neighbors even had to go begging or sell their daughters, times were so bad. So my parents thought I would have a better future in Gold Mountain."[3] Her fiancé said he was a clothing salesman in San Francisco and a Christian. He had a minister from Canton preside over the first "modern" wedding in his village. Law was eighteen and her husband, thirty-four. Nine months after the wedding, they sailed for America.

Born in 1902 to wealthy parents of the Toishan District, Guangdong Province (her family owned land and her father and uncle were successful businessmen in Australia), Jane Kwong Lee was able to acquire a Western education in the treaty port of Canton. There she was first exposed to American ideas of democracy and women's emancipation. During her last year in school, she was swept up by the May Fourth Movement, in which students agitated for political and cultural reforms in response to continuing foreign domination. At the time of her graduation from middle school, she observed that classmates were either entering technical institutions or getting married. "I thought otherwise," she said. "I enjoyed studying and I wanted to be economically independent. In that sense, it was clear in my mind that I had to have as much formal education as possible."[4]

Although she wanted to become a doctor, medical school was out of the question, as her father's remittances from Australia could no longer support both her and her younger brother's education. Arguing that graduates trained in American colleges and universities were drawing higher salaries in China than local graduates, Jane convinced her mother to sell some of their land in order to pay her passage to the United States. She then obtained a student's visa and sailed for America, planning to earn a doctorate and return home to a prestigious academic post. Jane Kwong Lee's class background, education, and early exposure to Western ideas would lead her to a different life experience in America than Law Shee Low and Wong Ah So, who came as obedient wives from sheltered and impoverished families.

The San Francisco Chinatown that the three women came to call home was different from the slum of "filth and depravity" of bygone days. After the 1906 earthquake and fire destroyed Chinatown, Chinese community leaders seized the opportunity to create a new "Oriental City" on the original site. The new Chinatown, in stark contrast to the old, was by appearance cleaner, healthier, and more modern with its wider paved streets, brick buildings, glass-plated storefronts, and pseudo-Chinese architecture. In an effort to establish order in the community, nurture business, and protect the growing numbers of families, the merchant elite and middle-class bourgeoisie established new institutions: Chinese schools, churches, a hospital, newspapers, and a flurry of civic and political organizations. Soon after the 1911 Revolution in China, queues and footbinding were eliminated, tong wars and prostitution reduced, and more of Chinatown's residents were dressing in Western clothing and adopting democratic ideas. Arriving in San Francisco's Chinatown at this juncture in time gave immigrant women such as Wong Ah So, Law Shee Low, and Jane Kwong Lee unprecedented opportunities to become "new women" in the modern era of Chinatown.

ESCAPING "A FATE WORSE THAN DEATH"

Upon landing in America, Wong Ah So's dreams of wealth and happiness vanished when she found out that her husband, Huey

Yow, had in fact been paid $500 by a madam to procure her as a slave.

> When we first landed in San Francisco we lived in a hotel in Chinatown, a nice place, but one day, after I had been there for about two weeks, a woman came to see me. She was young, very pretty, and all dressed in silk. She told me that I was not really Huey Yow's wife, but that she had asked him to buy her a slave, that I belonged to her, and must go with her, but she would treat me well, and I could buy back my freedom, if I was willing to please, and be agreeable, and she would let me off in two years, instead of four if I did not make a fuss.

For the next year, Wong Ah So worked as a prostitute for the madam in various small towns. She was also forced to borrow $1,000 to pay off Huey Yow, who was harassing her and threatening her life. Soon after, she was sold to another madam in Fresno for $2,500. Meanwhile, her family in China continued to write her, asking for money. Even as her debts piled up and she became ill, she fulfilled her filial obligation by sending $300 home to her mother, enclosed with a letter that read in part:

> Every day I have to be treated by the doctor. My private parts pain me so that I cannot have intercourse with men. It is very hard. . . . Next year I certainly will be able to pay off all the debts. Your daughter is even more anxious than her mother to do this. Your daughter will do her part so that the world will not look down upon us.

Then one evening at a tong banquet where she was working, Wong Ah So was recognized by a friend of her father's, who sought help from the Presbyterian Mission Home on her behalf. Ten days later, she was rescued and placed in the care of Donaldina Cameron, the director of the home. As she wrote, "I don't know just how it happened because it was all very sudden. I just know that it happened. I am learning English and to weave, and I am going to send money to my mother when I can. I can't help but cry, but it is going to be better. I will do what Miss Cameron says." A year later, after learning how to read Chinese and speak English and becoming a Christian, Ah So agreed to marry Louie Kwong, a merchant in Boise, Idaho.

Wong Ah So's story harks back to the plight of the many Chinese women who were brought to the United States as prostitutes to fill a specific need in the Chinese bachelor society. By the 1920s, however, the traffic had gone underground and was on the decline due to the Chinese exclusion laws, anti-prostitution legislation, and the efforts of Protestant missionaries. In 1870, the peak year of prostitution, 1,426 or 71 percent of Chinese women in San Francisco were listed as prostitutes. By 1900 the number had dropped to 339 or 16 percent; and by 1910, 92 or 7 percent. No prostitutes could be found in the 1920 census, although English- and Chinese-language newspaper accounts and the records of the Presbyterian Mission Home indicate that organized prostitution continued through the 1920s.[5]

Most well known for her rescue work in Chinatown, Donaldina Cameron was a product of the Social Gospel and Progressive movements, which sought to uplift the "uncivilized" throughout the world and eradicate political corruption and social vices in the nation's cities. Unable to work effectively among Chinatown bachelors and spurned by white prostitutes, Cameron found her calling among Chinese prostitutes and slave girls. In turn, some Chinese prostitutes, calculating their chances in an oppressive environment with few options for improvement, saw the Mission Home as a way out of their problems. Cameron made it her crusade to free them from "a fate worse than death" by first rescuing them, and then inculcating them with Christian moral values. Numerous accounts in newspapers and religious publications describe in vivid detail the dangerous raids led by Cameron, who was credited with rescuing hundreds of Chinese slave girls during her forty years of service at the Presbyterian Mission Home.[6]

Once rescued, the young women were brought back to the Mission Home to be educated, trained in the domestic arts and industrial skills, and, most importantly, indoctrinated with Victorian moral values. The goal was to regroom them to enter society as Christian women. While some women chose to return to China under Christian escort, others opted to enter companionate marriages, pursue higher education, or become missionary workers. Wong Ah So—a direct beneficiary of the efforts of Protestant missionary women—was among the last to be rescued, Christianized, and married to a Chinese Christian.

Newly-arrived Chinese women and children awaiting interrogation at the Immigration Station on Angel Island, near San Francisco, sometime after 1910. (Courtesy of California Historical Society, FN-18240.)

IMMIGRANT WIVES AS INDISPENSABLE PARTNERS

Immigrant wives like Law Shee Low also found their lives transformed by the socioeconomic conditions in Chinatown. They did not find streets paved with gold, but practically speaking, they at least had food on the table and hope that through their hard work conditions might improve for themselves and their families. Although women were confined to the domestic sphere within the borders of Chinatown, their contributions as homemakers, wage earners, and culture bearers made them indispensable partners to their husbands in their struggle for economic survival. Their indispensability, combined with changing social attitudes toward women in Chinatown, gave some women leverage to shape gender arrangements within their homes and in the community.

Upon arrival in San Francisco, Law Shee Low moved into a one-room tenement apartment in Chinatown with her husband, where she lived, worked, and gave birth to eleven children, eight of whom survived. While her husband worked in a restaurant that catered to

black customers on the outskirts of Chinatown, Law stayed home and took in sewing. Like other immigrant women who followed traditional gender roles, Law believed that the proper place for a woman was at home. As she recalls those days,

> There was no time to feel imprisoned; there was so much to do. We had to cook, wash the clothes and diapers by hand, the floors, and sew whenever we had a chance to sit still. It was the same for all my neighbors. We were all good, obedient, and diligent wives. All sewed; all had six or seven children. Who had time to go out?

Fortunately for Law Shee Low, her husband turned out to be cooperative, supportive, and devoted. Until he developed a heart condition in the 1950s, he remained the chief breadwinner, first cooking at a restaurant, then picking fruit in Suisun [California], sewing at home during the depression, and finally working in the shipyards during World War II. Although he refused to help with housecleaning or childcare, he did all the shopping, cooked the rice, and hung out the wash. In his own way, he showed concern for his wife. "When he was afraid I wasn't eating, he would tell me to eat more. Even though it was an arranged marriage, we got along well. I didn't complain that he went out every day. We hardly talked. Good or bad, we just struggled along as we had work to do."

As far as children were concerned Law Shee Low, like her neighbors, had not known how to interfere with nature. "We didn't know about birth control. We would become pregnant every year without realizing it. Even if we didn't want it, we didn't have the money to go see the doctor." All of Law's children were born at home, with the help of neighbors or the local midwife. Fortunately, her husband wanted children and was more than willing to provide for them all regardless of sex. "Other men would scold their children and beat them. One woman who had four children told me her husband would drag her out of bed and beat her because she didn't want to have any more children. We heard all kinds of sad stories like that, but my husband never picked on me like that."

It was not until her children were older that Law Shee Low went out to work in the sewing factories and to the Chinese movies on Saturdays, but she still did not leave the confines of Chinatown. Prior to that, she went out so seldom that one pair of shoes lasted her ten years. Since their first responsibility was to their families, many immigrant wives like Law found themselves housebound, with no time to learn English or to participate in social activities outside the home. Their husbands continued to be the chief breadwinner, to hold the purse strings, and to be their liaison to the outside world. But in the absence of the mother-in-law, immigrant wives usually ruled the household and assumed the responsibility of disciplinarian, culture-bearer, and of maintaining the integrity of their families. With few exceptions, they were hardworking, frugal, and tolerant, faithful and respectful to their husbands, and self-sacrificing toward their children. As such, they were indispensable partners to their husbands in their efforts to establish and sustain family life in America. And although they presented a submissive image in public, many immigrant women were known to "wear the pants" at home.

Overall, as compared to their predecessors, immigrant women in the early twentieth century were less tolerant of abuses to their persons and more resourceful in upgrading their status, thanks to the influence of the press,

the support of Protestant organizations in the community, and a legal system that was sympathetic toward abused women. Although most immigrant wives like Law Shee Low could not read the Chinese newspapers, they were affected by public opinion as filtered through their husbands, neighbors, and social reformers looking after their interests. Law noted that after the 1911 Revolution it was no longer considered "fashionable" to have bound feet, concubines, or slave girls. And as housebound as Law was, she was aware of the mission homes that rescued prostitutes, helped abused women, and provided education for children and immigrant women.

CHINESE WOMEN IN THE LABOR MARKET

Compared to Wong Ah So and Law Shee Low, Jane Kwong Lee had an easier time acclimating to life in America. Not only was she educated, Westernized, English-speaking, and unencumbered by family responsibilities, but she also had the help of affluent relatives who provided her with room and board, financial support, and important contacts that enabled her eventually to strike out on her own.

Arriving in the middle of a school semester and therefore unable to enroll in a college, she decided to look for a job. In spite of her educational background and qualifications, she found that only menial jobs and domestic service were opened to her. "At heart I was sorry for myself; I wished I were a boy," she wrote in her autobiography. "If I were a boy, I could have gone out into the community, finding a job somewhere as many newcomers from China had done." But as a Chinese woman, she had to bide her time and look for work appropriate for her race and gender. Thus, until she could be admitted to college, and during the summers after she enrolled at Mills College, Jane took whatever jobs were open to Chinese women. She tried embroidery work at a Chinatown factory, sorting vegetables in the wholesale district, working as a live-in domestic for a white family, peeling shrimp, sorting fruit at a local cannery, and sewing flannel nightgowns at home.

As was true for European immigrant women, the patterns of work for Chinese women were shaped by the intersection of the local economy, ethnic traditions, language and job skills, and family and child-care needs, but in addition, race was an influential factor. At the time of Jane's arrival, San Francisco was experiencing a period of growth and prosperity. Ranked the eighth largest city in the country, it was the major port of trade for the Pacific Coast and touted as the financial and corporate capital of the West. Jobs were plentiful in the city's three largest economic sectors—domestic and personal service, trade and transportation, and manufacturing and mechanical industries—but they were filled according to a labor market stratified by race and gender, with Chinese men occupying the lowest tier as laborers, servants, factory workers, laundrymen, and small merchants, while Chinese women, handicapped further by gender, worked primarily in garment and food-processing factories for low piece-rate wages. With inadequate child-care services in the community, most seamstresses worked with their children close by or had their babies strapped to their backs.

For Jane Kwong Lee, being Chinese and a woman was a liability in the job market, but because she spoke English, was educated, and had good contacts among Chinese Christians, she was better off than most other immigrant women. She eventually got a scholarship at Mills College and part-time work teaching Chinese school and tutoring Chinese adults in English at the Chinese Episcopal Church in Oakland. After earning her bachelor's degree in sociology, she married, had two children, and returned to Mills College, where she received a master's degree in sociology and economics in 1933. She then dedicated herself to community service, working many years as coordinator of the Chinese YWCA and as a journalist and translator for a number of Chinatown newspapers.

For most immigrant women, joining the labor market proved to be a double-edged sword: On the one hand, their earnings helped to support their families and elevate their socioeconomic status; on the other hand, they became exploited laborers in the factory system, adding work and stress to their already burdensome lives. On the positive side, however, working outside the home offered women social rewards—a new sense of freedom, accomplishment, and camaraderie. They were no longer confined to the home, they were earning money for themselves or the family, and they were making new acquaintances and becoming exposed to new ideas. As Jane Kwong Lee observed, having money to spend made the women feel more liberated in America than in China: "They can buy things for themselves, go out to department stores to choose their own clothes instead of sewing them."

FIRST STEPS TOWARD SOCIAL ACTIVISM

For working-class women like Law Shee Low, family and work responsibilities consumed all their time and energy, leaving little left over for self-improvement or leisure activities, and even less for community involvement. This was not the case for a growing group of educated and professional women like Jane Kwong Lee, who, inspired by Christianity, Chinese nationalism, and Progressivism, took the first steps toward social activism. Prior to the 1911 Revolution in their homeland, Chinese women in America followed the tradition of remaining publicly invisible. They seldom ventured out of their homes except perhaps to shop or go to the Chinese opera, where they sat in a segregated section apart from the men.

The Protestant churches and Chinese YWCA were the first to encourage Chinese women's participation in organized activities outside the home, as evidenced by the small but visible number of them at Sunday services, English classes, meetings, outings, and other church-sponsored programs. Some of the churches also helped organize Chinese women's societies to encourage involvement in Christian activities. Members of these groups met regularly to have lunch or socialize, and paid dues to help support the work of Bible women in their home villages in China.[7]

Aside from Christianity, the intense nationalistic spirit that took hold in the early twentieth century also affected Chinese women in far-reaching ways. Not only did the call for modernization include the need to improve conditions for Chinese women, but reformers also solicited women's active participation in national salvation work. Fundraising for disaster relief and the revolution in China opened up opportunities for women to become involved in the community, develop leadership abilities, and move into the male-dominated public sphere. The Tongmenghui, the revolutionary party founded by Dr. Sun Yat-sen to overthrow the Qing dynasty and establish a republic in China, was the earliest organization to accept women into its ranks. While women in China participated in benefit performances, enlisted in the army, and engaged in dangerous undercover work, women in San Francisco also did their share for the revolutionary effort—making patriotic speeches, donating money and jewelry for the cause, and helping with Red Cross work—sometimes under the auspices of Protestant churches, other times under the banner of the Women's Young China Society.

Although the success of the revolution and the establishment of a republic in China failed to bring peace and prosperity to the country, it did have a lasting impact on the lives of Chinese American women. As Jane Kwong Lee observed, "After the establishment of the Republic of China, Chinese women in this country picked up the forward-looking trend for equality with men. They could go to school, speak in public places, have their feet free from binding, and go out to work in stores and small factories if they needed to work."[8]

Arriving as a liberated woman at the time when she did, Jane did not hesitate to join other women in becoming socially active in the Chinatown community. In her capacity as a community worker at the Chinese YWCA, she made house visits, wrote articles that were published in the local newspapers, and implemented programs that benefited Chinese women in the community. She was particularly known for her loud and forceful speeches that she delivered in Chinese at churches and street corners in support of Christianity and nationalist causes, and before Chinatown organizations on behalf of the Chinese YWCA. Jane also made presentations in English to groups interested in learning more about Chinese culture, and traveled as a Chinese delegate to YWCA functions outside of Chinatown. On one of these occasions, she was so moved by a discussion on racial discrimination that she surprised herself and African Americans at a YWCA meeting by speaking up for them. "I said, you are all equal; nobody is inferior to another."[9]

CONCLUSION

As Sieh King King had advocated in 1902, Chinese women unbound their feet and began to unbind their lives in America during the first three decades of the twentieth century. Most, like Law Shee Low and Wong Ah So, had immigrated for a better livelihood but found themselves exploited as prostitutes or working wives at the bottom of a labor market stratified by race and gender. Some, like Jane Kwong Lee, had come from a privileged background yet still encountered discrimination in the workplace and in the larger American society. But like many other immigrant women before them, they not only persevered and survived, but took advantage of new circumstances to improve their lives and contribute to the well-being of their families and community. Even as immigrant women began to enjoy their new roles as emancipated women, economic depression set in and war loomed large in their homeland. The challenges of the 1930s and 1940s—economic survival and the war effort on two fronts—would lead to even greater dramatic changes in their lives, allowing them to take the first steps toward fuller participation in American society.

NOTES

1. *San Francisco Chronicle*, November 3, 1902, p. 7.
2. Wong Ah So's story is taken from "Story of Wong Ah So—Experiences as a Prostitute," *Orientals and Their Cultural Adjustment,* Social Science Source Documents, no. 4 (Nashville: Social Science Institute, Fisk University, 1946), pp. 31–35; and Donaldina Cameron, "The Story of Wong So," *Women and Missions* 2, no. 5 (August 1925):169–72.
3. Law Shee Low's story is based on her interview with Sandy Lee, May 2, 1982; and interview with author, October 20, 1988.
4. Jane Kwong Lee's story is based on her unpublished autobiography, "A Chinese American," in the possession of her daughter Priscilla Holmes.
5. See Lucie Cheng Hirata, "Free, Indentured, Enslaved: Chinese Prostitutes in Nineteenth-Century California," *Signs: Journal of Women in Culture and Society* 5, no. 1 (autumn 1979):3–29. The figures for 1900, 1910, and 1920 are based on my computations from the U.S. National Archives, Record Group 29, "Census of U.S. Population" (manuscript), San Francisco, California.
6. See Peggy Pascoe, *Relations of Rescue: The Search for Female Moral Authority in the American West, 1874–1939* (New York: Oxford University Press, 1990).
7. See Wesley Woo, "Protestant Work among the Chinese in the San Francisco Bay Area, 1850–1920," Ph.D. dissertation, University of California, Berkeley, 1983.
8. Jane Kwong Lee, "Chinese Women in San Francisco," *Chinese Digest* (June 1938):8.
9. Jane Kwong Lee, interview with author, November 2, 1988.

Zitkala-Ša (Gertrude Simmons Bonnin), ". . . this semblance
of civilization . . ."

Zitkala-Ša (1876–1938), whose mother was Sioux and father was Anglo-American, sought throughout her life to bridge the cultures of Native Americans and the United States. She was one of the first American Indian women who built an independent career as a writer; her voice, as the following selection from her early writing shows, could be simultaneously eloquent, sentimental, and bitter. Zitkala-Ša was eight years old when she left her home on the Yankton Sioux Agency in South Dakota for White's Indiana Manual Labor Institute in Wabash, Indiana, a training school funded by Quakers. She continued her education first at a teacher training school close to her home, then at Earlham College, and finally at the New England Conservatory of Music in Boston where she studied the violin.

After her marriage in 1901, Zitkala-Ša worked with her husband, Raymond Bonnin, who was an employee of the Bureau of Indian Affairs (BIA), advocating citizenship for Indians, exposing corruption in the BIA, and insisting on the dignity of Indian religions. In this stage of her life, she used her anglicized married name, Gertrude Simmons Bonnin. Bonnin lobbied for the Indian Citizenship Act of 1924; she founded the National Council of American Indians; and she sought to shape the Indian policy of the New Deal years.

When she wrote this memoir of her childhood in 1900 at age twenty-four, Zitkala-Ša had not yet taught at the Carlisle Indian School in Pennsylvania. The experience would strengthen her criticism of the practice of removing native children from their homes. It would also lead her to expose the corruption she found among the school's directors, who received federal money for each child they boarded and whose promotion of "Americanization" could be harsh and cruel. To what extent did her mother anticipate that the experience at the mission school would be difficult? What advantage did the educators think would result from cutting girls' hair? What evidence is there to suggest that she herself was involved in the process of acculturation? Compare Bonnin's education and geographic mobility to that of Sarah Winemucca (see Rose Stremlau's essay, pp. 227–237) and Wilma Mankiller (pp. 785–790).

The first turning away from the easy, natural flow of my life occurred in an early spring. It was in my eighth year; in the month of March, I afterward learned. At this age I knew but one language, and that was my mother's native tongue.

From some of my playmates I heard that two paleface missionaries were in our village. They were from that class of white men who wore big hats and carried large hearts, they said. Running direct to my mother, I began to question her why these two

Excerpted from "Impressions of an Indian Childhood," "The School Days of an Indian Girl," and "An Indian Teacher among Indians," by Zitkala-Ša, *Atlantic Monthly* 85 (January, February, March 1900): 45–47, 186–87, 386.

Zitkala-Ša, ca. 1898, posed in traditional dress.
This photograph is one in a series taken by the professional photographer Gertrude Käsebier, who had a studio on Fifth Avenue in New York City. In other images taken at the same sitting, Zitkala-Ša is in western dress (a white gown), and in some she holds in her lap a book, her violin, or an Indian basket. For interpretations of Käsebier's portraits of Zitkala-Ša and other Indians, see Laura Wexler, Tender Violence: Domestic Visions in an Age of U.S. Imperialism *(Chapel Hill: University of North Carolina Press, 2000), pp. 115–124, 177–208; and Elizabeth Hutchinson, "When the 'Sioux Chief's Party Calls': Käsebier's Indian Portraits and the Gendering of the Artist's Studio,"* American Art 16 *(Summer 2002), 40-65. (Courtesy of the Smithsonian Institution.)*

strangers were among us. She told me, after I had teased much, that they had come to take away Indian boys and girls to the East. My mother did not seem to want me to talk about them. But in a day or two, I gleaned many wonderful stories from my playfellows concerning the strangers.

"Mother, my friend Judéwin is going home with the missionaries. She is going to a more beautiful country than ours; the pale-faces told her so!" I said wistfully, wishing in my heart that I too might go.

Mother sat in a chair, and I was hanging on her knee. Within the last two seasons my big brother Dawée had returned from a three years' education in the East, and his coming back influenced my mother to take a farther step from her native way of living. First it was a change from the buffalo skin to the white man's canvas that covered our wigwam. Now she had given up her wigwam of slender poles, to live, a foreigner, in a home of clumsy logs.

Judéwin had told me of the great tree where grew red, red apples; and how we could reach out our hands and pick all the red apples we could eat. I had never seen apple trees. I had never tasted more than a dozen red apples in my life; and when I heard of the orchards of the East, I was eager to roam among them. The missionaries smiled into my eyes, and patted my head. I wondered how mother could say such hard words against them.

"Mother, ask them if little girls may have all the red apples they want, when they go East," I whispered aloud, in my excitement.

The interpreter heard me, and answered: "Yes, little girl, the nice red apples are for those who pick them; and you will have a ride on the iron horse if you go with these good people."

I had never seen a train, and he knew it.

"Mother, I'm going East! I like big red apples, and I want to ride on the iron horse! Mother, say yes!" I pleaded.

My mother said nothing. The missionaries waited in silence; and my eyes began to blur with tears, though I struggled to choke them back. The corners of my mouth twitched, and my mother saw me.

"I am not ready to give you any word," she said to them. "Tomorrow I shall send you my answer by my son."

With this they left us. Alone with my mother, I yielded to my tears, and cried aloud, shaking my head so as not to hear what she was saying to me. This was the first time I had ever been so unwilling to give up my own desire that I refused to harken to my mother's voice.

There was a solemn silence in our home that night. Before I went to bed I begged the Great Spirit to make my mother willing I should go with the missionaries.

The next morning came, and my mother called me to her side. "My daughter, do you still persist in wishing to leave your mother?" she asked.

"Oh, mother, it is not that I wish to leave you, but I want to see the wonderful Eastern land," I answered. . . .

. . . My brother Dawée came for mother's decision. I dropped my play, and crept close to my aunt.

"Yes, Dawée, my daughter, though she does not understand what it all means, is anxious to go. She will need an education when she is grown, for then there will be fewer real Dakotas, and many more palefaces. This tearing her away, so young, from her mother is necessary, if I would have her an educated woman. The palefaces, who owe us a large debt for stolen lands, have begun to pay a tardy justice in offering some education to our children. But I know my daughter must suffer keenly in this experiment. For her sake, I dread to tell you my reply to the missionaries. Go, tell them that they may take my little daughter, and that the Great Spirit shall not fail to reward them according to their hearts."

Wrapped in my heavy blanket, I walked with my mother to the carriage that was soon to take us to the iron horse. I was happy. I met my playmates, who were also wearing their best thick blankets. We showed one another our new beaded moccasins, and the width of the belts that girdled our new dresses. Soon we were being drawn rapidly away by the white man's horses. When I saw the lonely figure of my mother vanish in the distance, a sense of regret settled heavily upon me. I felt suddenly weak, as if I might fall limp to the ground. I was in the hands of strangers whom my mother did not fully trust. I no longer felt free to be myself, or to voice my own feelings. The tears trickled down my cheeks, and I buried my face in the folds of my blanket. Now the first step, parting me from my mother, was taken, and all my belated tears availed nothing.

Having driven thirty miles to the ferry-boat, we crossed the Missouri in the evening.

Then riding again a few miles eastward, we stopped before a massive brick building. I looked at it in amazement, and with a vague misgiving, for in our village I had never seen so large a house. Trembling with fear and distrust of the palefaces, my teeth chattering from the chilly ride, I crept noiselessly in my soft moccasins along the narrow hall, keeping very close to the bare wall. I was as frightened and bewildered as the captured young of a wild creature.

The first day in the land of apples was a bitter-cold one; for the snow still covered the ground, and the trees were bare. A large bell rang for breakfast, its loud metallic voice crashing through the belfry overhead and into our sensitive ears. The annoying clatter of shoes on bare floors gave us no peace. The constant clash of harsh noises, with an undercurrent of many voices murmuring an unknown tongue, made a bedlam within which I was securely tied. And though my spirit tore itself in struggling for its lost freedom, all was useless.

A paleface woman, with white hair, came up after us. We were placed in a line of girls who were marching into the dining room. These were Indian girls, in stiff shoes and closely clinging dresses. The small girls wore sleeved aprons and shingled hair. As I walked noiselessly in my soft moccasins, I felt like sinking to the floor, for my blanket had been stripped from my shoulders. I looked hard at the Indian girls, who seemed not to care that they were even more immodestly dressed than I, in their tightly fitting clothes. While we marched in, the boys entered at an opposite door. I watched for the three young braves who came in our party. I spied them in the rear ranks, looking as uncomfortable as I felt. . . .

. . . Late in the morning, my friend Judéwin gave me a terrible warning. Judéwin knew a few words of English; and she had overheard the paleface woman talk about cutting our long, heavy hair. Our mothers had taught us that only unskilled warriors who were captured had their hair shingled by the enemy. Among our people, short hair was worn by mourners, and shingled hair by cowards!

We discussed our fate some moments, and when Judéwin said, "We have to submit, because they are strong," I rebelled.

"No, I will not submit! I will struggle first!" I answered.

I watched my chance, and when no one noticed I disappeared. I crept up the stairs as quietly as I could in my squeaking shoes—my moccasins had been exchanged for shoes. Along the hall I passed, without knowing whither I was going. Turning aside to an open door, I found a large room with three white beds in it. The windows were covered with dark green curtains, which made the room very dim. Thankful that no one was there, I directed my steps toward the corner farthest from the door. On my hands and knees I crawled under the bed, and cuddled myself in the dark corner.

From my hiding place I peered out, shuddering with fear whenever I heard footsteps near by. Though in the hall loud voices were calling my name, and I knew that even Judéwin was searching for me, I did not open my mouth to answer. Then the steps were quickened and the voices became excited. The sounds came nearer and nearer. Women and girls entered the room. I held my breath, and watched them open closet doors and peep behind large trunks. Some one threw up the curtains, and the room was filled with sudden light. What caused them to stoop and look under the bed I do not know. I remember being dragged out, though I resisted by kicking and scratching wildly. In spite of myself, I was carried downstairs and tied fast in a chair.

I cried aloud, shaking my head all the while until I felt the cold blades of the scissors against my neck, and heard them gnaw off one of my thick braids. Then I lost my spirit. Since the day I was taken from my mother I had suffered extreme indignities. People had stared at me. I had been tossed about in the air like a wooden puppet. And now my long hair was shingled like a coward's! In my anguish I moaned for my mother, but no one came to comfort me. Not a soul reasoned quietly with me, as my own mother used to do; for now I was only one of many little animals driven by a herder. . . .

. . . Now, as I look back upon the recent past, I see it from a distance, as a whole. I remember how, from morning till evening, many specimens of civilized peoples visited the Indian school. The city folks with canes and eyeglasses, the countrymen with sunburnt cheeks and clumsy feet, forgot their relative social ranks in an ignorant curiosity. Both sorts of these Christian palefaces were alike astounded at seeing the children of savage warriors so docile and industrious.

As answers to their shallow inquiries they received the students' sample work to look upon. Examining the neatly figured pages, and gazing upon the Indian girls and boys bending over their books, the white visitors walked out of the schoolhouse well satisfied: They were educating the children of the red man! They were paying a liberal fee to the government employees in whose able hands lay the small forest of Indian timber.

In this fashion many have passed idly through the Indian schools during the last decade, afterward to boast of their charity to the North American Indian. But few there are who have paused to question whether real life or long-lasting death lies beneath this semblance of civilization.

CHANGE AGENTS

KATHRYN KISH SKLAR
Florence Kelley and Women's Activism in the Progressive Era

Florence Kelley was a remarkable woman who lived in a period when attempts to address the problems created by industrialization and urbanization generated both the early social sciences and the foundation of the welfare state. Kathryn Sklar, Kelley's biographer, provides in this authoritative and highly informative essay an account of a single individual that also illuminates the pursuit of social justice in which many progressive women of Kelley's generation were involved. Sklar reveals the factors that made it possible for these women to influence public policy even before they were allowed to vote. She also describes the changing political context that limited their influence following the Red Scare at the end of World War I.

What were the influences, personal and intellectual, that shaped Kelley's vision of social reform? What strategies did she employ in pursuit of that vision? What does Sklar mean when she says that Kelley used gender-specific legislation as a surrogate for class legislation? Precisely how did the Red Scare affect the political agenda of women's organizations? In what respects were at least three of the four significant features of women's power in the Progressive era that Sklar identified highly gendered? As we move into reading about the 1930s and beyond, think about which of the features persist and which do not.

One of the most powerful women in American history deserves to be better known today. Florence Kelley (1859–1932) was well known to her contemporaries as a leading champion of social justice legislation. For most of the 1890s she lived in the nation's leading reform institution, Hull House, a social settlement founded in Chicago by Jane Addams in 1889. Between 1899 and 1932 she served as head of the National Consumers' League in New York City.

Living collectively with other women reformers in Chicago and New York, Florence Kelley was able to make the most of her talents; for four decades she occupied the vanguard of social reform. Her forceful personality flourished in the combative atmosphere generated by her struggles for social justice. Jane Addams's nephew, who resided with Kelley at Hull House, was awed by the way she "hurled the spears of her thought with such apparent carelessness of what breasts they pierced." He thought her "the toughest customer in the reform riot, the finest rough-and-tumble fighter for the good life for others, that Hull House ever knew: Any weapon was a good weapon in her hand—evidence, argument, irony or invective." Nevertheless, he said, those who were close to her knew she was "full of love."[1]

Kelley's career, like that of many of her reform contemporaries, was responding to

Written expressly for *Women's America*. A revised version of this essay appears in Rima Lunin Schultz and Adele Hast, eds., *Women Building Chicago, 1790–1990: A Biographical Dictionary* (Bloomington: Indiana University Press, 2001.) Copyright © by Kathryn Kish Sklar.

profound changes in American social and economic life. Rapid industrialization was recasting the economy, massive immigration was reconstituting the working class, and sustained urbanization was making cities the focus of social change.[2] In this context, college-educated women reformers often achieved what men and male-dominated organizations could not.

Florence Kelley's life helps us understand how women reformers accomplished their goals. Her reform career exemplified four significant features of women's power in the Progressive era: their access to higher education; their prominence in early social science; the political autonomy of their separate institutions; and their ability to challenge American traditions of limited government. Having experienced these ingredients of women's power in her own life before 1899, thereafter, as the General Secretary of the National Consumers' League, she integrated them into her strategies for pursuing social justice.[3]

WOMEN'S ACCESS
TO HIGHER EDUCATION

When she graduated from Cornell University in 1882, Florence Kelley joined thousands of other young women in her generation who received college educations. Two changes in the 1860s and 1870s enabled white, middle-class women to attend college in sufficient numbers to become a sociological phenomenon. Elite women's colleges, such as Vassar, Smith, and Wellesley, began accepting students between 1865 and 1875, providing equivalents to elite men's colleges such as Harvard, Yale, and Princeton. And state universities, established through the allocation of public lands in the Morrill Act of 1862 and required to be "open for all," gradually made college educations accessible for the first time to large numbers of women in the nation's central and western states. By 1880 women, numbering forty thousand, constituted 33 percent of all enrolled students in higher education.[4] Though a small percentage of all women, they exercised an influence disproportionate to their numbers.

To Cornell Kelley brought a social conscience shaped by her family. Born into an elite Philadelphia family with Quaker and Unitarian political traditions, she grew up against the background of the Civil War and Reconstruction—dramas in which her father and her mother's aunt played major roles. Her father,

William Durrah Kelley, one of the founders of the Republican Party, was reelected to fifteen consecutive terms in the U.S. Congress between 1860 and 1890. As a Radical Republican, he advanced the cause of black suffrage and tried to forge a biracial Republican Party in the South. Her mother's aunt, Sarah Pugh, served as president of the Philadelphia Female Anti-Slavery Society almost every year between 1838 and 1870. In the 1860s and 1870s, Pugh accompanied her close friend, Lucretia Mott, to early woman suffrage conventions. To young "Florrie," Sarah Pugh was conscience incarnate, a full-time reformer who lived her beliefs, never wearing slave-made cotton or eating slave-produced sugar.[5]

During six mostly schoolless years before she entered Cornell, Florence systematically read through her father's library, imbibing the fiction of Dickens and Thackeray, Louisa May Alcott and Horatio Alger; the poetry of Shakespeare, Milton, Byron, and Goldsmith; the writings of James Madison; histories by Bancroft, Prescott, and Parkman; and the moral and political philosophy of Emerson, Channing, Burke, Carlyle, Godwin, and Spencer. These readings helped her reach out to her moody and distant father. For that purpose she also began reading government reports at the age of ten and, on trips to Washington, began using the Library of Congress by the time she was twelve.

A darker side of Kelley's childhood was shaped by her mother's permanent depression—caused by the death of five of her eight children before they had reached the age of six. Caroline Bonsall Kelley was a descendant of John Bartram, the Quaker botanist. Orphaned at the age of nine, she was raised in the Pugh family. With the death of her infants, Caroline developed a "settled, gentle melancholy" that threatened to envelop her daughter as long as she lived at home.[6] Florence grew up with two brothers, but no sisters survived. Keenly aware of the high social cost of infant mortality to nineteenth-century families, she developed a rage against human suffering that formed her lifelong career as a reformer.

WOMEN'S PROMINENCE
IN EARLY SOCIAL SCIENCE

Like higher education, the newly emerging field of social science served as a critical vehicle by which middle-class women expanded the space they occupied within American civic life between 1860 and 1890. Social science leveled the playing field on which women interacted with men in public life. It offered tools of analysis that enhanced women's ability to investigate economic and social change, speak for the welfare of the whole society, devise policy initiatives, and oversee their implementation. Yet at the same time, social science also deepened women's gender identity in public life and attached their civic activism even more securely to gender-specific issues.[7]

Kelley's early commitment to social science as a tool for social reform built on a generation of women's presence in American social science. Women came with the civic territory that social science embraced. Caroline Dall had been a cofounder of the association in 1865, and other women were especially active in the American Social Science Association's (ASSA) department of education, public health, and social economy, which gave them clear but limited mandates for leadership.

The question of "After college, what?" was as pertinent to Florence Kelley as it was to other women graduates.[8] Barred from admission to graduate study at the University of Pennsylvania because she was a woman, she faced a very limited set of opportunities. First she threw her energies into the New Century Working Women's Guild, an organization that fostered middle-class aid for self-supporting women. She helped found the Guild, taught classes in history, and assembled the group's library. Then, remaining a dutiful daughter, in 1882 she accompanied her brother when his doctor prescribed a winter of European travel to cure temporary blindness. In Europe she encountered M. Carey Thomas, a Cornell acquaintance, who had just completed a Ph.D. at the University of Zurich, the only European university that granted degrees to women. Thomas recommended that Kelley go to Zurich for graduate study.

Initially accompanied by her mother and younger brother, Kelley studied government and law at Zurich between 1883 and 1886. There she promptly befriended exiled socialist students from Russia and Germany. To the shocked amazement of her family and friends, in 1885 she married Lazare Wischnewetzky, a Russian, Jewish, socialist, medical student. She then gave birth to three children in three years.

Cloaked with her new personal identity as a European married woman, she stopped communicating with her family and began to forge a new political identity. Rejecting American public culture because it limited her opportunities for social service and because her father's career revealed so starkly that culture's tolerance of social injustice, she underwent a dramatic conversion to socialism, joined the German Social Democratic Party (SPD), and began to translate the writings of Friedrich Engels and Karl Marx. Outlawed in Germany, the SPD maintained its European headquarters in Zurich, where Kelley met many of its leaders. Since the death of Marx in 1885, Engels had become the chief theoretician of German socialism. Kelley's translation of his 1845 book, *The Condition of the Working Class in England,* is still the preferred scholarly version of that now-classic social science study. This project launched a close but troubled relationship with Engels that persisted until his death in 1895.[9]

When Kelley returned to the United States in 1886 with her small family, she searched without success for a political context capable of sustaining her newfound radicalism. Settling in New York City, within a year she was expelled from the Socialist Labor Party, predominantly a German-speaking immigrant group, for "incessant slander" against party leaders, whom she denounced for failing to recognize the importance of the writings of Marx and Engels.[10] Having reached a political dead-end, Kelley reoriented her use of social science as a vehicle for her activism. She resumed contact with her Philadelphia family and became a self-taught authority on child labor in the United States, as well as a sharp critic of state bureaus of labor, the agencies responsible for monitoring child labor. Writing articles on child labor that deployed both statistical and rhetorical power, she discovered that her most responsive publisher was the Woman's Temperance Publication Association, which printed her lengthy, hard-hitting pamphlet, *Our Toiling Children,* in 1889.

Lazare Wischnewetzky, meanwhile, never having managed to establish a medical practice, began battering her. After enduring this for more than a year, she borrowed money from a friend and fled with her children to Chicago. There she headed for the Woman's Temple, a twelve-story office building and hotel constructed by the Woman's Christian Temperance Union, where she was directed to an even more congenial place—Hull House, the nation's preeminent social settlement founded by Jane Addams and Ellen Gates Starr in 1889.

THE POLITICAL AUTONOMY
OF WOMEN'S SEPARATE INSTITUTIONS

"We were welcomed as though we had been invited," Kelley later wrote about her arrival at Hull House. "We stayed."[11] Addams arranged for Kelley's children, Nicholas, Margaret, and John, age seven, six, and five, to live with the family of Henry Demarest Lloyd and his wife, Jessie Bross Lloyd. That winter Kelley cast her lot with Addams and Hull House, remaining until May 1, 1899, when she returned to New York as a figure who had achieved national renown as a reformer of working conditions for women and children.

Chicago and the remarkable political culture of the city's women opened opportunities to Kelley that she had sought in vain in Philadelphia, Germany, and New York. Exploiting those opportunities to the fullest, she drew on the strength of three overlapping circles of politically active women. The core of her support lay with the community of women at Hull House. This remarkable group helped her reconstruct her political identity within women's class-bridging activism, and provided her with an economic and emotional alternative to married family life. Partly overlapping with this nucleus were women trade unionists. By drawing women and men trade unionists into the settlement community, she achieved the passage of pathbreaking legislation. Toward the end of her years in Chicago, she worked with the circle of middle-class and upper-middle-class women who supported Hull House and labor reform.

Florence Kelley's life in Chicago began with her relationship with Jane Addams. Julia Lathrop, another Hull House resident, reported that Kelley and Addams "understood each other's powers" instantly and worked together in a "wonderfully effective way."[12] Addams, the philosopher with a deep appreciation of the unity of life, was better able to construct a vehicle for expressing that unity in day-to-day living than she was capable of devising a diagram for charting the future. And Kelley, the politician with a thorough understanding of what the future should look like, was better able to invoke that future than to express it in her day-to-day existence. Addams

taught Kelley how to live and have faith in an imperfect world, and Kelley taught Addams how to make demands on the future.

At Hull House Kelley joined a community of college-educated women reformers who, like Addams and herself, sought work commensurate with their talents. Julia Lathrop, almost twenty years later the first director of the U.S. Children's Bureau, had joined the settlement before Kelley. Alice Hamilton, who arrived in 1897, developed the field of industrial medicine. These four, with Mary Rozet Smith, Jane Addams's life partner, became the settlement's main leaders. In addition to these women, Kelley forged close ties with Mary Kenney, a trade union organizer affiliated with the settlement, who lived nearby with her mother.

Since her father had lost most of his money before his death in 1890, Kelley had to support herself and her children. She first did so by working for the Illinois Bureau of Labor Statistics and the U.S. Department of Labor, collecting data for governmental studies of working conditions. A good example of the empowerment of her Hull House residence lay in her use of data collected for the U.S. Department of Labor, which in 1895 formed the basis of the maps published in *Hull House Maps and Papers*. She and four government "schedule men" collected responses to sixty-four questions on printed schedules from "each house, tenement, and room" in the ward surrounding Hull House.[13] From this data Carroll Wright, head of the Department of Labor, constructed scores of tables. But Kelley and Hull House associates, using only data about nationalities and wages in conjunction with residential information, created color-coded maps that displayed geographic patterns that told more than Wright's charts. Because the maps defined spatial relationships among human groups, they vividly depicted social and economic relationships: the concentration of certain ethnic groups in certain blocks; the relationship between poverty and race; the distances between the isolated brothel district and the rest of the ward; the very poor who lived in crowded, airless rooms in the rear of tenements and those with more resources in the front; and the omniscient observer and the observed. Expressing the democratic relationship among Hull House residents, *Hull House Maps and Papers* listed only "Residents of Hull House" as the volume's editors.

Kelley described the transformative effect of the Hull House community on her personal life in a letter to her mother a few weeks after her arrival. "In the few weeks of my stay here I have won for the children and myself many and dear friends whose generous hospitality astonishes me. It is understood that I am to resume the maiden name and that the children are to have it."[14] By joining a community of women, she had achieved a new degree of personal autonomy.

CHALLENGING TRADITIONS OF LIMITED GOVERNMENT

In the spring of 1892, Kelley used Hull House as a base to exert leadership within an anti-sweatshop campaign that had been launched in 1888 by the Illinois Woman's Alliance, a class-bridging coalition of women's organizations. At mass meetings that attacked the sweatshop system, Kelley shared the podium with Mary Kenney, Henry Demarest Lloyd, and other Chicago notables such as Reverend Jenkin Lloyd Jones, minister at All Souls' Unitarian Church, the most liberal pulpit in Chicago, and with young trade union organizers in the clothing industry such as Abraham Bisno.

Campaigns against sweatshops were widespread in American cities in the 1890s. These efforts targeted "predatory management" and "parasitic manufacturers" who paid such low wages to their workers as to require them to seek support from relief or charity, thereby indirectly providing employers with subsidies that enabled them to lower wages further.[15] Supported by trade unions, these campaigns used a variety of strategies to shift work from tenement sweatshops to factories. In factories, union organizing could more easily succeed in improving working conditions and raising wages to levels necessary to sustain life.

Outcries raised by anti-sweatshop campaigns prompted government inquiries, and in 1893, after intense lobbying in Springfield by Hull House residents and other well-known Chicago women, the passage of pathbreaking legislation drafted by Florence Kelley. That year Governor John Peter Altgeld appointed Kelley to a position the new statute created: Chief Factory Inspector of Illinois. Nowhere else in the Western world was a woman trusted to enforce the labor legislation of a city, let alone of a large industrial region the size of Illinois. With eleven deputies, five of whom were required to be women, and a budget of $28,000, for the next three years Kelley enforced the act's chief clauses. The act banned the labor of children under fourteen years of age; it regulated the labor of children age fourteen to sixteen; it outlawed the production of garments in tenements; it prohibited the employment of women and minors for more than eight hours a day; and it created a state office of factory inspection.

The statute's eight-hour clause made it the most advanced in the United States, equaled only by an eight-hour law for all workers in Australia. The limitation of hours, whether through statutes or union negotiations with employers, was the second most important goal of the labor movement between 1870 and 1910, the first being the recognition of the right of workers to form unions. Skilled workers had acquired the eight-hour day for themselves in many trades by the 1890s, but since women were not admitted to most skilled occupations, their hours remained long, often extending to twelve or even fourteen hours a day. In the late 1880s more than 85 percent of female wage earners were between the ages of fourteen and twenty-five and only about 5 percent were married.[16] Excluded from access to skilled jobs and presumed to leave the paid labor force upon marriage, they were crowded into a few unskilled occupations, where they were easily replaced, and employers exploited them by requiring long hours and paying low wages. Statutes that limited women's hours limited this exploitation. How to achieve such reduction of hours without reducing wages was a challenge that Kelley's office met by promoting the formation of unions among affected women workers, thereby helping them negotiate better wages for the hours they worked.

But the reduction of women's hours by statute had other beneficial effects: in many occupations it also reduced the hours of unskilled men, as was the case in garment-making sweatshops. In this and many other occupations, it proved impossible to keep men working longer than the legal limit of the working day for women. Therefore, hours statutes drove sweatshops out of business, since their profits could only be achieved through long hours. In the United States more than in other industrializing nations, the union movement consisted with few exceptions (miners being the chief exception) of skilled workers who shunned responsibility for the welfare of unskilled workers. Therefore, in the United States more than in elsewhere, gender-specific reforms like Kelley's 1893 legislation—undertaken by women for women—also had the effect of aiding all unskilled workers, men as well as women and children. In the United States, where labor movements were not as strong as they were elsewhere, gender-specific reforms accomplished goals that elsewhere were achieved under the auspices of class-specific efforts.[17]

In an era when courts nullified legislative attempts to intervene in the laissez-faire relationship between capital and labor, Kelley's enforcement of this new eight-hour law was inevitably challenged in the courts. In 1895 the Illinois Supreme Court found the eight-hour clause of the 1893 law unconstitutional because it violated women's right to contract their labor on any terms set by their employer. This setback made Kelley determined to change the power of state courts to overturn hours laws for women.

The high tide of Kelley's achievements between 1893 and 1896 ebbed quickly when Altgeld lost the election of 1896. His successor replaced her with a person who did not challenge the economic status quo, and she was unable to find work commensurate with her talents. German admirers came to her rescue. For fifty dollars a month she provided a leading German reform periodical with assessments of recent American social legislation. She also worked in the Crerar Library, a reference library specializing in economic, scientific, and medical topics.

Needing to reach beyond the limits of Hull House activities, Kelley began to work more closely with Ellen Henrotin. Wife of a leading Chicago banker, Henrotin had supported Kelley's legislation in 1892, and spoke vigorously at a rally to defend the law in 1894, urging those in attendance to "agitate for shorter hours for women because it means in the end shorter hours for all workers, men and women."[18] Henrotin's organization in 1893 of thirty women's congresses at the Chicago World's Fair catapulted her into the presidency of the General Federation of Women's Clubs (GFWC; founded 1890) from 1894 to 1898. By 1897 the GFWC served as an umbrella organization for more than five hundred women's clubs, including the powerful Chicago Women's Club. Fostering the creation of over twenty state federations to coordinate those clubs, Henrotin moved the GFWC in progressive directions by establishing national committees on industrial working conditions and national health. In this way she directed the path of what was to become one of the largest grass-roots organizations of American women beyond the minimal goals of good government and civil service reform to the more challenging issues of social inequalities and social justice.

Reflecting her growing awareness of the potential power of women's organizations as a vehicle for her social justice agenda, in 1897 Kelley began to work closely with Henrotin in organizing an Illinois Consumers' League. They built on the example of the New York Consumers' League, which had been founded in 1891 to channel consumers' consciousness toward political action on behalf of workers who made the goods that consumers purchased.

THE NATIONAL CONSUMERS' LEAGUE AND NEW STRATEGIES FOR SOCIAL JUSTICE

Kelley's work with Henrotin helped her make the biggest career step of her life when, in 1899, she agreed to serve as Secretary of the newly formed National Consumers' League, a position she held until her death in 1932. With a salary of $1,500 plus traveling and other expenses, the job offered financial stability and a chance to develop a more radical and more focused women's organization than the GFWC.

When she carried her formidable talents into the National Consumers' League in 1899, women's political culture gained a warrior with formidable rhetorical and organizational skills. She quickly made the National Consumers' League (NCL) into the nation's leading promoter of protective labor legislation for women and children. Between 1900 and 1904 she built sixty-four local consumer leagues—one in nearly every large city outside the South. Through a demanding travel schedule, which required her to spend one day on the road for every day she worked at her desk, Kelley maintained close contact with local leagues, urging them to implement the national organization's agenda and inspiring them to greater action within their states and municipalities. At the age of forty she had finally found a platform that matched her talents and goals.

In New York she lived until 1926 at Lillian Wald's nurses' settlement on Henry Street on Manhattan's Lower East Side. Her children moved east with her. Supported by aid from Jane Addams's life partner, Mary Rozet Smith, Nicholas Kelley graduated from Harvard in 1905 and then from Harvard Law School. Living in Manhattan, he became his mother's closest advisor. In a blow that caused Kelley to spend the rest of that year in retirement in Maine, her daughter Margaret died of heart failure during her first week at Smith College in 1905. After this bereavement Kelley maintained a summer home on Penobscot Bay, Maine, where she retreated for periods of intense work with a secretary each summer. John Kelley never found a professional niche, but remained close to his mother and joined her in Maine each summer.

THE WHITE LABEL CAMPAIGN:
NEW WAYS OF EDUCATING MIDDLE-
CLASS WOMEN ABOUT INDUSTRIAL
WORKING CONDITIONS

The national branch of the Consumers' League was formed in 1898 to coordinate the efforts of previously existing leagues in New York, Brooklyn, Philadelphia, Boston, and Chicago, all of which had conducted campaigns against sweatshops. At a convention of the local leagues called to coordinate their anti-sweatshop efforts, Kelley proposed the creation of a consumers' label as a way of identifying goods made under fair conditions. Her proposal galvanized the convention into creating a national organization "for the express purpose of offering a Consumers' League Label" nationally, recognizing that local efforts against sweatshops could never succeed until all producers were "compelled to compete on a higher level," and agreeing that the label could be a means of achieving that goal.[19] The NCL awarded its label to manufacturers who obeyed state factory laws, produced goods only on their own premises, did not require employees to work overtime, and did not employ children under sixteen years of age. To enforce the label, however, factories had to be inspected. Local leagues had employed their own factory inspectors; Kelley became the league's national inspector.

In determining whether local factories qualified for the label, local league members had to educate themselves about local working conditions. They had to pose and answer questions new to middle-class women, though painfully familiar to union organizers: Did the manufacturer subcontract to home workers in tenements? Were children employed? Were state factory laws violated? Could workers live on their wages, or were they forced to augment their pay with relief or charitable donations? How far below the standard set by the consumers' label were their own state laws? Even more technical questions arose when leagues came into contact with factory inspectors, bureaus of labor statistics, state legislatures, and courts. Should the state issue licenses for home workers? What was the relationship between illiteracy in child workers and the enforcement of effective child labor laws? Was their own state high or low on the NCL's ranked list showing the number of illiterate child workers in each? Should laws prohibit the labor of children at age fourteen or sixteen? Should exceptions be made for the children of widows? How energetically were state factory laws enforced? How could local factory standards be improved? These questions, recently quite alien to middle-class women, now held the interest of thousands of the most politically active among them. This was no small accomplishment. State leagues differed in the degree to which they worked with state officials, but wherever they existed they created new civic space in which women used their new knowledge and power to expand state responsibility for the welfare of women and children workers.

On the road steadily between 1900 and 1907, Kelley inspected workshops, awarded the label to qualified manufacturers, and strengthened local leagues. Her efforts were rewarded by the spectacular growth of NCL locals, both in number and location. The NCL's 1901 report mentioned thirty leagues in eleven states; by 1906 they numbered sixty-three in twenty states.

Flourishing local leagues sustained the national's existence, channeling money, ideas, and the support of other local groups into the national office. At the same time, locals implemented the national's agenda at the state level. Most league members were white, urban, northern, middle-class Protestants, but Jewish women held important positions of leadership. Catholic women became more visible after Cardinal James Gibbons of Baltimore consented to serve as vice president of a Maryland league and Bishop J. Regis Canevin of Pittsburgh encouraged members of that city's Ladies Catholic Benevolent Association to join. Two important reasons for the absence of black women from the NCL's membership and agenda were the league's focus on Northern urban manufacturing, and the residence of 90 percent of the nation's black population in the South, employed primarily in agriculture, in 1900.

10-HOUR LAWS FOR WOMEN: NEW USES OF SOCIAL SCIENCE

The work of educating her constituency being achieved by 1907, Kelley implemented a second stage of league work. With the use of social science data, the NCL overcame legal obstacles to the passage of state laws limiting women's hours. The overturning of Illinois's 1893 law by Illinois's Supreme Court in 1895 made Kelley determined to defend such laws before the U.S. Supreme Court. When an Oregon ten-hour law came before the court in 1907, she threw the resources of the NCL into its defense. This case, *Muller v. Oregon*, pitted the NCL and its Oregon branch against a laundry owner who disputed the state's ability to regulate working hours in non-hazardous occupations. For what became known as the "Brandeis Brief," Kelley's Research Director, Josephine Goldmark, gathered printed evidence from medical and other authorities (most of whom were British or European) to demonstrate that workdays longer than ten hours were hazardous to the health of women. Goldmark obtained the services of her brother-in-law, Louis D. Brandeis, a leading Boston attorney, who successfully argued the case on sociological rather than legal grounds, using the evidence that Goldmark had compiled. Thus at the same time that this case cleared the way for state hours laws for women, it also established the court's recognition of sociological evidence, a strategy that sustained the court's ruling against segregated schools in *Brown v. Board of Education* in 1954.

In the years immediately following the *Muller* decision, inspired by Kelley's leadership, and supported by other groups, local consumer leagues gained the passage in twenty states of the first laws limiting women's working hours. Also responding to the decision, nineteen other states revised and expanded their laws governing women's working hours.

The Supreme Court's 1908 opinion tried to block the possibility of extending such protections to men by emphasizing women's special legal status (they did not possess the same contractual rights as men) and their physiological difference from men (their health affected the health of their future children). Nevertheless, in 1917 Kelley and the NCL again cooperated successfully with the Oregon league in arguing another case on sociological grounds before the U.S. Supreme Court, *Bunting v. Oregon*, in which the Court upheld the constitutionality of hours laws for men in non-hazardous occupations. Viewing laws for women as an entering wedge for improving conditions for all working people, Kelley achieved that goal in the progression from *Muller* to *Bunting*. In this as in other aspects of her work with the League, though nominally focused on gender, her reforms had class-wide effects.

THE MINIMUM WAGE CAMPAIGN: NEW USES OF THE POWER OF WOMEN'S ORGANIZATIONS

As early as 1899, Florence Kelley had hoped "to include a requirement as to minimal wages" in the NCL's White Label. Australia and New Zealand had already organized wage boards as part of compulsory arbitration, but the path to an American equivalent did not seem clear until she and other Consumers' League members in 1908 attended the First International Conference of Consumers' Leagues, in Geneva, where they learned about the proposed British wage law of 1909, which that year implemented minimum wages for all workers in certain poorly paid occupations.

Almost immediately on her return, Kelley established her leadership in what became an enormously successful campaign for minimum wage laws for women in the United States. In her campaign she denounced the large profits made in three industries: retail stores, sweatshop garment making, and textile manufacturers. "Low wages produce more poverty than all other causes together," she insisted, urging that "goods and profits are not ends in themselves to which human welfare may continue to be sacrificed."[20]

Kelley argued that minimum wages would raise the standards in women's employment by recognizing their need to support themselves. "So long as women's wages rest upon the assumption that every woman has a husband, father, brother, or lover contributing to her support, so long these sinister incidents of women's industrial employment (tuberculosis, insanity, vice) are inevitable." She urged that "society itself must build the floor beneath their feet."[21]

Minimum wage legislation was much more difficult to achieve than maximum hours laws because, as one of Kelley's allies put it, wage legislation "pierces to the heart the classic claim that industry is a purely private affair."[22] For this reason, Kelley and the NCL were unaided in their efforts by their male-dominated equivalent, the American Association for Labor Legislation (AALL). When Kelley appealed in 1910 to their executive director, John Andrews, he loftily replied: "I question very seriously the wisdom of injecting the minimum wage proposal into the legislative campaign of this year, because I do not believe our courts would at the present time uphold such legislation, and I am afraid it would seriously jeopardize the splendid progress now being made to establish maximum working hours."[23] Two years later the AALL still opposed wage legislation as premature.

Kelley and the NCL were able to move ahead with this pathbreaking legislation because they could mobilize grass-roots support for it at local and state levels. The AALL had no local branches; instead, their power flowed from a network of male academic experts who advised politicians about legislation. If politicians were not ready to move, neither was the AALL. The NCL, by contrast, had in its sixty-four local branches enough political muscle to take the initiative and lead politicians where they otherwise wouldn't have gone.

In 1912 Massachusetts passed the first minimum wage law for women, followed in 1913 by eight additional states: California, Colorado, Minnesota, Nebraska, Oregon, Utah, Washington, and Wisconsin. By 1919 fourteen states and the District of Columbia and Puerto Rico had enacted minimum wage statutes for women. The success of these laws influenced the inclusion of a minimum wage for men *and* women in the Fair Labor Standards Act (FLSA) of 1938. In 1942, when the U.S. Supreme Court approved the constitutionality of the FLSA, the eight-hour day and the minimum wage became part of the social contract for most American workers. The class-bridging activism of middle-class women

in the NCL forged the way with these fundamental reforms.

GAINS AND SETBACKS IN THE 1920S

At Henry Street, Kelley continued to benefit from the same consolidation of female reform talents that had sustained her efforts at Hull House in Chicago. The creation of the U.S. Children's Bureau in 1911 sprang from her discussions with Lillian Wald. The Children's Bureau was the only governmental agency in any industrial society that was headed and run by women. Kelley thought that her most important contribution to social change was the passage in 1921 of the Sheppard-Towner Maternity and Infancy Protection Act, which first allocated federal funds to health care. She was instrumental in the creation of the coalition that backed the act's passage, the Women's Joint Congressional Committee, and in the coalition's successful campaign for the bill in Congress. Although limited to a program administered by the Children's Bureau to combat infant and maternal mortality, Kelley thought the Sheppard-Towner Act marked the beginning of a national health care program.[24]

After this high point in 1921, however, the decade brought a series of reversals that threatened to undo most of her achievements. In 1923 the U.S. Supreme Court in *Adkins* v. *Children's Hospital* found Washington, D.C.'s wage law for women unconstitutional. Many state wage boards continued to function during the 1920s and 1930s, however, providing ample evidence of the benefits of the law, but no new wage laws were passed. In 1926, Congress refused to allocate new funds for Sheppard-Towner programs, and responsibility for maternal and infant health returned to state and county levels.[25]

Just as important, by 1922 Kelley's strategy of using gender-specific legislation as a surrogate for class legislation had generated opposition from a new quarter—women who did not themselves benefit from gendered laws. The National Woman's Party (NWP), formed in 1916 by the charismatic leadership of Alice Paul and funded almost entirely by Alva Belmont, created a small coalition consisting primarily of professional women with some wage-earning women who worked in male-dominated occupations. Despite Kelley's strong objections over the damage they would do to gender-specific legislation, including the Sheppard-Towner Act, in 1921 the NWP proposed an Equal Rights Amendment to the U.S. Constitution (ERA). Although mainstream organizations such as the General Federation of Women's Clubs and the League of Women Voters continued to support gender-specific legislation, the NWP's proposed amendment undercut the momentum of such gendered strategies. In the 1920s most wage-earning women opposed the ERA because they stood to lose rather than benefit from it. By the 1970s changes in working conditions and protective labor laws meant that most wage-earning women stood to benefit from the amendment, and many more supported it.[26]

Even more damaging than these reversals, however, were the right-wing attacks launched by hyperpatriots against Kelley and other women reformers during the "red scare" of the 1920s. *The Woman Patriot* exemplified these attacks. Launched in 1916 and published twice a month, before the enactment of the woman suffrage amendment this newsletter was subtitled *Dedicated to the Defense of Womanhood, Motherhood, the Family and the State AGAINST Suffragism, Feminism and Socialism.* After 1920 the newsletter dropped its reference to suffrage, but continued its virulent attacks on the social agenda of women reformers. "SHALL BOLSHEVIST-FEMINISTS SECRETLY GOVERN AMERICA?" their headlines screamed, referring to the Sheppard-Towner Act. When *The Woman Patriot* referred to Kelley as "Mrs. Wischnewtzky" and called her "Moscow's chief conspirator," Kelley urged Addams to join her in a libel suit against them. Addams gently persuaded her to ignore the attacks. Kelley then wrote an impassioned series of autobiographical articles that established her lineage as an inheritor of American ideals and a dedicated promoter of American values.[27]

Attacks on women reformers in the 1920s were in part generated by supporters of American military expansion in the aftermath of World War I, when Kelley and many other women reformers were actively promoting peace and disarmament. For example, *The Woman Patriot* characterized the support that women reformers were giving to disarmament as "an organized internationalist Bolshevist-Feminist plot to embarrass the Limitation of Armaments Conference." Government employees joined the attack in 1924, when Lucia Maxwell of the Chemical Warfare Department of the Department of War issued a "Spider Web Chart" entitled "The Socialist-Pacifist Movement in America Is an Absolutely Fundamental and Integral Part of International Socialism." Depicting the connections between women's organizations and Congressional lobbying for social legislation and for disarmament, the chart sought to characterize as "pacifist-socialist" most women's organizations in the United States, including the National Consumers' League, the National League of Women Voters, the General Federation of Women's Clubs, the Woman's Christian Temperance Union, the National Congress of Mothers and Parent-Teachers Association, the National Women's Trade Union League, the American Home Economics Association, the American Association of University Women, the National Council of Jewish Women, the Girls' Friendly Society, the Young Women's Christian Association, and the National Federation of Business and Professional Women.[28]

Historians have not measured the effect of these attacks on the political agendas of women's organizations, but after these attacks the agendas of many women's organizations, for example that of the League for Women Voters, shifted from social justice to good government projects, from support for a Child Labor Amendment to the U.S. Constitution to advocacy for a city manager form of governance.[29] Such a shift was in keeping with the demise of the Progressive movement after World War I. But that demise was hastened by the rise of "red scare" tactics in American political culture.

Florence Kelley did not live to see many of her initiatives incorporated into federal legislation in the 1930s. Faced with the collapse of the American economy in the Great Depression of 1929–1939, policymakers drew heavily on the legacy of Progressive reforms initiated between 1890 and 1920. Florence Kelley's legacies, including the minimum wage and maximum hours legislation incorporated in the Fair Labor Standards Act of 1938, were strong enough to survive the reversals of the 1920s. In 1933, with the inauguration of Franklin Delano Roosevelt, Kelley's protégée Frances Perkins became the first woman to serve as a cabinet member. Reflecting the power of women's organizations in shaping a new social contract for American working people, Perkins was appointed Secretary of Labor.[30]

But Kelley's legacy reaches beyond any specific policies. U.S. Supreme Court Justice Felix Frankfurter said in 1953 that the nation owed Kelley an "enduring debt for the continuing process she so largely helped to initiate, by which social legislation is promoted and eventually gets on the statute books."[31] As Kelley shaped it during her long reform career between 1890 and 1930, that process relied heavily on women's organizations and their ability to act independently of the political status quo.

NOTES

1. James Weber Linn, *Jane Addams: A Biography* (New York, 1938), 138.

2. For an overview of social change in the Progressive era, see Steven J. Diner, *A Very Different Age: Americans of the Progressive Era* (New York, 1998).

3. For more on Kelley before 1900, see Kathryn Kish Sklar, *Florence Kelley and the Nation's Work: The Rise of Women's Political Culture, 1830–1900* (New Haven, 1995). Specific page references are provided for quotations used below.

4. Mabel Newcomer, *A Century of Higher Education for American Women* (New York, 1959), 37, 46. See also Barbara Miller Solomon, *"In the Company of Educated Women": A History of Women and Higher Education in America* (New Haven, 1985), 62–77.

5. For Kelley's childhood, see Kathryn Kish Sklar, ed., *The Autobiography of Florence Kelley: Notes of Sixty Years* (Chicago, 1986).

6. Sklar, *Autobiography of Florence Kelley*, 30.

7. Kathryn Kish Sklar, "Hull House Maps and Papers: Social Science as Women's Work in the 1890s," in Helene Silverberg, ed., *Gender and American Social Science: The Formative Years* (Princeton, 1998).

8. See Joyce Antler, "After College, What?: New Graduates and the Family Claim," *American Quarterly* 32 (Fall 1980):409–34.

9. See Dorothy Rose Blumberg, "'Dear Mr. Engels': Unpublished Letters, 1884–1894, of Florence Kelley (Wischnewetzky) to Friedrich Engels," *Labor History* 5 (Spring 1964), 103–33.

10. Sklar, *Florence Kelley*, 129.

11. Sklar, *Autobiography of Florence Kelley*, 77.

12. Jane Addams, *My Friend Julia Lathrop* (New York, 1935), 77.

13. Residents of Hull House, *Hull House Maps and Papers* (New York, 1895).

14. FK to Caroline B. Kelley, Chicago, Feb. 24, 1892, Nicholas Kelley Papers, New York Public Library.

15. Kathryn Kish Sklar, "Two Political Cultures in the Progressive Era: The National Consumers' League and the American Association for Labor Legislation," in Linda K. Kerber, Alice Kessler-Harris and Kathryn Kish Sklar, eds., *U.S. History as*

Women's History: New Feminist Essays (Chapel Hill, N.C., 1995), 58.

16. U.S. Commissioner of Labor, *Fourth Annual Report, Working Women in Large Cities* (Washington, D.C., 1889), 62–64.

17. For a full argument of this point, see Kathryn Kish Sklar, "The Historical Foundations of Women's Power in the Creation of the American Welfare State, 1830–1930," in Seth Koven and Sonya Michel, eds., *Mothers of a New World: Maternalist Politics and the Origins of Welfare States* (New York, 1993).

18. "Hit at Sweat Shops," *Chicago Tribune*, April 23, 1894; Sklar, *Florence Kelley*, 261.

19. Sklar, *Florence Kelley*, 309.

20. Florence Kelley, "Minimum Wage Boards," *American Journal of Sociology* 17 (Nov. 1911), 303–14.

21. Florence Kelley, "Ten Years from Now," *Survey*, March 26, 1910, 978–81.

22. Sklar, "Two Political Cultures," 60.

23. See, for example, John B. Andrews to Erich Stern, New York, Dec. 14, 1910, American Association for Labor Legislation Papers, Cornell University.

24. See Molly Ladd-Taylor, *Mother-Work: Women, Child Welfare, and the State, 1890–1930* (Urbana, Ill., 1994), 167–96.

25. See J. Stanley Lemons, *The Woman Citizen: Social Feminism in the 1920s* (Urbana, Ill., 1973), 169–76.

26. For the opposition of the progressive mainstream of the women's movement, see Kathryn Kish Sklar, "Why Did Most Politically Active Women Oppose the ERA in the 1920s?" in Joan Hoff-Wilson, ed., *Rights of Passage: the Past and Future of the ERA* (Bloomington, Ind., 1986).

27. *The Woman Patriot*, Vol. 5, no. 29, Nov. 1, 1921, 1. For the complete documents of this correspondence between Kelley and Addams, see Anissa Harper, "Pacifism vs. Patriotism in Women's Organizations in the 1920s: How Was the Debate Shaped by the Expansion of the American Military," in *Women and Social Movements in the United States, 1830–1930*, an Internet website edited by Kathryn Kish Sklar and Thomas Dublin, http://womhist .binghamton.edu. See also Nancy F. Cott, *The Grounding of Modern Feminism* (New Haven, 1987), 243–67.

28. The Spider Web Chart is reproduced in Helen Baker, "How Did the Women's International League for Peace and Freedom Respond to Right Wing Attacks in the 1920s?" in *Women and Social Movements* at http://womhist.binghamton.edu.

29. For example, see the furor aroused within the League of Women Voters over the proposed Child Labor Amendment to the U.S. Constitution in 1924, in Louise M. Young, *In the Public Interest: The League of Women Voters, 1920–1970* (New York, 1989), 97–98.

30. For Perkins see Susan Ware, *Beyond Suffrage: Women in the New Deal* (Cambridge, Mass., 1981), *passim*.

31. Felix Frankfurter, "Foreword," in Josephine Goldmark, *Impatient Crusader: Florence Kelley's Life Story* (Urbana, Ill., 1953), v.

ANNELISE ORLECK
From the Russian Pale to Labor Organizing in New York City

The pale of Jewish settlement was a territory within Russia to which Jews were restricted during the eighteenth and nineteenth centuries and where they were frequently subjected to ferocious outbursts of anti-Semitic violence. Crossing from the pale to the teeming streets of Manhattan's Lower East Side was a frontier crossing of major proportions. Yet two million European Jews who came to the United States between 1880 and 1924 made it across, among them the remarkable young women who are the subjects of Annelise Orleck's lively and informative essay.

Like so many of their fellow immigrants, Rose Schneiderman, Fannia Cohn, Clara Lemlich, and Pauline Newman gravitated to one of the earliest industries to employ women—the garment industry. Based in New York City, the industry had long provided countless married women with piecework to take back to dimly lit tenements, where they often enlisted the help of grandmothers and children. By the turn of the century, much of the work had been transferred to sweatshops and factories that were notorious for their low wages and squalid working conditions. Because so many of the female employees were young single women who presumably regarded their work as a temporary necessity until rescued by marriage, labor leaders usually assumed that the women were virtually unorganizable. Yet between 1909 and 1915, women garment workers in New York as well as in other cities exploded in labor militancy. By 1919, half of all women garment workers belonged to trade unions and many had joined the suffrage struggle as well. The role these four young women played in this process is the focus of Orleck's essay.

What experiences shaped their political consciousness and propelled their activism? As young girls forced to work and forego school and college, how did they educate themselves and for what purpose? Who were their allies and why were these alliances so necessary, yet so unstable? How was the balancing act required of the four with respect to male trade unionists and elite female reformers similar to that required of Charlotte Hawkins Brown, albeit in a different context (see Glenda Gilmore's essay, pp. 300–310)? What attracted these young working women to suffrage? What is meant by the term "industrial feminists"? You will find Pauline Newman's reminiscence of garment work in the documents that accompany this cluster of essays.

During the summer of 1907, when New York City was gripped by a severe economic depression, a group of young women workers who had been laid off and were facing eviction took tents and sleeping rolls to the verdant Palisades overlooking the Hudson River. While rising rents and unemployment spread panic among the poor immigrants of Manhattan's Lower East Side, these teenagers lived in a makeshift summer camp, getting work where they could

Excerpted from the prologue, and chs. 1 and 2 of *Common Sense and a Little Fire: Women and Working-Class Politics in the United States, 1900–1965,* by Annelise Orleck (Chapel Hill: University of North Carolina Press, 1995). Used by permission of the author and publisher. Notes have been edited and renumbered.

find it, sharing whatever food and drink they could afford, reading, hiking, and gathering around a campfire at night to sing Russian and Yiddish songs. "Thus we avoided paying rent or, worse still, being evicted," Pauline Newman later recalled. "Besides which, we liked living in the open—plenty of fresh air, sunshine and the lovely Hudson for which there was no charge."[1]

Away from the clatter of the shops and the filth of Lower East Side streets, the young women talked into the night, refreshed by what Newman called "the cool of the evening, glorious sunsets, the moon and stars." They shared personal concerns as well as shop-floor gripes—worries about love, about the future, and about the pressing problems of housing and food.

Their cliffside village meant more to Newman and her friends than a summer escape. They had created a vibrant alternative to the tenement life they found so oppressive, and their experience of it had set them to wondering. Perhaps the same sense of joy and comradeship could help workers transcend the drudgery of the garment shops and form the basis for effective organizing.[2]

At season's end, they emerged with strengthened bonds and renewed resolve to organize their communities around issues that the recent depression had brought into sharp relief: the need for stabilized rent and food prices, improved working conditions, and housing for the poor.[3]

The spirit of intimacy and solidarity that pervaded the summer of 1907 would inspire much of Pauline Newman's later organizing. Indeed, it became a model for the vision of change that Newman shared with her fellow Jewish immigrant radicals Fannia Cohn, Rose Schneiderman and Clara Lemlich. The four women moved to political struggle not simply by the need for better wages, hours and working conditions but also, in Newman's words, by a need to ensure that "poverty did not deprive us from finding joy and satisfaction in things of the spirit."[4] This essay examines the early careers of these four remarkable organizers and the role they played in building a militant working women's movement during the first decades of the twentieth century.

For even as girls, these marginally educated immigrants wanted to be more than . . . shop-floor drudges. They wanted lives filled with beauty—with friendships, books, art,

music, dance, fresh air, and clean water. "A working girl is a human being," Newman would later tell a legislative committee investigating factory conditions, "with a heart, with desires, with aspirations, with ideas and ideals." That image nourished Newman, Schneiderman, Lemlich, and Cohn throughout their long careers. And it focused them on a single goal: to reshape U.S. society so that "working girls" like themselves could fulfill some of their dreams.[5]

The four women moved through strikingly different cultural milieus over the course of long careers that would carry them in different directions. Still, they each bore the imprint of the shared culture in which they were raised, first in Eastern Europe and then in New York City. That common experience gave them a particular understanding of gender, class, and ethnicity that shaped their later activism and political thought.

All four were born in the Russian-dominated pale of Jewish settlement during the last two decades of the nineteenth century. Rose Schneiderman was born in the Polish village of Saven in 1882; Fannia Cohn was born in Kletsk, Poland, in 1885; Clara Lemlich was born in the Ukrainian village of Gorodok in 1886; and Pauline Newman was born in Kovno, Lithuania, around 1890.[6]

They were ushered into a world swept by a firestorm of new ideas, where the contrasting but equally messianic visions of orthodox Judaism and revolutionary Socialism competed for young minds. The excitement of living in a revolutionary era imbued these young women with a faith in progress and a belief that political commitment gave life meaning. It also taught them, at an early age, that gender, class, and ethnicity were fundamental social categories and essential building blocks for political change. Being born into turbulence does not in itself make a child into a political activist. But the changes sweeping the Russian Empire toward the end of the nineteenth century shaped the consciousness of a generation of Eastern European Jews who contributed, in wildly disproportionate numbers, to revolutionary movements in Russia and to the labor and radical movements in the United States.[7]

The four were exposed to Marxist ideas at a tender age. As Eastern Europe shifted uneasily from feudalism to capitalism in the latter part of the nineteenth century, class analysis became part of the common parlance of young people in Jewish towns and villages. "Behind every other volume of Talmud in those years, there was a volume of Marx," one union organizer recalled of his small Polish town. Clara Lemlich grew up on revolutionary tracts and songs; Fannia Cohn considered herself a committed Socialist by the age of sixteen.[8]

Their awareness of ethnicity was even more keen. As Jews in Eastern Europe, the four learned young that ethnic identity was a double-edged sword. It was a source of strength and solace in their bitterly poor communities, but it also enabled Tsarist authorities to single Jews out and sow seeds of suspicion among their peasant neighbors. Jews living under Russian rule were made painfully aware of their status as permanent "others" in the land where they had lived for centuries. Clara Lemlich's family lived not far from Kishinev, where in 1903 the Tsar's government openly and unabashedly directed an orgy of anti-Jewish violence that shocked the world. In cosmopolitan Minsk, where she had gone to study, Fannia Cohn watched with dismay as the revolutionary populist organization she had joined began mouthing the same anti-Semitic conspiracy theories spewed by the government they despised. Frustration turned to fear when her brother was almost killed in yet another pogrom.[9]

Sex was just as distinct a dividing line as class and ethnicity. Eastern European Jews had observed a strict sexual division of labor for more than a thousand years. But by the late nineteenth century, as political and economic upheaval jolted long-accepted ways of thinking, sex roles too were being questioned. And so the four girls' understandings of gender were informed both by traditional Jewish conceptions of womanhood and by the challenges issued by new political movements.

In traditional Jewish society, mothers were also entrepreneurs. Clara Lemlich, Pauline Newman, and Rose Schneiderman were all raised by mothers who were skilled businesswomen. Jewish mothers' success in this role grew out of and reinforced a belief that women were innately suited to competition in the economic sphere. In contrast to the image of the sheltered middle-class housewife then dominant in the United States, Eastern European Jewish religious tradition glorified strong, economically sophisticated wives and mothers.

But as much as women's entrepreneurship was respected, a far higher premium was placed on study and prayer. And that, religious tradition dictated, could be performed only by men. A woman was expected to be pious, to read the vernacular Yiddish—rather than ancient Hebrew—translation of the Bible, and perhaps to attend women's services at the synagogue. But her primary religious role was as keeper of the home. Formal religious education was offered only to males.[10] Because Eastern European Jewish women had to fight for every scrap of education they received, many began to see education as the key to independence from all masters. This view would strongly influence their political organizing once in the United States.

The four emigrated as part of the mass movement that brought two million Jews from Eastern Europe to the United States between 1881 and 1924. Schneiderman came in 1890, Newman in 1901, Lemlich in 1903, and Cohn in 1904. Like most of their compatriots, they arrived in New York Harbor and settled on Manhattan's Lower East Side, the largest settlement of Eastern European Jews in the United States.[11] The newcomers were tantalized by the exciting diversions that New York life promised: libraries, theater, music, department stores, and amusement parks. But they had neither time nor money to indulge in such pleasures, for all of them soon found themselves laboring long hours to support their families.

At an age when most girls in the United States were still in grade school, immigrant working girls like Newman spent twelve- to fourteen-hour days in the harshest of atmospheres. Their bodies and minds reeled from the shock of the shops: the deafening noise, the brutal pace, and the rebukes of foremen. Some children were able to slough off the hardship with jokes and games. Others, realizing that they were destined to spend their youth in dank factories rather than in classrooms or schoolyards, grew sullen and withdrawn.

Clara Lemlich, like so many others, was quickly disillusioned by her first job in a New York garment shop: "I went to work two weeks after landing in this country. We worked from sunrise to set seven days a week. . . . Those who worked on machines had to carry the machines on their back both to and from work. . . . The shop we worked in had no central heating, no electric power. . . . The hissing of the machines, the yelling of the foreman, made life unbearable."[12]

Newly arrived European women undergoing medical examinations at Ellis Island, ca. 1900.
"The day of the emigrant's arrival in New York was the nearest earthly likeness to the final day of Judgement, when we have to prove our fitness to enter Heaven." The words are those of a sympathetic journalist who shared the anxiety-ridden experience awaiting the immigrants at the port of entry. Failing the medical test could mean deportation. (Courtesy of Brown Brothers, Sterling, Pennsylvania.)

Anger drove young women workers like Lemlich and Newman to band together. Untrained and largely unschooled, these young women were drawn to Socialism and trade unionism not because they felt an ideological affinity but because they had a desperate need to improve their working conditions. "I knew very little about Socialism," Lemlich recalled. "[But] the girls, whether Socialist or not, had many stoppages and strikes." Newman too found that for most young women workers, political understanding followed action rather than precipitating it: "We of the 1909 vintage knew nothing about the economics of . . . industry or for that matter about economics in general. All we knew was the bitter fact that, after working seventy and eighty hours in a seven day week, we did not earn enough to keep body and soul together." These assertions reveal much about the political development of the tens of thousands of women garment workers who would soon amaze New York and the nation with their militancy.[13]

Shop-floor culture fed the young women's emerging sense of political identity. Working alongside older men and women who discussed Socialism daily, they began to feel a sense of belonging to a distinct class of people in the world: workers. This allegiance would soon become as important to them as their Judaism. The shops also provided an opportunity for bonding with other women. Slowly, out of their workplace experiences, they began to develop a complex political identity in which class, gender and ethnicity overlapped. Young women workers were moved by the idea of sisterhood. It captured their own experiences in the sex-segregated shops where they worked. The majority of New York's garment workers were little more than girls, and the relationships they forged with factory friends were similar to those of schoolgirls—intense, melodramatic, and deeply loyal. They were teenage confidantes as well as fellow workers, and they relied on shop-floor rapport to soften the harshness of factory life.[14] For young immigrant women trying to build lives in a new land, such bonds were powerful and lasting. From these shop-floor friendships would soon evolve the ties of union sisterhood.[15]

Pauline Newman and her co-workers at the Triangle Shirtwaist Factory literally grew up together. Only twelve when she first came to Triangle, Newman was assigned to a corner known as "the kindergarten," where workers as young as eight, nine, or ten years old trimmed threads from finished garments. They labored, Newman later recalled, "from 7:30 A.M. to 6:30 at night when it wasn't busy. When the season was on we worked till 9 o'clock. No overtime pay." Their only taste of a normal childhood came through the songs and games they invented to help pass the time, the stories they told and the secrets they shared.[16]

By the early twentieth century, New York State had passed laws prohibiting night work for children. But little attempt was made to enforce them. On the rare occasions when an inspector showed up at her factory, Newman remembered, "the employers were always tipped off. . . . 'Quick,' they'd say, 'Into the boxes!' And we children would climb into the big box the finished shirts were stored in. Then some shirts were piled on top of us and when the inspector came—No children." In a way it was fun, Newman remembered. They thought they were playing a game like hide and seek.[17]

But it wasn't really a game. Children who had to help support their parents grew up quickly. Rose Schneiderman was thirteen when her mother begged United Hebrew Charities, an organization run by middle-class German Jews, to find her daughter a "respectable job" at a department store. Retail jobs were deemed more respectable than factory work because the environment was more pleasant and sexual harassment was thought to be less common. Deborah Schneiderman worried that factory work would sully Rose's reputation and make her less marriageable. A job as a fashionable salesgirl, she hoped, would usher Rose into the middle class. The single mother who had fed her children on charity food baskets and had been forced to place them in orphanages was grimly determined to help them escape poverty.

But then as now, pink-collar jobs paid significantly less than industrial work. Anxious to free her mother from the rigors of maintaining their tenement building, Schneiderman left her job in Ridley's department store for the harsher and more morally suspect conditions of an industrial shop. Making linings for caps and hats, she immediately raised her weekly income from $2.75 to $6. As the sole supporter of her family, the sixteen-year-old hoped to work her way up quickly to a skilled job in the cap trade.[18]

Clara Lemlich's family also relied on her wages, particularly because her father was unemployed. She aspired to the skilled position of draper, one of the highest-paid positions a woman could attain in the dressmaking trade. Despite terrible working conditions, many ambitious young women chose garment work over other jobs because it seemed to offer their greatest chance to acquire skills and command high wages. When these hopes were dashed, some young workers grew angry. That anger was fanned and channeled by older women in the shops who were itching to challenge the authority of the bosses.[19]

That is what happened to Rose Schneiderman, who, like many skilled women garment workers, was blocked from advancement by the unofficial gender hierarchy at her factory. Finding that all the highest-paid jobs in her capmaking shop were reserved for men, Schneiderman asked around about ways to break through those barriers. When she approached fellow worker Bessie Braut with her concerns, Schneiderman was initiated simultaneously into trade unionism, Socialism, and feminism. Schneiderman recalled, "Bessie was an unusual person. Her beautiful eyes shone out of a badly pockmarked face and the effect was startling. An outspoken anarchist, she made a strong impression on us. She wasted no time in giving us the facts of life—that the men in our trade belonged to a union and were, therefore, able to better their conditions. She added pointedly that it would be a good thing for the lining-makers to join a union along with the trimmers, who were all women."[20]

Schneiderman, Braut, and several other workers called on the secretary-treasurer of the United Cloth Hat and Cap Makers to request union recognition for their fledgling local of trimmers and lining makers. Within a few days they had enough signatures to win a charter for their local, and Schneiderman was elected secretary.[21]

Surprising even herself, the once-shy red-head soon found she could be an eloquent and fierce advocate for her fellow workers. In recognition of her growing reputation, the capmakers elected her to the Central Labor Union of New York. Deborah Schneiderman was disturbed by the turn Rose's life was taking. She warned Rose that if she pursued a public life she would never find a husband. No man wants a woman with a big mouth, her mother said.[22]

In the flush of excitement at the praise and warmth suddenly coming her way, young Rose did not stop to worry. In organizing, she had found both a calling and a world of friends. She had no intention of turning back. "It was such an exciting time," she wrote later. "A new life opened up for me. All of a sudden I was not lonely anymore. . . . It was the beginning of a period that molded all my subsequent life."[23]

Fannia Cohn, too, chose garment work as her path to a career. And like Schneiderman, Lemlich, and Newman, she found a community there. Unlike the others, however, she did not enter a garment factory looking for work that paid well. She was a comfortable middle-class woman in search of a trade ripe for unionizing.

Cohn arrived in New York in 1904 and moved in with her affluent cousins. There was little about her early days in the United States that was comparable to the hard-pressed scrambling for a living that the Schneidermans, Lemlichs, and Newmans experienced. "My family suggested that I complete my studies and then join the labor movement but I rejected this as I did not want to come into it from 'without' but from 'within.' I realized then that if I wanted to really understand the mind, the aspirations of the workers, I should experience the life of the worker in a shop."[24] In 1905, Fannia Cohn became a sleevemaker. For a year she moved from shop to shop until, in the "white goods" trade, she found the organizing challenge she was looking for.

Shops that manufactured white goods—underwear, kimonos, and robes—were considered particularly hard to organize. Production took place in tiny sweatshops, not large factories, and the manufacturing process had been broken down into small tasks that required little skill. The majority of white goods workers were immigrant girls under the age of fifteen. And because they came from a wide range of backgrounds—Jewish, Italian, Syrian, Turkish, and Greek—it was difficult for them to communicate with each other, let alone organize. As a result, these workers were among the lowest paid in the garment trades.

At twenty, Cohn was an elder in the trade. With her high school education and fluency in three languages, she was seen as a mother figure by many of the adolescents in the shops. She and a handful of older women workers began to operate as mentors, meeting with the girls in each shop and identifying potential leaders. Cohn taught her co-workers to read, write, and speak in public, hoping they would channel those skills into the union struggle. Cohn had already created the role that she would play throughout her career: an educator of younger workers.[25]

Education was a primary driving force in the metamorphosis of all four young women from shop workers to union organizers. From the isolated towns and restive cities of Eastern Europe, where gender, class, and ethnicity stymied Jewish girls' hopes for education, the lure of free public schooling in the United States beckoned powerfully. Having to drop out of school to work was more than a disappointment for many Jewish immigrant girls; it was their first great disillusionment with the dream of America. And they did not give that dream up easily.

"When I went to work," Rose Schneiderman remembered, "I was determined to continue my studies." Her only option was to attend one of the many night schools then open to immigrant workers in New York. Having carried with her from Poland the ideal of education as an exalted, liberating process, she was disgusted by the mediocre instruction she encountered and felt betrayed by teachers who seemed to be patronizing her. "I enrolled and went faithfully every evening for about four weeks. But I found that . . . the instructor seemed more interested in getting one-hundred-percent attendance than in giving one-hundred-percent instruction. He would joke and tell silly stories. . . . I soon realized I was wasting my time." Schneiderman left the evening school but did not stop studying. She asked older co-workers if she could borrow books that she had discussed with them in the shop. In the evenings, she read with her mother at home. Serializations of Emile Zola's *J'Accuse* and other contemporary writings in the Yiddish evening paper *Abendblatt* gave Rose a taste for literature. "I devoured everything I could get my hands on."[26]

Clara Lemlich was an equally avid reader. At the end of each twelve-hour day stitching shirtwaists, she would walk from her factory to the East Broadway branch of the New York Public Library. There she read the library's entire collection of Russian classics. "I was so eager to learn things," she later recalled. When she tired of solitary study, Lemlich joined a free night school on Grand Street. She returned home late each night, ate the dinner her mother had kept warm for her, then slept for just a few hours before rising again for work.[27]

Not surprisingly, young women like Schneiderman, Newman, and Lemlich turned to radical politics to fulfill their desire for a life of the mind. If no other school was available, then what Pauline Newman called "the school of solidarity" would have to do. Membership in the Socialist Party and in unions, tenant organizations, and benevolent societies provided immigrant women with an opportunity to learn and study that most would never have gotten otherwise. And as Newman put it, "Because they were hitherto deprived of any tutorship, they at once became ardent students."[28]

Pauline Newman was just fifteen when she first knocked on the doors of the Socialist Literary Society. Although women were not yet allowed to join, she was permitted to attend classes. The Literary Society was a revelation to the young worker. There she was introduced to the writings of Shakespeare, George Eliot, and Thomas Hardy and personally met writers like Jack London and Charlotte Perkins Gilman, who came to speak there. Gratitude, however, didn't stop her from joining a successful petition drive to admit women to the society.

For Newman—as for Clara Lemlich, who attended Marxist theory classes at the Socialist Party's Rand School—studying was more than a distraction from work. The "desire to get out of the shop," Newman wrote later, "to learn, to understand, became the dominant force in my life." But unlike many immigrants, who saw schooling as a ladder out of the working class, both she and Lemlich were committed to helping others rise with them. So Newman and Lemlich formed study groups that met during lunch hours and after work to share what they were learning with their friends.[29]

"We tried to educate ourselves," Newman remembered of her co-workers at the Triangle Shirtwaist Factory. "I would invite the girls to my room and we took turns reading poetry in English to improve our understanding of the language." Because they had to steal the time to study, the young women approached everything they read with a heightened sensitivity. And when something they were reading struck a chord of recognition, seemed to reflect on their own lives, the catharsis was not only emotional; it was political.[30]

The evolution of Lemlich's study group illustrates how study often led to union activity. Older workers, who were teaching Lemlich the craft of draping, invited her to join their lunchtime discussion groups to learn more about trade unionism. Soon Lemlich and a group of young women waistmakers formed their own study group. Discussion quickly escalated to action, and they decided to form a union.[31]

Skilled male workers in the shirtwaist trade had been trying to establish a union since 1900. But after five years the union had managed to attract only ten members. The problem, Lemlich told her male colleagues, was that women workers had to be approached by an organizer who understood their particular needs as women. They bristled at the suggestion that this young girl might know more about their business than they did. But years later, one conceded that the failure of the first waistmakers' union was due at least in part to their ham-fisted tactics: "We would issue a circular reading somewhat as follows: 'Murder the exploiters, the blood-suckers, the manufacturers. . . . Pay your dues. . . . Down with the Capitalists!'" Few women or men showed up at their meetings.[32]

During the spring of 1905 the union disbanded and reorganized as Local 25 of the ILGWU, with Clara Lemlich and a group of six young women from her waistmaking shop on the executive board. Taking their cue from Lemlich, the new union used women organizers to attract women workers. Lemlich addressed street-corner meetings in English and Yiddish and found Italian women to address the Italian workers. Soon, like Schneiderman, Newman, and Cohn, she realized that she had found a calling.[33]

In the progressive atmosphere of early-twentieth-century New York City, influential people quickly noticed the militant young working women. Older Socialists, trade unionists, and middle-class reformers offered their assistance. These benefactors helped the young organizers sharpen their arguments, provided

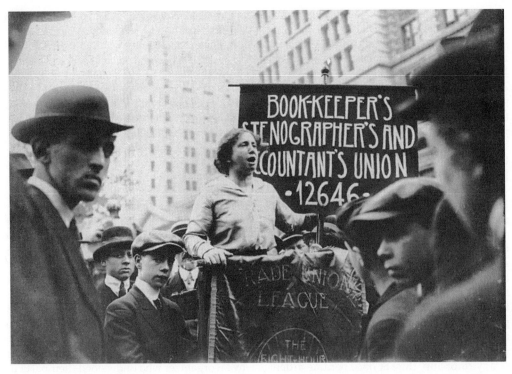

Rose Schneiderman addresses a street rally in New York City, probably 1910s. (Courtesy of Brown Brothers, Sterling, Pennsylvania.)

financial assistance, and introduced them to politicians and public officials. The protégés recognized the importance of this informal mentoring and would later work to recreate such networks in the unions, schools, and training programs they built for young women workers. Schneiderman, Newman, Lemlich, and Cohn were keenly aware that young working women needed help from more experienced and more powerful allies. But they also worried that the voices of women workers might be outshouted in the clamorous process of building alliances. From these early days, they battled to preserve the integrity of their vision.

Pauline Newman found her first mentors in the Socialist Party, which she joined in 1906 at the age of fifteen. Older women, including former garment worker Theresa Serber Malkiel, took her on as a protégé. Newman quickly blossomed under their tutelage. Before long she was running street-corner meetings. Armed with a sonorous voice and the certitude of youth, she would take "an American flag and a soapbox and go from corner to corner," exhorting the gospel of Socialism in Yiddish

and English. "I, like many of my friends and comrades, thought that socialism and socialism alone could and would someday fill the gap between rich and poor," Newman recalled. In a neighborhood crowded with sidewalk proselytizers, this child evangelist became one of the party's most popular street-corner attractions.[34]

In 1908, nine years before New York State gave women the vote, seventeen-year-old Newman was nominated by the Socialist Party to run for New York's Secretary of State. Newman used her campaign as a platform for suffrage. Her speeches were heckled by some Socialist men, and her candidacy provoked amused commentaries in New York City newspapers; some writers snickered at the prospect of a "skirted Secretary of State." It was a largely symbolic crusade, but Newman felt that she got people talking about the idea of women in government. The highlight of the campaign was her whistlestop tour with presidential candidate and Socialist leader Eugene V. Debs on his "Red Special" train.

The Socialist Party opened up a new world to Newman, who, after all, had never graduated from elementary school. Along with Debs, she met future Congressmen Meyer Berger and Morris Hillquit and leading Socialist intellectuals. Newman later wrote about the excitement of discussions that carried over from meetings and went into the night as she and her friends walked through Central Park, arguing till the sun came up. Those nights made her feel part of a historic moment.[35]

While Newman was being nurtured by the Socialist Party, Rose Schneiderman found her mentors in the United Cloth Hat and Cap Makers. At the union's 1904 convention she was elected to the General Executive Board; she was the first woman to win such a high-level post in the American labor movement. During the winter of 1904–5, Schneiderman's leadership skills were tested when owners tried to open up union shops to nonunion workers. The largely immigrant capmaker's union called for a general strike. The 1905 strike was a watershed event in Schneiderman's emerging career. Her role as the only woman leader in the union won attention from the press and lasting respect from male capmakers, including the future president of the union, Max Zaritsky, who became a lifelong friend and admirer.[36]

It also brought her to the attention of the newly formed Women's Trade Union League (WTUL), an organization of progressive middle- and upper-class women reformers founded in 1903 to help working women organize. Schneiderman had misgivings about the group because she "could not believe that men and women who were not wage earners themselves understood the problems that workers faced." But she trusted the League's best-known working-class member, Irish shirtmaker Leonora O'Reilly. And she could not ignore the favorable publicity that the WTUL won for the strikers. By March 1905, Schneiderman had been elected to the executive board of the New York WTUL. In 1906, the group elected her vice president.[37]

Schneiderman's entrance into the New York WTUL was an important turning point for both her and the organization. Three years after its founding, the WTUL remained dominated by affluent reformers who had dubbed themselves "allies" of the working class. Despite their genuine commitment to trade unionism, League leaders had credibility problems among women workers. Schneiderman had joined the League recognizing that working women lacked the education, the

money, and the political clout to organize effectively without powerful allies. Still, she remained ambivalent for a variety of reasons.[38]

The progressive reformers who dominated the League tried to steer workers away from radical influences, particularly the Socialist Party. Yet Schneiderman and O'Reilly, the League's leading working-class organizers, were Socialist Party members and saw unionism as a potentially revolutionary tool. As a result, the pair often felt torn by competing loyalties. Socialists distrusted their work with upper-crust women reformers. Union men were either indifferent or openly hostile to working women's attempts to become leaders in the labor movement. And the League women often seemed to Schneiderman and O'Reilly to act out of a patronizing benevolence that had little to do with real coalition building. The two grew angry at what they saw as attempts by wealthy allies to manipulate them. In January 1906, Leonora O'Reilly announced the first of her many resignations from the League, claiming "an overdose of allies."[39]

There were a few deep friendships between affluent WTUL leaders and working women like Schneiderman, O'Reilly, and Pauline Newman, who joined the League in 1909. Such bonds created hope that intimacy was possible between women of different classes; but cross-class friendships were the exception rather than the rule. Working women like Newman never lost sight of the ways their class background separated them from wealthy reformers. Sisterhood was exhilarating, but outside the WTUL, their lives and political agendas diverged sharply.[40]

Consequently, these women's relations with most wealthy League supporters were marked by deep ambivalence inasmuch as WTUL backers wanted to distance the League from radical working-class activism and to stake out a decidedly middle ground in the struggle for women's rights that was then gathering steam.

Schneiderman tried to counterbalance such influences by encouraging male union leaders to play a more active role in the League, but she had little success. She told them that the WTUL could help the labor movement by successfully organizing women workers, whose low wages might otherwise exert a downward pressure on unionized male wages. A *women's* trade union league was needed, she insisted, because women workers responded to different arguments than did men workers. The League could focus on the particular concerns of women, such as the double shift—having to perform household chores after coming home from long days in the factory. Her suggestions were greeted with indifference.

Addressing the First Convention of American Women Trade Unionists, held in New York on July 14, 1907, Schneiderman reported that she "was very much surprised and not a little disappointed that the attention of men unionists was so small." The truth is, she told her audience, working women needed more than unions. They needed political power. "The time has come," she said firmly, "when working women of the State of New York must be enfranchised and so secure political power to shape their own labor conditions." The convention passed a suffrage resolution, one of the first prosuffrage statements by any organization representing American working-class women.[41]

Schneiderman confronted middle- and upper-class allies with equal frankness. She told the NYWTUL executive board that they were having little success organizing women workers because they approached their task like scholars, not trade unionists. They surveyed conditions in the women's trades, noting which had the lowest salaries, the longest hours, and the worst hygienic conditions. Then they established committees to study the possibilities for unionizing each trade. Finally they went into the shops to explain their findings to the working women. Schneiderman suggested a simpler alternative: take their lead from women workers and respond to requests for aid from women workers who were already trying to organize. It was something they had never thought to do.[42]

Before long, requests for help were pouring in, mostly from immigrant Jewish women. In the dress trade, where Clara Lemlich was working, and in the white goods trade, where Fannia Cohn was organizing, women workers had launched a series of wildcat strikes. "It was not unusual for unorganized workers to walk out without having any direct union affiliation," Schneiderman later recalled.[43]

By 1907, long-simmering anger over speedups, wage cuts, and the requirement that employees pay for their own thread reached a boiling point. Foreshadowing its role in the decades to come, the Women's Trade Union League decided to champion women workers ignored by the male unions. The strike fever soon engulfed Brooklyn, where for two years Fannia Cohn had been struggling against male union leaders' indifference to organize white goods workers. So when three hundred workers in one shop decided to strike in 1908, they bypassed the UGW and called for help from Schneiderman and the WTUL.

Since the ethnic makeup of the Brooklyn white goods trade was far more diverse than any other in the garment industry, this strike raised a new challenge for Schneiderman: how to forge a sense of solidarity between working-class women of many religions and nationalities. Schneiderman decided that the best way to reach immigrant workers was through organizers who literally spoke their language.[44]

She decided to focus first on Italian workers because, after Jews, they comprised the single largest ethnic group in the garment trades. Recognizing the cultural as well as linguistic differences that separated her from Italian immigrant women, Schneiderman tried a strategy she would employ many times over the years to come: to identify and cultivate a leader from within the ranks of the workers. She began working with a Brooklyn priest on ways to approach young Italian women. She also got the League to hire an Italian-speaking organizer who assembled a committee of progressive New York Italians—including prominent women professionals and the editor of a popular evening paper *Bolatino de la Sera*—to popularize trade unionism among Italian women workers.[45]

The strategy proved successful. By 1909 enough workers had enlisted that the ILGWU finally recognized the Brooklyn white goods workers' union. The vast majority of its members were teenage girls; these young women elected their mentor, Fannia Cohn, then twenty-four, to the union's first executive board. Cohn, who stepped off the shop floor to a policy-making position, would remain a paid union official for the rest of her life.[46]

In 1909, Clara Lemlich—then in her twenties and on the executive board of ILGWU Local 25—enlisted Schneiderman's aid in her drive to organize shirt-waist makers. For the past three years, Lemlich had been zigzagging between small shops, stirring up trouble. Her first full-scale strike was at Weisen and Goldstein's Manhattan factory. Like the Triangle Shirtwaist Factory, where Newman worked, Weisen and Goldstein's was considered a model shop. The workrooms were modern and airy—a pleasant contrast to the dark basement rooms where most white goods workers labored. However, the advantages of working in a clean, new factory were offset by the strains of mechanization. In 1907 the workers at Weisen and Goldstein's went on strike to protest speedups.

Older male strikers proved critical to Lemlich's political education. Confused by an argument between workers at a strike meeting, Lemlich asked one to explain the difference between Socialist unionism and the "pure and simple trade unionism" of the American Federation of Labor (AFL). When the meeting ended, the man took Lemlich for a long walk. He explained Socialism in terms she could use with her fellow workers. "He started with a bottle of milk—how it was made, who made the money from it through every stage of its production. Not only did the boss take the profits, he said, but not a drop of that milk did you drink unless he allowed you to. It was funny, you know, because I'd been saying things like that to the girls before. But now I understood it better and I began to use it more often—only with shirtwaists."[47]

Lemlich returned to the picket line with a more sophisticated view of organizing. She became a regular at Socialist Party meetings and began attending classes at the Rand School. Through the Socialist Party she became friends with Rose Schneiderman, Pauline Newman, and other young women organizers. Both individually and in tandem, this group of radical young women organized strikes across the Lower East Side.

In 1909, after being fired from two more shops for leading strikes, Lemlich began working at the Leiserson shop. Brazenly, she marched uninvited into a strike meeting that had been called by the shop's older male elite— the skilled cutters and drapers. Warning them that they would lose if they attempted to strike without organizing the shop's unskilled women, Lemlich demanded their help in organizing women workers. They bridled at her nerve, but ultimately they helped her unionize the women.[48]

Lemlich's reputation as a leader grew rapidly during the fall of 1909 as stories of her bravery spread. During the Leiserson strike, which began that September, she was arrested seventeen times and had six ribs broken by club-wielding police and company guards. Without complaint, she tended to her bruises and returned to the line. By November 1909, when she stepped onto the stage in Cooper Union's Great Hall of the People to deliver the speech that would spark the largest women's strike the nation had yet seen, Lemlich was not the anonymous "wisp of a girl" that news accounts described. She was a battle-scarred veteran of the labor movement, well known among her fellow workers.[49]

Still, it is worth remembering that in this period, the four women activists were just barely adults. Newman, Schneiderman, and Lemlich still lived with their parents. During the Leiserson strike, Lemlich was so fearful that her parents would try to keep her home if they knew about her injuries that she hid her escapades and bruises from them. Later she explained the events to her grandson: "Like rain the blows fell on me. The gangsters hit me. . . . The boys and girls invented themselves how to give back what they got from the scabs, with stones and whatnot, with sticks. . . . Sometimes when I came home I wouldn't tell because if I would tell they wouldn't want me to go anymore. Yes, my boy, it's not easy. Unions aren't built easy."[50]

On November 23, 1909, New York City awoke to a general strike of shirtwaist makers, the largest strike by women workers the United States had ever seen. Overnight, between 20,000 and 40,000 workers—most of them teenage girls—silenced their sewing machines to protest the low wages, long hours, and dangerous working conditions. Though the magnitude of the strike amazed nearly everyone, including Schneiderman, Newman, Cohn, and Lemlich, the four knew that this was no spontaneous uprising: they had been organizing feverishly for almost three years and had noted a transformation in the working women they talked to, a growing sense of collective identity matched by an increasing militancy. They had laid the groundwork through a series of smaller strikes and had trained fellow workers to expect and respond to the violent and divisive tactics used by bosses to break the strike.

Despite their effectiveness, the strike was threatened by the escalation of police violence against the young women picketers. Two weeks after the strike call, Schneiderman and Dreier led ten thousand young waistmakers on a march to city hall to demand that Mayor

George McClellan rein in the police. He promised an investigation but did little. One month into the strike, there had been 771 arrests, many made with undue force.[51]

wtul leaders decided to try a different tack. They called a mass meeting of all the young women who had been attacked by police. The press and wealthy supporters were invited. One after another, adolescent girls rose to the stage to tell their stories. Mollie Weingast told a cheering crowd that when an officer tried to arrest her, she informed him that she had a constitutional right to picket. Minnie Margolis demanded that a policeman protect her from physical attack by her boss. When he refused, she took down his badge and precinct numbers. It was, she told the audience, an officer's job to protect her right to protest peacefully. Celie Newman, sixteen, said that police had manhandled her and dragged her into court, where her boss told a judge that she was an anarchist and should be deported. At another meeting earlier that week, seventeen-year-old Etta Ruth said that police had taunted her with lewd suggestions.[52]

Implying that picketers were little better than streetwalkers, employers often resorted to sexual innuendos to discredit the strikers. The workers clearly resented the manner in which middle-class standards of acceptable feminine behavior were used to manipulate them even though they enjoyed none of the advantages of middle-class birth. Then as now, society offered a limited range of cultural images of working-class women. They were either "good" girls who listened docilely to fathers, employers, and policemen, or "bad" women whose aggressive behavior made them akin to prostitutes. By walking on picket lines and going public with their demands, they'd forfeited their claims to femininity and respectability—and thus to protection.[53]

Such women were shown little deference by police and company thugs, who attacked them with iron bars, sticks, and billy clubs. And they received little sympathy in court when they attempted to press charges. One young woman appeared in court with a broken nose, a bruised face, and a head swathed in bandages. Yet the judge dropped her assault charge against police. "You are on strike against God and nature," one magistrate told a worker. Only the League's decision to invite college students and wealthy women onto the picket lines ended the violence. Alva Belmont

and Anne Morgan led a contingent of New York's wealthiest women in what newspapers dubbed "mink brigades," which patrolled the dirty sidewalks of the Lower East Side. Fearful of clubbing someone on the Social Register, police grew more restrained.[54]

The socialites' presence generated both money and press for the strikers. The move proved politically wise for the suffrage cause as well, because the constant proselytizing of suffrage zealot Alva Belmont, who often bailed strikers out of jail, got young workers talking about the vote. But rubbing elbows with the mink brigade did not blind workers to the class-determined limits of sisterhood. How far they were from the protected status of more affluent women was made abundantly clear by the violence they encountered at the hands of police and company guards and by the fact that the mink brigades were able to end police brutality simply by joining the picket lines.

Encounters in court and with feminist allies speeded the growth of group consciousness. Telling their stories in court, to reporters, and to sympathetic audiences of college and society women, the strikers grew more confident of their speaking abilities and of their capacity to interpret their world. They became more aware of the distribution of power in the United States. And finally, the violence directed against them intensified their bonds with one another.

For Schneiderman, Newman, and Lemlich, the 1909 shirtwaist uprising sped their maturation as organizers and political leaders. The strike breathed new life into a struggling immigrant labor movement and transformed the tiny ilgwu into a union of national significance. Still, it ended with mixed success for workers. Many won pay increases and union recognition; others did not. And the contracts hammered out by ilgwu negotiators left a devastating legacy, for without consulting the strikers, male union negotiators decided that safety conditions were less important than other issues. Their concessions would come back to haunt the entire labor movement two years later, when the Triangle Shirtwaist Factory burned.[55]

Flames from the volcanic 1909 uprising licked industrial cities from New York to Michigan. Within a matter of weeks, 15,000 women waistmakers in Philadelphia walked off their jobs. The spirit of militancy soon touched the Midwest. In 1910, Chicago women led a strike of 41,000 men's clothing makers. The following year, women workers and the wives of male workers played key roles in a bitter cloakmakers' strike in Cleveland. Meanwhile, in Muscatine, Iowa, young women button makers waged and won a long battle for union recognition. In 1912, corset makers in Kalamazoo, Michigan, launched a campaign for better working conditions that polarized their city and won national press attention. In 1913, a strike of underwear and kimono makers swept up 35,000 young Brooklyn girls and women. Finally, in 1915, Chicago dressmakers capped this period of women's labor militancy by winning recognition of their local union after years of struggle. They elected their organizer, Fannia Cohn, as the first woman vice president of a major American labor union.[56]

Cohn, Rose Schneiderman, Pauline Newman, and Clara Lemlich were at the center of a storm that by 1919 had brought half of all women garment workers into trade unions. Individually and in tandem, the four women participated in all of the major women's strikes between 1909 and 1915, arguably the most intense period of women's labor militancy in U.S. history. This wave of "uprisings" seemed to herald the birth of a working women's movement on a scale never before seen. And it catapulted the four young women into positions of leadership, forcing them, in conjunction with colleagues, to articulate a clearly defined set of goals for the new movement.[57] In the passion and excitement of the years that followed, Schneiderman, Newman, Lemlich, and Cohn would begin to mature as political leaders and to forge a vision of political change that originated in their years on the shop floor. Pauline Newman would later describe this new brand of activism as politics of the 1909 vintage, fermented during a brief era of young women's mass protest. That description expresses the importance of the 1909 strike as both symbol and catalyst for a new working women's politics.

"Industrial feminism," the phrase coined in 1915 by scholar Mildred Moore to describe working women's militancy over the previous six years, evokes the same spirit but focuses more broadly. It simultaneously captures the interaction between women workers and feminist activists and recognizes the profound influence that the shop floor had on shaping working women's political consciousness. Industrial feminism accurately depicts the contours of an emerging political movement that by decade's end would propel the problems and concerns of

industrial working women to the center of U.S. political discourse and make them players in the Socialist Party, the suffrage movement, and the politics of progressive reform.[58]

Industrial feminism was not a carefully delineated code of political thought. It was a vision of change forged in an atmosphere of crisis and awakening, as women workers in one city after another "laid down their scissors, shook the threads off their clothes and calmly left the place that stood between them and starvation." These were the words of former cloakmaker, journalist, and Socialist Party activist Theresa Malkiel, a partisan chronicler of women's labor militancy. Once an organizer, later a mentor for Newman, Lemlich, and Schneiderman, Malkiel told readers of the New York Call that they should not be surprised by the seemingly sudden explosion of young women workers' discontent. As hard as they might find it to take seriously the notion of a "girl's strike," she warned them, this was no outburst of female hysteria. "It was not . . . a woman's fancy that drove them to it," she wrote, "but an eruption of a long smoldering volcano, an overflow of suffering, abuse and exhaustion."[59]

Common sense, Pauline Newman would later say, dictated the most immediate goals of industrial feminists in the era of women's strikes. Given the dire realities of garment workers' lives, the first order of business had to be to improve their wages, hours, and working conditions. Toward that end the "girl strikers" of 1909–15 followed the most basic tenets of unionism. They organized, struck, and negotiated through their labor unions. But the "long-smoldering volcano" that Malkiel cautioned her readers to heed had been stirred to life by more than dissatisfaction over low wages and poor conditions.

The nascent political philosophy that began to take shape after the 1909 strike was more complex than the bread-and-butter unionism of AFL president Samuel Gompers. Why, young working women reasoned, should unions only negotiate hours and wages? They wanted to build unions that would also offer workers educational and cultural activities, health care, and maybe even a chance to leave the city and enjoy the open countryside.

Such ambitious goals derived largely from the personal experiences of industrial feminist leaders like Cohn, Schneiderman, Lemlich, and Newman. Political activism had enriched the four young women's lives, exposing them to more interesting people than they would have met had they stayed on the shop floor: writers, artists, professors, people with ideas. Through politics they had found their voices and a forum in which to raise them. The personal excitement and satisfaction they found in activism in turn shaped the evolution of their political vision: they wanted to create institutions that would provide some of the same satisfactions to any working woman who joined.

But alone, working women had none of the political or economic clout needed to open up such doors of opportunity. To build a successful movement, the four knew that they would have to win the support of more powerful allies. So they learned to build coalitions. From the time they left the shop floor until the end of their careers, they operated within a tense nexus of union men, progressive middle- and upper-class women, and the working women they sought to organize. These alliances shifted continuously, requiring the four women to perform a draining and politically hazardous balancing act. But each core group contributed an important dimension to the political education of the four organizers.

With their male counterparts and older women in the labor movement, they shared a class solidarity that would always remain at the heart of their politics. Traveling around the country, they met coal miners, loggers, and railroad workers who shared both their experiences of exploitation as laborers and their exhilaration in the economic and political strength that trade unions gave them.

From the middle- and upper-class women who joined them on the picket lines and lent them both financial and strategic support, they learned that trade union activism was not the only way to fight for improved work conditions. These allies would expose Newman, Cohn, Schneiderman, and Lemlich to a world of power and political influence, encouraging them to believe that through suffrage and lobbying, government could be put to work for their benefit.

Finally, as they began to think in terms of forging a national movement, they were forced to develop new techniques to reach women workers of different races, religions, and ethnicities. They learned from the women they sought to organize that just as women workers were best reached by women organizers, so Italian, Polish, and Hispanic immigrants and native-born black and white Protestant women were better reached by one of their own than by Jewish women steeped in the political culture of Eastern Europe and the Lower East Side. Though each of the four women had some success in bridging racial and ethnic divisions, they were forced to acknowledge their limitations. They could not do it all themselves; they had to nurture women shop-floor leaders from different backgrounds.

The work required to remain politically effective in this nexus of often-conflicting relationships yielded some real rewards, both strategically and personally. But sometimes the constant struggling wore on them. Conflicts and tensions were brought into sharp relief as the four exhausted themselves making speeches and giving pep talks to weary workers, when they themselves needed reassurance: although they had achieved recognition by the end of the 1909 strike, Schneiderman, Cohn, Newman, and Lemlich were still poor, uneducated, and young. Newman was only eighteen years old when the strike began, and Lemlich twenty-three. Even the elders in the circle, Cohn and Schneiderman, were only twenty-five and twenty-eight, respectively.

Letters between Newman and Schneiderman from that era reveal their vulnerability to slights and criticisms by male union leaders and female reformers. Life on "the battlefield," as Newman referred to it, was lonely. At an age when other women were contemplating marriage and family, they spent their nights in smoky union halls or the cheap, dingy hotel rooms that unions rented for their organizers. They sometimes questioned their life choices, for the reality of union work was far less glamorous than it had seemed in their shop-floor days. Indeed, Newman would quit several times before decade's end. Ultimately, though, their disillusionment did not drive the four women from the union movement. Instead, it fueled their desire to broaden the vision of U.S. trade unionism. When Schneiderman said "The working woman needs bread, but she needs roses, too," she was speaking from personal experience.[60]

NOTES

1. Pauline Newman, "Letters to Hugh and Michael" (1951–69), Box 1, Folder 3, Pauline M. Newman Papers, Schlesinger Library, Radcliffe College, Cambridge, Mass. (hereafter cited as Newman Papers).
2. Ibid.

3. Ibid.; *New York Times,* November 2, 25, December 3, 26, 1907.

4. Newman, "Letters to Hugh and Michael."

5. "The Testimony of Miss Pauline M. Newman," in *Hearings of the New York State Factory Investigating Commission* (Albany: J. B. Lyons Printers, 1915), 2868–71.

6. My estimate of Newman's age is based on evidence suggesting that she was around eighteen years old at the time of the 1909 shirtwaist strike. Newman, like many Jews of her generation, never knew for sure how old she was. Her birthdate was recorded only on the flyleaf of the family Bible. After the Bible was lost in transit, she could only guess at her age.

7. For analyses of the position of Jews in Russian society at the turn of the century, see S. Ettinger, "The Jews at the Outbreak of the Revolution," in *The Jews in Soviet Russia since 1917,* ed. Lionel Kochan, 3d ed. (Oxford: Oxford University Press, 1978), 15–30; see also Salo Baron, *The Russian Jew under Tsars and Soviets* (New York: Macmillan, 1976).

8. Sidney Jonas, interview by author, Brooklyn, N.Y., August 10, 1980; Paula Scheier, "Clara Lemlich Shavelson: Fifty Years in Labor's Front Line," *Jewish Life,* November 1954; Ricki Carole Myers Cohen, "Fannia Cohn and the International Ladies' Garment Workers' Union" (Ph.D. diss., University of Southern California, 1976), 5.

9. Newman, "Letters to Hugh and Michael"; Cohen, "Fannia Cohn," chap. 1; Scheier, "Clara Lemlich Shavelson"; Fannia M. Cohn to "Dear Emma," May 15, 1953, Fannia M. Cohn Papers, Astor, Lenox, and Tilden Foundations, Rare Books and Manuscripts Division, New York Public Library (hereafter cited as Cohn Papers).

In March 1903, gangs organized by Russian police rampaged through the Ukrainian town of Kishinev, killing 51 Jewish men, women, and children, and wounding at least 495 others. Edward H. Judge, *Eastern Kishinev: Anatomy of a Pogrom* (New York: New York University Press, 1992).

10. See Charlotte Baum, Paula Hyman, and Sonya Michel, *The Jewish Woman in America* (New York: NAL/Dutton, 1977), 55–91; Mark Zborowski and Elizabeth Herzog, *Life Is with People* (New York: Schocken, 1962); Jack Kugelmass and Jonathan Bayarin, *From a Ruined Garden: The Memorial Books of Polish Jewry* (New York: Schocken Books, 1985).

11. The Lower East Side continued to receive Jewish immigrants from Eastern Europe into the 1920s. See Ettinger, "Jews at the Outbreak of the Revolution," 19–22; Celia Heller, *On the Edge of Destruction* (New York: Schocken, 1980), 45–55; and Irving Howe, *World of Our Fathers* (New York: Harcourt Brace & Jovanovich, 1976), xix.

12. Clara Lemlich Shavelson to Morris Schappes, March 15, 1965, published in *Jewish Currents* 36, no. 10 (November 1982): 9–11.

13. Clara Lemlich, "Remembering the Waistmakers' General Strike, 1909," *Jewish Currents,* November 1982; Newman, "Letters to Hugh and Michael."

14. Much has been written about the importance of women's colleges to the various social reform movements of the Progressive Era. Stephen Norwood makes a similar argument for high schools. Norwood, *Labor's Flaming Youth: Telephone Workers and Labor Militancy, 1878–1923* (Urbana: University of Illinois Press, 1990).

15. Newman, "Letters to Hugh and Michael"; Pauline Newman, interview by Barbara Wertheimer, New York, N.Y., November 1976; Pauline Newman résumé, n.d., Newman Papers.

16. Pauline Newman, interview by author, New York, N.Y., February 9, 1984; Newman, interview by Wertheimer.

17. Joan Morrison and Charlotte Fox Zabusky, eds., *American Mosaic* (New York: E. P. Dutton, 1980).

18. See Rose Schneiderman, *All for One* (New York: Paul S. Eriksson, 1967), 35–42, and Susan Porter Benson, "The Customers Ain't God: The Work Culture of Department Store Saleswomen, 1890–1940," in *Working Class America,* ed. Michael Frisch and Daniel J. Walkowitz (Urbana: University of Illinois Press, 1983), 185–212.

19. Scheier, "Clara Lemlich Shavelson." See also Susan Glenn, *Daughters of the Shtetl: Work, Unionism and the Immigrant Generation* (Ithaca: Cornell University Press, 1990), 122–31.

20. Schneiderman, *All for One,* 48.

21. Ibid., 48–50.

22. Ibid.

23. Ibid.

24. FMC to Selig Perlman, December 26, 1951, Box 5, Cohn Papers.

25. Information on the problems of organizing the white goods trade is located in Minutes of the Executive Board of the NYWTUL, February 28, August 22, and November 26, 27, 1907, Reel 1, Papers of the New York Women's Trade Union League, Tamiment Institute Library, New York University (hereafter cited as NYWTUL Papers); information on Cohn comes from Cohen, "Fannia Cohn," 11–21.

26. Schneiderman, *All for One,* 39–40.

27. Scheier, "Clara Lemlich Shavelson."

28. Pauline Newman, "The White Goods Workers' Strike," *Ladies' Garment Worker* 4, no. 3 (March 1913): 1–4.

29. Scheier, "Clara Lemlich Shavelson"; Pauline Newman, Fragments 1958–61, Box 1, Newman Papers.

30. Newman, interview by Wertheimer; Newman, interview in Morrison and Zabusky, *American Mosaic.*

31. Scheier, "Clara Lemlich Shavelson."

32. Louis Levine [Lewis Lorwin], *The Women's Garment Workers: A History of the International Ladies' Garment Workers' Union* (New York: B. W. Huebsch, 1924), 148–49.

33. This information is pieced together from Scheier, "Clara Lemlich Shavelson"; Dora Smorodin, interview by author, Maplewood, N.J., March 12, 1991; and Levine, *Women's Garment Workers,* 148–49.

34. Newman, interview by Wertheimer; Newman, "Letters to Hugh and Michael."

35. Ibid.

36. Schneiderman, *All for One,* 58–60.

37. Ibid., 73–77; Minutes of the NYWTUL Executive Board, February 24, March 24, 1905. Reel 1, NYWTUL Papers.

38. Nancy Schrom Dye, *As Equals and as Sisters: Feminism, Unionism and the Women's Trade Union League of New York* (Columbia: University of Missouri Press, 1980), 110–22.

39. Ibid.; Minutes of the NYWTUL Executive Board, January 25, 1906, Reel 1, NYWTUL Papers.

40. Newman, interview by Wertheimer; Newman, interview by author, February 9, 1984, New York.

41. See also Alice Kessler-Harris, "Rose Schneiderman," in *American Labor Leaders,* ed. Warren Van Tine and Melvyn Dubofsky (Urbana: University of Illinois Press, 1987), 160–84.

42. Minutes of the NYWTUL Executive Board, February 24, 1905-February 1, 1909, Reel 1, NYWTUL Papers.

43. Schneiderman, *All for One,* 84.

44. Minutes of the NYWTUL Executive Board, February 28, August 22, November 26, 27, 1907, Reel 1, NYWTUL, Papers; Levine, *Women's Garment Workers,* 220.

45. Minutes of the NYWTUL Executive Committee, November 26, 27, 1907, Reel 1, NYWTUL Papers.

46. Levine, *Women's Garment Workers,* 220; Cohen, "Fannia Cohn," 36–43.

47. Scheier, "Clara Lemlich Shavelson."

48. Martha Schaffer, telephone interview by author, March 11, 1989; Joel Schaffer, Evelyn Velson, and Julia Velson, interview by author, Oakland, Calif., September 9, 1992.

49. Scheier, "Clara Lemlich Shavelson."

50. Clara Lemlich Shavelson, interview by Martha and Joel Schaffer, Los Angeles, Calif., February 2, 1974.

51. *New York Call,* November 30, December 4, 5, 6, 7, 8, 29, 1909.

52. *New York Call,* December 5, 7, 8, 1909.

53. *New York Call,* December 29, 1909. For complete coverage of day-to-day events on the picket line, see the *New York Times,* November 5, 6, and 14, 1909, and almost daily from November 23, 1909, through January 28, 1910.

54. Minutes of the New York Women's Trade Union League Membership Meeting, April 20, June 15, 1910, Reel 1, NYWTUL Papers.

55. See Meredith Tax, *The Rising of the Women: Feminist Solidarity and Class Conflict, 1880–1917* (New York: Monthly Review Press, 1980), pp. 230–240. Tax discusses the hierarchical union structure and the ways that union-appointed arbitrators undermined the women workers' control of the strike.

56. For information on the many women's strikes of the period, read the WTUL publication *Life and Labor,* which covered them all in some detail. The progressive magazine *The Survey* (1909–1914) also has good coverage of most of the strikes. See too, Pauline Newman, "The White Goods Workers' Strike," *Ladies' Garment Worker* 4, number 3 (March 1913): 1–4; on the Chicago strike see Mari Jo Buhle, *Women and American Socialism, 1870–1920* (Urbana: University of Illinois Press, 1981), 194–198. On the Kalamazoo strike see Karen Mason, "Feeling the Pinch: The Kalamazoo Corset Makers' Strike of 1912," in *To Toil the Livelong Day: America's Women at Work,* ed. Carol Groneman and Mary Beth Norton (Ithaca: Cornell University Press, 1987), 141–60. On the 1915 strike see *Chicago Day Book* cited in Winifred Carsel, *A History of the Chicago Ladies' Garment Workers' Union* (Chicago: Normandie House, 1940).

57. Gladys Boone, *The Women's Trade Union Leagues* (New York: Columbia University Press, 1942), 112–14.

58. Mildred Moore, "A History of the Women's Trade Union League of Chicago" (M.A. thesis, University of Chicago, 1915), cited in Diane Kirkby, "The Wage-Earning Woman and the State: The National Women's Trade Union League and Protective Labor Legislation, 1903–1923," *Labor History* 28, no. 1 (Winter 1987): 58–74.

59. Theresa Malkiel, "The Uprising of the 40,000," *New York Call,* December 29, 1909.

60. Pauline Newman, "From the Battlefield—Some Phases of the Cloakmakers' Strike in Cleveland," *Life and Labor,* October 1911.

Pauline Newman, "We fought and we bled and we died . . ."

One of the four young garment industry workers whose organizing activities emerged so vividly from the pages of Annelise Orleck's account, Pauline Newman had started out at the Triangle Shirtwaist Factory, which became the scene of one of the great industrial tragedies in New York City's history. Although the factory contained several elevators and two staircases, the eight-story wooden building had no sprinkler system; the doors to the fire escapes were locked to prevent outdoor relaxation. When fire broke out in 1911, 500 employees—many of them young Jewish and Italian women—were trapped behind locked doors. Some on the upper floors jumped to their deaths; others burned or asphyxiated while trapped inside. Altogether, the fire claimed the lives of 146 women. Viewing their charred bodies on the street, one reporter recalled that some of these same women had gone on strike only the year before to demand decent wages, more sanitary working conditions, and safety precautions.

The young women who died at the Triangle fire were buried together under a single monument. Hundreds of thousands of New Yorkers walked in the funeral procession in a driving rain. Not until 2011, a hundred years later, were they identified. The last living survivor of the fire, Rose Freedman, died in 2001 at the age of 107. She had saved herself by asking: what are the executives doing? She headed for their offices on the tenth floor, and then to the roof by way of the freight elevator, from which firefighters pulled them to safety. She never forgave the executives for saving themselves but leaving the doors locked, or, later, attempting to bribe her to testify that the doors were unlocked.

Unsafe buildings, blocked exits, and inadequate sprinkler systems threaten garment workers again today. The mass-market clothes that American women wear are often made in substandard conditions—in the United States when minimum wage, maximum hour, and occupational health and safety laws are unenforced, and abroad, in places where such standards barely exist. In an eerie reprise of the Triangle Fire, almost exactly 102 years later, in April 2013, the Rana Plaza factory in Dhaka, Bangladesh, collapsed, killing 1,129 workers, mostly women, who made cheap clothes for Western markets. (The United States suspended trade preferences for Bangladesh in recognition of labor rights violations and the persistence of safety problems, but unsafe factories continue to be used in that country and elsewhere.)*

*"100 Years Later, the Roll of the Dead in a Factory Fire is Complete," *New York Times*, Feb. 20, 2011; "Rose Freedman, Last Survivor of Triangle Fire, Dies at 107," ibid., Feb. 17, 2001; "Manufacturers in Bangladesh Resist Closing Garment Factories," ibid., June 26, 2014, pp. B1, B7.

Adapted from "Pauline Newman," in *American Mosaic: The Immigrant Experience in the Words of Those Who Lived It*, ed. Joan Morrison and Charlotte Fox Zabusky (New York: E. P. Dutton, 1980), pp. 9–14. Copyright © 1980 by Joan Morrison and Charlotte Fox Zabusky. Reprinted by permission of the publisher.

Educational director for the International Ladies' Garment Workers' Union until her death in 1986, Newman conveys in her own words what it was like to be a garment worker in the early twentieth century. What does she feel has been gained by organized labor? What does she feel has been lost over the years?

A cousin of mine worked for the Triangle Shirtwaist Company and she got me on there in October of 1901. It was probably the largest shirtwaist factory in the city of New York then. They had more than two hundred operators, cutters, examiners, finishers. Altogether more than four hundred people on two floors. The fire took place on one floor, the floor where we worked. You've probably heard about that. But that was years later.

We started work at seven-thirty in the morning, and during the busy season we worked until nine in the evening. They didn't pay you any overtime and they didn't give you anything for supper money. Sometimes they'd give you a little apple pie if you had to work very late. That was all. Very generous.

What I had to do was not really very difficult. It was just monotonous. When the shirtwaists were finished at the machine there were some threads that were left, and all the youngsters—we had a corner on the floor that resembled a kindergarten—we were given little scissors to cut the threads off. It wasn't heavy work, but it was monotonous, because you did the same thing from seven-thirty in the morning till nine at night.

Well, of course, there were [child labor] laws on the books, but no one bothered to enforce them. The employers were always tipped off if there was going to be an inspection. "Quick," they'd say, "into the boxes!" And we children would climb into the big boxes the finished shirts were stored in. Then some shirts were piled on top of us, and when the inspector came—no children. The factory always got an okay from the inspector, and I suppose someone at City Hall got a little something, too.

The employers didn't recognize anyone working for them as a human being. You were not allowed to sing. Operators would have liked to have sung, because they, too, had the same thing to do and weren't allowed to sing. We weren't allowed to talk to each other. Oh, no, they would sneak up behind if you were found talking to your next colleague. You were admonished: "If you keep on you'll be fired." If

you went to the toilet and you were there longer than the floor lady thought you should be, you would be laid off for half a day and sent home. And, of course, that meant no pay. You were not allowed to have your lunch on the fire escape in the summertime. The door was locked to keep us in. That's why so many people were trapped when the fire broke out.

My pay was $1.50 a week no matter how many hours I worked. My sisters made $6.00 a week; and the cutters, they were skilled workers, they might get as much as $12.00. The employers had a sign in the elevator that said: "If you don't come in on Sunday, don't come in on Monday." You were expected to work every day if they needed you and the pay was the same whether you worked extra or not. You had to be there at seven-thirty, so you got up at five-thirty, took the horse car, then the electric trolley to Greene Street, to be there on time. . . .

I stopped working at the Triangle Factory during the strike in 1909 and I didn't go back. The union sent me out to raise money for the strikers. I apparently was able to articulate my feelings and opinions about the criminal conditions, and they didn't have anyone else who could do better, so they assigned me. And I was successful getting money. After my first speech before the Central Trade and Labor Council I got front-page publicity, including my picture. I was only about fifteen then. Everybody saw it. Wealthy women were curious and they asked me if I would speak to them in their homes. I said I would if they would contribute to the strike, and they agreed. So I spent my time from November to the end of March upstate in New York, speaking to the ladies of the Four Hundred [the elite of New York's society] and sending money back. . . .

We didn't gain very much at the end of the strike. I think the hours were reduced to fifty-six a week or something like that. We got a 10 percent increase in wages. I think that the best thing that the strike did was to lay a foundation on which to build a union. There was so much feeling against unions then. The judge, when one of our girls came before him,

There was no morgue in New York City large enough to hold the bodies of the young women who had jumped from the burning buildings of the Triangle Shirtwaist Company in 1911. They were laid out on a pier for families to identify. Six of the victims were so badly burned that even relatives could not recognize them. (Courtesy of UNITE Archives, Kheel Center for Labor-Management Documentation and Archives, School of Industrial and Labor Relations, Cornell University, Ithaca, New York.)

said to her: "You're not striking against your employer, you know, young lady. You're striking against God," and sentenced her to two weeks on Blackwell's Island, which is now Welfare Island. And a lot of them got a taste of the club. . . .

After the 1909 strike I worked with the union, organizing in Philadelphia and Cleveland and other places, so I wasn't at the Triangle Shirtwaist Factory when the fire broke out, but a lot of my friends were. I was in Philadelphia for the union and, of course, someone from here called me immediately and I came back. It's very difficult to describe the feeling because I knew the place and I knew so many of the girls. The thing that bothered me was the employers got a lawyer. How anyone could have *defended* them!—because I'm quite sure that the fire was planned for insurance purposes. And no one is going to convince me

otherwise. And when they testified that the door to the fire escape was open, it was a lie! It was never open. Locked all the time. One hundred and forty-six people were sacrificed, and the judge fined Blank and Harris seventy-five dollars!

Conditions were dreadful in those days. But there was something that is lacking today and I think it was the devotion and the belief. We *believed* in what we were doing. We fought and we bled and we died. Today they don't have to.

You sit down at the table, you negotiate with the employers, you ask for 20 percent, they say 15, but the girls are working. People are working. They're not disturbed, and when the negotiations are over they get the increases. They don't really have to fight. Of course, they'll belong to the union and they'll go on strike if you tell them to, but it's the inner faith that people had in those days that I don't see today. It was a terrible time, but it was interesting. I'm glad I lived then.

Even when things were terrible, I always had that faith. . . . Only now, I'm a little discouraged sometimes when I see the workers spending their free hours watching television—trash. We fought so hard for those hours and they waste them. We used to read Tolstoy, Dickens, Shelley, by candlelight, and they watch the *Hollywood Squares*. Well, they're free to do what they want. That's what we fought for.

Crystal Eastman, Now We Can Begin

Crystal Eastman charts an agenda for feminists after the achievement of suffrage. For all humankind, what should we think of as being embraced by her observation that "freedom is a large word"? Most of her short essay focuses on how to achieve "woman's freedom" as she saw it through her particular early twentieth-century feminist frame. Do you agree that the issues she identifies needed to be prioritized in the 1920s? Are these issues still relevant today?

We invite you to do background research on Crystal Eastman and *The Liberator*, a magazine published in New York City starting in 1918 and named for William Lloyd Garrison's legendary abolitionist newspaper of the early nineteenth century. What things do you find most striking about Eastman's life? Who published *The Liberator* and for how long? Take a moment to open up the link to the digitized December 1920 issue so that you can see her short essay alongside other essays, artwork, and advertisements, imagining yourself as someone who moved in Eastman's circles in the 1920s.

Most women will agree that August 23, the day when the Tennessee legislature finally enacted the Federal suffrage amendment, is a day to begin with, not a day to end with. Men are saying perhaps "Thank God, this everlasting woman's fight is over!" But women, if I know them, are saying, "Now at last we can begin." In fighting for the right to vote most women have tried to be either non-committal or thoroughly respectable on every other subject. Now they can say what they are really after; and what they are after, in common with all the rest of the struggling world, is *freedom*.

Freedom is a large word.

Many feminists are socialists, many are communists, not a few are active leaders in these movements. But the true feminist, no matter how far to the left she may be in the revolutionary movement, sees the woman's battle as distinct in its objects and different in its methods from the workers' battle for industrial freedom. She knows, of course, that the vast majority of women as well as men are without property, and are of necessity bread and butter slaves under a system of society which allows the very sources of life to be privately owned by a few, and she counts herself a loyal soldier in the working-class army that is marching to overthrow that system. But as a feminist she also knows that the whole of woman's slavery is not summed up in the profit system, nor her complete emancipation assured by the downfall of capitalism.

Woman's freedom, in the feminist sense, can be fought for and conceivably won before the gates open into industrial democracy. On

Crystal Eastman, "Now We Can Begin," *The Liberator*, 3, no. 12 (December 1920), 23–4. For an open-access, digitized copy of the magazine issue, go to http://www.marxists.org/history/usa/culture/pubs/liberator/1920/12/v3n12-w33-dec-1920-liberator.pdf.

the other hand, woman's freedom, in the feminist sense, is not inherent in the communist ideal. All feminists are familiar with the revolutionary leader who "can't see" the woman's movement. "What's the matter with the women? My wife's all right," he says. And his wife, one usually finds, is raising his children in a Bronx flat or a dreary suburb, to which he returns occasionally for food and sleep when all possible excitement and stimulus have been wrung from the fight. If we should graduate into communism tomorrow this man's attitude to his wife would not be changed. The proletarian dictatorship may or may not free women. We must begin now to enlighten the future dictators.

What, then, is "the matter with women"? What is the problem of women's freedom? It seems to me to be this: how to arrange the world so that women can be human beings, with a chance to exercise their infinitely varied gifts in infinitely varied ways, instead of being destined by the accident of their sex to one field of activity—housework and child-raising. And second, if and when they choose housework and child-raising, to have that occupation recognized by the world as work, requiring a definite economic reward and not merely entitling the performer to be dependent on some man.

This is not the whole of feminism, of course, but it is enough to begin with. "Oh, don't begin with economics," my friends often protest, "Woman does not live by bread alone. What she needs first of all is a free soul." And I can agree that women will never be great until they achieve a certain emotional freedom, a strong healthy egotism, and some unpersonal sources of joy—that in this inner sense we cannot make woman free by changing her economic status. What we can do, however, is to create conditions of outward freedom in which a free woman's soul can be born and grow. It is these outward conditions with which an organized feminist movement must concern itself.

Freedom of choice in occupation and individual economic independence for women: How shall we approach this next feminist objective? First, by breaking down all remaining barriers, actual as well as legal, which make it difficult for women to enter or succeed in the various professions, to go into and get on in business, to learn trades and practice them, to join trades unions. Chief among these remaining barriers is inequality in pay. Here the ground is already broken. This is the easiest part of our program.

Second, we must institute a revolution in the early training and education of both boys and girls. It must be womanly as well as manly to earn your own living, to stand on your own feet. And it must be manly as well as womanly to know how to cook and sew and clean and take care of yourself in the ordinary exigencies of life. I need not add that the second part of this revolution will be more passionately resisted than the first. Men will not give up their privilege of helplessness without a struggle. The average man has a carefully cultivated ignorance about household matters—from what to do with the crumbs to the grocer's telephone number—a sort of cheerful inefficiency which protects him better than the reputation for having a violent temper. It was his mother's fault in the beginning, but even as a boy he was quick to see how a general reputation for being "no good around the house" would serve him throughout life, and half-consciously he began to cultivate that helplessness until today it is the despair of feminist wives.

A growing number of men admire the woman who has a job, and, especially since the cost of living doubled, rather like the idea of their own wives contributing to the family income by outside work. And of course for generations there have been whole towns full of wives who are forced by the bitterest necessity to spend the same hours at the factory that their husbands spend. But these bread-winning wives have not yet developed home-making husbands. When the two come home from the factory the man sits down while his wife gets supper, and he does so with exactly the same sense of fore-ordained right as if he were "supporting her." Higher up in the economic scale the same thing is true. The business or professional woman who is married, perhaps engages a cook, but the responsibility is not shifted, it is still hers. She "hires and fires," she orders meals, she does the buying, she meets and resolves all domestic crises, she takes charge of moving, furnishing, settling. She may be, like her husband, a busy executive at her office all day, but unlike him, she is also an executive in a small way every night and morning at home. Her noon hour is spent in planning, and too often her Sundays and holidays are spent in "catching up."

Two business women can "make a home" together without either one being over-burdened or over-bored. It is because they both know how and both feel responsible. But it is a rare man who can marry one of them and continue the homemaking partnership. Yet if there are no children, there is nothing essentially different in the combination. Two self-supporting adults decide to make a home together: if both are women it is a pleasant partnership, more fun than work; if one is a man, it is almost never a partnership—the woman simply adds running the home to her regular outside job. Unless she is very strong, it is too much for her, she gets tired and bitter over it, and finally perhaps gives up her outside work and condemns herself to the tiresome half-job of housekeeping for two.

Cooperative schemes and electrical devices will simplify the business of homemaking, but they will not get rid of it entirely. As far as we can see ahead people will always want homes, and a happy home cannot be had without a certain amount of rather monotonous work and responsibility. How can we change the nature of man so that he will honorably share that work and responsibility and thus make the home-making enterprise a song instead of a burden? Most assuredly not by laws or revolutionary decrees. Perhaps we must cultivate or simulate a little of that highly prized helplessness ourselves. But fundamentally it is a problem of education, of early training—we must bring up feminist sons.

Sons? Daughters? They are born of women—how can women be free to choose their occupation, at all times cherishing their economic independence, unless they stop having children? This is a further question for feminism. If the feminist program goes to pieces on the arrival of the first baby, it is false and useless. For ninety-nine out of every hundred women want children, and seventy-five out of every hundred want to take care of their own children, or at any rate so closely superintend their care as to make any other full-time occupation impossible for at least ten or fifteen years. Is there any such thing then as freedom of choice in occupation for

women? And is not the family the inevitable economic unit and woman's individual economic independence, at least during that period, out of the question?

The feminist must have an answer to these questions, and she has. The immediate feminist program must include voluntary motherhood. Freedom of any kind for women is hardly worth considering unless it is assumed that they will know how to control the size of their families. "Birth control" is just as elementary an essential in our propaganda as "equal pay." Women are to have children when they want them, that's the first thing. That ensures some freedom of occupational choice; those who do not wish to be mothers will not have an undesired occupation thrust upon them by accident, and those who do wish to be mothers may choose in a general way how many years of their lives they will devote to the occupation of child-raising.

But is there any way of insuring a woman's economic independence while child-raising is her chosen occupation? Or must she sink into that dependent state from which, as we all know, it is so hard to rise again? That brings us to the fourth feature of our program—motherhood endowment. It seems that the only way we can keep mothers free, at least in a capitalist society, is by the establishment of a principle that the occupation of raising children is peculiarly and directly a service to society, and that the mother upon whom the necessity and privilege of performing this service naturally falls is entitled to an adequate economic reward from the political government. It is idle to talk of real economic independence for women unless this principle is accepted. But with a generous endowment of motherhood provided by legislation, with all laws against voluntary motherhood and education in its methods repealed, with the feminist ideal of education accepted in home and school, and with all special barriers removed in every field of human activity, there is no reason why woman should not become almost a human thing.

It will be time enough then to consider whether she has a soul.

EMPIRE AND INTERNATIONALISM

LAURA WEXLER
A Lady Photojournalist Goes to the 1904 St. Louis World's Fair

How might *you* stage a world's fair, organizing the grounds, pavilions, and interior displays? With numerous nations and peoples showcased, there is inevitably a politics to how the various groups are represented. Laura Wexler's essay explores the gender, racial, and imperial politics of the 1904 World's Fair in St. Louis. Let's note two things about the timing of this fair.

First, many white Americans felt they were at a crossroads. At the previous world's fair, held in 1893 in Chicago, historian Frederick Jackson Turner had given a speech that quickly became famous, entitled "The Significance of the Frontier for American History."* He argued that the existence of a frontier, "a meeting place between savagery and civilization," and the availability of "free land" had been the crucial elements in shaping American society. The frontier experience of free land shaped the American people, particularly Euro-American men, fostering democratic and independent values. As much as his talk celebrated Anglo-American westward expansion, it also mourned what he understood to be the end of the frontier, as the 1890 census reported that pockets of settlement interrupted what had once been clear lines of division between Anglo-American and aboriginal settlement. Without the frontier, what would happen to democracy in the United States?

Second, during the last decade of the nineteenth century, the U.S. government engaged in a series of economic, political, and military endeavors to extend the American frontier beyond the continent. During this decade, the United States fought the Spanish-American War, thereby acquiring control over islands in the Caribbean. It also incorporated islands in the Pacific Ocean—Hawaii, Guam, Samoa, and the Philippines—that could serve as stepping stones or way stations for commercial and military endeavors. Nationalists in the Philippines, a colony of Spain, had supported the United States during the war, anticipating their own independence. However, once Spain was vanquished, the United States occupied and controlled the islands, refusing to recognize Filipino demands for independence. Filipino nationalists resisted; the United States responded with force. The three-year

---

* Frederick Jackson Turner, "The Significance of the Frontier in American History," Paper presented at the American Historical Association, Chicago, 1893; excerpts are available at http://nationalhumanitiescenter .org/pds/gilded/empire/text1/turner.pdf.

Excerpted from the introduction and ch. 7 of *Tender Violence: Domestic Visions in an Age of U.S. Imperialism* by Laura Wexler (Chapel Hill: University of North Carolina Press, 2000). Reprinted by permission of the author and publisher. Notes have been edited and renumbered.

guerrilla war that ensued resulted in the death of hundreds of thousands of Filipinos (some 20 percent of the population) and 4,000 Americans.[†]

The 1904 World's Fair in St. Louis provided an opportunity for the United States to display its new imperial possessions. Wexler's essay focuses on one of the white, middle-class female photographers who frequented and worked at the fair, Jessie Tarbox Beals. Becoming a lady photographer allowed a woman to travel and document (and hence interpret) the world around her. Wexler complicates this narrative of gender liberation, however, by emphasizing the racial impact of privileged white women's photography, especially given its embeddedness in an "Age of Imperialism" for the United States.

The first cohort of American women photographers to achieve serious public careers as photojournalists at the turn of the century often used the "innocent eye" attributed to them by white domestic sentiment to construct images of war as peace, images that were, in turn, a constitutive element of the social relations of United States imperialism during the era's annexation and consolidation of colonies. My term, "the innocent eye," designates a deeply problematic practice of representation that developed within the private domain of family photography at midcentury in the United States. At that time, white middle-class women, in both the North and the South, were regularly portrayed in family photographs as if looking out from within, without seeing the race and class dynamics of the household. [The "innocent eye"] . . . of domestic sentiment functioned to normalize . . . raced and classed relations of dominance during slavery and to reinscribe them after its legal end. As a representational practice, this private gaze took on a new national significance when in the late 1890s and early 1900s a certain group of American "New Women" photographers—among them Frances Benjamin Johnston; Gertrude Käsebier; Alice Austen; the Gerhard sisters, Emme and Mamie; and Jessie Tarbox Beals . . . —learned to turn it to their professional advantage by ensuring that from the panorama of foreign wars fought by white American men, white American women would construct visions of domestic peace.

When the World's Fair opened in St. Louis, Missouri, in 1904, thirty-four-year-old photojournalist Jessie Tarbox Beals was there— along with many other white, middle-class, American women photographers. The spectacle of the nineteenth century's great fairs and expositions held strong attractions for them,

and they often went to great lengths to photograph them. For the World's Columbian Exposition of 1893, for instance, Jessie (then Tarbox), a single, twenty-three-year-old, Canadian-born schoolteacher, had taken the train to Chicago from her home in Greenfield, Massachusetts. She stayed for twenty-five days in the women's dormitory, shooting photographs with her new little Kodak (she could not get a permit for a larger view camera with tripod) and developing her own film in the public darkroom facilities that the Exposition's photography department provided. After Chicago, no longer would her own life look the same to her.

She returned to small-town existence in western Massachusetts and to schoolteaching, writes her biographer Alexander Alland, "consumed with the desire to visit the foreign places whose makeshift villages she had seen and photographed at the exposition."[1] When she then discovered that she could make more money in one summer of selling freelance pictures than she could in a year of teaching school, she was spoiled for "protected" feminine domestic gentility for ever. Within seven years, Jessie Tarbox had married Alfred Beals, an Amherst College graduate who was working as a machinist in Greenfield, quit schoolteaching, and persuaded Alfred to give up his job, become her darkroom assistant, and set off to see what possibilities there were in earning their living as itinerant photographers. They started in Vermont, traveled for a year through Florida, and regrouped to upstate New York. Alfred, it turned out, had married a "lady" photographer. At the time, neither he nor she quite knew what that was going to mean. . . .

To the photographing woman, the fairs and expositions offered congenial stimulation and a way to gain recognition and make some money selling photographs. Simultaneously,

---

[†]This war was an early occasion in which U.S. military forces used waterboarding; see Paul Kramer, "The Water Cure: Debating Torture and Counterinsurgency—A Century Ago," *The New Yorker*, February 25, 2008.

they offered a way to construct a larger identity as a "lady photographer." If, as many scholars have proposed, the fairs performed the public function of remaking a national self-definition for a United States reunited a generation after the Civil War and newly emerging as an industrial world power, they also served the private purpose of self-making for white women photographers of the era. The fairs encouraged them to emerge from domestic confinement and to test just how far the designation "lady with a camera" would go.

St. Louis was very much a southern city at the start of the nineteenth century. From the time of the Missouri Compromise in 1820, through the 1857 *Dred Scott v. Sanford* decision, which ruled that a slave who lived in a free state or territory was still a slave, debates over slavery and abolition gave a veneer of political debate to St. Louis; meanwhile, slave auctions took place on the steps of the very courthouse where these decisions were handed down. The citizens of St. Louis defiantly elected a Secessionist governor before the Civil War, although the state of Missouri stayed in the Union. Because of strong economic ties to the north, St. Louis eventually became a center of Union support and a staging ground for Union troops, but many there never altered their allegiance to the South.

And now, at the turn of the century, the St. Louis World's Fair of 1904 invited the city and the world to contemplate the triumph of yet another new formulation of United States power. America's recent victory in the war with Spain highlighted the global ambitions of the new American state. More than 1,270 acres of Forest Park had been given over to display the nationalist fervor of a new imperial order. The fair transformed both the resistant sectionalism of the Old South and the resilient commercialism of the New beyond all possibilities of imagining earlier in the century.

Not that the voices of the Old South were stilled, by any means. Widespread Democratic anti-imperialist agitation built heavily upon the racist presumptions of men like Thomas Nelson Page, author of *Red Rock* (1898), and Thomas Dixon, author of *The Leopard's Spots* (1902), *The Clansman* (1905), and *The Traitor* (1907). Both these men argued against annexation of the Philippines on the grounds that imperial acquisition was unconstitutional and anti-republican and that Filipino self government was the only way to avoid burdening the United States with what Mrs. Jefferson Davis called "fresh millions of foreign negroes, even more ignorant and more degraded . . . than those at home."[2]

However, the thrust of the times was against them. Pro-annexation arguments were neither more egalitarian nor necessarily less racist. They simply alleged that in the Philippines "Caucasians were ushering in a new era in human history," an era in which "human culture is become unified, not only through diffusion but through the extinction of lower grades."[3] The cotton plantations of the Old South were a model for prospective fruit, sugar, and hemp plantations in Hawaii and the Philippines. Nineteen hundred four was one of the peak years of immigration to the United States by whites from western and eastern Europe, most of them poorly educated peasants looking for ways to better themselves and escape from lives of unremitting manual labor. Many blacks were also arriving from the West Indies, not all of whom were fully indoctrinated into the culture of American race relations. Nativist sentiment had not yet pushed Congress toward immigration restriction and overall quotas—that would take another twenty years—but its organization was growing. . . .

Above all else, then, the St. Louis World's Fair was advancing an argument for the vigor of the Caucasian culture of the Unites States and its capacity to incorporate the labor of such immigrants, since it had been able so successfully to discipline and assimilate its former slaves and aboriginal Others into a seemingly credible domestic "peace." In exemplifying how the United States had already dealt with similar tasks, the St. Louis World's Fair was addressing the greatest anxieties of its day, to indicate where and how white Americans could and would prevail. Industrial leaders believed that "the burden of humanity is already in large measure the White Man's burden—for, viewing the human world as it is, white and strong are synonymous terms."[4] They looked forward to shouldering America's load.

These particular views on race and national destiny were, in fact, the sentiments of Mr. W. J. McGee, one of the chief officers of the St. Louis Fair. McGee, the head of the Anthropology Department of the fair, reasoned that it was precisely the new global industrial opportunities that rationalized the horrific cost of the Civil War and the preservation of the Union. In the south, Reconstruction was over; its demise left a growing ambition to explore these new opportunities. McGee portrayed the field for action as nearly limitless: "It is the duty of the strong man to subjugate lower nature, to extirpate the bad and cultivate the good among living things, to delve in earth below and cleave the air above in search of fresh resources, to transform the seas into paths for ships and pastures for food-fishes, . . . and in all ways to enslave the world for the support of humanity and the increase of human intelligence."[5]

McGee and the rest of the team designed the St. Louis World's Fair to make the perspective of scientific racism and the imperative of United States imperialism seem equally valid and inevitable. . . . The St. Louis World's Fair was also the Louisiana Purchase Centenary Celebration. It commemorated the treaty which in 1803 had more than doubled the geographical size of the United States and simultaneously transformed the old Creole town of St. Louis into a booming American city, "the gateway to the West." It also celebrated a potent analogy constructed between pacification of "domestic" tribes of Native Americans and "foreign" tribes of Filipinos. As one of the official publications of the Exposition explained, "The time is coming when the purchase and retention of the Philippine Islands will seem as wise to our descendants as does the Louisiana Purchase seem to us who live today."[6]

In the brief nine months that it was open, St. Louis World's Fair of 1904 formulated for almost 19 million people who participated in its construction or visited its grounds a vision not only of the fruits of the past hundred years of expansion and conquest but also of the promising connection between that past and future acquisitions. The intertwined notions of imperialism and progress that the fair projected captured the spirit of the twentieth century as "The American Century," at its very moment of inception. . . .

Beals and her husband Alfred traveled to St. Louis from Albany, New York, where Jessie had been working as the "first official woman" staff photographer for the *Buffalo Courier*, with Alfred as her darkroom assistant. Beals regularly photographed suicides, murder trials, and fires for the paper when she could. When times were slow, she showed up where work crews met, or lingered at factory doors, or rode door-to-door on her bicycle, balancing twenty- to thirty-odd pounds of camera equipment and soliciting the chance to take portraits. Business was good. Her photographer's diary from the time is peppered with phrases such as "got a fine list of orders" and "Work has been booming–16 to 30 pictures taken daily. Poor Beals is kept busy developing and printing." When they left Albany on April 4, 1904, her departure was mourned in the Buffalo newspapers as the loss not simply of a newspaper photographer but of a *woman* newspaper photographer: "Buffalo lost one of its best professional women today when Mrs. Jessie Tarbox Beals, staff camera artist, departed on an early morning train for St. Louis." At the farewell party they hosted for her, . . . "the staffs of the two dailies Jessie worked for presented her with a parting gift—a gold enameled pin studied with pearls."[7] It was a gift particularly appropriate for the "woman" part of the equation, and it must have encouraged Beals about the viability of her plans to go to St. Louis as a "professional woman." . . .

"Lady" photographers had a larger official role at St. Louis . . . than at any other fair. . . . But what the presence of these [other] women meant in practice for Jessie Tarbox Beals was that when she arrived at St. Louis, at first all the doors were closed to her: "She had hoped her reputation in Buffalo would warrant an official press card. But officials at the exposition said that the Buffalo newspapers were regional and of no value to the national promotion of the fair. She applied to the St. Louis newspapers; they were fully staffed. She kept overhearing remarks that working on the crowded fairgrounds was too much for a woman to tackle."[8] This was the problem of tokenism. . . .

Beals solved this problem in a characteristic way. She transformed the fair officials' anxiety that a woman was of "no value to the national promotion of the fair" into evidence that the "nation" could be promoted by a women. First, she wrangled a "Pre-Exhibition Permit," which allowed her into the fair but limited her to making photographs "prior to the opening of the fair" and prevented her from selling any of the images or using them "in any other way except as ordinary illustrations . . . every negative made under the permit and not accepted as an illustration is to be destroyed."[9] The fair's officials were so eager to marshal all the images of the fair into the

Jessie Tarbox Beals taking pictures from a ladder at the St. Louis World's Fair, 1904, photographer unknown. The ladder is supported by her assistant, "Pumpkin." (Courtesy of the Schlesinger Library, Radcliffe Institute, Harvard University.)

grand educational (and commercial) scheme that Beals worked on pain of expulsion from the fairgrounds if she was found to violate these conditions.

If they were used to controlling the access of women photographers, the officials apparently didn't figure on Beals's next step: "Undaunted by the rules, Jessie roamed the fairgrounds as she saw fit, photographing what interested her. Most of the other photographers there concentrated on the sumptuous exhibits of the industrial nations; Jessie was drawn instead to the scenes of the daily lives of exotic, little-known peoples in their native habitats. She took pictures of the Igorots, the Bogobos, the Zulus, the Hottentots, the Eskimos, the Filipinos and other defenseless recipients of missionary barrels," writes Alland. Her multicultural pictures of domesticity read much like a precursor to [photographer Edward] Steichen's famous *Family of Man* exhibit.[10]

And then came some good luck. Regular hard work photographing the daily lives of

"exotic, little-known peoples" happened to put Beals at the scene when some "Patagonian Giants" of South America arrived at the "village" next door to the "Ainus of Japan." At first, she was the only photographer there. By the time the other photographers arrived, Beals had already made her interpretation of the event. As Alland reports, "An old Patagonian woman issued an edict that no black boxes were to be pointed at her people and she chased the camera men over a barbed wire fence. But Jessie had already made her images, and they were exclusives."[11]

What Beals had done was to show "Patagonian Giants" next to "pygmies," in a comparison by size that imaged the anthropometric premise of the fair—the belief that the essential information about where a group of people fell on the evolutionary ladder could be gleaned from their physical characteristics. Her pictures sold all over the country—providing the "national exposure" the Fair's officials craved—not only because they were positioned as "exclusive images" but [also] because they were images of

"*Pygmy and Patagonian Giant,*" *Jessie Tarbox Beals, photographer. (Courtesy of St. Louis Public Library.)*

an "exclusive" position that white Americans were constructing for themselves—as the physical golden mean and the evolutionary model.

Beals was rewarded for this work of making material the abstract racial premise of the anthropological "display." The next day's headlines trumpeted the news: "Woman Gets Permit to Take Pictures at the Fair." The story read, "The first permit to be issued to a woman authorizing the taking of photographs in the World's Fair Grounds has been given to Mrs. T. Beals. Mrs. Beals secured notice through her work in obtaining photographs of the double suicide of Mr. and Mrs. Pennell of Buffalo, who rode their automobile over a cliff into a quarry." The pygmy/Patagonian comparison showed the fair officials that Beals's eye was . . . good. . . . With it, Beals had become the "First Pictorial Journalist of Her Sex," even though she was not, as we have seen, the first woman licensed to take photographs in the "World's Fair Grounds."[12]

What really made Beals "first" . . . was that she had understood . . . that in St. Louis, juxtaposition was the clearest signifier of American size and strength. The St. Louis World's Fair was the largest international exposition ever yet presented. Its total exhibition space exceeded that of the Chicago Exposition of 1893

by more than one-third. The fair cost $15 million to produce, the same amount of money originally paid for the entire Louisiana Territory. The fair was so big that medical advisers warned "neurasthenic" patients to avoid the fair entirely, for fear of mental collapse, and "brain-fagged businessmen" and "men of affairs" were encouraged to spend "at least several weeks or months in order to avoid the almost certain breakdown that would result from a hurried visit."[13] It took a week merely to view the agricultural display. However, the real core . . . was the Department of Anthropology, . . . and the "exposition within an exposition," the U.S. government's Philippine Reservation. Other world's fairs, notably the one in Chicago, had featured anthropological divisions, but St. Louis's was by far the largest and the most central.

On the Anthropology Department's grounds and at the Philippine Reservation were displayed "specimens" of the peoples that American civilization had conquered and was now in the process of "educating," "disciplining," and "converting." The Philippine Reservation consisted of almost twelve hundred Filipinos living in villages on a 47-acre site that was deliberately called a "reservation" to make plain the parallel between the subjugation of the Native Americans and the domestication of the Philippines. The grounds were carefully laid out to represent "a sequential synopsis of the developments that have marked man's progress." In an essay entitled "The Trend of Human Progress," McGee explained that process as . . . "a trend of vital development from low toward the high, from dullness toward brightness, from idleness groveling toward intellectual uprightness. . . . It is a matter of common observation that the white man can do more and better than the yellow, the yellow man more and better than the red or black. . . . Classed in terms of blood, the peoples of the world may be grouped in several races; classed in terms of what they do rather than what they merely are, they are conveniently grouped in the four culture grades of savagery, barbarism, civilization, and enlightenment." McGee believed that at the turn of the century "perfected man is over-spreading the world." "Perfected man," in McGee's terms, meant "the two higher culture-grades—especially the Caucasian race, and (during recent decades) the budded enlightenment of Britain and full-blown enlightenment of America."[14]

To illustrate these "common observations," the Anthropology Department portrayed a "logical arrangement" of ethnological displays of "villages" of "non-white types" and "culture grades." Besides the twelve hundred Filipinos, these "types" included pygmies from the Congo, Japanese Ainu, Patagonian "giants," Kwakiutl Indians from Vancouver Island, and several groupings of Native Americans. Also on exhibit were the Apache leader Geronimo (under armed guard as a military prisoner), Chief Joseph of the Nez Percé, and Quanah Parker of the Comanche. The Indian School Building and the Philippine Reservation were carefully placed to make the instrumental relation between the two as plain as possible. Calling the Indian School building "designed not merely as a consummation, but as a prophecy," McGee explained the rationale behind its inclusion at the Fair: "now that other primitive peoples are passing under the beneficent influence and protection of the Stars and Stripes, it is needful to take stock of past progress as a guide to the future."[15] . . .

Beals played the woman's angle for all it was worth, which was considerable. She made many sets of "sympathetic" pictures of domestic life in the anthropology exhibits. Seen as "ethnological studies," they were eagerly bought by Harvard and Yale Universities and by natural history museums all over the country. Perhaps her most famous set of pictures was *Mother and Babe at the Exhibition;* but Beals made other sets of photographs as well, such as the *The Children of the Fair, Musical Instruments, Native Habitations, Strange Wedding Ceremonies, Head Dress, Dances of All Nations, Cooking Methods,* and *The Mutilation Practices.* In fact, Beals's work at St. Louis was taken as so good a model for ethnographic photography that in 1906 she was invited to exhibit some of it at a "women photographers" exhibition (the first ever in New England) at the Camera Club of Hartford, Connecticut, where confused critics singled out her work as "one of the best exhibits," crediting her with having "furnished several scenes in Japan (taken at the St. Louis World's Fair)."[16] . . .

As if all this were not recognition enough, Beal's photographs of the Philippine reservation were met with such consummate delight by the organizers of that exhibit that they brought them to the notice of Secretary of War William Howard Taft, previously governor-general of the Philippines. Much impressed, Taft offered Beals "a passport and a free round-trip to the islands . . . to bring back, as a contribution to science, pictorial records of the daily life of the little-known wild tribes."[17] Beals was elated, but unfortunately Alfred didn't want to go, quite possibly because he was aware that the fighting still continued in the Philippines.

Beals also exploited her angle of vision in a literal way, by choosing dramatic vantage points from which to photograph and allowing herself to be photographed and written about "as a woman" while in such stances. For instance, she climbed a twenty-foot ladder to photograph a parade. And just before the beginning of the International Balloon Race she climbed into one of the [balloon] baskets with her camera. One newspaper years later memorialized the event this way: "Just as one of the balloons was being set free, the huge crowd was thunderstruck to see a woman, a camera slung over her shoulder, grip the top of a basket and pull herself aboard. The balloon was off, and with it the intrepid woman photographer." Dr. David Francis, president of the Exposition, published the resulting panoramas of the fairgrounds, which Beals made from 900 feet aloft, in the official *Louisiana Purchase Exposition Bulletin.* Her bird's-eye view photographs were, he

"As the Lady Managers wanted to have them—Prime Christians," Jessie Tarbox Beals's satiric photograph of Filipinos (mis)representing their customary dress and lifeways, on the Philippine Reservation at the St. Louis World's Fair, 1904. (Courtesy of Missouri History Museum.)

wrote, "a view which I wish to remember."[18] This is perhaps not surprising, since, like the eye of the American eagle, they dominated what they surveyed.

But what exactly *was* the point of view of the "intrepid woman photographer"? The people in Beals's photographs were neither given derogatory names nor photographed as fetishes for the contemplation of nude bodily display. Her images are therefore less overtly racist than the productions of [other women's photographers such as] the Gerhard Sisters [Emme and Mamie]. Indeed, Beals made a photograph that explicitly mocked the sanctimonious (and highly publicized) efforts of the Board of Lady Managers to make the Igorots wear full sets of clothes rather than the loincloths that were their accustomed dress because it seemed to them that the male nudity was drawing

prurient looks, especially from "lady" visitors. In her hilarious but sharply pointed image, the Filipinos cooperate with Beals in performing a satiric pantomime of "'As the Lady Managers wanted to have them'—Prime Christians," which is how she captioned the photograph. Fully and awkwardly covered in heavy robes, coats, and wearing hats, but still barefoot, five Philippine Reservation inhabitants walk in a line, evidently performing one of their ceremonial dances the "Prime Christian" way.

Nor do Beals's images reproduce the sensational stereotypes of turn-of-the-century primitivism's imaginary [created by other women photographers at the fair] .... On the contrary, Beals felt that she had made "many new friends" among the "foreign" people she photographed and "would treasure their many parting gifts, particularly the pina fiber dress presented by the Filipino villagers and the exquisite bolt of Chinese silk given to her by Prince Pu Lun of China."[19] Given the American occupation of the Philippines, such "friendships" must have had a considerable component of fantasy.

Nonetheless, Beals seems to have been personally affected by the racial vision of the fair. The photographs she made are complexly complicit in keeping offstage any vision of the violence of the pacification of a people. While she was still at the fair, Beals made a collage of her photographs from the anthropological villages. The pictures are uniformly gracious and dignified domestic scenes, with their grass-rooted huts, their pastoral waterways, their smiling children, and their graceful young mothers. . . . [T]hey argue for the unharmed humanity of those they picture but without challenging the violent framework in which that humanity was concurrently differentiated, primitivized, and separated from the "higher" domestic forms of the "white race."

Thus, Beals's pictures extended sympathy, but they also fully eradicated any traces of the military surveillance that had accompanied the Filipinos to St. Louis. That is to say, first, they normalized the presence among the fair's Filipino delegation of several hundred members of the Philippine constabulary, a paramilitary force of Philippine collaborators set in place by the American occupation; one of them, photographed with an "innocent eye" by Beals, was included in the upper right-hand corner of her collage. Second, they remained oblivious to the fact that the Philippine villages were surrounded by high board fences and their inhabitants monitored by curfews, in a direct quotation of the so-called "relocation camps" in which thousands of their countrymen were being interned back in the Philippines at that very moment. And third, they avoided any view of the outer perimeter of the Philippine "reservation" itself, which was designed as a model of the old Spanish defense of the city of Manila. When walking through it to the ethnic villages, every visitor– and every Filipino inhabitant–re-created the heroic story of [Commodore George] Dewey's conquest and penetration of the city [in 1898] to gain access to the nation of "primitives" that supposedly lay beyond.[20] Even though during the whole time the fair was open in

St. Louis, Filipino insurgents were continuing to battle the United States occupation, and the United States was continuing to execute Filipino patriots as "outlaws," there is no sign of this activity in Beals's images. Her collage of domestic life in the Anthropological Department so completely illustrates the present success and bright future of the American rule of peace that it is no wonder that Taft himself, the author of the concept of "benevolent assimilation," longed to send her to the Philippines. . . .

Beals photographed the virtual geography of the fair by moving freely between the obviously "fake" Manila and the "obviously" real St. Louis, but it is difficult to distinguish the two in her photographs. This was, of course, the desired effect. The fact that Harvard and Yale Universities bought Beals's exposition images as ethnographic studies is one result of this confusion. . . . But the most significant reality effect of this simulacrum was that in construing the Philippine present as coterminous with the Southern past, the fair was portraying that past as the progressive and inevitable future of the American empire. Conversely, it was erasing actual Philippine history in order to rescript it as naturally consonant with the context of the American South.

In an essay entitled "The Sign as a Site of Class Struggle," Jo Spence identifies the ideological work of photographs as the production of an "imaginary coherence," one in which "images from . . . photography . . . are immediate yet appear to be retrospective," and in which "their presence confirms the absence of what appears to have been previously present."[21] This elegant formulation exactly describes what Beals's photographs accomplished. Their normalization of [the ethnic villages of the] St. Louis [Fair] as the Philippine future confirms the influence of the Southern past as constitutive of the Philippine's immediate reality. Never mind that it was a coherence that was patently corrupt; the conjuncture was made potent by Jim Crow—and rendered invisible by Jessie Beals.

However, the experience of working at the fair, with its emphasis on racial "diversity" and racial "progress," not only translated into photographs that configured the way that viewers were to see the coming American Century; it also prophesied a new Beals. After her work in St. Louis, Beals evolved into an even more ambitious photographer and an even less conventional woman. Beals was aware of its importance to herself. Some years after returning from St. Louis, Beals made another photographic collage, this time a narrative of her own life. The two panels document changes in a small-town girl's experience as she discovers photography. The world in the pictures steadily expands. In them, Beals and her camera conquer obstacles, travel, go to parties, and meet interesting and famous people. There are more photographs of Beals at the fair than at any other period of her life. In the photographs of St. Louis we see Beals in the balloon, Beals on the twenty-foot ladder, Beals working at the fair with her camera assistant named "Pumpkin," and Beals's hard-won press pass and photo ID card. Functioning as the fulcrum of Beals's autobiography, the fair separates her own experience into a "before," and "after." The collage demonstrates that as a sentimental indoctrination, the fair had apparently fulfilled an inner, as well as an ideological mission.

Indeed, life "before" was one thing, but life "after" was something else again. For a long time after St. Louis, nothing measured up for Jessie to the intensity of the nine months she had spent photographing the fair. Perhaps it was that Alfred Beals had dragged his feet about the trip to the Philippines and prevented her accepting the assignment from Taft. Perhaps it was that Jessie Beals was nearing forty and after many years of marriage she and Alfred still had no children. Her only infant, a girl born in 1901, had died only a few hours after birth. Perhaps it was simply that Beals had grown weary of the concept of "woman photographer" that juxtaposed her solely to Alfred or to other photographing women, when she had seemed in St. Louis to have the whole world as her counterpart.

NOTES

1. Alexander Alland, Sr., *Jessie Tarbox Beals: First Woman News Photographer* (New York: Camera/Graphic Press, 1978), 22. Other published sources of information on Beals include Jane Cutler, *Song of the Molimo* (New York: Farrar Straus Giroux, 1998).

2. Mrs. Jefferson Davis is quoted in Walter Benn Michaels, "Anti-Imperial Americanism," in *Cultures of U.S. Imperialism,* ed. Amy Kaplan and Donald Pease (Durham, N.C.: Duke University Press, 1993), 387 n. 1.

3. Robert W. Rydell, *All the World's a Fair: Visions of American Empire at American International Expositions, 1876–1916* (Chicago: University of Chicago Press, 1987), 161.

4. W. J. McGee, "Trend of Human Progress," quoted in Rydell, *All the World's a Fair,* 161.

5. W. J. McGee, "National Growth and National Character," quoted in ibid., 161.

6. W. J. McGee, quoted in ibid., 167.

7. Alland, *Beals,* 26, 40-41.

8. Ibid., 43.

9. Ibid.

10. Ibid. [In 1955 Steichen, as the director of photography at the Museum of Modern Art in New York, organized a monumental show of 503 photographs taken by 273 artists from 68 nations. The exhibit aimed to show life experiences and emotions shared across cultures. It went on a worldwide tour and became a best-selling book.]

11. Ibid.

12. Ibid., 43, 45.

13. Rydell, *All the World's a Fair,* 157.

14. McGee quoted in Ibid., 160, 161.

15. Ibid., 167.

16. Camera Club of Hartford, Conn., April 1906, quoted in Alland, *Beals,* 62.

17. Ibid., 52.

18. *Philadelphia Public Ledger,* January 26, 1921, and David Francis, both quoted in Alland, *Beals,* 48.

19. Ibid.

20. Beverly K. Grindstaff, "Creating Identity: Exhibiting the Philippines at the 1904 Louisiana Purchase Exhibition," in Donald Preziosi and Claire J. Farago, eds., *Grasping the World: The Idea of the Museum* (Aldershot, UK: Ashgate, 2003), 298–320.

21. Jo Spence, "The Sign as a Site of Class Struggle," in *Photography/Politics: Two,* ed. Patricia Holland, Jo Spence, and S. Watney (London: Commedia, 1986), 176.

LEILA J. RUPP
Sexuality and Politics in the Early Twentieth-Century International Women's Movement

We often imagine that in U.S. history "the sexual revolution" took place in the 1960s. Historians, however, perceive what they sometimes call a first sexual revolution, occurring early in the twentieth century (although this ignores changing ideas about sexual expression and gender roles in the 1700s and 1800s*). Two broad shifts were at work in mainstream American culture after the turn of the twentieth century, most notably in the 1920s. The first concerned homosociality, or the extent to which persons of one perceived sex spend most of their time with members of the same sex. For decades prior to 1920, women and men were expected largely to occupy different social realms. Around the period of the "roaring twenties," some Europeans and Americans began to pursue and celebrate heterosocial patterns of engagement, both in informal social activities and the organizations they joined. At the same time, heterosexual experimentation prior to and outside of marriage became more acceptable in some circles. One consequence of these shifts was that same-sex emotional and physical intimacy became increasingly stigmatized and labeled (pejoratively) as homosexuality.

Leila J. Rupp's essay tells us about the political alliances forged across national borders by women in Europe and the Americas, with the sexual revolution of the early twentieth century as a backdrop. These activists could afford to travel overseas and to devote themselves full-time to volunteer or paid work on the behalf of organizations such as the International Council of Women. They were often fluent in several languages. Some lived openly as same-sex couples. Others gloried in their heterosexual marriages or did not do much to hide their many affairs with men. Rupp reads personal correspondence and organizational records to find out how much sexual (or "affectional," as in where you place your most important affections) life choices factored in the political differences among the activists—such as over the issue of woman-only gatherings. She finds that national, class, and generational differences were just as important.

How do you think her insights about sexuality and politics might apply to activists today? Rupp's study focuses on transnational connections among women in the West. How might issues relating to sexual politics be similar or different if we examined transnational women's activism today between the global North and global South?

*For arguments about major shifts prior to 1830, see Richard Godbeer, *Sexual Revolution in Early America* (Baltimore: Johns Hopkins University Press, 2002); and Clare A. Lyons, *Sex Among the Rabble: An Intimate History of Gender and Power in the Age of Revolution, Philadelphia, 1730-1830* (Chapel Hill: University of North Carolina Press, 2006).

Excerpted from "Sexuality and Politics in the Early Twentieth Century: The Case of the International Women's Movement," by Leila J. Rupp, in *Feminist Studies* 23, no. 3 (Fall 1997): 577–605. Reprinted by permission of the author and publisher. Notes have been renumbered and edited.

In her autobiography, Lena Madesin Phillips, U.S. founder of the International Federation of Business and Professional Women, who lived for thirty-three years with a woman to whom she "lost her heart," reported that an Austrian colleague had once asked her about the large number of unmarried women in the organization. "You women seem quite content to have meetings without men present; to be happy though unmarried. . . . American women told us they had a splendid banquet where women had a fine meal, some speeches, and no men," the Austrian woman remarked with evident astonishment. Within the same international women's movement circles, Brazilian International Alliance of Women member Bertha Lutz expressed her disgust at the lobbying tactics of Inter-American Commission of Women head Doris Stevens, an American "emancipated woman" who worked for an international equal rights treaty by seeking the support of male government representatives to the Pan American Union. Lutz called Stevens a "nymphomaniac" and accused her of "paying the mexican delegates in kisses . . . [and] luring the haitians with a french secretary she has."[1]

These contrasting observations—about a surprisingly happy female world and a disturbingly (hetero)sexual one—alert us to some of the tensions that simmered beneath the seemingly placid surface of early-twentieth-century international women's organizations. In the industrialized societies of the Euroamerican arena, the first decades of the century marked a critical transition, sometimes graced with the label of "sexual revolution," from a world of privatized to a world of more public and commercialized sexuality. As the barriers between women's and men's public worlds began to break down in the decades on either side of 1900 and young women in Chicago and Harlem, London, and Copenhagen, laid assertive new claims to their own sexuality, increasingly rigid definitions of heterosexuality and homosexuality cast more and more suspicion on a whole range of women's relationships and forms of organizing.[2] Women might step over the line of respectable heterosexuality by cavorting with men outside of marriage, but women without men—whether "spinsters" or women in same-sex couples—came more frequently to earn the label "deviant." And, as I argue here, these moves had consequences for the politics of women's single-sex organizing.

Sexual respectability was not a new concern in the women's movement of the early twentieth century—one has only to think of the scandals that surrounded Mary Wollstonecraft or Victoria Woodhull [for Woodhull, see pp. 258–259]. But heightened attention to the deviant lesbian subject did transform the context in which women gathered in single-sex organizations. Before the categorization of the "female invert" or "lesbian" at the end of the nineteenth century, women in the women's movement could more easily form intense and passionate relationships as "romantic friends" or choose to live out their lives as single women without a diagnosis of abnormality.[3] Scholarship has long emphasized the importance of supportive relationships among women for the strength of the women's movement.[4] Although recent work has opened our eyes to the ease with which romantic friends in the nineteenth century and earlier could transgress what the counsel for the defense in a famous [Scottish] case called "ordinary female friendship," there is no question that coupled women had to trod ever more carefully as time wore on.[5]

The organizations making up the international women's movement provide a particularly interesting case study of such tensions, because these bodies came to life as shifts in the conceptualization of women's relationships proceeded. They also brought together women from a variety of cultures, if primarily middle-and upper-class women of European origin from the countries of Western Europe and North America. As we shall see, not only affectional but generational, class, and national differences—and their complex interplay in the lives of women—shaped responses to the practice of single-sex organizing.

My research concentrates on the three major transnational women's groups—the International Council of Women, the International Alliance of Women, and the Women's International League for Peace and Freedom—and the more narrowly focused bodies with which they interacted on a regular basis in the years between the emergence of international organizing in the 1880s and the conclusion of the Second World War, which marked the end of the first wave of the international women's movement (and the lull before the swell of the second). In this period all three organizations remained heavily elite and Euroamerican in composition and leadership. Not only did Europe and what have been called the "neo-Europes" contribute

Farewell banquet, International Council of Women, Quinquennial Congress at the Mayflower Hotel, May 13, 1925.
Reproduced from the Report on the Quinquennial Meeting, *Washington, D.C., 1925. (Image courtesy of Leila Rupp.)*

all but one of the national sections until 1923 but women from the United States, Great Britain, and Western and Northern Europe also served as the founders and leaders. This pattern perpetuated itself through the choice of official languages—English, French, and German—and the location of congresses primarily in Europe, with a few excursions to North America. Although women from Latin America, the Middle East, Asia, and Africa increasingly found their voices within the international organizations after the First World War undermined European dominance of the world system, their relative silence in the recorded debate about sexuality is testimony to their marginality in the organizational friendship circles.[6]

The International Council of Women (ICW), the most vaguely defined group, came together in 1888 and welcomed all women's organizations with whatever purposes, bringing in a huge number of members but forestalling commitment to controversial goals. The International Woman Suffrage Alliance (IWSA), later known as the International Alliance of Women (IAW), split off from the ICW in 1904 in order to take a position in favor of suffrage and remained a strongly feminist-identified

body, even after the increasing extension of the vote to women in the years after the First World War undermined the group's original rationale. The Women's International League for Peace and Freedom (WILPF), founded in 1915 by IWSA members who insisted on meeting despite wartime hostilities, consistently took quite radical positions on a range of issues.[7] These three groups, in conjunction with a wide array of bodies organized on a regional basis, or comprised of particular constituencies of women, or devoted to single issues, formed coalitions in the years between the wars to coordinate international collective action, especially lobbying at the League of Nations.

The transnational women's groups focused on issues of women's rights, peace, and women's work, paying minimal attention to questions of sexuality, with the exception of what they called "the traffic in women." The dialogue about sexuality and politics, then, must be ferreted out of the sources, read from assumptions and associations. As I explored discussions of difference between women and men, arguments about the appropriateness of single-sex organizing, and correspondence about personal relationships, I began to perceive tensions within the international organizations and patterns linking women's personal lives and cultural contexts to their political choices.

SAME-SEX LOVE, HOMOSOCIALITY, AND SEPARATISM

Within the international women's organizations, some women coupled with women in what seem to have been "lesbian" relationships or as "romantic friends," sometimes in relationships in which one woman served as a kind of caretaker for the other. Some women never formed intimate relationships with either women or men. None of these women can be easily categorized, but in one way or another all made their lives with other women.

We have no direct evidence that any of the women involved in the international women's movement identified as lesbians, but the concept of lesbianism was not unknown in their intellectual world. As early as 1904, in a speech to the Scientific Humanitarian Committee, the pioneering German homosexual rights group, Anna Ruhling associated lesbians ("Uranian women" in the terminology of the time) with the international women's movement, asserting that

> the homosexual woman is particularly capable of playing a leading role in the international women's rights movement for equality. And indeed, from the beginning of the women's movement until the present day, a significant number of homosexual women assumed the leadership in the numerous struggles and, through their energy, awakened the naturally indifferent and submissive average women to an awareness of their human dignity and rights.[8]

. . . That women in the international women's movement had some familiarity with the discourse of "homosexuality" as it emerged in the late nineteenth century is clear. . . . Discussion within international women's movement circles of "fairies," use of the terms "queer" and "perverse from a sexual point of view," [and] references to "Manly-Looking" women and women who "went about together at the Hague, hair cropped short and rather mannish in dress," . . . suggest that at least the European women had some familiarity with the work of the sexologists [such as Havelock Ellis].[9]

Despite such derogatory usages, women within the movement accepted women's couple relationships, conceptualizing them as romantic friendships or "Boston marriages" rather than lesbian love affairs. Anita Augspurg and Lida Gustava Heymann formed one such couple within the circle of internationally organized women. Augspurg, leading member of the radical wing of the German women's movement and the country's first woman lawyer, met Heymann, who had freed herself from the life of a daughter of a rich Hamburg merchant to become a social worker and trade union organizer, at an 1896 international women's conference in Berlin. In their memoirs, Heymann described her first vision of the woman she came to live with for over forty years. Arrested by Augspurg's powerful voice, she saw her at the lectern, dressed in a brown velvet dress. "Already graying short hair framed a high forehead, under which two clear-sighted eyes sparkled. A sharp profile contrasted markedly but not unharmoniously with a delightful small mouth, chin, and small ears."[10] Obviously it was a momentous meeting, and the physical description smacks of a "love at first sight" genre.

Although early on the two women decided not to live together, they happily broke that promise. "Every year brought us closer," Heymann wrote, "deepened our friendship, let us know that not only in questions of Weltanschauung [worldview] . . . but also in all the events of daily life . . . we stood in exquisite harmony." They moved to the country where they launched a series of ambitious, and successful, agricultural enterprises, a quite unusual undertaking for two women. As a result, they reported that their Upper Bavarian peasant neighbors viewed them with some suspicion. In the section of their memoirs entitled "Private Life," Heymann recounted that "it excited the envy and anger of the farmers that two 'vagabonds in petticoats' were successful, creative, and happy to organize their lives according to their own desires and inclinations." One day a cattle dealer came to call with proposals of marriage for both women, explaining that the farm was splendid and lacked only a man. "It took all our effort to remain serious and make clear to the man the hopelessness of his desire. As he left, we shook with laughter," Heymann commented.[11]

As such descriptions make clear, Heymann and Augspurg presented themselves in public, in their daily lives, and unselfconsciously as a couple, and that is certainly how they were treated within the international women's movement. Correspondents regularly sent messages to and received them from both women. Heymann sent "Heartfelt greetings from us both" to Rosika Schwimmer in 1919. . . . Augspurg and Heymann stayed in double rooms when they attended congresses, entertained movement friends at their home, and described a happy family life: "I had a very good journey home and found Anita and our dog in good health," Heymann wrote [to the French WILPF leader] on her return from a trip to Paris. When Heymann planned to travel to Geneva for a meeting in 1930, a WILPF staff member reported that "she is coming without Dr. Augspurg which is scarcely believable!"[12]

Heymann and Augspurg were enjoying a Mediterranean vacation in March of 1933 when Hitler came to power in Germany. As pacifists and feminists they had made themselves enemies of the Nazis, so they never returned to the land of their birth. Although in this way they stayed out of the Nazis' clutches, the regime seized all their property, including their books and personal papers, prompting WILPF friends to try to help them. Swiss WILPF cochair Clara Ragaz, hoping to arrange hospitality at headquarters in Geneva, commented about Augspurg, who suffered from heart disease, that "it is a very hard time for her friend—and of course for herself." When Heymann died in June of 1943, American Emily Greene Balch worked to raise money to support Heymann's "life-long friend and co-worker . . . , for whom she had cared so devotedly." But as it turned out, Augspurg did not survive long. "Did you notice that Lida Gustava Heymann and Dr. Anita Augspurg died within a few short weeks of each other?" Rosika Schwimmer asked a friend.[13]

Augspurg and Heymann made the acquaintance of another well-known couple, Hull House founder and WILPF president Jane Addams and Mary Rozet Smith, in the course of their work in the international women's movement. The German women enjoyed the hospitality of Addams and Smith when they came to the United States for the WILPF congress in 1924. . . . Like the German couple, Addams and Smith sent and received messages for one another, made arrangements for double-bedded rooms when they traveled, and took care of each other, although that responsibility fell more heavily on [the younger] Smith. . . .[14]

. . . Such relationships between older and younger, or more and less powerful, women [like Smith's devoted service to her more prominent partner] seemed to obscure the bond of love from the vision of outsiders. The relationship between Anna Howard Shaw, American minister, charismatic orator, and international leader, and Lucy Anthony, a niece of . . . Susan B. Anthony, falls into this category. Shaw had a reputation within suffrage circles for her "strong and passionate attachments to other women," some of which "have broken up in some such tempestuous fashion." Shaw described her "abiding love for home and home life" at her country house, Moylan, which she shared with Anthony. When Shaw fell and broke her foot and Anthony, at the same time, fractured her elbow, Shaw ruefully labeled them "rather a broken up couple." Yet Aletta Jacobs [Dutch IWSA leader and WILPF founder] saw Anthony as Shaw's "secretary, friend, and housekeeper," since Shaw paid her a salary. Anthony herself called Shaw, after her death, "my Precious Love," "the joy of my life."[15]

The same confusion greeted the relationship of International Woman Suffrage Alliance president Carrie Chapman Catt and New York suffrage leader Mary Garrett Hay. Catt's reserve and distaste for emotional display—one intimate friend likened her to "cold boiled halibut"—may have obscured the reality of her relationships, or the fact that Catt married twice may have led observers—as it has scholars—to undervalue her ties to women.[16] But Catt did not even live full time with her husband when he was alive, and when he died she and Hay set up housekeeping together. . . . Apparently rather authoritarian, Hay was not popular in international circles. Shaw, who detested her, ... did "not think there is any hope of breaking that affair off." . . . [W]hen Catt died in 1947, she was buried, at her request, not with either of her two husbands but next to her "unforgettable friend and comrade" Hay.[17]

More ambivalent, but following a similar pattern, was the relationship of Emily Greene Balch, Wellesley professor, WILPF leader, and winner of the Nobel Peace Prize, and her childhood friend Helen Cheever. Balch, like Catt, was a reserved woman; she described her Yankee background as one that valued "restraint not only of expression of emotion but of emotion itself." Cheever was a wealthy woman who financially supported Balch and wanted to live with her on a permanent basis. But Balch, who admitted that she both loved and was irritated by Cheever, balked. Perhaps, she wrote her sister, it was a result of Cheever's "giving me more love than I can quite digest." Yet when Balch was in Geneva as international secretary of WILPF, her coworkers eagerly anticipated, on Balch's behalf, a visit from Cheever. "I think she is homesick and it would be very good if her friend from America came soon to keep her company and also attend a bit to her physical health," Heymann confided to Jane Addams. Three years later Cheever wanted to resign her offices in the U.S. section of WILPF in order to go to Geneva where "my usefulness to the W.I.L. will be confined to being with Miss Balch." . . . [In the end] Balch resisted becoming part of a female couple and identified [instead] as an unmarried woman. . . . Unmarried women [found it] strange, [she later explained to Jane Addams, that] . . . "everything that is not concerned with the play of desire between men and women [is seen] as without adventure."[18]

The public defensiveness of single women may have originated in the awakened suspicion that women living without men might have perverse desires or it might simply have been provoked by popular assumptions that such women had no intimate ties. In a 1931 German anthology on the modern single career woman, Elisabeth Busse explained that such women were not "amazonian," "inverts," or "homosexuals," although "they lived in women's unions." So it is not surprising that ICW secretary Alice Salomon, a German Jewish pioneer in the world of social work who never married, apologized in her autobiography that "this book may sometimes seem as much a book about women as though I had lived in a harem." Actually, she assured her readers, "I always had men and women, old and young, rich and poor, and sometimes whole families as my friends." But, in fact, Salomon made her life in the female world of social reform and the women's movement. She apparently felt compelled to discuss why she never married, explaining that her work . . . "made me reluctant to form a union which could not combine love with common interests and convictions."[19]

In the ICW *Bulletin* of October 1932, Salomon published a defense of unmarried women, the first generation of independent women who pursued careers. She recognized that the discipline of psychology had changed attitudes toward single women—that they were reputed to be warped by celibacy—but quoted a woman of "international fame" to the effect that "they are alive, active, and they fully participate in present-day life by means of a thousand interests." Similarly, Lena Madesin Phillips recognized: "To live an old maid was . . . considered something to be greatly deplored"; but she insisted that she had "no complaints, no regrets, no fears" about her own unmarried, but woman-coupled life. Helen Archdale, a British equal rights advocate active in the international arena, reacted testily to a paean to marriage penned [by a friend] . . . . "What you say about the beneficial effects of marriage on one's life rather puzzles me. Why should 'spinsterhood' be gray?" Archdale shared a London flat and country home with Lady Margaret Rhondda, another international activist, in the 1920s, after which they "personally drifted very far apart."[20] Such defensiveness and defiance about living apart from men reflects the power of the intensified vision of married life as the only healthy alternative for women.

In the first decades of the twentieth century, then, overlapping frames of lesbianism, romantic friendship, devoted service, and singleness existed for women's choices in their personal lives. Women-only organizations offered an appealing haven for those who made their lives with other women, whatever the nature of their ties. But in a context in which homosociality often cast a pall of deviance, the desire to work apart from men grew more complex.

Almost all participants in the major international women's organizations accepted—or did not raise public objections to—an ideology of fundamental difference between women and men. The notion of difference underlay . . . "maternalist politics"—the construction of public positions on the foundation of women's biological and social roles as mothers.[21] But among women not involved in intimate relationships with men, belief in female values—read superior values—also led in a different direction: to the regular expression of anti-male sentiments in both private and public life. Heymann and Augspurg tried as far as possible to hire only women to manage their farm, and Heymann contrasted their satisfaction with their women employees to their displeasure with a male manager: "Vanity, thy name is man!" she proclaimed. "The customary judgment maintains, of course, that the female sex is the one enslaved by vanity, but this customary assertion is only a diversion and contradicts the law of nature among humans and animals."[22]

Similarly, Anna Howard Shaw had little use for men in her private life. When Lucy Anthony's broken arm failed to heal properly, Shaw announced that if a woman physician had treated Anthony everything would have been all right. During the First World War, Shaw complained about "male experts" wasting "millions of dollars on smoke and drink" while advising housewives to tighten their belts. "Men, I am convinced, never grow up and of all the animal creation are the least capable of reason."[23]

Such views spilled over into work in the international women's movement, merging especially with the common association of men with war and women with peace. The outbreak of the First World War unleashed a veritable barrage of anti-male proclamations. Shaw found men's "war madness and barbarism" "unthinkable" and claimed, despite her already low opinion of men, that "I have not half the respect for man's judgment or common sense that I used to have, that they are such fools as to go out and kill and be killed without knowing why." Heymann condemned men's "lies and hatred and violence" at the WILPF congress in 1919, proclaiming that the war would "never have come to pass had we women, the mothers of the world, been given the opportunity of helping to govern the people and join in the social life of nations." At the 1934 WILPF congress, Augspurg denounced the "world of men" as "built up on profit and power, on gaining material wealth and oppressing other people." Women "would be able to build a new world which would produce enough for all." According to Carrie Chapman Catt, "All wars are men's wars. Peace has been made by women but war never."[24]

Advocacy of separatist organizing logically flowed from such assumptions about women's moral superiority and potential efficacy in creating a peaceful world. It is not that women who built lives apart from men never associated or worked with them—both Heymann and Addams, for example, participated in political parties—but that they seemed particularly to value the women's world of the women's movement. Yet few women in the international women's movement explicitly defended the practice

of separatism. Emily Greene Balch seemed to prefer work with women but to feel that WILPF had to consider admitting men. In the first year after the [1915] Hague congress, she wrote that "my interest and belief in our woman's organization is as strong as ever." WILPF debated its commitment to separatism in the early 1920s but decided to remain a woman-only organization on the international level, in the process putting out a pamphlet that explained the reasons for keeping out men, one of the only public documents to defend the practice of separatism. . . .[25]

Given the persistence of all-female groups, the lack of vigorous defense of the principle of separatism is curious. Yet such silence speaks. It is possible that the need never occurred to those long committed to organizing in woman-only groups. But because the question of admitting men did arise, perhaps the silence was a sign of uneasiness over the old-fashioned associations of single-sex organizing in an increasingly heterosocial world. That separatist inclinations remained strong is clear from the apology of Eva Fichet, member of the mixed-gender Tunis section of WILPF, who planned to bring her member husband to the 1934 international congress. Noting that "his presence will offend some of our collaborators," she promised that "he will only make an appearance at public meetings, if there are any." Still, the comments of British suffragist and WILPF member Catherine E. Marshall, who never married, stand out in the records of the international women's movement: "It is always a pleasure to meet Women fellow workers. . . . I do like women best! Who was it said: The more I see of men the better I think of women!"[26] Such sentiments expressed the conviction that women had more in common with one another than with men and underlay the inclination to make both a personal and work life with other women.

HETEROSEXUALITY AND WORK WITH MEN

Some women within the international women's movement lived traditional married lives, while others engaged in more unconventional forms of heterosexual relationships. The model of the woman leader married to a supportive husband received a great deal of praise, but unorthodox heterosexuality crossed the line of respectability in a way that women's same-sex relationships did not and as a result met with disapproval. This difference probably reflects the generational divide that separated the predominantly older women of the international women's movement from younger cohorts more blasé about heterosexual expressiveness and more attuned to the sexual possibilities between women.

Lady and Lord Aberdeen, Scottish aristocrats, were without doubt the most lauded couple in international women's movement circles. The ICW regularly held them up as an exemplar of a couple committed to the same work, even though Lord Aberdeen in fact played no role in the organization. . . . Lady Aberdeen's devoted friend Alice Salomon described the Aberdeen marriage as modern and ideal and insisted that the ICW was as much a matter of concern to Lord Aberdeen as to Lady Aberdeen. The ICW president herself appreciated her husband's "never wavering support and . . . belief in the I.C.W." that had made possible everything she had accomplished. Emma Ender, the president of the German section of the ICW, responded that she knew from her own experience "what it means, to live at the side of a man who totally understands and supports the life work that we have taken on." Even after Lord Aberdeen's death, Lady Aberdeen referred to "the inestimable blessing of husbands who wish us to enter into all the fullness of life in service and responsibility."[27]

Aletta Jacobs, the first woman physician in the Netherlands and an international leader, and her husband, Carel Victor Gerritsen, also attracted favorable attention as a model couple within the international women's movement. Jacobs entered into [the] marriage, despite her perception of the institution's injustice, in deference to her husband's political career and their mutual desire to have a child. She described Gerritsen as "a feminist from the start," and when they married she kept her own name and they maintained separate quarters within the house they shared. Gerritsen actually took up Jacobs's cause by not only supporting her but by also speaking himself in favor of women's suffrage.[28] . . .

[Some] married women leaders [spoke] out on behalf of cooperation across the lines of gender. In her 1899 presidential address, Lady Aberdeen referred to separate women's organizations as a "temporary expedient to meet a temporary need" and hoped that they would not be allowed "to crystallise into a permanent

element in social life." Her successor as [ICW] president, American May Wright Sewall, also a married woman, agreed: "the Council idea does not stand for the separation of women from men, but rather for the reunion of women with men in the consideration of great general principles and large public interests." In a 1976 interview, Margery Corbett Ashby [president of the IWSA/IAW from 1923 to 1946] explained that the goal of women's organizations was to eliminate the need for women's organizations, although she admitted that it could be difficult for devoted members to accept this.[29]

. . . [Tension arose in the case of] women perceived as too involved—or in improper relationships-with men attracted harsh criticism. Martina Kramers, who maintained a long-term but unconventional liaison with a man, faced the censure of Carrie Chapman Catt in 1913. Bobbie, whom Kramers called her "left-handed husband," was a socialist and married man whose wife refused to divorce him. As president of the IWSA, Catt wrote to Kramers to recommend that she resign as editor of the organization's journal, *Jus Suffragii*, because her "moral transgressions" had provoked "horror and repugnance" among U.S. IWSA members. Kramers reacted with incredulity and defiance, refusing to give up either her man or her work and insisting to Catt that she was not a "propagandist of free love." She also implicitly equated the unconventionality but acceptability of her relationship with same-sex sexuality by comparing her situation to "the cases of Anita Augspurg [and] Kathe Schirmacher . . . accused by many gossipers of homosexual intercourse." . . . But to no avail. Catt managed, as Kramers put it, "to throw me out of the whole movement" by moving the office of *Jus Suffragii* to London and appointing a new editor. . . .[30]

[Controversy also swirled around Doris Stevens's work at] the Inter-American Commission of Women, as seen [in this essay's opening paragraph]. Stevens struck Bertha Lutz, a single woman who called herself Catt's "daughter," . . . as a "sex-mad psychopath" and a "mentally deranged woman." In fact, Stevens did engage in heterosexual activities outside of marriage, and in her work for the Inter-American Commission of Women she pursued flirtatious relationships with several Latin American diplomats. Far from [being] ashamed of such interactions, she remarked that women and men active in politics together were likely to find that the "deep personal bond takes the form of heterosexual love." . . . [But heterosexually active women like Stevens drew from some female comrades] strong criticism of [not only their allegedly] disreputable behavior but also [their] political [alliances] with men.[31] . . .

I do not mean to imply that the lines on the question of separatism ran strictly in accordance with sexuality or that no other factors shaped the political practices of separatist organizing. As the evidence presented here makes clear, women within the international women's movement in the first half of the twentieth century formed a variety of relationships, with both women and men, and cannot easily be categorized as "homosexual" and "heterosexual" in any case. There were married women such as Carrie Chapman Catt who lived with and loved women, and single women such as Alice Salomon who lavished devoted admiration on Lord and Lady Aberdeen. Coupled women's relationships might be characterized as lesbian partnerships, romantic friendships, loving caretaking, or some combination. In fact, given the variety of bonds, we might wonder whether internationally organized women managed to cross the boundaries of sexuality more easily than those of class, religion, and nationality.[32] Certainly the conflicts over sexuality within the movement tended to pit "respectable" against unconventional behavior rather than same-sex against heterosexual relationships.

And even if we could divide women into neat categories, the association would not be perfect. Rosika Schwimmer, who was married briefly in her youth but lived most of her life in close association with women, grew disgusted with separatist organizing in the 1930s. Mildred Scott Olmstead, a U.S. WILPF leader who maintained an intimate relationship with a woman throughout her married life, proposed in 1934 that the international organization admit men.[33] And the married women leaders and heterosexual renegades all continued to commit themselves to all-female groups, whatever their ideas about the proper way to organize.

Furthermore, affectional choices alone did not fashion the politics of separatism. National and generational differences, which helped to construct interpretations of sexuality, are particularly striking. European women seemed both more open to sexual expression and less interested in single-sex organizing than their Anglo-American colleagues. . . . [European women tended to associate separatism, like sexual prudery,] with the "New World." Danish women responded to the announcement of the Woman's Peace Party in the United States and a call for the formation of similar groups in other countries by asserting that "we preferred to work together, men and women, in the same organisation." At the 1915 Hague congress, Dutch women called for the concentration of all forces, female and male, working for peace. They noted that "a special women's movement is not necessary and therefore undesired. The force of a movement where two sexes cooperate will come to better results than an organisation of one sex only." Women trade unionists from Germany and Austria refused to send representatives to the second congress of the International Federation of Working Women in 1921, because they were "opposed to taking part in a separate women's trade union organisation" in the American fashion. . . .[34]

Similarly, women struggling side by side with men of their class or national group for justice or independence had reason to look critically at separatist organizing. . . . In 1935, Margery Corbett Ashby reported that the enormous difficulties facing the nationalist struggle in Egypt "bring the men and women nearer together" and found the leading Egyptian nationalist movement, the Wafd, "quite progressive as regards women's position." A Syrian woman, speaking at the Istanbul congress of the IAW in the same year, asserted her belief in the necessity of working shoulder to shoulder with men in her country for prosperity and freedom. "The economic and political situation of my country is so desperate that it is extremely difficult for us women to give our wholehearted energies to the cause of feminism alone."[35]

Generational differences on the question of separatism are also striking. Young women experiencing firsthand the breakdown between female and male social spheres in the twentieth-century world challenged women-only groups more readily than their older colleagues who clung to separatist organizing. . . . In 1931, Canadian Dorothy Heneker pointed out that young European women thought that women should work with men, and the IAW Youth Committee reported in 1938 that the general feeling favored a mixed organization of young women and men.[36] Generational, like national, differences on the question of separatism grew from distinctive patterns of homosocial versus heterosocial interaction, and so resistance to all-female groups came from both traditional and progressive sources.

The case of the international women's movement in this period illuminates the paradoxes of a women's world in an era undergoing profound change in the relations between the sexes. Internationally organized women, or at least some of them, knew about lesbianism but chose to view the same-sex relationships of their coworkers in an older frame, [not as pathologized]. Single women alternated between defiance and defensiveness, suggesting that the declining social segregation of the sexes in the industrialized Western world and the more insistent labeling of women without men as lesbians or old maids made a woman's choice of a female—or no—partner more suspicious and thus the women's world of separatist organizations more precarious. The . . . reservation of the strongest condemnation for women who challenged respectability through their sexual liaisons with men hints at the unease that spilled over from the transformation of social and sexual relations to the process of political organizing.

The story of the international women's movement also reveals how important it is to attend to the interaction of sexuality and politics. Conflict over sexuality and separatism added to the national, class, and generational tensions already bubbling within the international organizations and foreshadowed some of the contemporary critiques of lesbian separatism in the United States by working-class women and women of color.[37] At the same time, the silencing of the defenders of separatist organizing may have helped to undermine the potential power of a global women's movement in these years by questioning the validity of gathering apart from men in an increasingly heterosocial world. Whatever the case, the dynamics within the first wave of international organizing among women make clear that our contemporary struggles over sexuality and politics have a longer and more complex history than we sometimes think.

NOTES

1. Marjory Lacey-Baker, "Chronological Record of Events and Activities for the Biography of Lena Madesin Phillips, 1881–1955"; Lena Madesin Phillips,

"Unfinished History of the International Federation of Business and Professional Women," Phillips Papers, cartons 7 and 9, Schlesinger Library, Radcliffe College, Cambridge, Mass.; Lutz to Carrie Chapman Catt, 12 Feb. 1934, 7 July 1936, National American Woman Suffrage Association (NAWSA) Papers, reel 12, Library of Congress, Washington, D.C.

2. See Joanne J. Meyerowitz, *Women Adrift: Independent Wage Earners in Chicago, 1880–1930* (Chicago: University of Chicago Press, 1988); Kathy Peiss, *Cheap Amusements: Working Women and Leisure in Turn-of-the-Century New York* (Philadelphia: Temple University Press, 1986); Hazel V. Carby, "'It Jus Be's Dat Way Sometime': The Sexual Politics of Women's Blues," in *Unequal Sisters: A Multicultural Reader in U.S. Women's History,* ed. Ellen Carol DuBois and Vicki L. Ruiz (New York: Routledge, 1990), 238–49; Judith R. Walkowitz, *City of Dreadful Delight: Narratives of Sexual Danger in Late-Victorian London* (Chicago: University of Chicago Press, 1992); Birgitte Søland, *Becoming Modern: Young Women and the Reconstruction of Womanhood in the 1920s* (Princeton, N.J.: Princeton University Press, 2000).

3. On the emergence of the category and identity "lesbian" at the turn of the century, see George Chauncey Jr., "From Inversion to Homosexuality: Medicine and the Changing Conceptualization of Female Deviance," *Salmagundi,* nos. 58–59 (Fall 1982–Winter 1983): 114–46; and Lisa Duggan, "The Trials of Alice Mitchell: Sensationalism, Sexology, and the Lesbian Subject in Turn-of-the-Century America," *Signs* 18 (Summer 1993): 791–814.

4. See, for example, Mineke Bosch with Annemarie Kloosterman, *Politics and Friendship: Letters from the International Woman Suffrage Alliance, 1902–1942* (Columbus: Ohio State University Press, 1990); Ian Tyrrell, *Woman's World, Woman's Empire: The Woman's Christian Temperance Union in International Perspective, 1880–1930* (Chapel Hill: University of North Carolina Press, 1991), which discusses couples within the World Woman's Christian Temperance Union; and Johanna Alberti, *Beyond Suffrage: Feminists in War and Peace, 1914–1928* (London: Macmillan, 1989), which describes women's love for other women within the British women's movement; and Leila J. Rupp and Verta Taylor, *Survival in the Doldrums: The American Women's Rights Movement, 1945 to the 1960s* (New York: Oxford University Press, 1987), which emphasizes the centrality of coupled women in the U.S. women's rights movement.

5. In this early-nineteenth-century case, a well-connected girl accused her two schoolmistresses of engaging in sexual behavior, causing the ruin of the school; see Lillian Faderman, *Scotch Verdict* (New York: William Morrow, 1983). For more on the acceptability issue, see Martha Vicinus, "'They Wonder to Which Sex I Belong': The Historical Roots of the Modern Lesbian Identity," *Feminist Studies* 18 (Fall 1992): 467–97; Lisa Moore, "'Something More Tender Still than Friendship': Romantic Friendship in Early-Nineteenth-Century England," ibid., 499–520; and Marylynne Diggs, "Romantic Friends or a 'Different Race of Creatures'? The Representation of Lesbian Pathology in Nineteenth-Century America," *Feminist Studies* 21 (Summer 1995): 317–40.

6. The neo-Europes included Australia, New Zealand, the United States, and Canada. See Leila J.

Rupp, "Constructing Internationalism: The Case of Transnational Women's Organizations, 1888–1945," *American Historical Review* 99 (Dec. 1994): 1571–1600, and Rupp, "Challenging Imperialism in International Women's Organizations," *NWSA Journal* 8 (Spring 1996): 8–27.

7. *Women in a Changing World: The Dynamic Story of the International Council of Women since 1888* (London: Routledge and Kegan Paul, 1966); Arnold Whittick, *Woman into Citizen* (London: Athenaeum with Frederick Muller, 1976), on the International Alliance of Women; and Bosch, *Politics and Friendship*. On WILPF, see, for example, Gertrude Bussey and Margaret Tims, *Women's International League for Peace and Freedom, 1915–1965* (London: George Allen and Unwin, 1965); Lela B. Costin, "Feminism, Pacifism, Internationalism, and the 1915 International Congress of Women," *Women's Studies International Forum* 5, no. 3/4 (1982): 301–15; Catherine Foster, *Women for All Seasons: The Story of the Women's International League for Peace and Freedom* (Athens: University of Georgia Press, 1989).

8. Anna Ruhling, "Welches Interesse hat die Frauenbewegung an der Losing des homosexuellen problems?" [What interest does the women's movement have in the homosexual question?], in *Lesbian-Feminism in Turn-of-the-Century Germany*, ed. and trans. Lillian Faderman and Brigitte Eriksson ([Weatherby Lake, Mo.]: Naiad Press, 1980), 81–91 (quotation on 88).

9. Rosika Schwimmer to Wilhelmina van Wulfften Palthe, 29 July 1917, Schwimmer-Lloyd Collection, box A-90, Rare Books and Manuscripts Division, New York Public Library, Astor, Lenox, and Tilden Foundations; Marguerite Gobat to Vilma Glucklich [French], 27 Oct. 1924, Women's International League for Peace and Freedom Papers, reel 1; Aletta Jacobs to Rosika Schwimmer, 3 May 1909, Schwimmer-Lloyd Collection, box A-20; Helen Archdale to Anna Nilsson, 17 May 1933, Equal Rights International Papers, box 331, Fawcett Library, London Guildhall University.

10. Lida Gustava Heymann with Anita Augspurg, *Erlebtes-Erschautes: Deutsche Frauen kampfen fur Freiheit, Recht und Frieden 1850–1940*, ed. Margrit Twellman (Meisenheim am Glan: Anton Hain, 1972), 62. See also Regina Braker, "Bertha von Suttner's Spiritual Daughters: The Feminist Pacifism of Anita Augspurg, Lida Gustava Heymann, and Helene Stocker at the International Congress of Women at The Hague, 1915," *Women's Studies International Forum* 18, no. 2 (1995): 103–11.

11. Heymann with Augspurg, *Erlebtes-Erschautes*, 64, 74, 76.

12. Heymann to Schwimmer [in German], 3 Oct. 1919, Schwimmer-Lloyd Collection, box A-119; Emily Balch to Aletta Jacobs, 15 Nov. 1916, Jacobs Papers, box 2, Internationaal Informatiecentrum en Archief voor de Vrouwenbeweging, Amsterdam (hereafter, IIAV); Emily Hobhouse to Aletta Jacobs, 24 Apr. 1920, ibid., box 1; "List of individuals expected in Innsbruck" [German], [1925], WILPF Papers, reel 2; Heymann to Gabrielle Duchene, 17 Feb. 1926, Dossiers Gabrielle Duchene, Fol Res. 206, Bibliotheque de Documentation Internationale Contemporaine, University of Paris, Nanterre; Anne Zueblin to Jane Addams, 17 Jan. 1930,

Addams Papers, reel 21 (University Microfilms International).

13. Clara Ragaz to K.E. Innes and Gertrud Baer, 18 Apr. 1940, WILPF Papers, reel 4; Rosika Schwimmer to Alice Park, 7 Jan. 1944, Alice Park Papers, box 1, Hoover Institution, Stanford, California.

14. Heymann to Mary Rozet Smith [in German and English], 5 June 1924, Addams Papers, reel 16; Anne Zueblin to M. Illova, 10 June 1929, WILPF Papers, reel 19. On Addams and Smith, see Blanche W. Cook, "Female Support Networks and Political Activism: Lillian Wald, Crystal Eastman, Emma Goldman," *Chrysalis* 3 (Autumn 1977): 43–61. Addams described Smith as her "most intimate friend"; Addams to Heymann, 23 Feb. 1924, Addams Papers, reel 16.

15. For the theme of devoted service in these relationships, see Karin Lutzen, *Was das Herz begehrt: Liebe und Freundschaft zwischen Frauen*, translated from Danish by Gabriele Haefs (Hamburg: Ernst Kabel Verlag, 1990), 110–38. Shaw: Rachel Foster Avery to Aletta Jacobs, 14 July 1910, Jacobs Papers; Biography of Anna Howard Shaw, Dillon Collection, box 18, Schlesinger Library; Anna Howard Shaw to Aletta Jacobs, 19 Mar. 1914, Jacobs Papers; Aletta H. Jacobs, *Uithet leven van merkwaardige vrouwen* (Amsterdam: F. van Rossen, 1905), 37, quoted in Bosch, *Politics and Friendship*, 25; Barbara R. Finn, "Anna Howard Shaw and Women's Work," *Frontiers* 4 (Fall 1979): 21–25, quoted in ibid., 26.

16. Mary G. Peck to Carrie Chapman Catt, 6 Feb. 1929, quoted in Robert Booth Fowler, *Carrie Catt: Feminist Politician* (Boston: Northeastern University Press, 1986), 42. Catt also carried on a romantic relationship with Peck, who herself lived with another woman; see Catt to Frances Squire Potter, n.d., quoted in Bosch, *Politics and Friendship*, 38.

17. Anna Howard Shaw to Aletta Jacobs, 8 Feb. 1909, 7 Apr. 1911, and 14 Dec. 1908, Jacobs Papers, box 2; Rachel Foster Avery to Aletta Jacobs, 14 July 1910, ibid.; Anna Manus-Jacobi, tribute to Carrie Chapman Catt [in German], 11 Mar. 1947, Manus Papers, IIAV.

18. Quoted in Mercedes Randall, *Improper Bostonian: Emily Greene Balch* (New York: Twayne Publishers, 1964), 397, 299; Heymann to Addams [in German], 16 Sept. 1919, and Helen Cheever to Jane Addams, 13 Sept. 1922, both in Addams Papers, reel 12 and 15; Jane Addams, *Second Twenty Years at Hull House*, 197–98, quoted in Randall, *Improper Bostonian*, 399.

19. Elisabeth Busse, "Das moralische Dilemma in der modernen Madchenerziehung," in Ada Schmidt-Beil, *Die Kultur der Frau* (Berlin: Verlag fur Kultur und Wissenschaft, 1931), 594; Alice Salomon, "Character Is Destiny," 218 and 39–42, Alice Salomon Papers, Memoir Collection, Leo Baeck Institute, New York.

20. Alice Salomon, "The Unmarried Woman of Yesterday and Today," ICW *Bulletin* 11 (October 1932); Lena Madesin Phillips to Carrie Probst, 28 May 1935, Phillips Papers, carton 4, Schlesinger Library (on Phillips's relationship, see Rupp and Taylor, *Survival in the Doldrums*, 121–24); Archdale to Doris Stevens, 14 Feb. 1936, and Lady Rhondda to Doris Stevens [May 1928], both in Stevens Papers, cartons 4 and 5, Schlesinger Library. On Lady

Rhondda's relationships with women, see Shirley M. Eoff, *Viscountess Rhondda: Equalitarian Feminist* (Columbus: Ohio State University Press, 1991), 107–16.

21. See Rupp, "Constructing Internationalism." On maternalist politics, see the various contributions to Lynn Y. Weiner et al., "Maternalism as a Paradigm," *Journal of Women's History* 5 (fall 1993): 95–131; Seth Koven and Sonya Michel, "Womanly Duties: Maternalist Politics and the Origins of the Welfare States in France, Germany, Great Britain, and the United States, 1880–1920," *American Historical Review* 95 (October 1990): 1076–1108; and Karen Offen, "Defining Feminism: A Comparative Historical Approach," *Signs* 14 (Autumn 1988): 119–57.

22. Heymann with Augspurg, *Erlebtes-Erschautes*, 70.

23. Lucy Anthony to Aletta Jacobs, 10 Jan. 1915, and Anna Howard Shaw to Aletta Jacobs, 30 Aug. 1917, both in Jacobs Papers, box 2.

24. Anna Howard Shaw to Aletta Jacobs, 22 Aug. 1915 and 18 Apr. 1916, Jacobs Papers, box 2; speech of Lida Gustava Heymann, WILPF Zurich Congress, [1919], WILPF Papers, reel 17; Minutes, WILPF International Congress, 3–8 Sept. 1934, WILPF Papers, reel 20; "Man Made Wars," *Pax* 6 (May 1931).

25. Emily Greene Balch to Aletta Jacobs, 15 Nov. 1916, Jacobs Papers, reel 9.

26. Eva Fichet to Emily Balch [French], 19 Aug. 1934, WILPF Papers, reel 20; Catherine E. Marshall to Vilma Glucklich, 14 May [1923], Addams Papers, reel 15. On Marshall, see Jo Vellacott, *From Liberal to Labour with Women's Suffrage: The Story of Catherine Marshall* (Buffalo, N.Y.: McGill-Queen's University Press, 1993).

27. Alice Salomon, "To Lord and Lady Aberdeen on the Occasion of Their Golden Wedding, November 7th, 1927," *ICW Bulletin* 6 (November 1927); Lady Aberdeen to Emma Ender [in German], 31 Jan. 1928, Helene-Lange-Archiv, 78–315 (1), Landesarchiv Berlin; Emma Ender to Lady Aberdeen [German], 13 Feb. 1928, Helene-Lange-Archiv, 85–333 (2), Landesarchiv Berlin; "Lady Aberdeen's Response to Toast Proposed by Baroness Boel . . .," 13 July 1938, ICW, *President's Memorandum Regarding the Council Meeting of the ICW held at Edinburgh, (Scotland), July 11th to 21st 1938*, 15–17.

28. Aletta Jacobs to Rosika Schwimmer [in German], 18 Nov. 1903, Schwimmer-Lloyd Collection, box A-4; see Bosch, *Politics and Friendship*, 9–12, 53–55. Jacobs's reminiscences have been translated and published as *Memories: My Life as an International Leader in Health, Suffrage, and Peace*, ed. Harriet Feinberg, trans. Annie Wright (New York: Feminist Press, 1996).

29. Lady Aberdeen, "Presidential Address," ICW, *Report of Transactions of Second Quinquennial Meeting Held in London July 1899*, ed. Countess of Aberdeen (London: T. Fisher Unwin, 1900), v. 1, 49;

ICW, *Report of Transactions*, 1899, v. 1, 56; Margery Corbett Ashby interview, 21 Sept. 1976, conducted by Brian Harrison, Corbett Ashby Papers, cassette #6, Fawcett Library, London.

30. Catt to Kramers, 21 May 1913, box A-33; Kramers to Schwimmer [in German], 27 May 1913 and 2 June 1913, box A-32 and box A-33; Kramers to Schwimmer [in German], 31 May 1907 and 7 Oct. 1908, box A-12 and box A-17, all in Schwimmer-Lloyd Collection.

31. Lutz to Carrie Chapman Catt, 7 July 1936, 12 Feb. 1934, 15 July 1936, NAWSA Papers, reel 12; Doris Stevens, transcription of taped reminiscences, Stevens Papers, carton 3, Schlesinger Library. See Leila J. Rupp, "Feminism and the Sexual Revolution in the Early Twentieth Century: The Case of Doris Stevens," *Feminist Studies* 15 (Summer 1989): 289–309.

32. I am indebted to Susan Hartmann for this insight.

33. Rosika Schwimmer to Gabrielle Duchene, [1934], WILPF Papers, reel 20; Minutes, Eighth International Congress, Zurich, 3–8 Sept. 1934, WILPF Papers, reel 20. On Mildred Scott Olmstead's complex personal life, see Margaret Hope Bacon, *One Woman's Passion for Peace and Freedom: The Life of Mildred Scott Olmstead* (Syracuse: Syracuse University Press, 1993).

34. Elizabeth Baelde, "Impressions of the Visit of the I.C.W. to Canada," in *Our Lady of the Sunshine*, ed. Countess of Aberdeen (London: Constable, 1909), 310–34; Eline Hansen to Rosika Schwimmer, 12 Mar. 1915, and Edna Munch to Schwimmer, 18 Mar. 1915, both in Schwimmer-Lloyd Collection, box A-55 and A-57; "Report of Business Sessions," 29 Apr. and 1 May [1915], *International Committee of Women for Permanent Peace, International Congress of Women, The Hague—April 28th to May 1st 1915: Report*, 111–17, 162–63; "Stenographic Report of Second Congress," 17 Oct. 1921, International Federation of Working Women Papers, Schlesinger Library.

35. Margery Corbett Ashby to Josephine Schain, 5 Feb. 1935, Schain Papers, box 4 [Mrs. Bader Dimeschquie], "Delegates and Friends," 1935, International Alliance of Women Papers, box 1, both in Sophia Smith Collection, Smith College, Northampton, Mass.

36. Idola Saint-Jean to Helen Archdale, 15 Sept. 1931, Equal Rights International Papers, box 334; Minutes, Meeting of the International Alliance of Women for Suffrage and Equal Citizenship Board, Paris, 6–9 Dec. 1938, International Alliance of Women Papers, both at Fawcett Library.

37. For more on the national, ethnic, class, and generational tensions within the international women's movement, see Leila J. Rupp, *Worlds of Women: The Making of an International Women's Movement* (Princeton, N.J.: Princeton University Press, 1997).

SUFFRAGE AND CITIZENSHIP

ELLEN CAROL DUBOIS

The Next Generation of Suffragists: Harriot Stanton Blatch and Grassroots Politics

Campaigns to expand suffrage require that voters who are reasonably content with the status quo be persuaded to welcome new and unpredictable constituencies into the political arena. It is perhaps no surprise that the expansion of suffrage met severe resistance, in the North where there were considerable doubts about the immigrant vote and especially in the South where the franchise had been restricted (through literacy tests and poll taxes) to exclude African Americans and, in the process, many poor whites.

The campaign for woman suffrage presented a formidable challenge to established political theory that held a married woman's political interests were represented by her husband. It proceeded with a successful national mass mobilization at a time when even presidential campaigns hardly met that criteria. And it required brilliant street theater on a massive scale and, simultaneously, clever and delicate political maneuvering for which women were not noted. Although the accomplishment of woman suffrage in 1920 is well known, the complexity of the work that was required and the high level of political skill that women had to acquire is less appreciated than it deserves to be.

Harriot Blatch, the daughter of Elizabeth Cady Stanton, led the efforts of the Women's Political Union (WPU) to win suffrage for the women of New York State. From 1910 to 1915, the WPU lobbied state legislators to support the suffrage bill. They also targeted public support with parades, suffrage shops, and films. (See Photo Essay: "Women in Public," pp. 255–266.)

Ironically, many suffragists who demanded the vote were deeply skeptical about politics. Believing that women were more pure than men and that politics were corrupt, they insisted that if women had the vote, they would put an end to partisanship. In fact, their views were not so far apart from antisuffragists who resisted the vote precisely because they felt partisan politics would corrupt American womanhood. To their credit, Harriot Blatch and her colleagues understood that acquiring political skills and understanding partisanship were essential to acquiring the vote and, once acquired, using it effectively.

The battle for women's rights had begun in the state of New York, the birthplace of Elizabeth Cady Stanton and the longtime home of Susan B. Anthony. In Seneca Falls, New York, the Declaration of Rights and Sentiments had been rousingly proclaimed in 1848. In Albany, both Stanton and Anthony testified in the 1850s before the New York Senate's Judiciary Committee. There they argued, with some success, for changes in state law to establish women's guardianship rights over their children, grant property and earnings rights to married women, and deliver woman suffrage. In 1915, nearly seventy years later, the struggle, now led by a new generation, had come to focus on woman suffrage. Fittingly, Harriot Stanton Blatch, Elizabeth Cady Stanton's daughter, led this major effort to win woman suffrage in its home state. But even in the early twentieth century, success was uncertain.

Harriot Stanton, the second daughter and sixth child of Elizabeth Cady and Henry Brewster Stanton, inherited her role as defender of her sex from her mother. She was born in Seneca Falls in 1856, during a period when Elizabeth Cady Stanton was immersed in women's issues and the development of a convention movement to publicize concerns as revolutionary as liberalizing divorce.... While other Victorian girls followed their mothers into quiet lives based on family service, Harriot was taught to be assertive and independent.... Her mother prepared her daughters to go out into the world not only to make their individual marks on it but also to embody her convictions about women's untapped capacities....

... In 1874, [Harriot] enrolled at Vassar, the first all-female college established in the United States. There, she elected an unconventional course of study focused on science, politics, and history. Upon graduation, she became a member of the first generation of women college graduates, one of only a few thousand women in the United States who held a bachelor's degree....

[In 1882,] she met William Blatch, the handsome, accommodating son of a wealthy brewer from Basingstoke, Hampshire, England. Harriot and William married in 1882, and the couple's first child Nora (named after the heroine of Ibsen's *A Doll's House*) was born in England the next year. A second child, Helen, born in 1892, died of whooping cough in 1896. Like her mother but with fewer children, more money,

and a compliant husband, Harriot Blatch managed to combine marriage and motherhood with an energetic commitment to reform activities. She joined with veteran British women activists to revive the British suffrage movement.... In 1890, she joined the socialist Fabian Society, where she fought for, but failed to win, strong support for women's rights. For two decades as an [expatriate] in Edwardian England, she honed her political skills and updated her mother's feminist convictions, speaking at meetings, writing for suffrage journals, and becoming involved in local politics as a member of the Women's Local Government Society.

In 1902, with her daughter Nora grown and studying engineering at Cornell, and her husband Henry able to retire, Harriot Blatch moved permanently to New York to take up the task she had inherited—leadership of the American suffrage movement. She joined the Women's Trade Union League, a pioneering effort of elite settlement house women and female wage earners joined together to empower, not patronize, working women. There she came to see that to be modern and effective the suffrage movement in the United States must unite women across the classes in a militant effort. She also saw, as other women activists did not, that women's growing interest in electoral politics was crucial to the reinvigoration of the suffrage movement. Like the English suffragist Emmeline Pankhurst, she was committed to forcing the political parties to address the suffrage issue and winning from them the political support necessary to gain victory....

To enact her vision of a militant, democratic suffrage organization based on a coalition of working-class and middle-class working women, Harriot Blatch organized the Equality League of Self-Supporting Women in 1907, renamed the Women's Political Union (WPU) in 1910. Although it gradually moved away from reliance on wage-earning women for its most active participants, the WPU went on to spearhead a political effort to force the New York legislature to pass a bill authorizing a referendum to amend the state constitution to grant women suffrage.

The WPU suffrage campaign, which ran from 1910 to 1915, involved an exhausting and elaborate two-pronged effort: First, both houses of the state legislature had to pass a bill authorizing a referendum on woman suffrage, and then the state's all-male electorate had to approve the referendum. . . . [S]uffragists in New York took hope from a narrowly won suffrage victory in California in October 1911. . . . By 1912, California was the sixth state in which women were voting in the presidential election. Blatch and her followers were determined that New York women would do the same in the next presidential election. . . .

Harriot Blatch had a talent and taste for partisan politics that was unusual in the movement. Although many of the new generation of suffragists were college-trained professionals, Mary Beard, the historian and a close friend, wrote of Blatch that more than others, "she worked steadfastly to root the suffrage movement in politics, where alone it could reach its goal."[1] She certainly had the lineage. Her mother and Susan B. Anthony had immersed themselves in party politics. From them, from her father, and from her years in England, Harriot had come to see that if suffragists were ever to win, they would have to go behind the scenes and engage in precisely the political maneuvering and lobbying that women had traditionally repudiated as the unhappy consequence of the male monopoly of public life. While such openly political methods distressed many older women reformers, they invigorated Harriot.

In one episode, which became a staple of suffrage legend, Harriot and other WPU leaders tracked down a particularly elusive senator. By this time, opposition to suffrage had moved from ridicule to avoidance. "The chase led up and down elevators in and out of the Senate chamber and committee rooms." Finally, they ferreted out his hiding place and cornered him; he could no longer avoid the issue. The WPU account reversed the standard metaphors of gender to emphasize the senator's humiliation at the hands of women. "Of slight build," he was literally overpowered by the suffragists. "With Mrs. Blatch walking on one side with her hand resting ever so slightly on his sleeve [sic]," the women led him into the committee room and got his vote. "I'll never forgive this," he told Blatch. "Oh yes, you will," she responded, "some day you will be declaring with pride how your vote advanced the suffrage resolution."[2]

The WPU won a similar battle with Robert Wagner, the new Democratic majority leader of the state Senate and one of the most determined opponents of suffrage in the New York legislature. To prevent Wagner from once again employing the delaying legislative tactics of moving to table or returning the referendum resolution to committee for another year, Harriot arranged for three hundred New York City suffragists to go to Albany to pressure him to set a date for a vote. Some fifty or sixty women crowded into the committee room, with the rest gathered in the corridor outside. When Wagner moved to take his place in the chair at the front of the room, the aisle filled with suffragists. "There were no antisuffragists to rescue him," wrote Harriot later. "There were only all about him, the convinced and ruthless members of the Women's Political Union." He grudgingly agreed to set a date for the state Senate to vote on the suffrage resolution.[3]

In both episodes, the WPU's power rested not only in numbers but also in its willingness to exploit the gendered meanings of power. Wagner yielded because he could not afford to let it be known that he had been physically and politically outmaneuvered by women. The newspapers predictably reported what the women requested, and Wagner graciously granted a date for the Senate vote. But at a time in which accounts of British militant suffragists smashing windows were prominently featured in American papers, the sense of sexual warfare, of women besting men, was close to the surface and hard to overlook.

The Senate debate and vote took place on the date Wagner had guaranteed. Harriot and her followers watched from the gallery. Like good politicians, they had carefully counted their supporters, knew that they had just the right number of votes with not one to spare, and "were full of confidence" that the referendum would carry.[4] Across the hall, the lower house was giving them an unanticipated victory. It looked like the legislative battle might actually be won. But at the last moment a perfidious senator abandoned the public pledge he had given the WPU, shifted his vote, and denied them their victory.

With this undeserved defeat uppermost in her mind, Blatch went to the people. The WPU had organized parades twice before, but the 1912 New York City parade was by far the most carefully organized street demonstration in U.S. suffrage history. The WPU spared no effort at recruiting and educating a large number of marchers and alerting the public to the meaning and significance of the parade. Pledge cards were circulated, committing marchers to take to the streets. Newspapers eagerly covered the clever "stunts" that suffragists devised to advertise the parade: suffragists at the circus, "suffragette hats" for sale at department stores, recruitment booths behind the Public Library.

Harriot was determined that the parade give evidence of a massive, disciplined army of women with which politicians would have to come to terms. She paid great attention to the details of the march, the numbers of marching columns, and the spacing of the lines of marchers. Women were instructed to dress simply, walk erectly, and keep their eyes forward. The spectacle was to be an emotional and sensual evocation of women's power. Opponents, according to Blatch, should be converted through their eyes. "The enemy must see women, marching in increasing numbers year by year out on the public avenues, holding high their banner, Votes For Women." On the appointed day, more than ten thousand took to the streets: women college graduates in their academic gowns, working women by trades and industries, prominent wealthy women, even some men. The president of the national suffrage society marched with a banner that read "Catching Up with China"—a reference to reports that insurgent nationalists in one of China's provincial legislatures had declared women enfranchised. Public demonstrations of this sort were new and a bit daunting to many women. "I marched the whole length," one demonstrator proudly reported to a friend.[5]

In 1912, the emergence of a third national political party, the Progressives, affected the task of getting a suffrage referendum. While Progressive leaders begged women for their support, Blatch was disappointed with the tepid role the party had played in a woman suffrage referendum in Ohio earlier in that year. And former president Theodore Roosevelt, the party's candidate for president in 1912, repeatedly embarrassed himself and his party by sexist declarations that suffragists were "indirectly encouraging immorality."[6] Still, the Progressive Party's support was crucial for the WPU's plans in New York because of the leverage it gave in prying support out of the Republicans, who were struggling to keep voters from bolting to the new party. First the Progressives and then the Republicans endorsed the submission of the suffrage referendum to New York voters at their state conventions. . . .

[T]he Democrats followed the other two parties in urging submission of the referendum. Victory, at least in the legislature, was assured. The election of 1912 swept the Democrats . . . into power in the state, and, under the leadership of Woodrow Wilson, into the presidency as well.

There was a last-minute complication when the Republicans added a clause to the referendum subjecting immigrant women, who were citizens by marriage, to special requirements for voting, and the Democrats objected. The issue was a difficult one for Blatch. On the one hand, she had lost her American citizenship by virtue of her marriage to an Englishman and was sympathetic to women whose citizenship was altered by marriage. On the other hand, like her mother decades before, she had her own nativist prejudices, as did many of her middle-class followers. In the end, she decided the issue politically: Keeping the clause would gain the referendum more upstate Republican votes than it would lose downstate Democrats.

Party leaders followed her lead, and in January 1913, both houses passed legislation proposing an amendment to the state constitution striking out the word male and enfranchising citizens over twenty-one "provided that a citizen by marriage should have been an inhabitant of the United States for five years."[7] Blatch had worked three years for this moment, a long time for a single bill. And even with this victory, the most difficult task lay ahead—the winning of the referendum itself. Now the suffrage leaders would have to convince a majority of New York men to vote for woman suffrage.

Harriot Blatch and the leaders of the WPU had no illusions about how difficult this might be. "The task we must accomplish between now and election day 1915 [when the referendum would appear on the ballot] is a Herculean one, compared to that we have just completed," the Executive Committee of the Women's Political Union declared. Harriot had her misgivings about immigrant voters, with their "Germanic and Hebraic attitude toward women," but she counted on the democratic logic of the situation, believing that men who were being allowed to exercise the franchise could be convinced to vote in favor of women's demand to share it. [But a great deal was riding on the New York referendum. "If we win the Empire State all the states will come tumbling down like a deck of cards," she promised.[8]]

To cultivate the voters, the WPU played on its strengths. It based its suffrage advocacy on the proliferating devices of modern mass culture—forms of commercial recreation, methods of advertising, and the pleasures of consumerism. Californians had used billboards, automobile caravans, and suffrage postcards to bring their cause before the electorate in their successful campaign of 1911. New York women had to do the same. ["If we are to reap a victory in 1915, we must cultivate every inch of soil and sow our suffrage seed broadcast in the Empire state," Harriot declared.[9]]

Such an approach conformed to Harriot's view of democracy which, she believed, should be based on the heart rather than the head. Emotions were the key to popular democracy, not reason. "We learned . . . as we toiled in our campaign," she later wrote, "that sermons and logic would never convince. . . . Human beings move because they feel, not because they think."[10] This was not an expression of any special contempt for either women or working-class voters; on the contrary, she considered men (especially politicians) more irrational than women and the rich more prejudiced and conservative than the poor. She believed particularly that changes in women's status and in power relations between the sexes could never be reduced to rational arguments and dispassionate appeals, even to venerable principles of American democracy such as equality and civic virtue.

"Democracy was the keynote" of the grand suffrage ball that the WPU sponsored in January 1913 to inaugurate the referendum campaign. Extensively advertised, it took place in New York City's Seventy-First Street Armory, which was barely large enough for the eight thousand men and women who attended. Rich and poor, working-class and society women alike paid fifty cents to dance the turkey trot and other popular new dances. The event proved, as the WPU put it, "that love of liberty and democracy did not belong to one class or one sex but is deeply rooted in human nature itself."[11] . . .

Given Harriot's appreciation for the role of emotions in mass politics, she was especially intrigued by new technologies of mass communication. "I stand for the achievements of the twentieth century," she declared. "I will make use of . . . anything which civilization places at my command."[12] Lee de Forest, her former son-in-law (Nora's brief marriage to him had ended after a year), was one of the pioneers of modern radio broadcasting. . . . At his invitation, she delivered a radio talk on woman suffrage from the newly opened broadcasting station in downtown Manhattan.

Moving pictures represented another new technology with political possibilities. The WPU arranged for a commercial movie company to produce *The Suffragette and the Man,* a romantic comedy in which the beautiful young heroine, forced to choose between her suffrage principles and her fiancé, first picks principles and then overcomes an anti-suffrage competitor and wins back her lover.

In 1913, the WPU collaborated on a second movie entitled *What 8,000,000 Women Want.* This time the romantic triangle did not involve good and bad men fighting for a heroine's heart but good and bad politics fighting for the hero's soul. Newsreel footage of actual suffrage parades was interspersed with the dramatic action. Harriot played herself and brought to the screen her self-confident authority and her genuine pleasure at conducting the struggle. . . .

[In 1913, as in previous years, the most spectacular suffrage event was the parade organized by the WPU. Each year, the parades had become more stunning affairs, symbolically conveying both the diversity and the unity of modern women.] The 1913 parade was one of the high points of Harriot's suffrage leadership. "We will muster an army fifty thousand strong this year," she predicted. The marchers were arranged by divisions. At the head were two dozen female marshals mounted on horseback and dressed in stylish adaptations of men's evening wear, black cutaways and silk hats with streamers of green, purple, and white, the WPU's colors and those of the movement in England. Leading them, dressed in white and astride a white horse, was Inez Millholland, "the official beauty of the parade." The intention was to provide unforgettable visual images of all kinds of women marching shoulder to shoulder together. "In these times of class wars," Harriot observed, could men really afford "to shut out from public affairs that fine spirit of fellowship" that suffragism represented?[13]

The effectiveness of the parade as political propaganda infuriated antisuffragists, for whom the spectacular aspect of the movement was proof positive of the social and cultural upheaval that votes for women threatened. The antisuffragists charged that the bold stance of the marchers smacked of the deliberate exploitation of "sex appeal." . . . Harriot Blatch found the charges amusing. "Funny idea of sex appeal. Twenty thousand women turn out on a hot day. 87 degrees and march up Fifth Avenue to the blaring music of thirty-five bands; eyes straight to the front; faces red with the hot sun. . . . If it had been mellow moonlight. . . . But a sex appeal set to brass bands! That certainly is a new one."[14] The WPU was determined to finesse the conventional notions of female beauty that had so long restrained women's public activities. . . .

During the legislative lobbying years from 1910 to 1913, Harriot and the WPU had not faced much organizational opposition within the New York suffrage movement. The state suffrage organization was small and ineffective. But once the referendum campaigning began in earnest, the Woman's Political Union, led by the blunt, sometimes undiplomatic Blatch, came into direct conflict with the other great figure of New York suffragism, the moderate, circumspect Carrie Chapman Catt. Within the women's movement, Catt embodied the progressive faith in organizational structure and administrative centralization. In contrast, Harriot celebrated individual initiative, modern invention, and personal freedom. Notwithstanding lofty suffrage rhetoric about the unity of all womanhood and the solidarity of the sex, these two were bound to clash. . . . Catt was always more concerned to unify and reconcile all existing suffragists than to reach out and create new ones. While some activists believed that Blatch was autocratic and highhanded, the ever-diplomatic Catt prized harmony within the movement above all things. Catt's efforts went to creating internal order rather than tackling external obstacles. Unlike Blatch, Catt had little skill or interest in the intricacies of partisan politics and legislative maneuvers.

Catt's plan was to bring all the suffrage societies in New York . . . under one wing, but the Women's Political Union [crucial to her efforts and the richest organization in the state] refused to subsume itself under Catt's leadership. . . . By 1914, it was clear that two parallel suffrage campaigns would be conducted in New York, one by Catt's Empire State Campaign Committee and the other by Harriot Blatch's Women's Political Union. Both raised money for the referendum effort; both sent paid agents around the state; both set up separate offices, sometimes generating considerable conflict among activists in smaller communities in upstate New York. The suffrage movement had survived previous internal divisions and would face others in the future. . . .

In the last six months of the campaign, the WPU flooded the state with publicity-generating gimmicks and stunts. Suffragists played both ends of the gender divide to demonstrate that they could join in traditional male activities as good fellows and at the same time retain their female virtue. On Suffrage Day at the Polo Grounds, New York suffrage organizations competed with each other to sell tickets to a benefit baseball game between the New York Giants and the Chicago Cubs. . . . To counter the anti-suffrage claims that they were bitter women who wanted the ballot as compensation for their inability to find husbands, they even held a series of "married couple days," in which husbands and wives declared their mutual happiness and support of votes for women. . . .

Ten weeks before the end of the campaign, Harriot's single-minded attention to the cause was shattered by the sudden death of her husband, William Blatch, who was accidentally electrocuted. . . . Before leaving [for England to tend to her husband's estate], she took advantage of one benefit of widowhood and resumed her U.S. citizenship. Harriot's decision to leave the country so close to the end of the 1915 campaign is something of a puzzle. She could have postponed the trip a few months. Moreover, England was already at war with Germany, and the transatlantic trip was dangerous. Perhaps she was growing weary of the unrelenting labor of trying to convert New York voters, or perhaps she sensed that she was losing her position as New York's foremost suffragist to Carrie Chapman Catt. . . . By the time she returned in mid-October, the Empire State Campaign Committee . . . had taken over organization of the final suffrage parade. . . .

November 2, 1915, the day toward which Harriot Blatch, Carrie Catt, and thousands of other New York women had been working for years, was the kind of warm, sunny day for which hard-working campaigners pray. When the polls opened at 6 A.M., several thousand suffrage activists were in their places as poll-watchers, guarding against any effort to cheat them of their victory. . . .

By midnight, it was clear that the woman suffrage amendment had been defeated. Out of 1,200,000 votes cast across the state, woman suffrage had been defeated by 190,000 votes, about 16 percent of the total. All the boroughs of New York City voted against woman suffrage as well as fifty-six of the state's sixty-one counties.

Most New York suffragists kept the bitter disappointment they felt to themselves and declared the referendum a moral triumph. "On the whole we have achieved a wonderful victory," Carrie Chapman Catt proclaimed. "It was short of our hopes but the most contemptuous opponents speak with newly acquired respect for our movement."[15] Catt's wing of the campaign announced the day after the election that a second referendum campaign would begin as soon as state law permitted. . . .

Harriot Blatch was one of the few suffrage leaders who dared to react with open anger. She was "disgusted at the conditions which had forced women to campaign in the streets" and humiliated at having to appeal to immigrant men to gain her native-born rights as an American citizen.[16] She vowed she would never make another street-corner speech. Her retreat into this outraged elitism recalled her mother's reaction to her own crushing disappointment at the failure of the Reconstruction constitutional amendments to include women. Blatch also blamed the suffrage forces themselves for the defeat, at least the Catt wing of the movement, which she thought had neglected upstate New York. She believed a second referendum would be a mistake because the antisuffragists would be even better organized for the next round.

In this she was wrong. In 1917, a second voters' referendum was victorious in New York, thus winning an incalculably important political prize in the battle that was intensifying nationwide. Yet Harriot was correct in a larger way. The era of state suffrage referenda was over; with the exception of New York, no other state was won by this method after 1915. From this point on, attention, energy, and political initiative shifted to the federal arena, to the constitutional amendment Elizabeth Cady Stanton and Susan B. Anthony had first introduced and

which had been stalled in congressional committee for almost fifty years. In less than five years, the amendment was moved onto the floor, secured a two-thirds vote in the House and three years later in the Senate, and was ratified by three-quarters of the state legislatures to become the law of the land. . . .

NOTES

1. "Foreword" by Mary Beard, in Harriot Stanton Blatch and Alma Lutz, *Challenging Years: The Memoirs of Harriot Stanton Blatch* (New York: G. P. Putnam's Sons, 1940), p. vii.

2. Nora de Forest, "Political History of Women's Political Union," reel 1, Harriot Stanton Blatch Papers, Library of Congress, pp. 13–14; *Challenging Years*, pp. 162–63.

3. *Challenging Years*, pp. 163–64.

4. Ibid., pp. 169–70; Women's Political Union 1912–1913 Annual Report, pp. 7–8.

5. *Challenging Years*, p. 180; "Chinese Women Parade for Suffrage," *New York Times*, April 14, 1912, pt. 7, p. 5; Katherine Devereux Blake to Alice Park, n.d., Susan B. Anthony Memorial Collection, Huntington Library, San Marino, CA.

6. "Roosevelt Is for Woman Suffrage," *New York Times*, February 3, 1912, p. 7.

7. "Official Copy of Proposed Amendment," November 2, 1915, Blatch Papers, Library of Congress.

8. "The Referendum Policy of the Women's Political Union," p. 19, reel 1, Blatch Papers, Library of Congress. "Mrs. Blatch Plans Hot Fight to Win New York to Suffrage," *Chicago Tribune*, March 16, 1913. Blatch to Alice Paul, August 26, 1913, reel 4, National Woman's Party Papers: Suffrage Years.

9. Blatch, "Seed Time and Harvest," *Women's Political World*, June 16, 1913, p. 2.

10. *Challenging Years*, p. 192.

11. "Suffragists Tour City to Boom Ball," *New York Daily Mail*, January 11, 1913; "Charity Versus Votes," *Women's Political World*, January 15, 1913, p. 7.

12. "Barnard Girls Test Wireless Phones," *New York Times*, February 26, 1909, p. 7.

13. ". . . with Suffrage Workers," *New York Post*, March 7, 1913; "Eyes to the Front," *New York Tribune*, May 3, 1913; Blatch, "A Reviewing Stand," *Women's Political World*, May 15, 1913, p. 1.

14. "Answers Anti Attack," *New York Times*, May 13, 1913, p. 3.

15. Catt to Mary Grey Peck, December 12, 1912, Catt Papers, Library of Congress.

16. "Mrs. Blatch Pours Out Wrath . . . ," *New York Times*, November 4, 1915, p. 3.

DOCUMENTS

Chinese Exclusion: The Page Act and Its Aftermath

Named for the California congressman Horace F. Page, who was its most ardent supporter, the Page Act of 1875 was the nation's first federal exclusion of certain kinds of immigrants. Public and congressional debate on expanding the statute continued, and within seven years, the much more expansive Chinese Exclusion Act of 1882 barred virtually all but elite Chinese from entering the United States and reiterated the exclusion of women. "The Exclusion Act is clearly the pivot on which all American immigration policy turned," writes historian Roger Daniels, "the hinge on which Emma Lazarus's 'Golden Door' began to swing toward a closed position. It initiated an era of steadily increasing restrictions on immigration of all kinds that lasted until 1943."* Not until our alliance with China in World War II was the Chinese exclusion law repealed.

The Page Act, like the more capacious legislation that followed, was fueled by a mixture of policies: racist hostility to Asians; hostility to unscrupulous entrepreneurs who recruited unskilled workers, pressured them into multiyear contracts, brought them to the United States, and then undercut established wages; and authentic fears of prostitution rings. Knowledge that Chinese families practiced polygamy and foot-binding fueled generalizations about immorality and sexual exploitation. One San Francisco politician conceded that "as a class Chinese are intelligent," but insisted that among "the multitudes of Chinese women in our state there is not a wife or virtuous female in their number."†

The Page Act gestured in the direction of outlawing contract labor but actually focused on trafficking in women. It made the American consular officers in Chinese ports responsible for interrogating all prospective immigrants; in practice, any woman who wished to travel to the United States had first to persuade the consul that she was not a prostitute. Memories of this humiliating experience have been passed down over many generations in some Chinese-American families.

The impact of the law was quickly felt. In the two years between 1880 and 1882, some 50,000 Chinese men entered the United States, but only 220 Chinese women did so. In 1910 the gender ratio among Chinese in the United States was 14:1. The principle that prospective immigrant women had the additional burden of proving their morality persisted. The 1891 Immigration Act required all incoming pregnant women to prove that they were married. It also provided for the

*Roger Daniels, *Guarding the Golden Door: American Immigration Policy and Immigrants since 1882* (New York: Hill and Wang, 2004), p. 19.
†For a helpful overview, see Martha Gardner, *The Qualities of a Citizen: Women, Immigration, and Citizenship, 1870–1965* (Princeton, N.J.: Princeton University Press, 2005).

Page Act of 1875, 43rd Cong., 2nd sess., ch. 141.

expulsion of immigrants who became a public charge within a year of entry. That time limit was gradually expanded—to two years, then three, then five. In 1910, a new statute provided that alien women who turned to sex work could be deported at any time. In the debates over immigration policy in the early twenty-first century, shrill accusations against pregnant women seeking entry are again heard. Why do you think immigration officials and the American public are so concerned about female sexuality and reproductive capabilities?

The second gatekeeping mechanism in the Page Act (see the final paragraph) took on renewed vigor in later acts and with the construction of immigrant receiving stations—Ellis Island in New York Harbor in 1892 and Angel Island in San Francisco Bay in 1910. At the latter, Asian immigrant women tended to be detained longer than men, as well as grilled about their sexual character, plans to marry (if single), and ability to support themselves in the United States. See photograph on p. 341.

Be it enacted . . . that in determining whether the immigration of any subject of China, Japan, or any Oriental country, to the United States, is free and voluntary . . . it shall be the duty of the . . . consul of the United States residing at the port from which it is proposed to convey such subjects, in any vessels enrolled or licensed in the United States . . . to ascertain whether such immigrant has entered into a contract or agreement for a term of service within the United States, for lewd and immoral purposes; and if there be such contract or agreement, the said . . . consul shall not deliver the required permit or certificate . . .

. . . That the importation into the United States of women for the purposes of prostitution is hereby forbidden; and all contracts and agreements in relation thereto, made in advance or in pursuance of such illegal importation and purposes, are hereby declared void; and whoever shall knowingly and willfully import, or cause any importation of, women into the United States for the purposes of prostitution, or shall knowingly or willfully hold, or attempt to hold, any woman to such purposes, in pursuance of such illegal importation and contract or agreement, shall be deemed guilty of a felony, and, on conviction thereof, shall be imprisoned not exceeding five years and pay a fine not exceeding five thousand dollars . . .

. . . That it shall be unlawful for aliens of the following [two] classes to immigrate into the United States, namely, persons who are undergoing a sentence for conviction in their own country of felonious crimes other than political . . . and women "imported for the purposes of prostitution." Every vessel arriving in the United States may be inspected under the direction of the collector of the port at which it arrives, if he shall have reason to believe that any such obnoxious persons are on board. . . .

Mackenzie v. Hare, 1915

The persistent expansion of married women's property acts and the increasing popularity of woman suffrage make it tempting to conclude that the practice of coverture—women's legal and civic subordination to men—steadily dissolved over the course of the nineteenth and early twentieth centuries. But although it is true that some aspects of coverture eroded, others were sustained and even strengthened.

Mackenzie v. Hare, 239 U.S. 299 (1915).

Although Chief Justice Morrison R. Waite had been right when he observed in *Minor v. Happersett* (1874) (pp. 294–295) that "[t]here is no doubt that women may be citizens," he was wrong when he went on to claim that "sex has never been made one of the elements of citizenship. . . . [M]en have never had an advantage over women." According to the common law and early American practice, white women, like men, became citizens either by birth or by their own choice to be naturalized. But in 1855, following practices established in France by the conservative Code Napoleon (1804) and in Britain in 1844, the U.S. Congress extended the principle of marital unity to provide that "any woman who might lawfully be naturalized under the existing laws, married, or shall be married to a citizen of the United States shall be deemed and taken to be a citizen." That is, foreign women who married male citizens did not need to go through a naturalization process or even take an oath of allegiance. The law did not explain what should happen when a woman with U.S. citizenship married a noncitizen man. For the next fifty years, there was little consistency in how courts dealt with related cases that came before them. Often the principle of "marital unity" prevailed, meaning that women who were American citizens lost their citizenship by marrying a foreign national. In 1907, Congress passed a statute explicitly providing that women take the nationality of their husbands when they marry.

Expatriation—the loss of citizenship—traditionally has been a very severe punishment, usually reserved for cases of treason. If a married woman had to assume the nationality of her husband, she might become the subject of a king or czar in a political system that offered her even less protection than did the United States. She might even become stateless. If Americans claimed to base their political system on the "consent of the governed," could women's "consent" be arbitrarily denied? In time of war, the American woman who married, say, a German national could change her status overnight from a citizen to an alien enemy. President Ulysses S. Grant's daughter lost her citizenship when she married an Englishman in 1874; it required a special act of Congress to reinstate her citizenship when she returned from England as a widow in 1898.

Ethel Mackenzie, who had been born in California, married Gordon Mackenzie, a British subject, in 1909—two years after the passage of the Citizenship Act of 1907. She was active in the woman suffrage movement in California, and when it was successful in 1911 she worked in the San Francisco voter registration drive. It is not surprising that she herself should try to register to vote. When the Board of Election Commissioners denied her application, holding that upon her marriage to a British subject she had "ceased to be a citizen of the United States," she refused to let her husband apply for citizenship and instead challenged the law, claiming that Congress had exceeded its authority. She could not believe that Congress had actually *intended* to deprive her of the citizenship she understood to be her birthright. Why did the Supreme Court deny her claim? What "ancient principle of jurisprudence" did they rely on? Why did the Court think that the marriage of an American woman to a foreign man should be treated differently from the marriage of an American man to a foreign woman?

MR. JUSTICE MCKENNA:

. . . The question . . . is, Did [Ethel Mackenzie] cease to be a citizen by her marriage? . . . [Mackenzie contends] that it was not the intention [of Congress] to deprive an American-born woman, remaining within the jurisdiction of the United States, of her citizenship by reason of her marriage to a resident foreigner. . . . [She is trying to persuade the Court that the citizenship statute was] beyond the authority of

Congress.... [She offered the] earnest argument ... that ... under the Constitution and laws of the United States, [citizenship] became a right, privilege and immunity which could not be taken away from her except as a punishment for crime or by her voluntary expatriation....

[But the Court concludes:] ... The identity of husband and wife is an ancient principle of our jurisprudence. It was neither accidental nor arbitrary and worked in many instances for her protection. There has been, it is true, much relaxation of it but in its retention as in its origin it is determined by their intimate relation and unity of interests, and this relation and unity may make it of public concern in many instances to merge their identity, and give dominance to the husband. It has purpose, if not necessity, in purely domestic policy; it has greater purpose and, it may be, necessity, in international policy.... Having this purpose, has it not the sanction of power?

... The law in controversy deals with a condition voluntarily entered into.... The marriage of an American woman with a foreigner has consequences ... [similar to] her physical expatriation.... Therefore, as long as the relation lasts it is made tantamount to expatriation. This is no arbitrary exercise of government.... It is the conception of the legislation under review that such an act [marriage to a foreign man] may bring the Government into embarrassments and, it may be, into controversies.... [Marriage to a foreign man] is as voluntary and distinctive as expatriation and its consequence must be considered as elected.

The decision in *Mackenzie* angered suffragists and energized them; American women needed suffrage to protect themselves against involuntary expatriation and statelessness. The repeal of the Citizenship Act of 1907 was high on the suffragists' agenda, and they returned to it as soon as suffrage was accomplished (see Equal Suffrage [Nineteenth] Amendment). The Cable Act of 1922 provided that "the right of a person to become a naturalized citizen shall not be denied to a person on account of sex or because she is a married woman," but it permitted American women who married foreigners to retain their citizenship only if they married men from countries whose subjects were eligible for U.S. citizenship— that is, not from China or Japan. American-born women who married aliens from China or Japan still lost their citizenship. American-born women who married aliens not from China or Japan were treated as naturalized citizens who would lose their citizenship should they reside abroad for two years.

The Cable Act was extended by amendments well into the 1930s, but some exclusions remained, and the improvements were generally not retroactive. Thus, as late as the 1950s, some American-born women were denied passports because they had married foreign men before 1922. In 1998, 2001, and again in 2011, the U.S. Supreme Court upheld a practice of different rules for non-marital children born abroad. The child born to an unmarried citizen mother and a noncitizen man is a citizen at birth (so long as the mother has lived in the United States for at least one year). The child born to an unmarried citizen father and a noncitizen woman can be a citizen only if the father has met a number of requirements. Among them are that he must have lived in the United States for a specified number of years after he reached the age of fourteen. (The number of years changed when Congress revised the statute: until 1986 it was five years; then it was reduced to two years.) The father must also formally legitimize and financially support the child before the child reaches the age of eighteen.*

---

*Miller v. Albright , 523 U.S. 420 (1998); Nguyen v. Immigration and Naturalization Service, 533 U.S. 53 (2001); Flores-Villar v. United States, 131 S. Ct 2312 (2011). This note draws on Candice Lewis Bredbenner, A Nationality of Her Own: Women, Marriage and the Law of Citizenship (Berkeley: University of California Press, 1998).

In sustaining different rules for mothers and fathers, the Supreme Court majority emphasized the possibility of fraudulent claims of citizenship by unmarried noncitizen mothers and their children; the dissenting minority emphasized the ease with which men could avoid responsibility for the nonmarital children they had fathered.

Equal Suffrage (Nineteenth) Amendment, 1920

When the Fourteenth and Fifteenth Amendments (see p. 289) failed to provide for universal suffrage, a federal amendment was introduced into the Senate by S. C. Pomeroy of Kansas in 1868 and into the House by George W. Julian of Indiana in March 1869. Historian Ellen DuBois has observed, "Previously the case for suffrage had consistently been put in terms of the individual rights of all persons, regardless of their sex and race. Angered by their exclusion from the Fifteenth Amendment, women's rights advocates began to develop fundamentally different arguments for their cause. They claimed their right to the ballot not as individuals but as a sex. . . . The reason women should vote was not that they were the same as men but that they were different. That made for a rather thorough reversal of classic women's rights premises."*

Arguing for the vote on the basis of women's *difference* from men could be effective in strengthening women's sense of group consciousness, but it also was compatible with racist and nativist arguments that white women needed the vote to counteract the suffrage of black and immigrant men. The old alliance of woman suffrage and abolitionist activism eroded, even though voting rights for black men were under siege after Reconstruction. The suffrage efforts of 1870 to 1920 continued to display arguments on the basis of equality, but younger generations of activists were increasingly likely to emphasize difference—what one activist called "the mother instinct for government."

Woman suffrage was not accomplished easily. One scholar has counted 480 suffrage campaigns waged at the state level between 1870 and 1910, but in the end only seventeen referenda were held, with only two successes (in Colorado and Idaho).** Stanton died in 1902; Anthony in 1906. But a new, younger generation adopted new strategies. Americans were inspired by the militancy of the British suffrage movement. In 1902 Carrie Chapman Catt was simultaneously president of the International Woman Suffrage Alliance and the National American Woman Suffrage Association (NAWSA). By 1910 it was clear that a reinvigorated movement was under way, using door-to-door campaigns, street-corner speakers, and poll watchers on Election Day. For the first time, cross-class suffrage organizations, like New York's Equality League of Independent Women, were mobilizing

---

*Ellen Carol DuBois, "Outgrowing the Compact of the Fathers: Equal Rights, Woman Suffrage, and the United States Constitution, 1820–1878," *Journal of American History* 74 (December 1987): 848.

**Eleanor Flexner, *Century of Struggle* (Cambridge, Mass.: Belknap Press of Harvard University Press, 1959), 13; Rebecca Edwards, "Pioneers at the Polls: Woman Suffrage in the West," in *Votes for Women: The Struggle for Suffrage Revisited*, ed. Jean H. Baker (New York: Oxford University Press, 2002), pp. 90–101.

support for suffrage. Suffragists staged public parades that attracted tens of thousands of supporters.

Although many suffragists had claimed that when women got the vote, there would be no more American endorsements of war, Catt swung NAWSA behind Woodrow Wilson, American support for the allies, and, eventually, the nation's entry into World War I in April 1917. The more radical National Women's Party (NWP), under the leadership of Alice Paul, staked out a very public position protesting Wilson's failure to explicitly endorse a federal guarantee for women's suffrage. (For an image and more on the story of the NWP's picketing of the White House in 1917, see p. 261) Putting aside his states' rights approach, the president publicly endorsed a constitutional amendment in early 1918. One day later, the House of Representatives passed the suffrage amendment, barely achieving the required two-thirds majority. But despite a personal appearance from Wilson, it failed by only two votes to carry the Senate.

As state after state enacted woman suffrage for statewide elections, the number of members of Congress dependent on women's votes increased. With the federal suffrage amendment slated to come before Congress again and again, these men were likely to believe that they had no choice but to support it. In the fall 1918 elections, NAWSA targeted four senators for defeat; two of them failed to be reelected. Moreover, energetic campaigns in the states to elect prosuffrage candidates to Congress worked. When the amendment came up in the new Congress, according to Anne F. Scott and Andrew Scott, "224 of those voting yes came from suffrage states, and eighty from nonsuffrage states."[†] It squeaked by in the Senate. It was ratified by thirty-five states by August 1920; the final state was Tennessee, where, after a bitter struggle, it was ratified by a single vote, just in time to permit women to vote in the elections of 1920.

When Puerto Rican women attempted to register to vote in 1920, however, the U.S. Bureau of Insular Affairs decided that the Nineteenth Amendment did not automatically apply to U.S. territories. Suffragist groups mobilized in Puerto Rico, lobbying throughout the next decade both on the island and in Washington, D.C., with support from the NWP. In 1929 the territorial legislature granted suffrage to women restricted by a literacy requirement; not until 1935 was universal suffrage established in Puerto Rico.

Many southern states had excluded African American men from voting by using literacy tests, poll taxes, and intimidation; in those states black women could vote no more easily than black men, and suffrage was an empty victory. The state of Georgia effectively discouraged white women from voting as well by providing that any woman who did not choose to register to vote did not have to pay the poll tax. This law, which encouraged women—and their husbands—to see voting as an expensive extravagance, was upheld by the U.S. Supreme Court in 1937 (*Breedlove v. Suttles*, 302 U.S. 277).

Section 1. The right of the citizens of the United States to vote shall not be denied or abridged by the United States or by any State on account of sex.

Section 2. Congress shall have power to enforce this article by appropriate legislation.

[†]Anne F. Scott and Andrew MacKay Scott, *One Half the People: The Fight for Woman Suffrage* (Urbana: University of Illinois Press, 1982; orig. publ. Philadelphia: Lippincott, 1975), p. 45.

INDEX